The German Language

THE GREAT LANGUAGES

General Editor   L. R. Palmer, M.A., D.PHIL., PH.D.
*formerly Professor of Comparative Philology
in the University of Oxford*

THE FRENCH LANGUAGE   A. Ewert, M.A., LITT.D.

THE SPANISH LANGUAGE TOGETHER WITH PORTUGUESE, CATALAN, BASQUE   William F. Entwistle, M.A., LITT.D., LL.D.

THE CHINESE LANGUAGE   R. A. D. Forrest, M.A.

RUSSIAN AND THE SLAVONIC LANGUAGES
William F. Entwistle, M.A., LITT.D. *and*
W. A. Morrison, B.A., PH.D.

THE LATIN LANGUAGE L. R. Palmer, M.A., D.PHIL., PH.D.

THE SANSKRIT LANGUAGE   T. Burrow, M.A., PH.D.

THE ROMANCE LANGUAGES
W. D. Elcock, M.A., L.ES.L., D.DE L'U. TOULOUSE
(revised with a new introduction by John N. Green, M.A., D.PHIL.)

THE ITALIAN LANGUAGE
Bruno Migliorini, DOTT. IN LETTERE
(abridged and re-cast by T. G. Griffith, M.A., B.LITT.)

THE SCANDINAVIAN LANGUAGES   Einar Haugen

Other titles are in preparation

THE
GERMAN LANGUAGE

R. E. KELLER

HUMANITIES PRESS INC.

NEW JERSEY

First published in 1978
by Humanities Press Inc.
New Jersey
Printed in Great Britain

Library of Congress Cataloging in Publication Data

Keller, Rudolf Ernst.
The German language.
(The Great languages)
First–6th ed. by R. Priebsch and W. E. Collinson.
Includes bibliographies
1. German language–Grammar, Historical.
2. German language–History. I. Priebsch,
Robert, 1866–1935. The German language. II Title.
PF3101.K4 1977 430′.9 77–9109
ISBN 0–391–00732–7

© 1978 R. E. Keller

Contents

5 The Hohenstaufen Flowering

List of Maps and Diagrams

Preface

It cannot be said that there is a shortage of histories of the German language. If there is, nevertheless, room for a further historical description of the German language, the reason lies in the subject itself and in changing methodology. The field is vast and within it interest has turned to new aspects. Different methods of approach have developed. It has been my aim to describe the evolution of the German language by making cross-sections at four vital stages in the historical evolution of the language and by considering two prehistorical phases in the same way. It is hoped that the language in its various dimensions will come to life at these crucial epochs and will be seen as a functional entity. Continuity need nevertheless not suffer. The reader who wishes to follow through the development of a particular feature, for instance, phonology or word formation, may read the relevant sections successively, thus disregarding the synchronic cross-sections. In language synchrony and diachrony are always interwoven. It is hoped that by the present method justice may be done to both.

The student of German who wishes to inform himself of the historical evolution of the German language should acquaint himself, prior to embarking on his historical study, with the major concepts and methods of modern linguistics and phonetics. University courses in German frequently provide introductions in both fields.

It has unfortunately proved impossible to print the full bibliography and the detailed bibliographical references which the book was to have contained. The Select Bibliographies now provided at the end of each chapter are intended as an expression of acknowledgment to scholars to whose works direct reference is made. To a vast number of others whose works I have read with benefit I can regrettably only render anonymous thanks.

The maps on p. 36 by Professor Marija Gimbutas, on p. 221 by Dr. Rosemarie Schnerrer and on pp. 450–1 by Professor Gerhard Ising are reproduced by kind permission of The University Press of the University of Pennsylvania, the VEB Max

Niemeyer Verlag, Halle (Saale), and the Akademie Verlag, Berlin. I should like to thank Miss Elizabeth Anne Lowcock, chief cartographer of the Geography Department of the University of Manchester, for kindly drawing all the other maps. I also wish to thank the staff of the John Rylands University Library of Manchester for their willing and courteous assistance at all times. It is with great pleasure that I express my debt of gratitude to my friends and colleagues, Dr. David Blamires and Dr. Martin Durrell, who both read the whole typescript, and to Mr. David Allerton and Dr. Peter Skrine who read parts of it. Their comments were of great value to me. Finally, I must thank my wife, who typed the manuscript and assisted the growth of this book with patience, understanding and encouragement.

Manchester, December 1974   R. E. Keller

Abbreviations

Titles of periodicals which are referred to only very rarely are given in full. Grammatical terms, e.g. *genitive, accusative, masculine,* are abbreviated in the usual way where the context makes them easily readable, e.g. *gen., acc., m.,* although such traditional abbreviations are not included in the following list.

Alem.	Alemannic.
Bav.	Bavarian.
Beitr., from	*Beiträge zur Geschichte der deutschen Sprache und*
1955	*Literatur,* Halle, from 1955 also, Tübingen.
Beitr. (Halle)	
or *Beitr.* (Tüb.)	
BNF	*Beiträge zur Namenforschung,* Heidelberg.
CFr.	Central Franconian.
CGm.	Central German.
CUGm.	Central Upper German.
DU	*Der Deutschunterricht,* Stuttgart.
E	English.
ECGm.	East Central German.
EFr.	East Franconian.
ENHG	Early New High German.
EUGm.	East Upper German.
F	French.
Gm.	German.
Gmc.	Germanic.
Goth.	Gothic.
Gr.	Greek.
HAlem.	High Alemannic.
HG	High German.
IE	Indo-European.
It.	Italian.
JEGP	*Journal of English and Germanic Philology,* Ann Arbor.
Lg.	*Language.* Journal of the Linguistic Society of America, Baltimore.
Lat.	Latin.
LG	Low German.
Lgb.	Langobardic.

Lingua	*Lingua*. International Review of General Linguistics, Amsterdam.
Linguistics	*Linguistics*. An International Review, The Hague.
MHG	Middle High German.
MLG	Middle Low German.
Neuphil. Mitt.	*Neuphilologische Mitteilungen*, Helsinki.
NHG	New High German.
O	Old.
OE	Old English.
OF	Old French.
OFris.	Old Frisian.
OHG	Old High German.
OIcel.	Old Icelandic.
O. Ind.	Old Indic.
O. Ir.	Old Irish.
OLFr., OLFranc.	Old Low Franconian.
ON	Old Norse.
OS	Old Saxon.
PGmc.	Proto-Germanic.
PMLA	*Publications of the Modern Language Association of America*, New York.
Rh. Fr., Rhen. Franc.	Rhenish Franconian.
TPS	*Transactions of the Philological Society*, Oxford.
UGm.	Upper German.
WCGm.	West Central German.
WGmc.	West Germanic.
WUGm.	West Upper German.
Word	*Word*. Journal of the Linguistic Circle of New York, New York.
WW	*Wirkendes Wort*, Düsseldorf.
ZDA	*Zeitschrift für deutsches Altertum*, Wiesbaden.
ZDP	*Zeitschrift für deutsche Philologie*, Berlin, Munich.
ZDS	*Zeitschrift für deutsche Sprache*, Berlin.
ZfdMaa.	*Zeitschrift für deutsche Mundarten*, Wiesbaden.
ZfdWf.	*Zeitschrift für deutsche Wortforschung*, Strasbourg (to 1914), Berlin (1960–63).
ZMF	*Zeitschrift für Mundartforschung*, Wiesbaden.

Symbols and Spellings

*	reconstructed form, only used when indication is not otherwise clear, e.g. by abbreviations IE or PGmc.
>	becomes.
<	derives from.
−	superscript on a vowel indicates its length; in MSS superscript indicates an omitted *n* or *m*.
-x	x preceded by other element.
x-	x followed by other element.
-x-	x in medial position.
[ ]	phonetic or allophonic transcription.
//	phonemic transcription.
⟨s⟩	letter, written symbol or grapheme.
⟨⟩	allograph or graphemic variant.
ø	zero.

For transcriptions given in square brackets the symbols of the International Phonetics Association (IPA) are used. The signs between slant lines are generally the letters of the ordinary alphabet current at the linguistic stage under discussion. The traditional signs used in Germanic linguistics are: þ for the voiceless interdental fricative (E *th*), x for the voiceless velar fricative (Gm. *ach* sound), b, ð, g for the voiced fricatives.

In the Latin transliteration of Gothic the letters have their approximate Latin phonemic values with the following exceptions: ⟨aí⟩ and ⟨aú⟩ are approximately [ɛ] and [ɔ], ⟨ei⟩ is [iː]. Many authorities regard ⟨ai, au⟩ as representing diphthongs, others assume them to have been monophthongs of the *e*- and *o*-type. ⟨gg, gk, gq⟩ stand for the velar nasal plus a plosive in words which in other Gmc. languages have a velar nasal [ŋ], ⟨hʋ⟩ is a labiovelar fricative.

Introduction: the nature of language

1.1 | Why study the history of a language?

Students who have no great liking for history frequently ask: why should one study the history of a language? They learn a foreign language in order to be able to communicate with the native speakers of that language. If they are satisfied when they can order a glass of beer in Munich in German and ask the way to Nymphenburg, there is in fact no reason why they should proceed further. The intellectually curious will, however, not be able to restrain themselves from asking questions about the language. After all, there is so much in the language they are learning that is puzzling and calls for explanation. Why is it that the plural of German *Tag* is *Tage* but that of *Nacht* is *Nächte*, while English has a very regular formation *day – days, night – nights*? Variation in the root-vowel plays indeed a great role in the formation of noun plurals in German. But it is not entirely absent from English: *foot – feet*; *goose – geese*; *tooth – teeth*; *mouse – mice*; *louse – lice*; *man – men*. Indeed the German nouns which are etymologically related to these English nouns all show vowel variation too: *Fuß – Füße*; *Gans – Gänse*; *Zahn – Zähne*; *Maus – Mäuse*; *Laus – Läuse*; *Mann – Männer*. Some verbs also show vowel alternation, for instance *binden – band – gebunden*; *singen – sang – gesungen*, paralleled in English by *bind – bound – bound* but *sing – sang – sung*. German *bringen*, which on the face of it looks so similar, has however different forms: *brachte – gebracht* echoed by English *bring – brought*. What does it all mean?

Innumerable obvious links in word formation will appear intriguing: *wägen – Gewicht* (*weigh – weight*); *treiben – Trift* (*drive – drift*); *Freundschaft – friendship*; or *Haarbürste – hairbrush* but *Haaresbreite – hair's breadth*. Both within German and in the obvious relationship between English and German elusive links, analogies and differences incite the student to further probing. The examples so far are from the fields of inflection and derivation.

Other levels are no less perplexing and thought provoking. In phonology it is easy to draw up a list of sound correspondences between English and German in etymologically identical words such as *Weib – wife*; *Feile – file*; *Meile – mile*; *Seite – side*; *weiß – white*; *reiten – ride*; *Weile – while*; *beißen – bite*. But why does the correspondence formula: English [ai] – German [ae] break down, or rather, why is it replaced by a different formula, in the case of *Bein, Heim, allein, Seife, beide, Eiche, Speiche* – English *bone, home, alone, soap, both, oak, spoke* (German [ae] – English [ou])?

The syntactic use of the definite articles in German and in English is regulated by certain rules. Some usages in German appear anomalous, for instance, the absence of the article in *zu Bett, zu Hause, auf Erden, zu Wasser*, although they recall corresponding English phrases. Certain German rules of word order strike the English learner as being archaic: *Dies will ich tun*; *dort werde ich warten*, since they remind him of Biblical English (*this will I do*; *there will I wait*). Some usages of colloquial German seem strange, for instance the use of the definite article with proper names: *der Adenauer, der Springer*, and in South German usage also: *der Karl, der Hans*. Is there any significance in the fact that Italian has the same feature: *il Boccaccio*, and in sub-standard also, *il Giovanni, la Maria*? Or, for that matter, is there any significance in the fact that English, North German dialects, and French are averse to noun diminution while South German dialects and Italian are extremely favourably disposed towards the formation of diminutives?

In the lexicon, problems abound just as much. How has it come about that German shares the lexical items *Haus, Tor* with English (*house, door*) but *Fenster, Mauer* with French (*fenêtre, mur*)? Some etymologically identical words have identical meanings, for instance: *Hand – hand, Teig – dough, Daumen – thumb*; some differ subtly: *schwimmen – swim, Straße – street*; while others differ considerably: *Knabe – knave, tapfer – dapper, klein – clean*; even fairly recent loans can differ substantially: *eventuell – eventually, Promotion – promotion*. Each language structures its semantic fields in its own way. It is common European linguistic practice to differentiate in words of address between married women and unmarried women but not between married men and unmarried men: *Miss – Mrs* but *Mr*; *Fräulein – Frau* but *Herr*; *Mademoiselle – Madame* but *Monsieur*; *Signorina – Signora* but *Signore*. Present-day Germans have begun to use *Frau* for any lady over a certain age (most often thirty or increasingly less), especially if she is professionally active. Do they regard the earlier practice as unfair discrimination between the sexes, and have they departed from it in recent years for this reason ? Incidentally the German-speaking Swiss have not followed this innovation. But trying to keep in step with the spirit of the age, the head of the Swiss federal civil service proposed in October 1972 to introduce *Frau* as the uniform term of address for female civil servants and consulted Swiss women's organizations on his proposal. In Austria too, the civil service ruling since 1970 has been that *Fräulein* is no longer to be applied to women over eighteen but is to be replaced by *Frau*.

This raises the problem of regional distinctions. The English learner of German becomes familiar with two words for *Saturday*: *Samstag* (south) and *Sonnabend* (north). He will find large numbers of lexical differences even within the standard language: *Lehrstuhl* (Germany, Switzerland) – *Lehrkanzel* (Austria); *Treppe* (Germany, Switzerland) – *Stiege* (Austria); *Schornstein* (Germany) – *Rauchfang* (Austria) – *Kamin* (Switzerland). And, of course, he cannot remain unaware of the existence of regional dialects.

Explanations of linguistic facts are usually to be found in the historical evolution of the language. This is why the study of the history of a language is such a fascinating and rewarding topic. It is inconceivable that the study of the history of the German language should not form a large part of any serious academic study of German.

1.2 | **What is language?**

Language is the most important creation of the human mind. It is likely that both have evolved together. The functioning of the human mind could barely be conceived without language. Language is a system or code, or rather an extremely complex system of interlocking subsystems, by means of which individuals and social groups communicate. Language is systematic, for only thanks to this characteristic are we able to understand what we have never heard before, or are we able to say what we have never learnt before in our particular mother tongue or in a foreign language the 'system' of which we have also acquired. But language is a human system not an artefact like a system created by mathematicians or logicians. It thus shares features which circumscribe human life, above all, change. Language is thus not only systematic but also, although this may sound paradoxical, highly unstable; always on the move, always heterogeneous and continuously changing. It functions because it is systematic, and because it must. Instability, rate of change and type of change and its heterogeneity are never allowed to impair its prime function as a means of communication. Individuals and social groups may, however, change from one language as a means of communication to another, and in the process heterogeneity may seem exceptionally great.

1.2.1 | Content

Language exists on two planes: on the material plane of expression and on the conceptual plane of content or meaning. Expression consists of speech sounds (physical phenomena) and grammatical forms (morphs, words, sentences). *Content* is a relation or a symbolic value. When we pronounce the German word *Haus* we produce sounds or phones (transmitted as sound waves) in a particular linear sequence which on the one hand constitute a morph or form and on the other hand *mean* something. Content and form together are thus a sign or a symbol, not a reality. Meanings belong to the world of language, or rather a particular language, not to the world of reality. Meanings *refer* to the world of reality. Every language community creates its own world of meanings. It has often been said that the way speakers of a particular language look at the world of reality is determined by their language. And conversely that the way they create, in their language, a world of meaning reflects the way in which they look at the world of reality.

Examples are easy to find, although it is much more difficult to prove anything conclusive. Does an Englishman view the 'world' of time-pieces differently from a German because his language forces him always to distinguish automatically between *clock* and *watch*, while the German would normally refer to them indiscriminately as *Uhr*? Of course the German can discriminate if he wishes to by speaking of *Armbanduhr, Taschenuhr, Wanduhr, Turmuhr*, etc. but he does not do so unless the distinction seems important to him. Where the German says *ein Paket tragen, einen Hut tragen (in der Hand oder auf dem Kopf), Früchte tragen*, an English speaker must discriminate and use three different verbs whether he wants to or not. Language can be a straitjacket: *to carry a parcel, to carry a hat* or *to wear a hat*, as the case may be, *to bear fruit*. The ambiguity of the German *einen Hut tragen* is resolved in German by the addition of *in der Hand* while English with the duality of *wear* and *carry* does not allow the ambiguity to arise. Does the German see something special in *Schatten* because he does not discriminate between *shade* and *shadow* or does he render reality deficiently? This verbalizing of the world around us may alter in the course of time, too. The medieval form of *klein* combined the meaning of 'small' and the meaning of 'beautifully or delicately made'. Modern German employs two different words for the two different notions (*klein* and *zierlich*).

We have already seen that where a language has no word for a certain thing or concept, it can always use a paraphrase. In fact we can divide the lexicon into unanalysable 'labels', i.e. words which are unmotivated, explain nothing, and analysable 'paraphrases' which attempt to explain or describe the thing or concept. *Vagabond* is a 'label', *Landstreicher* a 'paraphrase'. This distinction has nothing to do with composition as such. Compounds can be just as much 'labels' as simple words. The meaning of *Großvater* or of *Eisbein* cannot be guessed at on the basis of the constituent elements. Words which are motivated at one time may become unmotivated at another. German or English *Nest – nest* are 'labels', i.e. unmotivated, but etymologists can point to a time when the formation was transparent: 'a place in which to sit down'.

1.2.2 | Expression

The *plane of expression* was for a time by some linguists regarded as the proper domain of linguistics while the plane of content was believed to belong to other disciplines such as philosophy or psychology. Few contemporary linguists now hold this view, but it is true that far more attention has been directed at the plane of expression, above all the *level of sound* and the *level of grammar*. On the level of sound, languages operate with something like two dozen to five dozen structural units. This is a manageable number, which no doubt accounts for the fact that phonology is the most thoroughly studied aspect of language. The level of grammar is usually subdivided into morphology (where the minimal forms, the morphemes within the word, are the structural units) and syntax (where the arrangement of morphemes into larger units, or words within the sentence, is the subject of investigation). On the level of grammar as a whole, language operates with a very much larger number of units or rules, perhaps thousands. While on the phonological and grammatical levels languages form relatively closed systems, the lexicon, both in its material aspect (the lexical items) and in its semantic aspect (the meanings), is open-ended.

This extremely brief and simplified account of what language is will have made it nevertheless clear that a complete description of a language on all its planes and levels is hardly capable of being achieved. If it were ever accomplished the result would probably overtax the patience and endurance of any reader. Even if the description of a language at only one given point in time were the aim, the selection of aspects to be treated would have to be extremely rigorous and judicious.

1.3 | The dimensions of language

Language does not exist in a vacuum. It is a human tool, as has already been stated, and as a human tool it is subjected to the same external conditioning factors as man. It is first defined by the natural dimensions of *time* and *space* and, secondly, it is defined by the social dimensions of the individual and the group, by the *user* and by the *use* to which it is put.

1.3.1 | Time

Even a casual glance at old documents will show that language changes along the axis of *time*. In some languages, or periods, change may be slow and the reader finds himself able to understand a text hundreds of years old. He can understand the older language if it is still more or less the same means of communication. We may therefore quite correctly say that he speaks an old language. If he can no longer understand as much of the old text as he would expect to understand of the text of a contemporary user of the language whom he is prepared to accept (if only just about) as a user of the same language, then we must conclude that the two forms are not the same medium. In this sense some languages are obviously older than others.

There is no need, at this point, to raise the question of why and how languages change or persist in the passage of time, except perhaps to hint at the changes any human being can observe in the course of his own life, in the subsequent generation and in the preceding generations. Like all human tools and institutions language is unstable even while serving its purpose as a means of communication.

It is traditional to divide the evolution of a language into periods along the time axis. Major linguistic changes tend to bunch together at certain periods of time and may hold good for a major part of the area of a language. Thus the so-called diphthongization of MHG long high-tongue or close vowels (MHG *ī, ū, iu* > NHG *ei, au, eu*) and the monophthongization of MHG diphthongs (MHG *ie, uo, üe* > NHG *ie* [iː], *u, ü*) are traditionally regarded as the indicators of the divide between MHG and NHG (actually ENHG). Objectors can point to the fact that either phenomenon can be found at the height of the MHG period, although in peripheral dialects only; and they draw attention to the fact that the former development has not taken place in High and Low Alemannic, while the latter is absent from all major Upper German dialects (Alemannic and Bavarian) even today. Indeed probably any division based exclusively on linguistic features can be faulted if the whole linguistic area is to be considered. Every dialect is a different mixture of archaisms and innovations. Thus usually recourse is also had to extralinguistic features such as cultural and political events. This is all the more justified since a connection between bundles of linguistic changes and profound historical events can often be established. Language change seems to be conditioned by an increase in the coincidence of linguistic systems. The more homogeneous a social group is and the more protected from contact with other social groups with different dialects or languages, the slower is the rate of linguistic change. The opposite is also true: the greater the clash of different linguistic systems the more rapid and far-reaching the rate and extent of linguistic change. In times of great historical upheavals, when populations are uprooted and the social order disturbed, the confrontation of linguistic systems is much increased and change tends to be accelerated and more profound. Linguistic geographers have shown that the innovating areas tend to be those of most intensive communication. Archaic features tend to be found along the periphery of a language area, although these peripheral dialects are also often typologically akin to neighbouring languages. The Age of the Great Migrations, just before the emergence of the German language in written documents; the breakdown of the Carolingian empire and its subsequent fragmentation and feudalization under the assault of external foes such as Vikings, Saracens and Magyars; the collapse of the Hohenstaufen empire and the great migrations to and colonization of the western Slav lands beyond the Elbe; finally the re-organization of the Empire by the Habsburgs, the Reformation, and the advance of science and technology (introduction of the printing press; general literacy); these great historical events coincide to a large extent with the major dividing lines and periods of the German language.

1.3.2 | Space

Linguistic maps using the same colouring for the area stretching say from Flensburg to the Matterhorn or from the Vosges to Vienna express a social, cultural and historical language reality. They do not truly reflect language along the axis of *space*. Wandering from village to village over those distances one would find a continuous variation in speech forms. Even if instead of listening to the spoken language one were to read the local newspapers written in the German standard language one would encounter regional variations. A language does not maintain a greater degree of homogeneity than the communicative needs of its speakers enforce. The normal split-up into dialects is thus a reflection of the communicative needs of social groups. The Bavarian or Swiss dialect speaker cannot possibly communicate in his dialect with a Luxemburg dialect speaker. The standard German language which they possess and which allows them to communicate, is a result of the long-range cultural and economic communicative needs. The Bavarian and Swiss dialect speakers can, however, communicate in dialect with a Swabian dialect speaker, presumably because the needs have kept the means alive. This variability and heterogeneity of language along the geographical dimension also mean that practically every speaker is familiar with linguistic systems other than his own. Most may be familiar with other systems only as hearers, many will also be able actively to use other systems or fragments of other systems. It is this fact which is to a large extent responsible for language change. German speakers of local or regional forms of the language which have the so-called feature of the unrounding of the rounded front vowels of MHG (e.g. *Glick, bees, Lait*) are aware that the standard language and other regional forms do not share this feature and they now go over rapidly and increasingly to those forms (*Glück, bös(e), Leut(e)*). The multi-system factor has not only to be reckoned with in the relations between dialects of one and the same language. It holds good across language barriers as well. Large numbers of linguistic features, mainly lexical, have in this way flowed across the Latin-German language barrier. For hundreds of years people who could write German also knew Latin. The Luxemburg dialects form the comparative of adjectives by means of the particle *méi* (*méi laang*) rather than by means of the suffix -*er* found in other German dialects (*länger*). No doubt the French analytical comparative (*plus long*) was the model. In this way, genetically unrelated languages which are in close communication with each other may acquire a typological relationship which can be as important as a genetic relationship.

It has already been stated that it is difficult to divide language into periods along the time axis. It is no less difficult to divide language geographically. Here, too, isoglosses (geographical boundaries between different linguistic forms, e.g. *ich/ik, Ziegel/Geiß*) tend to form bundles or fascicles where political, economic, religious divisions or topographical features impose a barrier to communication. But within the German language area no bundle of isoglosses is of such strength as to prohibit communication. As far as the dialects are concerned there is a continuum from the Alps to the North Sea and from the French linguistic boundary to the Polish, Czech and Hungarian boundaries. But the bundles of isoglosses which dialect geography has established allow the drawing-up of a map of German dialects. Although every dialect is in some respect a transition dialect it is nevertheless possible to set up major core areas. The continuum of the continental Germanic dialects is broken where German meets Danish; much less so where German meets Frisian. In the latter case the symbiosis of many centuries may have helped to create a measure of continuum where it may have once been less in evidence. In the former case we probably have an example of a rupture caused through migration. The gap has been seen by some scholars to have arisen through the emigration of the Angles and Saxons in the fourth and fifth centuries. In the north-west, political and cultural events have superimposed a language rupture on the dialect continuum. The Low Countries produced their own standard language, Dutch, the boundary of which against German tends to coincide with the state boundaries, whilst all other Germanic-speaking lands in north-western and central continental Europe eventually accepted the NHG standard language. The establishment of supraregional standard languages and the persistence and development of regional dialects show in operation the twin linguistic geographical processes of growing together and growing apart.

1.3.3 | Use
The social dimensions of use and user are to some extent the two sides of the same coin. When we analyse and classify a language according to the kind of *use* that is made of it, we find subcategories or varieties of language determined by the social circumstances and purposes of the users. Just as the German language is analysable along the axis of space into regional dialects, so it is analysable into social dialects or group languages. Even where there are no historical regional dialects, language varies according to the social class or occupation of its users. *Volkssprache, Umgangssprache, Hochsprache* are designations employed for

different uses of the German language. Where a speaker of *Hochsprache* discussing food and drink would use words like *Mund, essen, trinken,* a speaker using *Volkssprache* might say *Maul, fressen, saufen.* The following two sentences might be uttered by the same speaker – one, formally on the rostrum, the other, privately among friends – and refer to the same occasion:

'Ich kann mich mit dem Herrn Kollegen nicht in allen Punkten einverstanden erklären.'

'Na, was der wieder mal für einen Schmarren geschwätzt hat.'

Such a speaker would obviously make different use of the language, according to audience and circumstance.

Most speakers of German can express themselves in different varieties of German. In the family circle a man from Stuttgart might speak of his *Haisle,* at work of his *Häusle,* in a public speech of his *Häuschen.* The latter form he would, of course, also use in writing.

One important distinction is the one between the general language and specialist or technical languages (*Fachsprachen*). Every occupation or profession creates its own vocabulary or uses the general vocabulary with sharper precision, i.e. uses technical terms instead of common words. Lawyers, doctors, electricians, motor mechanics, printers and so on have their own *Fachsprachen.* While every speaker of German would understand *Fackelschein,* only coke-makers would know *Fackelrohr.* The man in the street would use the words *Füchsin* and *Wölfin* for the female of those species, a huntsman would use *Fähe.* To most Germans *Fahne* means 'flag' or 'banner', to the huntsman it also means 'bushy tail', for instance of a squirrel. To the post-office worker it also means a 'tie-on label' and to the printer and author of books a 'galley-proof'. It is well known that some words of OHG occur only in heroic poetry. This may mean that we have simply not a large enough documentation of the language to assess the full range of those words, or it may mean that we have here terms of the *Fachsprache* or specialist language of heroic poetry.

The most important distinction to be made according to use is that between spoken language and written language. Each medium creates its own forms. Basically language is, of course, spoken language, and a written language is a secondary, derived, visual representation. But a written language takes on an existence of its own and has its own history. Its raw material is letters and sounds.

Although letters are at some stage a reflection of sounds, once in existence they have their own evolution. Graphs and graphemes have a complicated relationship to phones and phonemes, and their own history. This is also true at the other levels: morphology, syntax, lexis. The genitive and the subjunctive present in modern German have a different existence in the spoken and the written medium. Written French has a tense which is no longer current in spoken French. Some words hardly ever leave the printed page; some others hardly ever appear on it, although here, too, practice may change with the passage of time.

We are now used to seeing a language employed for all purposes, in other words, to have a full range of varieties along the axis of use. In the history of both English and German there have been periods when this was not the case. In the early Middle Ages the language of church and state administration and of scholarship, or rather of the documentation thereof, was Latin. In England, at a somewhat later date, French or Anglo-Norman fulfilled a similar role and was in addition the spoken medium of at least part of the upper classes. Similarly, seventeenth-century aristocratic circles in Germany used French for polite conversation while reserving 'German for stable-boys'.

Where two clearly distinct forms of one and the same language are used in clearly delimited circumstances and fields, we speak of diglossia. A state of diglossia exists, for instance, in present-day German-speaking Switzerland, where standard German is the medium of school teaching, preaching, university lecturing, conversation with foreigners and the classical stage (quite apart from writing, of course) and Swiss German dialect is the medium of all informal conversation and of some public speaking. Diglossia is a relatively clearly defined state of affairs and is to be distinguished from the fluid state of ill-defined dialect mixing and adaptation to circumstances and interlocutor found in many parts of Germany and Austria.

1.3.4 | User

Language also takes on different forms according to the *user*. We have only to think of the language of children, schoolboys, criminals or any other social group. A text where words like *artfremd, kämpferisch, Leistungserziehung, Zersetzung, völkisch* occur is probably written by a Nazi. Another where we find: *Aktivist, Plansoll, Monopolkapitalismus, Klassenfeind, volkseigen* betrays a DDR pen. And where would one find constructions such as *die grasplatzungewohnten Spanier, die Briten-Prinzessin, Europas Hallstein, Wirtschaftswunder-Männer*, or a sentence like 'Kernpunkt des Kommissionskommuniqués war die Befürchtung, Deutschlands Mittvierzigerinnen würden nach der Bildblatt-Lektüre die Sprechzimmer der Frauenärzte stürmen, süchtig nach Östrogen-Spritzen und Pillen'? The journalists of *Der Spiegel* clearly wish to give their language a cachet of its own. Every individual has at his disposal a number of 'uses' of the language. He may use language as a technical language at one moment and as general language the next when he assumes that his partner would not understand the technical language. He will use a colloquial style on one occasion and a formal one on another. In German *noch was* would be perfectly appropriate on the former occasion, but would have to be replaced by *noch etwas* in formal literary style. Style in the narrow sense of the word, that is the free choice of linguistic items according to taste, predilection or inspiration, is clearly a phenomenon of the use of language determined by the user.

Social variations are just as much an intrinsic element of language as the better-known geographical variations. This does not mean that such variation is found equally on all levels of language. In German geographical variation is much more pronounced in phonology and lexis, somewhat less in morphology and is only slight in syntax. Social variation in use is greatest in lexis. Social variation by user contains a considerable phonological component.

One form of use very much determined by the will and inclination of the user is slang. It is a playful, ephemeral, hermetic use of vocabulary, found generally in tightly-knit groups. It has no special phonological or morphological form.

Language is an abstract notion which, in practice, is realized in the speech of an individual (an *idiolect*). An idiolect is, however, always based on and incorporates a language system. We can examine the German language and trace its history only through the idiolects in which it has taken shape. It would, however, be defeatist to say that we cannot know language as such simply

2

because we meet it only in the form of the speech of the individual. The two phenomena condition each other. Each exists only in and through the other. Our true aim must therefore be language even if the object of our investigation is an individual's idiolect.

1.3.5 | Diagram of dimensions

What has been said about language and its natural and social dimensions may be summarized in diagrammatic form on facing page.

How can one write the history of a language, itself an extremely complex system, with its dimensions of time and space, use and users? It is quite evident that nothing like a complete account is possible. All that can be hoped for is a selective but reasonable account which does some measure of justice to this immensely fascinating and many-sided story of the evolution of a language.

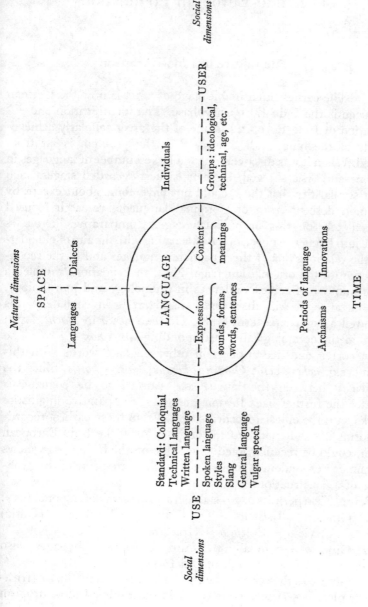

Fig. 1

The Indo-European Foundations

2.1 | The nature of Indo-European

The earliest identifiable stage of what is now the German language is the Indo-European phase. The identification and exploration of Indo-European is one of the great scholarly achievements of the nineteenth century. But the problem is far from solved. When it was discovered that a large number of languages in Europe and Asia showed, in their earliest recorded stages, such great similarities that these could not have come about except by common descent from one original language, research focused immediately on this original language. Comparative linguistics came into being as a new branch of learning with the aim of elucidating the relationships of these cognate languages and of the reconstruction of the original language. First, investigations revealed a large number of correspondences in phonology and morphology. For instance, it was discovered that sounds in cognate words followed a regular pattern: where German has *a* in *Nacht*, Latin has *o* in the etymologically corresponding word *nox – noctis*. The same correspondence appears in other cognate words with this sound, e.g. *acht – octo*; *Garten – hortus*; *Gast – hostis*. Since the similarity between the languages, assumed to be cognate, is greater the further back in time one goes, comparative linguistics works with the oldest recorded stages. From these earliest recorded forms it was hoped that the original form, the Indo-European form, could be reconstructed. The table on the facing page shows certain correspondences and serves to illustrate some of the problems of reconstruction.

Comparison permits us to establish a number of correspondences:

(1) Gmc. *a* = Latin *o* = Old Indic *a* = Lithuanian (Baltic) *a* = Old Slavic *o* = Celtic *o* = Greek *o*.

(2) Gmc. *n* = *n* in all other Indo-European languages; also Gmc. *m* = *m*; *l* = *l* (except in Old Indic); *r* = *r*.

(3) Gmc. *t* as the second element of a consonantal cluster (fricative or plosive +*t*) corresponds to *t* in most other Indo-European languages.

German	Nacht	acht	Garten	Gast	mahlen	Mähne
Oldest Gmc. form (Gothic)	nahts	ahtau	gards 'house' garda 'yard'	gasts	malan	mana (OHG)
Latin	nox, noctis	octō	hortus	hostis	molere	monīle 'necklace'
Greek	nuktós (gen.)	oktō	chórtos 'yard'	—	múllō	—
Old Indic	nák, naktam 'at night'	aṣṭau	gṛhá- 'house'	—	mṛṇāti	mányā 'neck'
Old Irish	-nocht	ocht	gort	—	melim	muin 'neck'
Welsh	nos	wyth Old W. oeth	garth 'paddock'	—	malu	mwn 'neck'
Lithuanian	naktìs	aštuonì	gařdas 'paddock'	—	malù	—
Old Slavic	noštĭ	osmĭ	gradŭ	gostĭ	meljǫ	monisto 'necklace'

Where individual languages depart from these correspondences this may be explained by:
(1) Internal or language-specific developments conditioned by various factors, e.g. phonological context, or analogy, or borrowing;
(2) 'root variation' or original alternation. This is one of the most important features of the inter-relationship of the Indo-European languages and will be more fully explained later.
Large numbers of words are found only in some individual languages. This poses further problems. They may have been lost in some languages with the passage of time, or their occurrence in the original Indo-European may have been dialectal, or they may have been formed at a later stage and may be shared only by some once contiguous languages. In fact it is quite rare that words with identical formation are found in a majority of Indo-European languages. In this respect the words in the above table are not representative at all of the attested Indo-European vocabulary. A handful of words are identical in formation, the majority though related, show the phenomenon provisionally named 'root varia tion'. In order to explain this we must first consider the structure

of most Indo-European words, at least the nominals (nouns and adjectives) and the verbs. The large majority of words are tri-partite in structure. The principle can also be explained with examples from modern German or English which show analogous structures.

Gen. sg. (des) *Fahrers*		(the) *driver's*
Dat. pl. (den) *Fahrern*	Gen. pl.	(the) *drivers'*

can be analysed as follows:

Fahr-er-s	*driv-er-'s* [draivəz]
Fahr-er-n	*driv-er-s'* [draivəz]

The element bearing the basic lexical meaning (*fahr-*, *driv-*) is the *root*. It is followed by the so-called *stem suffix* which is deriva-tional in character. In final position we find the *inflectional ending*. (The German example has two, the English only one which fur-thermore coincides with the inflectional ending of the plural. In spoken English the ambiguity of the inflectional ending is resolved contextually, whereas the written language marks the three func-tions visually.) In modern German and English stem suffixation plays a relatively modest part. Apart from *Fahrer* and *driver* we have *Fahrt*, *Fähre*, *fahren*, *führen*, *fertig*, *Furt* and *driven*, *driving*, *drift*. The English root etymologically identical with German *fahr-* shows a similar spread in stem suffixation: *fare* (verb and noun), *ferry*, (*way*)*farer*, *ford*.

In the Indo-European phase stem suffixation played a very large part indeed. It added classification and determination to the roots. Sometimes suffixes or formants were fairly clearly defined in function and meaning, such as those expressing the comparison of adjectives, but others were extremely vague. The reason is that the suffixes were active and meaningful at different periods. Once obsolete they are difficult to define. Thus in the above modern examples -*er* is an active suffix and relatively easily defined. Although here too, meanings are multiple. Compare *driver*, *Fahrer* (person who drives), with *washer* (washing machine), *Füller* (pen which can be filled), *sleeper* (railway coach in which one can sleep or the wooden planks to which rails are fixed or, in slang, a sleeping pill) and so on. The obsolete suffixes present greater difficulties, for instance -*t* (*Fahrt*, *Furt*, *drift*), -*m* (*seam* – *sew*; *Zaum* – *ziehen*). Several dozen nominal stem suffixes or for-mants have been identified for Indo-European. The individual recorded languages vary greatly in their word structures on account of different choices of stem suffixes. The infinitive of verbs, for instance, is formed with an *n*-suffix in Germanic, with an -*s*- > -*r*- element in Latin, with -*ti*- in Baltic and Slavic and with -*tum* in Sanskrit. The word for 'eye', German *Auge*, has an *s* stem suffix in Old Indic, an -*n*- element in Armenian and Germanic, a -*ph*- element in Greek (*ophthalmós*) with many variants in dialects, and an -*elo*- stem suffix in Latin (*oculus*).

From an IE root *st(h)ə- /st(h)ā-* with the meaning 'to stand' we get the verbal derivation Lat. *stāre*; with -*nt*- the present stem OE *standan*, E *to stand*, OHG *stantan*; with -*t*- the perfect stem E *stood*, Lat. *status*, the nominal derivations OHG *stad* 'shore', Gm. *Gestade*, from PGmc. *staðíz* : E *stead*, Gm. *Stadt, Statt, Stätte*, and in Sanskrit *sthíti* 'standing', in Lat. *statio*, in Greek *stásis*. With IE -*dh*-: OE *stōd* 'herd of breeding horses', E *stud*, Gm. *Stute*; with IE -*dhl*-: Lat. *stabulum* and probably Gm. and E *stall* < Gmc.*staðlaz*; with IE -*l*-; Gm. *Stuhl* and E *stool*, Russian *stol* 'table', Greek *stélē* 'pillar'; with IE -*m*-: Greek *stémenai* 'to stand', Lat. *stāmen* 'warp, fibre'; with -*mn*-: Greek *stámnos* 'earthen jar' and perhaps Gm. *Stamm*, E *stem*.

Stem suffixes frequently occur in multiples as, for instance, in modern German *freu-nd-schaft-lich* + an inflectional ending (-*e*, -*es*, -*er*, -*en*), and as in the modern example the inflectional endings always come last.

It is characteristic of the Indo-European languages that the stem suffixes and the inflectional endings become fused. This was already the case in the earliest recorded languages, and in modern German the historical distinction is no longer in evidence, although echoes of Indo-European stem suffixation are still morphologically functional. Mutation, for instance, as a plural marker (*Kunst – Künste*) is an echo of an Indo-European -*i*- stem suffix.

Stem suffixation is not the only factor which makes for divergence among the Indo-European languages. Vowel gradation or apophony (German *Ablaut*) within the root is just as important. It consists of a regular alternation of certain Indo-European vowels. Since this phenomenon plays a great part in Germanic morphology it will be more fully treated in the next chapter. Indo-European languages frequently differ from each other in showing different grades in otherwise identical roots. Thus the Germanic words *Fuß – foot* derive from a generalized long *ō*-grade; Greek has long *o*-grade in *pós* (nom.), short *o* in *podós* (gen.); Latin long *ē*-grade in *pēs*, short *e*-grade in *pedis* etc. The *e*-grade is found, too, in

Greek *pédon* 'ground', the *o*-grade in Old Slavic *podŭ* 'ground'. Modern English *foot, pedal, pedestrian* and *podium, tripod* all show therefore different Indo-European vowel grades of the same root. Differences in choice of vowel grades in cognate roots occur in the modern languages too, for instance, *singer* – *Sänger*; *drink* (noun) – *Trunk, Trank*. Apophony and the choice of different grades make for a great deal of divergence between the individual Indo-European languages. Different survival patterns have no doubt enhanced original variations in the use of different grades.

The reconstruction of original forms, indeed of the whole original Indo-European language, was the great ambition of nineteenth-century Indo-Europeanists. At one stage a fable was composed in the reconstructed language, to be re-written in the next generation, when the picture of Proto-Indo-European had substantially changed. The early optimism has gradually evaporated. It is realized that the historically attested Indo-European languages are a very long way from the common original. They themselves represent widely differing stages of linguistic evolution. Indeed the differences between the separate branches, themselves often sharply defined entities, are so profound that some scholars have reckoned with some form of interruption in the development (language mixture, replacement of former alien languages, and transference of Indo-European to alien cultures).

The earliest records which are accessible and form the basis for comparison are hundreds of years apart. Hittite documents date from about 1450 B.C., Mycenaean Greek from 1200 B.C., Vedic Sanskrit (Old Indic) from 1000 B.C. onwards, Ancient Greek from 800 B.C., Latin from 300 B.C. The oldest Celtic and Germanic scraps begin to appear in the first centuries of our era, but the literary tradition starts at the end of the fourth century for Germanic (Gothic), otherwise in the eighth (German, English) and at about the same time for Celtic (Old Irish) and Slavic. Baltic is not recorded before the sixteenth century, although one language, Lithuanian, is very archaic in character. We have traces of many more Indo-European languages (Venetic, Illyrian, Phrygian, Thracian) and reason to believe that others existed but vanished without a trace. Reconstruction naturally depends very much on the material available. Hittite, discovered after the nineteenth-century wave of reconstruction, has considerably affected and altered scholars' views of Indo-European.

2.2 | **The time factor**

When linguists say that certain languages are cognate they mean that they are related by descent from a common original source. The family-tree diagram shows schematically the lines of descent and the relative chronology of languages. It places the original language, Proto-Indo-European, at the bottom, sub-groupings such as *satem*-languages and *centum*-languages next, followed by other sub-groupings like Indo-Iranian, Balto-Slavic or Italo-Celtic. Then follow the earliest recorded languages (Hittite, Greek, Vedic Sanskrit) and reconstructed but unrecorded ancestors (Proto-Germanic, Proto-Celtic, Proto-Slavic), in the next generation further branches such as West-East-North Germanic, and in the subsequent generation the 'Old' forms (Old Irish, Old High German, Old English) followed by the 'Middle' forms (Middle English, Middle High German). Finally the structure culminates in the present-day descendants of Proto-Indo-European (Hindi, French, German, Russian, English, etc.). Assuming that the various stages bear some sort of relation to reality and are not just hypothetical constructs (e.g. Italo-Celtic), it can be said that the family-tree diagram gives an indication of the time axis. But of the time axis only. Now, we know that the space axis is just as real and as important. The family-tree pattern only approximates to reality if, say, a given language A (consisting of dialects $a_1 a_2 a_3 a_4$ etc.) were suddenly and permanently riven asunder so that $a_1 a_2 a_3 a_4$ etc. were able to develop in a vacuum and totally separated from each other. The dialects would eventually develop into divergent languages $A_1 A_2 A_3 A_4$ etc. That such an event would occur in reality is extremely unlikely. Normally language A (itself in contact with languages B C D etc.) would imperceptibly evolve in a continual process of give and take of the dialects $a_1 a_2 a_3 a_4$ etc. with one another.

One of the dialects might be a standard language thus occupying a specially prestigious place among the various forms of the language. It would nevertheless partake in the process of interchange. Periods of language divergence and convergence tend to follow upon each other as a result of historical circumstances. Thus, in prehistoric Italy the divergence of the Italic languages was followed by a period of convergence with Latin as the salient tongue from 200 B.C. onwards. After the decline of the Roman Empire a period of divergence led to the emergence of the Romance dialects. At the end of the Middle Ages a new phase of convergence, on a different geographical basis, produced the establishment of new national languages such as French, Italian and so on. Something analogous cannot be ruled out even for the evolution of prehistoric Indo-European. More violent mutations such as the development of pidgin languages and subsequent creolization cannot be discounted either, at least in parts of the early Indo-European world.

Factors of time and communication would lead to the eventual metamorphosis of language A into language A_1, (e.g. Middle English into Modern English) or of dialects $a_1 a_2 a_3$ etc. into mutually incomprehensible different languages (e.g. French, Italian, A being Latin).

When they emerge into the light of day the descendent Indo-European languages are widely divergent, pointing to a common source very distant in time. The separation need not have occurred, of course, at the same time for all. It is more than likely that the common original language, no doubt characterized by dialectal spread as soon as it was used by a certain minimum number of speakers, is to be located in time, at least two thousand, possibly several thousand years, before the appearance of the first records of Indo-European languages. Modern Icelandic is said to have hardly any dialect variation and to be a fairly uniform language. The Indo-European languages, being cognate, may have had, in the remote past, such a uniform source. That source may possibly have been very different from the language we believe we can reconstruct. In fact Indo-Europeanists claim that they can distinguish many phases and layers within the phase that precedes the individual languages. For instance, most descendent languages have three genders of nouns and we would reconstruct Proto-Indo-European as a language with three genders. But there are indications that one of the genders (the feminine) arrived fairly late on the scene. All we can hope to reconstruct to some extent, is a phase shortly before the 'break-up', remembering that the 'break-up' is not a chronologically fixed or ascertainable point in time. This phase is Proto-Indo-European. Before that we get an occasional glimpse at structures which may be termed Pre-Indo-European.

Many features seem to occur in one or two or a small group of Indo-European languages only. At one time this fact was interpreted genetically and descendent sub-groups such as Italo-Celtic or Balto-Slavic were set up. Perhaps the best-known early sub-grouping which was seen genetically is that of *satem* and *centum* languages. In the former group Indo-European velars, for instance *k*, developed palatal allophones which later became assibilated, that is developed to *s*-type consonants, while the other languages retained plosives. It seems clear now that here we have a development in one part of the Indo-European group: an isogloss separates the eastern languages from the western ones. In other words we see it as a spatial phenomenon which spread and finally embraced Indo-Iranian, Armenian, Albanian (or better its unknown ancient forerunner), Slavic and Baltic. While there is a *satem* group, sharing the *satem* isogloss, there is no *centum* group. To some extent it is, of course, true that an isogloss as a spatial feature and a common innovation as a feature of genetic relationship are only the two sides of the same coin. In this sense the genetic image of the family-tree and the spatial image of the wave (or isogloss) spreading across languages are both reflexions of reality. But only if seen together. Alone, the genetic image, above all, is easily a distortion.

The fair number of parallel features which have been discovered to exist between Celtic and Italic (or some languages of the Celtic group and some of the Italic group), between Slavic and Baltic, Baltic and Germanic, and Germanic and Italic are best seen in terms of isoglosses rather than as closer genetic links.

It used to be held that for a form or feature to be termed Indo-European it had to occur in more than two recorded languages, and preferably in both the eastern and western wings of Indo-European. This view is based on too simple a genetic view of the relationship. Indo-European is simply that which in a particular language predates the establishment of what we regard as the character of that language, and which is paralleled in one or more other Indo-European languages. Thus Lehmann (1961) has dated the inception of Proto-Germanic from the completion of its shift from free pitch accent to a stress accent fixed on the initial or root syllable of words. The linguistic geographer uses bundles of isoglosses to delimit one dialect from another. In the same way we may use bundles of changes on the time axis to delimit a later language from an antecedent one. It has been asserted that Proto-Germanic cannot be identified before about 500 B.C. What went before was

Pre-Germanic or Indo-European, not of course necessarily Proto-Indo-European, let alone Pre-Indo-European. For the Pre-Germanic or Indo-European phase we must reckon with at least a span of two thousand years. The reconstructed Proto-Indo-European must be located in the third millennium B.C. and the hypothetical uniform original language implied by the term 'cognate' must be even considerably more distant. Reconstructed Proto-Indo-European is in a way nothing but a system of hypothetical formulas. Basing ourselves on the correspondences which the surviving languages allow us to establish, we posit a form which explains most readily and easily those correspondences and the developments leading up to them. Thus for the first correspondence given on p. 22 we reconstruct a Proto-Indo-European *o* because this accounts for the presence of *o* in some languages and because the other reflex *a* is most easily explained as a development from *o*. The correspondence Latin *h-* = Greek *ch-* = *g-* in Germanic, Celtic, Slavic, Baltic is most satisfactorily accounted for by the assumption of *gh-* in Proto-Indo-European although this form is only attested in Indic.

What we call the Indo-European foundations of German may be features which go back to Pre-Indo-European, or may have developed later at any time in the direct antecedent of Germanic or in another Indo-European dialect and been borrowed from there, or they may have evolved independently in many Indo-European languages, including Germanic. The reconstruction of Proto-Indo-European and the investigation of whatever is discernible within the two or three thousand years' span which we must allot to this phase, is the task of the Indo-Europeanist. What concerns the student of German is the extent to which German is still shaped by its Indo-European past.

2.3 | The problem of location

One question which has always greatly exercised scholars' imagination is that of the original habitat of the speakers of common Indo-European. The majority of German scholars have always been enamoured of the idea that the North German plain from the Weser eastwards and the Jutland peninsula were the original homeland of the Indo-European language. There is no real reason why this should be so, although there were many reasons why they should have thought so. Most of these, happily, no longer prevail, and the question can thus be viewed dispassionately.

There are of course no direct sources which might inform us of the original homeland and none are ever likely to appear. Language itself must therefore provide a clue in its vocabulary. The examination of the lexicon with the aim of finding information on the culture, way of life, beliefs, ambience and social organization of the original speakers of Indo-European is called linguistic palaeontology. Words for animals, wild and domesticated, plants and climatic conditions are obviously of value in determining the original habitat. Indo-European languages have no shared words for lion, tiger, elephant, camel and ass, or for palm, vine, cypress, olive, oil and wine. This can be taken to eliminate Asia south of the Black Sea and the Caspian Sea, and the Mediterranean littoral.

Place-names and especially river names tend to cling to the topography with a pertinacity which often outlasts languages. While in Europe north of the Alps, with prolongation eastwards and westwards, there is no onomastic evidence for languages other than Indo-European, the southern regions and peninsulas show a strong non-Indo-European substratum. It has been concluded that the European Indo-European languages at least (Celtic, Italic, Germanic, Baltic, and others now extinct), must have been located at one time in this northern belt. The fact that these language groups enter history in or near this region is a further pointer. Both typological investigations and lexically based statistical examinations have shown these groups to be linguistically linked.

The common vocabulary shows the early Indo-European speakers to have flourished towards the end of the Neolithic age and to have had some acquaintance with the precious metals and one utilitarian one (cf. E *ore*, Gm. *ehern*). Both agriculture, that is crop-growing, and stock-rearing formed part of their way of life. The animal which characterized their civilization at a time

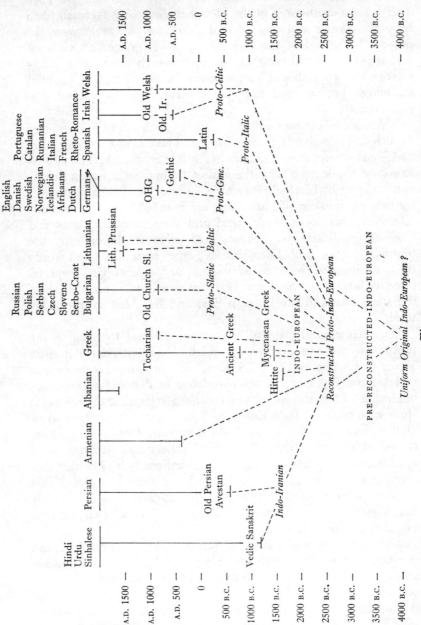

Fig. 2

Time-scale diagram of Indo-European

(1) On the top horizontal are listed some modern Indo-European languages, especially those which have become national languages, and those which are, or have been, neighbouring languages of German.

(2) In the vertical columns are recorded the earliest antecedents at the time they were first attested. The comparative method operates with these. They are not to be understood as direct lineal antecedents of the modern languages. They are merely nearer antecedents than any other languages.

(3) Some only fragmentarily recorded ancient languages, such as Gaulish, Venetic, Illyrian, Thracian (which may be a kind of antecedent of Albanian), Phrygian (which may be an antecedent of Armenian) are left out.

(4) Italicized forms indicate non-attested hypothetical languages.

(5) Reconstructed Proto-Indo-European is kept separate from 'Uniform Original Indo-European' because we must assume that the latter was a real, complete language, which the former quite obviously is not: only a fragment of the lexicon can be reconstructed; we can only form a vague impression of the syntax and even of the morphology. Furthermore, various developments prior to Proto-Indo-European can be detected. In other words Proto-Indo-European was only a phase in a continuous chain of evolution and the disparateness of the attested earliest stages is so great that we are forced to operate on a larger time-scale.

(6) Finally, the time-scale diagram must not be mistaken for a genealogical tree.

when it was still unknown to the civilizations of the Near East, was the horse. A variegated countryside permitting corn-growing and pasturing of cattle, and prairies providing a suitable habitat for the swift horse must have been available to these cultivators and herdsman-warriors, who had already invented a cart with wheels. The latter, as a chariot, played an important role in the earliest historic times. Theories based on arguments which are extremely narrow (the presence or absence of *one* word with this or that meaning) must be regarded as speculative. East-central Europe extending into the lands north of the Black Sea conforms perhaps best with the evidence of linguistic palaeontology. P. Friedrich, in his brilliant study *Proto-Indo-European Trees*, concludes (p. 16):

'In sum, from the foothills and steppe north of the western side of the Caspian westward through what is now the Ukraine and on north-westward into the north German plain there ran a fairly continuous and fairly homogeneous ecological zone – by and large one of temperate climate, open plains, and mixed hardwood forests. I assume that it was precisely in this east European area during the Atlantic period [c. 5500–3000 B.C.] that speakers of Proto-Indo-European were distributed in a block of dialects about three hundred miles wide and five hundred or more miles long: the area may have been only a third as large, but in any case probably included the central and eastern Ukraine. Subsequently, during the last of the late Atlantic and the first part of the Subboreal [c. 3000–800 B.C.], the speakers of at least three dialects (Celtic, Italic, and Germanic) entered, crossed or occupied central Germany and adjacent areas to the west, south, and north. (These three stocks, plus Baltic, Slavic, and Greek, yield most of the linguistic evidence on the arboreal system . . .).'

The only homeland, then, which we can locate, with reasonable certainty and on linguistic grounds, is the north-central-east European one of what were to become the European languages of Indo-European. Much points to the one-time northern habitat of these off-shoots prior to the dispersal, the results of which become apparent when these language groups enter history. To what extent the characteristics of these groups were already formed or foreshadowed while they were still in their northern habitats cannot be determined. It is more likely that they were formed in their new homelands to which Indo-European speakers migrated in powerful waves in the last half of the second millennium B.C.: Celtic in west-central Europe, Italic in the Italian peninsula, just as Greek arose in Greece and Germanic in North Germany and southern Scandinavia. It is likely that most of the eastern language groups were sited to the east of the European languages. They, too, would have acquired their specific characteristics after the dispersal, which probably predates that of the western groups. After all, the Anatolian and Indo-Iranian languages must have reached their historical habitats about 2000 B.C.

The uniform Original Indo-European which we must posit as long as we assume the cognation of the historical Indo-European languages must be dated back so far that to find a habitat for it must almost amount to a wild goose chase. On the other hand, if the theory of assimilation were to be adopted rather than that of genetic descent there would be no need to search for the small, tightly confined *Urheimat* of a unitary Original Indo-European. In either case an eastern centre of ultimate origin with subsequent westward expansion is inherently more likely.

Great store was once set by the findings of archaeology. The 'corded-ware' culture and the 'battle-axe' people of east-central Europe and the Danube basin were and still are by many believed to be Indo-European-speaking invaders from farther east, who eventually Indo-Europeanized earlier populations, for instance, the megalith builders of western and northern Europe. However, the identification of prehistoric cultures discovered by archaeologists and prehistoric languages and their speakers is extremely problematical and demands utmost care and not a little scepticism. The current archaeological view is most cogently propounded by Marija Gimbutas. She postulates a massive westward expansion of so-called Kurgan people, whom she considers to be Proto-Indo-European speakers, from north of the Black Sea and the lower Volga area. They brought with them certain foreign elements such as 'kurgans' (barrows), battle-axes, corded decoration on pottery, and others, which characterized many cultural areas in northern, eastern and central Europe during the centuries of the early Bronze Age. These cultural complexes, the Northern Area, Únětice (later Tumulus and Urnfield), the Baltic, and North Carpathian, appear to be the archaeological counterparts of the European Indo-European linguistic complexes.

The following map shows how an archaeologist, Marija Gimbutas, sees the rise and spread of Indo-European-speaking peoples.

(1) The earliest basis is the Kurgan Culture north of the Caspian Sea spreading to the regions north of the Black Sea.

(2) The first great expansion leads into the Balkans and east-central Europe, where the corded-ware (*Schnurkeramik*) and battle-axe culture arises.

(3) This latter subsequently penetrates the first northern or funnel-necked beaker culture (*Trichterbecherkreis* with megalith graves in part of the area) and spreads over central Europe north of the Alps.

(4) During the Bronze Age the Germanic complex forms in the Northern Area. The other European Indo-European language groups are sited in the north-central European regions (Únětice, Tumulus, Urnfield). They ultimately become Celtic, Italic, Illyrian and Venetic. Farther to the east, Baltic and Slavic (North Carpathian) gradually crystallize.

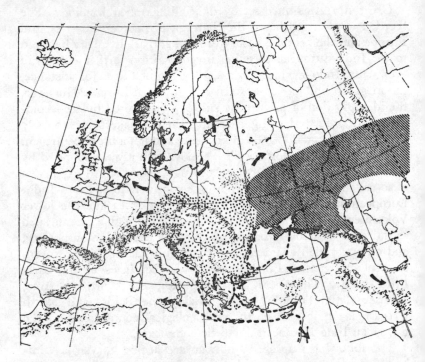

Fig. 3. Kurgan culture during the fourth and third millennia and the climax of expansions. *Solid grey area*: Kurgan culture in the Eurasian steppes. *Dotted area*: The area infiltrated not later than 4000–3500 B.C. *Arrows* show tentative movements after *c.* 2500 B.C. *Disconnected line and arrows* indicate possible sea-ways, raids, and destruction at *c.* 2300 B.C.

From Marija Gimbutas, 'Proto-Indo-European Culture', p. 193, in G. Cardona, H. M. Hoenigswald, A. Senn (eds.), *Indo-European and Indo-Europeans*, Philadelphia, 1970.

2.4 | The Indo-European heritage of German

Language evolution is characterized by two opposing forces: innovation and retention. The innovations of Germanic will form part of the next chapter. What we have to examine here are the retentions. They form the most obvious link in the chain from Indo-European to German.

2.4.1 | Phonology

In *phonology* there are a number of Indo-European features which German has retained. The most important is vowel gradation which, though no longer active, still permeates German morphology. It is responsible for such vowel alternations as *e – a – u – (o)* in *werfen – warf – Wurf – (geworfen)* (*o* and *geworfen* are bracketed because they arose through Germanic innovation from the same grade as that represented by *u* in *Wurf*); or *a – u* in *schaffen – schuf*; or *ei – i* in *beißen – bissen*. It is true, the realizations of the grades have greatly changed. The principle of vowel gradation is, however, an important Indo-European fossil.

Some vowels, although they are now incorporated in a different phonological system and derive, as phonemes, etymologically from varying sources, illustrate at least approximate phonetic retention:

a: *Acker*; IE: *ager* (Latin), *agrós* (Greek), *ájra-ḥ* (O. Ind.)
  Achse; IE: *axis* (Latin), *áxōn* (Greek), *ákṣa-ḥ* (O. Ind.)
e: *essen*; IE: *edō* (Latin), *édomai* (Greek), *édu* (Lith.)
  Sessel; IE: *sella* (Latin), *sedlo* (O. Slav.), *sedd* (Welsh)
i: *(ge)wiß*; IE: *video, vīsus* (Latin), *vitta-* 'known' (O. Ind.), *gwys* 'knowledge' (Welsh)
  Witwe; IE: *vidua* (Latin), *vidhávā* (O. Ind.), *vĭdova* (O. Slav.)
u: *jung*; IE: *juvenis* (Latin), *junŭ* (O. Slav.)
  Hund; IE: *kúōn, kunós* (Greek), *šuõ, šuñs* (Lith.), *ku* (Tocharian).

Such retentions are very rare. Indeed it is no accident that all these short vowels occur before consonantal clusters (*ss* was double, phonemically as well as graphemically, until fairly recently, at least into MHG). Short vowels before consonant clusters have been the least exposed to change of all vowels throughout the history of German, including the dialects.

Among the consonants we note the survival of the two liquids
(*l* and *r*) and the two ancient nasals (*m* and *n*):

l: *Licht*, *leuchten*; IE: *lux* (Latin), *leukós* 'bright' (Greek), *llug*
'brightness' (Welsh), *luk(k)*- 'to light' (Hittite).
Lauge; IE: *lavo* (Latin), *loúō* 'wash' (Greek).

r: *Erbe*; IE: *orbus* (Latin), *árbha*- 'small' (O. Ind.), *orphanós*
'orphan' (Greek).
Mord; IE: *mors*, *mortis* (Latin), *marati* 'dies' (O. Ind.),
marw 'dead' (Welsh).

m: *Meer*; IE: *mare* (Latin), *mor* (Welsh), *morje* (O. Slav.).
Mund; IE: *mandō* (Latin), *mástax* (Greek), *math*- 'eat' (O.
Ind.).

n: *Nase*; IE: *nāres* 'nostrils' (Latin), *nósis* (Lith.), *nasá* (O. Ind.).
Neffe; IE: *nepos* (Latin), *nápāt* (O. Ind.), *nei* (Welsh).

The semi-vowels [j, w] have been similarly persistent, although
the bilabial is now only dialectal, having otherwise become a
labiodental fricative within the last few centuries. *j*: *Joch*; IE:
iugum (Latin), *yugá*- (O. Ind.), *iau* (Welsh); *jung* (see above).
(*w*: *werden*; IE: *vertō* (Latin), *wrth* 'against' (Welsh), *vartati*
'turns' (O. Ind.); *Witwe* (see above).)

The one fricative of Indo-European (*s*) has changed its position
in the phonemic system and is usually voiced. Only in the medial
or final cluster with *t*, -*st*-, have we again a persistent feature:
Gast (Latin *hostis*). In the same position and as the second element
of the cluster [xt] *t* is the only plosive of venerable Indo-European
age, e.g. *Nacht* (Latin *noct*-), *acht* (Latin *octō*), *Haft* (Latin *captus*).

2.4.2 | Morphology

Among the Indo-European features of *morphology* there
are certain basic principles which are still in evidence in modern
German, for instance the close links of nouns and adjectives, both
of which have the categories of number and case, although now
only in rudimentary form. German still has three genders and
concord of noun and attributive adjective. The inflectional endings go back to a fusion of Indo-European stem suffixes and inflectional endings or to stem suffixes, cf. *Licht-er*: *gen-er-is*
(Latin); *Bot-en*: *hom-in-is* (Latin). Mutation (*Bach* – *Bäche*) is
also a reflex of an Indo-European stem suffix (-*i*- or *i*+vowel).

The only inflectional endings which can be said to be a last echo of Indo-European inflections are -s in the genitive singular of masculine and neuter and the nasal suffix in the dative plural (*Bach – Baches* < IE* -*so*/-*sio*; *Bäche – Bächen* < IE * -*mos*/-*mis*, for -*m* > -*n* see p. 169). It is also an Indo-European characteristic that the case endings are different in the singular and plural, unlike in some non-Indo-European languages where the same case marker is used in the singular and the plural. The function of the case inflection is still the same: to indicate the position or value of a word within a sentence, although its incidence is greatly diminished. Indo-European was a highly inflectional language, German is very much less so, although more than English.

The comparison of adjectives is still principally the same: by means of stem suffixation, and there are three grades (positive, comparative, superlative). The stem suffixes continue Indo-European suffixes with an -*s*- > -*r*- element in the comparative and an -*st*- element in the superlative. Indo-European had an *i*-element in front of both and this accounts for the incidence of mutation in many German adjectives (*arm – ärmer – am ärmsten*, for the forms with -*ō*- in OHG see p. 184).

The verb incorporates the categories of person and number (fused with each other), aspect or tense and mood, but not, for instance, gender (like some non-Indo-European languages). Beyond this we can merely say that the German verb makes use of Indo-European elements (vowel gradation; -*t*- suffix for past tense and past participle; mutation for mood distinction as a reflex of an Indo-European *i*-element; -*n* + dental plosive for present participle; -*n*- for infinitive), but it does so in a way which owes little to Indo-European. The clearest reflex of Indo-European is to be found in the personal endings of the present indicative: -*s*- of the second person singular, the dental of the third person singular and of the second person plural, and the nasal of the first and third persons plural. Both the dental plosive and the nasal have, of course, been subject to the phonological shifts which German has undergone. The difference between the endings of the present and the past of strong verbs, at least in the third person singular, -*t*/-*ø*: (er) *schwimmt*/*schwamm*, is also a reflex of a difference in the personal endings in Indo-European.

The German personal pronoun has retained the sex or gender distinction of the third person singular (but abandoned it in the plural) and has still asexual pronouns of the first and second persons. The first person has a nominative beginning with a vowel: *ich*, IE: *ego* (Latin), *egō* (Greek), *ahám* (O. Ind.), and oblique cases beginning with *m*-: *mich, mir, meiner,* IE: *mē, mihi* (Latin), *mām, mā* (O. Ind.).

The second person is well attested and fairly uniform throughout Indo-European: *du*; IE: *tū* (Latin), *tū* (O. Irish), *ti* (Welsh), *tù* (Lith.) etc.

As to derivation only obsolete, obscured suffixes remain of the Indo-European practice of derivation by means of suffixes and, to a lesser extent, prefixes, e.g. *t* in *Geburt – gebären*; *d* in *Freude – froh*; *n* in *Schwein – Sau*; *m* in *Blume – blühen*. But the method is basically preserved. There also remain fossilized forms in the derivation of verbs. For instance causatives could be formed in Indo-European by adding a suffix containing -*i*- to the *o*-grade of the root. This is reflected in such modern pairs as *trinken – tränken, sinken – senken*.

Composition was only one among many Indo-European means of distinguishing words from one another and of increasing the vocabulary. It has gained enormously in importance and is now by far the most important means in German. Many of the other methods of Indo-European have vanished altogether, for instance reduplication and stress alternation, or are found only as fossils (e.g. vowel gradation: *greifen – Griff*).

2.4.3 | Lexicon

The *lexicon* has always occupied an important position in Indo-European studies. The extent to which the Indo-European lexicon has been retained in German has frequently been described from a semantic and etymological point of view. Thus we find statements like: most kinship terms derive from Indo-European, e.g. *Vater, Mutter, Sohn, Tochter, Bruder, Schwester, Neffe* etc. Or, we are informed that animal names such as *Bock, Biber, Hahn* have Indo-European etymologies.

The following survey may give some idea of the semantic fields where we find substantial retention of Indo-European lexical items (on the plane of expression; the meanings are very much more problematic):

Man and his kin
Ahne (Enkel), Bruder, Erbe, (Bräuti)gam, Gast, Heer, Kind, König, Leute, Mann, Mutter (Muhme), Neffe, Nichte, Oheim, Schwager, Schwäher, Schwieger-, Schwester, Sohn, Tochter, Vater (Vetter), Waise, Wer(geld), Witwe.

The human body
Achsel, Ader, Arm, Auge, Bart, Braue, Ell(bogen), Fuß, Galle, Hals, Haupt, Haut, Herz, Hirn, Kehle, Kinn, Knie, Leib, Leiche, Mord, Mund, Nabel, Nagel, Nase, Niere, Ohr, Stirne, Tod, Zahn, Zunge.

Human habitation
Dach, Diele, Dorf, Garten, Giebel, Haus, Heim, Holz, Scheuer, Stall, Stuhl, Tor, Tür, Zimmer.

Animals
Aar, Biber, Bock, Eber, Elch, Ente, Ferkel, Fisch, Fohlen, Fuchs, Gans, Geiß, Hase, Hirsch, Hund, Igel, Kranich, Kuh, Luchs, Maus, Ochse, Otter, Sau, Schwein, Star, Stier, Vieh, Widder, Wiesel, Wolf. – Ei, Fell, Horn, Wolle.

Vegetation
Ahorn, Birke, Buche, Eibe, Eiche, Erle, Esche, Espe, Flachs, Föhre, Gerste, Hasel, Linde, Tanne.

The natural world
Acker, Ähre, Ast, Atem, Berg, Blatt, Blitz, Blume, Donner, Feuer, Flut, Furche, Halm, Heide, Jahr, Licht, Meer, Mond, Nacht, Nebel, Nest, Regen, Samen, Schatten, Schnee, Sommer, Stern, Strom, Wasser, Wind.

Tools and products
Achse, Ahle, Angel, Deichsel, Egge, Erz, Garn, Gold, Hammer, Joch, Korn, Malz, Met, Nabe, Nagel, Netz, Rad, Rechen, Ring, Ruder, Säge, Salbe, Salz, Teig, Zange, Zaun.

Some adjectives
alt, bar, dünn, eng, faul, gelb, (ge)mein, heil, jung, kalt, lang, lieb, mitten, nackt, neu, rot, sauer, süß, viel, voll, warm, weit.

Some verbs
(ge)bären, bauen, beißen, bieten, binden, brauen, decken, denken, dörren, drehen, essen, fahren, fangen, finden, flechten, fliegen, fließen, fragen, gehen, haben, hangen, heben, hehlen, heiraten, kann, kommen, lecken, leihen, lesen, liegen, mähen, mahlen, mahnen, melken, messen, mischen, nähen, nehmen, sagen, scheren, schwitzen, sehen, sitzen, spähen, speien, spinnen, stechen, stehen, steigen, sterben, streuen, suchen, trügen, tun, wachsen,

walten, weben, (be)wegen, werden, will, winden, (ge)winnen, wirken, wissen,
zähmen, zeigen, ziehen.

We shall now examine to what extent the words in a modern
German text are reflexes of Indo-European roots. The following
short text contains 115 roots or free morphemes, or 85 if those
occurring more than once are counted only once. Of these 85 roots
or free morphemes 61 are of undoubted Indo-European ancestry.
There are two kinds. The first (capitalized in the text) is composed
of more or less direct reflexes of probable Indo-European words.
The second kind, very much the larger numerically (italicized in
the text), consists of Germanic formations from Indo-European
roots.

ES jagte EIN*mal* EIN *König* IN EINem großen Wald, und jagte
EINem Wilde SO eifrig nach, DASS *niemand* von *sein*en *Leut*en *ihm*
folgen *konn*te; ZU*letzt* verIRRte ER *sich* und *fand* kein*en Ausgang.*
Da sah ER et*WAS auf sich* ZU*komm*en, DAS *ging wie* EINe ALTe
Frau, ge*bück*t und mit *wack*elndem Kopf, und *war ein*e ALTe Hexe.
*Der König red*ete *sie* AN und sprach: '*Zeigt mir doch den Weg durch den*
Wald.' 'O ja, *Herr König,*' ant*wort*ete *sie,* '*wenn* ihr *meine* TOCHTER
*heirat*en und ZUr *Frau König*in *mach*en *woll*t, *dann* soll'*s* ge*scheh*en,
sonst aber nicht, und ihr müßt HIER *bleib*en und *Hunger*s *sterb*en,
denn ihr *komm*t *nimmermehr ohne mich aus dem* Wald.'

Nearly all the remaining roots are Germanic: *jagen, von* (only
German and Dutch); *groß, Wald, und, Hexe* (West Germanic,
English: *great, weald – wold, and, hag*); *eifrig* (perhaps only
German). *Nach* (English *nigh – near – next*); *folgen (follow),*
sprechen (speak), wild, mit, sollen, aber, have some doubtful connections with roots in other Indo-European languages. *Kopf*
(English *cup, cop*) is a loanword from Latin *cuppa. Kein, sonst, ihr*
are German formations partly from Indo-European roots (see *ein,*
so, English *ye*); *müssen* may be a Germanic ō-grade derivation from
the root attested by *messen; ja* and *nicht* (Goth. *ni-waíht,* cf.
English *wight,* and negative particle *ni*) are Germanic.

A small, arbitrarily chosen sample can naturally not be ex-
ploited statistically. But it can show us how fundamental the Indo-
European lexical heritage is. The basic stock of roots from which
the German vocabulary is built up is to an overwhelming degree
Indo-European. If we take into account the natural rate of loss
with the passage of time and the new needs which arise through

the change of cultural and economic circumstances we can easily account for the present proportion of vocabulary inherited from Indo-European and of vocabulary the origin of which is not so identifiable. Furthermore, it must not be overlooked that comparative linguistics can only prove that a given lexical item *is* Indo-European in origin, never that it *is not*, on the basis of its occurrence in only one language.

2.4.4 | Onomastics

In *onomastics* (the study of proper names) the Indo-European foundations of German are, at least in two fields, also palpable.

In North Germany there are a number of river names with cognates in other Indo-European languages which show, through their participation in the later Germanic phonological developments, that they were current in the language in the Indo-European phase. If such roots exist also as appellatives there is of course no knowing at what time the names were coined, unless there is documentary evidence.

The name *Elbe* would seem to derive from an Indo-European root meaning 'white', attested in Greek and Latin (*albus*). *Saale* may contain an element meaning 'current' or 'flow', cf. Latin *salum* 'current'. *Weser* (oldest form *Visura*) probably derives from a root which occurs in Latin *vīrus* 'fluid' and corresponds to the English river name *Wear*. In many parts there are rivers called *Aa* or *Aach*, formed from the root which gives *aquā* in Latin. Krahe (p. 42) maintains that the word *Rhein*, OHG *Rīn*, formerly believed to be of Celtic origin, that is a loanword in German, is an autochthonous development of an Indo-European word meaning 'flow' (cf. Latin *rīvus*). The root vowel of hypothetical *Reinos*, *ei*, would become *ī* in Germanic, but *ē* in Celtic, whence the Latin form *Rhēnus*.

When German personal names were first recorded there appeared two types: a short form like *Otto* or *Karl* and a long dithematic form like *Friedrich* (< 'peace' + 'king') or *Wilhelm* (< 'will' + 'helmet'). It has been shown that the short form was affective and less formal, in fact more frequent in the lower strata of society than the long form, which may represent an aristocratic method of name-giving. The fact that both *Otto* and *Karl* were also names of kings is not an indication that the distinction was not of this kind at an earlier date. England too had its *Offa* beside *Edward* (< 'treasure' + 'protector'), and *Ethelred* (< 'noble' + 'advice'). The dithematic name is so widely current in many of the earliest attested Indo-European languages that it is assumed that it is the typical Indo-European form of personal name. For instance: Celtic *Caturix* (< 'fight' + 'king'), *Orgetorix* (< 'kill' + 'king'); Greek *Menelaos* (< 'support' + 'people'), *Nikandros* (< 'victory' + 'man'), *Demosthenes* (< 'people' + 'strength'). Monothematic names seem, however, to be just as old, and to be just as much Indo-European as the more aristocratic dithematic ones. The present practice of having *Fritz* beside *Friedrich*, or *Willy* beside *Wilhelm*, or *Bob* and *Robert*, *Bill* and *William*, may thus have a venerable age with roots in the Indo-European past.

Select Bibliography

H. Birnbaum, J. Puhvel, *Ancient Indo-European Dialects*, Berkeley, Los Angeles, 1966; G. Cardona, H. M. Hoenigswald, A. Senn (eds.), *Indo-European and Indo-Europeans*, Philadelphia, 1970; P. Friedrich, *Proto-Indo-European Trees*, Chicago, 1970; P. Hartmann, *Zur Typologie des Indogermanischen*, Heidelberg, 1956; H. Krahe, *Sprache und Vorzeit*, Heidelberg, 1954; W. P. Lehmann, *Proto-Indo-European Phonology*, Austin, 1952; id., 'A Definition of Proto-Germanic', *Lg.*, 37 (1961) 67–74; J. Pokorny, *Indogermanisches etymologisches Wörterbuch*, 2 vols., Berne, 1948–69; W. Porzig, *Die Gliederung des indogermanischen Sprachgebiets*, 2nd ed., Heidelberg, 1974; E. Pulgram, 'Indo-European Personal Names', *Lg.*, 23 (1947) 189–206; A. Scherer, *Die Urheimat der Indogermanen*, Darmstadt, 1968; F. Stroh, 'Indogermanische Ursprünge' in F. Maurer, H. Rupp, *Deutsche Wortgeschichte*, 3rd ed., Berlin, 1974, vol. 1, pp. 3–34.

The Germanic Basis

3.1 | The nature of Germanic

The Germanic phase is as obscure and hypothetical at its beginning as the Indo-European period. But it extends, at its close, almost to the confines of early history. While the layman would not regard the modern Indo-European languages such as Russian and English or Spanish and German as related, he would find so much affinity in the modern Germanic languages that he would readily accept them as members of a cognate group. The earliest recorded forms are so close to each other that to call them dialects is no exaggeration. Yet the problem is basically the same as with Indo-European. During a long period of probably two thousand years a language group formed which at the time of its emergence into history consisted of closely related languages. The earlier, genetic way of looking at language naturally saw these languages as descendants from one unitary original language, Proto-Germanic or *Urgermanisch*. There is no doubt, the degree of convergence is very great indeed. Yet, there is no proof that all passed through a uniform parent language. We must reckon with the spatial dimension in the case of Germanic as in any other language. Reconstruction remains a speculative exercise although less so than in the Indo-European phase. One early Germanic language (Gothic) has forms for the dual number in verbs. There is no certainty as to whether these are dialectal survivals from Indo-European or remnants of a dual number category existing in hypothetical Proto-Germanic. Some personal pronouns, e.g. German *er*, English *he*, are reflexes of Indo-European forms, but it is impossible to say what the Proto-Germanic form was unless we assert that the uniform parent language had more than one word for 'he'. Uniform languages do not usually have such a surfeit of forms.

Germanic is thus a linguistic phase and a linguistic complex with the usual dimensions of language rather than a uniform parent language ideally existing at a given point of time prior to the 'break-up' and the emergence of 'daughter languages'.

3.2 | Time and location

3.2.1 | The Germani

Scholars are in no doubt as to where this Germanic complex arose. Tacitus in his *Germania* expresses the view that the Germanic peoples were natives of their northern homeland and had been little affected by immigration or 'tainted by intermarriage', as he put it. The early historians of the Germanic peoples, Jordanes, Bede or Paulus Diaconus, were fully aware of the northern origins of their peoples. The Roman and Greek historians knew that the *Germani* had only relatively recently reached the Danube and the Rhine and started to cross them. Germany south of the Main and Bohemia were the homelands of Celtic peoples within their memory. The last few centuries B.C. were a period of great expansion which may have started around 750 B.C., when the rivers Vistula in the east and Ems in the west were reached. This was the Iron Age during which the contacts with the Celts and Illyrians were closest. The Bronze Age extending from before the middle of the second millennium B.C. to about 800 B.C. saw the actual formation of the Germanic (linguistically: Pre-Germanic) complex in southern Sweden, Denmark, Schleswig-Holstein and adjacent north-eastern Lower Saxony. North Germany between the rivers Weser (west), Oder (east) and the Harz mountains (south) was included early in their territory, probably by 1200 B.C. We saw in the last chapter that many archaeologists agree that the northern Stone Age funnel-necked beaker culture became the victim of an invasion towards the end of the Neolithic age, perhaps around 1800 B.C. The invaders were characterized by corded-ware and stone battle-axes and buried their dead in single barrows rather than in megalithic tombs which were characteristic of the northern zone of the previous culture. This invasion brought about the Indo-Europeanization of the north, according to many archaeologists. And the subsequent fusion produced the Germanic complex, which, again according to archaeologists, remained remarkably uniform and undisturbed throughout the Bronze Age.

Linguistic palaeontology has little to contribute to the question of the habitat. But it can confirm the importance of the sea, for much sea-faring terminology of the Germanic languages seems to have been formed in this phase. It can also confirm, on the basis of loanword traffic, that Celts and Finns were neighbours some time during this period.

The Romans called these people *Germani*. They received this name from the Gauls and it was apparently first the name of one tribe, the Tungri. It was subsequently extended to all the related northern peoples, when the Romans learnt to differentiate between the Celts and the *Germani*, in English also called the Teutons. Whether the word itself was Celtic or Germanic is uncertain. The Teutons appear not to have had a word to name their own tribes collectively.

3.2.2 | The periods

On the basis of external circumstances the Germanic period can be divided into two phases: the prehistorical and the early historical phase. On the basis of linguistic development we also arrive at two divisions. The earlier, Pre-Germanic, period is separated from the second, the Germanic period, by the bundle of linguistic changes which linguists regard as most characteristic of Germanic. The two kinds of divisions do not quite coincide. The linguistic dividing line predates the external division by 300 to 500 years.

First phase (external): prehistorical; only archaeological evidence; contacts with Celts and Finns.

Second phase (external): historical; Greek and Roman reports of an historical, ethnographical kind on the Germanic peoples, from 200 B.C. onwards.

First linguistic phase: Pre-Germanic, sharing isoglosses with Italic, Illyrian, Venetic, Celtic, Baltic, etc. Doubtful early loans to Finnish. Some loans from Celtic. Gradual restructuring of language, possibly under some substratum influence.

Second linguistic phase: Proto-Germanic, divided from the first phase by fundamental phonological changes (500–300 B.C.): accentual shift; consonantal shift (three Indo-European plosive series replaced by two Germanic fricative series and one plosive series). The earlier period of convergence is replaced by increasing divergence. The following sources date from the period of divergence (Late Germanic): loanwords in Finnish; lexical items (words and names) in classical sources; and the earliest inscriptions in the Germanic alphabet, the runes, from about A.D. 200; absorption of Latin loanwords during the Roman presence in northern Europe.

We assign a much longer space of time to the early periods, both linguistic and external, than to the later period. Scholars (e.g. Fourquet, Lehmann, van Coetsem) increasingly see Germanic as a relatively conservative Indo-European tongue which underwent fairly late the salient fundamental changes which characterize it, that is only a few centuries before the inception of historical records. Once all those features which we regard as typically Germanic were present, relative unity must soon have given way to divergence. Some, for instance *i*-mutation, seem to have taken place during the period of rapidly increasing differentiation. The separation of the individual tribal languages, developments of which finally saw the light of day with the advent of full literacy in the fifth century, in the case of Gothic, or the eighth century, in the case of German and English, must have taken place in the first centuries of our era.

3.2.3 | Time-scale diagram of Germanic

(1) On the top horizontal line are the contemporary standard or national languages. Those bracketed have not fully achieved this status but rank above dialects.

(2) Unbroken lines indicate an uninterrupted, more or less direct continuation from the earliest recorded form. A dotted line above a recorded language indicates a somewhat less direct or to some extent broken tradition; below a recorded language it indicates a conjectured line of development and may include sporadic recording, e.g. Runic, or words in classical sources.

(3) The development lines from the earliest recorded stages (OE, OLFranc., OHG, ON) onwards are simplified since the outcome was not predetermined. The reasons why in Britain only one Germanic standard language, in Scandinavia three and on the Continent two standard languages, German and Dutch, developed are political, economic and cultural. An observer in the late Middle Ages, aware of the intensifying trends towards unity, might have predicted that there would eventually (i.e. eighteenth–twentieth century) be one or three or four continental Germanic standard languages. Equally there are no *linguistic* reasons why the present state of affairs should persist.

(4) The ringed groupings show the geographical centres of Late Germanic although they cannot be placed in a geographically realistic manner

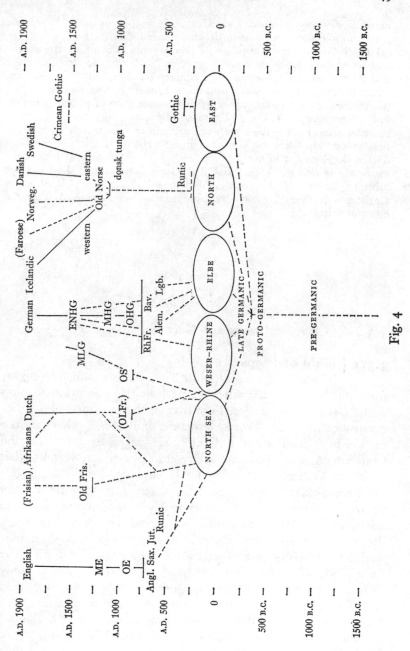

Fig. 4

in relation to one another. Late Germanic is the period of divergence prior to the emergence of the individual recorded languages.

(5) Proto-Germanic is the phase of convergence marked by the accentual innovation which delimits it against Pre-Germanic. Pre-Germanic and Proto-Germanic together are characterized by all those features which differentiate Germanic from other Indo-European tongues.

(6) While the western languages, with the exception of Frisian, are first fully documented between A.D. 700 and 850, the one eastern language recorded dates back to the fourth century and the northern branch to the twelfth century, although earlier Runic inscriptions throw some light on the development of early Norse and even on features of Late Germanic. It is also not immaterial that Gothic was recorded within the orbit of Greek and the western languages within the orbit of Latin Christianity, while the northern branch was more removed from the classical world.

3.3 | Classification of the Germanic languages

3.3.1 | Main divisions

There are two fixed points, nearly a thousand years apart, from which we can start when we wish to arrive at a classification of the Germanic languages. First there is the hypothetical point of greatest convergence, Proto-Germanic, and secondly there are the earliest fully documented individual languages. Starting from the later, more assured point we arrive at a tripartition. Scandinavian or North Germanic forms a clearly circumscribed, sharply defined complex from which both the much earlier Gothic and the various western dialects are obviously distinguished. But the relationship of the western dialects to one another and to Scandinavian and Gothic, and the relationship of Gothic and Scandinavian to each other are much more problematical. Till after the First World War, and often even later, the relationship was mainly seen as a genetic one. Proto-languages, such as West Germanic, East Germanic and North Germanic, were interposed between Proto-Germanic and the historical languages. The genealogical tree threw out its usual luxuriant growth of branches, for instance Anglo-Frisian and Proto-German from Proto-West-Germanic.

While the pattern remained basically the same there was no shortage of ingenious variations. Finally the impact of dialect geography added a new dimension and shattered the one-sided genetic view.

It can be shown that every early Germanic language is linked to others by certain shared innovations and retentions. Some links are strong, others are weak, some appear to have been formed early, some late. This is the sort of picture one would expect in the case of various degrees of dialect contiguity. In view of the fairly great mobility of early Germanic peoples the neighbourhood pattern must have altered in the course of time. The Roman and Greek reports show, for instance, the Langobards along the lower Elbe in the vicinity of the Saxons and other tribes of the North Sea littoral. A few hundred years later they are close neighbours of the Bavarians and Alemannians and their language appears to have been an OHG dialect. Old Saxon has features which place it in the vicinity of Anglo-Saxon and Frisian, and others which point to greater affinity with High German. Tribal movements must obviously have led to different contacts at different times. In fact it is unwise to separate the space and time axes.

F. Maurer has pointed out that the classical reports seem to agree – as much as they may disagree in detail and mention of individual tribes – in dividing Germania into five groups. A large central group on both sides of the Lower Elbe, later extending southwards into Bohemia and to the Danube, is termed *Suebi* or *Herminones*. Tribes belonging to this group were the Semnones, Hermunduri, Langobardi, Marcomanni, Quadi and others, while doubt exists as to whether the Chatti (Pliny) and the renowned Cherusci also belonged to this group. From the third century of our era onwards a new tribal league came into existence, the Alemanni. The Bavarians also, first mentioned even later, would appear to have derived from this central complex. This is Maurer's *Elbe-Germanic* group. It obviously occupied a most important position and retained strong links to the north before finally moving off into a southern and south-western direction.

East of the river Oder there was a group about which the classical writers knew less. But they agree that the Vandili, Lugii, Gutones, Burgundiones, Rugii and others belonged to it. The term East-Germanic is well established for this group. F. Maurer called them *Oder-Weichsel Germanen* or *Illeviones*. Jordanes relates that the Goths arrived from Scandinavia and then settled in *Gothiscandia* on the shore of the Baltic near the mouth of the Vistula. Although this is not the region in which the classical authors sited them, Jordanes' account was usually believed.

To the north of the central group come the tribes 'nearest the ocean' as Tacitus had it or Maurer's *North-Sea Germanic* group. Classical writers used the term *Ingvaeones* for a tribal, possibly religious league in this region and called a similar group worshippers of Nerthus, or Mother Earth. Among the tribes usually assigned to this group are the Saxones, Anglii, Eudoses, Cimbri, Teutoni and perhaps the Frisii.

The ancient writers knew hardly anything of the northernmost tribes in Scandinavia proper, except the name of the Suiones, the forebears of the Swedes.

The largest number of tribes that are named lived in the west nearest the Rhine. The name *Istvaeones* occurs in Tacitus and Pliny and has often been applied to the western group, which Maurer calls *Weser-Rhein Germanen*.

In the third century most of the tribal names current from Caesar onwards, of which some two hundred are recorded, went out of use. Large tribal leagues were now facing the Roman frontiers: the Saxons threatened the sea coasts, the Franks the Lower Rhine (Germania Inferior), the Alemannians the Upper Rhine (Germania Superior) and Danube frontiers. At this time communication with the Scandinavian tribes must have become tenuous. The formation of the Scandinavian group must be dated from the third or fourth century, while the contact between the Elbe, Weser-Rhine and North Sea groups was intensified and may have led to the spread of those linguistic features known as West Germanic.

If it was wrong to posit three proto-languages (West, North, East Germanic) it would now be equally wrong to see the five geographical complexes as sharply defined units. We must reckon with transitions in time and in space and see the groups primarily as centres of gravity. The 'Ingvaeonic' features and the 'Herminonic' features of Old Saxon, for instance, may indicate that Saxon was a border dialect between the North-Sea group and the Elbe group. Or they may indicate a geographical shift from one area to the other. A further complication arises from the tribal nomenclature. We do not know whether the third-century Saxons, the seventh- and eighth-century Saxons of England (e.g. Wessex), and the eighth-century Saxons of North Germany conquered by Charlemagne, were the same people or not. We do not know with what tribal background we have to reckon for Old Saxon recorded in the ninth century. Tribal names are easily detached from one people and attached to another. The same is true of languages. The Normans of the ninth century were Scandinavians speaking Norse. The Normans of the eleventh century spoke a French dialect. The large tribal league of the Franks is linguistically very problematical. It is to be assumed that most of the small tribes regarded as Istvaeonic or Weser-Rhine Germanic merged in the Frankish league. But did that produce a uniform dialect? The later linguistic development makes it seem more unlikely than likely. Yet, the suggestiveness of the tribal unity is great and even Ludwig Rösel who has given a sensible description of the Germanic linguistic relations assumes a Frankish linguistic unity. But we have no information on the linguistic composition and situation of the Frankish tribal league.

3.3.2 | Maps

Two maps will show the location of the most important Germanic tribes and the linguistic grouping:

Fig. 5 shows the location of some Germanic tribes in the first two centuries of our era, as mentioned by Tacitus, Pliny and Ptolemy. Only those are given whose subsequent history makes them important. Some of the names of the first two centuries, for instance, Anglii, Frisii and Langobardi, are also current in the subsequent centuries. Others, for instance, Semnones, Cherusci and Quadi, disappear. In their stead we have, from the third century onwards, the names of the Franks and Alemannians.

Fig. 6 shows the geographical-linguistic grouping of the first few centuries.

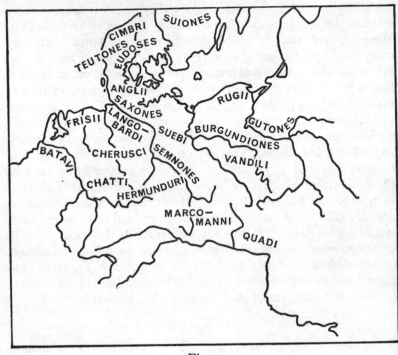

Fig. 5

Key to Fig. 6

Oder-Vistula Germanic or East Germanic (Illevionic).

Elbe-Germanic (Herminonic).

Weser-Rhine Germanic (Istvaeonic).

North-Sea Germanic (Ingvaeonic).

North Germanic (Scandinavian) was probably formed later after the great migrations had begun (third century).

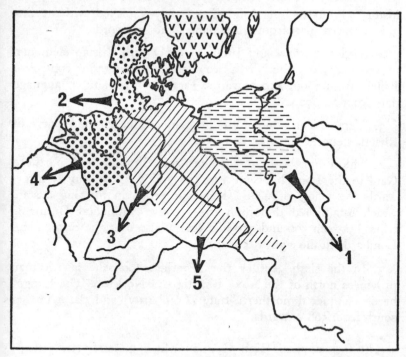

Fig. 6

The arrows indicate the direction of the subsequent migrations:

1. The Goths moved to the regions north of the Black Sea probably about A.D. 200. The kingdom they founded there was overwhelmed by the Huns towards the end of the fourth century. Some Goths sought refuge in the Eastern Roman Empire and embraced Christianity in the form of Arianism. Later two branches of the Goths, first the Visigoths, then the Ostrogoths, moved west and set up new kingdoms: the Visigoths in south-western France (Toulouse) and later in Spain (419–711), the Ostrogoths in Italy (488–552). The first bishop of the Goths, Wulfila (318–388), translated the Bible into Gothic (about 375), for which purpose he created an alphabet based mainly on Greek. It is a part of this Bible translation which has come down to us as the first substantial document in a Germanic dialect. While other East Germanic tribes such as the Vandals and Burgundians had no less a stirring

history of far-reaching migrations, they vanished without linguistic traces apart from a few names and loanwords.

2. Angles, Saxons, and Jutes, possibly with Frisian elements,
moved west along the North Sea coast and finally took control of
Britain from about 450 onwards. First records of their language
date from A.D. 700.

3. Alemannians conquered Germania Superior and parts of
Rhaetia between A.D. 300 and 450.

4. The Franks conquered Germania Inferior and northern
Gaul to the Loire between A.D. 400 and 500 and shortly afterwards the whole of Gaul. They succeeded in forming a state
which established dominion over many continental Germanic
tribes between 500 and 550 and finally also over the Saxons and
Lombards in the eighth century.

5. In the sixth century the Bavarians took the last Roman
provinces north of the Alps, Rhaetia and Noricum. The Langobards conquered northern Italy (Lombardy) and parts farther
south from 568 onwards.

The formation of High German which gradually took shape
between the third and eighth centuries must be seen as the result
of the convergence and fusion of tribal languages originally
belonging to the Elbe and Weser-Rhine groups. Its centre of
gravity lay in the former Celtic and Roman provinces along the
Danube and the Rhine. From quite early on it exercised influence
on the North-Sea dialects whose speakers had remained on the
continent and who eventually became united politically with the
tribes farther south. The Merovingian Frankish empire provided
the frame for the linguistic convergence which the migrations and
new settlements had prepared.

3.3.3 | Parallel texts

To illustrate some of the linguistic features of the early
Germanic dialects we shall consider a parallel text.

The Lord's Prayer

	Gothic	ON	OE	OFris.	OS	OHG (Rh.Fr.)	OHG (Alem.)
(1)							
(2)	atta	faþer	fæder	feder	fadar	fater	fater
(3)	unsar,	várr,	ūre	ūser,	ūsa,	unsēr,	unseer,
(4)	þu	(sa)þū	þū(þe)	thū(thi)	thu	thu	thū
(5)	is	ert	eart		bist		pist
(6)	in	ī	on	in	an	in	in
(7)	himinam,	hifne	heofonum,	himele	(them himila rīkea)	himilom	himile,
(8)	weihnai	helgesk	sī	ewīed sie	geuuihid sī	bist, giuuihit sī	uuihi
(9)	namo	nafn	þīn nama	thīn nama.	thīn namo.	namo thīn,	namun dinan,
(10)	þein	þitt	gehālgod;				
(11)	Qimai	Tilcome	Tōbecume	Kume	Cuma	queme	qhueme
(12)	þiudinassus þeins	þitt rike	þīn rīce;	thīn rīke.	thīn rīki.	rīchi thīn.	rīhhi dīn,
(13)	Wairþai	Verþe	Geweorþe	Werthe	Uuerða	uuerdhe	uuerde
(14)	wilja þeins,	þinn vile	þīn willa	thīn willa,	thīn uuilleo	uuilleo thīn,	uuillo dīn,

	Gothic	ON	OE	OFris.	OS	OHG (Rh. Fr.)	OHG (Alem.)
(15)	swe in himina jah ana airþai.	suā ā iǫrþ sem ā hifne.	on eorþan swā swā on heofonum.	on ertha alsa in himele.	sō sama an erðo, sō an them himilo rīkea.	sama sō in himile endi in erthu.	sō in himile sōsa in erdu.
(16)	Gif uns	Gef oss	Syle ūs	Jef ūs	Gef ūs	Gib uns	Kib uns
(17)	himma daga	ídag	tō-dæg	hiū-dega	dago	hiutu	hiutu
(18)		vārt dagligt	ūrne gedæg= hwāmlican	ūser degelik	gehuuilikes		
(19)	hlaif unsarana þana sinteinan.	brauþ.	hlāf;	hlef	rād,	broot unseraz emezzigaz.	prooth unseer emezzihic,
(20)	Jah aflēt uns	Ok fyrerlāt oss	And forgyf ūs	And forjef ūs	endi ālāt ūs	Endi farlāz uns	oblāz uns
(21)	þatei skulans sijaima,	ossar skulder	ūre gyltas,	ūsere skelda,	managoro mēnsculdio,	sculdhi unsero,	sculdi unseero,
(22)	swaswe jah	suā sem	swā swā	al sa	al sō	sama sō	sō

	Gothic	ON	OE	OFris.	OS	OHG (Rh. Fr.)	OHG (Alem.)
(23)	weis aflētam þaim skulam unsaraim.	vēr fyrerlātom ossom skuldo- nautom.	wē forgyfaþ ūrum gyltendum.	wī forjevath ūserum skeldichium.	uuē (ōðrum mannum dōan.)	uuir farlāzzēm scolōm unserēm.	uuir oblāzēm uns skuldikēm,
(24)	Jah ni briggais uns in	Ok inn leiþ oss eige ī	And ne gelǣd þū ūs on	And ne lēd ūs in	Ne lāt ūs (farlēdean lētha wihti,)	endi ni gileidi unsih in	enti ni unsih firleiti in
(25)	fraistubnjai, ak	freistne. (Heldr frels þū)	costnunge ac	forsēkinge(?) āk	ac help	costunga. auh	khorunka, ūzzer
(26)	lausei		ālȳs	ālēs		arlōsi	lōsi
(27)	uns	oss	ūs	ūs	ūs	unsih	unsih
(28)	af	af	of	of	uuithar (allun	fona	fona
(29)	þamma ubilin.	illo.	yvele.	evel.	uƀilon dādiun).	ubile.	ubile.

Comments

(1) a. The Gothic version is Matthew 6, 9–13 of the Uppsala *codex argenteus* (*c.* A.D. 500). A reproduction of part of the passage is found in W. Braune and E. A. Ebbinghaus, *Gotische Grammatik*, 16th ed. 1961.

b. The OE text is found in W. W. Skeat (ed.), *The Gospel according to St. Matthew in Anglo-Saxon*. It is in the West Saxon dialect of the tenth century.

c. No OFris. text has come down to us. The version given here is a word-for-word rendering to facilitate comparison.

d. The OS text is *Heliand*, 1600–1609, a free version in alliterative verse with several accretions which have been omitted. It dates from about A.D. 830.

e. The OHG versions are in the South Rhenish Franconian dialect of the *Weissenburger Katechismus* of about A.D. 800 and the Alemannic dialect of the *St. Gallen Paternoster* of about A.D. 790.

(2) The words for 'father' show

a. the preservation of Gmc. $\eth < \flat^1 <$ IE -t^1- in Gothic (the word *fadar*, $d = \eth$, is attested) and ON, while it is shifted to d in all western dialects;

b. western $d > t$ in OHG, which forms a step in the High German Sound Shift (see also 24a): ON $\flat$: OE, OFris., OS d:OHG t;

c. the Anglo-Frisian palatalization of a under certain conditions, cf. (18) *dæge* and OFris. *dega* or *dei*.

(3) The possessive adjectives show

a. a new development in ON, although the root corresponding to Gothic *unsar-* is found in *ossar* acc. pl. fem. and *ossom* dat. pl. masc.;

b. OE, OFris., OS show the so-called 'Ingvaeonic' loss of n before a fricative, while n is preserved in Gothic and OHG. Cf. *five*: *fünf*; *goose*: *Gans*; *other*: *ander*. When German dialect geography showed n-less forms in Alemannic (*öis, föif*) F. Wrede used it as evidence for his West Germanic theory, according to which an older West Germanic unity was broken up by a Gothic thrust into south-eastern German. High German appeared to him as a kind of 'gotisiertes Westgermanisch'. However, it has been shown that the Alemannic loss of n is much later and unconnected with the 'Ingvaeonic' phenomenon; the Alemannic OHG form *unseer* proves the loss to be post-OHG. The ON forms *ossar, ossom* and *oss* (17) also show loss of n. This loss is probably linked with the 'Ingvaeonic' phenomenon which may thus be dated back to the old close North-Sea Germanic and North Germanic link. The 'Ingvaeonic' features of continental dialects have been under pressure from HG ever since the latter's supremacy was established. Thus MLG has *uns* for OS *ūs*. In Dutch, which has *ons*, 'Ingvaeonic' forms survive dialectally.

(4) The Latin *qui es* inspired the ON and OE relative constructions *sa þū* and *þū þe*, while the other languages leave the relative element unexpressed.

(5) Only Gothic has the IE (Latin *es*) form. ON *ert* replaced an earlier *est*. OE and OHG continue different IE roots.

(6) OE *on* exemplifies the Anglo-Frisian rounding of *a* before a nasal in a closed syllable, see OE *Englalond* 'England'. Most of these forms were later changed to *a* again: *and, land, can* but *on* (German *an*).

(7) Most Gmc. versions (except ON and Alem.) follow the Semiticism of Greek and Latin and use the plural. The oldest form is Gothic *himin-s* (nom. sg.). Dissimilation of the two nasals in two different directions (*m > f* or *n > l*) may have led to the northern forms (ON, OE) and southern form (OHG) respectively. On the other hand *-l-* and *-n-* may be reflexes of different IE suffixes. OS demonstrates its position between OE and OHG by having both *heƀan* and *himil*.

(8) The Latin subjunctive passive *sanctificetur* and the corresponding Greek form are rendered in three different ways:

    a. Gothic has a weak class of verbs in *-nan* with inchoative meaning ('become holy');

    b. ON uses the newly formed synthetic passive (originally reflexive: *sik* (Gm. *sich*) added to the verbal root);

    c. the western Gmc. languages form a new synthetic passive with the verb 'to be' (here subjunctive present) and the past participle. But the Alem. author simply uses the subj. pres. of the active (hence *namo* in the acc.).

(9) a. Here and elsewhere we note that the Gmc. languages differ more in their unstressed forms than the stressed roots. Ever since the dynamic stress was fixed on the root syllable the unstressed elements were exposed to weakening.

    b. ON has again dissimilation *namn- > nafn*. Here this otherwise masc. noun is neuter, which is evident from the ending of the poss. adj.: *þîn + t* with typical ON assimilation of *nt > tt*.

(10) The Greek and Latin texts have the sequence noun plus poss. adj. (*pater noster, nomen tuum*). This was followed regularly by Wulfila and the OHG authors. OS, OE and ON have the more usual Gmc. word order, e.g. *þîn nama, þîn rîce, þîn willa*.

(11) The verb 'to come' has two different vowel grades in the Gmc. languages. Grade 1 (IE *e*) in Gothic *qiman* and OHG *queman* and zero grade (IE*m̥*) in ON, OE, OS (*koma, cuman*). In OHG *koman* and *cuman* are also attested.

(12) a. Gothic has an abstract noun from the root *þiuda* 'people', *þiudans* 'king', *þiudanon* 'to rule'. But it also has the word *reiki* (*ei* = [iː]), a common Gmc. loanword from Celtic (see p. 121).

    b. OHG *-ch-:-k-* in the other languages is a feature resulting from the Second Sound Shift, see 2b, 13a, 16b, 19b, 21a (see also pp. 167–77).

(13) a. As a corollary to the Second Sound Shift of OHG, Gmc. *th* became *d* via *dh* (*d* having become *t*). This occurred first in Upper German (Alem. and Bav.) and later in Rhen. Franc., hence we have (10) *thîn:dîn* (three times), (15) *erthu:erdu*, (22) *sculdhi:sculdi*, and here *uuerdhe:uuerde*. The Alem. scribe was aware of the graph ⟨*th*⟩ and used it without significance in (19) *prooth*, and in (4) *thu*, perhaps remembering such a spelling in MSS he had seen.

b. OE shows a phenomenon known as breaking or fracture: *e* > *eo*, e.g. before *r* +consonant, (15) *eorþan*, (5) *eart*, and before *o/a* of the next syllable: *heofonum* (7, 15).

(14) All WGmc. languages show doubling of consonants after a short vowel and before a following *j* or, less frequently, *r* and *l*. Cf. Gothic *wilja*: WGmc. *willa*. This change did not affect ON or Gothic, and attests to the powerful link between the WGmc. dialects at a certain point in time.

(15) ON also underwent 'breaking', caused by a former *-u*: *iǫrþ*.

(16) a. The Latin and Greek texts begin this sentence with the object phrase: *panem nostrum quotidianum da nobis hodie*. This order is also followed by the Gothic, OE and OHG translators, while the others begin with the verb phrase. In order to facilitate comparison I have rearranged all sentences in this way.

b. The OHG words show two phenomena connected with the Second Sound Shift: the Upper German spelling *k* indicating a voiceless stop for Gmc. *g* (see also the second *k* in *skuldikēm* and *khorunka*), and *b*, a stop for Gmc. *ƀ*, a fricative. Cf. English *give, live, seven, wife* and German *geben, leben, sieben, Weib*.

c. OE has the verb *giefan* as well. Initial *g* was a palatal fricative: an example of Anglo-Frisian palatalization. *Siellan* 'to endow' > *sell*, Gothic *saljan*, is another example of WGmc. doubling of consonants caused by *j* (see 14). It also shows *i*-mutation (see 29). For *ie* late OE spelt *y* (<*sielle, gief, giefaþ, ālies*).

(17) See (3b).

(18) a. See (2c).

b. The word for 'day' shows the tripartite division of the Gmc. languages: Gothic *dags* (*-s* < *-az*), ON *dagr, dagaR* (*r* < *z*), OE *dæg*, OFris. *dei* (endingless, with palatalization of *g*), OS *dag*, OHG *tag, tac* (endingless, OS with final fricative and OHG with shifted *d* > *t* and final voiceless plosive).

(19) a. The Gmc. languages have two synonyms for 'bread': Gothic *hlaifs*, ON *hleifr*, OE *hlāf* (*loaf*), OHG *leib* (*Laib*), probably relating to the shape and size or portion, and ON *brauþ*, OE *brēad*, OS *brōd*, OHG *brōt* cognate with 'brew' and probably referring to the process of making bread. OS *rād* 'support' is a free rendering. W. Krogmann (in L. E. Schmitt, *Kurzer Grundriß*, p. 217) made the ingenious suggestion that *rād* was a misunderstood, copied form from an earlier *brād* (=Frisian for 'bread') showing the strong Frisian element within OS.

b. Alemannic *p-* for WGmc. *b-* is part of the second step of the OHG Sound Shift: *b d g* > *p t k* of which *d* > *t* is general, *b g* > *p k* only early Alem. and Bav. See 5 *pist*, 2b, 13a, 16b.

(20) Cf. WGmc. *and–endi* (see 29) as against Gothic and ON.

(21) Gothic *lētan* 'to let', OE *lǣtan*, OFris. *lēta*, OS *lātan*, OHG *lāzzan* show

a. the OHG Sound Shift of *-t-* > *zz* (*ss*), cf. *-k-* > *-hh- -ch-* (12b), *-p-* > *-ff-* (*open–offen*);
b. Gothic *ē* as against WGmc. and ON *ā* with Anglo-Frisian palatalization *ā* > *ǣ, ē*.

(22) See 29.

(23) Gmc. *-z* is hardened to *-s* in final position in Gothic, in ON > *r*, in OHG (in pronouns) > *r*, but in North-Sea Gmc. it is lost, cf. 18b.

(24) Gothic uses the verb 'to bring' (*-gg-* is [ŋg]). The other verbs show
a. the ON *þ*: WGmc. *d*: OHG *t* correspondence (see 2b) with Rhenish Franconian remaining on the WGmc. level;
b. Gmc. *ai* > ON *ei*; > OE *ā*, or *ǣ* if mutated; >OS *ē* (*lēdean*); > OHG *ei*, or *ē* in certain cases.

(25) Latin *temptatio* is a Christian concept which poses the problem of the creation of a Christian vocabulary in the pagan Gmc. languages.

(26) Gmc. *au* > Gothic *au*; > OE *ēa*, and *ie* if mutated; >OHG *ou*, or *ō* according to certain conditions.

(27) and (17) show that OHG distinguished acc. pl. *unsih* from dat. pl. *uns* unlike the other Gmc. languages which had *uns, oss, ūs* although OE had a corresponding relic form *ūsic*.

(28) Only the continental Gmc. languages have the preposition OHG *fona*, OS OFris. *fan* while it is not found in Gothic, OE or ON.

(29) English *ill* is a loanword from ON *illr*; *evil* is the inherited word. While Gothic *ubils* shows no signs of *i*-mutation in its spelling, this had already taken effect in OE *yvel* and in OFris. *evel*. OE ⟨y⟩ was the graphic sign for mutated *u*. The later spelling ⟨e⟩ (*evil*) and OFris. *evel* show the next stage of unrounding of *i*-mutated vowels. OHG had probably reached the stage of allophonic split where /u/ was [y] before *i* and [u] before other vowels. Only one *i*-mutated vowel is indicated in OHG spelling: *e* (<*a+i, j*), cf. 20 *endi* (<*andi*).

3.3.4 | The Western Group

The study of German and Dutch dialects has revealed that there is a gradual but steady change of language type as one proceeds from south, that is High German, to north, and that the northernmost type of western Germanic is in fact English. In this section of the chapter on the classification of the Germanic languages we will first examine the features shared by all dialects of the western group and then conclude with a confrontation of those features of German and English which characterize their earliest stages and which may thus reflect the early distinction between North-Sea Germanic and Elbe Germanic.

(i) *West Germanic*

(1) Doubling of consonants, except *r*, caused by following *j*, and to a lesser extent, by following *r* or *l*: Gothic *satjan*, ON *setia*: OE *settan* 'to set', OHG *sezzen* (NHG *setzen*); Gothic *bidjan*, ON *biðia*: OE *biddan* 'to bid', OHG *bitten* (NHG *bitten*, ⟨tt⟩ is now only a spelling device); ON *eple*: E *apple*, Gm. *Apfel*. Early Latin loanwords were affected too: *putjus* (< *puteus*): OE *pytt* 'pit', Gm. *Pfütze*. Terminus post quem of this sound-shift may thus be about A.D. 200.

(2) Gmc. *ð* > *d*: Gothic *gards*, *garda* (⟨d⟩ = *ð* between vowels), ON *garðr* (hence the northern English name *garth*): OE *geard* 'yard', OHG *gart* (WGmc. *d* > HGm. *t*, *Garten*).

(3) Final Gmc. -*z* disappeared: Gothic *bairhts*, ON *biartr*: OE *briht* 'bright', OHG *beraht*; Gothic *hairdeis*, ON *hirðir*: OE *hierde* '(shep)herd', OHG *hirti*, NHG *Hirt*.

(4) 2nd pers. sg. pret. of strong verbs ends in -*i* and has the root vowel of the stem form of the pl.: Gothic *banst* (1st pers.: *band*, pl. *bundum*), ON *bazt*: OE *bunde* (1st pers.: *band*, pl. *bundon*), OHG *bunti* (1st pers.: *bant*, pl. *buntum*).

(5) Gen. and dat. of infinitive with a* -*ja*- suffix: OE *niman* 'to take': *nimannes*, *to nimanne*; OHG *neman* 'nehmen': *nemannes*, *nemanne*.

(6) No fourth class of weak verbs with inchoative meaning as found in Gothic, e.g. *waknan* 'to become awake'.

(7) Weak and strong declensions of the present participle.

(8) Masc. forms of the numeral 'two' with -*n*- element. Gothic *twai*: OE *twēgen*, OHG *zwēne*.

(9) The suffixes -*heit*/-*hood*, also -*schaft*/-*ship*, -*tum*/-*dom*: *Falschheit* – *falsehood*, *Freundschaft* – *friendship*, *Königtum* – *kingdom*.

(10) A common stock of words, e.g. *beide* – *both*; *Faust* – *fist*; *Flachs* – *flax*; *Geist* – *ghost*; *groß* – *great*; *Henne* – *hen*; *Herd* – *hearth*; *klein* – *clean*; *Knecht* – *knight*; *krähen* – *crow*; *kühl* – *cool*; *machen* – *make*; *mähen* – *mow*; *Nachbar* – *neighbour*; *Nachtigall* – *nightingale*; *sprechen* – *speak*; *Schaf* – *sheep*; *tun* – *do*; *wandern* – *wander*; and others.

(ii) *Differences between North-Sea Germanic (English in par-*

ticular) and German. (Again wherever possible modern examples are chosen as illustrations.)

(1) Long and short Gmc. *a* are palatalized in English in most conditions: *cat, that* [æ]: *Katze, das; year, sheep, eel: Jahr, Schaf, Aal.*

(2) Before a nasal long and short *a* become *o*: *long, on, comb*: *lang, an, Kamm* (but see p. 61) ; OE *mōna* 'moon', *spōn* 'spoon': OHG *māno* (*Mond*), *Span.*

(3) Gmc. *ai* > OE *ā* (later > *o*), OS *ē*: *home, bone: Heim, Bein; sore, soul: sehr, Seele* (split in German, see pp. 156-8).

(4) Gmc. *au* > *ēa* in OE, > *ā* in Fris., > *ō* in OS but > *ou* (later *au*) or *ō* in OHG (again split in German, see pp. 156- 8): *beam, seam, bean, bread: Baum, Saum, Bohne, Brot.*

(5) Gmc. *k* and *g* are palatalized before original palatal vowels: *chin, church, stitch: Kinn, Kirche, Stich* (*ch* < *k*); *yellow, yield, rain, slay: gelb, gelten, Regen, schlagen; ridge, hedge: Rücken, Hecke* (*gg* > *ck* in German). In OS there are only few traces of the palatalization of *k*.

(6) Gmc. medial and final postvocalic *ƀ* > *v* or *f*, but plosive *b* in German: *seven, self: sieben, selb.*

It is possible that the High German Sound Shift arose on the basis of an ancient 'Herminonic' consonantal correlation of intensity as opposed to an 'Ingvaeonic' correlation of voice.

(7) A Gmc. nasal before fricatives (*f, s, þ*) is eliminated: *south, soft, five, mouth: Sund(gau), sanft, fünf, Mund* (*th* > *d* in Gm.).

(8) Gmc. *j* in short verbal roots becomes *w*: *mow, sow, throw*: *mähen, säen, drehen* (MHG *mæjen, sæjen, dræjen*).

(9) Frequent occurrence of *r*-metathesis in NWGmc.: *burn, third, horse, -bourne: brennen, dritt, Roß, -brunn* (cf. *Schönbrunn* (South German) and *Paderborn* (North German)).

(10) One ending for all three persons of pl. pres. indic.: OE *we, ge, hie maciaþ*, modern Low Saxon dialect *wi, ji, si mak(e)t*: OHG *wir machōmēs, ir machōt, sie machōnt.*

(11) Voiceless *th* in the ending of 3rd pers. sg.: *he maketh* (now archaic): *er macht* (Gm. *t* < WGmc. *d* < Gmc. voiced *ð*).

(12) No reflexive pronoun corresponding to German *sich.* Dutch has *zich*, possibly from a southern dialect, and Low German later formed an analogous *sik.*

(13) Personal pronouns *he, him*: Gm. *er, ihm.*

(14) Pronouns without *-r* (< Gmc. *-z*): *we, who, me, thee, ye*: *wir, wer, mir, dir, ihr.*

(15) Consequential non-distinction of acc. and dat. in pers. pron. of 1st and 2nd pers.: *me, thee: mich, mir, dich, dir.*

(16) One important noun class has pl. ending (nom. and acc.) in -*s*: OE *dagas* 'days', *stānas* 'stones': Gm. *Tage, Steine.*

(17) Numerous lexical items are specifically North-West Germanic or 'Ingvaeonic' and contrast with different German words: *bark: Rinde; barm: Hefe; bell: Schelle, Glocke; brain: Hirn; brine: Salzwasser; brink: Rand, Anhöhe; bull: Stier; busy: fleißig, tätig; clay: Lehm; to cleanse: säubern; clover: Klee; to creep: kriechen; down(s): Hügel; ebb: –; elder: Euter; film: Häutchen; gloom: Dunkelheit; hatch: kleine Tür; helm: Steuerruder; heel: Ferse; hook: Haken; hoop: Reif; hunk: Stück; to hire: mieten; how: wie; key: Schlüssel; lane: Seitenweg; luke(warm): lau; left (<'weak'): links; mist: Nebel; oast: –; oats: Hafer; pith: Mark; rafter: Sparren, Balken; to rend: zerreißen; Saturday: Samstag* (for *Sonnabend* see p. 220); *to scald: abbrühen; to scream: schreien; scythe: Sense; sedge: Rietgras; shallow: seicht; stairs: Stiege; steam: Dampf; thus: so* (MHG *sus*); *Wednesday: Mittwoch; whey: Molken.* Some of these 'Ingvaeonic' words are also found in Norse. What is most characteristic of the continental counterparts is their regression. While some extend over most of the Netherlands, Flanders, and Low Germany, others are confined to the coastal regions. This may be, in some cases, the result of the northward thrust of High German.

3.4 | The earliest records and the art of writing

3.4.1 | The Negau inscription

The earliest inscription in Germanic came to light when a hoard of some two dozen bronze helmets was found in the last century near Negau in Styria. One of the helmets bears the inscription, in a North Etruscan alphabet running from right to left: HARIXASTITEIVA /// IP or IL. The text seems to consist of three well-attested Indo-European etyma in unmistakably Germanic phonological form: IE *k* > *h, gh* > *X* or *Kh(g), d* > *t*, *st* > *st*, *o* > *a*, *ei* > *ei*. The change of *ei* > *ī* has now been shown by van Coetsem to be fairly late. In the case of *d* > *t* the evidence of the spelling is ambivalent since the North Etruscan alphabet had no *d*.

The last two letters have never been quite satisfactorily explained. The first two words constitute a compound, the third is separate. HARI- is Gothic *harjis*, Gm. *Heer*, E *Here-* in *Hereford*, Latinized Celtic *Corio-*. XASTI is Gothic *gasts*, Gm. *Gast*, E *guest*, Latin *hostis*; and TEIVA, if we read it as a word, is ON *Týr*, OE *Tiw(es dæg)* 'Tuesday', OHG *Ziu*, cf. modern Alem. dialect *Zischtig*, Sanskrit *dēva-ḥ*, related to Latin *deus*.

It is when we turn to the grammatical forms and the meaning of the inscription that the difficulties begin. *Harigasti* could either be a name, e.g. of the owner of the helmet or of a god, or it could be a descriptive epithet of the god ('the army's guest or friend'). *Teiva* could have the meaning 'god' in general like Latin *deus* or be the name of the god of war like ON *Týr*, OE *Tiw*, OHG *Ziu*. The grammatical endings throw little light on the question. *Teiva* could be either nom. **teiwaz* or acc. **teiwam*. The latter form would be most easily acceptable, since the loss of -*z* in WGmc. is usually dated fairly late (second century A.D.), and in Gothic it would be -*s*, in Norse -*R*. The loss of the earlier acc. -*m* in *Harigasti* would also be easiest to accept. But the ending -*i* could also be plausibly explained as a gen. or dat. deriving from an IE instrumental -*ī*. Since a North Etruscan alphabet had no obvious way of spelling -*z*, the nom. cannot be ruled out either. Many readings have been proposed and a definitive interpretation is perhaps unattainable. Maybe an invocation (acc.) to *Harigasti* (the army's guest), the God of War (*Teiwa*), is linguistically the most satisfactory.

The dating of the inscription must obviously depend on the chronology of the North Etruscan alphabets and the helmets. Epigraphers hold the view that the North Etruscan script was largely superseded by the Latin alphabet by 90 B.C. It would therefore appear that the Negau inscription must belong to the second century B.C. On archaeological evidence the hoard has, however, been dated as late as A.D. 100. Linguistically, either date makes this the earliest Germanic inscription. However, this is not the end of the story.

The archaeological-historical approach sees the helmets as

belonging to auxiliaries serving in the Roman army early in the first century A.D. It claims that we do not know how long the North Etruscan or North Italic alphabets lingered among the barbarians of the Alps. The sort of inscription a Roman auxiliary would most likely have had made in his helmet would give his name, patronymic and his unit. F. van Tollenaere, who has written a comprehensive treatise on this problem, therefore accepts the reading: HARIGASTI TEI (filii) V(exillarius) or V(exillatio) A(larum) III IL(lyricarum), i.e. '(belonging to) Hereguest, Teus' son; detachment formed from three Illyrian squadrons' or perhaps 'standard-bearer of the third Illyrian squadron'. As to the date, he assumes that the inscription 'belongs to the first half of the first century B.C.', preferring this to the more precise dating of A.D. 6 to 9. We would thus be left with the name of a Germanic mercenary, Harigast (Hereguest). And the inscribed name would be of no more significance than the Germanic names quoted by Caesar or Tacitus or those given in other Latin inscriptions.

3.4.2 | Words in Latin sources

An indirect source for our knowledge of Germanic is further to be found in the Greek and Roman reports and inscriptions. The Germanic words and names quoted are naturally seen through a Latin or Greek filter, but they are nevertheless a valuable testimony, lexically more so than phonologically. There are far more names than appellatives that have come down to us. It is uncertain to what extent the name elements were also current as appellatives. The early Romance dialects attest hundreds of words of Germanic origin. There is no doubt that the overwhelming majority were borrowed from the individual tribal dialects after the final invasions which led to the establishment of Germanic realms on Roman soil. But some particularly widely current words may have been borrowed from Late Germanic into Vulgar Latin.

The following list drawing from the above sources is intended to give some impression of the earliest recorded Germanic words:

Word	Source	Comments
ala-	3rd cent.	Gothic *ala-* in compounds, *alls*; E, Gm. *all*.
alces	Caesar	<**algiz* with sound-substitution, >ON *elgr* (with *i*-mutation). OHG *elaho* <**elh-* (vowel grade *-e-*) >Gm. *Elch*, >E *elk*.
asci-	Tacitus	*Asci-burgium*, now *Asberg* (Lower Rhine), <**askiz*, >OHG *ask*, OE *æsc* >E *ash*, Gm. *Esche* (mutated vowel from pl.).
-avia	Pliny	<**awjō* >ON *ey* 'island', >OHG *ouwa* 'land by water' >Gm. *Au*, *Aue* (place-name).
Bācenis (silva)	Caesar	Contains the Gmc. root **bōk-*, either before IE *ā* > *ō* or with Latin substitution for Gmc. [ɔ:]. Cf. OE *bœce* > E *beech*, OHG *buohha* > *Buche*.
-bardi	Tacitus	In tribal name *Langobardi* 'longbeards', from WGmc. **barda-*, E *beard*, Gm. *Bart*.
barditus	Tacitus	Perhaps *barritus*: a war chant. Has never been satisfactorily explained.
biber	Polemius Silvius	With Latin *-b-* for Gmc. *ƀ*, E *beaver*, Gm. *Biber*.
blank-	Romance	The Gmc. word for 'white', 'shining', cf. ON *blakkr* 'white horse', probably from Gmc. cavalry into Vulgar Latin.
brāca	Romance	From Gmc. **brōk-* > OHG *bruoh*, OE *brōc* 'trousers', cf. E *breeches*.
brūn-	Romance	Another Gmc. colour term. E *brown*, Gm. *braun*.
brūtis	3rd-cent. inscriptions	From Gmc. **brūđiz* 'newly married woman', with Latin *t* for the fricative. Correctly classified as *i*-stem. E *bride*, Gm. *Braut* – *Bräute*.
-burgium	Tacitus	In place-names *Asciburgium* and *saltus Teutoburgiensis*, 'a fortified place', later for 'town', cf. *Würzburg, Shrewsbury, Loughborough*.
falwa-	Romance	A Gmc. colour term. E *fallow*, Gm. *fahl*.
framea	Tacitus	'Spear'. Probably related to Gmc. **framjan* >OHG *fremmen* 'to carry out, to thrust', OHG *fram* 'forwards', cf. E *from*.
-furdum	Ptolemy	In *Lupfurdon* (Greek), the place at a ford in the river Lippe. Gm. *Furt*, E *ford*.
ganta	Pliny	'Goose'. OE *ganot*, OHG *ganzo* 'gander'.

Word	Source	Comments
glaesum *glesum*	Pliny } Tacitus }	'Amber'. OE *glær* 'resin'. With different vowel grade Gm. *Glas*, E *glass*.
grīs	Romance	Gm. *greis* 'old', in Romance 'grey'.
-haemum	Tacitus	In the place-name *Boiohaemum*, < **haima*, E *home*, Gm. *Heim*.
haribergo	Romance	The non-mutated *a* of Romance (F *auberge*) points to early borrowing, 'army shelter', Gm. *Herberge*, E *harbour*.
harpa	Venantius Fortunatus	An important Gmc. musical instrument. Gm. *Harfe*, E *harp*.
lango-	Tacitus	In tribal name *Langobardi*, showing Gmc. *a* < IE *o*, 'long'.
mannus	Tacitus	'The author of their race.' Also in *Alamanni* ('all men') and *Marco-manni* ('frontier men'). Gm. *Mann*, E *man*.
marka	Tacitus and Romance	'Frontier territory', cf. E *Welsh Marches*, Gm. *Ostmark* etc.
melca	Apicius	'Milk dish', cf. E *milk*, Gm. *Milch* < **meluk-*.
sahs-	Pliny	In *Saxones* < **Sahsonez*, **sahsa* 'sword' or 'stone'; Gregory of Tours: 'cum cultris validis, quos vulgo [i.e. the Franks] scrama-saxos vocant'.
sāpo	Pliny	'A cosmetic cream to dye hair', < **saipōn-* > Gm. *Seife*, E *soap*. The Romance words, F *savon*, It. *sapone* derive from the Gmc. loan-word in Latin.
sigi- *segi-*	Tacitus	In names like *Segimērus*, cf. Gm. *Sieg*.
suppa	Romance	From the Gmc. root **sūpan* > Gm. *saufen*, E *to sup*. Borrowed back into Gm. as *Suppe*, E *soup* from F.
Thingsus	Votive stone on Hadrian's Wall.	*Mars Thingsus* is the Latinized form of the Gmc. God of War: **Tiwaz* (cf. *dies Martis* = E *Tuesday*), protector of the 'thing', the assembly of warriors, hence Gm. *Dienstag* (<*Dingstag*).
ūrus	Caesar	OHG *ūro* > Gm. *Auer(ochse)*.
vargus	Sidonius Apollinaris	'A thief'. ON *vargr*, OE *wearg*, OHG *warg* 'outlaw'.

3.4.3 | Words in Finnish

A further indirect source is provided by Finnish. The age of the oldest loanword stratum has been much discussed. It now appears that these words stem from the first two centuries of our era and represent an influence of East Germanic. As far as the linguistic features of this material are concerned it is, for our purpose, important that they afford a glimpse of Late Germanic, that is that they predate the historically attested Germanic languages, but include all those changes which we regard as characteristic of Germanic. Owing to the conservative character of some Finnish dialects these oldest loanwords preserve a form more archaic than that of any recorded Germanic language. The list of loanwords has often been amended but a basic stock is undisputed. It is from these words that a sample may illustrate the early Germanic features:

autio 'empty, deserted': Gothic *auþ(ei)s*, OE *ieðe*, OHG *ōdi* > Gm. *öde*; sound-substitution of Finn. *t* for Gmc. *þ*; Gmc. *au*.

jukko 'yoke': -*kk*- for Gmc. *k* is regular, Gothic *juk*, Gmc. *u* (later *o*), no conclusions can be drawn from -*o*.

kana 'hen': <Gmc. **hanan*- with sound-substitution of Finn. *k*- for Gmc. *h*- (*x*-), Gm. *Hahn*.

kaunis 'beautiful': Gothic *skauns*, Gm. *schön*; Gmc. *au, i* and final -*z* (>Finn. -*s*) preserved.

keihäs 'spear': <Gmc. **gaizaz*, Gm. *Ger*; with sound-substitution of -*z*- > *h*, but final -*z* > -*s*.

kuningas 'king': <Gmc. **kuningaz*, OE *cyning*, OHG *kuning*, ON *konungr*. The Finnish form is more archaic than the ON, OE or OHG forms.

lammas, gen. *lampaan* 'sheep': <Gmc. **lambaz*-; Goth., OE, OHG *lamb*; note the preservation of the -*s* of the *s*-stem.

mallas, gen. *maltaan* 'malt': <Gmc. **maltaz*, in voiced surroundings not every Gmc. *t* > Finn. *tt*; Gmc. *a* < IE *o*.

miekka 'sword': <Gmc. **mēkia*-, Gothic *mēki*; Finn. -*ie*- from Gmc. -*ē*-, *ē¹* thus preserved, not yet > *ā* (N and WGmc.).

mitta 'measure': cf. Gothic *mitan*, OE *metan*, Gm. *messen*, *e > i* before *a* in the next syllable is only found in Gothic. -*tt*- normal from Gmc. -*t*-.

murha 'murder': <Gmc. **murþa*-, Gm. *Mord*; Gmc. *u* before *a* not yet > *o*.

paita 'shirt': Gothic *paida*, OE *pād*, OHG *pjeit*. Gmc. *d* > Finn. *t* is regular.

pelto 'field': < Gmc. **felþ-*; usual sound-substitution Gmc. *f*, *þ* > Finn. *p*, *t*; may show loss of *-m* in Gmc. or perhaps only in transition to Finn.

raippa 'whipping with a rope': Gothic *-raip*, OE *rāp*, ON *reip*, OHG *reif*. Lex Salica (about A.D. 500) has Frankish-Latin *reipus*, *rēpus*.

rengas 'ring': < Gmc. **hrengaz*, IE *o* > Gmc. *a*, *e* still preserved before *n*+cons., cf. OE, OHG *hring*, ON *hringr*, *-as* < Gmc. *-az*.

ruhtinas 'prince': < Gmc. **druhtinaz*, OHG *truhtin*, OE *dryhten*; see retention of Gmc. ending.

runo 'poem': < Gmc. **rūnō-* 'mystery, secret' cf. Gm. *raunen*, with preservation of Gmc. *ō* (>*o*), which became *-u* in OE and early ON and *-a* in Gothic and OHG, cf. *sakko* 'a fine', OE *sacu*, OHG *sahha* > Gm. *Sache*, ON *sǫk* (<*saku*).

saippua 'soap': < Gmc. **saipiōn-*, *-pp-* is the normal correspondence of Gmc. *-p-*, the ending attests Gmc. *-iō-* stem: Alem. *Seipfe*, while other forms, e.g. OE *sāpe* > E *soap*, derive from an *-ō-* stem.

sairas 'sick': < Gmc. **sairaz*, OE *sār* > E *sore*, ON *sārr*, Gm. *sehr*; Gmc. *-ai-*, *-az* (>*-as*).

varas, gen. *varkaan* 'thief': < Gmc. **wargaz* > ON *vargr*, with pre-ON ending, cf. p. 70 Latin *vargus*.

3.4.4 | The runes and runic sources

The earliest direct sources of Germanic, written by native speakers themselves, are the runic inscriptions. They extend over a thousand years in time. But only the inscriptions from the third to the sixth centuries of our era can be regarded as a testimony of Germanic or, more precisely, of Late Germanic. Since the majority are from Scandinavia and show, while clearly predating Old Norse, some North Germanic features, their language is usually called Runic Norse. Some twenty very short inscriptions are from the third century and something over twice this number from the Age of Migrations. The great bulk of the five thousand or so runic inscriptions are, however, from much later. They are predominantly in Old Norse or even in early forms of the Scandinavian languages. Apart from Norse only Old English is represented in runic inscriptions to any great extent. The later English and Scandinavian phases of the runic script do not concern us here. The alphabet itself had by then undergone considerable changes. While in England the original common Germanic alphabet of twenty-four letters was extended, in Scandinavia it was reduced to sixteen letters.

The Germanic runic script is alphabetic, that is it assigns letters to the sounds, like Greek and Latin. But its signs or letters are arranged in a manner quite different from that of the alphabets of the classical languages. Its name, *fuþark* (*þ* = *th*), derives from the first six letters. It is now commonly held that the Germanic fuþark does not derive from the Greek or Latin alphabets, but from one of the several closely related North Italic or North Etruscan alphabets which were current in the Alpine regions of northern Italy before the final victory of the Latin alphabet in the last century B.C. It is the letters of the North Italic alphabets, themselves deriving from Greek like the Latin alphabet, that the runes resemble most closely. Since it need not necessarily be assumed that the creator of the Germanic runes had to copy a foreign script as nearly as possible, similarity in itself is of course no final proof. Wulfila did not slavishly copy the Greek alphabet when he translated the Bible into Gothic. On the face of it one would perhaps assume that the Latin script of the Roman Empire facing the Germanic peoples all along the Rhine and Danube frontiers from the last century B.C. onwards would be the obvious source for a Germanic alphabet. After all, it was the Roman world with which the northern peoples were now in increasingly close contact as traders, slaves or mercenaries. But strange as it may seem, at no time before the great missionary efforts in the eighth century was the Latin alphabet itself used for writing Germanic. And if the runic fuþark had been an adaptation of the Latin script one would expect to find the earliest traces along the Rhine and Danube frontiers. This is not so: Denmark and eastern Europe are the regions of the earliest finds. The runes not only look very similar to the letters of the North Italic alphabets but they also follow the same practice of the free direction of writing, while both Greek and Latin adhered strictly to the left to right rule. It was from the moribund writing tradition of northern Italic peoples, then, that the fuþark was created, probably in the first century B.C. If the earliest finds date from three hundred years later, the reason is probably to be found in the writing material used. Tacitus (*Germania*, ch. X) tells us of the *notae* (runes ?) on strips of wood, and Venantius Fortunatus, admittedly at the end of the sixth century, mentions the barbaric rune painted on ash-wood tablets (*barbara fraxineis pingatur rhuna tabellis*). It is thus far away from the Roman world and several centuries after the original creation that the runes first come to light.

The name given the signs is *runa* which means 'mystery, secret' in Gothic, OE and OHG. ON and OE also give us the words *stafr* and *rūnstæf* for the letters. German *Buchstabe* still shows the connection. English has preserved the two verbs expressive of the new craft: *to write* < 'to carve', Gm. *reißen, ritzen*, and *to read* < 'to interpret', Gm. *raten*. There is little doubt that the art of writing runes was used in magic and sortilege as well as for carving the owner's or maker's name on objects, such as fibulas, spears, swords and coins. Stone inscriptions belong mainly to the later phase. The names which the runes bore probably had religious and magical significance. Although they were not recorded before the ninth century, the names in Old English and Old Norse correspond remarkably well and must be of considerable age. They recall the Germanic world of gods, giants and natural forces. The first letter stands for **fehu* 'cattle, wealth' cf. E *fee*, Gm. *Vieh*; the second for **ūruz*, Gm. *Auerochse* (see p. 70) the wild ox of northern Europe; the third for **þurisaz* 'giant' although in Christian England the word *þorn* 'thorn' was substituted; the fourth stands for **ansuz* 'god'. The letter for H had the meaning 'hail', that for N the name 'need', that for I the name 'ice' and that for T the name **teiwaz*, that is the God *Tiw* or *Ziu*. In each case the letter was the first of the respective name.

The Germanic world was definitely a preliterary society. It must have made very limited use of this new invention and it was only in the second phase of the fuþark from the ninth century onwards that longer inscriptions, sometimes of a literary character, were made. Yet the fuþark was an ingenious tool, well adapted for the phonology of the Germanic languages. It had, for instance, signs for [θ, ŋ, w], sounds for which only a long process of experimentation finally produced the graphs ⟨th⟩, ⟨ng⟩ and ⟨w⟩ in the Latin alphabet used for English and German.

Many inscriptions are not easy to interpret. Among those of which the reading is generally agreed we find the following:

(1) Spearhead of Kowel, about A.D. 250: TILARIDS 'attacker' cf. OE personal name *Tilred*; final -*s* and *ī* for N and WGmc. *ā* suggest a Gothic or East Gmc. origin.

(2) Spearhead of Dahmsdorf, second half of 3rd century:

RANJA 'runner, assailant', an agent noun from the verbal base *ran- cf. Gm. *rennen* (with later *i*-mutation).

(3) Spearhead of Øvre Stabu, about A.D. 200: RAUNIJAR 'essayer, tester', an -*ia*- agent noun derivation from a verbal root which in ON is *reyna* with final -*ʒ* represented by a rune which is usually transliterated by -*R*, indicating a sound between *ʒ* and *r*.

(4) Fibula 2 of Himlingøje, about A.D. 200: WIDUHUDAR, probably a man's name: 'wood'+'hound'; OE *wudu* < *widu*, cf. Gm. *Wiedehopf* 'hoopoe'; *hundaʒ*, Gm. *Hund*, N is sometimes omitted.

(5) Stone of Einang, about A.D. 350: DAGAR ÞAR RUNO FAIHIDO 'I, Dagr ('Day' personal name) painted these (?) runes'. *Runo*, acc. pl. later ON *runar*; *faihido*: 1st pers. sg. pret. of *faihian*, ON *fā* 'to paint', cf. Venantius Fortunatus' *pingere*. The first two words are rather mutilated and have also been read: ...DAGASTIR, a man's name with 'guest' as second element.

(6) Stone of Kjølevik, about A.D. 450: HADULAIKAR EK HAGUSTADAR HLAAIWIDO MAGU MININO. A gravestone in memory of Hadulaikar; the man's name can be compared with OE *Heaðolāc* < 'fight'+'play'. One would expect spelling with þ rather than D. 'I Hagusta(l)dar (note the alliteration of the two names) buried my son'. *hlaiwido* is 1st pers. sg. pret. of *hlaiwian* 'to bury' < *hlaiwa, OHG *hlēo*, OE *hlāw* 'hill', E *low* in place-names. *Magu*, acc. sg., Gothic *magus*, OHG *magu* 'son', cf. Gaelic *mac-*. *Minino*, acc. sg. masc. cf. Goth. *meinana*, ON *minn*.

(7) The Golden Horn of Gallehus, about A.D. 400: EK HLEW-AGASTIR HOLTIJAR HORNA TAWIDO 'I Leeguest, (son of) Holt made the horn'. Dithematic name with well-attested second element, cf. *Harigast* (Negau), *Arbogast* (a Frank); *holtijaR*: probably patronymic -*ia*- derivation from *holta* (note alliteration). It is interesting that the *o* < *u* before *a* is retained even before an *i*-suffix. *Horna* acc. sg. ending is older than comparable acc. sg. in any other Gmc. dialect. *Tawido*: 1st pers. sg. pret. < *taujan, Gothic *taujan*, OE *tawian*, E *to taw* 'to prepare skins'; *tool* is an *l*-derivation from the same root.

(8) Fibula of Freilaubersheim, probably from between A.D. 550 and 600: BOSO WRAET RUNA ÞK DAÞENA GODA 'Boso wrote (the) runes, to you, Dathena gave (this)'. This is the only

runic inscription in sentence form and relatively easy to read which has come down to us from the territory of the German language. The fibula was found in a Frankish cemetery. The language may be the regional pre-OHG Frankish tribal dialect. *Boso* is an attested man's name of the short type in *-o* known from OHG. *Wraet*: 3rd pers. sg. pret. of the strong verb **writan* with Gmc. *ae* diphthong (*ei* in OHG), *t* preserved, i.e. not > OHG *z*. *Runa* is probably acc. pl. but it could be acc. sg. as well. *ÞK* is probably abbreviated from *þik*, Gm. *dich*. *Daþena* is presumably the name of the woman who gave the fibula to the unnamed recipient. *Gōda* probably pret. *gōdda* < **gōdjan* 'to present with goods'.

These few words and sentences must suffice as specimens of Late Germanic of the last few centuries before the individual languages in the west and north first emerged into history.

3.5 | Phonology

3.5.1 | Accent

The accent shift is the phenomenon which is generally regarded as providing the dividing line between Pre-Germanic and Proto-Germanic. Pre-Germanic had the Indo-European so-called variable accent, that is the accent could theoretically fall on any syllable in the word. At one time Indo-European must have had a predominantly dynamic or stress accent based on intensity of articulation. During this phase the so-called vanishing grade or zero grade must have arisen (see 3.5.3). This sort of effect of a strongly dynamic stress can be seen when comparing for instance English *drama* [ˈdraːmə] with *dramatic* [drəˈmætik] where [aː] alternates with [ə] according to the incidence of stress. At another time Indo-European must have had a predominantly musical or pitch accent. This is presupposed by the Indo-European *e/o* vowel gradation (see 3.5.3) and by the evidence of a pitch accent in many Indo-European languages. In Pre-Germanic accent must have become predominantly dynamic until finally it was permanently established or fixed on the first or root syllable of the word. In what later appeared as verbal compounds the stress accent was on the verbal root syllable not the prefix. All Germanic languages show this phenomenon of the initial or root stress. Even modern English and German exemplify it, at least in their inherited Germanic vocabulary: *Váter, Váters, Väter, Våtern, våterlich, Våterschaft; fáther, fáther's, fáthers, fátherly, fátherhood* but compare Gm. *Paternität; E patérnal*. In languages with different accentual systems the stress may also be borne by inflectional endings. See for instance Latin *ámō, amátis, amāvérunt*.

This fixation of the stress on the first syllable established a hierarchy among the syllables and deprived them of their former autonomous status. Two far-reaching consequences ensued which characterized the development of the Germanic languages for the next thousand years: (a) the mutations of the root vowels through anticipation of articulatory features of the subsequent vowels, (b) the gradual withering of the unstressed elements. Germanic words were progressively shortened until the monosyllabic root became the characteristic word form, in English more so than in German, in many German dialects to a greater extent than in standard German.

Most of these consequences worked themselves out in historical times. Some consonantal developments (see pp. 87–8) are only explicable in terms of the Indo-European accent. For these reasons the epoch-making accent shift must be dated fairly late, probably in the last two or three centuries B.C.

3.5.2 | The stressed vowel system

The Pre-Germanic or Indo-European system which must be assumed as the starting point for the subsequent developments is:

(I) (i)   (u) /ī/   /ū/ (ei eu
     /e/ /ə/ /o/   /ē/ /ō/   oi ou
     /a/   /ā/   ai au)

(a) *i, u* exist phonetically as vocalic allophones of the sonants or resonants /j/ and /w/.

(b) The diphthongs show by their subsequent evolution that they are clusters consisting of the vowels /e, o, a/ plus the sonants /j, w/.

(c) /ə/ and /a/ coalesce in a number of Indo-European languages, including Germanic.

(d) /a/ and /o/, /ā/ and /ō/ coalesce in Germanic. The same phenomenon is found in adjacent Baltic and Slavic. But Greek and Latin keep them apart.

(e) At some stage, difficult to place chronologically, the vocalic allophones of the Indo-European sonants /l, r, m, n/ become clusters consisting of $u + l, r, m, n$. i and u must now be regarded as phonemes.

This leads to Stage II, the Proto-Germanic system ($e - a$ phase):

(II)   /i/   /u/   /ī/   /ū/   (ei   eu
     /e/   /å/   /ē/   /ā̊/   åi   åu)

If a system consists of few phonemes these tend to have a wide phonetic latitude. Stage II is based on the contrasts high : low and back : front or rounded : spread. The further development is easier to understand if we posit an alternative to the above system:

   /i/   /u/   /ī/   /ū/
     /e/   /ē/
       /å/   /ā̊/

The short vowel system is now subjected to a rearrangement of the front vowels and to mutations, in the case of Gothic caused by consonantal contexts, in the case of the other languages caused by vowels in the subsequent syllable or, more rarely, also by consonants.

(a) /i/ and /e/ coalesce in /i/ in Gothic with allophones [i] and [e], the latter only before r, h, hʸ (= hw). /u/ develops allophones [u] and [o], the latter again before r, h, hʸ. Later this allophonic distribution is disturbed and leads to new phonemes /i/-/e/-/u/-/o/ (Gothic of Wulfila's Bible).

(b) In the other languages there is a powerful tendency to rearrange /i/ and /e/ in the following manner:

[i] before nasal plus consonants, cf. Lat. *ventus* – *Wind*.

[e] before *a* (*a*-mutation) and before *e*, *ō*: cf. Lat. *vir* – OHG *wer* (cf. *Wergeld*), *edo* – OHG *ezzan* (*essen*).

[i] before *u* (*u*-mutation): cf. Lat. *pecus* – OHG *fihu* (*Vieh*).

[i] before *i, j* (*i*-mutation): cf. Lat. *medius* – Gm. *mitten*, E *mid*.

If no morphological interference had occurred and if all mutations had been equally effective over the whole area, we should be able to posit one phoneme with the allophones [i] and [e] in complementary distribution. It has been shown that Old Icelandic provides evidence that the /i/–/e/ contrast before *a* was always maintained – in its particular antecedent. Old English and Old Norse also preserved distinct reflexes of IE /i/ and /e/ before *u*: OE *eo/io*, OIcel. *iǫ/y*. It is nevertheless possible that somewhere in the Proto-Germanic area a complete merger occurred. But even Old High German, where *u*-mutation is most in evidence, provides exceptions to the pattern of complementary distribution, notably the past participles of the first class of strong verbs (*giritan* not **giretan*). The early loss of final -*a*, -*e* may also have interfered with the tendency, and the question of merger or not can now probably no longer be solved.

(c) /u/ developed an allophone [o] before *a* (*a*-mutation) and before $\bar{e}^1$, $\bar{o}$ (see Stage III) but was [u] before nasal plus consonant even if *a* followed, and before *i, j, u*.

We thus get Stage III of the short vowel system with a hypothetical variant (a) and a realistic variant (b) attested in the historical languages:

(III)
(a) /i–e/   /u–o/   (b) /i/   /u–o/
          /a/   /e/
                                              /a/

The long-vowel system is now affected by the appearance of a further long mid-front vowel, $\bar{e}^2$, in a large part of Germania (though not in Gothic) in addition to the existing $\bar{e}^1$:

(a) /ī/   /ū/   (b) /ī/   /ū/
        /ē¹/   →/ē²/   /ō/
              /ā̄/   (/ē¹/)   (/ā̄/)
                                                    /æ/

(c) /ī/   /ū/
        /ē/   /ō/
              /æ/

The appearance of /ē²/ has long been one of the tantalizing riddles of Germanic philology. F. van Coetsem and E. H. Antonsen have recently given a plausible explanation by considering the phenomenon as part of the mutations discussed above. The diphthongal clusters were affected by the same mutations and each element reacted as a single vowel. The cluster *eu* developed new variants *iu* and *eo* under conditions in which the single vowels underwent the same changes to *i* or *o*. If we assume that this mutation also affected the parallel diphthong *ei*, we get *ii* and *ee* as positional variants. The former fused with existing /ī/, which has long been recognized, and the second is the new /ē/ or $\bar{e}^2$. Contractions and loans further increased the incidence of this new phoneme.

The Proto-Germanic vowel system (second phase) is therefore:

(IV)

/i/		/u–o/	/ī/			/ū/	
	/e/			/ē/	/ō/		/iu–eo/
	/a/			/æ/		/ai/	/au/

In view of the fact that this system explains the systems of West and North Germanic adequately but fits Gothic less well, one ought perhaps to regard it as characteristic of Late Germanic rather than of Proto-Germanic. The criterion which has been used by W. P. Lehmann to determine the end of the Proto-Germanic phase is the loss of -*e* and -*a* in weakly stressed final syllables. This led to the establishment of [u] and [o] as separate phonemes. Since the relative chronology and geographical incidence of these phenomena of the second phase of Proto-Germanic are not clear, it is advisable not to press too hard the terminological distinction between Proto-Germanic and Late Germanic.

The *i–e* and *u–o* phenomena of Proto-Germanic have produced numerous word pairs with a vowel alternation: *Erde – irden, Berg – Gebirge, Nest – nisten, wägen – Gewicht, geben – gibt, vor* (<*fora*) *– für* (<*furi*), *über – ober, Geburt – geboren, Zorn – zürnen, Gold – gülden*. Owing to levelling in different directions or the action of different contexts we have a fair number of words in English and German which are differentiated on the basis of these Proto-Germanic phenomena: *stick – Stecken, stilt – Stelze, liver – Leber, quick – keck, lick – lecken, live – leben, seven – sieben*; *buck – Bock, ford – Furt, fox – Fuchs, storm – Sturm, wolf* (OE *wulf*) *– Wolf, full – voll, dull – toll*.

One kind of mutation, *i*-mutation, led to further important allophonic developments in Late Germanic. Other kinds of mutations, e.g. further *u*-mutation, became important in North Germanic but are not in evidence in German.

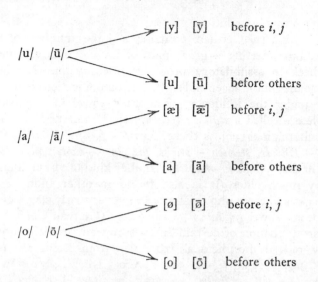

/o/ could, of course, only have this allophonic distribution after it was analogically introduced into positions before *i* or *j*. There are indications that this happened early. See *holtijaR* on the Golden Horn of Gallehus, about A.D. 400.

It can be assumed that the diphthongs /ai/ and /au/ were similarly affected by *i*-mutation. It was only in the next phase, that of the individual languages, that these *i*-mutations were to have structural consequences.

One further allophonic development occurred before /n/ plus /h/. In this position /a, i, u/ developed nasalized allophones [ã, ĩ, ũ]. After the loss of /n/ and compensatory lengthening, the resulting long vowels were denasalized and joined corresponding long vowels. It is this process which accounts for the modern irregular forms *brachte – brought* and *dachte – thought*, the past tenses of *bringen – bring*, *denken – think* respectively.

The Late Germanic vowel system of direct relevance to German is:

(V)

/i/   /u/ /ī/   /ū/   /iu/

   /e/   /o/   /ē/   /ō/   /eo/

     /a/   /ā/   /ai/   /au/

3·5·3 | Vowel gradation

Modern German contains a large number of vowel alternations affecting a great part of its vocabulary. One kind goes back to assimilatory processes operative in Germanic in consequence of the accentual shift. Such modifications of a stressed vowel under the influence of another vowel in a subsequent syllable are called *mutations* (see 3.5.2). Mutations have brought about alternations such as these: *Kraft – Kräfte, Kunst – Künste, Haus – Häuser, stechen – sticht, graben – gräbt, voll – füllen – völlig* or *Hof – höfisch – hübsch*. Another kind of vowel alternation is very much older. It is also found in other Indo-European languages and came into existence in the very early stages of Indo-European. Vowel *gradation* or *apophony* (German *Ablaut*) is the regular alternation of certain Indo-European vowels in etymologically related morphemes. Examples from Latin are *tego* 'I cover', *toga* 'dress', *tēgula* 'tile'; *precor* 'I beg', *procus* 'wooer'; *sedimus* 'we sit', *sēdimus* 'we sat'; *meditor* 'I reflect', *modus* 'measure'; or compare Greek *pétesthai* 'to fly', *poté* 'flight', *ptésthai* inf. aorist, *pōtâsthai* 'to flutter'. The alternations are thus both quantitative and qualitative. Indo-Europeanists regard the former kind as the result of a dynamic stress which was phonemic at one time and resulted in a vowel *e* being realized as *e* under normal stress, being reduced to *ə* or nothing when stress was absent, or being lengthened to *ē* under conditions of stress and with absorption of unstressed elements. Long vowels resulting from contractions of vowel plus laryngeal (an *h*-type consonant) were also subject to reduction when unstressed. Thus we get three different quantity grades (German *Abstufung*): Normal Grade (*Vollstufe*), Reduced Grade (*Reduktionsstufe*) or Zero Grade (*Schwundstufe*) according to the phonetic surroundings, and Lengthened Grade (*Dehnstufe*).

At another, later stage, Indo-European is assumed to have been characterized by a predominantly musical or pitch accent. This accent resulted in qualitative gradation or *Abtönung*. Under chief pitch accent *e, ē* remained, but under secondary pitch accent they became *o, ō*. The vowels chiefly involved in the Indo-European gradation pattern were thus *e – o – ē – ō*, and to a lesser extent also *a* and *ā*. They formed a number of series, such as *e – o – ē – ō – Ø, a – o – ā – ō – Ø, ā – ō – ə, ē – ō – ə* and combined also with the resonants: *e+j – o+j – i* (reduced grade), *e+w – o+w – u*, or

$e+r - o+r - r/\underset{.}{r}$ etc. Very rarely do we get full series. Subsequent phonological developments greatly complicated and altered the originally simple gradations. In Germanic the gradation series are put to morphological use and greatly restructured.

The following table illustrates some of the patterns:

	Normal Gr. I	Normal Gr. II	Lengthened Gr. I	Lengthened Gr. II	Red. or Zero Gr.
IE	e	o	ē	ō	ə –
Gmc.	e/i	a	ǣ	ō	—
	genu (Lat.)	*gónu* (Greek)			*Knie*
	pedis (Lat.)	*podós* (Gr.)	*pēs* (Lat.)	*fōtus* (Gothic) 'foot'	
OHG	*geban* 'to give'	*gab*	*gābum*		(*gigeban*)
IE	ei	oi			i
Gmc.	ei > ī	ai			i
Goth.	*greipan* 'to grip'	*graip*			*gripans*
E	*ride*	*rode, road*			*ridden*
IE	eu	ou			u
Gmc.	iu/eo	au			u
Gm.	*riechen*	*Rauch*			*Geruch/ gerochen*
Gm.	*fließen*	*Floß*		*Flut*	*Fluß/ geflossen*
IE	e+r+cons.	o+r+cons.			r/$\underset{.}{r}$
Gmc.	er-	ar-			ur-
Gm.	*werden*	*ward*			*wurden/ geworden*
IE	e+n+cons.	o+n+cons.			n/$\underset{.}{n}$
Gmc.	in-	an-			un-
Gm.	*klingen*	*Klang*			*geklungen*
	binden	*band/Band*			*Bund/ gebunden*
IE	a	o	ā	ō	ə
Gmc.	a	a	ō	ō	a
		sāgio (Lat.)	*sōkjan* (Gothic) 'to seek'		
Gm.	*Hahn*		*Huhn*		
	fahren		*fuhr*		
	Stall		*Stuhl stōls* (Gothic) *Statt*		

As can be seen, the infinitive and the present of primary verbs appear in normal grade I, the singular of the past tense (Germanic) or the perfect (Indo-European) is marked by normal grade II and derivative verbs, such as causatives, have this grade as well. Verbal nouns are derived from normal grade II or zero grade, cf.

Normal Gr. I	Normal Gr. II			Red. or Zero Gr.
schwimmen	schwamm, schwemmen	—	—	der Schwumm (dialectal)
schießen	schoß Geschoß	—	—	Schuß geschossen

Both *u* (*Schuß*) and *o* (*geschossen*) are reflexes of PGmc. *u*, the zero grade of the diphthongal base with *w*, or of PGmc. *U* developed from IE *l̥, r̥, m̥, n̥* (see pp. 87, 82–3). The subsequent split, exemplified also by *Fluß – geflossen*, *Geruch – gerochen*, *wurden – geworden*, occurred in Late Gmc. (see pp. 79, 80).

The PGmc. *au* of the normal grade II of the same diphthongal base also split in pre-OHG (> *ou/ō*, see pp. 156–8), hence *Rauch* but *Floß*. The modern German form *schoß* with short *o* is the result of levelling in favour of the short vowel in *geschossen* and *schossen* (MHG *schuzzen*), see also *floß* from *fließen*, but with long vowel *bot* from *bieten*. MHG had *scōz* and *vlōz*.

The modern forms *Flut, Huhn, fuhr, Stuhl* derive their root vowel from OHG *uo* < PGmc. *ō* (see p. 157). *Hahn* and *fahren* with their long root vowels go back to medieval forms with short *a* (see p. 272).

In the past participle OHG *gigeban* the root vowel is not a reflex of the IE reduced or zero grade but derives analogically from normal grade I. A root variant *gb- was avoided for obvious reasons and Gmc. verbs always have a vowel between the initial and the root-final consonants.

E *rode* and *road* derive from the OE pret. sg. *rād* and the noun *rād*. In both cases OE *ā* was a regular development of PGmc. *ai*, the normal grade II of the diphthongal base with *j*.

3.5.4 | The consonant system

Indo-European had three classes of phonemes: vowels, sonants or resonants, and consonants or obstruents. A fourth class, the laryngeals, is less easily identifiable. In Germanic the class of the laryngeals is no longer in evidence, and the sonants form a sub-group of the consonants. In Indo-European they could either function as syllabics or as non-syllabics. In Germanic they eventually split between the vowels and the consonants according to their previous functions, as follows:

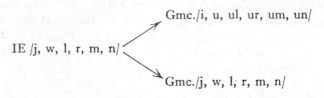

Gmc./i, u, ul, ur, um, un/

IE /j, w, l, r, m, n/

Gmc./j, w, l, r, m, n/

The Indo-European obstruent system or consonant system, in the narrow sense of the word, consisted predominantly of plosives which formed oppositions of voice and aspiration:

(I) /p/   /t/   /k/   /kʷ/   1
     /b/   /d/   /g/   /gʷ/   2
     /bh/   /dh/   /gh/   /gʷh/   3
     /s/

Of the three series of plosives 1 contrasted with 2 on the basis of voice and with 3 on the basis of voice and aspiration. 3 contrasted with 2 on the basis of aspiration only. It appears that it was this uneven distribution of correlations which first gave rise to a shift. J. Fourquet has propounded the theory that the first step was a switch from a correlation of voice (1–2) to a correlation of aspiration. The critical factor in the equation is series 3. Its nature is very much in dispute. Its reflexes in the individual Indo-European languages perhaps only suggest the distinctive feature of voice (hence the notation /B etc./ below, avoiding an over-precise definition). It is, however, preferable to see series 1 and 2 linked in the next step of development, for otherwise we would hardly get a credible system. The traditional view of the Germanic Sound Shift, also known as Grimm's Law, sees the shift of /b d g gʷ/ as the last step, largely because it neglects the system as a whole, but also, not very convincingly, because certain loanwords would seem to suggest that this shift came last. Following Jean Fourquet we thus posit an intermediate system:

(II) /ph/   /th/   /kh/   /kʷh/   1
      /p(b̥)/ /t(d̥)/ /k(g̥)/ /kʷ(gʷ)/   2
      /B/   /D/   /G̥/   /Gʷ/̥   3
      /s/

The correlation of aspiration of plosives (1–2) must now have been replaced by one of friction versus occlusion. What is remarkable is that the system of three series with four points of articulation was preserved in its entirety although it was subject to such profound phonetic changes. With one context restriction (Stage II 1 did not become Stage III 1 after obstruents) this is the system of Pre-Germanic:

(III) /f/   /þ/   /x/   /xʷ/   1
       /p/   /t/   /k/   /kʷ/   2
       /B/   /D/   /G/   /Gʷ/   3
       /s/

Latin providing the examples for Indo-European, and Gothic for Germanic, we get the following correspondences:

(1) p > f   *piscis – fisks* 'fish'
              pater – fadar 'father'
     t > þ   *tres – þreis* 'three'
              tongēre 'to know' – *þagkjan* 'to think'
     k > x   *capere – hafjan* 'to heave' (*h < x*)
              canere 'to sing' – *hana* 'cock' cf. *hen*
     kʷ > xʷ   *quod – hƴa* 'what'
              sequor 'to follow' – *saíƕan* 'to see'

The clusters *pt* and *kt* become *ft* and *xt*, that is, the second plosive remains unshifted. The plosive in second position is also preserved in *sp, st, sk* (*spuo* – E *to spew*; *est – ist*; *piscis – fisks*), presumably because there was neutralization and subsequent reassignment.

(2) b > p   *scabere* 'to rub' – *gaskapjan* 'to shape'
              lābī 'to glide' – *slēpan* 'to sleep'
     d > t   *domus* 'house' – *timbrja* 'carpenter' cf. *timber*
              duo – twai 'two'

g > k   *gūstus* 'taste' – *kustus* 'test'
        grānum – *kaúrn* 'corn'
gʷ > kʷ *nūdus* (< **nogwedos*) – *naqaþs* 'naked'
        venire (< **gʷ-*) – *qiman* 'to come'

(3) bh > b *fero* (< **bh-*) 'I carry' – *baíran* 'to bear'
          findere (< **bh-*) 'to cleave' – *beitan* 'to bite' (Latin
          has an *n* infix in pres. The perfect tense is *fidi*.)
    dh > d *foris* (< **dh-*) – *daúrō* 'door'
          fingere (< **dh-*) 'to form' – *digan* 'to knead', cf.
          dough (Lat. with *n* infix)
    gh > g *longus* (< **gh-*) – *laggs* 'long'
          haedus (< **gh-*) – *gaits* 'goat'
    gʷh > gʷ IE **sengʷh-* – *siggwan* 'to sing'
      > w   *ninguit* (< **gʷh-*) 'it is snowing' – *snaiws* 'snow'

When the new Germanic fricatives *f*, *þ*, *x* and the inherited *s* were not in initial position or immediately preceded by stress they became voiced in voiced surroundings: *ƀ đ g ʒ*. As long as the Indo-European stress system was in existence, voiced and voiceless realizations can be regarded as allophones of the one fricative series. If /B D G/ had already been fricatives it seems likely that they would have been drawn into this distributive pattern. This is, however, not the case. The discoverer of the occurrence of voicing or non-voicing of the Pre-Germanic fricatives is Karl Verner. The phenomenon is called after him, Verner's Law. ('Eine Ausnahme der ersten Lautverschiebung', *Zeitschrift für vergleichende Sprachforschung*, iii (1877) 97–130.) It explains for instance the apparently irregular correspondence of Gothic *d*/*þ* or Old English *d*/*þ* or German *t*/*d* to Lat. *t* in the corresponding Latin words *pater* and *frater*: *fadar* – *brōþar*, *fæder* – *brōþor*, *Vater* – *Bruder*. Those languages which still had the Indo-European accent such as Greek and Sanskrit show that in the case of the word for 'father' the stress occurred after *t*, in the case of 'brother' immediately before. Hence we see that the Indo-European accent had the following effect in Germanic:

IE ´t- > PGmc. ´þ- > þ
    -t´ >   -þ´ > ð

Since different forms within the same paradigm or grammatical categories could have different stress patterns as long as the Indo-

European variable accent was in existence consonantal alternations arose: *f*, *þ*, *x*, *s*: *ƀ*, *ð*, *g*, *z*. The historical Germanic languages, in particular also German, still showed reflexes of this, for instance in the stem forms of strong verbs. The phenomenon is known as Grammatical Change (an alternation of consonants, which has nothing to do with grammar). In the subsequent centuries these consonantal alternations were greatly reduced through phonological developments and analogical levelling. But even the modern languages have traces. For instance English in *was – were* (*r* < *z*), *lose – forlorn, seethe – suds, sodden* (*d* < *ð*); German in *schneiden – schnitten, ziehen* (*h* < *x*) – *zogen* (*g* < *g*), *verloren – Verlust*.

When the accent was finally shifted to the root syllable in Germanic the voiced and voiceless realizations of the fricatives became separate phonemes. The voiced variants then coalesced with the voiced fricative allophones of the phonemes / B D G Gʷ /. It used to be assumed that IE /bh dh gh gʷh/ became voiced fricatives in Germanic: /b ð g gʷ/. W. G. Moulton has shown that all individual Germanic languages except OHG had both fricative and plosive realizations of this Indo-European phoneme series and that they were in complementary distribution (plosives: initially (except probably /g/), after nasals and when doubled).

The Proto-Germanic system has therefore the following form:

(IV)   /f/   /þ/   /s/   /x/   1
        /p/   /t/   /k/   2
        /b–ƀ/   /d–ð/   /z/   /g–g/   3
        /m/   /n/
                          /l/
                          /r/
        /w/   /j/

The only series which was still unimpaired in incidence was the voiceless plosive series /p t k/. Between series 1 and 3 there had been a partial coalescence. The series of labiovelars was dissolved in at least part of Germania, including that part out of which German grew.

In Late Germanic /x/ developed the allophones [h] in initial position and [x] in other positions. German *Horn* and *Nacht* show a last reflex of this dual distribution, cf. Latin *cornu – noctis*, IE /k/ > Gmc. /x/. By a process known as rhotacism /z/ became *r* in North and West Germanic.

The allophonic distribution of the phonemes of the third series was eventually to lead to an important difference between German and English. /d–ð/ became /d/ everywhere in West Germanic (later > *t* in German): *daughter – Tochter, deaf – taub, yard – Garten.* /b–ƀ/ and /g–g/ became uniformly /b/ /g/ in German, at least in the Upper German dialects, but retained plosive and fricative articulations in English, hence: *bind – binden, rib – Rippe* but *seven – sieben, wife – Weib; yell – gellen, finger – Finger, way – Weg, rain – Regen* with irregular correspondences in *give – geben, guest – Gast.*

The cause and detailed process of the Germanic Sound Shift have been the subject of innumerable investigations and speculations. Neither psychological motivation (the great vigour of the Teutons!) nor substratum theories have proved helpful. No entirely satisfactory reasons for this phenomenon of extraordinary consistency and regularity, other than those inherent in the accentual and systematic features of Indo-European and Germanic phonology, have ever been proffered. The time of the occurrence has been determined with greater success. Since no Latin loanwords were affected by the Germanic Sound Shift and since all Germanic words quoted by classical authors show the results of it, it must have occurred before and been completed by the time of the first contact with Rome in the second half of the last century B.C. On the other hand certain Celtic loanwords were affected by the shift. The contact with the Celts was not likely to have been very close before the middle of the last millennium B.C. The Germanic Sound Shift is therefore most likely to have taken place in the early part of the last half millennium B.C.

3·5·5 | The development of vowels and consonants in final unstressed syllables

The accent shift brought about as one of its most far-reaching consequences the progressive reduction of final unstressed syllables, as has already been stated. Such syllables were mainly inflectional endings. The consequences were therefore not just phonological but also morphological. Morphology operates in paradigms. Although the phonological process of progressive reduction is essentially syntagmatic or linear, because of the morphological or paradigmatic implications the developments were far from simple. The *Auslautsgesetze* of the neo-grammarians' handbooks are some of the most forbidding chapters. They are, however, a good example of the competition and conflict between syntagmatic-phonological and paradigmatic-morphological trends. Only some of the salient features can be mentioned.

Of the IE final consonants *r* is preserved, for instance, in the kinship terms: *Tochter*, *Vater*, *Mutter* etc. Final nasals were lost early. Hence the distinction between plural and singular in the chief neuter class of nouns (nom. and acc.) was undermined and, in fact, no longer existed in West Germanic. The nom./acc. distinction in the vocalic masculine and feminine stems also disappeared (cf. Latin *servus/servum*; *silva/silvam*; *turris/turrem*) after West Germanic lost its final -*z* (< -*s*) as well. Final -*s* was still preserved in Gothic and had become -*R* (> *r*) in ON, hence we posit *-*z* for Proto-Germanic. Final IE *t* also disappeared early. Only where IE *s* and *t* were once followed by a vowel were they still preserved in Germanic. This accounts for the endings *-is*, *-iþ* (*-ið*), *-eþ* (*-eð*) in the 2nd, 3rd pers. sg. and 2nd pers. pl. pres. ind. of the regular verbs (OHG *gibis*, *gibit*, *gebet*) and the 'endingless' 3rd pers. sg. pres. of the modern modal auxiliaries (*soll*, *kann* etc.), subjunctive (*er gebe*), and preterite (*er gab*).

The originally short vowels IE *e*, *o*, *a* (> Gmc. *e*, *a*) were lost at the end of the Proto-Germanic phase, but *i*, *u* only after long root syllables in West Germanic, that is, after roots with a long vowel or diphthong, or a short vowel plus more than one consonant. Since a large class of weak verbs formed the past tense with the suffix *-iða*, this loss or preservation of unstressed *-i-* according to the length of the root syllable had far-reaching consequences in West Germanic. The long-stem verbs of this class had no mutation in the past, the short-stem ones had. Even today English and German have a few echoes of this phenomenon, known as *Rückumlaut* (see weak verbs in the following chapters): *sell – sold, tell – told*; *kennen – kannte, brennen – brannte*.

The original long vowels and the long vowels resulting from contractions were shortened in Germanic in the first instance. Where the historical languages had unstressed long vowels these resulted from contractions. They were shortened one stage later.

3.6 | Morphology: Inflection

3.6.1 | Noun inflection

Three grammatical categories were distinguished in Germanic nouns: case, number, and gender. Even in Indo-European they did not form separate patterns but were interlocking and overlapping. The history of the noun in Germanic was determined by the internal conflict or 'contradictions' between these interwoven categories, and the motive power behind the evolution was the new accent pattern with its consequential weakening of the very means for expressing those three categories. Case and number were traditionally indicated by inflectional endings. Gender was unevenly distributed among the inflectional classes but became from time to time a factor in the evolution of the classes. The classes themselves were originally based on the Indo-European stem suffixation, that is the formants such as -o-, -ā-, -i-, -u- etc. which were added to the roots (see pp. 24–5). As the formants and roots progressively fused, the classes sorted themselves out on the basis of case and number formation. If Gothic is taken as the closest reflexion of Proto-Germanic we must conclude that case and number held an even balance. But even in Gothic there was a portent of what was to happen. Two important classes (f. ō-stems and m.f.n. n-stems) did not distinguish the nom. and acc. cases in the plural, but sg. and pl. were clearly differentiated. The West Germanic languages, recorded some four hundred years later, show that the balance had already significantly shifted in favour of number distinction. In fact only gen. and dat. and nom./acc. were still fairly clearly distinguished whilst the number distinction was somewhat better maintained. It is true, here too, significant coalescences had occurred: sg. and pl. nom./acc. were no longer distinguished in the case of n. a-stems and f. ō-stems (with exceptions in OE) but i-mutation became an indication of future possibilities.

The function of the cases was predominantly grammatical, i.e. to express sentential relations. Relations of space (locative) and manner (ablative or instrumental) were largely assigned to other syntactical devices and the cases expressed mainly the relations between various phrases within the sentence.

Indo-European had a very large number of nominal classes. One of the first features to be eliminated was the possible occurrence of vowel gradation within nominal paradigms. There are no traces within Germanic of vowel gradation in noun roots within paradigms. Different grades may have survived dialectally in inflectional endings. In the gen. sg. of *a*-stems Runic Norse -*as* and OE -*æs* appear to derive from PGmc. *-asa* (< *-oso*) while Gothic -*is* and OHG -*es* are reflexes of *-esa* (< *-eso*). In other words, the dialectal variants appear to be based on the Indo-European *e*/*o* gradation. In roots, too, dialects may occasionally have reflexes of different grades which may testify to levelling in different directions, or perhaps more likely, simply go back to roots with different grades, e.g. OHG *rehho* – OE *raca*, *Rechen* – *rake* (IE *e*/*o* grades); *Kuchen* – *cake* (IE *ō*/*o* or *ā*/*a* grades); *Liebe* – *love*, OHG *lioba* – OE *lufu* (IE *u*/*eu*); OHG *brust*, Gothic *brusts* – OE *brēost*, OS *briost*, *Brust* – *breast* (IE *u*/*eu*). The fact that there are not many such cases would indicate that elimination of gradation took place early. Equally, the effect of the shifting accent was removed very early from nominal paradigms. There were no cases of grammatical change, deriving from Verner's Law, within the Germanic nominal declensions. But there are echoes dialectally, e.g. OHG *haso* – OE *hara*, *Hase* – *hare*, the former representing Gmc. *hásan-*, the latter *hasán-* > *házan-*.

Owing to the fusion of unstressed elements and the operation of accent-generated gradual reduction a powerful tendency to concentration set in within Germanic. There is a small number of vital noun classes acting as a magnet for remnants in other classes. On the one hand there is polarization on the dichotomy regular *vs.* irregular, to the extent that OHG *tag* – *tages* (nom.-gen.) is regular but OHG *snēo* – *snēwes* an irregularity within the *a*-stems rather than an independent class of *wa*-stems. On the other hand there is an incipient opposition within the 'regular' field between vocalic and consonantal stems or between 'weak' and 'strong' declensions.

The restructuring and reorganization in Germanic was carried out on an Indo-European material basis and the classes are easily paralleled:

(1) *a-stems*: IE -*o*- > Gmc. -*a*-, masc. and neuter (feminines eliminated in Gmc.), cf. Latin *servus* – Gmc. *kuningaz* (Finn. *kuningas*).

(2) *ō-stems*: IE -*ā*- > Gmc. -*ō*-, only fem., cf. Latin *silvā* – Gmc. *rūnō* (Finn. *runo*).

Both these classes had extensions with -*j*- (>*ja*, *jō*) which caused mutation and constituted a powerful link with the *i*-stems.

(3) *i-stems*: IE -*i*- > Gmc. -*i*-, originally all three genders with uniform declension. In Gmc. elimination of neuter and differentiation between fem. and masc. declensions. Cf. Lat. *hostis* – Gmc. *gastiz (Runic -*gastiR*). This class is characterized by the attraction of the *a*-class on the one hand and the functionalization of the incipient *i*-mutation.

(4) *u-stems*: IE -*u*- > Gmc. -*u*-, originally all three genders with uniform declension. This class was probably small in IE. Attraction to other classes made itself felt. Cf. Lat. *exercitus* – Gmc. *handuz (Gothic *handus*).

(5) *n-stems*: IE -*en*- (with vowel gradation) > Gmc. -*en/an*-, masc. and fem. with few neuters. Cf. Lat. *homo, hom-in-is, natio, nati-on-is* – OHG *zunga* – *zungun*. An expanding class.

(6) *s-stems*: IE -*es/os*- > Gmc. -*ez/az*-, only neuters. Cf. Lat. *genus, gen-er-is* (*r* < *s*) – Gmc. *lambiz, pl. *lambizo > -*ir*. In Gmc. this class was moribund with only very few examples, but its chance of survival arose out of the incipient *i*-mutation and the persistence of -*r* (see p. 179).

(7) *r-stems*: IE -*ter*- (with vowel gradation) > Gmc. -*r*, an ancient class of kinship terms, m. and f. Cf. Lat. *māter* – Gmc. *mōðer. A small class subject to early erosion.

In addition to these vocalic classes (1–4) and consonantal classes (5–7) there were a number of further small relic classes of no further consequence in the evolution of the declensional system.

3.6.2 | Adjective inflection

The inflection of adjectives followed originally that of nouns and the same stem classes can be distinguished, cf. Latin *parvus* – *parva* – *parvum* (IE *o*- and *ā*-classes > Gmc. *a/ō*) and *brevis* – *breve* (IE *i*-class). Gmc. -*ja*- and *u*-stems also existed. Beside these vocalic stems there were the consonantal *n*-stems. What characterized this word class was the indication of gender and the comparison. In Germanic the adjective became a much more clearly distinct word class, first by the adoption of pronominal elements in the inflection, and secondly by the introduction of a new, dual system of declension. The declension was now no

longer based on the stem classes, although as a fossil the stem
classes (e.g. *a/ō*-stems and *-ja*-stems) can still be identified, cf.
OHG *guot* (*a/ō*), *gruoni* (*ja*). They were now used in a functionally distinct way: a so-called strong declension (historically
vocalic stems) was in opposition to a so-called weak declension
(historically consonantal *n*-stems). Every adjective was declined
in either way according to semantic and syntactic criteria. The
pronominal elements are found in the strong declension, e.g.
gutem (:*dem*), *guten* (:*den* acc. masc.), *guter* (:*der* dat. fem.).

The Germanic system arose possibly on the basis of an earlier
phase of substantivization. The *n*-stem formation was specialized
for the purpose of substantivization (cf. Lat. *-o/-onis*, *Naso* 'the
one with the nose') and thus acquired the semantic notion of
definiteness ('the tall one'). It must then have been drawn into
an opposition with the indefinite form ('tall man' = *any* tall man),
hence renewed adjectival use became possible: 'tall man' indef.
(strong declension) *vs*. 'tall-one man' def. (weak declension).

3.6.3 | Verb inflection

Indo-European had a very large number of present
stems, some were primary, others secondary, that is derived
from other verbs or from nouns. Some stems had root stress,
others had an unaccented root. Some were characterized by a so-
called theme, i.e. *e/o* vowel grades added to the root, others lacked
a theme. They are called athematic. Still others had various
suffixes, often with a *-j-* or *-n*-element, or even an infix *-n-*. In
Germanic reflexes of these Indo-European stems are still found,
for instance the nasal infix in English *stand – stood*, OHG *stantan –
stuat* (dialectally); or double consonants which are the product of
the assimilation of suffixes (e.g. *-n-*) in OHG *spinnan* 'to spin';
fallan 'to fall'; or we have reflexes of a *-j-* suffix element, for
instance in German *sitzen* (< **sitjan*), *stemmen* (< **stamjan*). But
such survivals are nothing but fossils. What is characteristic of
Germanic is the almost total remodelling of the inherited verbal
system. The Indo-European system of numerous stem classes
organized loosely in an aspectual system with subordinate tense
indication was replaced by a system which centred on the opposition of the tenses preterite: : non-preterite or present. In the

process the original stem classes were regrouped in three verbal types on the basis of the relationship between present and preterite. By far the largest and the only active or productive type, from Germanic to the present day, is the type usually known as 'weak'. It was so called by Jacob Grimm because it was the newest type and because it lacked many of the archaic features of the other types. Archaic he equated with 'strong'. It would be better to name it the *dental-suffix type*: *leben – lebte, live – lived*. The past participle is also marked by means of a dental suffix: *gelebt, lived*.

This dental-suffix type of verb formation is a Germanic innovation. Its origin is one of the most discussed problems of Germanic linguistics. One solution looks to the Indo-European suffix *-to-* found mainly in participles, cf. Latin *amatus, finitus, monitus*; and the Germanic forms attested by ON *ð*, OE *d*, OHG *t* correspond to the formula *-to- > -þa- > -ða*. It is likely that the participial suffix was the starting point for the development of the new form of the preterite, or the dental element may have been combined with a suffix *-ē-* or *-ō-*. Another major theory sees the origin of the dental preterite in a periphrastic construction with Indo-European **dhē*, English 'do'. Many languages provide examples for analytic constructions giving rise to new synthetic forms, for instance the French future: *je chanterai < cantare habeo*. Although in principle this possibility cannot be ruled out for the Germanic dental preterite, there are numerous difficulties in practice, listed in the specialist literature, which make this the less likely origin for Germanic as a whole. Analogy with the forms of the verb 'to do' is, however, probably responsible for the Gothic preterite endings.

The Indo-European stems which were principally absorbed in this new Germanic type were the causatives in **-éje/éjo-* with suffix stress and o-grade of the root vowel; denominatives in Gmc. *-ō-* (cf. Latin *plantāre*); formations in *-ē-* (cf. Latin *monēre*); and inchoatives. These form in fact the basis of the classes into which the dental-preterite type of verbs is first divided in Germanic:

I	Goth. *hausjan*	OHG *hōren*	'to hear'
II	Goth. *bi-raubōn*	OHG *roubōn*	'to rob (of clothes)'
III	Goth. *liban*	OHG *lebēn*	'to live'
IV	Goth. *fullnan* 'to become full'. Not a separate class in OHG.		

What is more important, however, than the Indo-European background of this formation is the fact that this is the open-ended Germanic verb type in which we are eventually to find thousands of verbs.

The second type, known as 'strong', is interesting above all for historical reasons. It would be better to call it the *apophonic* type. It consists of a core of about two hundred and thirty verbs which are found more or less in all ancient Gmc. languages plus perhaps another hundred which are only fragmentarily or dialectally attested. It includes many of the semantically most basic verbs. Everywhere it has suffered losses in the course of history. But even in English it is much in evidence and forms one of the strongest links with the Germanic and Indo-European past. The apophonic verbs are as much a salient feature of Germanic as the dental-suffix verbs.

While the ancient Indo-European feature of apophony was eliminated from the nominal paradigm and the present stem of verbs and would possibly only have survived as an etymological-lexical feature, the establishment of the present: : preterite tense opposition as the hall-mark of the verb system saved apophony in Germanic and made it into a most distinctive feature. The Indo-European perfect which yielded the basis of the new Germanic preterite tense was marked by (a) different vowel grade from the present stem; (b) vowel alternation in the root, differentiating singular and plural; with root stress in the singular and suffix stress in the plural; (c) reduplication in the root in many verbs, cf. Latin *cado – cecidi*; (d) distinctive personal endings especially in the singular: *-a, *-tha/-te, *-e. Vowel gradation proved more productive than reduplication. Its incidence was therefore increased and that of reduplication progressively reduced. In fact the Germanic system was in flux with regard to reduplication. It was still in evidence in Gothic providing the basis for a separate class, and there are traces in West Germanic where reduplication had otherwise been eliminated as a class-forming device. It may well be that the fixed root accent clashed with the principle of reduplication and helped to eliminate it. The traditional classification of the Germanic apophonic verbs found in the handbooks is based on the Indo-European vowel gradation patterns. In many ways this historicizing view has obscured the true structural typology of Germanic. F. van Coetsem has pointed the way to a more adequate classification, and the following table is based on his systematization.

Classification of the Germanic apophonic verbs

Structural types		Proto-Germanic stem grades				Traditional class
		pres.	sg.pret.	pl.pret.	p.p.	
e-diphth.	e+j+C	ei	– ai	– i	– i	I
+ ɪC	e+w+C	eu	– au	– u	– u	II
e+2C	e+L/N+C (e+CC)	e	– a	– u	– u	III
e+ɪC	e+L/N	e	– a	– ē	– u	IV
	e+C	e	– a	– ē	– ø	V

		N–WGmc.		Gothic		
		pres. pret. p.p.		pres. pret.		
a-diphth.	a+j+C	ai	– ei(>ē²)			
+ ɪC	a+w+C	au	– eu			
a+2C	a+L/N+C	a	– e(>ē²)	R		VII
a+ɪC	a+L/N	a	– ō	a – ō		VI
	a+C					
ē+ɪC		ē	– ei(>ē²)	R		VII
ō+ɪC		ō	– eu			

C = consonant, L = liquid, N = nasal, R = reduplication.

Examples from Gothic, for comparison with the OHG correspondences see p. 187:

I	dreiban	draib	dribum	dribans	'to drive'
II	sliupan	slaup	slupum	slupans	'to slip'
IIIa	waírpan	warp	waúrpum	waúrpans	'to throw'
IIIb	spinnan	spann	spunnum	spunnans	'to spin'
IV	stilan	stal	stēlum	stulans	'to steal'
V	ligan	lag	lēgum	ligans	'to lie down'
VIIa	haitan	haíhait	haíhaitum	haitans	'to be called'
VIIb	aukan	aíauk	aíaukum	aukans	'to ıncrease'

VIIc	falþan	faifalþ	faifalþum	falþans	'to fold'
VI	skaban	skōb	skōbum	skabans	'to shave'
VIId	lētan	lailōt	lailōtum	lētans	'to let'
VIIe	flōkan	faiflōk	faiflōkum	flōkans	'to lament'

The first group or *e*-group is based directly on the Indo-European *e/o* apophony, appearing typically in three grades: Normal Grade 1, Normal Grade 2 and Zero Grade. In the third sub-group we have an anomalous *ē* in the plural of the preterite, another much discussed conundrum of Germanic philology. There may be Indo-European sources for this apparent lengthened grade, or analogy with the long vowel grades of the preterite of the *a*-group may also be possible. Zero Grade in the past participle of Class V appears to have been replaced analogically by other grades.

The second or *a*-group is a Germanic innovation. It contains, together with the very small *ē*- and *ō*-groups, verbs in transition from the reduplicating class to a new apophonic type modelled largely in analogy to the inherited *e*-group. It has typically only two vowel grades, thus reflecting the new polarization on the present : preterite axis. In this light the sg. – pl. vowel contrast of the preterite of the *e*-group is an archaism. It, too, was eventually eliminated although not for another fifteen hundred years. West Germanic, it is true, appears to have made a first step in this direction, when the 2nd pers. sg. came to be based on the root of the plural:

	Gothic	OE	OHG
1st, 3rd sg.	halp	healp	half
2nd sg.	halpt	hulpe	hulfi
1st pl.	hulpum	hulpon	hulfum

A predominantly historicizing view saw in this West Germanic form a survival of an IE aorist form. More recently opinion has swung round to seeing in it a new analogical formation based on the optative.

Another feature going back to Indo-European conditions is the so-called Grammatical Change resulting from the operation of

Verner's Law (see p. 87). It is remarkably well preserved in Classes I–III but appears only sporadically in other classes. This may be an indication that the Indo-European feature of accent switch from singular (root stress) to plural (suffix stress) held good only in the first three classes. On the other hand it must not be overlooked that this is again a regressive feature of Germanic.

The third type of verb in Germanic is traditionally known as preterite-presents. A synchronically more adequate label would be *apophonic dental-suffix type*. It straddles in fact the other two types and may well have played an important role in the formation of the dental-suffix type. It included originally just over a dozen verbs, but was numerically weakened even further. Semantically and functionally this type includes some of the most basic verbs of the language, the modal auxiliaries of German and English. It is interesting that the Germanic verbal system appears to rest on a tripartition with increasing and decreasing semantic importance and formal novelty and regularity:

I	dental-suffix type: open-ended	semantically least defined, diffuse	newest
II	apophonic type: restricted	semantically more concrete, primary and basic	archaic-remodelled
III	apophonic dental-suffix type: most restricted	semantically and functionally most basic, attitudinal, auxiliaries	most archaic

Any 'neat' pattern tends to have fuzzy edges, and the above is no exception. It leaves out of account certain exceptions within the classes, e.g. the presence of the verb 'to have' in the first type; the verb 'werden' also becoming an auxiliary; the absence of apophony in certain verbs of type III. The most anomalous verbs of Germanic, those for 'to be', 'to go', 'to stand' and 'to do' cannot be said to constitute a type except on the basis of their anomaly. But as a type IV they would not be out of place and would fit into the semantic-formal pattern.

The apophonic dental-suffix verbs constitute a type on the following basis: (a) internal vowel gradation in the present; (b) inflectional endings in the present corresponding to those of the preterite of apophonic verbs; (c) a dental-suffix preterite of a specially archaic kind, i.e. without a medial vowel; (d) they are often defective with regard to past participle and infinitive. Historically speaking they go back to Indo-European perfects which, in Germanic, function as presents. Their preterite may be based on an Indo-European preterite formation with the suffix *-to-. They would thus have formed an important bridgehead for the expansion of the dental preterite. They are not entirely alone in this function. Several other verbs, belonging to the other types, also have such an ancient *-to- suffix without medial vowel. Of these *bringen – brachte* (an apophonic verb with dental preterite), *denken – dachte* (a dental-suffix verb), and English *seek – sought, work – wrought, buy – bought* are modern reflexes.

The following table of Gothic examples illustrates some of the points:

	Apophonic type	Apophonic dental-suffix type	Dental-suffix type
Infinitive	brinnan	kunnan	brannjan
Present			
1st sg.	brinna	kann	brannja
2nd sg.	brinnis	kant	branneis
3rd sg.	brinniþ	kann	branneiþ
1st pl.	brinnam	kunnum	brannjam
2nd pl.	brinniþ	kunnuþ	branneiþ
3rd pl.	brinnand	kunnun	brannjand
Preterite			
1st sg.	brann	kunþa	brannida
2nd sg.	brant	kunþēs	brannidēs
3rd sg.	brann	kunþa	brannida
1st pl.	brunnum	kunþēdum	brannidēdum
2nd pl.	brunnuþ	kunþēduþ	brannidēduþ
3rd pl.	brunnun	kunþēdun	brannidēdun
Past participle	brunnans	kunþs	branniþs

The dual of Gothic is of no further consequence for the history of German and is therefore not given. The above indicative forms are everywhere paralleled by optatives. Gothic also has a passive present, again of no further consequence for German. In the first class of the dental-suffix type some of the Gothic personal endings have variants according to the length of the root. In the history of the West Germanic languages this distinction between short roots and long roots acquired great importance once syncopation led to a differentiation in the preterite suffixes, e.g. *-da* (syncopated after long root), *-ida* (unsyncopated after short root). See 4.5.3 (i). For the 2nd pers. sg. pret. of the apophonic type West Germanic has a different stem form, e.g. OHG *brunni* (see p. 98). The Gothic dental suffixes show much greater affinity with the forms of the verb 'to do' than do the corresponding suffixes of other Germanic languages.

A further feature distinguishing the apophonic and dental-suffix types is the suffix of the past participle: *-n-* in the case of the former, *-þ-* > *-ð-* > WGmc. *-d-* (OHG *t*) in the latter.

The Germanic personal endings of the 2nd and 3rd singular and plural pres. ind., e.g. 3rd sg. OE *-eþ*, OHG *-it*, do not all correspond but appear to form two dialectal groups. The endings of one group, to which OE belongs, have usually been explained as being based on an IE suffix accent, while those of the other group including OHG would have resulted from the IE root accent. R. D. King has shown that by the application of a set of ordered rules on the generative grammatical model, common Proto-Germanic endings with generalized root-accent can be postulated.

3·7 | Morphology: Word Formation

3·7.1 | Derivation and composition

In the Germanic languages we can distinguish three kinds of words. First, there are those which are unconnected such as *Stadt* and *Land*, secondly there are words which are connected such as *Stadt* and *städtisch*, *Land* and *ländlich* or *Stadt* and *Landstadt*. The process by which words are 'connected' is called word formation. It has existed in this language group for as long as we can go back either with the aid of records or reconstruction. Two kinds of word formation can be distinguished: *composition*, in which two (or more) free morphemes are linked together (*Landstadt*), and *derivation*, in which a bound or affix morpheme is added to a free morpheme (*länd-lich, städt-isch*).

Earlier types of formations may become so obscure that the difference between 'connected' and 'unconnected' becomes obscured as well. Are *nähen* and *Nadel* connected? Are English *sew* and *seam* connected? That *Landstadt* is composed of two free morphemes, *Land* and *Stadt*, is clear. But are *Flugzeug*, *Werkzeug* or *Schuhwerk* composed in the same way, or are *-zeug* and *-werk* on the way to becoming dependent elements like *-isch* and *-lich*? These examples point to the all-important fact that synchrony and diachrony are interwoven but nevertheless need to be distinguished if we wish to arrive at a satisfactory description of word formation at any given stage. Not only can the difference between 'connected' and 'unconnected' be fluid but also that between derivation and composition. What a synchronic account of word formation must therefore first of all aim at, is a clear distinction between what is productive and what is no longer productive. We must distinguish the sort of historical derivation represented by *nähen – Nadel* from the productive derivation represented by *Land – ländlich*. Productive is a relative term. A productive suffix is a suffix which can be used analogically to form words from bases or certain bases. There are probably no suffixes which are productive in the sense of being completely freely usable. Modern German *-er* is probably one of the most productive means the language has known. Yet it is not entirely free. Although Germans say *Rufer*, *Kläger*, it is doubtful whether anybody would say *Weiner* or *Bitter* from *rufen, klagen, weinen, bitten*. A particular type of derivation may have been active a very long time ago. As long as a sufficient number of words exemplify that particular type it may be re-employed analogically even if the original derivational suffix or means of derivation has long become obscure. Feminine nouns in *-e* represent such an ancient type in German, for instance *die Bahre, die Lage* from the apophonic verbs OHG *beran* (*ge-bären*), *ligan* (*liegen*). Even the modern language can imitate the type: *die Liege, die Durchreiche*, although purists who tried to replace *Propaganda* by *die Werbe* have not been successful. The term 'productive' seems therefore to cover two possible phases: an active one when the affix is 'alive' and a purely imitative one when the earlier semantic function is usually no longer understood and has become blurred by mechanical imitation. The adjectival suffix *-bar* carried the connotation 'bearing' in its first active phase (*fruchtbar, dankbar*) but has become semantically quite different in its imitative phase (*gangbar, reizbar*). If this imitation is extensive, the affix may enter a new phase of being 'alive', as has happened with -*bar* in modern German.

How then can one determine what derivative morphemes were active at a prehistorical stage? The phonological shape of any given type is an indicator of at least relative chronology. If there is evidence of the occurrence of Verner's Law or of vowel gradation we are obviously referred back to the formative stage of Proto-Germanic itself. Comparative linguistics can only operate with the assumption that what is present in all descendent languages must also have been present in the antecedent stage and what is present in only some must have undergone some form of change or developed later.

As regards derivation we find Germanic in a particularly fluid state. On the one hand the extraordinarily richly developed derivation of Indo-European had left Germanic strewn with numerous transparent formations, some in limited groups, others in sizeable groups. On the other hand few of those Indo-European formations were still active or productive in the individual Germanic languages, although some were more numerously represented than those which had newly become productive, for instance the **-ti* abstract nouns from verbs compared with the feminine **-ungō* derivations (*Zucht* as against *Ziehung*). Germanic appears to have been at a stage when the dead but probably still recognizable system of derivation far exceeded the active, productive system. Among the completely dead formations we find, for instance, adjectives in -*t* (originally the Indo-European participial suffix -*to*- added to verbal roots): *alt* – *old, kalt* – *cold, tot* – *dead* (cf. *to die*), *schlecht* – *slight, recht* – *right* (cf. Latin *regere*), *laut* – *loud* and so on; or nouns in -*m* formed from verbal roots: *Saum* – *seam* (*to sew*), *Samen* (*säen*), *Zaum* – *team* (*ziehen*), or *Schwarm, Qualm, Strom, Traum* (*trügen*), *Helm, Schirm, Schleim*.

3.7.2 | Noun derivation

In the most ancient Germanic stratum the following noun derivations must have been productive:

(i) **-ti*: this formed feminine abstracts from apophonic verbs, usually from the grade of the past participle, i.e. the reduced or vanishing grade. There were also masculine *-tu derivations from normal grade I, but only the feminines have survived, forming a sizeable category:

Flucht – fliehen, Pflicht – pflegen, Sicht – sehen, Tracht – tragen, Trift – treiben, Schuld (OHG *skal > soll*), *Haft – heben, Geburt – gebären* (cf. *birth – to bear*), *Schlacht – schlagen, Fahrt – fahren, Last – laden* (*st* developed in many words where there was a dental in the root), also *Wurst, Gunst, Kunst, Geschwulst,* and with a *p > f* glide between *m* and *t* in *Vernunft* (*nehmen*), *Kunft, Ankunft* (*kommen*), OHG *fernumft, kumft.*

(ii) *-ō/-ōn*: feminine verbal nouns were formed with these two originally distinct suffixes, but confusion set in early. Vowel gradation is a characteristic of this early class: *Binde, Grube, Schlinge, Winde, Bahre, Falle, Lehre, Reise.* This formation became productive again later when weak verbs formed the basis: *Klage, Hetze.* Denominative weak verbs, e.g. OHG *salbōn* from *salba,* yielded a new pattern corresponding to that of the earlier pattern based on the vowel gradation of the strong verbs.

(iii) Masculine verbal abstracts derived from the apophonic verbs. In the verb classes I–IV they are formed with the vowel grade of the past participle, in classes V–VII from the basic grade which is usually found in the infinitive, present, and past participle. Modern German still has for instance the following: *Biß, Bund, Bruch* (*Ver*)*druß, Fall, Fang, Fund, Flug, Fluß, Gang, Genuß, Guß, Griff, Halt, Hang, Hieb, Hub, Kniff, -laß, Lauf, Lug,* (*Ver*)*lust, Pfiff, Rat, Riß, Ritt,* (*Ge*)*ruch, Ruf,* (*Unter*)*schied, Schlich, Schliff, Schluß, Schmiß, Schnitt, Schreck, Schritt, Schub, Schuß, Schwund, Schwung, Schwulst, Schwur, Sitz, Sproß, Spruch, Sprung, Stand, Stich, -stieg, Stoß, Strich, Suff, Trieb, Tritt, Trunk,* (*Be*)*trug, Wuchs, Wurf, Zug.* The group is so large and so marked that it has remained active and now also includes nouns from weak verbs such as *Dank, Brauch, Druck, Kauf, Kuß.*

(iv) *-an/-jan-*: these form masculine agent nouns, for instance: OHG *helfo* 'helper', *loufo* 'runner', *scirmeo* 'protector', *scuzzeo* 'a shot' (Modern German *Schütze*) and Gothic *waúrstwja,* OE *wyrhta,* OHG *wurhteo* 'wright' or 'worker'.

(v) *-l*: denotes instruments, agents or diminutives. Some are very old and obscure, e.g. *Nagel, Sattel, Vogel, Stuhl,* others form a more clearly defined group of derivations from apophonic verbs: *Büttel – bieten,* cf. *beadle,* OHG *tregil – tragen* 'carrier', E *cripple – creep; Sessel – settle, Bendel – binden, Bügel – biegen, Griffel – greifen, Schlegel – schlagen, Schlüssel – schließen, Stößel – stoßen, Würfel – werfen, Zügel – ziehen, Flügel – fliegen, Stachel – stechen.* E e.g. *stool, tool, spool, towel, riddle, shovel, spindle.* Here, too, extension to weak verbs occurred: *Bengel, Deckel, Pickel.*

(vi) *-īn-*: indicating 'descent', 'belonging to', 'what is small'. Both nouns and adjectives could be formed by means of this suffix which derives from Indo-European and corresponds to Latin *-īnus.* The nouns are neuter: OHG *fulin – folo*: *Füllen – Fohl(en)*, E *filly – foal*; Gothic *gaits* 'goat' – *gaitein* 'kid'. Adjectives denote mainly materials, e.g. OHG *guldin*, OE *gylden – gold*; *irden – Erde.* A feminine noun derivation was possible from masculines: OHG *bero* 'bear' – *birin* 'she-bear', *got* 'god' – *gutin* 'goddess'. An English survival is *fox – vixen.* This suffix became very productive later in German in the extended form *-inne, -inna.*

(vii) *-isk-*: this is an adjectival suffix denoting 'origin' or 'descent'. Relatively few words show early phonological features, such as MHG *hof – hübisch* (> *hübsch*), Gothic *funisks* 'fiery': *fōn – funins*; OHG *diot* 'people' – *diutisc.* The really productive phase appears to be Late Germanic: *englisch – English* and many other name derivatives.

What characterizes all these early Germanic formations is their close link with vowel gradation which is the distinguishing mark of the strong verbs. They thus clearly belong to the stage when Germanic apophony came into being. Another feature is the presence of reflexes of the Germanic *e-i* rearrangement and the allophonic split of Proto-Germanic /u/. In all these early derivations the root morpheme is thus clearly involved. The types which become productive in Late Germanic depend much more on suffix derivation and leave the root morpheme unaffected except for one phenomenon, *i*-mutation. In word formation, too, we therefore can distinguish an earlier, more synthetic phase, and a later, more analytic phase.

The noun suffixes of the Late Germanic phase are:

(i) *-arius*: this is a loan suffix from Latin which entered Germanic first with loanwords like *molīnārius* but soon established itself as a means of forming masculine agent nouns in competition with the inherited types (iv, v above) which it eventually ousted. Examples: Gothic *bōkareis* (*ei* = [iː]) 'Pharisee', *laisareis* 'teacher',

OE *bōcere, wrītere*, OHG *puahhāri, lērāri*. The Latin *-ā-* appears to have remained long in some Germanic dialects, while it had a short reflex in others.

(ii) **-inga (-unga)*: a masculine derivative suffix functioning as the expression of 'connection with' or 'bearing the characteristics of', also 'descent', giving rise to patronymics. The earliest Germanic settlement names contain this suffix: *Sigmaringen* 'the settlement of the descendants of Sigmar', *Godalming* 'the settlement of the descendants of Godhelm'. Or see the dynastic names: *Merowinger, Karolinger*. Denominative derivations are OHG *ediling* 'nobleman', *kuning* 'king'. Names for coins were also formed with this suffix: Gothic *skilliggs* 'shilling', English *sterling*. An early extended form is *-ling*: *Lehrling, Häuptling, darling, changeling*. Gothic had few such derivations, but in all other old Germanic languages this suffix was highly productive.

(iii) **-īn-*: functioned to form abstract nouns denoting 'quality' from adjectives. E.g. Gothic *hauhei, gōdei, managei* – OHG *hōhī, guotī, menigī*: *Höhe, Güte, Menge*.

(iv) **-iþō-*: functions as a substantivizer of adjectives in all Germanic languages, forming feminine abstracts: Gothic *diupiþa* 'depth', *hauhiþa* 'height'; OHG *frewida* 'Freude', *heilida* 'healing' cf. E *health*. This suffix was in competition with *-īn-*. It has survived better in English than in German, e.g. *depth, length, strength, filth*.

(v) **-sal*: forms mainly neuter nouns denoting tools or neuter abstracts. It developed mainly in North Germanic, but German has a few survivors: *Scheusal, Rätsel*.

(vi) **-assu- (-issu-, -ussu-)*: functioned as suffix forming neuter or feminine abstracts from verbs, later also from nominals. It was most productive when, under the impact of Latin, large numbers of abstracts were formed. Since it was added almost exclusively to stems with an *n* formant it became *-nassu-* etc. very early. Examples: Goth. *þiudinassus* 'rule, dominion' from *þiudanōn* 'to rule'; cf. E *goodness, forgiveness, likeness*; Gm. *Geheimnis, Finsternis, Verständnis*.

(vii) **-ungō, -ingō*: feminine deverbal abstracts with few examples at first but vast expansion in the individual languages on the impact of Latin. Used mainly with weak verbs at first, German preferring *-u-* but ON, OE and Dutch favouring *-i-*: OHG *warnōn > warnunga* 'warning'.

(viii) *ga-(root)-ja: among the ja-stem class there was a type originating as a compound with ga-. This element lost its independent status very early and the result was a composite affix, which functioned to form neuter collectives. While OE had many examples, the erosion of the prefix ge- led to the disappearance of this means from English. In German it became extremely fertile, cf. Gefilde – Feld, Gebirge – Berg, Geäst – Ast, Gewölk – Wolke.

(ix) West Germanic *-haid: the Germanic languages had a noun (Gothic haidus 'manner', OE hād 'rank, manner', OHG heit 'rank') which became a suffix forming abstracts from nominals. They were masculine in OE but feminine in OHG: mennischeit 'humanity', kindheit 'childhood'.

(x) *-skap- (or with *-ti suffix -scaft-): here, too, the second element of a compound became a suffix: Freundschaft – friendship, Bürgerschaft – citizenship. Although predominantly West Germanic this suffix, forming abstracts principally from personal nouns is also found in Norse.

(xi) West Germanic *-dōm: the noun OHG tuom, OE dōm 'judgment, rule, power' developed into a suffix. In function this derivation competed with the other denominal abstract formations such as *-haid and *-skap. Examples: OHG wīstuom 'wisdom', herizogen-tuom 'dukedom'. It is also found in Norse, but was perhaps borrowed from West Germanic.

3·7·3 | Adjective derivation

That the originally very close link between nouns and adjectives became gradually looser can also be seen in the development of purely adjectival suffixes. The early suffix *-īn- (see p. 105) was shared by adjectives and nouns. The following were only adjectival:

(i) *-ag-/-ig-: transforms nouns into adjectives. Cf. Gothic mōdags 'angry', ON mōðugr, OE mōdig, OHG muotig from the noun Gothic mōþs, ON mōðr, OE mōd, OHG muot. Cf. mutig – moody; blutig – bloody; witzig – witty.

(ii) *-isk-: (see p. 105 for phonological implications) added to nouns to indicate relationship, especially frequent with names in the earliest period: OHG frenkisc, diutisc, walahisc, englisc; E French, Dutch, Welsh, English; and kindisch – childish.

(iii) *-līk-: this suffix appears to have evolved from a noun, Gothic *leik*, ON, OS, OE *līc*, OHG *līh* 'body', with the early function 'having the shape of'. The phase of productivity started in the individual languages: *männlich – manly, freundlich – friendly, tödlich – deadly* etc.

(iv) West Germanic: *bāri-: originally a deverbal adjective meaning 'bearing, capable of bearing', it became a frequent second element of compounds in OE and eventually a suffix of some importance in OHG. Its greatest period of productivity occurred later in German.

(v) *-sama: formed adjectives from abstract nouns. The earliest parallel is Gothic *lustusama*, OE *lustsumlic*, OHG *lustsam* 'pleasant'. It became productive in West Germanic and even more so in German when it was also added to verbal and adjectival stems: *fulsome, winsome; langsam, duldsam*.

Prefixation played only a minor part in nominal derivation. It is true the close links with the verbal system gradually introduced the verbal prefixes into the nominal derivation. Originally only *ga-* and the negative particle *un-* were important, and in OHG we also have a few examples with *ur-* and *ant-*. *Ga-* appears to have been unstressed. The other nominal prefixes bore the main stress. Examples: Gothic *un-hulþa* 'devil', OHG *un-holdo* (*der Unhold*), OE *un-holda*; Gothic *un-kunþs* 'unknown', cf. *unkund – uncouth*; OHG *antwurti* 'answer', *urteil* 'judgment'.

3.7.4 | Verb derivation

It is characteristic of the Germanic languages that suffix derivation is above all a feature of the nominals. With verbs it is much more restricted. What is typical of the verbs is particle prefixation, which in old Germanic was an important element of composition. As far as verb derivation is concerned we can again distinguish two phases: an early analytical phase when the classes of weak verbs with their specific semantic or functional aspects (causatives, inchoatives, iteratives) and the strong, apophonic classes were formed (see 3.6.3). To the same phase belong also a number of fossilized suffix derivations, e.g. with -s-, cf. OHG *blāsan – blāen* 'to blow'; with -k-, cf. *hören – horchen* and *hear – hark; tell – talk; to snore – schnarchen*; and others.

In the second, more synthetic phase, in Late Germanic, with survival and further development in the individual languages, we have the following verbal suffixes:

(i) *-r-: OHG had a number of verbs with an r-suffix which were derived from nouns or adjectives (also comparatives) ending in -r. But in addition there were verbs with iterative function often alongside verbs without the r-suffix. Since verbs of this kind occur also in English and the Scandinavian languages they may go back to a common base in Late Germanic. Cf. German *glitzern – gleißen*, E *to glitter*; *schlittern* – MHG *slīten*, E *to slide, to slither*; *schimmern, schlabbern, flüstern, schnattern*; E *shimmer, slobber, chat* and *chatter*. Compare also German *winden – wenden – wandern* (also *wandeln*) with English *to wind – wend – wander*. Since there is a strong onomatopoeic aspect to such verbs, many may also have arisen independently in the individual Germanic languages.

(ii) *-l-: Verbs with this element appear to have arisen in the same way. In addition to being iteratives many have diminutive connotation. German: *klingeln – klingen, tröpfeln – tropfen, funkeln, hüsteln*; English *scribble, dribble, drizzle, haggle, handle, suckle* etc.

(iii) *-atjan-: Gothic -atjan- corresponds to OHG -azzen, OE -ettan. This suffix conveyed iterative-intensive meaning and was productive especially in West Germanic and played some part in the early periods of German and English, e.g. OHG *heilazzen* – OE *hālettan* 'to bid hail'.

(iv) Consonant gemination was productive to form intensive, expressive verbs in West Germanic and North Germanic. Various assimilations may have originally led to this formation and the semantic connotation may have resulted from the meaning differentiation of the basic and derived verbs. German has still: *ziehen – zucken, zücken*; *triefen – tropfen*; *biegen – bücken*; *stoßen – stutzen*. Compare English *tie – tuck*, but this formation is no longer productive.

3.7.5 | Nominal composition

Proto-Germanic inherited *composition* as a means of increasing its vocabulary from Indo-European. But as it possessed an extensive system of derivation it does not appear to have made as much use of composition as subsequent phases. Two questions are of interest: first, what types of composition existed and were productive? second, what compounds existed, that is, can be reconstructed from the extant parallel compounds of the several descendent languages?

We again note a fundamental difference between nominals and verbs.

Nominal composition means primarily the linking of two nominals. Only primary composition, where the first element appears in the pure stem form without a case ending, existed in Proto-Germanic. But secondary compounds, where the first element has a case ending, gradually emerged as closer units from syntactic groups. The earliest attested example is Gothic *baúrgswaddjus* 'town wall', while the West Germanic loan translations of the Latin names of the days of the week, cf. *dies Solis* and OHG *sunnun-tag*, probably date from the third or fourth century.

The most productive type of noun composition is the compound consisting of two nouns. Composition of adjective plus noun or adjective plus adjective was only in its infancy and the verb was not drawn into the orbit of nominal composition until the formation of the individual languages. Apart from the highly productive type and the emergent types we also have moribund types. The whole material has been most carefully assembled and examined by C. T. Carr, who has also reconstructed the likely common stock of Germanic nominal compounds. What is of most importance for the further evolution is the degree of productivity of the various types of composition.

(i) *Copulative composition*, where the two parts are added together, is very sparsely attested by noun plus noun compounds only, e.g. OHG *sunufatarungo* 'son and father'. It is not a productive type, and this one example can hardly be said to be fully understood and explained.

(ii) *Exocentric composition*, where reference is made to a third element which is separate from the two parts of the compound, is exemplified by a typical but dying class of adjectives, e.g. OHG *einhenti*, OE *ānhende* 'one-handed', OHG *barvuoz*, OE *bærfōt* 'bare-foot(ed)'. The second element was a noun but the whole functioned as an adjective. With the increasing growing-apart of these two parts of speech this type of composition, known as adjective *bahuvrīhi* (a Sanskrit term for this kind of exocentric or possessive compound), was gradually replaced by a formation with an adjectival suffix, cf. German *einhändig*, but still *barfuß*. The latter is in fact the only German survival of this type. Other kinds of exocentric compounds began to emerge, e.g. noun *bahuvrīhis*: *Langobardi* 'long-beards' < 'they have long beards'. It is likely that this type always existed and was indeed the starting point for the adjective *bahuvrīhis*. It is, however, scantily attested and did not really become productive before the fourteenth century.

(iii) *Determinative composition*, where the first element determines or restricts the second element, of the type noun plus noun, is by far the most productive. A large number of such compounds are so widely attested that they can be postulated for Proto-Germanic, e.g. Gothic *manleika* 'effigy', OHG *manalīhho*, OE *manlīca*, or Gothic *augadaúro* 'window', OHG *augatora*, OE *eagduru*, or in their modern forms: *Bräutigam* – *bridegroom*, *Ellenbogen* – *elbow*, *Hagedorn* – *hawthorn*, *Haselnuß* – *hazel-nut*, *Regenbogen* – *rainbow*, *Stegreif* – *stirrup*, *Stiefvater* – *stepfather*.

The type adjective plus noun is also attested but was not yet firmly established. Its development lay still in the future. An old example is Gothic *midjungards*, OHG *mittingard* or *mittilgarto* 'earth', OE *middangeard*, ON *miðgarðr*.

The type noun plus adjective seemed to be restricted to certain adjectives which had the tendency to become suffixes, see **-sama* (p. 108), **-laus-* e.g. OHG *scamalōs*, OE *scamlēas*, ON *skammlauss* 'shameless – *schamlos*'. This type became very productive in German and English when the second element had become the suffix *-los/-less*.

A third emergent type has some early English – German parallels, although it is not Proto-Germanic: verb plus noun cf. OHG *wezzistein*, OE *whetestān* '*Wetzstein* – *whetstone*'. This type probably arose through misinterpretation of the first element when it was a verbal noun or where the root was both nominal and verbal.

3.7.6 | Verbal Composition

While nominal composition consisted primarily of the linking of two nominals, verbal composition means prefixation.

Some fifteen particles, which were originally free morphemes mainly indicating place, formed what was still a loose union with verbs. They remained pretonal, that is the primary stress fell on the verbal root. They could be separated from the verbal root either by other particles or used postpositionally after other phrases. The following prefix particles, given in their Gothic and modern German forms with an example from German, were current in Germanic: (i) *af-*, *ab-* 'away' *abgeben*; (ii) *ana-*, *an-* 'on, to' *angeben*; (iii) *anda-*, *ent-* 'against' *entgehen*; (iv) *at-* (cf. Latin *ad*) Gothic *at-standan* 'to stand by'; (v) *bi-*, *be-* 'at, about' *begehen*; (vi) *faír-*, *ver-* 'about' *verheißen*; (vii) *faúr-*, *ver-* 'past, gone' *vergehen*; (viii) *fra-*, *ver-* 'away' *vertreiben*; (ix) *ga-*, *ge-* 'complete' *gefrieren*; (x) *in-* 'into' replaced by *ein-*, *eingeben*; (xi) *dis-*, *zer-* 'apart' *zerschneiden*; (xii) *uf-*, *ob-* 'under, over' *obliegen*; (xiii) *ufar-*, *über-* 'over' *übergehen*; (xiv) *uz-*, *er-* 'out' *erlösen*. In West Germanic we also find (xv) *miss-* 'opposite' *mißbrauchen, mislead*; (xvi) OHG *umbi-* OE *ymb-* 'about' *umgehen*.

In German many more local particles came into use in this way, e.g. *durch, unter* etc. but six became a special category of inseparable prefixes: *be-, ent-, er-, ge-, ver-, zer-*.

3.8 | Syntax

If we wish to find out how sentences were constructed in Germanic an examination and comparison of the sentence types in the individual recorded Germanic languages afford the only starting point. Yet the difficulties are very great. The early prose texts are nearly all translations from the Greek or Latin and often strongly influenced by those languages. The poetic texts while in the truly Germanic medium of alliterative verse represent a literary tradition which may be representative of one kind of stylized diction only. Alliterative verse was, however, the product of the specific Germanic accentual system and being archaic may offer us the only chance of a glimpse of Germanic sentence construction. We know that the few hundred years which had elapsed since the introduction of the Germanic root accent had already had a profound effect on the unstressed inflectional endings by the time West and North Germanic dialects were written down. Their syntax appears to have been in flux and it underwent considerable changes in the first few centuries of written records. The originally synthetic verb and noun phrases came to rely more and more on function words, such as subject pronouns in lieu of personal endings and prepositions in lieu of case endings. Demonstratives were evolving into articles. These changes affected the weight of the elements of the sentence and the rhythm of the whole sentence and may be presumed to have affected the relative positioning of the elements or phrases within the sentence. Statements and yes-or-no interrogative sentences were probably originally marked only by means of intonation and synthetically by enclitic particles, cf. Latin *-ne*. The Gothic interrogative particle *-u* is a last reflex of this earlier practice: *ni wisseduþ* 'you did not know' – *niu wisseduþ?* 'did you not know?' At some stage the two sentence types came to be differentiated by word order as they are in modern English and German.

Word order, or better, the positioning of the elements of the sentence relative to each other, is generally determined by four factors: (i) it may be absolute, i.e. grammatically determined. Modern German has for instance the grammatically determined order *das weiße Haus* and does not permit **das Haus weiße*. (ii) It may be determined by emphasis or the focus of attention. In *Der Bauer pflückt die Äpfel* we have a sentence which is neutral as to emphasis. Emphasis is expressed by means of stress and intonation and can fall on subject, verb or object:

Der Bauer pflückt die Äpfel.

Der Bauer pflückt die Äpfel.

Der Bauer pflückt die Äpfel.

But we can also have a word order which expresses emphasis: *Die Äpfel pflückt der Bauer.* In other words the German word order is sensitive as to the positioning of the object, but not as to the positioning of the subject or the verb. It is obviously important to distinguish between a neutral order and an emphatic order. (iii) Word order may be rhythmically determined. Thus in German one says *Land und Leute, bei Nacht und Nebel* and inverts the order in *er schenkte seiner Tochter ein Auto* when the direct object is a pronoun: *er schenkte es seiner Tochter*, or *er schenkte es ihr*. But the rule appears to be less mandatory if both pronouns have a similar weight: *er schenkte ihn* (*einen Pelzmantel*) *ihr* or *er schenkte ihr ihn*. In fact the determining factor, rhythm, may also be called 'weight', although weight need not necessarily be coupled with rhythm. We may therefore regard it as the fourth factor. (iv) Many languages have different arrangements according to weight. In French a noun object follows the verb: *il a vu l'homme* but a pronominal object precedes: *il l'a vu*.

It is not always easy to determine what factors are present in a given word order, especially when dealing with dead languages. Authorities differ as to whether the initial position of the verb in Germanic was emphatic or neutral.

Among the earliest sentences we find the following:

(i)   OE   *Song hē ærest be middangeardes gesceape*
              'He first sang about the creation of the world'
      Gothic *urrann gagrefts fram kaisara Agustau*
              'went out a decree from Caesar Augustus'
              gahailida managans af saúhtim
              'He healed many of illnesses'
      OHG   *holōda inan truhtin* 'the Lord fetched him'
              gab her imo dugidi 'He gave him accomplishments'

(ii) Runic   *DagaR þar runo faihido* 'D. painted these runes'
      Norse   *Ek HlewagastiR HoltijaR horna tawido*
              'I ... made the horn'
      OE   *he him āþas swōr* 'he swore oaths to him'
      OHG   *ih inan infahu* 'I receive him'
              gode lob sageda 'he gave praise to God'
      Gothic *aþþan ik in watin izwis daupja*
              'but I dip you in water'

(iii) Runic   *Ek Hagusta(l)daR hlaaiwido magu minino*
      Norse   'I H. buried my son'
      Pre-OHG *Boso wraet runa* 'B. wrote (the) runes'
      OS   *Ik gedōn that* 'I'll do that'
      OHG   *Mīn sēla lobot got* 'my soul praises God'

(iv) OHG *einan kuning weiz ih* 'I know a king'
         in anaginne was wort 'in the beginning was the
            word'

   OE   *þā ārās he from þæm slæpe*
         'then he arose from his sleep'
         And þȳ īlcan geare hīe sealdon Cēolwulfe . . . rīce
         'and in the same year they gave Cēolwulf the
         kingdom. . . .'

These sentences represent four different types:

(i)   V(erb) + S(ubject) + C(omplements) or V + C(+ S)
(ii) S + C + V   or C + V
(iii) S + V + C
(iv) C + V + S   or C + S + V

Basically they can be reduced to the formulas:

   the verb in initial position;
   the verb in final position;
   the verb in medial position.

When we ask ourselves which of these types is the oldest the difficulties begin. Every position has found its proponent and scholars have frequently disagreed as to the interpretation of the relative positions and their implications.

Some scholars consider Type (i) as the basic and oldest type. The nominal subject would only precede the verb if specially emphasized. The pronominal subject is secondary anyway. Certain unstressed particles especially *þā* (OE) or *dō* (OHG) and the negative particle *ni* were permitted proclitically and should therefore be distinguished from heavier elements introducing Type (iv). Old English, at any rate, made such a distinction and Type (iv), other than *þā*-sentences, follows the pattern C + S + V . . . Here we have of course the starting point of the basic difference between German: *Heute morgen ging er in die Stadt*, and English: *This morning he went to town*. Type (iv) with its head position of a complement would, of course, be an emphatic version of Type (i). We frequently find in language that what is emphatic at one time becomes standard and neutral later. This is what, according to some scholars, happened to Type (iii). The new neutral sentences beginning with a nominal or pronominal subject (after this became

5

necessary), the old *þā*-sentences and those of Type (iv) beginning with an emphatic complement would together establish a new pattern with the verb in second position. This pattern is already dominant in Old High German.

J. Fourquet considers the initial position of the verb as emphatic and refuses to reduce the other types to an original Type (i). But he is also against the other thesis which considers the final position of the verb as original. He sees the verb as constituting the core of a predicate round which the other elements are grouped. The more closely linked elements of the verb phrase precede the verb: *horna tawido*. But the elements to which separate attention is drawn follow the verb: *hlaaiwido magu minino*. Again the more emphatic position becomes the normal one, at a later stage. In Old High German this was already generally the case, greatly increasing the incidence of the second position of the verb. J. Fourquet traces the gradual but profound transformation and elimination of Type (ii) in Old English in great detail. There it was not, as in German, the dominant second position of the verb which was analogically extended. First the heavy complement was regularly relegated to the originally emphatic position and only light elements (particles and pronouns) continued to be tolerated before the verb. The 'light' verb 'to be', was the first to be regularly followed by all complements. Eventually, by analogy, all other verbs came to have the same pattern, so that English arrived at the neutral order S + V + C.

All authorities are in agreement that Germanic originally had no different word order in the subordinate clause and the main clause. But as the light elements predominated in the subordinate clause, Type (ii) (S + C + V) tended to dominate numerically. The subject is more often than not pronominal in a subordinate clause. For rhythmical reasons it was attracted into preverbal position. Thus the distinction arose in German that the verb was found in second position in the main clause but further back in the subordinate clause. The absolute final position of the verb did not become the rule until very much later.

In conclusion one can therefore say that all the Germanic languages have departed from the earliest types with the verb in initial or final position and that they first evolved parallel to each other, but that they finally went their own ways, although related features are still evident.

3·9 | Lexicon

3.9.1 | The inherited stock

Indo-European languages have a relatively small number of complete words in common, such as *Tochter, Vater, Bruder, Fisch*; and even here usually only some languages share such complete words, hardly ever all. But many Indo-European languages share a high proportion of roots. From these they built up or developed their words. In this sense Germanic is overwhelmingly Indo-European. The individual Germanic languages, on the other hand, share complete words not only roots. The formation of much of the vocabulary of every Germanic language thus dates back to the period of greatest convergence, that is Proto-Germanic. In so far as the 'new' Germanic vocabulary was built on Indo-European lexical material there is linguistically nothing unusual about it. A certain proportion, however, appears to have no Indo-European source. This fact has given rise to much speculation concerning a non-Indo-European admixture in the form of a substratum or superstratum. If however one distinguishes clearly between 'new' vocabulary built with Indo-European roots and new vocabulary without a known Indo-European etymology, there is little need to look for a strong foreign element. For instance, Germanic has a common nautical terminology which is 'new' but predominantly built up of Indo-European elements. The following words have Indo-European cognate roots, though usually of a non-nautical meaning: *Bord, Damm, Eis, Floß, Flut, Hafen, Kiel, Klippe, Luke, Mast, Nachen, Netz, Reede, Reise, Schiff, schwimmen, Segel, Stange, Steuer, Strand, Sturm, Sund, Zeit*. And even the directions *Nord, Ost, Süd, West*, so clearly of Germanic creation and borrowed by other European languages, are built up of Indo-European elements. Only relatively few are not identifiable as going back to Indo-European roots: *Brise* – breeze, *Ebbe* – ebb, *See* – sea, *Takel* – tackle, *Tau* – tow, etc.

Even in the modern languages the strong common element of words is clearly evident, as the list on p. 118 may show.

Most of the common everyday words of Germanic have survived and are still found in the modern languages. But many have died out. Germanic also had a richly developed specialist vocabulary reflecting the way of life, mentality and activities of its

German	Dutch	Swedish	Danish	English
Erde	aarde	jord	jord	earth
Feld	veld	fält	mark	field
Frost	vorst	frost	frost	frost
Gras	gras	gräs	graes	grass
Hagel	hagel	hagel	hagl	hail
Heide	heide	hed	hede	heath
Heu	hooi	hö	hø	hay
Licht	licht	ljus	lys	light
Mond	maan	måne	maane	moon
Regen	regen	regn	regn	rain
Regenbogen	regenboog	regnbåge	regnbue	rainbow
Salzwasser	zout water	saltvatten	saltvand	salt water
Sand	zand	sand	sand	sand
Schnee	sneeuw	snö	sne	snow
Sommer	zomer	sommar	sommer	summer
Sonne	zon	sol	sol	sun
Stern	ster	stjärna	stjerne	star
Sturm	storm	storm	storm	storm
Tal	dal	dal	dal	valley (dale)
Tau	dauw	dagg	dag	dew
Wasser	water	vatten	vand	water
Wasserfall	waterval	vattenfall	vandfald	waterfall
Welt	wereld	värld	verden	world
Wetter	weer	väder	vejr	weather
Wind	wind	vind	vind	wind
Winter	winter	vinter	vinter	winter

speakers. The native heroic poetry is the only source for this specialist vocabulary. Most of it has died out. Germanic had dozens of words for warriors, war, weapons, armour and so on. They formed the intricate word-fields of a barbarous world. Specialist studies have attempted to retrace them.

What is more important for the German language, and for English, is the extent of the Germanic lexical heritage today. As a sample we shall trace the fate of the well-attested Germanic words beginning with the letter *h-* as listed in F. Holthausen's *Gotisches Etymologisches Wörterbuch* (first four pages). A comparison based on the etyma or lexical items (*Wortkörper*) is relatively easy to make. A comparison of the meanings would demand an extremely extensive investigation, for meaning is based on general lexical convention and particularized by the context. The meaning of one word is determined by the meanings of other words and such elusive factors as style, connotation and implication intended by the users. The following comparison is therefore confined to the material plane of the survival of lexical items. OE and OHG forms are given where the words have not survived.

Gothic		German		English
haban		haben		have
hafjan		heben		heave
haftjan		heften	OE	hæftan
hafts		Haft	OE	hæft
hagl		Hagel		hail
hāhan		hangen		hang
haidus		–heit		–hood
haifsts 'struggle'	OHG	heisti	OE	hǣst
hailags		heilig		holy
hailjan		heilen		hcal
hails		heil		whole
haims 'village'		Heim		home
haírda		Herde		herd
haírdeis		Hirt		(shep)herd
haírto		Herz		heart
haírþra 'intestines'	OHG	herdar	OE	hreðer
haírus 'sword'	OS	heru	OE	heoru
haitan		heißen		(he hight)
haiþi		Heide		heath
haiþno		heidn(isch)		heathen
hakuls 'coat'	OHG	hahhul		hackle
				'cloak, straw covering'
halbs		halb		half
haldan		halten		hold
halja		Hölle		hell
hals		Hals	OE	heals
halts 'lame'	OHG	halz		halt
-halþei		Halde	OE	hielde
hana		Hahn	OE	hana
handugs 'wise'	OHG	hantag 'wild'	OE	hendig 'dexterous'
handus		Hand		hand
hansa 'crowd'	OHG	hansa	OE	hōs
hardus		hart		hard
hariggs		Hering		herring
harjis		Heer	OE	here
harpa		Harfe		harp
haspa		Haspe		hasp
hatan		hassen		hate

Gothic		German		English
hatjan		hetzen	OE	hettan
haþus 'fight'	OHG	hathu-	OE	heaðu-
haubiþ		Haupt		head
hauhs		hoch		high
hauniþa 'humility'	OHG	hōnida	OE	hienðu
haunjan 'humiliate'		höhnen	OE	hienan
haúrds 'door'	OHG	hurt-Hürde	OE	hyrd-hurdle
haúrn		Horn		horn

This small sample, chosen at random, can hardly yield more than pointers. It would seem to confirm that modern German has retained more of its inherited Germanic vocabulary than English. But with a loss of approximately one fifth in German as against one third for English, the difference is perhaps surprisingly small. Rather characteristically it is mainly culture words ('sword', 'fight', 'coat') which have been lost. It must, of course, not be overlooked that Gothic, although the earliest recorded Germanic language, is not identical with Proto-Germanic itself.

3.9.2 | Borrowed vocabulary

Apart from developing its own lexical resources Germanic, like all languages, also made use of foreign sources. Three strands of loans can be distinguished in the Germanic period. Certain words are identifiable as loans on account of their isolation, cultural circumstances or linguistic features. Some of these are from unknown sources, some from Celtic. These two strands are early loans and are characterized by having undergone most of the Proto-Germanic sound changes. By far the most important group, the third strand, entered Germanic during the Late Germanic stage, i.e. after the Proto-Germanic sound changes but before any marked later developments, such as the High German or Second Sound Shift, had taken place. These are the Latin loanwords borrowed during the existence of the Roman Empire.

(i) Early loans of uncertain origin. According to Herodotus the Greek word *kannabis* was a recent import in the Greek of his time. Somewhat later presumably, but before the First Sound Shift it reached Germanic ($k > x, h; b > p$). The North-Sea Germanic forms show mutation, hence E *hemp* (<*henep*), Dutch *hennep* but German *Hanf* ($p > f$ as a result of the High German Sound Shift).

Also found in Greek is the possibly Thracian word *baitē* 'a shepherd's coat' which is recorded in Germanic as Gothic *paida*, OE *pād*, German dialectal *Pfeit* (Austro-Bavarian *pfoat*) 'shirt'. This is the first known loanword from the field of clothing, which has continuously proved susceptible to importing fashionable foreign terms.

German *Pfad*, English *path* are isolated words with cognates in Iranian languages from which they were probably borrowed after the Germanic Sound Shift.

The common Germanic word *Silber* – *silver*, also attested in Slavic and Baltic, probably reached the northern Indo-European languages from some Middle Eastern source.

Erz, OHG *aruzzi*, OS *arut*, related to Latin *raudus* and Slavic and Iranian forms, is probably a loan derived from Sumerian *urudu* 'copper', borrowed by a number of Indo-European languages.

English *ore* derives from a Germanic root from which the adjective *ehern* is now the only survival in German. This Germanic root is also found in other Indo-European languages, for instance *aes* in Latin, and may be one of the earliest words for copper or bronze. It probably goes back to the name *Ajasja*, the older name of the island of Cyprus. The later name, of course, underlies the Latin *cuprum* from which our *copper* – *Kupfer* comes.

Linse and Latin *lens-lentis* (whence English *lentil* via French) seem to derive from some unknown eastern source as well. *Rübe* and Latin *rapa*, *Affe* – *ape* are also very early loanwords of eastern origin.

(ii) A small group of loanwords derive from Celtic. This is not surprising seeing that the Celts were the neighbours to the south-west and south during the flourishing Celtic Bronze and Iron Ages when they were also politically at their zenith. Political supremacy is suggested by some of these loanwords, for instance Gothic *reiks* 'ruler', *reikeis* 'powerful' attested in all other Germanic dialects (*Reich, reich*). It belongs to an Indo-European root which is directly represented in Germanic by *recht* – *right*. Latin has *rēx* 'king' and Indian *raja*. Indo-European *ē* became *ī* in Celtic (*-rix* in Gaulish names) which proves the Germanic words with *ī* to be loanwords and not directly inherited words.

German *Amt* has been compared with Gaulish *ambactos* 'servant', a compound containing the roots **ambi-* 'about' and **ag-* 'to act'. The neuter noun *Amt* is to be seen as a Germanic development from the loanword with the meaning 'servant, follower'.

Eid – oath, while deriving from an Indo-European root with the meaning 'to go', developed a specialized juridical meaning in both Celtic and Germanic. The assumption of a semantic loan from Celtic is therefore quite likely. A similar link in legal terminology is provided by *Geisel* 'hostage'.

Celtic and Germanic also share the word for iron (German *Eisen*), but both possibly borrowed it from the Illyrians, the creators of the northern European Iron Age (*Hallstattkultur*).

(iii) By far the greatest influence on the Germanic vocabulary was brought about by the confrontation of the Germanic tribal world with the Roman Empire. Caesar's appearance on the banks of the Rhine halted the Germanic expansion westwards for several centuries. Those tribes which had already crossed the river were subjugated and incorporated in the newly founded Roman provinces; others further east were now exposed to commercial and political penetration, in the first century also to military expeditions. Later they reversed the direction of those military exploits. At all times mercenary service and trade contacts promised a share of the products of Mediterranean civilization. A large number of Roman cities and trading posts sprang up along the Rhine, Moselle, Meuse and Danube. The Roman way of life, cities with stone-built houses, industrial enterprises, a productive large-scale agriculture, horticulture and viticulture spread across the provinces: to be seen, admired, envied, copied or ransacked by the barbarian tribesmen. In all matters of material life, warfare and economic production, in the arts and crafts the Romans were superior. Many hundreds of Latin words in these fields were borrowed by the tribesmen. The Goths who left their homeland along the shores of the Vistula towards the end of the second century share a number of early loanwords with their western neighbours. Many words betray by their phonological form that they were borrowed early. By and large the Anglo-

Saxons absorbed the same words as their continental kinsmen. We therefore conclude that this loan traffic occurred between the beginning of our era and the beginning of the fifth century. Although the Romans enjoyed superiority not only in material things – after all they possessed a literate administration and reached the highest achievements in law and literature, thought and science – the barbarians had no use for such accomplishments. The Romans, of course, were not proselytizers. The barbarians remained barbarians, not even Roman literacy was adopted.

The research of Theodor Frings and others has shown that the Roman infiltration took place from Gaul across the Lower and Middle Rhine. Germania and Italy were separated by the Alps which allowed for few contacts. Thus it was that Northern Gaul, Britain and Roman Germania formed an economic and cultural unit within the Empire. Rhenish dialects contain a last reflex of this to the present day.

Phonologically the Latin loanwords of this period are of great interest. They tell us a good deal about Late Germanic.

(i) The Roman Imperial loanwords underwent the High German Sound Shift (see pp. 169–77), i.e. their adoption occurred before it took place. Compare Lat. *piper* – Gm. *Pfeffer*, E *pepper*; *tēgula* – *Ziegel, tile*.

(ii) They show evidence of the West Germanic doubling of consonants (see p. 64): *puteus* (> *putjus*) – *Pfütze, pit* (OE *pytt*); *vicia* (> *wikja*) – *Wicke, vetch*; *cuprum* – *Kupfer, copper*.

(iii) They partake in the *e-i* rearrangement (see pp. 78–9) *sināpi* – *Senf* 'mustard', OE *senep*; *secula* – *Sichel, sickle* (it may, however, have been borrowed in a Vulgar Latin form **sicila*); *bicārium* – *Becher, beaker*; *menta* – *Minz, mint*. These examples cannot easily be used to date the *e-i* rearrangement. Sound-substitution must be taken into account. After the rearrangement *e* would not have occurred before *n* + consonant and Latin *menta* would have become *mint* simply by sound-substitution as happened to the much later loanword *census* > *Zins*. As with the Late Germanic *e-i* rearrangement we have irregular developments, e.g. *pice(m)* – *Pech* but *pitch*; *cista* – *Kiste* but *chest*.

(iv) They adopt Germanic stress: *flagellum* – *Flegel, flail*; *monēta* (> *munita*) – *Münze, mint* ('coins').

(v) They undergo Germanic *i*-mutation: *catīnus* – *Kessel, kettle*; *molīna* (> *mulina*) – *Mühle, mill*.

(vi) Latin *o* becomes Germanic *u* (see p. 79) in some cases: *pondo* – *Pfund*, *pound* (Germanic had only *u* before *n* + consonant); Vulgar Latin *cocīna* (< *coquīna*) – *Küche*, *kitchen* with change of *o* > *u*, but *coquere* became OHG *kochōn* with *o* preserved before *ō*. Gmc. /u/ must at least have undergone the allophonic split by the time of borrowing even if [o] had not yet become an independent phoneme. But examples like *postis* – *Pfosten*, *post*, *corbis* – *Korb* indicate that the phonemicization of [o] predates the introduction of these loanwords.

(vii) Latin *au* becomes Gmc. *au* before the latter developed to OHG *ou*, *ō* or OE *ēa*: *caupo* – *kaufen*, *cheap*; *caulis* – *Kohl*, though English *cole* does not show the normal development of Gmc. *au*: but *pāvo* – *Pfau*, *pea*(*cock*) does.

(viii) Latin *ae* becomes Gmc. *ai* in the early loanwords: *Caesar* – *Kaiser*.

These loanwords also throw an interesting light on the Latin of the time of borrowing:

(i) The early loans have Gmc. *k* < Lat. *c* even before palatal vowels where it was affricated in Vulgar Latin. Thus we have German *Kaiser*, *Kalk* (< *calcem*) – E *chalk*; *Kirsche* (< *cerēsia*).

(ii) Latin *v* was borrowed as Gmc. /w/, in other words had still its early bilabial value, e.g. *Wall* (< *vallum*) – *wall*, *Wein* – *wine* < *vīnum*.

(iii) The classical Latin short vowels were still preserved in *asilus* (< *asinus*), *Esel*; *camera* > *Kammer*.

(iv) But in *speculum*, *brevis*, *febris* the short *e* had become long so that it was assimilated to Gmc. *ē*² and developed with the native *ē*² to *ia* in OHG, later to *ie*: *Spiegel*, *Brief*, *Fieber*. The consonants, too, show later Latin developments: *c* > *g* and *v* > *f*.

(v) Some Latin words died out early without traces in the Romance languages but were borrowed into Germanic: *cāseus* – *Käse*, *cheese* (*formāticum* is the basis of the modern Romance words, *fromage*, *formaggio*); *pondo* – *Pfund*, *pound* replaced early by *libra* in Latin.

(vi) The names of the days of the week go back to pagan Roman forms, not the later Christian replacements, e.g. *dies Solis* > *Sonntag*, *Sunday*, or *dies Saturni* > *Saturday*, *Zaterdag* in Dutch and adjacent Low German dialects. The Christian *dies dominica* (Fr. *dimanche*, It. *domenica*) was not borrowed but *sambatum* is responsible for South German *Samstag*.

The early medieval Germanic languages contained many early Latin words which have now died out or survive only dialectally. In the following list only such words are included which are still current today in the standard language. In comparing them with the Latin words it must not be forgotten that they were borrowed from the spoken Latin of the frontier settlers, not from Classical Latin, and usually from the oblique forms not the nominative, thus *Kette* presupposes a vulgar form **cadina* rather than *catēna* and *Kalk* is borrowed from *calce* or *calcem* not *calx*. The following semantic fields are of special importance:

Administration and warfare
Drache (*dracō*), *Kaiser* (*Caesar*), *Kampf* (*campus*), *Kerker* (*carcer*), *Kette* (**cadina* < *catēna*), *Meile* (*mīlia passuum*), *Pfahl* (*pālus*), *Pfalz* (*palātia*), *Pfeil* (*pīlum*), *sicher* (*sēcūrus*), *Straße* (*via strāta*), *Wall* (*vallum*), *Zoll* (*toloneum* < *telōneum*).

Building and domestic objects
Arche (*arca*), *Becher* (*bicārium*), *Büchse* (*buxis*), *Estrich* (*astracum*), *Fenster* (*fenestra*), *Kalk* (*calcem*), *Kammer* (*camera*), *Keller* (*cellārium*), *Kessel* (*catīnus*), *Kiste* (*cista*), *kochen* (*coquere*), *Korb* (*corbis*), *Küche* (*cocīna*), *Mauer* (*mūrus*), *Pfanne* (*patina*), *Pfeife* (*pīpa*), *Pfeiler* (*pīlāre*), *Pflaster* (*plastrum*), *Pforz(-heim)* (*porta*), *Pfosten* (*postis*), *Pfühl* (*pulvīnus*), *Pfütze* (*puteus*), *Sack* (*saccus*), *Schemel* (*scamellum*), *Schindel* (*scindula*), *Schrein* (*scrīnium*), *Schüssel* (*scutella*), *Semmel* (*simila*), *Sims* (*sīmātus*), *Söller* (*sōlārium*), *Speicher* (*spīcārium*), *Spiegel* (*spegulum* < *speculum*), *Stube* (**stuba*), *Tisch* (*discus*), *Ziegel* (*tēgula*).

Commerce
Esel (*asinus*), *Karren* (*carrus*), *kaufen* (*caupo*), *Kupfer* (*cuprum*), *-menge*, OHG *mangari*, E *-monger* (*mango*), *Maultier* (*mūlus*), *Mühle* (*molīna*), *Münze* (*monēta*), *Pfeffer* (*piper*), *Pferd* (*paraverēdus*) *Pfund* (*pondo*), *Saumtier* (*sauma* < *sagma*).

Agriculture, horticulture and viticulture
eichen (*aequāre*), *Eimer* (*amphora*), *Essig* (*acētum*), *Flaum* (*plūma*), *Flegel* (*flagellum*), *Frucht* (*fructus*), *impfen* (*imputāre*), *Kelch* (*calicem*), *Kelter* (*calcatūra*), *Kirsche* (*ceresia*), *Kohl* (*caulis*), *Kümmel* (*cumīnum*), *Kürbis* (*cucurbita*), *mausern* (*mūtāre*), *Minz* (*menta*), *mischen* (*miscere*), *Most* (*mustum*), *Pfau* (*pāvō*), *Pfirsich* (*persica*), *pflanzen* (*plantāre*), *Pflaume* (*prūnum*), *pflücken* (*piluccāre*), *pfropfen* (*propagāre*), *Rettich* (*rādicem*), *Sichel* (*sicula, sēcula*), *Trichter* (*trāiectōrium*), *Weiher* (*vīvārium*), *Wein* (*vīnum*), *Winzer* (*vīnitor*).

Days of the week
They are not loanwords but loan translations. The Latin words
for sun and moon were translated into Germanic, the Latin gods
and names of planets were rendered by the names of Germanic
gods nearest to them in significance. Thus the God of War
(Mars) was given as *Tiw* or *Ziu* among some tribes (Anglo-Saxons
and Alemannians) but the Franks equated him with *Thingsus*, the
god presiding over the assembly of warriors (the 'thing'). The
Bavarians adopted a loanword from Greek (Ares, the God of
War). Jupiter (or Jovis), the god of thunder, corresponds to
Germanic *Donar* or *Thor*, and the Latin goddess of love (Venus)
was identified with the Germanic *Frija*. For Saturnus the Germanic peoples had no translation. Whether the various dialects
once had a common name for Wednesday and Saturday and
diversified later we now cannot tell. That there was considerable
pressure in favour of the Christian terms at later stages is certain.

Sonntag (*Sōlis diēs*); *Montag* (*Lūnae diēs*); *Dienstag* (*Martis diēs*, *Mars
Thingsus* > *Dingstag*, Alem. *Zyschtig* – E *Tuesday*, Bav. *Ertag* < *Ares*);
Mittwoch, translation of *hebdomas media* (Christian Lat.), but classical
Mercuriī diēs > *Wednesday*, also in Dutch (*Woensdag*) and N.W. Gm.
dialects (*Gudestag*, *Gōnsdag*); *Donnerstag* (*Iovis diēs*, OHG *Donarestag*,
Bav. *Pfinztag* < Gr. *pente*); *Freitag* (*Veneris diēs*); *Samstag* (< Gr.
sambaton), N.W.Gm. *Saterdag*, Dutch *Zaterdag*, E *Saturday* (< *Saturni
diēs*), *Sonnabend* (< OE *sunnanǣfen*) in North Germany.

The Christian church
Relatively few Christian words are Late Germanic, that is predate
the developments of the individual Germanic languages, for instance High German. Seeing that Christianity became established
earlier in the Greek half of the empire than in the Latin half, it is
not surprising that the earliest loanwords derive from Greek
rather than from Latin. But over what route they reached the
Germanic tribes is still uncertain. Both Greek Christian con-
gregations in the Rhenish cities, above all Trier, and early Gothic
missionary activities have been claimed as possible sources for
those Greek loans. They are *Kirche – church* (< *kyriakon*), *Bischof –
bishop* (*ebiscopus* < *episkopos*), *Engel* (< *angelos*), *Teufel – devil*
(< *diabolos*). The large majority of the Christian terminology
belongs, of course, to the next phase of the German language.

3·9·3 | Onomastics

(i) Among the *geographical names* we find as the oldest stratum the river names. In the territory held by the Germanic peoples during the Proto-Germanic and Late Germanic periods all the larger rivers have names of Indo-European and Germanic ancestry. They represent the oldest type of name, consisting of a single word, a descriptive epithet referring to the flow or colour of the river or to its natural surroundings: *Elbe, Oder, Weser* or *Aller* ('alder swamp'), *Saale, Hase* ('grey'), *Havel, Hunte, Unstrut, Bever, Gande.* Their gender is feminine. The earliest compounds, those with *-apa* and *-aha* both meaning 'water', probably also go back to common Germanic types although they became most productive during the period of Frankish colonization. In the western and southern territories into which the Germanic peoples expanded in pre-Roman times and after the fall of the Roman Empire the larger rivers retained their foreign, Celtic or Illyrian, names, e.g. *Main (Moenus), Maas (Mosa), Mosel (Mosella), Lahn (Logona), Isar (Isara), Neckar (Nicer), Nahe (Nava), Saar (Saravus), Sieg (Sigona), Lech (Licus), Donau (Danuvius).* The Latin forms are of course adaptations of the unrecorded Celtic or Illyrian names. The smaller rivers were named or re-named in the centuries of colonization and forest clearing. Linguistically these names also represent the new type. They are usually compounds, for instance with *-bach (Ottenbach, Sulzbach),* and the first element may be the name of a settler, a settlement or a natural feature.

Apart from the Germanic river names very few other geographical names date from Germanic antiquity. The Roman and Greek sources yield not much more than a dozen names. The reason is no doubt that settlements were mainly named after the people. This is confirmed when we compare the dearth of place-names in classical sources with the wealth of tribal names. It is also confirmed by comparative reconstruction. The earliest and most widely current type of Germanic settlement name consists of a personal name plus the suffix **-ing- (Reading, Hastings, – Reckingen, Reutlingen, Tuttlingen)* with the meaning 'the descendants of –', or 'the people of –'. Most of the modern regional names also derive from tribal names rather than from topographical names: *Hessen, Schwaben, Franken, Sachsen* (< dative plural 'among the Saxons' etc.). The relative scarcity of topographical names, either nature names or habitation names, for settlements is thus an important feature of the Germanic period. But it is nevertheless significant that hints of this other type, possibly not very productive in Germanic times, exist. Among the names recorded by Romans and Greeks we find compounds with -*burg* (*Asciburgium*), -*furt* (*Lupfordon*) ,-*heim* (*Boiohaemum*, see pp. 69 f.). This type of dithematic name with -*burg*, -*heim*, -*stadt* etc. must be assumed to go back to Late Germanic. But probably more important was the derivation with the suffix *-*ing*- denoting 'the people of –'. Especially in the northern homeland it also occurs with nature names, e.g. *Roringen* 'people or place near sedge', *Solingen* 'people or place near a pool'. The Germanic migrations west and south spread, as the most typical habitation name, that in *-*ing*-, overwhelmingly and typically with a personal name as the first element. These earliest Germanic settlement names of the migratory period are found in western and southern Germany, in England, France, Italy and Spain.

During the later centuries of the Age of Migrations the second type of Germanic settlement name is also frequent. As we have seen, it consisted of the settlers' name or a nature name plus a basic noun denoting 'homestead, hamlet, village or fortified place'. It is possible that the Franks who forged the closest links with the Romance population came to favour this second type. If so, they may well have been influenced by the Latin mode of name-giving where the settlements were named (by means of *villa*, *vīcus* or *curtis*) rather than the settlers as in the Germanic -*ing*- formations. At any rate, it is clear that fashion and imitation were important. While in some areas *-*ing*- names were extremely popular, for instance in Lorraine, parts of Baden and in Swabia and in parts of Bavaria, in others -*heim* names were no less predominant, e.g. in Alsace and the Palatinate. Apart from -*heim* the following second elements also occurred: -*burg* (*Würzburg*, *Aschaffenburg*, *Hamburg* (A.D. 715 *Hamanaburg*, OS *ham* 'bay'), *Straßburg*, *Salzburg*, and the translations *Augsburg*, *Regensburg*); -*sel* (cf. OS *seli*, OE *sele* 'hall, building', e.g. *Wallisellen*, *Dagmarsellen*); OHG -*stat*, -*stete*, E -*stead*, ON -*steðir* (*Darmstadt* < *Darmundestat*, *Eichstätt*); in the east of the OS area -*leben* (OHG *leiba*, OS *lēva* 'patrimony', *Aschersleben*, *Molschleben* < *Magolfeslebo*); -*dorf* (*Düsseldorf*). In England and adjacent areas on the continent -*tūn* > -*ton* (*Brixton*, *Teddington*) belong to the same type.

Frequently *-heim* was added to older *-ing-* names (*Besingheim,
Effingham*). Some foreign elements were also adopted in the early
period, e.g. E *-chester* (< *castra*), Gm. *-kesteren*; E *-wich* (< *vīcus*),
Gm. *-wiek, -wich* (*Bardowiek*) and Gm. *-weiler* (< *villare*).

In the former Roman provinces the foreign names of the larger
towns were retained, the most notable exceptions being perhaps
Straßburg (*Argentoratum*) and *Salzburg* (*Juvavium*): *Nimwegen*
(*Noviomagus*), *Aachen* (*Aquis*), *Remagen* (*Rigomagus*), *Bonn*
(*Bonna*), *Köln* (*Colonia*), *Neuß* (*Novaesium*), *Jülich* (*Juliacum*),
Zülpich (*Tolbiacum*), *Koblenz* (*Confluentes*), *Andernach* (*Antun-
nacum*), *Zabern* (*Tavernae*), *Worms* (*Bormetia* < *Borbetomagus*),
Mainz (*Maguntia* < *Mogontiacum*), *Zürich* (*Turicum*), *Basel*
(*Basilia*), *Winterthur* (*Vitodurum*), *Kempten* (*Cambodunum*), *Bregenz*
(*Brigantium*). Sometimes we have partial translation, such as
Regensburg (*Regina castra*), *Augsburg* (*Augusta*). Among the Latin
place-name-forming suffixes, *-acum/-iacum* > Gm. *-ach/-ich* is
found especially frequently, e.g. *Breisach* (*Brisiacum*), *Lörrach*
(*Lauriacum*), *Metternich* (**Martiniacum*). Many *-acum/-iacum*
names were later reinterpreted as *-ingen* names. *Civitas Aurelia
Aquensis* or its short form *Aquis* was translated as *Baden* (*-Baden*).

Two foreign tribal names borrowed in Germanic times have
been productive. The Celtic tribal name *Volcae* became Germanic
**walha-* with an adjectival derivation **walhisk-*. From denoting
the Celtic neighbours it was transferred on the continent to the
Romance peoples generally, hence *Welsche, Welschland, wallonisch,
Wallachei, Walnuß* cf. E *Welsh, Wales, Cornwall* and *walnut*.
The name of the *Venethi* (Tacitus) or *Venedi* (Pliny) was borrowed
and was used as a German name for the Slavs (OHG *Winida*, OE
Wenedas): *Wenden, wendisch*.

(ii) Germanic *personal names* retained the Indo-European
dithematic and monothematic types. The few hundred names
recorded up to A.D. 500 in classical sources and runic inscriptions
are of course overwhelmingly names of leading figures. This may
explain the early predominance of the dithematic names and must
be borne in mind when examining the actual name-giving technique and the use of various appellatives in name composition.
Such an investigation is complicated by the fact that the signs of
mechanical imitation were already very prevalent in the first
centuries of our era and that the ethical and possibly religious
ideas which had once given rise to this particular kind of name-

giving were already blurred. With this reservation in mind it is nevertheless possible to ascertain certain principles:

(1) The dithematic names consisted of two nominal elements, nouns or adjectives.

(2) Monothematic names were of two kinds. There were genuinely monothematic ones like *Horsa* or *Karl* (OE *Ceorl*) and hypocoristic, that is familiar shortened forms from a dithematic name such as OE *Cutha* for *Cuthwulf* or Gothic *Totila* with diminutive suffix *-il-*.

(3) Male names had a masculine noun as second element, female names a feminine noun. But primary masculine names could be made into secondary feminine names, e.g. m. *-fridus* (< *-friþu- 'peace') > f. *-freda*. Neuter nouns were thus excluded from second position in the compound. Adjectives could of course take either masculine or feminine endings, but some adjectives were typically more 'male', e.g. *-bald-* 'bold', *-hard-* 'hard', *-mār-* 'famous', and others typically more 'female', e.g. *-flād-* 'beautiful', *-swinþ-* 'swift, strong'.

(4) The two elements never alliterated with each other. But names within a family frequently alliterated, e.g. *Gunther – Gernot – Giselher – Grimhilt* (*Kriem-*). In the royal house of Essex (the East Saxons) all names with one or two exceptions alliterated in *S-* deriving from their progenitor *Seaxnete*, a son of Woden. Alliteration stayed alive for over a thousand years, at least in parts of Germania.

(5) Certain name elements became established in particular noble lines, e.g. see the Burgundian kings *Gundaharius – Gundevechus – Gundobadus*, the Merovingians *Theodericus – Theodebertus – Theodebaldus*, or the constant use of the initial elements *Aethel-* and *Ead-* in the royal house of Wessex.

(6) Alliteration and basic words could be combined to produce a pattern of variation. The Merovingian *Chlotharius I* had a brother *Childebertus* and sons *Charibertus*, *Sigebertus* and *Chilpericus* and grandsons *Childebertus* and *Chlotharius II*. Both front and end variation were often practised for many generations. Among the Merovingians straightforward repetition occurred frequently: there were five called *Chlotharius*.

(7) The second elements did not begin with a vowel, thus the elements **Aran-* or **Arnu-* 'eagle' and **Eƀura-* 'wild boar' occurred only as first elements.

(8) The semantic relationship between the two elements is doubtful. While perhaps some of the values of the appellatives were wished upon the child (e.g. the strength of a bear), the compounds cannot be seen as either copulative or determinative compounds. But alliteration and variation were productive and significant principles.

(9) The two elements derive from certain semantic spheres and may at one time have had a particular magical or religious significance, but that time must already have been distant in Late Germanic times. The shifting patterns of popularity of certain elements may have been purely mechanical or may have reflected certain beliefs. But it is doubtful whether the popularity of the *hraban-* element ('raven') in Frankish and High German had anything to do with the cult of Woden. The popularity of certain themes in particular families must have reflected a certain attitude towards blood-relationship and noble lineage.

(10) The chief semantic fields from which the name elements were drawn were (the forms are mainly those found in OHG):

(a) Fighting, battle: *badu-, hadu-, gund, hild, wīg* all 'battle', *sigu-* 'victory', *fridu-* 'peace'.

(b) Army: *hari-/heri-, folc-*.

(c) Weapons: *brand-* 'sword', *ask-* 'spear', **agjō-* 'point', *gēr-* 'spear', *helm-* 'helmet', *lind-* 'shield', *ort-* 'point', *rand-* 'shield'.

(d) Ruling: *rīh-* 'ruler', *bodo-* 'one who bids', *ward, mund* 'protector', *wald-* 'ruler'.

(e) Wealth and fame: *hruod-, hlodo-, mār-* all 'famous', *ōt-* (OE *ēad-*), *uodal-* 'treasure, heritage', *rāt* 'help'.

(f) Kith and kin: *kuni-* 'kin', *liut-* 'people', *diet-* 'people', *gast, win-* 'friend'.

(g) Qualities: *adal-/edil-* 'noble', *bald-* 'bold, brave', *ballo-* 'splendid', *berht* 'bright', *kuon-* 'brave'.

(h) Animals: *wolf, bero-/bern-* 'bear', *ebur-* 'wild boar', *ar-/arn-* 'eagle' and *swana-* 'swan' as first element for female names.

(i) Religious concepts: *alb-* 'elf', *ans-* (OE *os-*) 'god', *got-, irmin-* 'name of a god'. It is characteristic that the names of the gods *Woden, Tiw/Ziu* or *Thor/Donar* are never found in names in early times.

Although some names or name elements were more common in some tribes than in others, for instance 'eagle' and 'raven' were not well attested in Old English or Old Saxon, many elements were extremely common throughout the Germanic tribal world. To the population of the Roman Empire they represented a totally new cultural feature. After the conquests they became a new fashion and the names of the conquerors were eagerly and widely adopted by the conquered. It has been estimated that in the sixth century fifty per cent of the names in Gaul were Germanic. The Romance languages still have many traces, for instance French *Bertrand* (*Berhtrand*), *Roger* (*Hrodgerius*), *Guillaume* (*Wilhelm*), *Thierry* (*Dietrich, Theodoricus*), *Henri* (*Heinrich*), *Thiebaut* (*Dietbald, Theodobaldus*), *Gautier* (*Walthari*). In the Germanic languages these names represent as much a part of the common heritage as any other feature of these languages, although they were later supplanted by other modes of name-giving.

Select Bibliography

E. H. Antonsen, 'On Defining Stages in Prehistoric Germanic', *Lg.*, 41 (1965) 19–36; K. R. Bahnick, *The Determination of Stages in the Historical Development of the Germanic Languages by Morphological Criteria*, The Hague, 1973; C. J. E. Ball, 'The Germanic Dental Preterite', *TPS* (1968) 162–88; H. Benediktsson, 'The Proto-Germanic Vowel System' in *To Honor Roman Jakobson*, The Hague, 1967, vol. 1, pp. 174–96; C. T. Carr, *Nominal Compounds in Germanic*, Oxford, London, 1939; F. van Coetsem, 'Zur Entwicklung der germanischen Gemeinsprache' in L. E. Schmitt (ed.), *Kurzer Grundriß der germanischen Philologie*, vol. 1, Berlin, 1970, pp. 1–93; id., *Das System der starken Verba und die Periodisierung im älteren Germanischen*, Amsterdam, 1956; id. and H. L. Kufner, *Toward a Grammar of Proto-Germanic*, Tübingen, 1972; K. Düwel, *Runenkunde*, Stuttgart, 1968; R. W. V. Elliott, *Runes*, Manchester, 1963; J. Fourquet, *Les mutations consonantiques du germanique*, Paris, 1948; id., 'Die Nachwirkungen der ersten und der zweiten Lautverschiebungen', *ZMF*, 22 (1954) 1–33, 193–8; id., *L'ordre des éléments de la phrase en germanique ancien*, Paris, 1938; T. Frings, *Grundlegung einer Geschichte der deutschen Sprache*, 3rd ed., Halle, 1957; id., *Germania Romana* (now Mitteldeutsche Studien, 19) Halle, 1966–8; H. Fromm, 'Die ältesten germanischen Lehnwörter im Finnischen', *ZDA*, 88 (1957/8) 81–101, 211–40, 299–324; L. L. Hammerich, 'Die germanische und die hochdeutsche Lautverschiebung', *Beitr.* (Tüb.), 77 (1955) 1–29, 165–203; W.

Herrlitz, *Historische Phonologie des Deutschen*, i *Vokalismus*, ii *Konsonantismus*, Tübingen, 1970/72; O. Höfler, 'Stammbaumtheorie, Wellentheorie, Entfaltungstheorie', *Beitr.* (Tüb.), 77 (1955) 30–66, 424–76; 78 (1956) 1–44; R. D. King, *Historical Linguistics and Generative Grammar*, Englewood Cliffs, 1969; F. Kluge, W. Mitzka, *Etymologisches Wörterbuch der deutschen Sprache*, 21st ed., Berlin, 1975; W. P. Lehmann, 'The Conservatism of Germanic Phonology', *JEGP*, 52 (1953) 140–52; G. Lerchner, *Studien zum nordwestgermanischen Wortschatz*, Halle, 1965; E. A. Makaev, 'The Morphological Structure of Common Germanic', *Linguistics*, 10 (1964) 22–50; F. Maurer, *Nordgermanen und Alemannen*, 3rd ed., Berne, 1952; H. Moser, 'Deutsche Sprachgeschichte der älteren Zeit' in W. Stammler (ed.), *Deutsche Philologie im Aufriß*, 2nd ed., Berlin, 1957, vol. I, 621–854; W. G. Moulton, 'The Stops and Spirants of Early Germanic', *Lg.*, 30 (1954) 1–42; id., 'Zur Geschichte des deutschen Vokalsystems', *Beitr.* (Tüb.), 83 (1961) 1–35; E. Prokosch, *A Comparative Germanic Grammar*, Philadelphia, 1939; L. Rösel, *Die Gliederung der germanischen Sprachen nach dem Zeugnis ihrer Flexionsformen*, Nuremberg, 1962; R. Schützeichel, *Die Grundlagen des westlichen Mitteldeutschen*, 2nd ed., Tübingen, 1976; E. Seebold, *Vergleichendes und etymologisches Wörterbuch der germanischen starken Verben und ihrer Primärableitungen*, The Hague, 1970; F. de Tollenaere, 'De Harigasti-inscriptie op helm B van Negau', *Mededelingen der Koninkl. Nederl. Akad. van Wetenschapen/Letterkunde*, 30, 11, Amsterdam, 1967; W. F. Twaddell, 'The Inner Chronology of the Germanic Consonant Shift', *JEGP*, 38 (1939) 337–59; J. B. Voyles, 'Simplicity, Ordered Rules, and the First Sound Shift', *Lg.*, 43 (1967) 636–60; H. B. Woolf, *The Old Germanic Principles of Name-Giving*, Baltimore, 1939; F. Wrede, 'Ingwäonisch und Westgermanisch', *ZfdMaa.*, 19 (1924) 270–83.

The Carolingian Beginning

4.1 | **The Regnum Francorum
and the lingua theodisca**

4.1.1 | The linguistic territory

When the turbulent centuries of the Age of Migrations
gave way to more settled conditions towards the end of the sixth
century, the territory inhabited by the western Germanic peoples
had changed very markedly since the days of the *Pax Romana*
(see the map on p. 147). In the north it extended as far as the river
Eider. The peninsula itself had, however, been taken over by the
Scandinavian-speaking Danes. In the east, the vast expanse of
territory between the Vistula and the Elbe and Saale rivers was
now inhabited by Baltic and Slavic peoples. So was Bohemia.
Skirting the Bohemian Forest the boundary reached the Danube
at the mouth of the river Enns and followed the course of the
Enns into the Alps. Carinthia was an area of mixed Slovene and
Bavarian settlement. At not a few places Slavic speakers were found
even west of the Elbe and Saale. In the south, Bavarians and
Alemannians had settled the pre-Alpine lands of the former
Roman provinces of Germania superior, Rhaetia and Noricum
and were pushing into the Alpine valleys where the Romance
population had retained a foothold. While Alpine Rhaetia with
its capital Chur was a Romance-speaking area reaching as far
north as Lake Constance (Bodensee) – the only surviving Roman
province north of the central Alps – the Lombards formed a
Germanic-speaking outpost south of the Alps. For over two centuries after their conquest of Lombardy from 568 onwards their
legal codes contained Germanic words. But we do not know how
numerous the Lombards were or how long a substantial proportion of their people retained their Germanic speech. It is unlikely
that Lombardic survived much beyond the end of the independent
Lombardic kingdom in 774, and it must have completely disappeared in the course of the tenth century. In the meantime
Bavarian settlers had crossed the Brenner pass and formed the

one substantial German-speaking area south of the Alps in what is now known as South Tyrol.

In the west, Alemannians settled solidly up to the northern end of the Jura and to the crest of the Vosges. In the course of the ninth century they crossed the northern range of the Alps and pushed into the upper Rhone valley. Known as *Walser*, they continued the colonization of the highest Alpine valleys for several centuries. From the Vosges to the sea the linguistic boundary was probably at first very ill-defined. Franks had penetrated in strong numbers to the Seine and to some extent up to the Loire. But it must not be assumed that they ever constituted more than a small minority of the population west of the Meuse except along the sea coast. On the other hand sizeable Romance populations were still found farther east especially in the valley of the Moselle. Romance speakers may also still have inhabited the ruined Roman cities of Trier, Cologne and Mainz. While this extensive mixture of populations was the result of the migrations and settlements linked with the fall of the Western Roman Empire, the stabilization and subsequent formation of a clear-cut linguistic boundary was the consequence of the history of the one successful successor state of the Roman Empire: the Kingdom of the Franks.

4.1.2 | Conquest and conversion

In the sixth century the Merovingian kings of the Franks succeeded in incorporating the majority of the Germanic peoples dwelling in central Europe in their kingdom and in asserting their hegemony over the rest. Rhine Franks (including the Hessians), Thuringians, Alemannians and Bavarians thus formed the eastern half of the Merovingian kingdom. The frontier against the Frisians in the north-east tended to advance or retract according to the strength of the Frankish dynasty. Even the Saxons paid tribute when the power of the Merovingians was impressive enough to extract it. The Lombards in Italy, also paying tribute at one time, were made aware of the might of their northern neighbours. Merovingian Frankish power rested on two closely-linked advantages, which the Merovingian kingdom enjoyed alone of all the Germanic kingdoms on Roman imperial soil. First the Merovingians and their Franks shared the orthodox Catholic Christian faith of their Latin subjects right from the moment of conquest. Secondly, in consequence of this, they commanded the co-operation and support of the powerful educated lay and clerical Roman provincial magnates. They therefore based their supremacy on the Roman provincial church and administration. Latin was their sole official and written linguistic medium. The eastern Germanic and barbarous half of their kingdom was allowed to remain barbarous, and church and state administration stayed rudimentary. Just as the Roman Empire had not produced literacy among the Germanic tribes, the Merovingian dominion did not bring it about either. In fact literacy was to be the gift not of the state but of the church. And then it was intended to be literacy in Latin. Written German appeared by reason of the educational needs of Latin, at least at first. But the fact remains, it was a child of the conversion, and the conversion to Roman Christianity was finally the achievement of the *Regnum Francorum*.

During the declining decades of the Merovingian dynasty it appears to have been the preaching of Irish missionaries more than the efforts of the established Christian church in Gaul which led to the first wave of conversion in the eastern half of the Frankish kingdom. In particular, the Alemannians and Bavarians were converted in the seventh century and the beginning of the eighth. They, like the Rhine Franks, lived in former Roman provinces where traces of Christianity may never have completely disappeared. Two areas of paganism were more persistent: the centre of the eastern kingdom, Hesse, which had never been Roman, and the north-east, Frisia and beyond, Saxony.

When the long-haired scions of the house of Merovech were no longer able to wield power in their much divided kingdom the reins were assumed by the mayors of the palace of Austrasia, the eastern part of the kingdom. The descendants of Arnulf, bishop of Metz, and of Pepin of Landen, had their power-base in the western Rhinelands, between Aachen and Metz. But it was not until Charles Martel seized power in 719 that the decline of the kingdom was arrested. The tribal duchies which had acquired a degree of independence were once more reduced to provinces. There were expeditions against the Saxons, and independent northern Frisia was finally conquered. It was now that the missionary activities, which Anglo-Saxons had already begun, received more and more Frankish encouragement. The gospels were to supplement the sword. The earliest Anglo-Saxon foundation was the monastery and abbey of Echternach in present-day Luxemburg, founded in 698 by Willibrord, who became 'the apostle of the Frisians'. While Willibrord from Northumbria was active in the north-east, becoming the first archbishop of the newly founded metropolitan see of Utrecht, Winfrith of Wessex, whose church name was Boniface, worked in central and southern Germany. The Anglo-Saxon church had particularly close connections with the pope, and Boniface had been specially commissioned for his task of converting the pagans of Hesse and Thuringia. It was he who became the first organizer of the Frankish church in Germany, the founder of the Abbey of Fulda (744) and the first archbishop of Mainz, whose province covered the major part of Germany. He also organized the church in Bavaria for its semi-independent duke Odilo. In close collaboration with Rome the Carolingian house promoted the organization of the church and the foundation of a large number of monasteries which often retained close links with the dynasty. The Rhenish sees, Chur (in Rhaetia), Constance and Strasbourg (in Alemannia), Speyer, Worms, Trier and Cologne (in the Frankish Rhinelands), and Augsburg (on the border of Alemannia and Bavaria) date from the Merovingian era, with tenuous links even to late Roman times in some cases. The Bavarian and Franconian sees and the two dozen most important monasteries were all founded during the reigns of Charles Martel and Pepin the Short, grandfather and father respectively of Charles the Great. The conversion of the Germans within the kingdom of the Franks and the organization of their church was thus the work of the eighth century, where it had not already been achieved before. But nowhere was the supremacy of Latin challenged, nor had the political centre of power yet shifted decisively to the German-speaking Rhinelands. Pepin the Short, when he was finally encouraged by the pope to assume the title of King of the Franks after the deposition of the last Merovingian, was crowned at Soissons. He died in 768 and was buried at St Denis. It was during the long reign of his son, Charles the Great (768–814), that politically the weight was shifted to the east. It was he who in thirty years of brutal warfare finally subdued the heathen Saxons and made them Christian subjects of his *Regnum Francorum*. Along the Slav frontier he established military border commands, the so-called Marches (Nordmark, Sorbische Mark,

Ostmark, Mark of Friuli). In the south-east he broke the power of the Avars in Hungary, thus facilitating the advance of Bavarian settlers into what is now Upper and Lower Austria. With papal encouragement he conquered the kingdom of the Lombards and made himself *rex Francorum et Langobardorum* (774). It was during his reign that further German metropolitan sees, in addition to Mainz, were established: Cologne (replacing Utrecht), Trier and Salzburg. Although his court remained peripatetic it was in the Rhinelands that he built new palaces, at Nymegen, Ingelheim and Aachen, which became his favourite and preferred residence, with its famous palace chapel. The illustrious court academy which he founded and staffed with scholars from all corners of his far-flung empire was mainly set the task of Christian education and Christian renewal. Its greatest luminary, Alcuin of York, the third great Anglo-Saxon churchman in Frankish service after Willibrord and Boniface, was a teacher and reformer. Most of the effort and zeal of these scholars went into the renewal of the sources of their faith: the Bible, the commentaries, the establishment of an authoritative liturgical manual, a collection of the canons, a new edition of the rule of St Benedict, liturgical chant and the renewal of the art of writing. It was above all the aim of a better-educated clergy and a better-instructed laity which led Charles and his circle to give encouragement also to the use of the German vernacular as a written medium. Thus it was during his reign that the German language first became a written literary medium. While he no doubt shared all the ideals of the Latin-Christian renewal pursued so vigorously by the members of his court academy, he was no bigot. Einhard, his biographer, tells us: 'At the same time he directed that the age-old narrative poems, barbarous enough, it is true, in which were celebrated the warlike deeds of the kings of ancient times, should be written out and so preserved. He also began a grammar of his native tongue' (L. Thorpe, *Einhard and Notker the Stammerer*, London, 1969, p. 82). Nothing of this has come down to us. But his attitude to the German language must have been widely known. The unknown copyist who wrote down the one preserved heroic poem, the *Hildebrandslied*, may well have been encouraged by the king's expressed opinion. Not only were translations for educational and religious purposes inspired, but the few original compositions which we possess must equally have benefited from this favourable climate, although they were written long after Charles's death.

4.1.3 | The lingua theodisca

The language thus encouraged was known to the Carolingian ecclesiastical authorities, who of course wrote only in Latin, as *lingua theodisca*. The meaning of this expression has been much discussed, naturally enough since it contains the earliest recorded form of the word *deutsch* from Germany itself. The etymology is clear enough. It is a Latin loanword from Germanic: Gothic *þiuda*, OE *þēod*, OHG *thiot(a)* mean 'people', and *theodiscus* is based on an adjectival derivation in *-*isk*-. In its meaning three aspects can be distinguished. It can quite simply mean 'vernacular' in contrast to Latin. In fact, in the first recorded occurrence of the word, in a report by the papal legate George of Ostia, written to the pope possibly by the Frankish abbot and chaplain to Charles, Wigbod, it refers to English. The text states that the resolutions of the Anglo-Saxon Synod of Corbridge were read at the Synod of Cealchyd in 786 'both in Latin and in *theotisce* so that all might understand', in other words in the language of the people or the vernacular. Since there was another 'vulgar language' (< *vulgus* 'people'), the *lingua Romana*, to be distinguished from Latin, the *lingua theodisca* had naturally the narrower meaning of the 'vernacular of the Germanic peoples'. Other, later, references in fact include the Goths and the Langobards. The linguistic unity of the Germanic peoples was thus recognized by Carolingian scholars. The third shade of meaning arises through specific reference to all the peoples of the eastern kingdom of the Franks. The word thus gradually acquired the narrower meaning of *deutsch*, including, however, the language of the Netherlands, especially Flemish, until modern times. Hence the English word *Dutch* with its specialized meaning. *Lingua theodisca* was very typically a word of the Carolingian age. Towards the end of the ninth century it was generally replaced by *teutonica*, just as, significantly, the eastern kingdom was styled *regnum Teutonicorum*, from the time of its renewal under a different dynasty in about 920.

4.1.4 | Regional variants

Early medieval German was of course no uniform, normalized written language. For that the political and educational conditions simply did not exist. Regularized written standard languages with which we are familiar in our age, and which the ancient world knew in Latin, were not part of the medieval scene. With a struggle and some lapses the Middle Ages retained a dead language as a regularized fixed written medium. German was written in local forms in a relatively small number of places, mainly in about two to three dozen monasteries where scriptoria were maintained. As far as the written records are concerned it is useful to distinguish between two kinds of documents. Firstly, there are documents written in Latin which contain individual German words either as quoted technical terms, e.g. *morganegyba* 'wedding gift to the bride', *leudes* 'retinue of warriors', *herisliz* 'desertion from the army', cf. German *Morgengabe*, *Leute*, **Heer-schlitz*, or as glosses written or scratched into a Latin codex for the purpose of translation or explanation. Secondly, there are those documents in which German is the main medium or purpose of composition. Here we find complete glossaries, translations of whole texts and original works. The earliest document of the second category dates from about 770 while documents of the first category link up, backwards in time, with the recordings of Late Germanic words in Roman and Greek reports. Records in German depend very much on the circumstances of the time and on the vicissitudes of later survival. Lombardy and West Francia (Neustria) were no longer in a position to react to the Carolingian cultural impulses in favour of German owing to advanced Romanization. From there we only have documentation of the first kind. Saxony and Frisia were still too backward and undeveloped. Our documents thus come overwhelmingly from Franconia, Alemannia and Bavaria. But the history of survival is very much more favourable in the case of Alemannia and Bavaria than in that of Franconia, at least the Rhenish part.

The language written in those relatively few ecclesiastical centres may be said to consist of a number of 'monastery dialects'. But many factors contribute to these dialects:

(i) The circumstances of the foundation of the institution and the traditions arising from it. Anglo-Saxon features in orthography and lexicon at Echternach, Würzburg and Fulda are an example.

(ii) The seat of the scriptorium is obviously important. Linguistic features of the 'monastery dialect' may to this extent reflect the linguistic features of the local dialect, e.g. in St Gall the Alemannic dialect of the Carolingian Thurgau.

(iii) The provenance of the monks. Many of the first generation of monks of Fulda, for instance, including its abbot Sturmi, hailed from Bavaria.

(iv) Although every centre tended to evolve its own orthographic tradition, the training and educational background of every scribe and writer may be of some importance. Otfrid of Weissenburg and Walahfrid Strabo, later abbot of Reichenau, were educated at Fulda.

(v) Copying played a far greater part than original composition. The provenance of the original to be copied is obviously important. Every shade of possibility can occur: faithful copying, partial adaptation to the local linguistic tradition, far-reaching translation from the 'foreign' practice into the local convention.

(vi) There may be multiple copying in different centres and the facts may remain obscure, thus allowing a free rein to speculation or ingenuity of interpretation.

(vii) Regional traditions existed, e.g. the spelling ⟨p, t, k⟩ in Bavarian scriptoria for WGmc. /b–ƀ, d, g–g/ or ⟨uo⟩ in East Franconia for WGmc. /ō/. In the course of time tendencies of levelling made themselves felt, e.g. Franconian features began to prevail in Alemannic scriptoria (⟨uo⟩ for earlier ⟨ua⟩, ⟨b, g⟩ replacing earlier ⟨p, k⟩).

It is, however, the practice to refer to the individual monastery dialects by the names of assumed tribal regional dialects. If the designation is taken to indicate the geographical location of the particular scriptorium the practice is harmless. There may, however, also be a linguistic justification. The tribes had a historical existence and significance from the third century onwards. Although they were amalgams of disparate populations, probably continually changing in composition, and engaged in conquest and colonization for much of the time, they had no doubt developed some linguistic characteristics. The historical situation in which they found themselves would tend to lead to much levelling, to regional large-scale dialects rather than sharply subdivided local dialects. In fact language must have had the features of settlers' dialects or of colonial languages in general. Although some very

few salient features of present-day German dialects (the Alemannic – Rhine Franconian *pf-/p-* contrast; the High German – Low
German *-ss-/-t-* contrast etc.) go back to early medieval times, the
overwhelming number of dialect differences of today are of much
later origin, e.g. Bavarian – Alemannic *au/ū, Haus – Huus*. To
approach the early medieval dialects with the dialects and dialect
map of today in mind may thus be very misleading. The dialect
differences may very well have been much smaller than they were
to become in the fragmented and stabilized world of the later
Middle Ages. In the Carolingian empire the tribal units continued to have some existence although they were under pressure:
the tribal laws were written down in the eighth century (*Lex
Alamannorum, Lex Baiuvariorum* etc.); the army was composed
of tribal levies; tribal duchies under local magnates formed or reformed whenever the central power weakened; some sees were
clearly constituted on a tribal basis, e.g. the province of Salzburg
for Bavaria, the see of Constance for central Alemannia. All these
facts indicate that we cannot be far wrong if we speak of tribal
dialects, and always remember that the written monastery dialects
are at best only a partial reflection and may well be a confused
reflection of the spoken regional dialects.

Early medieval German, as a linguistic phase, extends in time
from about 750 to 1050. Documentation, as far as individual words
are concerned, begins before and, of course, does not come to an
end or alter abruptly in linguistic type. But literary output reached
a climax in the ninth century and fell off very considerably in the
tenth. Much of the work of the eleventh century already prepared the way for a new linguistic type: German of the High
Middle Ages. A synchronic description of early medieval German
is therefore best based on the language of the middle of the ninth
century. This also holds good for the individual dialects when they
are characterized in comparison with one another. In reality they
are, of course, in flux throughout the period.

In this sense we distinguish the following early medieval
German dialects:

Sources	Main scriptoria	Salient features
(i) *Alemannic* Glosses from St Gall and Reichenau; Rule of St Benedict; Murbach hymns; onomastic material; the work of Notker Teutonicus (early 11th century). Murbach origin of the Isidore translation (before 800) is assumed by some, disputed by others.	St Gall in eastern Switzerland; Reichenau, an island in Lake Constance; Murbach in the southern Vosges; Strasbourg, Alsace.	(a) WGmc./p-, t-, k-/ spelt *pf*, *z*, *ch*. (b) WGmc. medial and final /p, t, k/ spelt *ff*, *f*; *zz*, *z*; *hh*, *h*. (c) WGmc. /p, t, k/ after liquids and nasals shifted: *pf*, *z*, *ch*. (d) WGmc. /b-ƀ, d, g–g/ spelt *p*, *t*, *k* (*b* and *g* becoming more general later). (e) WGmc. /þ/ > *d* in 8th century. (f) Notker in 11th century has a special law of initial consonants. (g) WGmc. /ē²/ > *ea*, *ia*. (h) WGmc. /ō/ > *ua*, later *uo*. (i) WGmc. /ai/ > *ei* or *e* (before *r, h, w*). (j) WGmc. /eu/ > *iu*; *io* (before dent. +*a, e, o*). (k) Prefix: *ka-*, (*ke-*).
(ii) *Bavarian* The oldest alphabetically arranged glossary: *Abrogans*; numerous other glosses; *Exhortatio*; Wessobrunn Prayer; *Muspilli*; Monsee Fragments; copy of Otfrid's *Liber Evangeliorum*.	Salzburg, Monsee in present-day Austria. Freising, Regensburg (St Emmeram), Wessobrunn, Tegernsee in Bavaria.	(a) (b) (c) (e) as Alem. (d) *p, t, k* spellings more widespread and persistent than in Alem. (g) WGmc. /ē²/ spelt *e* in 8th century. (h) WGmc. /ō/ spelt *o, oo* into first half of 9th century. (i) WGmc. /ai/ spelt *ai* till *c.* 800, then *ei* except where >*e*. (j) As Alem. (k) *ka-*
(iii) *Lombardic* Personal names and appellatives in Latin documents, notably *Edictus Rothari*		(a) WGmc. /p-, k-/ spelt *p, c*. (b) probably shifted (see Alem.) WGmc. /t/ spelt *s* or *z*, *tz*. (d) *p* and *t* spellings. (e) *d, th* and *t* spellings for WGmc. /þ/.

Sources	Main scriptoria	Salient features

(643), *Historia*
Langobardorum
by Paulus
Diaconus.

(g) WGmc. /ē²/ spelt *e* or *i*.
(h) WGmc. /ō/ spelt *o*.
(i) WGmc. /ai/ spelt *ai*, later *e, a*.
(j) WGmc. /au/ spelt *au*.

(iv) *East Franconian*
Translation of   Fulda,
Tatian's gospel Würzburg,
harmony.   Bamberg.
Confessions,
glosses.

(a) and (c) as Alem. with the
     exception: /k/ > k.
(b) as Alem.
(d) WGmc. /b-ƀ, d, g-g/ spelt *b, t, g*.
(e) WGmc. /Þ/ > d (initial *th*
     spellings).
(g) WGmc. /ē²/ > *ia, ie*.
(h) WGmc. /ō/ > *uo*.
(i) as Alem.
(j) WGmc. *eu* > *io* bef. *a, e, o,* > *iu*
     bef. *i,* (*j*)*, u*.
(k) Prefix *gi-*.

(v) *South Rhenish Franconian*
Catechism,   Weissenburg
charters,   (Wissembourg)
Otfrid's *Liber* on the river
Evangeliorum   Lauter on the
(863–71),   northern border
onomastic   of Alsace.
material.

(a) WGmc. /p-, t-, k-/ spelt *p, ᴢ, k*.
(b) as Alem.
(c) as Alem. but /k/ > k.
(d) WGmc. /b-ƀ, d, g-g/ spelt *b, d-/*
     -t-/-t, g.
(e) WGmc. /Þ/ spelt *th/-d-*.
(g) WGmc. /ē²/ > *ia*.
(h) WGmc. /ō/ > *ua*, later *uo*.
(i) as Alem.
(j) WGmc. /eu/ > *iu, io* or *ia* as EFr.
(k) *gi-*.

(vi) *Rhenish Franconian*
Strasbourg   Mainz, Lorsch,
Oaths, *Ludwigs-* Worms, Speyer.
lied, glosses and
charters. Charles
the Great's
names of months
and winds. The
Isidore transla-
tion is located
within the wider
western
Franconian
region by many
scholars.

(a) (b) (c) as SRh.Fr. but *-pp-* and *-mp-*
     remain.
(d) WGmc. /b-ƀ/, d, g-g/ spelt *b, d/-t, g*.
(e) WGmc. /Þ/ spelt *th-/-dh-*.
(h) WGmc. /ō/ > *uo*.
(i) (j) (k) as SRh.Fr.

Sources   Main scriptoria Salient features

(vii) *Central Franconian*

Mainly glosses, Echternach,   (a) (b) (c) as Rh.Fr. but with *-rp-*,
earliest in   Cologne,   *-lp-* spellings.
Maihinger   Trier.   (d) WGmc. /b–ƀ, d, g–g/ spelt *b, d, g*
Evangeliar   but with *-v-* and *-h, -ch* spellings,
(Echternach).   increasing later.
Trier Capitulary.   (e) WGmc. /þ/ usually *th*. Otherwise
                            like Rh.Fr. The modern dialectal
                            'relic words' *dit, dat, wat, it, -et*
                            (*allet*) 'this, that, what, it, all' are
                            only rarely recorded.

All the above written dialects together constitute Old High German in the period from the eighth to the eleventh century.

(viii) *Old Low Franconian*

Some glosses,   Flanders,   Earliest form of Netherlandish.
onomastic   Limburg.
material, psalm
fragments.

(ix) *Old Saxon*

Heliand,   Werden,   (a) (b) (c) WGmc. /p, t, k/ spelt *p, t, k*
Genesis,   Essen,   (c).
glosses.   Merseburg,   (d) WGmc. /b–ƀ, d, g-g/ spelt *b/ƀ, v, f*;
             Freckenhorst,   *d*; *g* (also *-gh, -ch*).
             but none of the (e) WGmc. /þ/ spelt *th* or *ð*.
             sizeable works (g) WGmc. /ē²/ spelt *e* (but also *ie*).
             can be traced (h) WGmc. /ō/ spelt *o* or *uo*.
             to any centre (i) WGmc. /ai/ spelt *e*; /au/ spelt *o*.
             with certainty. (j) WGmc. /eu/ spelt *io* (bef. *a, e, o*) or
                            iu (bef. *i, j, u*).
                    (k) Prefix *gi-*.

The following samples show some of the representative dialectal spellings, which of course are never exclusive.

Alem.	Bav.	EFr.	SRh.Fr. & Rh.Fr.	CFr.	OS
pruader 'brother'	proder	bruoder	bruoder, bruodher	broder, bruder	brothar
cotes 'God's'	kotes	gotes	godes	godes	godes
chirihcha 'church'	chirihha	ch-, kirihha	ch-, kirihha	kiricha	kirika

Alem.	Bav.	EFr.	SRh.Fr. & Rh.Fr.	CFr.	OS
ze kebanne 'giving'	ze kepanne	ze gebanne	ze gebanne	ce gevene	te gebanne
kap, kab, gab 'gave'	kap	gab	gab	*gaf	gaf
in erdu 'on earth'	in erdu	in erdu	in erdhu, in erdu	an erthe	on erðu
haben 'to have'	hapen	haben	haben	havan	hebbian
selbo 'self'	selpo	selbo	selbo	selvo, self	selbo
tiuf 'deep'	tiuf	tiof, teof	diaf, diof	def, dief	diop
liup 'dear' ('lief')	liup	liob	liab, liob	lef, lieb	liof
kepuazzen 'to atone'	kipuazzen	gibuoz(z)en	gibuaz(z)en -uo-		gibotian
kilauba 'belief'	calaupa	gilouba	gilouba	*gilova, *gilouba	gilobo

Old Saxon is accorded the position of a distinct Germanic language by most authorities. On purely linguistic grounds a case can no doubt be made out. There are a large number of features which separate Old High German and Old Saxon, and many which link Old Saxon more closely with other Germanic languages, for instance, above all the absence of the consonantal shift (the Second Sound Shift). The question whether a particular cognate dialect is an independent language or a dialect of another language is, however, not to be decided on the basis of linguistic criteria alone, but much more on the basis of political, economic and cultural factors. The *lingua theodisca* of the Carolingian empire of the ninth century lacked a standardized norm and consisted only of a number of dialects. Influences and conventions spread among these, thus testifying to a unifying tendency, however weak it may have been. Old Saxon, at least as far as most written documents are concerned, was also exposed to this unifying tendency. From the beginning of records it can thus be said to have been a 'dialect of German', or of the *lingua theodisca* of the eastern kingdom.

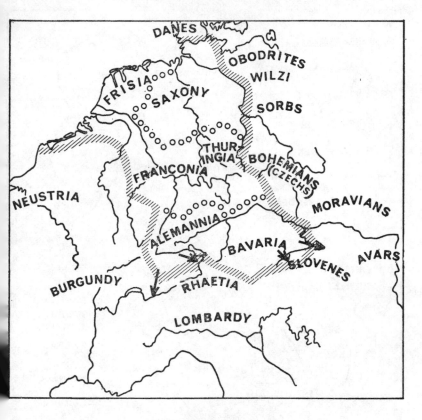

Fig. 7

The German linguistic territory within the empire of Charles the Great. Territorial names are used for areas within the empire, tribal names for areas outside the empire. Arrows indicate areas of German linguistic expansion.

4.2 | The written records

Linguistically the Carolingian empire, like many largely illiterate and primitive societies, was characterized by a situation of functional bilingualism. Where such a state of affairs prevails two, or possibly even more, linguistic media share the functions of

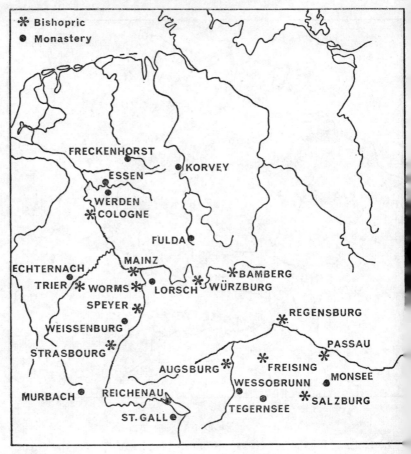

Fig. 8

Main Carolingian Scriptoria.

communication. These two media, in the eastern Carolingian kingdom, were Latin and the German dialects. The former was the written medium of state and church, of education, the law, learning and literature. The latter was the spoken medium of everyday life, of oral literature, jurisdiction and preaching. Contacts between the two media, or points where the sharp functional distinction was liable to break down, existed in initial education, religious instruction of novices and lay people, and jurisdiction. Once German was committed to writing, the further contact in the *genre* of literature (German oral literature – Latin written literature) could, with encouragement, form a bridge between the two media. The sources of early medieval German, flowing naturally extremely meagrely in this given situation of functional bilingualism, correspond exactly to the points of contact and can in fact be classified accordingly.

(i) Individual German words occur in legal and historical documents.

(ii) Individual translations of difficult Latin words for the sake of comprehension or instruction are inserted between the lines, above or beside the Latin words, or at the margin. Finally, whole glossaries are composed by translating a Latin dictionary (e.g. *Abrogans*), or by extracting words from Latin works (the Bible, Virgil etc.), either ordering them alphabetically or thematically, and translating them into German. A very large part of the early medieval German vocabulary known to us derives from *glosses* and *glossaries*. Glosses are preserved in nearly a thousand manuscripts, most of course copies or repeated copies.

(iii) Interlinear glosses may grow into interlinear *translations*. These and relatively freer translations form the bulk of texts which we have of this period. We can distinguish:

(a) Liturgical texts (Lord's Prayer, Catechism, Baptismal Vows, Confessions, hymns, *Exhortatio*);

(b) Biblical texts (Gospels, Psalms, Song of Songs);

(c) Theological texts (Rule of St Benedict, Isidore's tract *De fide catholica*, commentaries (Notker));

(d) Texts of late antiquity, e.g. Boethius.

(iv) Poetic compositions of four kinds:

(a) those based on the Gospels, e.g. Otfrid's *Liber Evangeliorum* (Otfrid of Weissenburg is the first German poet known by name), *Heliand*, OS *Genesis*, *Christ and the Samaritan Woman*;

(b) those based on other Christian themes (*Muspilli*, *Wessobrunn Prayer*, *Memento mori*);

(c) those based on personalities (*Ludwigslied*, *De Heinrico*, *Georgslied*);

(d) poems of Germanic antiquity (*Merseburg Charms* and other charms, *Hildebrandslied*).

(v) Prose texts of contemporary utility: *Strasbourg Oaths*, fragments of a conversational handbook for foreign travellers to Germany.

The vast bulk of early medieval German writing thus arose

out of the process of Christianization and the absorption of Christian Latin civilization. It required a tremendous effort of linguistic adaptation. The only sources which are a testimony of native spontaneity and ease are the accidentally recorded remains of oral Germanic literature and the few pieces of contemporary spoken German. For a brief span of time in the ninth century German also became a medium of written literature, when the two epics, *Heliand* and Otfrid's *Gospel Book*, and a number of short poems were created.

4.3 | The art of writing

When eighth- and ninth-century clerics felt the need to commit their German vernacular to parchment they naturally resorted to the Latin alphabet in which they were already literate. The runes had vanished by 700. They belonged to the world of Germanic paganism. Even if they were still known to the German clerics they must have appeared an undesirable tool. Alcuin and perhaps Hrabanus Maurus at Fulda and other Carolingian clerics showed scholarly and antiquarian interest in them, but as a vehicle for literacy in German there could be none other than the Latin alphabet. The adoption and adaptation of this foreign alphabet presented the scribes with innumerable difficulties.

An alphabetic script provides signs or letters for sounds. It thus presupposes a segmentation of the phonic level of language. From the infinitely variable realizations of speech sounds this segmentation singles out the functional or distinctive units. An alphabetic script is thus ideally a phonemic script. It matches the phonemes of a language with graphemes, and a one-to-one correspondence is the goal it envisages but is unlikely to reach. Admittedly, given the ability to establish a phonemic segmentation and complete freedom to invent the required graphemes, the creator of an alphabetic script for a hitherto unrecorded language is likely to succeed. The many unknown German clerics who attempted this task in the eighth and ninth centuries, and even

later, had no such advantages. The medium they were to use had
been created for and adapted to Latin, a foreign language with its
own phonemic system. The letters were thus graphemic correspondences of the phonemes of another language, not their own.
What is more, that language was regarded as a sacred language
and possessed immeasurable cultural prestige. For centuries
there had existed a regularized and rigid system of orthography.
But the language for which this orthography had been fixed had
now changed. Classical Latin had given way to Vulgar Latin and
between the sixth and the eighth centuries the classical orthography
had been severely affected by the decline in education: ⟨e⟩ and
⟨i⟩, ⟨o⟩ and ⟨u⟩, ⟨b⟩ and ⟨p⟩, ⟨d⟩ and ⟨t⟩, ⟨g⟩ and ⟨c⟩ were frequently confused and had become interchangeable. Spellings
such as *bago* or *paco* for *pago* were now common, or *ropustus*
(for *robustus*), *caudens* (*gaudens*), *persuna* (*persona*), *denicat*
(*denegat*), *eridis* (*heredes*) etc. Many phonetic changes had occurred,
and the way the German learners heard Latin pronounced by the
Romance population of the Merovingian empire was not at all the
way with which the classical orators had been familiar. ⟨c⟩ before
⟨i⟩ and ⟨e⟩ was [ts], so was ⟨-ti-⟩ in medial position. ⟨b, d, g⟩
between vowels were now pronounced as voiced fricatives [v, ð, γ].
Unstressed *e* in ⟨ea, eu⟩, e.g. *vinea*, *puteus*, was now [j], *vinja*,
putjus. The old Latin vowel system of three heights to which the
vowel signs had exactly corresponded: ⟨i–e–a–o–u⟩, had now
given way to a system of four heights [i–e–ɛ–a–ɔ–o–u] so that the
letters no longer matched the sounds. The old diphthongs *ae*, *oe*,
au had become monophthongs [ɛ, e:, o:] and had partly coalesced
with other sounds. The spelling was now confused, sometimes
the traditional orthography prevailed, sometimes new spellings
were attempted. In Merovingian Gaul many of the old long vowels
were now diphthongized, *ē* > *ei*, *ō* > *ou* and former short vowels
in open syllables had become long. Neither diphthongization nor
lengthening were generally indicated in contemporary spelling
until Old French was finally written. This did not happen until
nearly a century after German writing began. Since Merovingian
Latin incorporated numerous Germanic names and not a few
appellatives, certain spelling conventions for foreign, Germanic
sounds had become established, e.g. ⟨ch⟩ for [h] and [x], e.g.
Charibertus (*Herbert*), *Chuni* (*Huns*); ⟨th⟩ for [θ] *Theodericus*,
heodisca; but also ⟨eu⟩ for [eo] *Theudebertus*; ⟨o⟩ for [w] *Alboinus*

(*Albwin*, E *Alfwin*). ⟨h⟩, a spare letter in Latin orthography, was also occasionally used to indicate that ⟨g⟩ and ⟨c⟩ before ⟨e⟩ or ⟨i⟩ were plosives: ⟨gh, ch⟩, as otherwise these letters before ⟨e⟩ and ⟨i⟩ were pronounced as affricates.

The German creators of an orthography for German were thus not only working with bricks ill-suited for their purpose, they were also building on shifting sand. To some extent the confused state of Merovingian Latinity must have encouraged experimentation with the letters. This can be clearly seen in the case of the rendering of long vowels. Latin spelling did not distinguish between long and short vowels although it marked double consonants by double letters, e.g. *calidus* 'warm', *callidus* 'experienced', or *curo* 'I care', *curro* 'I run'. There was therefore no difficulty in German with regard to single consonants and geminates. For instance, *stelan* 'to steal' and *stellen* 'to stand' were nearly always clearly distinguished. In the early period we find that doubling of vowels was not infrequent, e.g. in the translation of the Rule of St Benedict, in Isidore, or in the early St Gall documents. The translator of Isidore's tract usually marked a long vowel in a closed syllable by a double letter, but left it single in an open syllable. He thus experimented where Latin orthography was ambiguous and unhelpful but followed Latin orthographic rules where the contemporary vulgar Latin pronunciation shed sufficient light on his German practice.

When the Carolingian reform brought about a return to a more regularized Latin orthography, experimentation in German seemed to diminish as well and such an un-Latin spelling device as double vowel letters became rare. Perhaps for the same reason the sporadic use of the circumflex accent never became widespread in German during Carolingian times. On the whole German spelling must be seen against the background of contemporary Latin. When in Central Franconian documents the voiced fricatives [v, γ] are most frequently spelt with ⟨-b-, -g-⟩ the reason is probably that these letters had, in contemporary Latin, between vowels, the value of voiced fricatives. On the other hand, the early Upper German practice of spelling ⟨p, k⟩ for the voiceless lenis plosives must probably be seen as a wish to indicate clearly the plosive character of the sounds, which the spelling with ⟨b, g⟩ would not have achieved. Thus *geban* may be interpreted as Central or perhaps also Rhenish Franconian [gɛvan], and *kepan* as Upper

German [g̊ɛb̥an]. Under Franconian influence Alemannic scriptoria later adopted ⟨b, g⟩ spellings.

Spellings with ⟨o, oo⟩ for later OHG *uo*, ⟨eu⟩ for *eo*, ⟨au⟩ for *ō* must always be seen in the full and possibly complicated context in which they are found. They do not necessarily indicate the earlier stages of phonological processes which are attested in OHG. One experimental orthography may have been changed simply because an influential and more important scriptorium had a different spelling. Early Alemannic ⟨ua⟩ probably made way for Franconian ⟨uo⟩ for this reason. When some OS manuscripts spell ⟨uo⟩ for PGmc. *ō* and ⟨o⟩ for PGmc. *au* the scribes no doubt wished to differentiate between two different values and to indicate a contrast neglected by other scribes who spelt ⟨o⟩ indiscriminately. But ⟨uo⟩ does not necessarily stand for the same sort of diphthong as in the Franconian documents from which the spelling was no doubt borrowed. Not only the older Merovingian Latin and the newer Carolingian Latin must be taken into account but also the continuous influence of one German scriptorium and spelling convention on another. Seeing that copying was much more frequent than original composition there can be no great surprise when spelling is often a most confusing and confused puzzle. What is perhaps more surprising is that in fact a certain spelling type evolved although with regional variants, and that whole spelling systems show remarkable regularity, for instance that of the Isidore translation, of the *Tatian*, of Otfrid's and Notker's compositions and of the better *Heliand* manuscripts.

Although spelling is the most important source for our knowledge of the phonology it must never be accepted uncritically. Spelling changes may but need not indicate phonological changes. The relationship between letters and sounds is extremely complicated and philologists have sometimes shown too much readiness to exploit spellings beyond what they can reasonably yield.

Some sounds were particularly trying for the scribes. [w] could not satisfactorily be expressed by Latin ⟨v⟩, since this now stood for a labiodental fricative or, of course, together with the rounded letter ⟨u⟩, for the vowel *u*. The Anglo-Saxon scribes had therefore borrowed a runic sign and the *W*-rune is occasionally also found in the Anglo-Saxon missionary centres in Germany. More often, however, the letters ⟨u⟩ or ⟨v⟩ were combined to express [w]. Since either letter could also stand for [u] and [f], they were hard worked: *uueiz, uveiz, vueiz, vveiz* '(he) knows', but also *varan* or *uaran* 'to travel', *huaz* (=*huuaz*) 'what', *uuurm* 'worm'. Small wonder that Otfrid, in the Latin dedication of his work to Archbishop Liutpert of Mainz, found the task of matching German sounds and Latin letters daunting. Complaining about the barbarous nature of this tongue – *inculta et indisciplinabilis* – he mentioned that the spelling sometimes demanded 'three *u*'s of which the first two would seem to me to be consonants, and the third would express the sound of a vowel'.

Since ⟨c⟩ represented both [ts] and [k] in contemporary Latin it was also used for those two sounds in German. But these sounds were differently distributed in German and contrasted. The spellings *cit* 'time' and *cuo* 'cow' might have been unambiguous, but for [tsuo] 'to' some other letter was clearly needed. Thus ⟨z⟩ was most generally used for [ts], *zuo* 'to', but also for the new dental fricative which had developed postvocalically from PGmc. *t: thaz* 'that'. For [k] both ⟨k⟩ and ⟨c⟩ were employed. Combined with ⟨h⟩ (⟨kh, ch⟩) they usually indicated the velar affricate. But ⟨ch⟩ before ⟨i⟩ or ⟨e⟩ may also stand for the plosive. [x] was usually spelt ⟨h⟩ before consonants (*naht* 'night') or finally (*sioh* 'sick') and ⟨hh⟩ or ⟨ch⟩ between vowels (*sprehhan* or *sprechan* 'to speak').

For [θ] the Anglo-Saxons had retained the rune ⟨þ⟩ and also used a modified *d*: ⟨ð⟩. Both signs are found in German manuscripts from scriptoria with an Anglo-Saxon tradition, but only in OS were they used extensively. Upper and Central German documents usually have the Latin ⟨th⟩ or a newly developed analogical ⟨dh⟩.

Spellings are often only tendencies, usually generalized by helpful editors of medieval texts. The scribes permitted themselves a greater latitude of usage. Throughout the period the relationship between the graphemic and the phonemic levels remained one of uneasy compromise, improvisation, ingenious inventiveness and careless irregularity.

4·4 | Phonology

4.4.1 | The stressed vowel system

The Late Germanic vowel system to which all German developments can be traced back is Stage (V) given in 3.5.2:

/i/		/u/ /ī/		/ū/	/iu/
/e/	/o/		/ē/	/ō/	/eo/
/a/			/ā/	/ai/	/au/

The incidence of these phonemes was not entirely identical in the various earliest German dialects. Thus we get variants within OHG such as *fugal – fogal* 'bird', *fehu – fihu* 'cattle', *truhtin – trohtin* 'lord', *skif – skef* 'ship', *skirm – skerm* 'protection', *ubar – obar* 'over', *konda – kunda* 'could', *stimna – stemna* 'voice'. Between OHG and OS the differences were even more numerous: *neman – niman* 'to take', *geban – giƀan* 'to give', *sturm – storm* 'storm', *fuhs – fohs* 'fox', *furt – ford* 'ford', *fol – ful* 'full', *joh – juk* 'yoke', *wolf – wulf* 'wolf', *goma – gumo* 'man', and OS had *fugal, fehu, stemna*. Within OS we find both *skild* and *skeld* 'shield'. It is however in the incidence of /iu/ and /eo/ that the most marked dialectal difference is found: Central German (Franconian) and OS had /eo/ before Gmc. *a, e, o* and /iu/ before Gmc. *i, j, u* in the following syllable. Bavarian and Alemannic had /eo/ only if a dental or Gmc. *h* stood between the diphthong and *a, e, o* of the following syllable. In other words, labials and velars ensured the survival of the labio-velar element of the PGmc. diphthong /eu/. Thus we have

OS	Franc.	Bav. Alem.
siok 'sick'	*sioh*	*siuh*
liof 'dear'	*liob*	*liup*
diop 'deep'	*tiof*	*tiuf*
liogan 'to tell a lie'	*liogan*	*liugan*
biodan 'to bid'	*biotan*	*biotan*
liudi 'people'	*liuti*	*liuti*

The developments which characterized the phase from Late Germanic to OHG are a conditional *monophthongization* of the low diphthongs, a *general raising* of the diphthongs, the *diph-*

thongization of the mid long vowels and the first step in the *phonemicization* of the *i*-mutated allophones.

The relevant distinctive features of the system were tongue height and lip position, i.e. rounded *vs.* unrounded. Important allophonic developments had occurred through anticipatory assimilation caused by */i, j/ in the following syllable. All rounded vowels had both back and front allophones, the latter before a following */i, j/. So had the lowest vowel, which was neutral with regard to lip position. It would appear that the low diphthongs underwent a contact assimilation to something like [æi] and [ɒu]. Further palatalization in the case of the first and rounding in the case of the second diphthong now brought about an allophonic split through loss of the *i*-glide before Gmc. /r, w, h/ and in final position, and of the *u*-glide before Gmc. /h/, all dentals (/þ, d, t, s, n, r, l/) and in final position. Labials and velars protected the *u*-glide. The allophonic development was thus schematically:

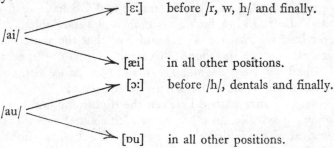

[ɛː]	before /r, w, h/ and finally.
[æi]	in all other positions.
[ɔː]	before /h/, dentals and finally.
[ɒu]	in all other positions.

What allows us to arrive at a relative dating is the circumstance that the new [h] resulting from Gmc. /k/, although coinciding with the existing /h/, is preceded by [ɒu] < */au/, not by [ɔː] and by [æi] < */ai/, not by [ɛː]. Therefore the allophonic split must predate the consonantal shift (Second or High German Sound Shift). It was this consonantal shift, in fact, which led to the phonemicization of the two allophones:

Gmc.	Phonetic phase	OHG	OS
aik- 'oak'	[æik-]	*eih*	*ēk*
laih- 'he lent'	[lɛːx-]	*lēh*	*lēh*
auk 'also'	[ɒuk]	*ouh*	*ōk*
hauh- 'high'	[hɔːx-]	*hōh*	*hōh*

It is perhaps tempting to assume that the consonantal shift establishing the phonemic status of the previous positional variants
put an end to the process of contact assimilation. The completion
of the monophthongization found in OS (Gmc. /ai/ > OS /ē/;
Gmc. /au/ > OS /ō/ except before the semivowels /j, w/), where
the consonant shift did not occur, might lend support to such an
assumption. The contrast, however, between the newly established
OHG phonemes rested on a very slender basis, even after it was
gradually widened through further developments. Dialect geographers, however, have generally assumed that monophthongization, being much more widespread in the north, began there and
spread into OHG to the limited extent to which it is attested.
What the political or economic circumstances favouring such a
north to south thrust were, is difficult to see. And why a spontaneous change in the north should be taken over as a conditioned
change in the south is linguistically no less difficult to comprehend.
Seeing that in Gothic *r*, *h*, *hʸ* were also inimical to high tongue elements (**i* > [ɛ] spelt ⟨ai⟩, *raíhts* 'right'; **u* > [ɔ] spelt ⟨au⟩, *haúrn*
'horn') it was most likely the phonetic character of inherited Gmc.
r, *h* (and other factors) which favoured this monophthongization.

In English Gmc. /au/ changed uniformly to /ēa/ unless affected
by *i*-mutation. The spelling is still retained in many cases and the
Pre-German phonemic split emerges clearly from a comparison
between etymologically related words:

German:	Bohne	Ohr	Lot	tot	rot	Kloß	Brot
English: {	bean	ear	lead	dead	red	cleat	bread
{	beam	seam	dream	cheap	leap	leaf	sheaf
German:	Baum	Saum	Traum	kauf-	lauf-	Laub	Schaub (dial.)

It has been stated that the new monophthongs, /ɛ̄/ and /ɔ̄/ may
have exerted pressure on the other mid long vowels, /ē/ and /ō/,
and thus caused them to change. In OS new and old *ē/ō*-type
monophthongs continued to exist side by side. In most documents
throughout the Middle Ages they were both spelt ⟨e⟩ and ⟨o⟩.
But occasional orthographic distinctions, e.g. OS ⟨e – ie⟩, ⟨o–uo⟩,
probably borrowed from Franconian orthography, and modern
dialects show that they were kept apart. In OHG Gmc. /ē/, i.e.
ē², and /ō/ became diphthongized to /ie/ and /uo/. Early spellings
were ⟨ea, ia⟩ and ⟨oa, ua⟩. To some extent these spellings, occurring mainly in the eighth century, marked the phonetic path of

change. There were also dialectal differences. The most frequent mid ninth-century spellings were probably the result of a good deal of orthographic levelling. After this diphthongization the new monophthongs were free to take up the mid position in a system of three heights.

Here, too, dialect geography has drawn a picture of sweeping movements. Diphthongizations in Old French and other Romance languages were brought together with the OHG diphthongization and Frings saw 'eine einheitliche Welle von Tours bis nach Fulda' (p. 111). Within OHG the starting point was seen in Franconian (Frings, Brinkmann) and Alemannic and Bavarian were at the receiving end. More recent research has led I. Rauch (p. 95) to state: 'Each dialect had within its structure the potentiality to diphthongization and developed it more or less in a regular manner'. Since the dialect-geographical theories were more characterized by their lack of sound scepticism than by the presence of cool cogency this conclusion has much to recommend it.

The OHG vowel system after the monophthongization and diphthongization and the general raising of the existing diph-thongs due to contact assimilation, but without regard to the results of i-mutation, was therefore:

(VI)   /i/   /u/ /ī/   /ū/
    /e/   /o/   /ē/   /ō/
                     ↑   ↑
      /a/   (Gmc. *ai*) /ā/ (Gmc. *au*)

(Gmc. $ē^2$)→/ie/   /io/   /iu/   /uo/←(Gmc. *ō*)
                 ↑
    /ei/ (Gmc. *eo*)   /ou/
     ↑   ↑
  (Gmc. *ai*)   (Gmc. *au*)

Examples:

   dih 'thee'   *dīh!* 'thrive!'
   reht 'right'   *dēh* 'throve'
   dah 'roof'   *gedāht* 'piety'
   doh 'yet'   *zōh* 'pulled'
   zuht 'breeding' *būh* 'belly'

dieh 'thigh' *sioh* 'sick'   *buoh* 'book'
eih 'oak'   *ziuh* 'pull'   *gouh* 'cuckoo'

The OS system differed in the long vowel and diphthongal system:

/ī/   /ū/   /io/   /iu/

    /ē/   /ō/   [ie, ia, eo]

      /ɛ̄/   /ɔ̄/   /eu/
       ↑   ↑

(Gmc. *ai*) /ā/ (Gmc. *au*)   /ai/   /au/

Examples:

> *thīh!* 'thrive!'   *siok* 'sick'
> *lēt* pret. 'to let'   *tiuh!* 'pull!'
> *ēk* [ɛ:] 'oak'   *ei* 'egg'
> *thāhta* pret. 'thought'   *heu* 'hewed'
> *bōk* 'book'   *hrau* 'repented'
> *rōk* [ɔ:] 'smoke'
> *hūs* 'house'

The final problem of the vowel system concerns the position of *i*-mutation. As a phonetic phenomenon *i*-mutation is assumed to be a feature of Late Germanic (see pp. 80–1). It belongs to those extremely important assimilatory processes which linked the vowels of the unstressed and those of the stressed syllables in Germanic in consequence of the accentual shift. Of the effect of *i*-mutation we have in OHG and OS, before the early eleventh century, only one indication: Gmc. /a/ was spelt ⟨e⟩ under conditions of *i*-mutation except in some cases where ⟨a⟩ was spelt, e.g. *gast – gesti* 'guest' sg. – pl., *lamb – lembir* 'lamb' sg. – pl., *kraft – krefti* 'strength' sg. – pl. and nom./acc. sg. – gen./dat. sg., *faran – feris, ferit* 'to travel' inf. – 2nd/3rd pers. sg. But *naht – nahti* 'night' nom./acc. sg. – gen./dat. sg., *wahsan – wahsit* 'to grow' inf. – 3rd pers. sg., *kraftlīh* 'powerful', *magad – magadi* 'maid' sg. – pl. The older view was that in OHG and OS only one *i*-mutation had taken place, that of short *a*, although it was prevented by certain consonantal clusters, e.g. -*ht*-, -*hs*- and others, and had not taken place if the mutating factor occurred in the second syllable after the stressed one. Some words showed no evidence of a mutating factor, e.g. *ende* (Gothic *andeis*), *sezzen* (Gothic *satjan*), *wecken* (Gothic *wagjan*). Where the mutating factor had been a *j* this had thus already disappeared in OHG. This mutation of Gmc. short *a* was called 'primary *umlaut*'. Where evidence of mutation of short *a* was found later (MHG *nähte, mägede* etc.) a 'secondary *umlaut*' was posited. Occasionally this term is also used for all those other mutations (*ü, ö, öü*) for which orthographic evidence appears from the eleventh century onwards.

It is one of the finest achievements of American linguists (W. Freeman Twaddell, Herbert Penzl, James W. Marchand, William G. Moulton and most recently Elmer H. Antonsen) to have provided an explanation both comprehensive and logically coherent. Three separate questions arise, after it has been accepted that *i*-mutation is an allophonic development of Late Germanic.

(a) Why did the scribes indicate one result of *i*-mutation, that of short *a* except before certain consonants, as early as the inception of German writing?

(b) When did the palatal allophones become phonemes?

(c) Why did the medieval scribes not express the new palatal sounds in their orthography until long after they had become phonemes? (Even fifteenth-century manuscripts and early prints frequently omit to distinguish between *ü/u, ö/o, äu/au*.)

(a) Mutation of short *a* must have led to at least three allophones:

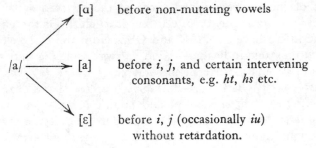

[ɑ]   before non-mutating vowels

/a/ ———→ [a]   before *i, j*, and certain intervening consonants, e.g. *ht, hs* etc.

[ɛ]   before *i, j* (occasionally *iu*) without retardation.

[ɛ] would be the result of a raising and fronting which went through the major stages [a – æ – ɛ]. Now, somewhere in the process this allophone of /a/ must have become an allophone of /e/:

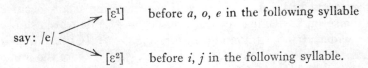

say: /e/

[ɛ¹]   before *a, o, e* in the following syllable

[ɛ²]   before *i, j* in the following syllable.

Continuing assimilation would have raised the allophone before the palatals [ɛ²] higher than the allophone before the mid or low vowels [ɛ¹]. In this way this former allophone of /a/ bypassed all other allophones of /e/. What OHG scribes spelt was therefore not so much a mutation as the fact that one result of a mutation had coalesced with the phoneme /e/ or, without anticipating the question of its phonemic status in OHG, that it had become an e-type vowel for which the Latin alphabet provided a letter. Careful rhyming in MHG shows that the two allophones (ɛ¹ and ɛ²) had become separate phonemes by then. Modern Upper German dialects confirm this and also show that the former mutation of Gmc. /a/ is higher than the reflex of Gmc. /e/.

Compare Alem. *štelə* 'to stand' < OHG *stellen* < **staljan*
         štælə 'to steal' < OHG *stelan* < **stelan*.

That this raising was only possible, without confusion arising, as long as the conditioning factor was present, is obvious. The so-called 'secondary *umlaut*' was not drawn into the orbit of the e-sounds but remained a palatal allophone of /a/ until it was phonemicized.

(b) It is sometimes alleged that scribes do not spell allophones because they are not even aware of them but that they do spell phonemes. The late indication of other products of mutation would therefore suggest that they were phonemicized fairly late, perhaps only in the eleventh century. At that time the unstressed so-called full vowels (*a, e, i, o, u*) were about to coalesce, in so far as they had not already done so, in a neutral [ə]. This removed finally all factors conditioning these allophones. But the process had started in prehistoric times. The earliest records yield words without conditioning factors present: *ende* 'ends' dat. pl. *endum*; *hella* 'hell' [e] – *helfa* 'help' [ɛ]; *stunta* 'hour' – *sunta* 'sin' cf. *Stunde* – *Sünde*; *sunna* 'sun' – *brunna* 'armour' cf. *Sonne* – *Brünne*; *slāfes* 'sleep' gen. – *kāses* 'cheese' gen. cf. *Schlafes* – *Käses*; *swertes* [ɛ] 'sword' gen. – *hertes* [e] 'hard' gen. m.; *guotes* 'good' gen. m. – *muodes* 'tired' gen. m. cf. *gutes* – *müdes*. Mutated and unmutated sounds were thus in contrast owing to the loss of Gmc. /j/, in other words, they were phonemes from this loss onwards. It is true, in a majority of cases they continued to be conditioned, cf. *tag* – *taga*, *gast* – *gesti*; *mūs* – *mūsi* cf. *Maus* – *Mäuse*; *hōh* – *hōhī* cf. *hoch* – *Höhe*; *skōno* – *skōni* cf. *schon* – *schön*. This state of affairs has been called 'phonemic indeterminacy' (E. Haugen). One could also say that the rounded palatal and non-

palatal sounds were in contrast in a relatively small but rapidly
increasing number of cases, but were neutralized in a large number
of contexts. Not only the loss of Gmc. /j/ led to early phonemicization. Morphological resistance to mutation, which may be assumed,
also contributed to early phonemicization. Masculine *n*-stem
nouns had *i* in the gen. and dat. sg. ending in Upper German
dialects and the resultant paradigm of *hano* 'cock' would thus be:
nom. *hano*, acc. *hanun*, gen. *henin*, dat. *henin*. These mutated
forms are, however, very rare and occur only in the earliest documents. The normal form *hanin* thus contributed to phonemicization of the mutated vowels. In other cases, e.g. *poto – potin* 'messenger', *ouga – ougin* 'eye', we simply cannot tell whether mutation was ever present or not. Still, it is clear that the palatal variants
were phonemicized from the beginning of OHG, that neutralization played a large part until the disappearance of the /i/ – /e, a, o,
u/ contrast in unstressed syllables, and that we must distinguish
two phases of phonemicization: the first before the beginning of
OHG literature, the second towards the end of the OHG phase.

(c) Those who cling to the older view of mutation and wish to
date it, except for the 'primary *umlaut*' of short *a*, to the late OHG
period to coincide with the appearance of the first orthographic
indication of the mutation of *ō*, *ū*, *ā*, etc. usually point to the many
excellent and phonetically perceptive scribes such as the translator of Isidore or Notker Teutonicus of St Gall. If even a Notker
did not spell the mutation of *ā* then it simply could not have
occurred, so the argument goes, cf. Notker *nāmen* and *nāmin*,
but cf. (sie) *nahmen – nähmen*. But all that mutation need mean is
that there was a front and a back *ā*, say [aː] or [æː] and [ɑː]. For
such a distinction the Latin alphabet had only the letter ⟨a⟩.
What Notker's spelling does however indicate is that the mutated
ā was an *a*-type and not an *e*-type vowel. Further, we must remember that the Latin alphabet provided no letters for [y, ø, øy] or the
distinction between [e] and [ɛ] and [a] and [ɑ], and that the widespread neutralization before ⟨-i⟩ may have played its part in the
preservation of an orthography which did not mark the mutated
vowels. It is true, it was the contemporary practice of the Anglo-
Saxons to use the letters ⟨y⟩ and ⟨œ⟩ and this might have pointed
the way for OHG scribes. The greater conservatism of German
phonology retained the status of 'phonemic indeterminacy' for
longer. German literacy never reached the degree of independence

from Latin that contemporary Anglo-Saxon civilization attained
with its laws, royal writs, its chronicle writing in Old English (the
Anglo-Saxon Chronicle, the Old English translation of Bede's
Ecclesiastical History of the English People), and its secular epic
Beowulf. It is only by accident that late OHG provided the sign
⟨iu⟩ for [y:]. After the second phase of the phonemicization of the
mutated vowels the pressure for the indication of the mutated
vowels became greater and it is from that time onwards that the
orthography became more responsive. But not until New High
German did the spelling of mutated vowels become regular. There
was therefore always a great gap between the evolution of the
phonology and the adaptation of the orthography.

Before we can establish the OHG phonemic system the question of a possible /ø/ phoneme must be examined. If there had
been no morphological interference with the phonological evolution, *o* would not have occurred before *i* and there could therefore have been no mutation of *o* (see 3.5.2). Some OHG examples
show the alternation which is to be expected: *loh* – *luhhir* 'hole' or
gold – *guldīn*. The former alternation did, however, not persist
and analogical *lohhir* became the rule, hence *Loch* – *Löcher*; but
Gold – *gülden* has survived. The greater the morphological pull,
we must assume, the greater the tendency to level phonologically.
That sometimes *o* came thus to occur before *i* while mutation was
still in its phonetic phase seems likely, although the majority of
ö-forms may be the result of analogy rather than of active *i*-
mutation. Whether this *ö* had already phonemic status in OHG is
doubtful since there cannot have been strong morphological
pressure for the analogical introduction of *o* before *j*. But *forhten*
besides *furhten* 'to be afraid' < **furhtjan* is attested, and forms
like *oli* – gen. *oles*, dat. *ole* 'oil' may suggest an unconditioned
[ø], unless we assume alternation of [ø] before *i* and [o] before *e*
within the paradigm. Once the conditioning factor *i* disappeared
as well as *j*, in late OHG, [ø] was undoubtedly established as a
phoneme.

The Old High German vowel system of the ninth century:
(VII)

/i/			/ü/		/u/	/ī/	/ǖ/	/ū/
	/e/		/ö/	/o/		/ē/	/ȫ/	/ō/
		/ë/						
			/æ/	/a/		/ǣ/	/ā/	

/ie/   /iü/   /iu/   /üö/   /uo/
/io/   (üe)
/ei/   /öü/   /ou/

Unless we assume that words ending in -i in the nominative singular, with mutated root vowels (e.g. *māri, scōni*), had unmutated root vowels before the genitive ending -*es*, examples in the genitive (masc. and neuter) of nouns and adjectives afford unconditional cases of the mutated vowels:

/i/	*bizzes*	'bite'	/ī/	*nīdes*	'hatred'	/ie/	*zieres*	'fine'
/e/	*bettes*	'bed'	/ē/	*sēres*	'pain'	/io/	*liodes*	'song'
/ĕ/	*gibetes*	'prayer'				/iu/	*liutes*	'people'
/æ/	*gislahtes*	'lineage'	/ǣ/	*māres*	'famous'	/iü/	*tiures*	'dear'
/a/	*bades*	'bath'	/ā/	*māles*	'time'	/uo/	*guotes*	'good'
/o/	*gibotes*	'command'	/ō/	*rōtes*	'red'	/üö/	*muodes*	'tired'
/ö/	*oles*	'oil'	/ȫ/	*ōdes*	'empty'	/ei/	*steines*	'stone'
/u/	*nuzzes*	'use'	/ū/	*hūses*	'house'	/ou/	*rouhes*	'smoke'
/ü/	*nuzzes*	'useful'	/ǖ/	*kūskes*	'chaste'	/öü/	*giroubes*	'loot'

4.4.2 | The unstressed vowels

One of the most obvious and characteristic differences between ninth-century German and the later stages of the language lies in unstressed vowels. One need only compare the following modern words with their uniform final -*e* [ə]: *Hase, Hirse, Steine, Friede, Sünde, Tiefe* with the corresponding OHG forms: *haso, hirsi, steina, fridu, sunte* (later *sunta*), *tiufī*. The modern ending -*en* in the dative plural of nouns, e.g. *Steinen, Betten, Tauben* corresponds to OHG: -*um* (*steinum*), -*im* (*bettim*), -*ōm* (*tūbōm*); in the infinitive of verbs it corresponds to OHG -*an* (*wegan* 'to weigh'), -*en* (*weggen* 'to move'), -*ēn* (*wegēn* 'to assist'), or -*ōn* (*wegōn* 'to assist'). OHG had a fully developed system of unstressed vowels. But it was not a stable system. In time and in space everything was in flux. While most of the stressed root vowels if unaffected by *i*-mutation, by and large, appear stable throughout the period and over the whole territory, the vowels not bearing the main stress show a great deal of variation from one document, or one copy of it, to the next and from one region to another. As far as we can see the *ī* in *zīt* 'time' was uniform from the coast to the Alps, while in the modern period its reflex varies extraordinarily from one dialect to another. Moving only from the Moselle to the Rhine and the Danube we can now hear [æi, i, iː, ai, əi, ɔi, ɛi] in the dialect words for *Zeit*. The vowel in *Kind*, seemingly uniform in OHG, appears in modern dialects, over the same stretch of territory, as [a – e – u – o – i]. In the OHG period dialectal variation was most characteristically found in the unstressed vowels. The effect of the Germanic fixation of stress, the most likely cause of the various mutations, was now leading to the erosion of the system of the unstressed vowels. Large-scale dialectal differentiation of the root vowels would seem to have occurred only in the next phase of the evolution of the German language.

For vowels not under chief stress we must distinguish four situations: (i) occurrence in verbal prefixes; (ii) occurrence in derivational suffixes; (iii) occurrence in medial syllables; (iv) occurrence in final, chiefly inflectional syllables, where they may be either in absolutely final (*sihu* 'I see') or in preconsonantal position (*sihit* 'he sees').

(i) In the verbal prefixes corresponding to NHG *be-*, *emp-/ent-*, *ge-*, *ver-*, and *zer-* the East Franconian Tatian translation has *bi-*, *int-*, *gi-* but differs according to scribe in the case of *ar-/er-* and *for-/fur-* thus probably reflecting the different dialectal cackgrounds of the various scribes. In early texts of Alemannic provenance we find *ka-* and *ke-*, later *gi-* becomes more general. In Bavarian texts *ka-* (or *ca-*) persists longest. It is thus a dialectal distinguishing mark in the ninth century. It is idle to try to establish a system of unstressed vowels in pretonal position since the material is too scant and possibly arbitrary. But we note that in the first half of the ninth century most dialects had at least two vowels in this position, a palatal and a velar, and that towards the end of the century there was generally only one, for instance in Otfrid who spelt it ⟨i⟩ with the variant ⟨y⟩ before *r*. In no other position were the vocalic differences obliterated so early. P. Valentin (*Phonologie*, p. 53) is no doubt correct in stating that since these prefixes were sufficiently distinguished by their consonants, the vowels were functionally unimportant and in consequence exposed to neutralization.

(ii) If vowels in pretonal position were in the vanguard of the evolution those in derivational suffixes formed the rear and remained largely unaffected, e.g. *-īn*, *-inna* (*lewīn* 'lioness'), *-isc* (*kindisc* 'young'), *-ing* (*ediling* 'nobleman'), *-unga* (*warnunga* 'preparation'), *-nissi* (*fir-stantnissi* 'understanding'), *-heit* (*gotheit* 'divinity') etc. The more such a suffix remained productive the less it was affected by phonetic erosion. As a derivational suffix it no doubt attracted a secondary stress. Derivational suffixes which were less protected by secondary stress came to be treated as medial syllables, e.g. *-il* (*sluzzil* 'key'), *-ag*, *-ig*, *-īg* (*bluotag* 'bloody', *sitig* 'modest') etc. Here too dialectal differences developed. In Upper German *-līn* and *-līh* probably retained their long vowels, hence NHG *-lein*, *-līh* being shortened later (> NHG *-lich*). In Franconian they were shortened earlier, hence NHG *-chen* (< *-chin* < *-kīn*).

(iii) In medial syllables OHG had not only three to five short vowels but also long vowels. The circumstances are very complicated, all the more so as there were also so-called intrusive or *svarabhakti* vowels between *r* or *l* and *h*, e.g. *forhta* and *forahta* 'fright', *durh* and *duruh* 'through', and in Upper German also between *r* and certain other consonants, e.g. *berg* and *pereg* 'mountain'. In Franconian, especially in the language of Otfrid, we frequently get assimilation, whereby medial vowels change to become similar to the subsequent inflectional vowel, e.g. *mihhil* > *mihhala* 'big'. Before *l* or *r* the medial vowel could be dropped if the preceding syllable was long, e.g. *andere* and *andre* 'others'. However much the circumstances may vary from one document to another it is clear that OHG, even of the ninth century, already tolerated only a reduced number of vowel phonemes in medial position.

(iv) In final position vowels were overwhelmingly inflectional vowels. Morphology and phonology together therefore played their part in the further evolution. When for instance an early final *-e* in *sunte* 'sin' was later replaced by *-a* (*sunta*) there can be no question of a phonological development. In analogy to the much more frequent final *-a* of the feminine ō-class the nouns of the jō-class were given *-a* for *-e*. If the first wavering in the verbal system is found in the 3rd pers. pl. ind. pres. where the strong verbs had originally *-ant* and the weak verbs of class I *-ent*, we may assume that the reason was phonological. The heavy consonantal ending was a clear enough carrier of the meaning. If the verbs of the class II of weak verbs nevertheless retained their distinctive ending *-ont* the reason was also phonological. The ō was long, as is indicated by Notker, and therefore withstood levelling longer than the short *a* and *e*. The only documents which indicate vowel length in unstressed positions are the Alemannic Rule of St Benedict and the works of Notker of St Gall. We thus know that Alemannic had a long – short contrast in unstressed position. It is however very uncertain that Franconian had any long vowels in unstressed final position apart from the probable -*ī*, e.g. in feminine *ī*-stems, cf. *hōhī* 'height', *tiufī* 'depth'. In this case we have, of course, characteristically, a derivational suffix, bearing in all probability a secondary stress. For Franconian of the early ninth century we therefore posit the following system of unstressed vowels:

$$
\begin{array}{ccc}
/i/ & & /u/ \\
/e/ & & /o/ \\
& /a/ &
\end{array}
$$

There is no reason to assume that *e* < *ja (*sunte* < *suntja) was generally distinguished from earlier *e*. The contrast between /u/ and /o/ showed signs of being tenuous. The next contrast to weaken was that between /i/ and /e/. Notker in the eleventh century had only three short phonemes /e/–/a/–/o/. But spelling fluctuations in many directions indicate that the process of reduction followed several different courses. Scribes, we must assume, echoed their different dialects in this way.

4.4.3 | The consonant system

The Proto-Germanic system of plosives and fricatives given in 3.5.4 is:

(IV) /f/   /þ/   /s/   /x/
      /p/   /t/   /k/
      /b–ƀ/ /d–ð/ /z/   /g–g/

The further changes in the West Germanic languages (see pp. 88–9) led to the following Late Germanic system:

(V)   /f/   /þ/   /s/   /h–x/
      /p/   /t/   /k/
      /b–ƀ/   /d/   /g–g/

With the exception of the velar fricatives these sounds are still observable in Modern English:

*f*ind	*th*ing	*s*ing	*h*orn-ni*ght* (⟨gh⟩ < x)
*p*ound	*t*in		*k*ing
*b*ind-sie*v*e	*d*eer		long(er)-*y*ield

In the dialects which were later to form the southern area of High German the remaining voiced fricatives became plosives, so that the Late Germanic system on which the subsequent developments were based was:

(Va) /f/ /þ/ /s/ /h–x/
      /p/ /t/ /k/
      /b/ /d/ /g/

An important feature of the consonant system was gemination or doubling of consonants especially in medial position after short vowels, but also occasionally after long vowels and diphthongs, and in final position after the loss of certain final vowels. Some geminates had resulted from assimilation, some from affective gemination, even more came into being through the West Germanic doubling of consonants (see 3.3.4). Beside every single consonant there was a double. Although the geminates were probably originally clusters of two identical phonemes, the frequency of their occurrence must have had structural consequences. The opposition of voice was gradually replaced by an opposition of quantity or length. The next, still pre-OHG, phase may therefore be assumed to have been:

(VI) /f/ /þ/ /s/ /h/   /ff/ /þþ/ /ss/ /hh/
      /p/ /t/ /s/ /k/   /pp/ /tt/   /kk/
      /b̥/ /d̥/ /g̥/   /b̥b̥/ /d̥d̥/   /g̥g̥/
      /m/ /n/   /mm/ /nn/
           /l/   /ll/
           /r/   /rr/
      /w/   /j/ /ww/   /jj/ (semi-vowels)

The liquids, nasals, and semi-vowels which were unaffected by the further shift can be attested from OHG:

imo	'him'	*spanan*	'to tempt'	*stelan*	'to steal'	*meri*	'sea, mere'
stimma	'voice'	*spannan*	'to span'	*stellen*	'to stand'	*merren*	'to mar'
wurm	'worm'	*kiuwan*	'to chew'	*jār*	'year'		(geminate semi-vowels were no longer in evidence.)

There were some changes in incidence: *-m* in an inflectional element began to change to *-n* from the beginning of the ninth century, e.g. *steinum > steinun* (see 4.5.1); *w-* before *r* and *l* was lost before the earliest documents, e.g. Gothic *wrakja*, OHG *reccho* 'a banished person', cf. E *wretch*. Initial *h-* before *l, n, r, w* also disappeared in the ninth century, for example earliest OHG *hlauffan* 'to run', *hnīgan* 'to bow', *hros* 'horse', *hweizi* 'wheat' > later *laufan, nīgan, ros, weizi*.

The fricatives can also be attested although in the ninth century examples for the interdental fricative can only be found in the Franconian dialects:

nevo	'nephew'	*nidhar*	'nether'	*risi*	'giant'	*slahan*	'to slay'
heffen	'to raise'	*fethdhah*	'wing'	*missen*	'to miss'	*lahhēn*	'to laugh'

The geminate fricatives were extremely rare except for *ss* so that the functional load of this opposition was at best minimal. The interdental geminate fricative is hardly attested at all and may be disregarded. The later reflex was *-tt-*.

It was the Germanic series of voiceless stops that appeared fundamentally altered when OHG was first recorded. They had become affricates and fricatives, as a rapid comparison between English and German still shows:

*p*ound:*Pf*und *t*in:*Z*inn *k*ing:*K*önig (but OHG *kh-* i.e. [kx] in UGm.)
shi*p*:Schi*ff* eat:e*ss*en ma*k*e:ma*ch*en

This sound shift is easiest to understand if we assume that first an allophonic split occurred (taking the dental plosive as example):

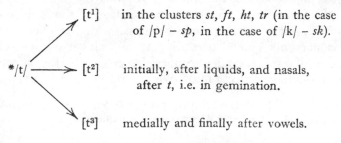

[t¹] in the clusters *st, ft, ht, tr* (in the case of /p/ – *sp*, in the case of /k/ – *sk*).

*/t/ [t²] initially, after liquids, and nasals, after *t*, i.e. in gemination.

[t³] medially and finally after vowels.

What the shifting factor was we do not know for certain. Its effect was most radical in context 3: a fricative; less so in context 2: an affricate; and without consequence in context 1. Examples, where possible from the modern languages, illustrate this:

	Context 1	Context 2	Context 3
	S*t*uhl–s*t*ool	*z*ehn–*t*en	has*s*en–to ha*t*e
Gmc.	Gif*t*–gif*t*	Her*z*–hear*t*	hei*ß*–ho*t*
/t/			
	Toch*t*er–daugh*t*er	Sal*z*–sal*t*	
	*T*rog–*t*rough	grun*z*en–to grun*t*	
		se*tz*en–to se*t*	
		(OE se*tt*an)	
	s*p*innen–to s*p*in	*Pf*anne–*p*an	ho*ff*en–to ho*p*e
		Har*f*e–har*p*	tie*f*–dee*p*
		OHG har*pf*a	
Gmc.		hel*f*en–to hel*p*	
/p/		OHG hel*p*fan	
		stum*pf*–stum*p*	
		A*p*fel–a*pp*le	
	schaben–to shave	kühn–keen*	bre*ch*en–to
	OHG s*c*abēn–OE s*c*afan	OHG *ch*uoni–OE *c*ēne	brea*k*
		star*k*–star*k*	Bu*ch*–boo*k*
	As*ch*e–ash	OHG star*ch*–OE stear*c*	
Gmc.	OHG as*c*a–OE æs*c*e	Wer*k*–work	
/k/		OHG wer*ch*–OE weor*c*	
		dan*k*en–to thank	
		OHG dan*ch*ōn–OE þan*c*ian	

The opening effect of surrounding vowels could clearly produce such a pattern, but so could increasingly strong aspiration. Although aspiration explains the shift in part of context 2 (initial position) it is less satisfactory in context 3. The opening effect of vowels is most plausible in context 3. Whether the more advanced stage, the fricatives, passed through the stage of the affricates is not certain, but it has frequently been assumed. The effect of the shift is not only graded according to the phonetic context. It worked itself out in a graded manner also geographically, affecting the southernmost dialects most, the central dialects less and the

* In context 2 the shift of Gmc. /k/ is not found in modern standard German. In OHG, Bav. and Alem. documents illustrate it.

northernmost dialects (OS, OLFranc.) not at all. The shift affects all Upper German and Central German dialects in context 3. In context 2 only the southernmost for all three plosives, then tapering off northwards in descending order for velar and then labial plosives, while the dental plosive is shifted in context 2 to the HG/LG boundary. The grading may be shown diagrammatically, using simplified present-day dialectal forms:

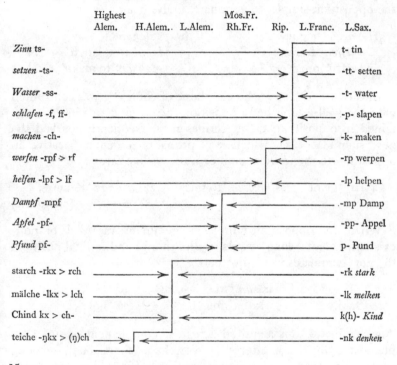

	Highest Alem.	H.Alem.	L.Alem.	Mos.Fr. Rh.Fr.	Rip.	L.Franc.	L.Sax.
Zinn ts-							t- tin
setzen -ts-							-tt- setten
Wasser -ss-							-t- water
schlafen -f, ff-							-p- slapen
machen -ch-							-k- maken
werfen -rpf > rf							-rp werpen
helfen -lpf > lf							-lp helpen
Dampf -mpf							-mp Damp
Apfel -pf-							-pp- Appel
Pfund pf-							p- Pund
starch -rkx > rch							-rk *stark*
mälche -lkx > lch							-lk *melken*
Chind kx > ch-							k(h)- *Kind*
teiche -ŋkx > (ŋ)ch							-nk *denken*

Notes:

(1) Italicized examples are present-day standard German, others dialectal.

(2) The Rhenish, Moselle, and Ripuarian Franconian 'relic forms' *dat, wat, it, allet* 'das, was, es, alles' are regarded as resulting from lenition (Gmc. *t* > *d* in unstressed position hence subsequently unaffected by Second Sound Shift, thus Fourquet (see p. 132), Bruch, Schützeichel (see p. 133), Höfler (see p. 133).

(3) In Rip. and Moselle Franc. context 1 also includes WGmc. -*t*- before *d* in the past part. of wk. vbs., e.g. Luxemburgish *späizen–gespaut* 'to spew', *setzen–gesat* 'to set', *schwätzen–geschwat* 'to talk', which would indicate early loss of medial -*i*- (WGmc. *-id*). There has, however, been much local levelling.

It seems clear that structurally and phonetically this was an extraordinarily coherent and consistent shift although its final realization varied regionally.

The allophonic developments of the Germanic voiceless plosives had important structural consequences:

(i) The labial and velar allophones of context 3 absorbed the very few examples of the geminates *ff and *hh and thus maintained the opposition simple vs. geminate. OHG examples are:

/f/	*nevo* 'nephew'		/h/	*slahan* 'to slay'
/ff/	{ *heffen* 'to raise' < *ff		/hh/	{ *lahhēn* 'to laugh' < *hh
	{ *offan* 'open' < *p			{ *mahhōn* 'to make' < *k

In the case of Gmc. *t* the allophone of context 3 was confronted with the well-established opposition /s/:/ss/ and was itself maintained in opposition. OHG scribes most frequently marked the new sound as ⟨zz⟩, which was probably a dental fricative in opposition to the more palatal or more *sh*-like /s:ss/:

/s/ *risi* 'giant'   /ss/ *missen* 'to miss'   /zz/ *wizzan* 'to know'
(cf. to *wit*)

Where the opposition simple vs. geminate was weak or non-existent, i.e. after long vowels or diphthongs and in final position, the new geminates were shortened:

slāfan 'to sleep'	*wīzan* 'to reproach'	*rīh(h)i* 'kingdom'
scif 'ship'	*wīz* 'white'	*loh* 'hole'

The geminates thus acquired a regular complement of two allophones: a 'long' one after short vowels, a 'short' one after long vowels, diphthongs, and in final position. Since they contrasted with the simple consonants not only on the basis of quantity but also on the basis of intensity (fortis vs. lenis) the distinctive feature now became intensity rather than quantity.

The system of the fricatives and plosives after the first step of the shift would thus be:
(Stage VII)

/f/	/þ/	/s/	/h/		/ss/	
/pf–ff/	/ts–zz/	/kh–hh/	/ppf/	/tts/	/kkh/
/b̥/	/d̥/	/g̊/	/b̥b̥/	/d̥d̥/	/g̊g̊/

(ii) The new affricates and fricatives remained allophones of one phoneme /pf–ff/, /ts–zz/, /kh–hh/, as long as the contexts in which they had arisen remained unaltered. There was, however, one context where conditions must have changed early. That was the position after an identical phoneme, i.e. the geminate: *pp > ppf, *tt > tts, *kh > kkh. These geminate affricates occurring medially and finally were not in contrast with any simple affricates and were thus reduced: > pf, ts, kh. They now formed a contrast with the new fricatives:

scaffōn 'to shape'	*wizzan* (*zz*) 'to know'	*rehhan* 'to revenge'
scepfen 'to create'	*wizzi* (*ts*) 'wits'	*strecchen* 'to stretch'
slaf 'lazy'	*scuz* (*z*) 'shot'	*loh* 'hole'
slipf 'slip'	*scaz* (*ts*) 'treasure'	*bock* 'buck'

In other words, the new allophones of Gmc. /p t k/ were now phonemicized.

The remaining plosives still contrasted on the basis of simple *vs.* geminate, but took up the whole phonological space of each respective place of articulation. Hence the widespread fluctuation in spelling between ⟨b–p⟩, ⟨bb–pp⟩, ⟨g–k⟩, ⟨gg–kk(ck)⟩, especially in Upper German documents. In the case of the somewhat over-loaded dental order a reduction set in early in Upper German: *d* > *t* (coalescing with the remaining allophone [t] of Gmc. */t/), *þ* > *d*. Modern German and English still show the reflexes of this additional shift:

Gmc. *t* (context 1): s*t*erben–s*t*arve; tüch*t*ig – dough*t*y;
Gmc. *d*: *T*eil – *d*eal; Fal*t*e – fol*d*; lei*t*en – to lea*d*;
Gmc. *þ*: *D*orn – *th*orn; Er*d*e – ear*th*; Le*d*er – lea*th*er.

Whether *d moving to *t* initiated the development of *þ to *d* or whether the shift from *þ to *d* caused *d to move to *t* is difficult to decide. That the two moves were however linked is evident. The Rhenish Franconian texts which preserve *þ* longer than the Upper German documents also retain *d*. The lenis plosives and the fortis geminate plosives only contrasted medially and finally. A similar contrast lenis/fortis was thus introduced in initial position in the case of the dental through the development of Gmc. *þ*, *d* > Upper German *d*, *t* and through the borrowing of Latin words with initial *p*- and *k*-. This in turn led to the native *b̥*, *g̊* becoming increasingly spelt with ⟨b⟩ and ⟨g⟩.

The lenis/fortis contrast only existed in voiced surroundings. In a cluster of fricatives or plosives it was neutralized, e.g. *luft, lust, zuht.*

The OHG consonant system of the Upper German region of the middle of the ninth century may thus be set up as follows:

(VIII)

/f/	/s/		/h/	lenis
/ff/	/ss/	/zz/	/hh/	fortis
/pf/	/ts/		/kh/	affricates (could be regarded as clusters)
/b̥/	/d̥/		/g̥/	lenis
/p/	/t/	/tt/	(/k/)	fortis
/m/	/n/			
/mm/	/nn/			
	/l/			
	/ll/			
	/r/			
	/rr/			
/w/	/j/			

Examples in medial position for fricatives and plosives:

/f/	*nevo*	/s/	*risi*			/h/	*slahan*
/ff/	*scaffōn/ slāfan*	/ss/	*giwissi*	/zz/	*wizzan/ wīzan*	/hh/	*mahhōn/ rīh(h)i*
/pf/	*scepfen*	/ts/	*wizzi*			/kh/	*strecchen*
/b̥/	*sibun* 'seven'	/d̥/	*bruoder* 'brother'			/g̥/	*nagal* 'nail'
/p–pp/	*sippa* 'sib' ('relation')	/t/	*snita* 'slice'	/tt/	*snottar* 'clever'	(/k–kk/	*rucki* 'back')

In initial position:

/f/	*fallan* 'to fall'	/s/	*sagēn* 'to say'	/h/	*halb* 'half'
/pf/	*pfaffo* 'priest'	/ts/	*zagel* 'tail'	/kh/	*chalt, kalt* 'cold'
/b̥/	*bad* 'bath'	/d̥/	*danne* 'than'	/g̥/	*gān* 'to go'
/p/	*palma* 'palm'	/t/	*tag* 'day'	(/k/)	*kelich* 'chalice'

This system was unbalanced at three points.

(a) The old dental geminate fricative /ss/ had, unlike the new geminate fricatives, no fortis allophone. The others, while contrasting with the lenis fricatives, had geminate allophones after short vowels [ff, zz, hh] and fortis allophones [f, z, h] after long vowels, diphthongs, and finally.

(b) The dental plosives alone maintained a three-way contrast. Simple fortis and geminate fortis, otherwise allophonically distributed (see (a)) were here in contrast, i.e. different phonemes.

(c) The velar affricate was maintained in the southernmost dialects. In present-day High Alemannic [kx–g̊–kk] – [štrekxə, nag̊əl, rukkə] are parallel to [pf – b̥ – pp] and [ts – d̥ – tt]. But it is doubtful whether foreign k- was introduced initially parallel to p- and the existing t-. Most likely foreign k- became /kh-/, cf. modern Alem. *chalt* and *Chelch*. In more northern dialects we find an aspirated velar plosive which fused with the fortis from former geminate g̊g̊ and with foreign k-. In most OHG dialects there was thus one velar geminate plosive (either affricated or aspirated) and modern German *strecken* and *Rücken* exemplify the coalescence of Gmc. **kk* and **gg*, but High Alemannic still distinguishes [štrekxə] < **kk* and [rukkə] < **gg*.

It is the Second or High German Sound Shift, more than any other phenomenon, which separates High German from the other Germanic languages. It occurred in the preliterary centuries between the fall of the Roman Empire and the emergence of the written vernacular. The early Latin loanwords borrowed during the centuries of the Roman Empire, including some Christian terms borrowed presumably in the fourth century (OHG *pfaffo* < **papo* < Gr. *papas*; *kirihha* < Vulgar Latin **kyrikon*), show the effects of the sound shift. That is, they were present in the language when the sound shift occurred. The name of Attila, who died in 453, was *Etzel* in later German. It too must have been borrowed before the shift and thus became affected by it. We need, however, not assume that the shift took place everywhere at the same time. In fact the OHG evidence from Upper German and Franconian dialects concerning the consequential shift of Gmc. *d* and *þ*, clearly shows the southern dialects to have been chronologically in advance. The earliest attested shifted forms are from the middle of the sixth century. It is therefore reasonable to assume that the shift took place between 500 and 700 over most of the High German territory, in the northern part possibly somewhat later than in the southern. Any attempt at closer dating must amount to extracting from the scant evidence more than it can give.

Dating of sound changes as opposed to dating of orthographic changes must take into account the system as a whole. If it is maintained that the shift of Gmc. $t > z$, zz in Alemannic occurred in the fifth to the sixth centuries, that of $p > pf$, f, ff; $k > kh$, h, hh one or two centuries later, and the shift of Gmc. $d > t$ in the eighth century, we would have to posit a most unlikely system for the intervening centuries.

Since the sound shift was in all probability chronologically ahead in the south and since it was also carried further in the south and shows a tapering towards the north and did not affect Old Saxon or Low Franconian at all, the question of 'spread' has frequently been raised. It was above all in the period between the twenties and fifties of this century that dialect geography, at the zenith of its achievements, propounded the view of a grandiose linguistic thrust from the south (either Bavaria, Lombardy or latterly Alemannia) carrying the Second Sound Shift across Franconia eventually as far as the present-day dialect boundary between High German and Low German (the Benrath Line). If 'spread' merely means a chronological lag in the completion of the shift, which itself took place spontaneously and polygenetically, there is nothing to be said against such an assumption. If it means imitation of an extraneous sound pattern, the borrowing of a foreign phonological structure, we should have to examine the historical circumstances as well as the phonological-structural facts. We have already seen that the sound shift was structurally coherent wherever it took place, that is in Central Franconian and Rhenish Franconian as much as in Alemannic and Bavarian. The graded structural picture is more likely to be the result of a co-herent, although regionally varying autochthonous sound change, than the outcome of large-scale phonological borrowing. Further-more, it has now been shown that the sound shift was in existence in parts of Central Franconian by the early eighth century. The historical circumstances, that is the Frankish hegemony, however tenuous it was during the Merovingian period, make such a lin-guistic sweep of unprecedented speed, originating in the subjected south, highly improbable. It is therefore much more likely that the language that Charles the Great and his Alemannic and Bavar-ian contemporaries spoke had spontaneously undergone every-where, in the previous preliterary centuries, a profound but regionally, structurally, and chronologically varying consonantal sound change. It is possible to distinguish a Franconian type of sound change and a Bavarian-Alemannic type. We can also distinguish a Lombardic type, although we do not know Lombardic as extensively as we would wish. Polygenesis is linguistically and historically much more likely than the sort of large-scale borrowing posited by the dialect geographers.

The possible cause of the Second Sound Shift has led to no less speculation than the cause of the First. It is most likely that the consonant change was the result of an internal shift of distinctive features, that is from a correlation of voice to a correlation of intensity linked to the gradually increasing incidence of gemination. It cannot be ruled out that interlanguage contact, i.e. the effect of a substratum, also played a part. After all it may be no coincidence that the former non-Germanic territories along the Middle and Upper Rhine and the Danube (not forgetting the River Po) were the lands where the Second Sound Shift occurred. The prime cause is, however, most likely to be found in the structural conditions of the consonantism itself.

4·5 | Morphology: Inflection

4·5·1 | Noun inflection

The declension of the noun in OHG was determined by stem class, gender, case, and number. Of these the last three had syntactic support: gender, number, and case through agreement within the noun phrase and number also through concord with the verb. In addition to their grammatical functions these three categories had semantic support. Stem class had neither. It was simply a relic or fossil from the Indo-European past. In most handbooks, however, the nominal declensional system is based on this most irrational of all four determining factors. The reason is mainly that they take a historical, diachronic view, but also that stem class was most clearly in evidence in the basic form, the nominative singular, and that case and number were formally shaped by stem class. That is, they are diachronically comprehensible only in terms of class. The declensional suffixes themselves were the products of an inextricable fusion of stem class, case, and number elements. The suffix -*i*, for instance, could occur in nom. acc. sg. masc. and neuter, gen. dat. sg. fem., nom. acc. pl. masc., fem. and neuter. Only one suffix, -*es*, was functionally clearly circumscribed. It could not be anything but genitive singular masc. and neuter, although class ensured that it was not the only gen. sg. masc. and neuter suffix.

The case system rested overwhelmingly on a contrast between nom./acc. on the one hand, and gen./dat. on the other. A form marking a distinct instrumental existed only for masc. and neuter sg. in the vocalic declensions. While in the singular, nom. and acc. shared a form in most declensions, there were one or two notable exceptions. In the plural there was a common nom./acc. form in all declensions and gen. and dat. were also clearly distinguished both from each other and from the common case nom./acc. This clear case system characterized the plural in contrast to the singular where, on the one hand, there existed a remaining nom. – acc. distinction and where there was on the other hand, in one class, a lack of distinction between gen. and dat. and, in the case of feminines even between nom./acc. and the other cases. In the nom. sg. an OHG noun could either be endingless, e.g. *tag* (m.) 'day', *scuz* (m.) 'shot', *kalb* (n.) 'calf', *lioht* (n.) 'light', *birin* (f.) 'she-bear', *hūt* (f.) 'skin', or end in a vowel: *namo* (m.) 'name', *melo* (n.) 'meal, flower', *diorna* (f.) 'girl', *hella* (f.) 'hell', *fehta* (f.) 'fight', *herza* (n.) 'heart', *situ* (m.) 'custom', *fihu* (n.) 'cattle', *wini* (m.) 'friend', *gibirgi* (n.) 'mountains', *hōhī* (f.) 'height'. Neither the genders nor the classes were unambiguously marked in the nom. sg.

The inflectional endings contained either a consonant plus a vowel, or a vowel only. Since they were unstressed there was a conflict between their important grammatical function and the accentual system of the language based on strong root stress. This conflict led to much dialectal variation and also to the extensive changes which occurred widely and fairly quickly during the OHG period. They affected the vowels, but left the consonants unscathed except for the gradual replacement of -*m* by -*n*.

It is difficult to present stable paradigms, for even within one text, e.g. Tatian or Otfrid, there was fluctuation. A historical description based on the stem classes can take account of these dialectal variations and fluctuations in time. But it hardly leads to a satisfactory synchronic picture. A functional, synchronic view of the OHG declensional system of the nouns in the middle of the ninth century is best obtained if we base it on the most clearly profiled grammatical category: number. On the basis of plural forms OHG distinguished three declensions each with subgroups according to gender.

I. *a-plural*

		M.	N.	F.	M.	N.	F.
Pl.	Nom. acc.	-*a*	-*ø*	-*ā*	steina	(barn, kelbir)	zalā
	Gen.	-*o*		-*ōno*	steino		zalōno
	Dat.	-*um*		-*ōm*	steinum		zalōm
Sg.	Nom. acc.	-*ø*		-*a*	stein	(barn, kalb)	zala
	Gen.	-*es*		-*a*	steines		zala
	Dat.	-*e*		-*u*	steine		zalu
	Instr.	-*u*			steinu		

Notes:

(1) The following masc. nouns had -*i* instead of zero in the nom./acc. sg.: *hirti* 'shepherd', *rucki* 'back', *hueizzi* 'wheat', *hirsi* 'millet', *tilli* 'dill', *kāsi* 'cheese', *pfuzzi* 'well'. In Franc. texts these nouns had -*im* in dat. pl., thus forming a bridge between the *a*-pl. and *i*-pl. types. In early texts -*i*- may also occur before the endings -*o*, -*e*, -*u*.

(2) Masc. nouns ending in -*ar*- before the pl. ending also had -*i* in nom./acc. sg., e.g. *fiskara–fiskari* 'fisherman'. The -*a*- was probably long in some dialects (Alem.), possibly short in others (Franc.).

(3) Neuter nouns of the *barn* and *kalb* types are listed here on the principle of complementary distribution. Neuter nouns ending in -*ir*- before the pl. ending (-*ø*, -*o*, -*um*) dropped -*ir*- in the sg. and there was an alternation of mutated vowels in the pl. and unmutated in the sg. Where ⟨e⟩ stood for /e/ in the pl. it alternated with ⟨a⟩ in the sg. In the case of *ehir* 'ears of corn' the sg. usually retained this stem form, although the regular *ah* is also attested. In the sg. n.=m.

(4) Masc. nouns whose root ended in -*w*- in the pl. changed it to -*o* in the nom./acc. sg.: *hlēwa* 'graves' – *hlēo*, *scatwa* 'shadows' – *scato*. Where the root vowel was -*u*- the -*w*- disappeared.

(5) Neuter nouns ending in -*o* before zero had -*w*- as the final root element before inflectional endings: *kneo* 'knee' – *knewum* (dat. pl.), *horo* 'dirt' – *horwum*.

(6) Fem. nouns ending in -*innā* in the pl. reduced this to -*in* in the nom. sg. but originally not in the acc. sg. This irregularity led to early levelling.

(7) The fem. pl. endings had long vowels according to Alem. texts. Whether this was also the case in Franconian is not known. At any rate

in the subsequent history of the written language they developed in the same way as the masc. and neuter endings.

(8) The kinship terms *fater, bruoder, muoter, tohter, swester* followed this declension in the gen. and dat. pl. but were otherwise endingless throughout the paradigm, except for *fater* which followed the *a*-plural declension but had endingless alternatives in gen. and dat. sg. Similar irregularities were also attested for *man* m. and *naht* f. 'night'.

Historically this OHG *a*-plural declension was formed by the Gmc. masc. and neuter *a*-stems, the masc. *ja*-stems, the masc. and neuter *wa*-stems, fem. *ō*- and *jō*-stems, the neuter IE *s*-stems and the *r*-stems (see 3.6.1.).

II. *i-plural*

		M. N. F.	M.	N.	F.
Pl.	Nom. acc.	*-i*	slegi	betti	hūti
	Gen.	*-o*	slego	betto	hūto
	Dat.	*-im*	slegim	bettim	hūtim
Sg.	Nom. acc.	*-ø -i -ø*	slag	betti	hūt
	Gen.	*-es* *-i*	slages	bettes	hūti
	Dat.	*-e* *-i*	slage	bette	hūti
	Instr.	*-u* (*-iu*)	slagu	bettu	

Notes:

(1) Mutation was a feature of the pl. of all three genders but only in masc. was it in contrast to an unmutated sg. Where the pl. masc. had ⟨e⟩ for /e/, the sg. had ⟨a⟩. All neuters had, where appropriate, mutation in pl. and sg. The feminines had ⟨e⟩ for /e/ in the gen. and dat. sg. where they had it in the pl. but not in the nom. acc. sg.

(2) A few masc. nouns ended in *-i* instead of zero in the nom. acc. sg.: *wini* 'friend', *risi* 'giant', *quiti* 'statement'.

(3) Two fem. had also *-i* instead of zero in the nom. acc. sg.: *turi* 'door', *kuri* 'choice'. One fem., *hant* 'hand', had *-um* in dat. pl. *hantum*.

(4) The fem. abstracts in *-ī*, e.g. *hōhī* 'height', followed this declension in the dat. pl. (*hōhīm*) and retained *-ī* throughout the sg.

(5) A few masc. ended in *-u* in the nom. acc. sg. They were: *situ* 'custom' (the only one with pl. forms). Others, without pl. forms, had the regular gen. and dat. sg. endings of the *a*- and *i*-pl. declensions: *hugu* 'mind', *sigu* 'victory', *witu* 'wood' and also *fihu* n. 'cattle'.

(6) In the gen. pl. there were alternatives, chronologically usually earlier, in *-io*, *-eo*. The neuters *heri* 'army' and *beri* 'berry' had *-i-* regularly before the endings *-o*, *-es*, *-e*.

Historically the OHG *i*-pl. declension arose on the basis of the Gmc. masc. and fem. *i*-stems, the neuter *ja*-stems, masc. fem. and neuter *u*-stems, and the fem. *īn*-stems.

III. *n-plural*

		M.	N.	F.	M.	N.	F.
Pl.	Nom. acc.	-on/-un	-un	-ūn	namon	herzun	diornūn
	Gen.		-ōno		namōno	herzōno	diornōno
	Dat.		-ōm		namōm	herzōm	diornōm
Sg.	Nom.	-o	-a	-a	namo	herza	diorna
	Acc.	-on/-un	-a	-ūn	namon	herza	diornūn
	Dat. gen.	-en/-in	-en/-in	-ūn	namen	herzen	diornūn

Notes:

(1) The masc. endings -*on* and -*en* were more northern (Franc.) and chronologically, later; -*un* and -*in* were Alem. and earlier.

(2) Masc. and fem. nouns were very numerous but there were only four neuters: *ouga* 'eye', *ōra* 'ear', *wanga* 'cheek' beside *herza* 'heart'.

Historically this *n*-pl. declension continued the Gmc. *n*-stems.

It is evident from the tables that the distinction between the *i*- and *a*-declensions rested on the differences between unstressed vowels. It is true, mutation existed as a subsidiary factor, operative only, of course, where the root vowels were susceptible to mutation. Words like *gift* f. 'gift', *scrit* m. 'stride' depended on the vocalic markers only. Since mutation, at least in the case of the large masc. class, was tied up with the number distinction, it became functionalized when the distinction between the unstressed vowels was no longer kept alive. In Old English, mutation in the corresponding class was not confined to the plural and was therefore never functionalized to the same extent as in German.

Neuter nouns were strongly represented only in the two vocalic declensions. In both declensions there was no number distinction in nom. and acc. There was, however, one small group of neuter nouns where a number distinction existed by virtue of the suffix -*ir*. One could in fact set up this small group as a fourth declension. But if we base our declensional system on the plural, the pattern -*ø*, -*o*, -*um* corresponds exactly to the *a*-declension of neuters and a simple deletion rule leads to the singular forms. Nine nouns belonged regularly to this sub-group: *kalb* 'calf', *lamb* 'lamb', *hrind* 'heifer', *huon* 'hen', *farh* 'young pig', *ei* 'egg', *hrīs* 'twig', *blat* 'leaf', *luog* 'lair', and another six usually: *hol* 'cave', *rad* 'wheel', *grab* 'grave', *loub* 'leaf', *krūt* 'herb', *bret* 'board'. Here was the nucleus of a neuter declension with number distinction, resistant to suffix weakening owing to the consonant *r*, with supplementary *i*-mutation in the plural. No wonder it attracted an increasing number of neuter nouns.

The *n*-declension being consonantal was equally resistant to phonological change. Thanks to this resistance the one nom.–acc. distinction was to survive and the declensional system of later stages was to centre on the opposition consonantal *vs.* vocalic, i.e. weak *vs.* strong.

Feminine nouns bridged the contrast as the large number of nouns in the *a*- and *n*-pl. declensions already shared the gen. and dat. pl. The weakening of the final vowels was to deprive the feminine nouns of the vocalic classes of case distinction in the sg. There were numerous nouns which showed adherence to more than one declension. It is not quite clear to what extent dialectal differences explain this fluctuation between declensions and to what extent there was genuine polymorphism.

The evolution of the noun declension was dominated by the increasing importance of number distinction, the decreasing importance of case and class distinction, the resistance of consonantal endings to phonological change, the gradual elimination of vocalic distinctions in inflectional endings, and by the functionalization of mutation.

4.5.2 | Adjective inflection

Six categories determined the form of an adjective in OHG: stem class, gender, number, case, definiteness, and comparison. Stem class was only in evidence on the lexical level, i.e. in the termination of the unmarked form. Adjectives ended in a consonant or in the vowels *-i* or *-o*: (a) *jung* 'young', *ubil* 'evil', *irdin* 'earthen', *diutisc* 'German', and the past participles, *gisalbōt* 'anointed'; these derived historically from the *-a/-ō*-stems; (b) *scōni* 'beautiful', *dunni* 'thin', *swāri* 'heavy', and the present participles, *nemanti* 'taking'; historically these continued the *-ja/-jō*-stems; (c) *gelo* 'yellow', *kalo* 'bald', *grāo* 'grey'; before inflectional endings *o* changed to *w*. In some cases contraction occurred, e.g. *frō* 'glad', and *w* before endings no longer appeared. Adjectives in *-o* are a reflex of the *-wa/-wō*-stems.

Gender, number, and case were expressed in two paradigms. These two paradigms were governed by the notion of definiteness. The strong paradigm expressed a degree of 'indefiniteness' and the weak paradigm expressed 'definiteness'. The weak paradigm was identical with the *n*-pl. declension of the nouns (see 4.5.1), although differentiation owing to varying degrees of weakening in the two word classes set in fairly early. The comparative and superlative had only the weak paradigm. Historically the weak paradigm is a reflex of the *n*-stem class.

The strong paradigm resembled both the *a*-pl. declension of the nouns and the pronominal declension. In the masc. and fem. nom. sg., neuter nom. and acc. sg. and the nom. pl. of all three genders, forms deriving from the nominal and the pronominal declension existed side by side. In predicative usage the inflected forms of the pl. predominated in early OHG but tended to give way later; in the case of past part., inflected forms persisted longer than in the case of adjectives.

In attributive position either sg. form was used, but in the pl. the pronominal or inflected forms were the rule. For example: *jung kuning* or *junger kuning, der kuning ist jung* or *junger*, but *junge kuninga, die kuninga sint jung* or *junge*.

The strong paradigm

		M.	N.	F.
Sg.	Nom.	*-ø, -ēr*	*-ø, -az*	*-ø, -iu(-u)*
	Acc.	*-an*	*-ø, -az*	*-a*
	Gen.	*-es*		*-era*
	Dat.	*-emo*		*-ero*
	Instr.	*-u*		
Pl.	Nom. acc.	*-ø, -e*	*-ø, -iu(-u)*	*-ø, -o*
	Gen.		*-ero*	
	Dat.		*-ēm*	
Sg.	Nom.	jung, junger	jung, jungaz	jung, jungiu
	Acc.	jungan	jung, jungaz	junga
	Gen.	junges		jungera
	Dat.	jungemo		jungero
	Instr.	jungu		
Pl.	Nom. acc.	jung, junge	jung, jungiu	jung, jungo
	Gen.		jungero	
	Dat.		jungēm	

Notes:

(1) For *-ø* read *-i*, *-o* where lexically required.

(2) The ending *-iu* was diphthongal in Alem., but probably *-*ju* > -*u* in Franc. with consequential earlier weakening.

(3) *-emo*, *-ero* were *-emu* and *-eru* in very early texts. In gen. and dat. sg. fem. there was a tendency to let the cases fall together.

(4) Final *-m* tended to change to *-n*.

In the comparison there was the luxury of two suffixes: *-ir-* or *-ōr-* in the comparative, and *-ist-* or *-ōst-* in the superlative. Adjectives in *-i* preferred the *i*-forms: *suozi – suoziro – suozisto* 'sweet'. Polysyllabic adjectives and adjectives with derivational suffixes (*-līh*, *-īg* etc.) had the *ō*-suffix: *sālīg – sāligōro – sāligōsto*. Others fluctuated. The *j*-suffix introduced mutation into comparison, hence modern German *arm – ärmer – am ärmsten*, but *haltbar – haltbarer – am haltbarsten*.

4.5.3 | Verb inflection

The morphology of the verb in OHG was characterized by three different systems. First there was the division into classes based on the formation of the two simple tenses. Secondly there were the inflectional endings expressing person and number and, in part, tense and mood as well. Thirdly there were the periphrastic forms which had recently come into existence or were being created during the OHG period. As a new feature the permanent accretion of the perfective prefix *ga-/gi-* to the stem of the past participle in OHG has also to be recorded. This prefix had formerly either expressed the semantic feature of 'together' or had added the aspect of completion to the basic meaning of the verb. In OHG it had become a part of the past participle inflection except in a few verbs which were perfective in themselves, such as *queman* 'to come', *findan* 'to find', *bringan* 'to bring', *werdan* 'to become', and except in the case of the verbs with inseparable prefixes.

(i) The Germanic division into *three main classes*, the weak verbs (dental-suffix type), strong verbs (apophonic type), and preterite presents (apophonic dental-suffix type), was fully maintained. The *weak verbs* consisted of four classes:

	Inf. Pres.	Pret.	Past Part.
Ia	-*en* (mutation)	-*ta* (no mutation)	-*it* (mutation)
			-*tēr* etc. (no mutation)
	brenn-en 'to burn'	*bran-ta*	*gibrenn-it* (*gibrant-*)
	sezz-en 'to set'	*saz-ta*	*gisezz-it* (*gisazt-*)
	lōs-en 'to loosen'	*lōs-ta*	*gilōs-it* (*gilōst-*)
Ib	-*en* (mutation)	-*ita* (mutation)	-*it* (mutation)
	den(n)-en 'to stretch'	*den-ita*	*giden-it* (*gidenit-*)
	fer(r)-en 'to ferry'	*fer-ita*	*gifer-it*
	uuel(l)-en 'to choose'	*uuel-ita*	*giuuel-it*
II	-*ōn*	-*ōta*	-*ōt*
	bad-ōn 'to bathe'	*bad-ōta*	*gebad-ōt*
III	-*ēn*	-*ēta*	-*ēt*
	lirn-ēn 'to learn'	*lirn-ēta*	*gilirn-ēt*

Classes Ia and Ib derived from the Gmc. -*jan* class of weak verbs. They are usually, for historical reasons, taken together and called class I. Mutation caused by *i* or *j* occurred where the root vowels were mutable; *j* also caused gemination of a single consonant after a short vowel (in Upper German apparently also after a long vowel). Not all Gmc. verbs had -*i*- in the preterite (see p. 101). Syncopation of medial -*i*- after long or polysyllabic roots in West Germanic greatly increased the number of verbs without an *i*-element and hence subsequently without mutation in the preterite and the declined forms of the past participle. 'Long roots' were roots with a long vowel or diphthong, or a short vowel plus more than one consonant. In OHG former Gmc. *p*, *t*, *k* became geminates thus making the root long. Where Gmc. *d* and *l* (geminated before *j* in the present and infinitive) preceded the dental suffix, medial -*i*- also tended to be syncopated (*retten* 'to save': *ratta* or *retita*, *zellen* 'to tell': *zalta* or *zelita*). Thus the incidence of short roots, where medial -*i*- in the preterite remained, was greatly reduced. By far the greater number of former *-jan* verbs had the OHG suffix -*ta* in the preterite and no mutation. Class Ib with -*ita* contained only about thirty-five verbs, not counting the compounds derived from them. The absence of mutation, in OHG spelling, of course, only in evidence in the case of verbal root vowel -*a*-, is generally known by Jacob Grimm's designation *Rückumlaut*. Vowel alternation on the basis of mutation had thus become a major feature of a large class of weak verbs. By affecting only verbs with the appropriate root vowels, and seen against the background of all weak classes, this vowel alternation was an irregularity. Class Ia, however, remained a well established class as long as the other weak classes were marked as separate entities by medial *-i-*, *-ō-*, *-ē-* respectively. A further anomaly existed in the second and third persons sg. and the imperative of many verbs, where a single consonant varied with a geminate caused by former *j* in the infinitive and the other forms of the present. Thus *zellen* but *zelis*, *zelit* or *den(n)en* but *denis*, *denit*. Where the root was originally long this alternation did not occur: *brennen*, *brennis*, *brennit*. Nor was it found where the root had an affricate: *setzen*, *setzis*, *setzit*, although the affricate was phonologically not germane to the second and third persons. Levelling set in quite early especially in Franconian: *denen*, *zelen*.

Both dialectally and chronologically there was a considerable amount of fluctuation in the membership of the weak classes. The numerical strength of the *ō*-class was specially characteristic of OHG. Semantically the classes were not sharply separated although in the classes Ia and Ib there were many causatives, e.g. *tiuren* 'to make dear', *sougen* 'to cause to suck', and in class III there were many inchoatives, e.g. *fūlēn* 'to become rotten', *bleichēn* 'to grow pale'.

The *strong verbs* had the same pattern of stem formation as in Germanic but various sub-classes had evolved in consequence of phonological developments. (See pp. 97–8 for the Gmc. classification and Gothic examples.)

The structural types with the IE base vowel *e* (classes I–V) continued the inherited pattern remarkably faithfully. Between classes IV and V there had been some interchange. Some verbs of type *e* + consonant, notably those with OHG *hh* < Gmc. *k*, had joined class IV, e.g. *brechan* – *gibrochan* 'to break'.

In class II there were three verbs with *ū* in the inf. stem: *sūgan* 'to suck', *sūfan* 'to drink, to sup', *lūchan* 'to lock'.

In class V three verbs reflected a former *j*-stem element in the inf. and pres.: *liggen* 'to lie', *sitzen* 'to sit', *bitten* 'to beg', and in class VI also three: *heffen* 'to lift', *swerien* 'to swear', *skepfen* 'to create'.

Classification of the Old High German apophonic verbs

Traditional class	Inf. pl. pres.	3rd sg. pres.	Sg. pret.	Pl. pret.	P.p.
Ia	ī	ī	ei	i	i
	trīban	trībit	treib	tribun	gitriban
b	ī	ī	ē	i	i
	zīhan	zīhit	zēh	zigun	gizigan
IIa	io	iu	ou	u	o
	sliofan	sliufit	slouf	sluffun	gisloffan
b	io	iu	ō	u	o
	siodan	siudit	sōd	sutun	gisotan
IIIa	e	i	a	u	o
	werfan	wirfit	warf	wurfun	giworfan
b	i	i	a	u	u
	spinnan	spinnit	spann	spunnun	gispunnan
IV	e	i	a	ā	o
	stelan	stilit	stal	stālun	gistolan
V	e	i	a	ā	e
	geban	gibit	gab	gābun	gigeban
VIIa	ei	ei	ia		ei
	heizan	heizit	hiaz	hiazun	giheizan
b	ou(ō)	ou(ō)	io		ou
	loufan	loufit	liof	liofun	giloufan
c	a	a(e)	ia		a
	faldan	faldit	fiald	fialtun	gifaltan
	(-t-)	(-t-)	(-t)		
d	ā < Gmc.ē	ā	ia		ā
	lāzan	lāzit	liaz	liazun	gilāzan
e	uo < Gmc.ō	uo	io		uo
	hruofan	hruofit	hriof	hriofun	gihruofan
VI	a	e	uo		a
	skaban	skebit	skuob	skuobun	giskaban

The structural types with Gmc. base vowel *a* and those with *ē* and *ō* were considerably affected by the phonological changes, so that it is best to rearrange them in two new classes: VII, characterized by the diphthongs *ia* or *io* in the whole preterite, which were to coalesce in late OHG, and VI with the alternation *a – uo*. The former class is usually called the 'Reduplicating Class'. It consisted of a relatively small number of verbs in each sub-class with a great variety in the root vowels of the present stem.

The $\bar{e}$ and $\bar{o}$ apophonic classes (see p. 97) had suffered the greatest losses in the transition from Germanic. The verbs with roots ending in a vowel, the so-called *verba pura*, had become weak, and now belonged to the OHG class Ia. E.g. *blāen* 'to blow', *drāen* 'to turn', cf. E *to throw*, *knāen* 'to know', *krāen* 'to crow', *māen* 'to mow', *nāen* 'to sew', *sāen* 'to sow' and with Gmc. $\bar{o}$: *bluoen* 'to flower', *gluoen* 'to glow', *gruoen* 'to grow', *luoen* 'to low'. The modern reflexes have mutated vowels, e.g. *mähen*, *nähen*, *blühen*, *glühen*. In contrast to German some of the English correspondences are still strong.

Grammatical change (see p. 88) occurred in about two dozen verbs, in particular the following alternations between:

d:t *snīdan– sneid – snitun – gisnitan* 'to cut'
s:r *friosan – frōs – frurun – gifroran* 'to freeze'
h:g *ziohan – zōh – zugun – gizogan* 'to pull'.

The *preterite-presents* (or the apophonic dental-suffix type) numbered nine in OHG with two further rare forms. In the present tense they echoed the gradation of the preterite of the strong classes.

The OHG preterite-presents

	Inf.	1st, 3rd sg. pres.	2nd sg. pres.	Pl. pres.	Pret.	
I	wizzan	weiz	weist	wizzun	wissa/ wessa	'to know'
II	—	toug (impersonal)	—	tugun	tohta	'it is useful'
III	unnan	an	—	unnun	onda	'to grant'
	kunnan	kan	kanst	kunnun	konda	'can'
	durfan	darf	darft	durfun	dorfta	'to need'
	—	gitar	gitarst	giturrun	gitorsta	'to dare'
IV	scolan	scal	scalt	sculun	scolta	'shall'
V	magan/ mugan	mag	maht	magun/ mugun	mahta/ mohta	'can'
VI	—	muoz	muost	muozun	muosa	'may'

There was a good deal of regional fluctuation in these forms. The preterite forms are specially interesting, being formed by the addition of the dental suffix to the reduced grade stem without medial vowel. Both consonantal developments ($t + t > ss$, $g > h$) and vocalic changes (Gmc. $u > o$, $i > e$ before a) show that these

forms are old. *Konda* and *scolta* derive their *d* and *t* from IE
t > *þ* under differing stress conditions: *'þ* > WGmc. *þ* (OE
cūðe) > OHG *d* (*konda*); *þ'* > *ð* > WGmc. *d* (OE *sceolde*) >
OHG *t* (*scolta*).

Here may be added the irregular verbs:

wellen	willu, wili, wili	wellemēs (-ēn)	wolta	'to want'
wesan	bim, bist, ist	birun, -ut, sint	was, wārun	'to be'
tuon	tuon, tuos(t), tuot	tuomēs	teta, tātun	'to do'
gān	gām(-n), gās(t), gāt	gāmes (gān)	giang	'to go'
stān	stām(-n), stās(t), stāt	stāmes (stān)	stuont	'to stand'

The last two verbs represented short forms of the strong verbs
gangan and *stantan* and had two regional forms: with *-ā-* in
Alemannic while in Franconian and Bavarian *-ē-* predominated.

(ii) The *inflectional personal endings* were still shaped by the
original Indo-European division into primary and secondary
endings and those of the perfect (see pp. 39, 90, 96). These
differences were now, however, meaningless and a tendency to
eliminate class differences but to maintain person, number, and
mood differences made itself felt during the OHG period. There
was much dialectal and chronological fluctuation and levelling,
but the following tables may serve as an indication of the prevailing patterns in the middle of the ninth century.

	Ind. pres.			Subj. pres.		
	I	II	III	I	II	III
1st sg.	-u	-ō-m	-ø	-e	-o (-ōe)	-i
2nd sg.	-i-s(t)	-ō-s(t)	-t, -st	-ē-s(t)	-ō-s(t) (-ō-ēs(t))	-is
3rd sg.	-i-t	-ō-t	-ø	-e	-o (-ōe)	-i
1st pl.	-e-mēs (-ēn)	-ō-mēs (-ōn)	-un	-e-mēs (-ēn)	-ō-mēs (ōēm) (-ōn)	-in
2nd pl.	-e-t	-ō-t	-ut	-ē-t	-ō-t (ō-ēt)	-it
3rd pl.	-e(a)-nt	-ō-nt	-un	-ē-n	-ō-n (ō-ēn)	-in

Inf.:	neman	badōn	kunnan	neman	badōn	kunnan
	nimu	badōm	kan	neme	bado	kunni
	nimis(t)	badōs(t)	kanst	nemēs(t)	badōs(t)	kunnis
	nimit	badōt	kan	neme	bado	kunni
	nememēs	badōm	kunnun	nememēs	badomēs	kunnin
	(-ēn)	(-ēs)		(-ēn)	(-ōn)	
	nemet	badōt	kunnut	nemēt	badōt	kunnit
	nement	badōnt	kunnun	nemēn	badōn	kunnin

Notes:

(1) Suffixes listed under I apply to strong verbs and weak verbs of classes Ia and Ib (-*jan* verbs). Suffixes under II are for the weak classes II (*ōn*-verbs) and III (*ēn*-verbs). The latter have -*ē*- for -*ō*- throughout. In the 3rd pers. pl. the strong verbs had -*ant* originally and the *jan*-verbs had -*ent* but confusion set in early. The suffixes under III are those of the preterite-presents. In the 2nd pers. sg. some had -*t*, others -*st* (see p. 188).

(2) In the 2nd pers. sg. the earlier ending was -*s* but in analogy to the preterite-presents with -*st* (and *bist*) and owing to agglutination of the dental in inversion (*nimis-du* > *nimist du* - *du nimist*) -*st* became general in the ninth century.

(3) In the 1st pers. pl. the original ending was vowel +*m* as in 1st pers. sg. II (*badōm*). Then the mysterious ending: vowel (-*e*-, -*a*-, -*u*- apart from ō(*ē*)) plus -*mēs* spread, perhaps to effect a number differentiation. Some scholars have seen in it a pronominal form related to *wir*, others have suggested an extension from the 2nd pers. sg. subjunctive in adhortative use. In the second half of the ninth century forms with -*n* spread rapidly and gradually ousted the -*mēs* forms.

(4) The 1st pers. sg. was clearly distinguished as to class in the indicative present only. This led to levelling in either direction: vocalic ending or nasal ending (-*m* or later -*n*) in both I and II. Finally the vocalic ending became general in the written language. But the modern Alemannic dialectal *i nime(n)* with -*n* before vowels is a reflex of levelling in the opposite direction.

(5) The subjunctive is usually called optative in OHG grammars, because it does not correspond to the IE subjunctive. As it is, however, the forerunner of the modern German subjunctive, the term subjunctive is here preferred. Only the 3rd pers. sg. and pl. are clearly marked. The bracketed longer forms with the -*ē*- mood theme also in II (-*ō*- is replaced by -*ē*- in the *ēn*-verbs) was especially Alemannic. Franconian had almost exclusively short forms. In the 2nd pers. sg. -*t* was added later than in the corresponding indicative form. In the 1st pers. pl. the extended indicative form became also fairly widespread in the subjunctive for a time. Finally the subjunctive forms -*ēn* etc. spread to the indicative.

(6) The declined forms of the infinitive add -*nes* (gen.), -*ne* (dat.).

	Ind. pret.		Subj. pret.	
	I	II	I	II
1st, 3rd sg.	-ø	-ø-ta	-i	-ø-ti
2nd sg.	-i	-ø-tōs	-ī-s	-ø-tī-s
1st pl.	-u-mēs	-ø-tu-mēs	-ī-mes	-ø-tī-mēs
2nd pl.	-u-t	-ø-tu-t	-ī-t	-ø-tī-t
3rd pl.	-u-n	-ø-tu-n	-ī-n	-ø-tī-n

I	II	I	II
nam	branta/badōta	nāmi	branti/badōti
nāmi	brantōs/badōtōs	nāmīs	brantīs/badōtīs
nāmumēs(-un)	brantumēs/badōtumēs	nāmīm(es)	brantīm(ēs)/badōtīm(es)
nāmut	brantut/badōtut	nāmīt	brantīt/badōtīt
nāmum	brantun/badōtun	nāmīn	brantīn/badōtīn

Notes:

(1) I means strong verbs, II means weak verbs. For -ø in II read -i- (weak class Ib), -ō- (weak class II), -ē- (weak class III).

(2) The strong verbs had different stem forms for 1st/3rd sg. and for 2nd sg. and the persons of the pl. On the WGmc. form of the 2nd pers. sg. see p. 98.

(3) The weak verbs changed the 2nd sg. -tōs, -tīs to -tōst, -tīst. But this change was later than the intrusion of -t in the ind. pres.

(4) In the ninth century the characteristic OHG 1st pers. pl. ending -mēs occurred in the pret. as well, but later it gave way again to -un, -īn.

(5) In Alem. documents all weak verbs (II) had -ō-: brantōn, brantōt, brantōn.

(6) Weak verbs showed no mutation in the subj. pret.: *branti, zalti*, not *brenti, *zelti. In Alemannic the suffix -i was long. It may have attracted the kind of secondary stress that belonged to derivational rather than inflectional suffixes which could explain the absence of mutation.

In the 2nd pers. sg. of the imperative there was a further marked difference between strong and weak verbs. The former ended in the final consonant of the root (*nim!*) while the weak verbs always ended in a vowel (*brenni! bado!* etc.).

(iii) It is not unreasonable to assume that when the simple West Germanic verbal system of two synthetic tenses and moods was confronted with the highly developed system of Latin with its preterite/perfect distinction, its pluperfect, its future and its passive voice, the impulse for the creation of additional systemic distinctions must have been increasingly felt by the German clerics. The rise of *periphrastic forms* was thus very much a feature of Old High German. The verbs which were employed as function verbs were *wesan* 'to be', *werdan* 'to become', *habēn* 'to have' and as a variant in the pl. *eigun* 'to own'. The non-finite parts were the present participle and the past participle, both of which were initially frequently declined as adjectives. The infinitive was used with the preterite-presents as function words but such forms constituted a verbal phrase rather than a tense or voice form. The periphrastic forms can be listed as follows. Their use is a matter for syntax.

	Passive		*Perfect*	
wesan ⎫	(fact, state, duration)	*wesan* ⎫		
⎬ +past participle (trans. verbs)	⎬ +past participle			
werdan ⎭	(process, inception)	*habēn/eigun* ⎭		

Present state (active)

wesan ⎫
⎬ +present participle ⎰ (duration)
werdan ⎭   ⎱ (inception)

4.6 | Morphology: Word Formation

4.6.1 | Noun derivation

The prime function of derivation is lexical. By means of derivation speakers extend the vocabulary of their language, either within a word class, e.g. *Liebe – Liebling – Liebschaft*, or by conversion of one word class into another, e.g. *warm – wärmen – Wärme*. Adjectives are thus made into nouns or verbs, nouns into verbs or adjectives, verbs into adjectives or nouns. It is often not easy to decide which form was the starting point, and synchronically it is irrelevant. What matters, however, synchronically is to determine what derivational means are active and productive.

Old High German was a period of high activity. The enormous richness of the Latin vocabulary was a challenge to Carolingian glossators and translators, and their works show clearly the extent to which they responded in the field of word formation. What concerns us here are the derivational means which they employed. On the basis of a survey of the translation of the Rule of St Benedict (BR) and of Otfrid's *Gospel Book* (O) the following noun suffixes can be said to have been productive in the ninth century:

(i) *-o*: deriving from former *-*an* (predominantly deverbal) and *-*jan* (predominantly denominal) this suffix forms *nomina agentis*, e.g. *gebo* 'giver'. It is especially frequent with prefixes or in compounds: *giferto* 'companion', *gimazo* 'companion at table', *giteilo* 'comrade'; *betti-riso* 'paralytic', i.e. 'one who has taken to his bed', *man-slago* 'killer', *widarwerto* 'adversary'.

(ii) *-āri*: although numerically not much less frequent than *-o*, (in BR 14 *-o*, 13 *-āri*; in O 29 *-o*, 22 *-āri*), it often appears to be more restricted to the new world of the church, e.g. *bredigāri* 'preacher', *buachāri* 'evangelist', *fisgāri* 'fisherman', *gartāri* 'gardener', *heilāri* 'healer', *scribāri* 'writer', *skualāri* 'pupil', *zuhtāri* 'teacher'. It seems to owe its spread to its use to form uncompounded agent nouns from weak verbs mainly in imitation of Latin agent nouns in *-tor*, *-sor*, as well as *-arius*, while *-o* formations, belonging to the older part of the vocabulary, are above all Germanic-type compounds from strong verbs. Weinreich (p. 210) states that of forty-three *-(e)o-* derivations in the OS *Heliand*, thirty-two are compounds whereas all five *-āri*-derivations are simple nouns. Only loanwords appear to denote things, e.g. *karkāri* 'prison'.

(iii) *-in*: although hardly attested in the texts mentioned, this suffix was undoubtedly the chief means of forming nouns denoting females, e.g. *kuningin* 'queen' from *kuning*, *esilin* 'she-ass' from *esil*, *fiantin* (BR) Lat. *inimica*.

(iv) *-ī*: this is by far the most frequently occurring suffix in the two texts investigated. It formed abstract feminine nouns from adjectives. In frequency it outweighed its nearest competitor *-ida* by seven to four in BR and by seven to one in O. It was added freely to adjectives of all kinds, e.g. short ones *snellī* (O) 'bravery' from *snel* 'brave', *rīffī* (BR) 'ripeness' from *rīffi* 'ripe'; derivative adjectives *smāhlīhhī* (BR) 'slightness' from *smāhlīh* 'slight', *gisuntī* (O) 'well-being' from *gisunt* 'well'; compound adjectives *geginwertī* (O) 'presence' from *geginwert* 'present', *ubarmuatī* (BR) 'pride' from *ubarmuati* 'proud'; past participles *farlāzzanī* (BR) 'forgiveness' from *farlāzzan* 'forgiven', *far-tragani* (BR) 'sufferance' from *fartragan* 'suffered'.

(v) *-ida*: this is next in frequency. It formed abstract nouns, in O only from adjectives, and was often in direct competition with an *-ī* formation, e.g. *beldida* and *baldī* 'boldness' from *bald* 'bold', *heilida* 'health' and *heilī* 'salvation' from *heili* 'healthy', *lūtida* 'loudness' and *lūtī* 'sound' from *lūt* 'loud'. It is more frequent in BR, where it is also used with verbal roots, than in O, e.g. *kehenkida* 'agreement, consensus' from *kehenkan* 'to agree', *pihaltida* 'observation' from *pihaltan* 'to observe'. It often gives the impression of having been used in response to a Latin abstract noun, e.g. *ordo, ordinatio* > *kisezzida, antreitida*; *misericordia* > *arma-herzida*; *ignorantia* > *unwizzida*.

(vi) *-nissi*: there is a great deal of fluctuation in the OHG documents with regard both to gender (e.g. n. in O, f. in Isidore) and to the vowel in the suffix (*a, u*, apart from the more frequent *e* (Tatian f. and n.) and *i*). E.g. *stuncnissī* f. (BR) 'contrition', *kernnissa* f. (BR) 'devotion'. In O this suffix is often in competition with *-ī* and *-ida*, e.g. *finstarnissi* beside *finstrī* 'darkness', *suaznissi* 'sweetness' beside *suazzī*, also from adj. are *stilnissi* 'stillness', *wārnissi* 'truth'. There are also derivations from verbs and nouns, e.g. *irstantnissi* 'resurrection' from *irstantan, gotnissi* 'deity'.

(vii) *-unga*: fem. abstract verbal nouns denoting an action or the result of an action are formed by means of this suffix. O has only four, e.g. *samanunga* 'the coming together' from *samanōn* 'to gather', *manunga* 'reminding, admonition' from *manōn* 'to admonish', but in BR *-unga* abstracts are fairly frequent. Here Latin abstracts in *-atio* etc. seemed to have led to increased use in learned prose, e.g. *auhhunga* 'growth' Lat. *augmentatio*, from *auhhōn* 'to add', *īlunga* 'hurry', Lat. *festinatio*, from *īlen* 'to hurry', *scauwunka* 'consideration' from *scauwōn* 'to consider'. Such derivations were frequent from weak verbs, especially *-ōn* verbs, but much more rare from strong verbs where older abstract formations were available, see pp. 103, 106.

(viii) *-ōd, -ōdi*: m. verbal derivations have generally *-ōd* or *-ōt*, e.g. *wegōd* (O) 'advocacy' from *wegōn* 'to assist, advocate', *rīhhisōd* (BR) n. 'dominion' from *rīhhisōn* 'to rule'; denominal derivations have usually *-ōdi* or *-ōti* f. or n., e.g. *ebenōti* (O) 'plane' from *eban* 'even', *hērōti* n. (O) 'lordship, dignity' from *hēr* 'old, honourable'.

(ix) *gi-i*: this composite derivational device is one of the most

fertile in OHG. It forms neuter nouns often with collective meaning but also often with little semantic differentiation. The base is a
noun. E.g. *giknihti* (O) 'disciples' from *kneht* 'young man',
gizungi (O) 'language' from *zunga* 'language, tongue'. In words
like *gibendi* 'bands' the presence of both the noun *bant* and the
verb *bintan* prepared the later extension of this derivation to
verbal roots.

(x) Other nominal suffixes, e.g. *-ahi* forming collectives of
things, e.g. *boum* 'tree' > *boumahi* 'group of trees', *stein* 'stone' >
steinahi 'stony land', or *-isal* forming nouns from verbs, e.g.
wertisal n. (O) 'injury' from (*ir*)*werten* 'to hurt', or *-ing* (*-ling*), e.g.
kataling m. (BR) 'parent', *zehanning* m. (BR) 'deacon', do not
show themselves, by the test of frequency, to have been particularly productive. The same applies to diminutive suffixes, e.g.
kindilīn (O) 'little child'.

(xi) *-heit*: fem. abstracts denoting 'nature, kind' were formed
with nouns and adjectives as the basis and the noun *heit* 'kind,
figure', which had developed into a suffix. E.g. *deoheit* (BR)
'humility', *kewonaheit* (BR) 'use, custom' from *kiwon* 'usual',
bōsheit (O) 'wickedness', *gimeitheit* (O) 'arrogance' beside *gimeitī*
'arrogance' from *gimeit* 'arrogant'.

(xii) *-scaf*: fem. abstracts denoting 'state, condition'. BR has
for instance *lantscaf* 'region', but words with personal nouns are
more typical: *kinōzscaf* 'community', *fiantscaf* 'dissension';
Otfrid has *botascaf* 'message', *bruaderscaf* 'brotherhood, frater-
nity', *drūtscaf* 'friendship', *fiantscaf*, *heriscaf* 'host, crowd'.

(xiii) *-tuom*: m. or n. denoting 'status, degree', e.g. BR *meistar-*
tuam m. Lat. *magisterium*, *ēwarttuam* Lat. *sacerdotium*, O: *altduam*
n. 'old age', *hēriduam* m. 'authority', *thiarnuduam* m. 'virginity',
wīsduam n. 'wisdom'.

(xiv) *-tag* (*-tago*): denotes mainly a 'disagreeable state'. Otfrid
has *nakotdag* m. 'nakedness'.

Prefix nouns were also a characteristic feature of OHG. Those
with *un-* with the meaning 'negative' were especially frequent, e.g.
in Otfrid we have among many *unfruati* 'ignorance', *unfrewida*
'unhappiness', *ungiwitiri* 'bad weather, storm'. In view of the
increased interchange between the word classes of the verbs and
the nouns the originally characteristically verbal prefixes were
now also found in large numbers with deverbal nouns, e.g.
ablāzi 'indulgence', *ākust* 'lack', *anawalt* 'refuge'. Some pre-

fixation with nouns is not dependent on verbal prefixation, e.g. *abgrunti* 'abyss' with different class from *grunt*, *antluzzi* 'face' with a prefix which with verbs has the unstressed form *int-*.

4.6.2 | Adjective derivation

Adjectives shared with nouns the characteristic feature of suffix derivation. The following suffixes were most productive in OHG in particular in BR and O:

(i) *-līh*: this was by far the most frequent suffix. It was attached to nouns and adjectives making the latter frequently somewhat more abstract than the basic adjective. E.g. from nouns *lastarlīh* (BR) 'reprehensible', *ābandlīh* (O) 'in the evening'; from adjectives *frīlīh* (BR) 'free', *woroltlīh* (O) 'worldly'; from past participles *unerrahōtlīh* 'untold'; from compounds *got-kundlīh* (O) 'divine'. Very often adverbs in *-līcho* occur beside the adjectives.

(ii) *-ig* (*-ag*): formed adj. from nouns and adj. and occasionally from verbs. The form *-ag* was very much less frequent. We have for instance *ōtag* (BR) 'rich', *slaaffag* (BR) 'sleepy' and *nōtag* (O) 'needy', *iāmarag* (O) 'pitiful'. Beside *heil* 'saved' we have in BR *heillīh* and *heilīg*; or *wintirig* (O) 'wintry'.

(iii) *-isc*: O and BR share *himilisc* 'heavenly' and *chindisk* or *kindisg* 'childlike'. We also have derivations from names which are typical for this suffix: *rumisk* (BR) 'Roman', *kriahhisg* (O) 'Greek'.

(iv) *-īn*: added to nouns it indicates 'belonging to, made of', e.g. *girstīn* (O) 'of barley', *skāfīn* 'of sheep', *steinīn* 'made of stone'.

(v) *-al*: this suffix expressed 'inclination', e.g. *filu-ezzal* (BR) 'inclined to eat much', *slāfal* (BR) 'somnolent', *trunchal* 'inclined to drink'.

(vi) *-sam*: this suffix was originally an adjective, English '*same*'. It was used mainly with nouns but was not very frequent, e.g. *hōrsam* (BR and O) 'obedient', *leidsam* (BR) 'abominable', *fridusam* (O) 'peaceful'.

(vii) *-haft*: formations with *haft* were also originally compounds, with the old past participle *haft* (< **hafjan*) added to nouns and later to verbs with the meaning 'possessing', e.g. *ērhaft* (BR) 'honourable', *wurzhaft* (BR) 'with roots', *lībhaft* (O) 'living', *wārhaft* (O) 'true'.

(viii) *-bāri(g)*: this suffix derives from a verbal adjective meaning 'bearing', and several of the formations convey this meaning, e.g. *dancbāri* 'grateful', *unlastarbārig* (O) 'blameless'. It has been found that the semantic content of this suffix was already so weakened in the ninth century that it had become a purely formal element indicating merely the part of speech. It was little differentiated from the competing derivations in *-līh*, *-ig*, *-sam* or *-haft*, although with a total of only fourteen formations compared with nearly nine hundred with *-līh*, over a hundred with *-haft* and forty-seven with *-sam* it was only sparingly employed.

With the following suffixes we are on the border between derivation and composition. By the criterion of relative frequency the following two may also be considered as derivational suffixes:

(ix) *-muoti*: for instance in BR *luzzilmuati* 'dispirited', *klatamuati* 'glad', *ubarmuati* 'arrogant' and O has *dump-muati* 'stupid', cf. Gm. *stumpfsinnig*, *einmuati* 'unanimous', cf. Gm. *einmütig*, *fast-muati* 'constant, firm-minded', and others. While forms with *-haft* and *-bāri* have greatly increased in the language those with *-muati* have decreased, apart from having changed to *-mütig*. *-muati* was on the way to becoming a derivational suffix, in fact can be regarded as such in OHG, but its further evolution was eventually brought to a halt, unlike that of the other two suffixes or of *-lōs*.

(x) *-lōs*: 'without', e.g. *ruahhalōs* (BR) 'negligent', *drōstolōs* (O) 'protectionless', *goumilōs* (O) 'unwatched', *suntilōs* (O) 'innocent'.

The only prefix which was widespread in adjective derivation was *un-*, which negated adjectives, e.g. *unfrō* 'unhappy', *ungiwar* 'unaware'. Other prefixes such as *gi-* or *ur-*, *urwāni* (O) 'hopeless', spread in the wake of the adjectivization of other word classes.

4.6.3 | Verb derivation

By far the most important process in verb derivation was the conversion of nouns, adjectives or verbs into weak verbs, especially of the *-ōn* and *-ēn* classes, but also of the **-jan* class. Only one or two loan forms joined the strong class, e.g. *scrīban* 'to write' (see 4.5.3). As far as suffix derivation is concerned we have the following means:

(i) *-ilōn* (*-olōn*): iterative verbs were formed mainly from other verbs, e.g. in O: *grubilōn* 'to peruse', cf. *graban* 'to dig', *quitilōn* 'to narrate', cf. *quedan* 'to speak', *quiti* 'saying', *skrankolōn* 'to stagger' from *skrankōn* 'to fall', *spurilōn* 'to find out' from *spurien* 'to trace'.

(ii) *-isōn*: there were a number of verbs formed by the addition of this suffix to nouns, adjectives or other verbs, but it is difficult to judge to what extent this was a productive derivation rather than a lexical sub-class. O has *rīhhisōn* 'to rule' beside *rīhhi* noun 'power' or adj. 'rich, powerful', cf. *hērisōn* 'to rule' beside *hērī* 'dignity' or *hēr* 'old'.

(iii) *-izen* (or *-izōn*): this is an inherited type of iterative or intensive formation which, although not attested in O, may have been productive in Upper German dialects, e.g. *heilazen* 'to hail', *līhhizen* 'to feign', cf. *gilīh* 'alike'.

It is debatable whether prefixation forms part of derivation or of composition. The larger part of verbal prefixation is undoubtedly composition, but a very important, more restricted section, where the prefixes are bound morphemes, could justifiably be included in derivation. For the sake of uniformity of treatment the whole prefixation is dealt with under composition.

4.6.4 | Nominal composition

In sheer quantity derivation probably exceeded composition in OHG, but the significance of nominal composition, mainly of the noun plus noun type lies in the fact that this was one of the most characteristic devices of the Germanic languages and one which was largely lacking in Latin. It was therefore the native genius of the language which was responsible for such forms in BR as *ābantmuas* for Latin *cena*, *morkanlob* for *matutinus*, *wāthūs* for *vestiarium*, *nahtwahha* for *vigiliae*.

As far as the form of nominal composition is concerned we can distinguish the following types:

(i) The most productive type was: noun + noun. Here primary composition, i.e. composition with the first element in the stem form without a case ending, far exceeded secondary composition with an inflected first element. But the two kinds had already become confused owing to the weakening of the medial vowels and owing to the general loss of unstressed vowels after long roots. The two kinds of composition can only be clearly distinguished in the case of the presence of a gen. sg. *-es* or *-un* (*-en*). All other medial elements must be viewed with some suspicion. We obviously have primary composition in cases (all in O) like *erdgrunt* 'earth', *lantliut* 'inhabitants', *kornhūs* 'cornstore' or with final vowel *bettiriso* 'paralytic', *dagamuas* 'midday meal', *heristrāza* 'highway', *hugulust* 'mentality'. But the significance of the medial vowel is less clear in *arnogezīt* 'harvest time' or *nōtigistallo* 'companion in need'. Beside *brūtlouft* 'wedding' we have *brūtigomo* 'bridegroom' which could be an inflectional compound or a compound with the root vowel preserved despite the length of the root. Examples of secondary composition in O are: *sunnūnāband* 'Saturday', *sunnūnlioht* 'sunlight', *dageszīt* 'time of the day', *wintesbrūt* 'whirlwind'.

It is characteristic that the first element is generally a simple word, neither with a derivational suffix nor itself a compound. Otherwise the syntactic-semantic connection between the two elements is unrestricted, but all are of the determinative type.

(ii) Adjective plus noun: certain formations are quite frequent, e.g. those with *alt* and *ala* but otherwise this type is not much developed, e.g. *alagāhī* 'all speed', *altgiscrib* 'Old Testament'. By far the most popular first element in O is *worolt* 'world', e.g. *woroltruam* 'worldly fame', *woroltmagad* 'virgin of this world'. Although itself a noun it appears to function as a kind of adjective determiner.

(iii) Among the adjective compounds we can distinguish two kinds:

(a) determinative compounds consisting of noun or adjective plus adjective, e.g. BR *cotchund* 'divine', *filuezzal* 'greedy', *wīntrunchal* 'inclined to drink', *kakanwart* 'present', O *managfalt* 'manifold', *ubilwillig* 'malevolent';

(b) exocentric compounds (see 3.7.5(ii)), e.g. in O *armherzi* 'compassionate', *ebanreiti* 'on the same journey', *einluzzi* 'single', *einstimmi* 'unanimous', *elilenti* 'exiled', BR *einstrīti* 'obstinate'. The *-muoti* derivations (see 4.6.2(ix)) could, of course, also be regarded as exocentric adjective compounds.

4.6.5 | Verbal composition

There are two kinds of verbal composition: prefix or particle composition, which is inherited and extensive, and noun plus verb composition which appears both new and relatively rare and unimportant.

(i) Of the noun plus verb type we have in O for instance *fuazfallōn* 'to fall at somebody's feet', *halsslagōn* 'to hit, to box', in BR *castluamen* 'to be a guest', *welaqhuedan* 'to bless', *ābandmuasōn* 'to dine'. All these, except one, are really verbal derivations from nominal compounds, e.g. *castluamī* 'hospitality' etc., although they were to set a pattern for future developments. *Welaqhuedan* is best regarded as a loan translation of Latin *benedicere*.

(ii) Verbal prefixation. The particles which could be prefixed to verbs in Germanic had from the beginning an adverbial and a prepositional function. They were generally unstressed. By OHG times functional and accentual differentiation had brought about a division into two classes of prefixes. An older class included particles which were always unstressed and had become reduced, although the vowels varied dialectally (e.g. *gi-, ge-, ga-*). Some historically separate particles had become fused, e.g. Gothic *faír-, fra-, faúr-*: OHG *fir-* or Gothic *and-, in-*: OHG *in-*. These always maintained their position before the verb, and the past participle of the verb did not take *gi-*. On the whole they were semantically vague. They did not clearly correspond to any Latin prefix particles. A newer class of prefix particles were much more strongly adverbial in function, semantically more sharply defined; they could be stressed. As prefixes they had the same phonological form as they had as independent words. They preceded the verb in the infinitive and the past participle, but were separated by *gi-* from the verb in the past participle and by *zi-* if the infinitive required this particle. They also preceded the verb in the subordinate clause but followed it in the main clause. The majority of particles clearly belonged either to the one class ('inseparable') or the other ('separable') but a few could belong to either.

(a) Inseparable (all examples from O): *bi- biborgēn* 'to be careful'; *int- (in-) intfliahan* 'to escape'; *ir- irbaldēn* 'to embolden'; *gi- gibeiten* 'to urge'; *fir- firneman* 'to hear'; *zi- zibrechan* 'to destroy'. The following also always preceded the verb: *duruh thuruhstechan* 'to pierce'; *hintar hintarqueman* 'to be surprised'; *missi missidrūēn* 'to mistrust'.

(b) Separable: *aba-* 'off' (not in O) (BR) *abasnīdan* 'to cut off', Lat. *abscisio*; *after afterruafan* 'to call after'; *ana* 'to' *anablāsan* 'to blow', Lat. *inspirāre*; *fram framgangan* 'to go forth', Lat. *procedere*; *fora* (BR) *forachunden* 'to announce', Lat. *pronuntiāre*; *furi furibringan* 'to bring forth'; *in ingān* 'to go in'; *hera* 'to' *herafuaren* 'to move'; *hina* 'away' *hinaneman* 'to take away'; *miti* 'with' *mitiloufan* 'to accompany'; *nāh* 'after' *nāhloufan* 'to run after'; *nidar* 'down' *nidarfallan* 'to fall down'; *dana* 'away' *thanasnīdan* (O for *aba-* see above); *ubar* 'over' *ubarwinnan* 'to defeat', Lat. *superāre*; *ūf* 'up' *ūfgangan* 'to rise'; *umbi* 'about' *umbirītan* 'to surround on horseback'; *ūz* 'out' *ūzirdrīban* 'to drive out'; *widar* 'against' *widarwerban* 'to return'; *zua* 'to' *zuaruafan* 'to call to sb.'; *ubar, untar, umbi* and *widar* occurred in both the separable and the inseparable classes.

Parallel Latin-German constructions are found most frequently with the more clearly defined particles of place and verbs implying movement. Some are obvious imitations, e.g. in BR *anathionōn* for *inservīre*, *untarambahten* for *subadministrāre*, *zuahelfan* for *adiuvāre*, while others could easily have been formed spontaneously in OHG, e.g. *umbikangan* for *circumvenīre* or *zuaneman* for *adsumere*.

4·7 | Syntax

It appears that in syntax, too, profound changes occurred between Late Germanic and the advent of literacy in Carolingian times. Thus in the ninth century the basic features of German syntax both in the ordering of elements within the sentence and in the structure of the phrases were already present, although in the details many changes were yet to occur. The study of early German syntax is vitiated by the fact that the texts were overwhelmingly either translations from Latin, with a strong tendency to imitation, or poetry in alliterative or end-rhyming verse, where departure from 'normal' syntax was no less usual than in modern poetry.

4.7.1 | The position of the verbal phrase

The position of the phrases within the clause relative to each other was dominated by the verbal phrase. This consisted, as now, of a finite verb or of a finite verb plus non-finite parts. On the basis of the position of the finite verb we can distinguish the following sentence types:

(i) *Initial position of finite verb* is found regularly in independent interrogative sentences without an interrogative particle:

Forsahhistū unholdūn? 'Will you forsake the devil?' and in adhortative and imperative sentences:

Dua noh hiutu unsih wīs 'Tell us today!' In conditional sentences without conjunction of condition (*if* etc.):

Quimit hē gisund ūz, ih gilōnōn imoz
'If he emerges hale, I shall reward him'.

These sentence types are unchanged in modern German.

(ii) *Second position of the finite verb* is numerically the most frequent in independent statements. The first position may be occupied by the subject (nominal or pronominal), an object, an adverbial complement or a non-finite form of the verbal phrase. Sentences where another clause occupies the first position were, however, relatively rare.

First position	Second position		English
subj.	finite verb		'the king rode
Ther kuning	*reit*	*kuono*	bravely'
obj.			'I know a certain king'
Einan kuning	*uueiz*	*ih*	
adv.			'since that time he be-
Sīdh	*uuarth*	*her guot man*	came a good man'
non-finite verb			'our presence is
Giskerit	*ist*	*thiu hieruuist*	determined'

Initial position gave emphasis to all phrases except the subject. Both in poetry and in prose in imitation of Latin, but perhaps also as an echo of Germanic practice, the finite verb is also found in initial position:

Lietz her heidine man obar sēo līdan
'He caused heathen men to come over sea'

Quad tho Maria (*Dixit autem Maria*)
'Mary then spoke'.

It was, however, an anomalous position, tolerated in poetry for emphasis, but otherwise in the process of being eliminated in the course of the OHG period. Even in the earliest texts, e.g. the Isidore translation, Latin initial position of the finite verb was frequently not followed in the German version but was replaced by what was the typical OHG position of the finite verb: the second position, e.g.

Isidore (15, 18) *fecit deus hominem:got chiworahta mannan*. (17, 12) *dedi spiritum meum super eum: ih gab ubar inan mīnan gheist*.

A position later than the second was also anomalous even in the early texts although it may again have echoed earlier Germanic possibilities, e.g. Isidore (17, 11) *ih inan infāhu* 'I receive him'. Sometimes it is difficult to decide whether one or two adverbial complements are present, e.g. Isidore (5, 3) *sō dhār auh ist chiscriban* 'as there is written'.

(iii) *Retarded position of the finite verb* was characteristic of dependent or subordinate clauses. Where the clause contained few or only light complementary elements retarded position amounted to the final position of the finite verb, so characteristic of the modern German subordinate clause. But heavy complements, especially prepositional adverbial groups were usually placed after the finite verb. The more elements there were the less likely was the final position of the finite verb. Objects were usually placed before the finite verb. The non-finite parts of the verbal phrase were frequently put after the finite verb, infinitives more so than past participles.

The examples not only illustrate the relatively free arrangements in third position, which appear often dictated by rhythmical considerations, but also the existence of several kinds of subordinate clauses, e.g. with conjunctions, with *daz* 'that', and relative clauses. Most of the conjunctions were in a state of development, often in imitation of Latin, and differed considerably from the conjunctions with which we are familiar in modern German. The actual incidence of subordinate clauses differed also strongly from the modern practice. Parataxis was frequent where later stages of the language preferred subordination, e.g. *fon thero burgi thiu hiez Nazareth* cf. *von der Stadt. Die hieß Nazareth,*

1st pos.	2nd pos.	Ret. pos. of fin. vb. and pos. of complements
conj.	subj.	f.v. compl.
Sō	*thaz*	*uuarth al gendiōt*
		'when this was all ended'
		obj. compl. inf. f.v.
Ob	*her*	*arbeidi so iung tholōn mahti*
		'if he could bear such tribulations so young'
		f.v. ob.
Wio	*er selbo*	*druag thaz kruzi*
		'as he himself bore the cross'
		compl. f.v. p.p.
dhazs	*dhiz*	*fona Cyre Persero chuninge sii chiforabodōt*
		'that this was prophesied of Cyrus, king of the Persians'
subj.		
rel. pron.	compl.	f.v. p.p.
dher	*fona*	*uuard chisendit*
	uuerodheota	
	druhtīne	'who was sent by the lord of the hosts'

and the more usual *von der Stadt, die Nazareth hieß*. In particular we have to note the absence of subordinate causal clauses (e.g. *weil*-clauses). The chief particle introducing causal clauses was *wanta* with a non-subordinate word order, e.g. *Want ira anon warun thanana* (Otfrid I, 11, 27) 'for her ancestors were from there', corresponding to modern German *denn*-clauses.

4.7.2 | The verbal phrase and the noun phrase

It has already been shown that the *verbal phrase*, consisting of a finite verb and a non-finite element, had, in the subordinate clause, not yet attained the modern order. In the independent clause the non-finite elements were often in final position as in modern German:

f.v.   inf.

Musp.   *dar scal er vora demo rihhe az rahhu stantan*
         'there he will have to render account before the king'

f.v.   past. part.
denne uuirdit untar in uuic arhapan
'then the battle between them will begin'.

But, for rhythmical reasons or in imitation of the Latin, complements could also follow the non-finite elements:

f.v.   inf.
Her ūzgangenti ni mohta sprehhan zi in
Egressus autem non poterat loqui ad illos.

Wessobrunn   f.v.   inf.
Predigt   *Uuir ne sculun nieth uoben die irdisgen acchera durh*
werltlīchen rīhtuom
'we should not cultivate our earthly fields for the
sake of worldly riches'.

The *noun phrase* has the usual order, no doubt inherited from Germanic: what is to be determined is preceded by what determines it. Hence we have the order: adj. + noun, poss. adj. + noun, noun in genitive + governing noun. Even the different Latin order was usually not allowed to affect the German:
thie heilago geist:spiritus sanctus:'the holy ghost'
in sīn hūs:in domum suam:'in his house'
in themo sehsten mānūde:in mense sexto:'in the sixth month'
mannes sunu:filius hominis:'man's son'
himilo rīhhi:regnum coelorum:'the kingdom of the heavens'
gotes thiu:ancilla domini:'God's maid'
Post-position is found in poetic diction and where the genitive group is heavy: *in nemin fateres enti sunes enti heilages gheistes: in nomine patris et filii et spiritus sancti.* The partitive genitive also followed the governing noun, and this practice gradually gained ground, until in modern German *der Kahn des Fischers* contrasts with English *the fisherman's boat*.

In late OHG a state was reached where, as in modern English, a distinction was made between personal nouns (genitive precedes regularly) and non-personal nouns (genitive begins to follow), cf. English *our neighbour's garden* but *the size of the garden*.

OHG had a characteristic construction in the phrase where the article of the governing noun preceded the genitive, e.g. *thiu himilrīches guatī* 'the goodness of the kingdom of heaven', *in theru druhtines brusti* 'in the Lord's breast'.

4.7.3 | The articles

OHG used the definite article extensively even in texts translated from the Latin which had no article. Yet, in detail the use differed substantially from modern German. In general the definite article expressed definiteness, either in referring back to an earlier mention or in specifying in some other way. Where specification was expressed by other verbal means the article could be dispensed with or, somewhat tautologically, could be used as well. Indefiniteness was at first left unexpressed, but the use of the numeral *ein* as an indefinite article increased rapidly within the OHG period. Earlier it had distinguished 'one of its kind' from 'a specific individual' (pointed to by means of the demonstrative pronoun which had gradually become the definite article). Abstracts, unique objects (*hella* 'hell', *sunna* 'sun'), nouns governed or defined by a preposition, nouns occurring in pairs or formulas (*tag und naht*) lacked the definite article, but practice varies in the different texts and the use of the article increased gradually with the passage of time.

As an example we may take the Tatian translation of John, 4, 6–9:

Uuas dār *brunno* Jacobes. *Der heilant* uuas giuueigit fon *dero uuegeferti*, saz sō oba *themo brunnen*, uuas thō *zīt nah sehsta*. Quam thō *wīb* fon Samariu sceffen *uuazzar* . . . Sīne iungoron giengun *in burg*, thaz sie *muos* couftin. Thō quad imo *uuīb thaz samaritanisga*. . .

brunno: unique, defined by J., but NHG *der Brunnen Jakobs.*
der heilant: 'the saviour', def. article implies that he is 'well-known to us', 'mentioned before'.
dero uuegeferti: the journey has already been mentioned.
demo brunnen: the specific, above mentioned well.
zīt sehsta: the sixth hour, precise by definition.
wīb: indefinite.
uuazzar: indefinite.
in burg: NHG *in die Stadt*, but E *to town*. German still has many expressions without article, e.g. *zu Bett.*
muos: 'food', indefinite.
uuīb: is defined by the apposition 'the Samaritan'.

4.7.4 | The subject pronoun

Until the demonstrative pronoun developed into an anaphoric definite article in Late Germanic the noun was unaccompanied. Similarly, the verb was originally self-sufficient and expressed the categories of person and number by its own suffixes. Gothic on the whole only used the subject pronoun for emphasis, just like modern Italian. OHG already made extensive use of the subject pronoun and the reason is most likely that what was emphatic at an earlier stage had become neutral and normal later. However, its use was much less absolute, i.e. grammatically determined, than now, and made some allowance for context. Poetic needs and imitation of Latin further reduced the incidence of the subject pronoun. But its use increased continuously, although certain formulas persisted for a long time, e.g. *neweiz* '(I) don't know', *quad* '(he) spoke'.

In the *Ludwigslied* we find one verb without a subject pronoun: *fand her thia Northman:gode lob sageda* 'he found the Northmen, (he) gave praise to God' where the context supplies the information. But we also have repetition, e.g.

Thō nam her godes urlub,   Huob her gundfanon ūf,
Reit her thara in Vrankon   Ingagan Northmannon.

'Then he took leave from God, he raised the war banner, he rode there into France, against the Northmen.'

4.7.5 | The nominal cases

In its use of articles and subject pronouns OHG was innovating and well on the way to becoming an analytical language. In its use of the nominal cases it possessed an archaic feature. But in many ways cases were losing their independent status and were being supplemented or replaced by prepositions or other syntactical devices. If we examine for instance the *Ludwigslied* we find a large number of uses of cases which differ from modern German practice, such as the predicative nom.: *Kind uuarth her faterlōs* (*als Kind wurde er vaterlos*); an inflectional acc. with a name: *Hiez her Hluduīgan ... rītan* (*er hieß Ludwig ... reiten*); the vastly more extensive use of the gen.: *lōnōn* 'to reward' with dat. of person and gen. of thing (*ihn dafür belohnen*); other verbs with gen. object *buoz uuerdhan* 'to recompense', *brūchan* 'to enjoy, to make use', *korōn* 'to test' gen. of pers., *manōn* 'to warn', *sih gibuozzen* 'to atone', *ingelden* 'to suffer punishment', *beidōn* 'to wait', *bitteres līdes skenken* 'to pour bitter wine' (partitive gen.); after adjectives *fol lōses* 'full of loose living', *thegeno gelīh* 'like warriors'; the marked inflectional gen. pl. *czala uuunniōno* 'the number of delights', or after *wē: wē ... thes lībes* 'woebetide their lives'.

The oldest texts also show the use of the instrumental, e.g. (*Hildebrandslied*) *nu scal mih suasat chind suertu hauwan* 'now my own son is to strike me with his sword' and in the pl. the dat. is used similarly: *her frāgēn gistuont fōhēm uuortum* 'he began to ask in a few words'. In late OHG the instrumental was usually supplemented by the preposition *mit*.

The greater independent use of the cases and the wide range of the genitive in particular contribute considerably to the strangeness that OHG has for modern German speakers.

4.7.6 | The periphrastic verb forms

To some extent the expansion of the noun phrase by means of form words such as articles and prepositions was paralleled by the evolution of the periphrastic verb forms.

The starting point was provided by the existence of two verbal adjectives, the present participle and the past participle, both inherited from Germanic and ultimately from Indo-European. The pres. part. was active in meaning and the past part. passive in the case of transitive verbs but neutral in the case of intransitive verbs, e.g. *pflückend*, *kommend* (active), *gepflückt* (trans., passive), *gekommen* (intrans., neutral). As adjectives these participles were at first firmly in the orbit of the noun phrase, but with verbs denoting existence or possession ('to be', 'to have') they were attracted into the verbal phrase. To use modern examples again:

(a) eine Blume ist / (eine) gepflückt(e)——→eine Blume ist
    gepflückt /
    eine Blume wird / (eine) gepflückt(e)——→eine Blume wird
    gepflückt

(*sein* is a static or factual verb of existence, *werden* an ingressive verb of existence);
(b) ich habe / eine gepflückte Blume (Blume gepflückte)———→
    ich habe / eine Blume / gepflückt;
    er ist / gekommen (cf. er ist / alt)———→ er ist gekommen /;
(c) * er ist / pflückend———→*er ist pflückend/
    * er ist / kommend———→* er ist kommend /.

These potentialities were present in Germanic. In the emergent
Germanic languages they became realized in differing degrees,
often plainly under the impact of Latin or Greek with their highly
developed verbal systems, in some cases perhaps spontaneously.
OHG thus possessed:
(a) a periphrastic passive:

> Isid.   *nu ist ... chiquhedan got chisalbōt*
> ecce deus unctus ... dicitur ('is called')
> *endi dor ni uuerdant bilohhan*
> et portae non claudentur ('are not being closed').

OHG thus had the possibility of distinguishing between a state or
fact and a process or result. An example of the original nominal
use of the past part. is

> Ludw.   *Sume sār verlorane Uuurdun sum erkorane*
> 'some then became condemned, some chosen'.

(b) a periphrastic perfect and potentially a pluperfect although
this was even more rarely used than the perfect:

> Exh.   *ir den christaniun namun intfangan eigut*
> qui christianum nomen accepistis 'have received'
> Ludw.   *Heigun sa Northman Harto biduuungan*
> 'the Northmen have oppressed them sorely'.

The use of the English perfect is not to be taken as an indication
that the functions of the OHG and English perfect are the same.
They are not. For past time in general OHG used its past tense.
The rarely used perfect indicated a certain actuality or particular
relevance, although simple past and periphrastic perfect were never
sharply delimited. In late OHG a perfect with 'to have' began
also to be formed in the case of intransitive verbs with durative
meaning (*hat geslāfen*) while perfective intransitives continued to
form their perfect with the forms of 'to be' (*was irstantan*).

(c) a periphrastic durative:

Tat.   *inti uuas thaz folc beitōnti Zachariam*
Latin *et erat plebs expectans Zachariam*
       'and the people were waiting for Zacharia'

This is the clearest case of the imitation of Latin. The Vulgate and other texts of late Latinity abounded in such constructions inspired by New Testament Greek. In OHG the periphrastic durative was characteristic of scholarly prose. *Heliand* and other native texts lack this construction, and in Otfrid the convenience of rhyming is frequently responsible for its use:

1.9.10 *Sih uuarun sie einonti, uuio man thaz kind nanti*
        'they decided (were deciding) what the child was to be called'.

Despite its foreign origin this construction flourished in written German for several centuries.

Future time was not indicated by any tense form in Germanic. In response to the Latin future the Germanic languages eventually developed a periphrastic form, but since this was done by means of the modals or in later German by the ingressive verb *werden* such aspects as obligation, intention, and probability are difficult to disentangle from pure futurity. The OHG auxiliary was *sculan* and, less frequently, *wellen*, e.g.

Isid.   *miin gheist scal wesan undar eu mitten*
             'my spirit shall dwell amongst you'
Otfr. II, 3, 68 *so thu hiar nu lesan scalt*
             'as you shall read here'.

4.7.7 | Negation

Negation illustrates the evolutionary position of OHG very characteristically. From Indo-European and Germanic it inherited the particle *ni*. This was primarily prefixed to verb forms with which it formed a unit, e.g.

Ludw. *mih selbon ni sparōti* 'I would not spare myself'
       thō ni uuas iz burolang 'then it was not very long before ...'.

But it also attached itself to certain other words, e.g. *alles* 'all' > *nalles*; *io* 'ever' > *nio*; *ein* 'one' > *nihein* (*nih* cf. Latin *nec*); *man* 'man' > *nioman* (< *ni+io*); *wiht* 'thing, spirit', cf. E *wight*, > *niowiht* (< *ni+io*) and others. Where such negated forms were combined with a verb the verb was frequently negated as well. But throughout the OHG period practice varied and double negation never became the rule, cf.

Musp.   *denne ni kitar parno nohhein* 'then no child dares'
         imo nioman kipagan ni mak 'no one can fight against
         him'
Wess. Pr. *Do dar niuuiht ni uuas* 'then there was nothing'
Otfr.   *Ni habes ... fazzes uuiht* 'you have not any vessel'
         thoh sies uuiht ni uuestin 'yet they did not know it'.

In the course of OHG the simple particle *ni* was gradually more and more automatically coupled with the emphatic *niowiht*, later *nieht*, *niht*, until finally the function of negation rested primarily on *niht*. Eventually, but not for many centuries, *ni* was completely replaced by *niht*.

4.8 | Lexicon

Ideally, the language historian would like to have three questions answered concerning the lexicon of a former stage of the language. First, how does the word stock of that former period compare with the lexicon of the present day language? In other words, he would like to know to what extent the vocabulary has survived, or which part of it has survived, and where losses or changes have occurred. Secondly, he would like to know how the content of the then extant lexical items compares with the content of the surviving words. This is by far the most difficult question. It can best only be answered for a few individual words the semantic history of which has been subjected to close scrutiny. Thirdly, he would like to know what role borrowing from foreign languages played at that period, what shape it took and what lexical material was actually borrowed.

8

4.8.1 | The native stock

We must naturally take into account that the documentation of OHG is limited, and that of OS even more so. This affects
above all the open-ended part of the vocabulary, the stock of weak
verbs, of common nouns, and adjectives. As far as the closed part
of the lexicon is concerned, what is remarkable is above all the
very high survival rate.

The stock of personal pronouns has remained, although the
phonological evolution has led to coalescences, e.g. fem. sg. *siu*
(nom.) and *sia* (acc.) > *sie*; in the pl. *sie* (m.), *sio* (f.), *siu* (n.) >
sie; *ira* (gen.) and *iru* (dat.) > *ihr*; and the forms *uns*, *iu* (dat.) and
the derivative forms *unsih*, *iuwih* have also coalesced (> *uns*, *euch*).
The demonstrative pronouns, functioning also as def. art. and
rel. pron., interrogative pronouns, and the reflexive pronoun have
survived equally well. The indefinite pronouns were then and are
now to a large extent compounds and, characteristically, have
changed greatly. But the basic forms *man* (relatively new in OHG)
and *ioman* (> *jemand*), *nioman* (> *niemand*), *dehein* (with assimilation > *kein*) have survived, while the simple form *sum* (cf. E
some) has disappeared. The numerals have survived with one or
two exceptions: *zehanzug* 'a hundred' has been replaced by
hundert and the ordinal 'second' OHG *ander* by *zweite*. The
ordinals from thirteen to nineteen are now compounds consisting
of cardinal plus ordinal, e.g. *dreizehnte*, while the OHG formation
consisted of ordinal plus ordinal, e.g. *drittozehanto*. Again characteristically, compound numerals, e.g. OHG *einfalt*, *zwifalt* or
fiorstunt have survived least well (> *einmal*, *zweimal*, *viermal*).
The basic simple prepositions (*ab*, *an*, *auf*, *aus* etc.) are also still
present although there have been two noteworthy losses: OHG
fram 'forwards' and *after*, while modern needs have led to a
great increase in the prepositional stock through conversion from
nouns, e.g. *dank*, *trotz*, *hinsichtlich*. Among the preterite-present
verbs only those particularly restricted in forms and use, e.g.
eigun 'they have', *genah* 'it is enough', *gitar* 'I dare' have vanished
and the OHG impersonal *toug* 'it is useful' has become an ordinary weak verb (*taugen*) as has *an* (and *gi-an*) > *gönnen*. The
others have survived and constitute the important group of the
modal auxiliaries. Semantically, of course, they have changed
much.

The strong verbs also belong to the closed part of the vocabulary, although to the least grammaticalized section of it. Generally, the only sporadically or dialectally attested ones have been lost. A number, especially of the traditional sixth and seventh classes, have become weak, e.g. *gnagan* or *nagan* > *nagen*, *malan* > *mahlen*, *bannan*, *spannan*, *faldan* > *falten*, *spaltan*, *waltan*, *salzan*. Among the losses the most noteworthy are perhaps: *bītan* 'to wait' cf. *to abide* (the str. vb. was in competition with the wk. vb. *beiton*, and later both with *warten*); *sīgan* 'to sink', *rīsan* 'to fall' (both may be deemed to have been semantically superfluous on account of the existence of *sinken* and *fallen*); *klīban* 'to cleave' (replaced by the related weak verb *kleben*); *lūchan* 'to lock' (succumbed to the competition of *schließen*); *belgan* 'to become angry'; *bāgan* 'to fight'; *dwahan* 'to wash' (ousted by the synonym *waschen*). The best attested OHG strong verbs which have been lost are undoubtedly *quedan* 'to say', cf. *to bequeath*, and *jehan* 'to state'. In a word field still amply represented by the surviving *sprechen*, *sagen*, *reden*, (*er*)*zählen* and the later additions *schwatzen*, *plaudern* and the numerous compounds (*aussagen*, *vorsagen*, etc.) they were obviously not indispensable. The total loss of strong verbs since OHG would seem to amount to about one fourth. One verb was added in the early Carolingian period on the basis of analogy: *scrīban* 'to write' < Lat. *scribere*.

Closed lexical systems are that part of the lexicon which is most strongly embedded in grammar or most clearly circumscribed by grammatical functions. They have the highest survival rate from OHG to the present day. When we look at the vocabulary as a whole we further note that the simple words, the unmotivated elements of the vocabulary have survived much better than the derivational and compound or motivated forms. The motivated part of the vocabulary appears therefore much more strongly tied to time while the unmotivated, fully lexicalized part would seem less period-bound.

We can exemplify this by looking at dictionary entries. The simple words beginning with *n*- in R. Schützeichel's OHG dictionary and the NHG etymological correspondences show:

the survivals		the losses	
(gi)nāda	Gnade	naffezen	'to fall asleep, nap'
nāen	nähen	(ga)nah	'he has sufficient'
nagal	Nagel	nant	'impertinence'

8-2

the survivals		*the losses*	
nāh	nahe	neimen	'to refer to'
nāh	nach	neizzen	'to punish'
naht	Nacht	nenden	'to risk, to brave'
nackot	nackt	nesso	'worm'
nāmi	(ge)nehm	ni	'not'
namo	Name	ginindan	'to take upon o.s.'
narro	Narr	niot	'desire'
nasa	Nase	niumo	'jubilation'
nātara	Natter	niusen	'to try'
natura	Natur	nol, nollo	'hill'
naz	naß	nōz	'beast'
nebul	Nebel	nūen	'to smash'
nefo	Neffe	(ge)nuscen	'to link'
neigen	neigen		

the survivals

nein	nein	nio	nie
neman	nehmen	niozan	(ge)nießen
nemnen	nennen	niun	neun
nerren	nähren	niuwi	neu
(gi)nesan	(ge)nesen	noh	noch
nest	Nest	nord	Nord
nezza, -i	Netz	nōt	Not
nīd	Neid	(gi)nōz, -o	Genosse
nidar	nieder	nu	nun
nīgan	neigen	(gi)nuog	(ge)nug
nicchen	nicken	nuohtarnin	nüchtern
nicchessa	Nixe	nuz	Nutzen

When we turn to the derivations and compounds we are faced with a different picture. Although some exist today as well, a large number are without counterparts. And the modern language is of course full of recent derivational and compositional formations or neologisms. For instance, from the simple word OHG *naht* we have the following derivations and compounds of which the corresponding modern forms are: *nächtlich, nachts, Nachtlicht, Nachtrabe, Nachtwache.* But we also find: *nahtfarewa* 'blackness of night', *nahtfinsteri* 'darkness of night', *nahtforhta* 'fear of night', *nahtlob* 'night service', *nahtmuos* 'evening meal', *nahtol* 'god of night', *nahtsculd* 'night crime', *nahtsterno* 'evening star', *nahttimberi* 'darkness of night', *nahtwig* 'night fight'. From *neman-nehmen* we have prefix verbs also existing today with: *ab-*, *be-*, *ver-*, *hin-*, *über-*, *unter-*, *aus-*, *zu-*, but also now extinct formations with *gi-*, *abage-*, *dana-*, *danage-*, *furder-*, *misse-*, *samant-*, *wider-*. The adjective *truobi*, NHG *trübe*, had the adj. derivations *truobal*, *truobmuotig*; the nominal derivations *truobī*, *gitruobida*, *gitruobnessi* and the two weak verbs *truoben* (also *gitruoben*) 'to disturb', 'to make dim' (NHG *trüben*) and *truobēn* 'to become dim or disturbed'.

Many derivations and compounds were ad hoc formations created for the needs of translation, and this accounts to some extent for the more transitory character of this part of the vocabulary. The disappearance of so many of the neologisms of OHG specialist language is partly also a reflexion of the broken tradition. The links between the various scriptoria were tenuous and the Carolingian activity was followed by the recession of German letters in the subsequent century and a half. Among the simple words which died out there are many which appeared to be rare or regional even in OHG. The driving force behind new derivation and composition was the need to render the large number of alien Christian and classical Latin concepts which were then entering the German world. Of course many were simply left in their foreign garb and they constitute the significant loanword element of Carolingian German (see 4.8.2). But perhaps more interesting was the attempt to adapt and develop the native resources in order to incorporate the foreign concepts.

In this process we can distinguish four different approaches. First, an existing word could be employed with a new meaning derived from a foreign word (*semantic loan*). Secondly, the foreign word, if it was a derivational or compositional formation could be imitated and translated mechanically part-by-part (*loan translation*). Thirdly, a partial or approximate translation could be made (*loan rendition*), and, fourthly, the foreign concept could be rendered in a linguistically independent way by a new formation (*loan creation*). What distinguishes these four methods from direct borrowing is the employment of native resources. The studies of W. Betz have shown that they were used in Carolingian times in his descending order of frequency. He estimated that about 10 per cent of the total OHG vocabulary consisted of loan formations (loan translations, loan renditions, loan creations) and 5 per cent of semantic loans. In the OHG Tatian there are 258 words of religious significance and it has been estimated that 59 per cent were semantic loans, 17 per cent loan translations, 7 per cent loan renditions and 2 per cent loan creations, while 11 per cent were outright borrowings, i.e. loanwords (the remaining 4 per cent are difficult to classify). Otfrid's religious vocabulary consists, according to W. Betz, of 388 words of which he considers 300 to be semantic loans, 27 loan translations, 18 loan renditions and 37 loanwords.

For a diachronic assessment of the OHG lexicon such studies are invaluable. The synchronic approach is bound to apply different criteria. Only formal or semantic distinctiveness would afford a scale for classification. It is doubtful whether many of Otfrid's semantic loans, after two hundred years of Christianity in Weissenburg, would have been identifiable as such to him or his contemporaries. To us a word like *Gleichheit* can only be an historical semantic loan (from eighteenth-century French *égalité*), unlike *Verbalphrase*, which is a contemporary semantic loan from English *verbal phrase*, with German *Phrase* acquiring a new hitherto non-existent semantic facet from English *phrase*. The foreign influence on the development of the native vocabulary of OHG can therefore only be considered diachronically.

W. Betz also found that of all these innovations the direct borrowings had the highest survival rate while in the Benedictine Rule, for instance, about a third of the semantic loans survived into MHG, less than a third of the loan translations and only one tenth of the loan renditions. The last two categories proved ephemeral no doubt because they were so often personal and artificial. The cultural significance of loan adaptation has been enormous. Ever since the European languages adopted the terminology of Greco-Roman Christianity and of much of classical civilization, down to the present age with its *iron curtain* (*Eiserner Vorhang,* *le rideau de fer*), *cold war* (*Kalter Krieg*) and *people's republic* (*Volksrepublik*) loan adaptation has been responsible for the creation of a common European vocabulary.

Semantic loans occurred above all in the adoption of the central and more general ethical and religious concepts. Most of these were expressed by existing words of ethical, religious and often legal implication, but in nearly all cases the new Christian meaning so overshadowed and finally ousted the pre-Christian meanings that we have only faint and often dubious impressions of their former significance. The word which all Germanic languages adopted for the Christian *deus* was *Gott* – *God*, one of several Gmc. designations for deities. It undoubtedly was originally neuter and only became masculine under the influence of *deus*. It presumably meant a depersonalized spirit or abstract idea and received anthropomorphic connotations by being christianized. For *dominus* the most frequent WGmc. word was OHG *truhtin*, OE *dryhten*, while its counterpart in Gothic, *frauja*, was relatively rare in the west (OHG *frō*, OE *frēa*). *Truhtin* derived from the designation of the leader of the Germanic warrior-band (Gmc. **druht-*, OE *dryht*). But so successful was the process of christianization that the word gradually lost all secular, military connotations and finally became almost a name, i.e. meaningless in itself. For this reason it received strong competition in late OHG from a word which had secular, feudal connotations and allowed figurative usage: OHG *hērro* > *Herr*, cf. also E *lord* for earlier *dryhten*. OHG *hērro* was a contraction of the comparative *hēriro* < *hēr* 'old' which itself was a semantic loan from Latin (Romance) *senior* 'lord' < *senior* 'older' < *senex* 'old'. Further ethical terms belonging to the Germanic world of the *comitatus* or warrior-band were *triuwa*, *trōst*, *huldi*, *milti*, *ēra*, *heil*. That the christianization of these and other terms of Germanic warrior society occurred both in England and in Germany is significant. Mutual influence no doubt played a part, on the other hand the similarity of the conditions could also easily lead to the same semantic developments. *Himil* and *hella*, Gmc. designations for the sky and the underworld, were filled with the meaning of *caelum* and *infernum*. *Ātum* 'breath' was the earliest attempt to render Latin *spiritus*, Greek *pneuma*. It was later replaced by *geist* which appears to have had pagan meanings such as 'ecstasy, emotion', perhaps 'ghost'. For the Christian *anima* the word *sēla*, *soul* was adopted which appears to have been the word for the disembodied spirits of the dead, possibly connected with a sacred lake (Gm. *See*). Semantic adaptation we also have in *beten*, *Gebet*; *Beichte* (OHG *bijiht* < 'statement', where the ancient *-ti* derivation shows that it cannot be a Christian loan formation for *confessio*); *Buße* (cf. E *boot* 'advantage', *bootless* related to *better*, OHG *buoza*) and *hriuwa* (cf. E *rue*) were terms for *satisfactio* and *poenitentia*; *ewig*;

Glaube for *fides* (from the same etymon as *lieb*); *Gnade* (OHG *gināda* for *gratia*, *misericordia*); *Heil* (*salus*, *salutare* from pagan 'success and prosperity in this life'); *taufen* 'to baptize' originally 'to dip in water'; *fasten* 'to fast'; *Heide* 'heathen' (originally literally 'living in the wilderness') took the meaning 'non-Christian' from Latin *paganus*, itself derived from *pagus* 'open countryside'. *Rīhhi*, originally 'powerful', was gradually given the additional meaning of Latin *dives*, especially in translations.

Many attempts to infuse a new meaning into an existing word did not succeed. For *crux* 'cross' the loanword *krūzi* prevailed over the native *galgo* 'gallows', cf. English *cross* and *rood* (related to Gm. *Rute*); *ēwart(o)* lit. 'the protector of the law' for the Christian priest (*sacerdos*) was finally ousted by the loanwords *Priester*, *Pfaffe* or *Pfarrer*; *zimbrōn*, cf. *zimmern*, was given the metaphorical meaning of *aedificare* 'to edify' but the usage did not succeed; *samanunga* lit. 'the getting together' served for *congregatio* but gave way later; *rūna* or *girūni*, cf. *raunen*, for *sacramentum* or *mysterium* were replaced by *Sakrament* in the technical sense and *Geheimnis* in general usage.

For many technical terms different authors made different adaptations. Thus in Tatian *virtus* is given as *megin* (cf. E *main*), by Otfrid as *kraft*, finally by Notker as *tuged*. The Bavarian form with *-end* eventually established itself as the technical term, NHG *Tugend*. The concept of *gratia* was infused into several native words: *anst* (south-east), *gināda*, *trōst* (Upper German), *geba* (in the Anglo-Saxon missionary field), *huldī* (in the Franconian Rhinelands), of which *Gnade* carried the day. Very often semantic loans existed side by side with various loan formations, e.g. for *salus* we have *heil*, *heila*, *heilī*, *heilida* and *heilhaftī*, as well as ad hoc translations in glossaries.

Loan translations, i.e. exact part-by-part translations of Latin terms, were especially frequent for the less general, more precise Latin terminology of religion. For example *trinitas* > *drīnissa*, cf. OE *þrīnes*; *decanus* > *zehaning* ('the man in charge of ten'); *praedicere* > *forasagēn*; *propheta* > *forasago*; *pervenire* > *duruhqueman*; *subiectus* > *untarworfan*; *spiritalis* > *ātumlīh*; *misericordia* > *armaherzida*; *praepositus* > *furigisazter*; *providentia* > *forascauwunga*, cf. OE *foresceawung*; *superfluere* > *ubarfliozzan*; *superfluitas* > *ubarfleozzida*; *acceptabilis* > *antfanclīh* with the meaning of English 'acceptable' not Gm. *empfänglich*; *partici-*

patio > *teilnemunga*; *omnipotens* > *almahtig*; *praeiudicare* > *forasuanen*. Many such loan translations have persisted, e.g. *Gewissen* (*conscientia*), *bekehren* (*convertere*), *Wohltat* (*beneficium*), *Gemeinde* (*communio*), *Himmelreich* (*himilrīh* < *regnum caelorum*). It is, of course, not surprising that many loan translations were regionally confined. For *temptatio* the term *kostunga* occurred in the northern missionary districts, while *korunga* was south-eastern.

Loan renditions, i.e. approximate renderings of a Latin term, are particularly arbitrary and tend to compete with other forms. Examples are: *communio* > *gimeinsamī*; *divinus* > *gotkund* (*gotelīh* is a loan translation); *oratorium* > *betahūs*; *remissio* > *forlāznessi*; *oboediens* > *hōrsam* (NHG *gehorsam*), cf. OE *hiersum*; *-sam* indicates 'a characteristic' and was not added to verbal roots, except in this case which clearly proves this word to be a loan rendition. A. Lindqvist has shown that for some terms there were very numerous translations, many quite ephemeral, e.g. eleven for *redemptio* (NHG *Erlösung*), twelve for *temptatio* (NHG *Versuchung*), twelve for *resurrectio* (NHG *Auferstehung*): *arstantnessi, urstendida, urstendi, urstant, urstendī, irstandini, urstodalī, urstendidi, ūfferstende, erstantnunga, urrist, urrestī*. For *ascensio* or *ascensus* we have *ūffart* and *himelvart*, both of which are loan renditions.

Loan creations are free versions but the meaning must be regarded as borrowed. Examples are: *zwelifboto* for *apostolus*; *findunga* for *experimentum*; *wīhrouh*, lit. 'holy smoke' for *incensum*.

Many German idioms can be traced back to OHG translations, e.g.

den Mund auftun: *os aperire*: (Notker) *munt uf intduon*;
den Mund halten: *os custodire*: *munt ... haltan*;
Gebote erfüllen: *praecepta ... adimplere*: *gibot ... erfullen*;
auf Herz und Nieren prüfen: *scrutans corda et renes*: *scauuonti herzun inti lenti*;
die Seele erheben: *exaltari animam meam*: *er huab sela mina*;
Antwort geben: *responsum reddere*: *antwurti ... keban*.

Carolingian German consisted of dialects of scriptoria and scribes' and authors' idiolects. It is therefore only to be expected that we find much more regional variation than in periods of a unitary language. T. Frings (*Germania Romana*, p. 3) has stated

that there are about 360 words in *Heliand* not known in HG which
link OS to Frisian and English. Even in the East Franconian
Tatian he identified about 120 such words. It is possible that
obsolescent words were taken up by Anglo-Saxon missionaries
and used because they reminded them of OE words. For *pati*,
passio Tatian has *druoēn, druounga*, cf. OE *þrōwian, þrōwung* and
G. de Smet explains: 'Mit dem letzten Denkmal des angelsächsischen Einflusses verschwand auch die künstlich wieder-
belebte Wortsippe aus der deutschen Überlieferung, um nie
wieder aufzutauchen'. In contrast to such North Sea affiliations
we have the no less tangible existence of a South German church
language. And it too appears to have received support from outside (see Gothic, Romance, and Irish influence, 4.8.2). Frings
characterized the following words as belonging to these southern
innovations: *dulden, sich freuen, klagen, trauern* (Tatian still had
mornēn 'to mourn'), *zeigen, zweifeln, Trost, Erbarmen, Gnade,
Demut*.

The political unification of Germany was the work of the
Carolingian dynasty. It has been shown that the legal terminology
spreading during this period reflects the role of the Frankish state
administration. In Bavaria and the south in general the word for
iudicium 'judgment' was *suona*, for 'judge' *suoneo, suonari* and for
'witness' *chundari*. The older word *tuom*, OE *dōm*, was still
recorded but was only really current north and east of the Franconian Rhinelands. In the Franconian heartland west of the
Rhine the legal terminology included the words *urteili* 'judgment',
irteilen 'to pass sentence', *urkundo* 'witness', *urkundi* 'testimony'.
In the course of the Carolingian period these terms spread into
the other parts of Germany, and one word, *ordāl* with the new
meaning 'iudicium dei', i.e. NE *ordeal*, even reached England,
while OE *dōm* (NE *doom*) remained in the traditional sense of
'judgment'. It has recently been shown by R. Schnerrer that *tuom*,
suona, urteili were also the usual terms for the Last Judgment,
with the corresponding words *tuomestag* and *suontag*, and that
they had the same characteristic regional distribution, as the
following map shows.

Regional differences which have persisted into the present are
exemplified by the words *Samstag – Sonnabend* and *Ziege – Geiß*.
In OHG a southern form *Samstag* confronted the northern
Saterdag. In clerical circles there was also current *Sonnabend*

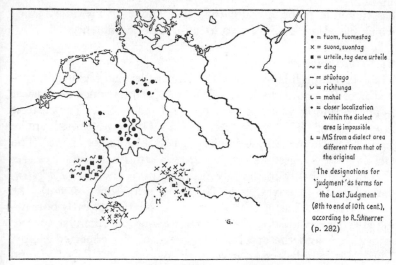

Fig. 9

first for part of the day only, i.e. the time after vespers. In the course of time it succeeded in confining *Saterdag* to a relatively small north-western dialectal region of Germany. The latter word survived in Dutch and English. But against *Samstag* it was less successful so that modern German can be said to have two standard words: southern *Samstag* and northern *Sonnabend*. *Ziege* owes its position as the standard word to the spread of OHG *ziga*, a Franconian dialect word which gained ground in consequence of superior stock-breeding in the more advanced western regions. The south has retained *Geiß* as its native dialect word.

4.8.2 | Borrowed vocabulary

Borrowing in Carolingian times meant borrowing from Latin. Especially the concrete objects, the new Christian buildings, the institutions, and offices of the church were designated by their foreign Latin names. But forces other than the Frankish-Roman church with Latin as its medium also took part in the long process of the conversion of the German tribes. The missionary activities of Irish monks and Anglo-Saxon clerics are well attested and well known. Their possible linguistic influence on German has therefore to be investigated. It is above all lexical evidence which has also led scholars to look for Gothic influence.

(i) *Gothic influence*

The OHG church language of the Upper German regions, in particular of Bavaria, contained a number of words which are easiest to understand if we assume borrowing from Gothic. The clearest case is that of OHG *pfaffo* 'clergyman'. Greek *papas* had unlike Latin *papa* the meaning of 'cleric', not 'bishop' or 'pope'. The OHG form suggests Gothic *papa* as an intermediary stage, borrowed probably in the late fifth century. The word *Pfingsten*, too, ultimately derives from Greek < *pentēkostě* (*hēméra*) 'the fiftieth day after Easter'. Its shifted *pf* < *p* indicates early borrowing and the assimilation points to borrowing into popular speech, rather than into the specialist language of the educated clergy. The Bavarian dialects derive their names for 'Tuesday' and 'Thursday', *Ertag* and *Pfinztag*, and the OHG *pferintag* 'Friday' also from Greek, most probably via East Germanic intermediaries. They also have the words *Maut* < Gothic *mōta* 'customs post', and *Dult* < Gothic *dulþs* 'fair'. Further direct borrowings are doubtful, but *taufen*, Gothic *daupjan*, seems to presuppose an understanding of Greek *baptízein* 'to immerse'. The use of this Gmc. word (a semantic loan) may well have been inspired by the Gothic example. The German translation of the Benedictine Rule contains the word *mias* 'table', which is clearly reminiscent of *mēs*, the usual Gothic word for table. Perhaps the occurrence of OE *mēse* suggests widespread borrowing of Vulgar Latin *mēsa* < classical *mēnsa*. The Gothic word for 'holy' was *weihs* and the fact that *wīh* in OHG was particularly Bavarian (e.g. *der wīho ātum* 'the holy spirit') may suggest a link, perhaps less likely on the basis of borrowing than on that of usage. A few parallel loan formations show the same suggestive geographical distribution, e.g. Gothic *armahaírtei*, southern OHG *armherzī* for *misericordia*, Gothic *armhaírts*, OHG *armherz* for *misericors*; Bavarian *stuatago* 'Last Judgment' (only Gothic *stōjan* meant 'to punish' or 'to judge', while OHG *stuēn* meant 'to accuse'); the usage of *fullen – irfullen* was paralleled by Gothic *fulljan – usfulljan* and is easiest to understand on the basis of Greek, not of Latin.

The historical circumstances behind these Gothic loan influences are rather enigmatic. We have no direct evidence of any

Gothic-Arian mission among the South Germans. It is true, they lived under Gothic protection and suzerainty for a few decades at the beginning of the sixth century. Some Arian influence in the region is attested. The Lombards were converted to Arianism in their Danubian lands before they moved into Italy. We have evidence of an Arian Alemannic duke Gibuld in the fifth century. Whatever influence there was was thoroughly routed after the establishment of Frankish hegemony by those who regarded Arianism as a heresy. But the fact remains that faint traces of Gothic influence form a constituent part of the early South German church vocabulary.

(ii) *Irish missionaries' influence*

History has drawn a veil over any possible Gothic-Arian mission in South Germany. It also reveals next to nothing about the survival of Christianity in the former Roman centres, e.g. Augsburg, or in the surviving Romance enclaves in Bavaria, Alcmannia, and above all Rhaetia. Some scholars have therefore attributed a major role in the formation of the well documented early South German church language to the Irish missionaries. One word only is, however, generally assumed to derive from the Irish: *Glocke*, OHG *glocka* from Old Irish *clocc*, a new word for a new object imported by the Irish monks. Perhaps their role is best seen as promoting the growth of a native South German Christian terminology while any direct linguistic influence remains perforce intangible.

(iii) *Anglo-Saxon influence*

The Anglo-Saxon missionaries themselves possessed a richly developed native Germanic Christian terminology. Their early church, in many ways more tolerant and accommodating than the Frankish-Roman church they were helping to strengthen and organize, had already solved and was still tackling the same problem of transplanting the Latin Christian terminology into a Germanic vernacular that faced the German clerics. It is therefore not surprising if we find innumerable parallel semantic loans and loan formations. Anglo-Saxon influence becomes palpable in two ways: (a) German words corresponding to words in OE are used within the Anglo-Saxon missionary sphere as religious terms although not in the rest of Germany, and (b) German words are coined in imitation of Anglo-Saxon words.

German words which would seem to have benefited from
Anglo-Saxon support were for instance: *tuom* 'judgment', *tuomen*
'to judge', *tuomo* 'judge', cf. OE *dōm, dēman, dēma* and *tuomestag*
'doomsday'; *druoēn, druounga* 'to suffer', cf. OE *þrōwian, þrōwung*
(see p. 220); *wuofen* 'to weep, to lament' for southern *klagōn*;
dolēn as a church word 'to suffer patiently' for southern *dultēn*;
mornēn 'to mourn' for southern *trūrēn*; *fluobra* as the German term
for *consolatio* for southern *trōst* (OE *frōfor*); *gimunt* 'memory', cf.
OE *gemynd* but southern *gihugt*; *gifehan* 'to rejoice', cf. OE
gefēon for southern *sih frewen, sich freuen*; *wizzago* 'prophet',
cf. OE *witega* against Rhenish Franconian *forasago*; *geba* for
gratia, cf. OE *gifu*, and southern *ginā́da*. It has been suggested
that the OHG preference for *truhtin* 'lord' rather than for *frō*
(Gothic had *frauja*) may have been inspired by OE usage (*dryhten*
rather than *frēa*). It is possible that the Tatian word *postul* 'apostle'
was borrowed from OE *postol*. It will have been noticed that none
of these preferences has been of lasting significance for German.
This however is not so with the following three words, where
Anglo-Saxon support has in fact led to the permanent establishment of these words in the language: *heilig, Geist, Ostern*. We
have already seen how the South German church language
favoured *wīh* (Gothic *weihs*) for *sanctus* and *ātum* (Gothic *ahma*)
for *spiritus*. The OE use of *hālig* and *gāst* led to the introduction of
heilag and *geist* first into the Anglo-Saxon missionary sphere and
gradually to the whole of Germany at the expense of the older
expressions *wīh* and *ātum*. *Der wīho ātum* thus became *der heilago
geist*. The connection between OE *ēastor-* and OHG *ōstrūn*,
current in the church province of Mainz, is not entirely clear.
A direct borrowing of OHG from OE is not excluded, but perhaps the phonological form of the OHG word suggests the existence of a German word hailing from the pagan past (the name of
a spring or fertility feast or goddess) which came to be used for the
Christian feast in imitation of OE usage and with the encouragement of Anglo-Saxon clerics.

Among the loan adaptations which were probably inspired
by earlier Anglo-Saxon forms we have for instance *drīnissa*, cf.
OE *þrīnis*, 'trinity'; *gitruobnessi*, cf. OE *gedrēfnes* 'suffering, sadness'; altogether it would seem that the Fulda predilection for the
suffix *-nessi* had something to do with its popularity in Anglo-
Saxon; *gotspel* 'gospel' from OE *gōdspell*, an Anglo-Saxon loan

translation of *euangelium*, lit. 'good message', and reinterpreted as 'message from God', OE *gōd* or *god* > OHG *guot* or *got*; *miltherzi* and *miltida*, cf. OE *mildheort*, *misericors*, *misericordia* for southern *barmherzi*, *irbarmida*; *ōdmuotī*, OE *ēaðmōd*, for 'humility' which is southern *deomuotī* > *Demut*, but see Dutch *ootmoed*; *gotkund* 'divine', cf. OE *godcund*; *Heiland* 'saviour', cf. OE *hǣlend*, competing with *neriand*, *haltant* in OHG; *sunnūnāband*, cf. OE *sunnanǣfen*, originally 'the time after vespers on Saturday', > *Sonnabend*.

With the exception of the last two words, *Heiland* and *Sonnabend*, all traces of this kind of Anglo-Saxon influence eventually vanished as well.

(iv) *Latin influence*

The earliest Christian loanwords were borrowed from Greek and date back to Late Germanic times (see p. 126). The occupation of the Rhenish and Danubian provinces brought the Germans into closer contact with Roman Christianity. A few Latin Christian loanwords show, by being affected by the Second Sound Shift, that they were borrowed early, probably before the seventh century: OHG *opfarōn* – NHG *opfern* < **opprari* < Lat. *operari*, a word of the South German church language, while the north (incl. the Netherlands and England) borrowed Lat. *offerre* > E 'to offer', OS *offrōn*; OHG *seganōn* – NHG *segnen* < Lat. *segnare*, *signare*; OHG *munistri* – NHG *Münster* < **munisterium* < Lat. *monasterium* with the semantic specialisation 'church of a monastery', finally 'large church'; OHG *tuom* < Lat. *domus episcopalis* hence a bishop's main church, NHG *Dom* either from LG or scholarly reborrowing from Lat. *domus*; OHG *farra* or *pfarra* < Lat. *parochia* 'parish'. A number of words for clerics also show features of early borrowing, probably in the Danubian provinces, from the local Romance population or through contact with Italy, e.g. *chlīrih* < *clericus*; *knunih* < *canonicus*; *munih* (NHG *Mönch*) < *municus* < *monicus* < *monachus*; *nunna* (NHG *Nonne*) < *nonna*; *techan* (NHG *Dechant*) < *decanus*, also OHG *iacuno*, *iachono*. Two adjectives also belong to this old South German loanword stratum: OHG *sūbar*, NHG *sauber* < Lat. *sobrius* 'sober'; OHG *chūski*, NHG *keusch* < Lat. *conscius* 'knowing', i.e. 'instructed in the Christian way of life'.

It is, of course, often impossible to say whether a Latin loan-

word entered German in the earliest days of Christianity before
the Carolingians or later during the great period of the foundation
of Christian churches and monasteries in the eighth century in the
reigns of Charles Martel and Pepin the Short or even during the
reforming years of Charles the Great.

Other OHG loanwords from Latin are therefore given on a
thematic basis:

Churchmen and the Bible

abbat < *abbas, abbatem*, NHG *Abt*; *antichristo* 'Antichrist'; *postul,
apostol(o)* < *apostolus*, NHG *Apostel*; *bābes* < *papa*, OFrench *papes*,
NHG *Papst*; *disco* 'pupil' < *discipulus*; *filleol* 'godchild'; *krist,
christanheit* < *cristianitas*; *martyr(a)* < *martyra*, also *martar-tuom* <
martyrium and the verbs *martirōn, martolōn*, NHG *Märtyrer, martern*;
mesinari < **masionarius* < *mansionarius*, NHG *Mesner*; *piligrīm* <
pelegrinus < *peregrinus*, NHG *Pilger*; *priast* and *priester* < *presbyter*;
probist, -ōst < *propos(i)tus* < *praepositus*, NHG *Propst*; *satanas* <
satanas.

The church and church objects

altari < *altāre*, NHG *Altar*; *ampla* 'oil lamp' < *ampulla* 'flask', NHG
Ampel; *fundament* < *fundamentum*; *gimma* < *gemma* 'jewel', NHG
Gemme, reborrowed; *kancella* 'special place for the clergy' < *cancelli*
'barrier', NHG *Kanzel*; *kapella* < *cap(p)ella*; *kentila* < *candēla* 'can-
dle'; *klostar* < *claustrum* originally the closed-off part of the monastery,
NHG *Kloster*; *klūsa* < *clūsa* 'hermitage', NHG *Klause*; *chrismo* <
chrisma 'ointment'; *krūzi* < *crux, crucem*, NHG *Kreuz*; *crystalla* <
crystallum, NHG *Kristall*; *chōr* < *chorus* 'communal singing', NHG
Chor; *līra* < *lyra*, NHG *Leier*; *oli* < *olium* < *oleum*, NHG *Öl*;
organa < *organa*, NHG *Orgel*; *sīda* < **sēda* < *sēta*, NHG *Seide*;
tempal < *templum*, NHG *Tempel*; *tunihha* < *tunica* 'coat', NHG
Tünche 'whitewash', metaphorical extension from 'to coat, to cover';
cella < *cella*, NHG *Zelle*; *zinseri, -a* < *incensum* 'incense' for 'incense
burner'; *zitera* < *cithara*, NHG *Zither*.

The church and its service

alamuosan, elimuosina < *alemosyna* < Gr. *eleemosyna* 'alms', NHG
Almosen; *ēvangeliō* < *euangelium*, NHG *Evangelium* reborrowed; *fern* <
infernum 'hell'; *vespera* < *vespera* 'evening time', NHG *Vesper*;
fīra < *fēria*, NHG *Feier, Ferien* reborrowed from *feriae*; *canon* <
canōn 'rule', NHG *Kanon*; *cantico* < *canticum* 'song'; *chestiga,
chestigōn* < *castigatio, castigare* 'to reproach', NHG *kasteien* 'to
torture'; *kurz, churtnassi* < *curtus* 'shorn, shortened', NHG *kurz*; *missa,*

messa, < *missa*, NHG *Messe*; *nuohtarnīn* 'not having consumed anything' < *nocturnus* 'at night', NHG *nüchtern* 'sober'; *paradīs* < *paradisus*, NHG *Paradies*; *peh* 'pitch, hell' < *pix, picem* 'tar', NHG *Pech*; *pīna*, *pīnon* 'punishment' < *pēna* < *poena*, NHG *Pein*; *prediga, predigunga, predigōn*, also with *b*- < *praedicare, praedicatio* 'to announce publicly', NHG *Predigt* 'sermon', and reborrowed as *Prädikat*; *psalm, salm* < *psalmus*, also *psalteri* < *psalterium*, NHG *Psalm, Psalter*; *purpurīn, purpura* < *purpura*, Greek *porphyra*, NHG *Purpur*; *sancti* < *sanctus*, NHG *Sankt*.

The scriptorium, education and learning

arzat < *archiater* < Greek *archiatros*, NHG *Arzt*; *brief* < *breve* (scriptum) 'short piece of writing' > 'document', NHG *Brief*; *krīda* < **crēda* < *crēta* 'chalk', NHG *Kreide*; *kōsa* 'matter before the court' < *causa*; *curs* 'spiritual exercise' < *cursus*, NHG *Kurs* reborrowed; *labōn* 'to wash' < *lavare*, NHG *laben* 'to refresh'; *lectia, lekza* < *lectio* 'a reading', NHG *Lektion* reborrowed; *libel* 'book' < *libellus*; *magister, meistar, meistarōn* < *magister*, NHG *Meister* etc.; *metar* < *metrum* 'metre'; *murmulōn, murmurōn* < *murmurāre*, NHG *murmeln*; *musica* < (*ars*) *musica*; *natura* < *natura*; *ordo, ordena* 'order, sequence', *ordinōn* < *ordo, ordinare*, NHG *Orden, ordnen*; *pergamin* < *pergamen(t)um*, NHG *Pergament* reborrowed; *prosa* < *prōsa*, NHG *Prosa*; *regula* < *regula*, NHG *Regel*; *scrīban* < *scribere*, NHG *schreiben*; *scrībo* 'writer, scribe', NHG *Schreiber*; *scuola* < *scola*, NHG *Schule*; *scuolari* < *scolaris*, NHG *Schüler*; *sillaba* < *syllaba*, NHG *Silbe*; *spentōn* < *spendere, expendere* 'to give out, weigh out', NHG *spenden*, cf. E *to spend*; *spīsa* < *spēnsa, spēsa* 'expense, food', < *expēnsa* 'expense', NHG *Speise*; *temprōn* 'to regulate' < *temperare* 'to measure'; *tihtōn, dihtōn* 'to write down' < *dictāre* 'to dictate', NHG *dichten*; *tincta* < (*aqua*) *tincta* 'coloured liquid', NHG *Tinte*, reborrowed as *Tinktur*; *titul* < *titulus*, NHG *Titel*; *tradunc* < *translatio*; *trahtōn* 'to consider' < *tractare*, NHG *trachten*; *vers, fers* < *versus*, NHG *Vers*.

Exotic animals and plants

balsamo < *balsamum*, NHG *Balsam*; *cēdarboum* < *cedrus*, NHG *Zeder*; *cullantar* 'coriander seed' < *coriandrum*, NHG *Koriander*; *fīga, fīgboum* < *fīga* < *fīcus*, NHG *Feige*; *helphant, helfentbein* < *elephantus* 'elephant, ivory', NHG *Elefant, Elfenbein*; *lattuh* < *lactuca*, NHG *Lattich*; *lōrberi, lōrboum* < *laurus*, NHG *Lorbeer*; *mandala* < *amandula* < *amygdala*, NHG *Mandel*; *mirra* < *myrra*, NHG *Myrrhe*; *mūrberi, mūrboum* < *mōrum*, NHG *Maulbeere* 'mulberry'; *narda* < *nardus*, NHG *Narde*; *olbenta* 'camel' < *elephantus* (?); *palma* < *palma*, NHG *Palme*; *rosa* < *rosa*, NHG *Rose*; *salbeia* < *salvegia*, NHG *Salbei*;

scorpio(n) < *scorpio(nis)*, NHG *Skorpion*; *timiām* < *thymus*, NHG *Thymian.*

Many of these loanwords clearly moved straight from a Latin text on to a German written page. Others entered German through the spoken language and contact with Romance speakers. Many reveal the date of their entry into the language by their phonological form: no traces of the Second Sound Shift, [ts] for Latin *c* before palatals, Latin *ō* and *ē* often become OHG *ū* and *ī*. All testify to the profound influence which the Mediterranean world exercised on Germany during the Carolingian age.

4.8.3 | Onomastics

(i) There are basically two kinds of *geographical names*: names for human habitations and names for natural features, e.g. rivers, mountains, valleys, forests, fields, ditches and so on. Human habitations were characteristically named after the settlers in the Germanic languages and the oldest type appears to be that composed of a personal name plus the suffix *-ing-*. The place of the suffix could also be taken by a word signifying 'home' or 'place', e.g. *-heim*, *-statt* (*-stedt*, *-stetten*), *-sel*, *-burg*, and this possibly more modern type became increasingly more prolific as, with settled conditions after the Age of Migrations, the naming principle shifted from being based on people to becoming based on places. When human habitations became disused a former habitation name might become a nature name. The opposite development is much more frequent: when a settlement is established the nature name of the place can become a habitation name, e.g. *Eschenbach, Rheinau, Frankfurt* (A.D. 792 *Francono furd* 'ford of the Franks'), *Bremen* (A.D. 937 *Bremun* < *brēm* 'swampy bank'), *Hannover* ('*am hohen Ufer*'), *Bocholt* (< *bōc-* 'beech' + *holt* 'wood'), *Wittenberg* ('white hill'), *Zweibrücken, Osnabrück, Innsbruck* (cf. E *Cambridge* 'bridge over the river Granta'), *Schweinfurt, Herford, Fürth* (< OHG *furti* 'ford'), cf. E *Oxford, Neckargemünd, Gmunden*, cf. E *Weymouth, Bournemouth.* An intermediate type of habitation name arose on the basis of an appellative plus *-ing-* or a 'home' or 'place' element, e.g. *Dornheim, Blaubeuren* (< OHG *būr* 'house', cf. E *bower*), *Bochum* (< *bōc-* 'beech' + *hēm* 'home'), *Talheim, Altenburg.* Nature names, too, may contain a personal name as first element, e.g. *Ezzilenbuohhun* 'Ezzilo's beeches', *Geroldsbach*.

It has proved possible to distinguish two chronological phases in the German onomastic material which was first recorded from about A.D. 700 and increasingly during the Carolingian period. The first phase is characterized in North Germany by particularly archaic, often obscure names, e.g. *Hadamar*, *Geismar* ('swampy spring'), *Goslar* ('pasture on the river Gose'), *Wetzlar*, *Hemert* (A.D. 850 *Hamariti*). In South and West Germany this phase is characterized by the style of the migration period: personal name (monothematic or dithematic) plus *-ing-* or plus words like *-heim*, *-stadt*: *Freising* (A.D. 770 *Frigisingun* < *Frigis*+ *-ing-*); *Ermatingen* (< *Herimuot*+*-ing-*); *Rüdesheim* (< *Hruodines-heim*), *Hildesheim*; *Heriolfes stat* A.D. 800 (Fulda document). On the whole the more flourishing, populous villages on the best soils bear such names. In many areas *-heim* remained popular longer than *-ing-*.

The second period is marked by the names of settlements originating in the wave of internal colonization during the Merovingian and Carolingian age. Such settlements on the whole occupy less desirable, more remote, higher sites, often on less fertile land. The villages tend to be smaller. The second elements of the names are: *-hausen* (*-husen*), *-hofen*, *-weiler* (*-weier*, *-weil*, *-wil*), *-felden*, *-büttel* only in North Germany especially Dithmarschen, and *-leben* in parts of Thuringia around Erfurt. While these names became the fashion during the Carolingian and Ottonian periods of internal colonization, *-dorf*, *-stadt*, and *-burg* continued to be used without forming particular centres of popularity. Names in *-hausen* and *-hofen* have sometimes, like the *-heim* names, an *-ing-* form as their basis, e.g. *Recklinghausen*, *Billinghausen*, *Iringshofen*. In Switzerland *-inghofen* became *-ikon*, e.g. *Hombrechtikon*, and in Bavaria *-kofen*, e.g. *Rempelkofen* (< A.D. 980 *Reginpoldinchova*). In northern Germany *-husen* often became shortened to *-sen*: *Lütmarsen* (< *Lutmereshusa*), *Herbsen* (< *Heriwardeshusen*). Most of these names contain a personal name as their first element, e.g. *Lüttringhausen* (< *Luthelminchusen*), *Gelnhausen* (< *Geilanhusen*). One of these fashionable elements, *-weiler*, was of foreign origin. OHG *wīlari* < late Latin *villare*, is first found in Merovingian times: A.D. 696 *Audoneuillare*, i.e. *Ōtwini*+*villare* > *Ottweiler* in Alsace. In France the names with

-villers generally date from this time. But in Germany the *-weiler* names did not become popular till the Carolingian colonization period. Then they became very widespread throughout the west and south, but they are relatively rare in the areas farthest removed from the Franks, e.g. Saxony, Hesse, Bavaria, Thuringia (see A. Bach, II, 2, § 484). There are regional variants: *-weier, -weil, -wil* but the last two may also derive from Latin *villa*.

Although names tend to go in groups and to be fashionable in certain areas only, it has proved untenable to link names with tribal settlement areas. Name types are not only restricted regionally but also in time and they may be in fashion and go out of fashion at different times in different regions.

Most of the habitation names of this second period, the period of internal colonization under the Merovingian and Carolingian dynasties, have as their first element a personal name, i.e. they are genuine habitation names. But it must be assumed that the secondary habitation names, that is those that were originally nature names, were on the increase. In fact it has proved possible to delineate zones of early occupation and colonization from zones of later expansion on the basis of a predominance of primary or secondary habitation names. In the St Gall documents from A.D. 700 to 920 S. Sonderegger has found that seventy per cent of all names were primary habitation names and up to twenty per cent were secondary habitation names, the rest being nature names and regional names.

It is to be noted that the names connected with intensive, large-scale forest clearings, e.g. in *-rod, -reute, -rüti* etc., *-scheid, -hagen, -schwand*, do not belong to the Carolingian period, but to the twelfth and thirteenth centuries.

Apart from the basic type of personal name plus 'home, place' or the secondary habitation names, there were also in the Carolingian period names reflecting the new Christian society, such as in *-kirchen* (A.D. 800 *Steinkiricha*); or *-münster* (*Kremsmünster*); or with reference to saints: *ad sanctos* > *Xanten*; *St Goar, St Florian, St Gallen, St Pölten* (A.D. 950 *abbatia ad sanctum Yppolitum*), *Weihenstephan, Heiligenstadt*. Such names are usually elliptical, a word like 'abbey', 'monastery', or 'cell' having been dropped. However, most of the saints' names date from later centuries. Further Christian place-names are: *Pirmasens* < A.D. 820 *Pirminiseusna* < *Pirminisensna*, possibly 'Pirmin's hermitage'; *Korvey*, a name transferred A.D. 816 from the monastery at Corbie on the Somme; *Benediktbeuren* < *būr* 'house'; *Pfäffikon* with OHG *pfaffo* as first element (+*inghofen* > *-ikon*).

Water mills first spread in the Carolingian era, hence mill names first date from this period: *Mühlheim*, *Mühlhausen* (Thuringia, 967 *Mulinhuson*), *Möllenbeck* (see A. Bach II, 2, § 484). The political organization of the empire is reflected in the many *-gau* 'district' names recorded first in this era. They are based either on major old cities, e.g. *Zürichgau* or on river names, e.g. *Aargau*, *Thurgau*, *Saargau* (OHG *Sarahgewi*). A smaller political and legal unit was the hundred: OHG *huntari*, e.g. *Waldrammishuntari* (see A. Bach II, 2, § 485).

Political events such as resettlements are echoed in such names as *Frankenhausen*, *Sachsenheim*, *Geiselwind* (*-wind* < *Wenden*, i.e. Slavs). The name of *Lothringen* derives from one of the Carolingian emperors: *Lothar*, a grandson of Charles the Great. But the new OHG and afterwards MHG name for France, *Karlingun*, *Kerlingen*, after Charles the Great, did not succeed in becoming the German name for France.

(ii) The remarkable fact about *personal names* in the OHG period is that christianization had hardly any effect on personal name giving. The Germanic system of single monothematic or dithematic personal names survived practically unimpaired beyond the year A.D. 1000. This is all the more surprising as the names which have come down to us are overwhelmingly those of monks. There is no basic difference between the names of laymen recorded in various legal documents and the names of monks contained in the books of monks' vows, necrologies, or the very important *libri confraternitatum*. The latter were lists of monks at other monasteries who were to be included in the prayers of the brothers of a given house. In this way extensive links were forged between the various monasteries of the Frankish Empire. The name material thus recorded is vast: the St Gall *liber confraternitatum* contains about 9,000 names mainly of the ninth century, that of Salzburg about 8,000 names of the eighth and ninth centuries and the largest, that of Reichenau, even 40,000 names of the late eighth and the ninth centuries from the whole Frankish Empire.

The majority of the names, sometimes more sometimes less latinized, were those of the type: *Gērmuot*, *Sigemunt* (masc.) or

Raathilt, Rīchtrūd (fem.), in a Lorsch document of A.D. 802. The monothematic names were either primary, e.g. *Ernust* (*Ernist*), *Karl*, or 'nursery names' such as *Tetta, Nanna, Woppo*, or they were secondary, that is shortened from dithematic ones, e.g. *Benno* (<*Bernger, Bernhard*), *Eppo* (<*Eberhard, Eberwin*), *Otto* (<*Audobreht*). The proportion of short forms to long forms tends to vary somewhat from place to place and also from one type of document to another. Formal legal documents have more dithematic names, informal name lists often a higher proportion of short ones. It has also been noted that freemen tend to have dithematic names and bondsmen a higher proportion of short names. But there can be no question of a strict social ordering. In Zürich material over two thirds of the freemen had dithematic names, under one third had short names. In the case of bondsmen rather more than half had dithematic names and under half had short names.

The situation was however not static and there are many indications that the Germanic system of name giving was weakening: (a) Many name elements were no longer current in appellative usage or were obsolescent, e.g. *ans-* 'god', *brand-* 'sword', *gund, hadu-* 'fight', *hruod-* 'fame'. (b) The naming technique was no longer understood, as is shown by false contemporary etymological explanations, e.g. *Richmund* ('powerful' + 'protector')=*potens bucca* ('powerful' + 'mouth'), *Richmir* ('powerful' + 'famous')= *potens mihi* ('powerful' + 'to me'). (c) Phonological developments had led to coalescences, e.g. *-bald, -wald* > *-old* or had obscured the second element, e.g. *beraht* > *-berht, -breht, -bert, -wolf* > *-olf, -hart* > *-art, -hraban* > *-ram*. This led to a further weakening of the second element, which was in itself restricted (see 3.9.3(ii)). (d) There was increasing predilection for hypocoristic forms in *-izo* (m.), *-iza* (f.), e.g. *Hugizo* < *Hugbert, Imiza* < *Irmintrud, Bliza* < *Blithilt*, cf. modern German *Heinz, Lutz, Fritz, Götz*, in *-l, -lin* or *-k, -kin, -chin*, e.g. *Sigilin* < *Sigi-, Hildelin* < *Hilde-*, in *-man* or *-wip*, e.g. *Karlman, Hereman, Guotwip, Reginuuif*. (e) Although the use of *cognomina* did not become general or widespread practice, it did exist, e.g. *Notker Balbulus, Notker Teutonicus, Godofridus niger cognominatus* (see A. Bach I, 2, § 335). There were also nicknames like *Subar* 'clean', *Buobo* 'boy', which clearly fell outside the inherited system. (f) In some areas the use of short names did increase very greatly. While the system of dithematic names had allowed an indication of kinship by means of alliteration, repetition of themes, and variation, this possibility was now diminished by an increased use of short names. In St Gall S. Sonderegger counted 480 dithematic names among 668 personal names, 110 secondary short names, 40 primary short names, 35 foreign names and 3 typically Christian names (such as *Gotesscalh*; similarly there are also *Godedanc, Gotesthiu*). But R. Schützeichel found in a Cologne list of the eleventh century that of 400 persons bearing 230 names, about two thirds of the persons had short names and that half of all the names were short names. This shows an already considerable decline of the dithematic Germanic name-giving system.

Foreign names and names inspired by Christianity played a very small part in the incipient erosion of the existing system. A few biblical names were current in OHG times, e.g. *Abraham, Adam, David, Isaac, Johannes, Petrus* and for women *Judith, Elisabeth, Susanna* (see Bach I, 2, § 285). But they were never numerous. Even ecclesiastical authorities generally bore Germanic names. Of the first twenty-five bishops of Strasbourg only seven had foreign names. Among the ninth-century canons of Basle 220 had Germanic and only seven had foreign names. It was no different in Anglo-Saxon England. Among the twenty-seven abbots of Glastonbury from A.D. 601 to the Norman Conquest not one had a biblical foreign name and only four had short names.

In personal-name giving the Carolingian age remained firmly Germanic.

4·9 | **Specimen Text**

The OHG Tatian

The OHG text generally regarded as preceding, in its dialectal form, modern German more directly than any other is the OHG translation of the Latin version of Tatian's gospel harmony. A copy of Victor of Capua's Latin version is in Fulda. The only complete manuscript of the OHG version is in St Gall and dates from the second half of the ninth century. Its dialect is not that of

St Gall and it is generally assumed that the original translation was made in Fulda *c.* A.D. 830. The Latin text accompanying the OHG version was probably not the text or not the only text from which the translation was made but it is very close to the original version. Cf. Matthew 14, 23–33.

81, 1. Abande giuuortanemo eino uuas her thar. Thaz skef in mittemo seuue uuas givvuorphozit mit then undon: uuas in uuidaruuart uuint.

2. In thero fiordun uuahtu thero naht gisehenti sie uuinnente quam zi ín ganganter oba themo seuue inti uuolta furigangan sie. Inti sie gisehente inan oba theme seuue gangantan gitruobte vvurdun quedente, thaz iz giskin ist, inti bi forhtun arriofun. Inti sár tho ther heilant sprah ín quedenti: habet ír beldida, ih bím iz, ni curet íu forhten.

3. Antvvurtenti thó Petrus quad: trohtin, ob thúz bist, heiz mih queman zi thir ubar thisiu uuazzar. Thara uuidar her thó quad: quim! Inti nidarstiganter Petrus fon themo skefe gieng oba themo uuazare, thaz her quami zi themo heilante.

4. Gisehenti hér thó uuint mahtigan forhta imo, inti so her bigonda sinkan, riof quedanter: truhtin, heilan tuo mih! Inti sliumo ther heilant thenenti sina hant fieng inan inti quad imo: luziles gilouben, bihiu zuehotus thú? Inti so sie thó gistigun in skef, bilán ther uuint, inti sár uúas thaz skef zi lante zi themo sie fuorun.

5. Thie thar in themo skefe uuarun, quamun inti betotun inan quedante: zi uúare gotes sún bist. (Tatian, ed. E. Sievers, 2nd ed., Paderborn, 1892).

Select Bibliography

E. H. Antonsen, 'Zum Umlaut im Deutschen', *Beitr.* (Tüb.), 86 (1964) 177–96; W. Betz, *Deutsch und Lateinisch. Die Lehnbildungen der ahd. Benediktinerregel*, 2nd ed., Bonn, 1965; id., 'Lehnwörter und Lehnprägungen im Vor- und Frühdeutschen' in F. Maurer, H. Rupp, *Deutsche Wortgeschichte*, 3rd ed., Berlin, 1974, pp. 135–63; W. Braune, 'Althochdeutsch und Angelsächsisch', *Beitr.*, 43 (1918) 361–445; id., H. Eggers, *Althochdeutsche Grammatik*, 13th ed., Tübingen, 1975; H. Brinkmann, 'Sprachwandel und Sprachbewegungen in althochdeutscher Zeit', now in *Studien zur Geschichte der deutschen Sprache und Literatur*, Düsseldorf, 1965, vol. 1, pp. 9–236; R. Bruch, 'Die Lautverschiebung bei den Westfranken', *ZMF*, 23 (1955) 129–47; E. S. Coleman, 'Zur Bestimmung und Klassifikation der Wortentlehnungen im Ahd.', *ZDS*, 21 (1965) 69–83; H. Eggers (ed.), *Der Volksname Deutsch*, Darmstadt, 1970; J. Fourquet, 'The two e's of MHG', *Word*, 8 (1952) 122–35; K. F. Freudenthal, *Arnulfingisch-karolingische Rechtswörter*, Göteborg, 1949; T. Frings, 'Germanisch ō und ē', *Beitr.*, 63 (1939) 1–116; D. H. Green, *The Carolingian Lord*, London, 1965; E. Gutmacher, 'Der Wortschatz des ahd. Tatian in seinem Verhältnis zum Altsächsischen, Angelsächsischen und Altfriesischen', *Beitr.*, 39 (1914) 1–83, 229–89, 571–7; W. Krogmann, 'Altsächsisch und Mittelniederdeutsch' in L. E. Schmitt (ed.), *Kurzer Grundriß der germanischen Philologie bis 1500*, vol. 1, Berlin, 1970, pp. 211–52; A. Lindqvist, 'Studien über Wortbildung und Wortwahl im Ahd. mit besonderer Rücksicht auf die nomina actionis', *Beitr.*, 60 (1936) 1–132; H. Penzl, *Geschichtliche deutsche Lautlehre*, Munich, 1969; id., *Lautsystem und Lautwandel in den ahd. Dialekten*, Munich, 1971; id., 'Umlaut and Secondary Umlaut in OHG', *Lg.*, 25 (1949) 223–40; I. Rauch, *The Old High German Diphthongization: A Description of Phonemic Change*, The Hague, 1967; F. Raven, *Die schwachen Verben im Ahd.*, 2 vols., Giessen, 1963/67; I. Reiffenstein, 'Geminaten und Fortes im Ahd.', *Münchner Studien zur Sprachwissenschaft*, 18 (1965) 61–77; id., *Das Ahd. und die irische Mission im oberdeutschen Raum*, Innsbruck, 1958; R. Schnerrer, 'Altdeutsche Bezeichnungen für das Jüngste Gericht', *Beitr.* (Halle), 85 (1963) 248–312; R. Schützeichel, *Ahd. Wörterbuch*, 2nd ed., Tübingen, 1974; id., 'Die Kölner Namenliste des Londoner MS Harley 2805', in *Namenforschung. Festschrift für A. Bach*, Heidelberg, 1965, pp. 97–126; G. de Smet, 'Die altdeutschen Bezeichnungen des Leidens Christi', *Beitr.*, 75 (1953) 273–96; S. Sonderegger, 'Ahd. Sprache' in L. E. Schmitt (ed.) *Kurzer Grundriß der germanischen Philologie bis 1500*, vol. 1, Berlin, 1970, pp. 288–346; id., *Ahd. Sprache und Literatur*, Berlin, 1974; id., 'Aufgaben und Probleme der ahd. Namenkunde', in *Namenforschung. Festschrift für A. Bach*, Heidelberg, 1965, pp. 55–96; id., 'Die ahd. Schweiz', in *Sprachleben der Schweiz. Festschrift R. Hotzenköcherle*, Berne, 1963, pp. 23–55; P. Valentin, *Phonologie de l'allemand ancien*, Paris, 1969; id., 'Ahd. Phonemsysteme', *ZMF*, 29 (1962) 341–56; O. Weinreich, *Die Suffixablösung bei den Nomina agentis während der ahd. Periode*, Berlin, 1971; J. Weisweiler, W. Betz, 'Deutsche Frühzeit' in F. Maurer, H. Rupp, *Deutsche Wortgeschichte*, 3rd ed., Berlin, 1974, pp. 55–133.

The Hohenstaufen Flowering

5.1 | The period and the linguistic territory

5.1.1 | The period

A biological metaphor is rarely appropriate if applied to a language. But there is one aspect of language, its use in written records, where such a metaphor can be meaningfully employed. In this sense, the German language flourished during the Hohenstaufen period as it had never done before. For the first time it became a written medium which could be used for a wide range of cultural activities, although it still had to share most with Latin.

The period, during which this efflorescence came about and during which all those linguistic and cultural features most characteristic of it came into being, can be dated from 1050 to 1350. This three-hundred-year period falls naturally into three phases of about a hundred years each. In the first, during the rule of the Salian dynasty, the theocratic system of the previous age was increasingly challenged by a reformed Church. Gradually a secular class of professional mounted warriors became the mainstay of imperial government. This class received its ethical and religious support and justification in the ideas of the code of chivalry and of the *militia Dei*, realized most forcefully in the crusades. These developments came to fruition in the middle century, the period of the Hohenstaufen dynasty, when a secular literature in German first arose. But new forces, epitomized in the growth of the towns and the emergence of a new class of territorial princes, eventually altered this order. The last century of our period, after the fall and disappearance of the Hohenstaufen dynasty, was dominated by a competition of these new forces. The first wave of secular literature in German, that of chivalry, gave way to writings catering for the needs of burghers and of clerics, especially those of the new orders. Still further fields were thus opened for the use of the German language.

5.1.2 | The linguistic territory

If being spoken by more people than before amounts also to a flowering of a language, then our biological metaphor applies in a further sense. The period of 1050 to 1350 was characterized by a very great increase in population and a consequential wave of expansion, both internal and external. As a period it is sharply delimited by a staggering drop in population after 1350 owing to catastrophic epidemics, of which the Black Death raged most savagely. It has been estimated that the German population at the end of the Carolingian age amounted to about two millions. By 1350 it had risen to about fifteen millions. Between the year 1000 and 1350 the population appears to have increased about fivefold. No wonder the world of the High Middle Ages was a world almost unrecognizably different from that of the Carolingian age. Enormous, towering Romanesque and Gothic cathedrals had taken the place of the modest stone and wooden churches of the Carolingian age. Ten thousand strongholds or *Burgen* covered the German lands, usually looking out from hilltops over the strategic highways of the kingdom. Nearly all were built between the years 1000 and 1300. In the same period the primeval forests and moors were cleared and drained and innumerable new villages established. The habitation names of this period testify to the massive wave of internal colonization (see 5.8.3(i)). The total number of villages and hamlets of the modern age, although not their size, was approximated in the thirteenth century.

Rural settlement was matched by momentous urban developments. In the first one hundred and fifty years of our period the legal status of the German town was established. Burghers, merchants and artisans organized themselves in communes which gradually succeeded in wresting a form of autonomous self-government from their clerical or secular feudal overlords (bishops, abbots, counts). By 1200 about fifty German cities, most of them with episcopal sees or royal palaces, many originally Roman foundations, had acquired city status through the grant of privileges and charters. Most strove for the desired status of a free imperial city. In the thirteenth century there followed an unheard-of expansion: a tenfold increase meant that by 1300 another five hundred new towns had joined the already established cities. Some markets and *Burgen* had simply grown in size and had finally acquired the legal status of a town. Many were new foundations. The twelfth and the thirteenth centuries were a time of unprecedented town planning and town foundation. The territorial magnates realized the economic value of towns and headed the great wave of foundations. Thus the Dukes of Zähringen founded Freiburg im Breisgau in 1120, Villingen in 1130, Rottweil in 1140, Berne in approximately 1152. The Welf Duke Henry the Lion founded Munich in 1158, and Lübeck in 1143/1159; the House of Wettin founded Leipzig in 1160; the Hohenstaufen the city of Hagenau in 1164, Chemnitz (now Karl-Marx-Stadt), Altenburg and Zwickau in 1165, and Eger in 1180. These were the precedents for the innumerable thirteenth-century foundations.

Internal colonization and the establishment of new cities were two results of the increase in population. A third, perhaps the most momentous, was the expansion into the Slav lands of the east. Eastward expansion had, in fact, started under the Ottonian dynasty in the tenth century, and then, as later, the missionary aim of converting the heathens and the desire of acquiring land went hand in hand. But a great Slav rebellion towards the end of the tenth century led to the loss of the subjugated territory between the Elbe and the Oder. Only the new Mark of Meissen and that of Lusatia were retained. The eastward move was arrested for nearly a century. In the meantime Poland and Bohemia became Christian, which gave these two states recognition and a degree of security, but exposed the smaller heathen Slav tribes between the Elbe and the Oder and the pagan Baltic Prussians along the coast to even greater pressure. In 1134 Count Albert the Bear (Albrecht der Bär) was enfeoffed with the North Mark by Emperor Lothar. He and his successors of the Ascanian house succeeded in creating a large and strong principality with its centre in Brandenburg, between the Elbe and the Oder, reaching eastwards as far as the Vistula. No less important was the grant of the Mark of Lusatia, in 1136, to Conrad of Wettin who already held the Mark of Meissen. The third great leader in the eastward drive was the Saxon Duke Henry the Lion who subjected the Obodrites in 1158 and refounded Lübeck in 1159. At the time of the Second Crusade the Saxons received papal assurance that a war against the pagan Slavs would count as fulfilment of a vow to undertake a crusade. Thus the Saxons were able to substitute an immediately profitable drive to the east for the hazardous and wearisome journey to remote Palestine and still to acquire the everlasting glory which was the due reward for crusading. The duchies of Pomerania and Silesia were opened to Christianization and Germanization by their own Slav princes. In Silesia in less than a century and a half a hundred and twenty towns and over twelve hundred villages were settled and developed, often with Slav inhabitants taking part. An event of particularly far-reaching consequences occurred in 1226 when Duke Conrad of Masovia granted the Teutonic Knights, the militant order of St Mary's Hospital at Jerusalem, a base in Culmerland on the lower Vistula, and Pope Gregory IX and Emperor Frederick II promised them full sovereignty over all the land they would conquer from the heathen Prussians. In the course of a hundred years they established a strong, extremely well-administered ecclesiastical principality in the eastern Baltic.

These moves of course only afforded the political framework for the intensive colonization which was undertaken by German noblemen, monks, peasants and artisans who flocked east in their hundreds of thousands. Cistercians and Premonstratensians founded monasteries which played a big part in opening up the land. The clearing of the vast forests was now tackled. Moors and swamps were drained, and it is known that Flemings and other Netherlanders were among the colonizers and applied their already well-known expertise in reclaiming land. In Brandenburg, Pomerania, Meissen, Lusatia, and Silesia hundreds of towns were founded. The majority had been Slav settlements or strongholds. Most retained their Slav names, others received the name of the home town of the original settlers, e.g. Frankfurt an der Oder. The Slav princes were no less eager to encourage German settlement of their underpopulated lands than the German rulers. After the final subjugation of the Prussians the Teutonic Knights founded something like fourteen hundred villages in western and eastern Prussia and in Pomerelia. German towns, such as Reval, Riga, and Dorpat, were founded amidst an alien population. Distant enclaves were also formed in Slovakia (Zips) and in Transylvania (Siebenbürger Sachsen).

Before the end of the Middle Ages the Prussians had become Germanized, but Pomerelia which had been under German rule for only about a hundred and fifty years remained largely Slav. Thus originated the Polish Corridor. Little is known of the details of Germanization. Slav enclaves of Wends and Sorbs have survived to the present day. Everywhere it was characteristic of the eastern linguistic boundary that it was ill-defined. There was a wide belt of territory where Slavs and Germans lived intermingled, with numerous enclaves and mixed settlements. By and large the colonization came to an end in the fourteenth century, and the German linguistic territory, as it existed at the beginning of the twentieth century, was thus already formed in the fourteenth.

What was linguistically of the greatest importance was that the settlers were of mixed provenance. Although the north was largely settled by Saxons and became Low German speaking and the centre was largely Central German, everywhere large-scale levelling and mingling took place. The German linguistic territory was therefore not only vastly expanded, but its dialectal map was also significantly altered by the addition of extensive colonial dialects. These became all the more important as a significant shift in political power ensued in the subsequent period. The Hohenstaufen dynasty had its German power base in the western duchies of Swabia and Franconia, although it did not lack an eastern foothold, in the Vogtland and in Eger. In so far as the German language had a regional focus, it lay in the south-west. After the fall of the Hohenstaufen, political and economic power shifted decisively to the east. The margraves of Brandenburg, and the dukes of Meissen-Saxony were from now on powerful new political figures. When dynasties established themselves again in the fourteenth century, first with the Luxemburgers, then with the Habsburgs, these were eastern dynasties; the former as kings of Bohemia, the latter as dukes of Austria, Styria, and Carinthia.

Compared with the vast expansion of the linguistic territory in the east other changes were minor. The Burgenland, on the Austrian frontier, was settled in the twelfth century. Beyond the southern boundary Bavarians established small linguistic islands in Italy in the thirteenth century, the so-called Seven Communes and Thirteen Communes, whose dialect became erroneously known as Cimbrian. The biggest settlement was set up in Slovenia, south of Ljubljana, about 1325 by Carinthians and Tyroleans. Known by its capital, Gottschee, it grew to a colony of about two hundred villages. Bavarians also played a big part in the settlements in southern Bohemia and Moravia. In the south-west the Walser migrations led to the foundation of villages in the highest valleys of Piedmont, in Grisons among the Rheto-Romance population, and in Vorarlberg.

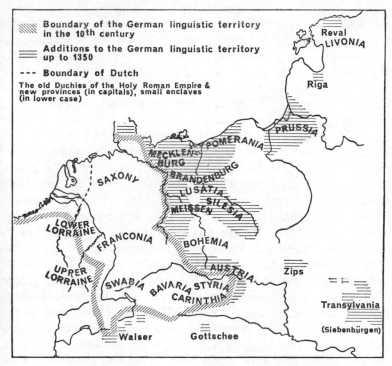

Fig. 10

The German linguistic territory (A.D. 1000–1350)

The western linguistic boundary appears to have been stable during this period. In the Netherlands, particularly in Flanders and Brabant, the written language, Middle Dutch, acquired a degree of independence that characterizes it as a separate language.

5.2 | The range of the literary language

During the High Middle Ages the established pattern of functional bilingualism was fully maintained. But German made significant and considerable gains. It was not that Latin ceased to function as a written medium in any of its established fields, but that German was now also used in many of them and that there were some new fields where German predominated decisively. The secular society of knights and burghers had cultural needs which only German could fulfil. As long as a monastic-clerical society possessed exclusively the accomplishment of literacy the German language was needed for writing only exceptionally. When knights and burghers acquired a degree of literacy and had leisure for cultural pursuits their mother tongue had to serve as a medium. Up to the beginning of the Hohenstaufen era only didactic and religious poetry was composed in German, as had been the intermittent practice since Charles the Great. About the year 1140 the first secular epic appears to have been written by a cleric, Pfaffe Lamprecht. It was a translation and adaptation of the adventures of Alexander the Great. Somewhat later the French *Chanson de Roland* was translated into German. Both were tales of chivalrous exploits in distant lands and must have appealed to knights called upon to fight for God and the King in lands equally distant. New worlds were opened at the same time with the first glimpses into the romantic, Celtic ambience of Tristan and the no less romantic, classical scene of Aeneas and Dido. Towards the end of the century the glorious life of French chivalry, idealized in the society of King Arthur and his knights, was presented to an eager German audience. In the meantime the French and Provençal practice of courtly love poetry had inspired a German lyric poetry which became the twin of the courtly romance as literary achievements of German knighthood. The secular epic, once firmly established with foreign motifs, was finally extended to include the native, heroic traditions of Germanic antiquity (Nibelungen, Dietrich).

In the thirteenth century, especially the second half, German prose grew to be an equal partner of the earlier German poetry. It is true, prior to 1300 almost all German prose works were translations from Latin. Prose now served for didactic, annalistic, historical, legal, medical, astrological, edificatory and religious writings. Chronicles, deeds and charters, sermons, mystical treatises, religious dramas and new versions of the Gospels and of Old Testament books appeared in German and reflected the aspirations of the burghers just as much as the more idealistic epics and lyrics of half a century before had been an expression of knighthood at its zenith. Not that these were not still also cultivated. Troy and King Arthur lost nothing of their fascination, and the lyric was at least parodied, once *Minnedienst* belonged to the vanished world of true chivalry. Later, the worthy burghers became Mastersingers and avid readers of prose romances.

Latin was still the official written language of state and church, of law and science, of learning and serious literature. But German could be used alongside it, and was used. In fact it already dominated in not a few fields, where knights and burghers found it a more convenient medium. The most significant advance that German made in the thirteenth century was in the field of legal documentation. The rise of the German *Urkundensprache* has been the subject of a number of studies. It has to be seen in the context of the progress of the vernacular languages everywhere in western Europe. In Spain, Provence and Italy the native languages asserted themselves as written languages of law even earlier than in Germany. It is no coincidence that the western and southern regions, the valleys of the Rhine and the Danube, were to lead the way in Germany. Up to the year 1300 the overwhelming number of the over four thousand legal documents in German which have been preserved are from these western and southern regions. In central Germany the vernacular became usual only by about 1330 and in northern Germany by 1350 or even later. The movement began in the south-west towards the end of the first third of the thirteenth century, at a time when the nobility and the burghers were already quite familiar with a rich secular literature in German. It took the rest of the century for legal documentation in German to become usual. There must have been considerable feeling that for a contract to be official it had to be in Latin. Yet the lower nobility and the mass of the burghers can only have had a limited knowledge of Latin. It was thus the needs of a whole new class of clients which encouraged the use of the vernacular, now that they became participants in the rapidly expanding documented legal processes. That these new classes did in fact play a decisive part in the move from Latin to German can be seen in the type of document which first appeared in German: proclamations of the king's peace and city laws and charters. The need for the widest possible publicity clearly led to the use of German in such cases. Emperors and princes wanted to ensure that their attempts to establish peace in the land became known everywhere. Cities wanted all their burghers, and their neighbours, to be aware of their newly won freedom, their constitutions and laws. These may well have been read out aloud to the citizens on certain occasions. Many cases of the translation of city laws into German are known from the thirteenth century: Brunswick by the middle of the century, Lübeck before 1267, Freiburg i. Br. by 1275, Winterthur before 1284, Strasbourg by 1296. One of the earliest treaties in German was a pact of reconciliation between the archbishops of Trier and Cologne on the one hand and the Count Palatine of the Rhine on the other. It is dated 17th November 1248. Episcopal chanceries were generally the last to abandon Latin. But where wide publicity was desirable German obviously was a more useful medium. It is understandable that law court decisions, especially those of the king's court, and other private documents, were for a considerable time still predominantly in Latin. It has been estimated that about half a million original legal documents in Latin are preserved from the period of 1230–1300. The over four thousand original documents in German thus form but a modest if nevertheless important beginning.

For the linguist they are of the greatest importance because they alone give us, by the end of our period, a more or less complete coverage of the whole German linguistic territory. They show what the *written* language was like over the length and breadth of the land, and they are clearly dated, unlike most of the literary manuscripts. But they need to be handled cautiously and carefully by the dialectologist who hopes to use them as sources of information on the medieval dialects. For one thing, they are only specimens of local and regional *writing* traditions. These may or may not reflect dialectal features, or may do so only sporadically. The question of the place of origin has also to be considered carefully. On the whole it was the beneficiary of the document who had the copy made out, usually by a local or neighbouring municipal or monastic scriptorium. The place mentioned as where the document was given is, of course, the home of the person who had to affix his seal and signature and may thus not be the place where the copy was actually made. The scribe may not himself have been a native of the place of the scriptorium; he may have learnt a different writing tradition. A strong personality in a scriptorium with a weak writing tradition would to some extent impose his own mode of writing. In a well-established scriptorium with a firm tradition the individual scribe, wherever he came from, would however be unlikely to assert himself. All this means that the optimism of the dialectologist who hopes to draw a map of the thirteenth- and fourteenth-century dialects has to be tempered with caution and scepticism.

The earliest legal document is the common law book by Eike von Repgow known as the *Sachsenspiegel*. The spoken language of legal proceedings and of jurisdiction had always been German. But all the Merovingian and Carolingian codifications of German law had been in Latin. Now in *c.* 1220–30 a common law book was written in German, although there was a prior draft in Latin. Its impact must have been enormous. No fewer than about two hundred and seventy manuscripts have come down to us. Only the *Schwabenspiegel*, an adaptation of it for southern Germany, with about three hundred and eighty extant manuscripts, is numerically more strongly represented. These two law books thus surpass any literary work, for *Parzival* by Wolfram von Eschenbach, which heads the list of literary manuscripts, is preserved in only eighty-five copies and fragments. Other prose works, such as the veterinary handbook by Meister Albrant (*Roβarzneibuch*), and the medical treatise of Meister Bartholomäus, also date from the Hohenstaufen era and count among the most prolifically copied works, with one hundred and ninety-six and over one hundred copies respectively. Owing to their great literary merit, lyric poetry and romances have overshadowed these more humdrum productions. But it must not be overlooked that the prose works of everyday life with their wide distribution are of no less significance for the development of the German language in the Middle Ages.

5.3 | The written language and the dialects

5.3.1 | The written records

Although the records of the German language from the High Middle Ages may have increased a hundredfold over those from the Carolingian age, the linguistic situation is basically the same. Authors of literary works can usually be localized, if only approximately. The author of *Tristan und Isolde* lived and worked in Strasbourg, Heinrich von Veldeke hailed from the region of Maastricht, Wolfram had his home at Eschenbach near Ansbach in East Franconia. Of Hartmann von Aue we know at least that he was from Alemannia, and Walther von der Vogelweide was most likely an Austrian. Of Friedrich von Hausen, who was an early Minnesinger, many of the salient biographical facts are still traceable. Internal evidence and external references allow us also to date most of the literary works, at least within a decade or two and often much more precisely. However, virtually no autographs have survived. The bulk of the literature of the age has in fact come down to us in copies of the fourteenth and fifteenth centuries. It may be an extreme case if *Erec* by Hartmann von Aue, dated to about 1180–5, is known to us, apart from two small fragments, exclusively from a copy made by the customs official Hans Ried of Bolzano or Bozen in the South Tyrol between 1504 and 1515 for Emperor Maximilian. The heroic epic *Kudrun*, from about 1240, and the courtly *Märe Moriz von Craun* from the end of the thirteenth century, have also only survived thanks to Hans Ried's *Ambraser Heldenbuch*. Works of which we have manuscripts written not more than about a generation (approximately thirty years) after the original composition, e.g. *Tristan und Isolde*, *Rolandslied*, and *König Rother*, are an exception at the other end of the scale. The handsome manuscript B (Giessen) of *Iwein*, dating probably from the first decade of the thirteenth century, certainly not later than 1220, is perhaps the copy nearest the time of the composition of an early original. The earliest datable manuscript of a given work may, of course, well be a fragment or a less carefully made copy than a later one. The place of the scriptorium where a particular manuscript originated is hardly ever known. Dating of manuscripts is often only possible to within half a century. Manuscripts are now usually known by the place where they are preserved or where they were first discovered in modern times, for instance Heidelberg, Munich or Berlin. Such designations say nothing about the place of origin. Literary documents can usually not be localized except by such loose descriptions as Bavarian, Swabian, Central Franconian or Alemannic. This is generally done on the basis of some recurrent linguistic features which have been shown to be indicative in documents which can be localized, for instance legal documents.

If numerous copies of a particular work have come down to us
they are nearly always 'contaminated', that is the copyist worked
with more than one manuscript when he made his copy and chose
from either or several what seemed to him preferable. Furthermore, manuscripts were very frequently written by several
scribes, which is usually evident not only from the various hands,
but also from linguistic or orthographic differences. Some scribes
worked as exact copyists, subject only to human error; others,
and this was more often the case, took it upon themselves to
'improve' or alter the version they were copying. Many worked
in a slip-shod manner, perhaps sometimes copying from memory,
with only an occasional glance at the work which they were
copying. Thus, where the manuscript tradition is rich, it is usually
also extremely complex. The number of copies which precede an
extant manuscript, or separate it from its ultimate source, is
generally not known, although the minimum number can sometimes be guessed at with fair assurance. Copies tend to shade off
into different recensions or versions. Where the borderline between a copy and a recension is to be drawn, it is often impossible
to say, or at any rate left to the subjective judgment of each
modern editor. Manuscripts can, of course, not only be contaminated with regard to the literary version but also linguistically or
dialectally. Seeing that each scriptorium or region had, to some
extent, its own orthographic and linguistic tradition, it must be
expected that the works to be copied were adapted to its own convention, sometimes rigorously, sometimes in such a manner that
the older copy was allowed to show through the new copy. A copy
may very often have been commissioned by a literary patron in
order to obtain a work in the regional form which he found
acceptable and with which he was familiar. Rewriting into the
regional or local convention, and contamination are, so to speak,
the synchronic or spatial dimension of our problem. There is
also the diachronic dimension: modernization was often felt to be
necessary, either in orthography, e.g. sixteenth-century ⟨ei⟩, ⟨au⟩
spellings for thirteenth-century ⟨i⟩, ⟨u⟩, or in grammar and
vocabulary. Loss or replacement of inflectional endings (*alliu* >
alle) and the substitution of current words for archaic words
(*grōz* for *michel* or *meinen* for *wænen*) are thus regular features of
the later manuscripts. But basically, manuscripts remain a blend
of archaic and innovatory features, just as much as they tend to be

a blend of regional linguistic or orthographic traditions. A really 'good' manuscript would be one of which the place and date of manufacture are known, antecedents of which would belong to the same region and would not be greatly different in age, and finally, one which would use its letters to differentiate as many of the phonemes of the language as possible. The reality of the manuscript tradition of our period is far removed from this ideal postulate. For instance, in a few lines of the Heidelberg manuscript of *König Rother* we find the Central Franconian forms *zo*, *plach*, *gaf*, *got*, *penning*, *irhauen* (NHG *zu*, **pflag* (=*pflegte*), *gab*, *gut*, *Pfennig*, **erhaben* 'begun') and the Upper German forms *daz*, *guot*, *getan*, *lebine* (with *b* not *v*), *tac*, *pfunde*, *gab* (NHG *daß*, *gut*, *getan*, *leben*, *Tag*, *Pfunde*, *gab*). Sheer inconsistency of spelling is a general characteristic. Thus in the same text (*König Rother*) we find the following spellings for the word for 'good': *guth*, *gut*, *guot*, *got*, and even rhymes can be spelt divergently, e.g. *guot*:*not*. In many texts the fricative [x] is spelt ⟨g⟩ or ⟨ch⟩ without any consistency.

Lyric poetry represents a special but not unsymptomatic case. The poems of over a hundred and fifty known poets from the middle of the twelfth century to the end of the thirteenth have come down to us in five codices. These vary in size and as to the poets included. Many poems are attributed to different authors in the various codices. Codex A, the *Kleine Heidelberger Liederhandschrift*, the oldest, dates from the end of the thirteenth century and was probably written in Strasbourg. It contains thirty-four authors. Codex B, the *Weingartner Liederhandschrift*, was probably written about 1300 in Constance and contains thirty-one poets. Codex C, the *Große Heidelberger Liederhandschrift* or *Manessische*, from between 1310 and 1330, was written in Zürich and includes one hundred and forty-one poets. With its beautiful miniatures of individual poets this constitutes one of the artistic treasures of the age. The *Würzburger Liederhandschrift* (Codex E) from about the middle of the fourteenth century includes above all some of the poetry of Walther von der Vogelweide, and Codex J, the *Jenaer Liederhandschrift*, written in the second half of the fourteenth century in eastern central Germany, is famous for the melodies which it contains, apart from the poetry of thirty mainly central and northern German didactic and gnomic poets. The manuscripts A, B and C and, to a lesser degree, E, are linked in so far as they derive, in differing degrees, from the same or related earlier collections. They testify to the great interest that the *Minnesang* of the previous hundred and fifty years still evoked in the south, in particular in southern Alemannia. It also means, of course, that lyric poetry, wherever the poets themselves hailed from, be it Thuringia, Austria, the Rhinelands, Swabia, Bavaria, or what later became Switzerland, has come down to us mainly in southern, Alemannic and East Franconian, garb.

The same regions play no less important a role in the tradition of many of the best-preserved, most complete and most carefully written manuscripts of the great courtly and heroic epics. The manuscripts A, B and C of the *Nibelungenlied* are Alemannic, so is the Giessen MS B of *Iwein*; Munich Cgm. 18 containing *Parzival* G and Munich Cgm. 51 containing Tristan M, are both from the same Alemannic scriptorium, probably in Strasbourg. The other great *Parzival* recension, MS D, forms part of the great Alemannic St Gall miscellany in which we also find the *Nibelungenlied* MS B. These are but a few of the most noteworthy works.

The language historian finds the manuscript material which is his sole information on the language of the period extremely confused evidence, especially the literary texts. The literary historian has not helped. Wishing to present the masterpieces of the age in as readable a form as possible for the enjoyment and study of the texts as literature, he has often eagerly listened to those who have postulated the existence of a courtly standard language in the Hohenstaufen age. It was Karl Lachmann and his followers who created, in the first half of the last century, a normalized, standardized Middle High German. This polished and purified orthography and grammar graces many of the numerous volumes of the *Altdeutsche Textbibliothek* and *Deutsche Klassiker des Mittelalters* while the series *Deutsche Texte des Mittelalters* adheres more rigidly to the manuscript versions. Primers and grammars, for obvious didactic reasons, also generally cling to the normalized 'standard' Middle High German. Most of our classical texts are most easily available in such editions, while the actual manuscript versions are less readily obtainable in the occasional diplomatic reprints or the more demanding facsimile editions. For many texts one would actually have to go to the manuscripts. In more recent times the climate has been much more critical of and unfavourable to the wholesale reconstruction of 'original' poets' versions from the extant manuscripts. The latter are more appreciated as genuine witnesses of the language and literary culture of the Middle Ages and the word 'corrupt' is used, if at all, with less opprobrium and in a more factual sense.

One reason why the reconstruction of the assumed original text, usually, but not necessarily, in normalized 'classical' Middle High German, is so tempting and attractive is that often none of the extant manuscripts, with gaps and nonsensical emendations, can possibly represent the poet's own work. This is clearly the case with the *Nibelungenlied*. None of the oldest three manuscripts, A, B or C, is more than a somewhat divergent copy of an archetype which itself was probably already removed from the original. Even later manuscripts may occasionally provide a more convincing reading. Where so little authority adheres to any one manuscript – and the case of the *Nibelungenlied* is by no means an extreme one, rather the opposite – it is difficult to see why the literary editor should renounce his critical, philological abilities and simply reproduce a manuscript of somewhat doubtful literary value. Where the linguist cannot even date or localize the manuscript, its service as a linguistic document is equally dubious, except in demonstrating the medieval reality and spontaneity of German writing practice. Hence the case for reconstructing a text, rather than leaving it as it has been transmitted to us, is often very strong.

The differences of manuscript copies and a reconstructed critical text edition in normalized 'classical' MHG orthography can be seen in the following examples, chosen at random, from the *Nibelungenlied*.

(a) Munich MS A from the second half of the thirteenth century:

939   Die blůmen allenthalben   von blůte waren naz.
      do rang er mit dem tode.   vnlange tet er daz,
      wan des todes zeichen   ie ze sere sneit.
      sam můst ersterben ŏch   der reke kůne vnde gemeit.

(b) St Gall MS B, generally regarded as the best MS, written about 1260–70:

995   Di blvmen allenthalben   von blvte wrden naz.
      do rang er mit dem tode.   vnlange tet er daz,
      want des todes waffen   ie ce sere sneit.
      done moht niht reden mere   der recke chv̊n gemeit.

(c) Donaueschingen MS C, the oldest extant MS, probably from the first half of the thirteenth century, generally regarded as a slightly modernizing version:

1009 Die blume*n* allenthalben   von blv̄te warn naz.
     do ranger mit dem tode.   vnlange tet er daz,
     wande in des todes wafen   al ze sere sneit.
     do mohte reden niht mere   d*er* reche chv̊n un̄ gemeit

(d) The critical text, based on B, by K. Bartsch, from the 13th edition by H. de Boor, Wiesbaden, 1956:

998 Die bluomen allenthalben   von bluote wurden nz.
     dô rang er mit dem tôde.   unlange tet er daz,
     want des tôdes wâfen   ie ze sêre sneit.
     dô mohte reden niht mêre der recke küen' unt gemeit.

Two of the other manuscripts have *degen* in the last line instead of *recke* and one has *held*, apart from other divergences.

It will be noticed that the editor performed two different tasks: textual emendation and normalization of the orthography to make it conform to Lachmann's spelling system. Although he took B as the basis of his edition he rejected the B reading of the first half-line of the fourth line, presumably for rhythmical reasons, and preferred the reading of C. The validity of the B reading is, however, supported by the archaic double negative device *ne – niht*, and many editors might now hesitate to make such an emendation for rhythmical reasons. As to spelling, the alterations comprise: the indication of vowel length by means of a circumflex; the introduction of ⟨uo⟩ for ⟨v⟩ where it is historically justified, and ⟨üe⟩ for ⟨v̊⟩. In fact, MS B is not very discriminating in its use of ⟨v⟩, e.g. 979 *Der brvnne der vvas chvle lvter vnd gvt*: *Der brunne der was küele, lûter unde guot*, where the graph ⟨v⟩ stands for no fewer than four different phonemes of classical MHG: /u, ū, üe, uo/. Although /üe/ is sometimes written ⟨v̊⟩, as in our passage, this is by no means regular and the same graph may also stand for /ü/, e.g. *kv̊nich*, just as ⟨v⟩ may here do service for a fifth phoneme: /ü/, e.g. *chvnich*. Other regularized spellings are well supported by the orthography of the MS, e.g. ⟨ei, ie, æ, ov, ev⟩ and the indication of mutated vowels, although not regular, is not as rare as in other MSS, e.g. ⟨bôsen⟩. The reduction of ⟨ff⟩ in *waffen*, and also for instance in *lieffen*, although in

keeping with the regularized classical orthography, may, in an
Upper German text, well amount to an unjustified interference
with the language (see 5.4.4).

5.3.2 | A Middle High German standard language?

What gave impetus originally to regularization was
Grimm's and Lachmann's belief that there had been among poets
in the thirteenth century 'ein bestimmtes, unwandelbares Hochdeutsch' with only few dialectal features, but that uneducated
scribes had allowed this language to become corrupted. Ever since
that time the question of a MHG *Schriftsprache* has held scholars'
attention. Their discussions were often bedevilled by the ambiguity of the German term *Schriftsprache*, which can mean both
written language and *standard language*, terms which need to be
clearly distinguished. There can be no doubt that there was a
written language with its long established tradition and with its
orthographic, syntactical and stylistic conventions. Writers did not
transliterate their spoken dialects. When they wrote, they employed
the written language which had long acquired characteristics and a
separateness of its own. But medieval written languages did not
possess the extreme degree of exclusive normalization which
marks modern languages. They possessed an amplitude which
permitted regional and local traditions to evolve, which tended to
rest on certain dialectal features. And they even allowed a fairly
free hand to personal idiosyncrasies, especially where a scribe
was isolated and not a member of a well-established scriptorium.
Nor was consistency a characteristic feature. Where the personal
involvement of the scribe with the written language was slight on
account of his lack of education, lack of frequent practice, limitation
of texts to be copied to purely local documents, the resultant text
can be expected to be much closer to the local dialect than would
be the case with texts of supra-regional significance manufactured
in a large, well-established scriptorium in a large town, for instance
Freiburg i. Br. or Strasbourg. It is an important characteristic of
written medieval German that it was more responsive and adaptable
to regional dialectal and to phonetic features and changes than the
modern language (compare the spellings *tages* – *tac, limperc*
'Lindberg'). Tolerance existed in matters of regional and phonetic

features and in orthographic conventions. Many differences in orthography were based on local traditions and had nothing to do with local dialects, e.g. when ⟨k⟩ in initial position became a feature of Alemannic orthography but ⟨ch⟩ of Bavarian, or when ⟨a⟩ remained the usual graph even after the corresponding sound had become an o-type vowel in many areas. Despite regional variation we have good reason for stating that most variants of the MHG written language were actually nearer to the regularized 'classical' MHG than to the spoken local dialects.

This amounts to the same thing as to state that there *was* a degree of standardization and a unifying trend. Although there was no uniform standard language there was a tendency towards standardization. This manifests itself on two levels: first, in the preference given in many parts of Germany to certain orthographic and linguistic usages of the south-west, the Rhine-Main-Danube region, and secondly in the existence of a courtly idiom, the *höfische Dichtersprache*, with the same regional basis and the same exemplary character.

It has been noted by G. Korlén that the thirteenth-century texts written in Eastphalia reveal a more or less strong southern influence, for instance, in the adoption of the graphs ⟨ie⟩ and ⟨uo, û⟩ for dialectal *ē* and *ō*, ⟨b⟩ for *v*, *von* for *van*. In Westphalian texts of the same period, too, and in Brandenburg texts, HG features are noticeable, e.g. the suffixes -*schaft* and -*unge* for native -*scap* and -*inge*. In the Central Franconian regions spellings like *halb*, *geben*, *wib*, -*g*, *t*-, *ie*, *û* beside *half*, *geven*, *wif*, -*ch*, *d*-, *e*, *u*/*o* testify to early southern influence. Beside the regional *dat*, *dad* the form *daz* occurs early and gradually increases in use.

Thuringia and Saxony, too, were exposed to very strong southern influences and we do well to remember H. Bach's conclusion (vol. i, p. 34):

'Betrachten wir nun die sprachform der hier untersuchten denkmäler, so wie also in den kanzleien Thüringens und Sachsens um das jahr 1300 geschrieben wurde, so tritt uns alles in allem eine gleichartige sprache entgegen, die nicht weit von dem "normalmhd." entfernt ist. Sehr viele wörter treten immer mit derselben lautform auf, die rechtschreibung kann eher wechseln. Wir betrachten diesen lautstand nicht als den ursprünglichen für dieses gebiet, sondern als durch starke beeinflussung aus dem süden, also aus dem oberen Main-gebiet entstanden.'

Here again the graphs ⟨ei⟩ and ⟨ou⟩ persisted against a dialectal background of monophthongs *ē*, *ō*, which are occasionally attested by ⟨e⟩, ⟨o⟩ spellings. For MHG *ie* the graph ⟨i⟩ shows dialectal monophthongization which led to a coalescence with lengthened MHG *i* for which we find inverted spellings with ⟨ie⟩, e.g. *gechrieben* for *geschriben* 'written'. But in some documents the southern graph ⟨ie⟩ for MHG *ie*, dialectal [iː], is strongly represented (H. Bach, vol. i, p. 82). Further features of the southern written language which occur despite a divergent dialect background are the sharp differentiation between initial ⟨d⟩ and ⟨t⟩, medial ⟨b⟩, initial ⟨pf⟩ (H. Bach, vol. ii, pp. 72–3, 90, 95).

Many widespread dialectal features occur only sporadically in the written language, e.g. the velarization of *nd/nt* > *ng*, the spelling is almost invariably ⟨nd/nt⟩ (*hinten* not *hingen*); in certain words of the written language, e.g. *zins*, the Alemannic loss of a nasal before a fricative (*öis* or *üs* for *uns*) is frequently not shown (Boesch, p. 177); in Alemannic the unstressed vowels were uniformly spelt ⟨e⟩, e.g. *lenge* 'length', although the former long vowels had still distinct reflexes and had not coalesced with those of the former short vowels; the Bavarian dialectal personal pronouns *es* and *enk* only turn up sporadically towards the end of our period. Initial ⟨b⟩ is also found in Austrian texts quite frequently although the regional tradition had a characteristic initial ⟨p⟩; ⟨w⟩ for *b*, e.g. *gewurt* for *geburt* never became more than a fairly widespread regionalism. On the whole the forms of the Alemannic-East Franconian written language had a wider currency than any other forms, although naturally many regional features were strongly entrenched, e.g. the Bavarian ⟨ai⟩ for MHG *ei*, or the Central Franconian, in particular Ripuarian, indication of vowel length by means of ⟨i⟩ or ⟨e⟩, e.g. *groiz* for MHG *grōz*. The very fact that documents from remote places show more dialectal features than those from the major centres is a kind of negative proof for the existence of a unifying tendency.

Although there was no centralization in MHG there was an early and persistent convergence. It is even doubtful whether the degree of convergence was greatest during the Hohenstaufen century and was replaced by a resurgence of the dialectal forms of the written language in the subsequent century and a half. What is certain is that only little written material has actually come down to us from before 1220 and that there was an immense increase in the late thirteenth and fourteenth centuries. This mass of material does show a great degree of regional divergence. To some extent divergence was greater simply because more was written in many more places than before. But whether we are actually faced with a genuine reduction of the incipient convergence and an increase in divergence is difficult to judge.

The second clear indication of a degree of standardization is to be found in the existence of a courtly idiom of supraregional significance. A common literary form, the court epic and the courtly lyric, led to a common mode of expression based on a stock of rhyming words, and a syntactical, lexical and stylistic convention. The degree of uniformity which came into being owed much to the language of Hartmann von Aue. The *höfische Dichtersprache* was also characterized by a stock of common key words, e.g. *zuht*, *vuoge*, *hōher muot*, or standing epithets like *minneclich*, *lobesam*, *klār*, and many foreign words such as *ors*, *amīe*, *massenīe*. The rhymes were predominantly etymological which made them acceptable over a wide area, e.g. *wīb* and *līb* would also rhyme in their Central Franconian forms *wif* and *lif* or their Bavarian forms *weib* and *leib*. It has been shown how poets such as Hartmann von Aue increasingly eschewed rhymes which they learnt to recognize as regional. This language of courtly literature with its strong unifying tendency was in many ways regarded as exemplary and found imitators in many parts of Germany. North Germans, e.g. Eilhart von Oberg and Albrecht von Halberstadt, who wished to take part in the fashionable courtly literature of the age chose High German as their medium, usually in its Central German form. Prose and the language of the legal documents were equally indebted to the written form of courtly literature which many scribes practised. Many of the copies of the *Schwabenspiegel* and the sermons of Berthold von Regensburg are in 'good', average MHG.

There was thus a *written language* in many regional forms, which were in no way identical with the spoken dialects, but which nevertheless tended to echo some dialectal features. And there was also a tendency towards a *standard language*, in so far as the written language of the courtly literature of the south-west was exemplary for poets far and wide as a mode of expression and for scribes in general as a commendable vehicle to be imitated, or by which they were influenced.

5.3.3 | Regional variants

There can, of course, be no question of doing for medieval German what dialect geography has done for modern German. On the basis of local and regional linguistic traditions we can, however, establish a grouping of written regional forms. These can be compared with modern dialects. In doing so we must concentrate on salient features which together constitute dialect types. Dialect boundaries had better be left out of account. Modern isoglosses have an uncertain age. Medieval dialectal evidence stems from manuscripts which are for the most part, except for original legal records, contaminated and usually written in an inconsistent orthography. In fact, they are written idiolects, and it is from these that we must attempt to draw conclusions as to the characteristics of medieval dialects. The geographical extension of these dialects will, in any circumstances, remain approximate. So will their forms. Precise descriptions of the language of individual manuscripts can be given. The salient characteristics of the dialects have to be abstracted from these. The descriptions in the grammars and handbooks tend to be an uneasy amalgam of information extracted from the modern dialects and from the spellings of the medieval manuscripts.

The following account is based only on the record of the medieval manuscripts. For each dialect a representative sample is given and a few typical features are mentioned, even if, in view of the brevity of the sample text, not all actually occur in the passage. These features are most often – but it must be remembered never exclusively – encountered in the respective dialects. The location and grouping of medieval German dialects are indicated on the map on p. 257. Contemporary commentators were aware of these *lantsprachen* as they called them, just as much as they regarded them all as forms of one language which they called *tiutsch* or *dutsch*.

(i) *Alemannic*
   (a) South Alemannic

> Wa vunde man sament so manig liet.
> man vunde ir niet.
> in dem kúnigriche.
> als in zúrich an bûchen stat.
> des prûuet man dike da meister sang.

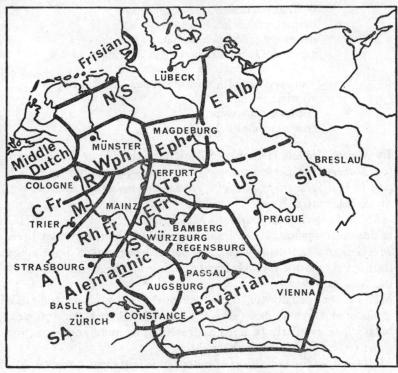

Fig. 11

German written dialects in the High Middle Ages. (cf. the maps in Paul-
Moser-Schröbler and *Kl. Enzykl.* i, p. 152)

			SA	South Alemannic
Upper	Alemannic		A	Alsatian
German			S	Swabian
	Bavarian			Bavarian

MHG		East	EFr.	East Franconian
Middle		Franconian		
High			Rh.Fr.	Rhenish Franconian
German	Central	West Central		M	Moselle Franconian
	German	German	CFr.	R	Ripuarian
			T	Thuringian
		East Central	US	Upper Saxon
		German	Sil.	Silesian

MLG			Wph.	Westphalian
Middle	Low		Eph.	Eastphalian
Low	German		NS	North Saxon
German			EAlb.	East Albingian

> dˢ Manesse rank.
> darnach endeliche.
> des er dú liederbûch nu hat.
> gegen sim houe mechten nigin die singere.
> sin lob hie prûuen vn andirswa.
> wan sang hat bŏn, vn̄ wúrzen da.
> vn̄ wisse er wa.
> gût sang noch were.
> er wurbe vil endelich darna.

By Meister Johans Hadloub of Zürich, in the *Große Heidelberger* (or *Manessische*) *Liederhandschrift*, *c.* 1310–30, written in Zürich (see F. Pfaff, *Die große Heidelberger Liederhandschrift*, Heidelberg, 1909, col. 1216).

In the following comparisons MHG means the 'classical' MHG as described for instance in Paul-Moser-Schröbler, and elsewhere.

MHG *ie, uo, üe*: usually ⟨ie, ů ǔ,⟩, i.e. preserved as diphthongs (but see p. 250 for the divergent spelling in the Alem. MS B of the *Nibelungenlied*).

MHG *ei, ou*: usually ⟨ei, ŏ⟩, *öu* variously ⟨ŏi, ȯ, v̇⟩. In the Lake Constance area we find ⟨ai⟩, ⟨æi⟩ for *ei* (see Boesch, pp. 106–14).

MHG *ī, ū*: regularly ⟨i, u⟩, i.e. preserved as monophthongs; for *iu*: ⟨ú⟩ or ⟨v̇⟩ are most frequent.

MHG *ü, ö, œ*: the indication of mutation is fairly usual, e.g. ⟨ú, ŏ⟩.

MHG *ë, e, ē*: usually ⟨e⟩.

MHG *ä, æ* ⟨æ⟩ in the eastern part, ⟨e⟩ in the western part.

MHG *a, ā*: generally ⟨a⟩.

MHG *b, p, pp, pf*: usually ⟨b, p, (pp), pf or ph⟩.

MHG *d, t*: ⟨d, t⟩.

MHG *k-*: predominantly ⟨k⟩, but with many ⟨ch⟩.

MHG *s* and *z*: early coalescence (but *Nibelungen* MS B distinguishes them).

MHG *m* in final position or at the end of a syllable very frequently ⟨n⟩, e.g. *boum* ⟨bŏn⟩.

Verbs *gan, stan* for 'to go' **and** 'to stand', but poetic texts also use *gen, sten*; past tense *kam* or less frequently *kom* 'came'; *dur* for *durch*; *har* for *her*; *kilche* for *kirche*; the abbreviations *dc, wc* for *daz, waz* are specially characteristic of Zürich and central and western Switzerland; *ener* for *jener*; *nit* for *niht*; 2nd pers. pl. ind. pres. in *-ent* (also imp. and later pret.); *tüeje, tüege* subj. pres. of *tuon* 'to do'; *unz* for 'until'.

(b) Alsatian (or Low Alemannic)

s us chom er vnde sin frŏwe ysot.
z em brunnen vnde des bŏmes schate.
v il heinliche vnde ze gŏter state.
i n ahtagen vnde ahtstunt.
d az ez nieman wart chunt.
n och ez dechein ŏge nie gesach
w an eines nahtes ez geschach.
d o tristant aber des endes gie.
d o wart sin melot ine weiz wie.

From *Tristan* by Gottfried von Strassburg, from the Munich MS Cgm. 51, first half of the thirteenth century, probably written in Strasbourg (see Petzet-Glauning, *Deutsche Schrifttafeln*, vol. iii, xxxii).

Linguistically similar to South Alemannic, but with the following differences: MHG *ā* sometimes ⟨o⟩; MHG *ei* sometimes ⟨e⟩ reflecting the dialectal monophthongization; MHG *ie* occasionally ⟨e⟩ reflecting the Strasbourg dialect; ⟨ch⟩ for MHG *k-* is an archaism which was later replaced by ⟨k⟩. The graph ⟨ŏ⟩ for both MHG *ou* and *uo* is usually a primitive feature but may, in a Strasbourg text, indicate the monophthongal and palatalized character of both sounds, cf. modern dialect [ø:] in MHG *guot* and [œ:] in MHG *koufen*. Gottfried has only etymological rhymes.

(c) Swabian

– Dar nach sol der Herzoge von Tekke·vnde Graue Albreht von Haigerloch vnde alle ir helfer · gånzelich versv̊net sint · vnde vrv̊nde sin · mit dem vorgenanten Eberh [art von wirtenberch] vnde mit allen den sinen·vnde geschåhe zewúschen in kainerlaige bruch dar umbe sv̊len die zewo vorgenante bv̊rge niht phant oder behaft sin·Vnde wurden mir oder vnser Stette helfent dem Herzogen·oder Grauen Albreht·oder aber aim andern·Swaz schaden denne Eberȟ von wirtenberch·oder die sinen da wider tåten in dem vrlv̊ge dar umbe Sv̊len die bv̊rge niht behaftet sin·Hilfet er ŏch sinen vrv̊nden darumbe sv̊len ŏch die bv̊rge niht beheftet sin Der vorgenant Eberȟ·der sol ŏch mit gûten trv̊wen gelten·baide Cristan·vnde Juden alles das dez er in Schvldige ist·vnde sol ŏch vns antwúrten die Stat Stûtgarten zerbrechende·alse da geredet ist. –

Extract from a treaty concluded on 10th November 1286 outside Stuttgart (see Wilhelm *et al.* vol. ii, no. 844).

The major differences from South Alemannic are: MHG *ei*: ⟨ai⟩; *æ, ä*: ⟨å⟩, both features are also north-eastern South Alem.; ⟨au⟩ for *ā* especially in the fifteenth century; the Bavarian ⟨av⟩ spelling for MHG *ou* reaches Augsburg in the last quarter of the thirteenth century. An intrusive vowel between *z* and *w*, e.g. *zewúschen, zewo*, is found elsewhere in Alem. ⟨g⟩ for [j], e.g. in *kainerlaige*, is characteristically Alem.

(ii) *Bavarian*

> Do pylat*u*s gesampt daz levt di f*ů*rste*n* vnd di maisterschaft vnd daz levt. Do sprach er zv in. Ir habet. mir braht disen menschen alz
> 10 einen verlaitter vnd fragt ich in vor evr vnd vinde dehein schvlde an im an den dingen. vnd ir in r*ů*get noch avch herodes. nv sant ich evch hintz zv im vnd wart in niht vertailt da er an schvldich were. Ich z*ů*htig in vnd lazze in. es waz avch durch den hiligen tag. in einen. zu lazzen. Do rvft di menig alsam. hab in. vnd lazze
> 15 vns barrabam, Der waz dvrch einen streit gevangen. Der da ergangen waz. in der stat. vnd vmb ein manslaht waz er gevangen. vnd geworfen in einen charcher. pylat*u*s sprach ab*e*r zv in. vnd welt ir ich lazze ev Jesum. Si rvften in aber an. chr*ů*zige chr*ů*zige in, er sprach ze dem dritten mal zv in. waz hat er *ů*bels getan.
> 20 Ich vinde dehein schvlde des totes an im. Ich wil in straffen vnd lazzen. Si stvnden vf vnd rvften lavt vnd paten daz er chrevtzte in.

From a MS book of pericopes from the monastery of Oberaltaich, Bavaria, probably written towards the end of the thirteenth or the beginning of the fourteenth century. (See Petzet-Glauning, *Deutsche Schrifttafeln*, vol. ii, plate xxviii.)

MHG *ie, uo, üe* remain diphthongal, although only ⟨ie⟩ is regular. ⟨*ů*, v, *ů*⟩ render the other two diphthongs.

MHG *ei, ou, öu* are usually ⟨ai, æi, av, ev⟩, frequent exceptions are *ein, dehein*.

MHG *ī, ū, iu* are usually ⟨ei, av, ev⟩, also ⟨î, *ů*⟩.

MHG *ü, ö, œ*: indication of mutation by ⟨*ů*⟩ or ⟨ô⟩, but not regular.

MHG *ë, e, ē*: usually ⟨e⟩.

MHG *ä, æ*: often ⟨æ⟩.

MHG *a, ā*: *a* and *o* before *r* occasionally confused. *ā* sometimes ⟨o⟩. Shortening of *ā* in *slāfen, strāfen* is characteristic.

MHG *b*- very often ⟨p⟩, sometimes ⟨w⟩.

MHG *k-* predominantly ⟨ch⟩, also ⟨-ch, -kch⟩, which points to an affricate.

Occasionally, dialectal sound changes are indicated, e.g. diphthongization of MHG *ō* > *ou* or monophthongization of MHG *ou*, Bav. ⟨av⟩, to *a*, unrounding of MHG *ü* to *i*, cf. *prout, gelaben, ibel* for NHG *Brot, glauben, übel*. The suffix -*lich* contains a long vowel, hence -*leich* in the thirteenth century; -*age-* > *ei*, e.g. *meit*, Alem. *maget* 'girl'; occasionally *mier, dier* for *mir, dir*.

Verbs *gen, sten* but also *gan, stan* in court epics; past tense *kam*; *vor* with gen. of pers. pron.; early apocope and syncope (*fragt, vertailt*).

(iii) *East Franconian*

185   Es kunde so vil wunders
                Kein meister nie von Lunders,
                Von Bruck, Paris und Dolet;
                Sin sin alda begriffen het
                Nuwer wunder dannoch mere.
190   Auch waz die sule gezirt so her
                Mit bilden[1] wol durch gniten,[2]
                Us flader holtz[3] gesniten,
                Buchsbum, aloe, cipressen,
                Daz knie, bein und hessen[4]
195   Heten so recht gelenke gar,
                Daz ich ez niht wol sagen tar.
                Ir zen, ir augen und ir gran:
                Dar uz vil manig stein bran
                Ye nach der selben varbe,
200   Als ez erwunschet garbe
                Von meisterlicher kunste were.

[1] statues carved in wood;   [2] formed;   [3] wood with a marked grain;
[4] back of the knee.

From *Die Minneburg*, composed towards the middle of the fourteenth century by an unknown poet, probably from Würzburg or its region, the best manuscript of which, Heidelberg P, from about 1400, has also been located in Würzburg (see H. Pyritz (ed.), *Die Minneburg*, Deutsche Texte des Mittelalters, vol. 43, Berlin, 1950).

The edition distinguishes the letters *u, v, i, j* according to their consonantal or vocalic functions, not in the fashion of the MS.

Pyritz has also introduced modern punctuation. These arrangements also apply to the following texts: v-vii.

MHG *ie*: ⟨i, ie⟩; *uo, üe*: both indiscriminately ⟨u, ů⟩, i.e. they are
monophthongized.

MHG *ei, ou, öu*: usually ⟨ei, au, eu⟩.

MHG *ī*: ⟨i⟩; *ū* and *iu* indiscriminately ⟨u, ů⟩, with an occasional
euch for *iuch*, *ewern* for *iuwern*.

The signs ⟨ô⟩ and ⟨û⟩ stand for both mutated and unmutated
vowels. Mutation is thus not reliably indicated.

MHG *ë, e, ē, ä, æ*: ⟨e⟩, but the reflexes of MHG *ē* and *æ* are not
rhymed.

MHG *ā* often spelt ⟨o⟩.

The consonantal spellings are very close to those of Alemannic
and NHG. Initial ⟨k⟩ is regular. But in *verba pura* (e.g. *blühen*)
the dialect has -*w*- not UGm. -*j*-; *rw* > *rb*; *hs* > *ss* (*hesse* for
hahse); -*n* in the infinitive is frequently dropped. Syncope and
apocope are general. The infinitive of 'to come' is *kumen*, pret.
quam beside *kam, kom*; *gen* and *sten* with *gan, stan* only in rhymes;
sul 'shall' for UGm. *sol*.

(iv) *Rhenish Franconian*

585   Do medea vurnam
                 Daz er Iason dar quam
                 Sie was is fro vñ gemeit
                 Ir was vō siner hubisheit
                 Harte vil da vor gesaget
590   Des hette er ir vil wol behaget
                 E sie in ie gesehe
                 Des was ir harte gehe
                 Sie ginc in ein schone gadem
                 Vñ nam ir helfenbeinē ladē
595   Da ir zirde inne was
                 Vñ streichte ir schonē vaz
                 Ir scheiteln sie berichte
                 Die szoppe sie slichte
                 Siden far was ir har
600   Ir ǒgen luter vñ clar

From the *Liet von Troye* by Herbort von Fritzlar, written shortly
after 1210. Only one complete MS, now at Heidelberg, from the
first third of the fourteenth century, written in Hesse, has been

preserved (see the diplomatic reprint by K. Frommann, Quedlin-
burg and Leipzig, 1837, repr. Amsterdam, 1966).

MHG *ie*: usually ⟨ie⟩ with rare ⟨i⟩ and ⟨e⟩ spellings, but before
consonantal clusters regular ⟨i⟩, indicating shortening of the
monophthong, e.g. *dinst, ginc, licht.*

MHG *uo, üe*: ⟨u⟩, rarely ⟨o⟩, e.g. *zo.*

MHG *ei, ou, öu*: usually ⟨ei, ou, eu⟩.

MHG *ī*: ⟨i⟩; *ū* and *iu*: ⟨u⟩.

MHG *ü, ö, œ*: no indication of mutation, ⟨u, o⟩.

MHG *ë, e, ē, ä, æ*: all spelt ⟨e⟩, with rhymes *ēre: wære.*

MHG *a, ā*: generally ⟨a⟩, but before *g* frequently ⟨au⟩, e.g.
klaugen, waugen, NHG *klagen, wagen*; this probably indicates
the widespread dialectal development of *-ag- > -aw-*, e.g.
Waawe NHG *Wagen.*

MHG *i* and *e* are occasionally conflated, e.g. *is* MHG *ez.*

MHG *u* is ⟨o⟩ before *l, r, ch,* e.g. the rhyme *holt: schult*; *gebort*
'birth'; the inverted spelling *wurt* 'word'.

MHG *b, p, pp, pf*: usually ⟨b, p, (pp), ph or pf⟩, e.g. *phile* 'arrows',
kampf 'fight', but *szoppe* NHG *Zöpfe.*

MHG *d, t, g*: ⟨d, t, g⟩.

The orthographic consonantism, as well as the fairly consistent
⟨ie⟩, are powerful indications of the trend towards standardization on the Alem.-EFranc. pattern. In the dialect the shift to *pf*
did not occur, WGmc. *d* remained *d* except in final position, and
medial and final *b* and *g* were probably fricatives, which is indicated by such rhymes as *lobe:houe* NHG *Lobe:Hofe*; *liebe:brefe*
NHG *liebe:Briefe*; *geschah:lach* NHG *geschah:lag*. Non-literary
texts show many of these dialectal features.

MHG *s* and *z*: kept apart fairly regularly.

MHG *hs*: ⟨ss⟩, e.g. *vaz* MHG *fahs* 'hair'.

Verbs *gan, stan,* past tense *quam*; *her* beside *er*; *leren, keren*
with *Rückumlaut* in pret. *larte, karte*; *sal* for UGm. *sol*; the suffix
-schaf not *-schaft*; *otmvtig* for NHG *demütig*; *bit* for UGm. *mit,*
bis 'until'.

(v) *Central Franconian*

Der are gelichit deme heligen Kriste,
wir sin di jungen indeme neste,
di mudir di uns vûdit,
630   dat is sin gnadi di uns hûdit,

dir vadir, di uns minnit
undi inbovin uns swingit –
Moyses sagit uns dat:
'Sicut aquila provocat',
635   dat quid: 'alse der are locke'
    sine jungire zu vlocke,
    also hat unse scepere,
    der himil konic herre,
    sine vlugile gispredit,
640   da mide he uns leidit
    in sinis vadir riche,
    da leth he uns algiliche.

Die vier Schiven by Werner vom Niederrhein from a Hanover MS miscellany written in the thirteenth century (ed. P. F. Ganz, *Geistliche Dichtung des 12. Jahrhunderts*, Berlin, 1960, p. 59).

MHG *ie, uo, üe*: usually ⟨i, u⟩ also ⟨ů⟩; inverted spellings ⟨ie⟩ for lengthened MHG *i* (e.g. *viele*) not infrequent. Lengthening of originally short vowels in open syllables must therefore be assumed.

MHG *ei, ou, öu*: generally ⟨e, u⟩ also ⟨o⟩, occasional ⟨ei⟩, also as inverted spelling.

MHG *ī, ū, iu*: ⟨i, u⟩.

MHG *ü, ö, œ*: usually no indication of mutation. *ü* and *u* are ⟨o⟩ before certain consonants (*son* UGm. *sun* NHG *Sohn*), and *i* and *e* are also sometimes conflated.

MHG *ë, e, ē, ä, æ*: all ⟨e⟩.

MHG *a, ā*: generally ⟨a⟩, but *greve* NHG *Graf*. A feature which is common, above all in Ripuarian, is the use of *i* or *e* to indicate vowel length, e.g. *wair* NHG *wahr*. It is absent in this text.

MHG -*b*-: usually ⟨v⟩, also ⟨b⟩.

MHG -*g*, -*b*: ⟨-ch, -f⟩.

MHG *pf*: ⟨p⟩, i.e. unshifted, in Ripuarian also after *l* and *r*.

MHG *d* and *t* both ⟨d⟩, except in final position where hardening to *t* is general.

MHG *k*-: ⟨k⟩.

MHG *ck* also ⟨ck⟩, *pp* ⟨pp⟩.

Verbs *gan, stan* with 2nd and 3rd pers. sg. pres. ind. *geis, geit* also *deis, deit* of 'to do'; past tense *quam*; *dat, dit* for MHG *daz, diz*; *he* for *er*; *is* for *ist*; *unse* for *unser*. Vowels in unstressed syllables predominantly ⟨i⟩; apocope, such as is general in UGm., has not taken place, e.g. *are, deme, jungiren, vlugile. Sal* for UGm. *sol* 'shall'; often *inde* for 'and', *tusschen* for 'between'.

(vi) East Central German

(for OHG and ENHG versions of the same text see 4.9, 6.4.3 and 6.4.4)

Matthew, 14,23–33

23. Und her liz di schar, her steic uf einen berc alleine zů betene. Abir do iz vesper wart, do was her do alleine. 24. Abir daz schiffelin was mitten in dem mere und wart geworfin von den ůnden, wan der wint was en widerwertic. 25. Und in der virden wache der nacht quam her zů en wandernde uf dem mere. 26. Und si sahin en uf dem mere wandernde und sint betrubit und sprachin: 'Wan iz ist ein getrok' und scrieten vor vorchten. 27. Und zůhant redete mit en Jhesus und sprach: 'Habit getruunge, ich bin iz, vorchtet uch nicht!' 28. Abir Petrus antworte und sprach: 'Herre, bistu iz, so heiz mich zů dir kůmen bobin den wazzeren.' 29. Und her sprach: 'Kům!' und Petrus steic nider von dem schiffeline und wandirte uf den wazzeren, biz daz her queme zů Jhesum. 30. Und her sach einen grozin wint, her vorchte sich und do her begonde zů sinken, do rufte her und sprach: 'Herre, mache mich heil!' 31. Und zůhant reichete Jhesus uz sine hant und begreif en und sprach zů ime: 'Cleines gloubin, warummc zwivcldes du?' 32. Und do her uf gesteic in daz schiffelin, do liz der wint abe. 33. Und di in dem schiffelin waren, di quamen unde anebétten en und sprachin: 'Werlichen, du bist gotes sun!'

From the Gospel translation made for Matthias von Beheim in Halle in 1343, by an unknown translator who claimed: 'Uz der byblien ist dise ubirtragunge in daz mittelste dutsch mit einvaldigen slechtin worten uz gedruckit.' For the reprint of the one MS see: R. Bechstein (ed.), *Des Matthias von Beheim Evangelienbuch in mitteldeutscher Sprache, 1343*, Leipzig, 1867 (repr. Amsterdam, 1966).

MHG *ie, uo, üe*: generally ⟨i, u⟩ with some ⟨ie⟩ and frequent ⟨ů⟩.

MHG *ei, ou, öu*: ⟨ei, ou, eu⟩, sporadic ⟨e⟩, ⟨o⟩ (in ECGm. texts) testify to the dialectal monophthongization.

MHG *ī, ū,* and *iu*: ⟨i⟩ and ⟨u⟩, rarely ⟨ů⟩.

MHG *ü, ö, œ*: no indication of mutation.

MHG *ë, e, ē, ä, æ*: ⟨e⟩.

MHG *a, ā*: ⟨a⟩. Some texts show ⟨o⟩ for *ā*.

MHG *i* is ⟨e⟩ in the pers. pron. *en, eme,* otherwise sporadically in most ECGm. texts. ⟨i⟩ is frequent in unstressed suffixes.

MHG *u* is ⟨o⟩ before certain consonants, especially *r*: *vorhte, worm, begonde* but *vurste, durch, sun.*

There is very little trace of apocope or syncope, cf. *reichete.* The orthographic consonantism of this text is again a testimony to the strength of the south-western, the Alem.-EFranc., tradition. Hardening in final position is also common. Other features include: *lt* > *ld, alden, mb* > *mm*; exact distinction of *s* and *z* with the use of *cz* or *zc* for [ts] to correct the ancient ambiguity of ⟨z, zz⟩; *s* before *l, r, m, n, w* remains; ⟨w⟩ or ⟨h⟩ or zero for UGm. ⟨j⟩ in the *verba pura*; predilection for *Rückumlaut* in verbs; *gen, sten, kumen* – *quam,* the pers. pron. *her* 'he'; the suffix *-lin* in the diminutive; *vregen* for NHG *fragen, greve* for NHG *Graf*; *ich gebe* for UGm. *ich gibe*; *sal* for UGm. *sol.*

(vii) *Middle Low German*

Do de grote könnich Otte sinen ende genam,
sin sone her Otte na eme an dat rike quam.
ein eddel vrouwe was sin moder, Edith genant,
de was, als ek an dem boke wol hebbe bekant,
1695   von vadere to vadere von negen[1] könnigen geboren.
idoch hadde se einen högern vader gekoren:
dat was an er er vil mannichvaldich eddele mot,
de itwelken minschen bat geboren dot,
denne eft[2] dusent könnige ere vedere weren.
1700   Seit,[3] nu is de könnich an den könnichliken eren;
to allerhande dögeden was he bereide genoch,
över de armen barmhertich gemöte he droch,
to einem vadere makede he sek wedewen unde weisen,
vredebrekere dede he vor sinen handen eisen,[4]
1705   unde an godem vrede stunden alle de lant.

[1] nine   [2] if   [3] see   [4] tremble

From Priest Everhart's rhymed chronicle of Gandersheim written in 1216–18 at Gandersheim and preserved in a sole fifteenth-century manuscript copied at Gandersheim (see the edition by L. Wolff, *Die Gandersheimer Reimchronik des Priesters Eberhard,* Halle, 1927).

The editor made slight emendations; in particular he used the diacritic marks to indicate mutation. In the MS superscript *e, o,* or two strokes are applied to originally short vowels to indicate mutation and to long *ō, ū* to indicate vowel length.

Where MHG has *ie, uo, üe* MLG has ⟨e, o⟩, here also ⟨ô⟩.

MHG *ei, ou*: MLG ⟨e, o⟩, or ⟨ei⟩ where WGmc. *ai* was mutated.

MHG *ī, ū, iu* correspond to MLG ⟨i, u⟩, here also ⟨ű⟩.

For MHG *ë, e, ē, ä, æ* MLG has ⟨e⟩. Where the sign stands for short vowels they rhyme. But among the several long vowels expressed by the one graph ⟨e⟩ there are dialectally varying values which do not rhyme.

MHG *a, ā* correspond to MLG ⟨a⟩.

MHG *u, ü* and *i* in open syllables correspond to ⟨o, ô⟩ and ⟨e⟩.

The shifted MHG consonants *z, zz*; *pf, ff, f*; *ch*; *t*; medial and final *b, g* correspond, of course, to unshifted *t, p, k*; *d*; *v, f*; ⟨g⟩ (fricative), *ch*. Hardening in final position is responsible for spellings such as *mot*, MHG *muot*, or *lant* for 'land'.

Among many other features are the verbs *gan, stan* with *geit, steit* in 3rd pers. sg. pres. ind.; *komen – quam*; *hebben* for MHG *hān*; *is* and *sal*; the pronouns *he* and *gi* for UGm. *er* and *ir*.

The Eastphalian dialect of Gandersheim has certain affinities with HG, e.g. *von* for usual MLG *van*, while *t* in *gemöte, Otte* or *der, sagen, ist, han, vrouwe* for LG *vruwe* are HG loans.

After this – limited and much abbreviated – dialectal *tour d'horizon* it must be evident that the phonological and grammatical description of the German language of this period must either be based on the idiolect of one written source or on as many representative idiolects (or their abstractions, the written dialects) as are available, or on the traditional classical Middle High German of our textbooks. The first course would be arbitrary and restrictive, the second limitless and exhaustive, in more than one sense of the word. The third is practicable and acceptable, in so far as the medium is a justifiable and representative abstraction, as has been shown. It is the third course which will be followed.

5.4 | Phonology

5.4.1 | Letters and sounds

In the last chapter orthographic aspects such as convention and innovation, inconsistency and variation – regional and chronological – were to the fore. Now the feature of regularity must be considered. It stands to reason that any workable orthography must also, to a minimum extent, be systematic. In any alphabetic script there must be an acceptable degree of correspondence between the graphemic and the phonemic levels. In Middle High German the graphemic distinctions, corresponding to phonemic distinctions, which were observed were as follows:

(i) *Vowels*

Here the basic degrees of openness or closeness, front or back indicated by the Latin letters ⟨a, e, i, o, u⟩ were distinguished except in regions where a phonemic merger had occurred or where phonetic similarity complicated the task of the scribe. No distinction was made for vowel quantity, although this was undoubtedly phonemic. Two diphthongal graphs were regular: ⟨ei⟩ (regionally ⟨ai⟩) and ⟨ie⟩. It is surely no coincidence that it is these graphs which have survived into the modern language. Other diphthongal values were expressed with a fair degree of regularity by means of diacritics, e.g. ⟨ů, ŏ⟩. Some of the degrees of openness in front vowels, additional to the ones for which the Latin alphabet made provision, were also expressed by means of diacritics, e.g. ⟨å⟩ or by a digraph ⟨æ⟩. But this indication was generally confined to the Bavarian and some Alemannic, mainly eastern and Swabian, areas. Vowel sounds combining the features of rounding and fronting were the least likely to be graphemically represented. Systems nearest to classical MHG tended to employ diacritically marked graphs: ⟨ú, ŏ, ŏi, ů⟩, others left such vowels undistinguished. ⟨iu⟩, a traditional graph representing formerly a diphthong, is also met with as a spelling for a close rounded front vowel. Four signs, ⟨i, j⟩ and ⟨u, v⟩, stood for both vowels and consonants. The distribution of ⟨v⟩ and ⟨u⟩ (or of ⟨j, i⟩) was often used to mark word boundaries: ⟨v⟩ initially and ⟨u⟩ medially.

The MHG graphemic system of vowels was thus characterized by the non-indication of vowel length and the use of diacritical marks for diphthongs and mutated vowels beyond anything that the modern language has adopted. The constructed standard MHG distinguishes vowel length, indicates the rounded front vowels (generally by means of diacritics) and uses diphthongal signs:

short		*long*			*diphthongal*		
i ü	u	ī iu	ū		ie	üe	uo
e (ë)ö	o	ē œ	ō		ei	öu	ou
ä		æ					
a		ā					

The sign ⟨ë⟩ is generally only used in grammars to distinguish the more open *e*-sound from the more close (⟨e⟩), while text editions use ⟨e⟩ for both phonemes and, of course, for the unstressed neutral vowel [ə]. (For the phonetic values of the letters see 5.4.2.)

(ii) *Consonants*

In MHG orthography consonants were regularly distinguished as to place of articulation: ⟨b, d, g⟩, ⟨p, t, k⟩, ⟨l, r, m, n⟩, ⟨s, z, f, ch, sch⟩, but other distinctions such as those of intensity (lenis – fortis), voice or even manner of articulation (plosive – fricative, fricative – affricate) were treated more cavalierly. Thus the labiodental lenis fricative could be spelt ⟨v, u⟩ or ⟨f⟩, the corresponding fortis ⟨f⟩ or ⟨ff⟩, but in word final or preconsonantal position ⟨f⟩ was general, indicating neutralization of the contrast. The signs ⟨z, zz⟩ served for both the dental fricative and the affricate. For the latter ⟨tz⟩ and ⟨cz⟩ and ⟨c⟩ initially, were alternatives. In many manuscripts ⟨h⟩ was used before consonants and ⟨ch⟩ intervocalically and finally for the velar fricative. But both signs could also represent other values: ⟨h⟩ initially and intervocalically the glottal fricative, and ⟨ch⟩ the velar plosive or affricate, alternating with ⟨k⟩ initially and with ⟨ck⟩ or ⟨kh⟩ elsewhere. The *sh*-sound tended to be written historically, i.e. ⟨sc⟩ or ⟨s⟩ according to origin and surroundings, but these graphs competed with the new signs ⟨sch⟩ and ⟨sh⟩.

In word final or syllable final preconsonantal position the signs ⟨p, t, f, c, *or* ch⟩ alternated in many of the best manuscripts with the signs ⟨b, d, v/u, g⟩ in intervocalic position, thus indicating hardening or neutralization, e.g. *wibes – wip* 'woman', *bades – bat* 'bath', *houes – hof* 'court', *dinges – dinc* 'thing'.

While doubling of vowel signs was most uncommon, gemination of consonants was quite usual. This is probably a reflection of Latin spelling habits. Phonologically German demanded both. Nasal and liquid geminates were distinguished from their simple counterparts with a fair degree of regularity, e.g. *sune* 'son' dat. – *sunne* 'sun', *helec* 'secret' – *helle* 'hell', *ar(e)* 'eagle' – *karre* 'cart'. But among fricatives the lenis – fortis geminate distinction ⟨f–ff⟩, ⟨z–zz⟩, ⟨s–ss⟩ or among the dental plosives the fortis–fortis geminate distinction ⟨t–tt⟩ was less regular and was reasonably consistent only in the best manuscripts. After long vowels and diphthongs the fortis geminates were frequently reduced, e.g. *slafen, slaffen* 'to sleep', *groze, grozze* 'big'. Before further consonants and in final position doubling of consonants was unusual in early texts, e.g. *mannes – man* 'man'.

The MHG graphemic system of consonants was thus more responsive to phonetic factors and to position within the word and less systematic than the modern German system. It also expressed consonantal length with some regularity. In NHG, where there are no long consonants, doubling in spelling indicates solely the shortness of the preceding vowel.

Standard MHG utilizes and systematizes these inherent tendencies of the spelling systems of the manuscripts:

	labial		dental		postdental		velar	glottal
plosive	b	p/pp	d	t/tt			g/gg k/ck	
affricate		pf/ph		z²/tz			ch/ck/kh	
fricative	v/f	f/ff¹	z²	z/zz	s	s/ss	h/ch	
						sc/sch/sh		
nasal	m		mm	n	nn		n+g/n+k	
liquid				l	ll	r	rr	
semi-consonants	w					j(g)		h³

¹ Strictly speaking labiodental.

² In initial position ⟨z⟩ was always the affricate [ts], but medially and finally it was ambiguous, e.g. ⟨heizen⟩ NHG *heißen* and *heizen*, ⟨nuz⟩ NHG *Nutzen* and *Nuß*. Some regularized texts use ⟨ʒ, ʒʒ⟩ for the fricative as opposed to ⟨z, zz⟩ for the affricate.

³ Perhaps pharyngeal rather than glottal.

5.4.2 | The stressed vowel system

In OHG a vowel system of twenty-six vowels came into being (Stage VII pp. 163–4), of which no fewer than ten vowels remained in a state of phonemic indeterminacy as long as a contrast of /i/– /a, e, o, u/ in unstressed syllables persisted. This contrast had disappeared by MHG times and with it phonemic indeterminacy had been resolved (see 5.4.3).

In classical MHG three mergers had reduced the number of phonemes to twenty-three:

OHG /ie/ (< *ia*) and /io/   > MHG /ie/
OHG *hier* (*hiar*) *tior*   > MHG *hier*, *tier*
OHG /iü/ and /ū/ and /iu/   > MHG /iu/ [y:]
OHG *hiuti mūsi biutu*   > MHG *liute, miuse, biute*.

Stage VIII, the classical MHG stage, was thus:
(using the conventional orthography, see 5.4.1(i))

/i/	/ü/	/u/	/ī/	/iu/	/ū/	/ie/	/üe/	/uo/
/e/	/ö/	/o/	/ē/	/œ/	/ō/			
/ë/						/ei/	/öu/	/ou/
/ä/	/a/		/æ/	/ā/				

bit	'prayer'	*wīt*	'far'	*liet*	'stanza'
bette	'bed'	*sēr*	'sore'	*kleit*	'dress'
bëte	'request'	*wæte*	'dress'	*güete*	'goodness'
geslähte	'lineage'	*liut*	'people'	*höut*	'(he) hits'
nütze	'useful'	*tœten*	'to kill'	*bluot*	'blood'
götze	'idol'	*trūt*	'dear'	*schout*	'(he) sees'
butte	'rosehip'	*tōt*	'death'		
bote	'messenger'	*tāt*	'deed'		
bat	'bath'				

This system was most probably that of Hartmann von Aue and of his Alemannic contemporaries. In other areas and later in the thirteenth century different systems prevailed. The major divergences and developments affected (i) the *e*-vowels; (ii) the diphthongs /ie, üe, uo/; (iii) the short vowels in open syllables; (iv) the long vowels /ī, iu, ū/; and (v) the rounded front vowels /ü, ö, iu, œ, üe, öu/.

(i) The somewhat overweighted series of three *e*-sounds was nearly everywhere reduced to two (in Upper German) or even one (in later Central German). In Alemannic and early Central

German /ë/ (open) and /ä/ (very open) coalesced and contrasted with /e/ (close), the reflex of the primary *umlaut*. In later Central German these remaining two coalesced as well in a mid [ɛ], but in Alemannic a contrast of a close [e] and a rather open [ɛ] or [æ] or [a] has remained to the present day. A three-way contrast has survived in isolated pockets of Alemannic. In Bavarian /ë/ before most consonants, but notably not before *r*, *l*, *ch*, has merged with /e/. The reflex of the secondary *umlaut* is still sharply distinguished from the close reflex of the earlier coalescence. Upper German dialects have also generally preserved the contrast between the two long *ē*-vowels while Central German has merged them.

(ii) The diphthongs /ie, üe, uo/ prevailed in Upper German and have generally survived in those dialects, except for coalescences owing to unrounding (*üe* > *ie*). But Central German, first East Central German, then also most of East Franconian and Rhenish Franconian, developed long monophthongs as early as the eleventh and twelfth centuries. These new long monophthongs did not coalesce with the old /ī, iu, ū/ and were probably more open. For Central Franconian different reflexes of Gmc. *ē²*, *eo*, and *ō*, the bases of these MHG diphthongs, must be assumed.

(iii) In the northern dialects of MHG short vowels in open syllables were generally lengthened, as in the adjacent Low Saxon and Low Franconian areas. They usually merged with the old long vowels, but in the case of the close vowels with the products of the Central German monophthongization (*siben*, *lieben* = [iː]: *wiben* = [iː]).

(iv) By the end of the thirteenth century the old long /ī, iu, ū/ had become diphthongized in all Bavarian dialects. Orthographic indication of this diphthongization is first found in Carinthian documents which, of course, does not prove that the sound change started in Carinthia. Bilingual scribes first became aware of the discrepancy between the traditional phonetic values of the Latin letters and the phonetic realizations in the relevant words. In the subsequent centuries a similar diphthongization can be noted in Swabian, East Franconian, East Central German and, finally, in the sixteenth century, also in most of West Central German (Rh. Fr. and Moselle Fr.). The extent to which this widespread diphthongization was the result of diffusion remains unknown. Of course, in the written language the phenomenon was overlaid by the growth of standardization and the rise of the NHG standard language. But for the dialectal development it is perhaps safer to reckon with polygenesis, i.e. spontaneous diphthongization in many areas; after all similar diphthongizations are also found in Dutch and English (cf. MHG *wīz, brūn* – NHG *weiß, braun*, E *white, brown*).

The new diphthongs were mostly kept distinct from the reflexes of the old diphthongs /ei, öu, ou/. MHG Bavarian distinguished ⟨ai⟩ (< MHG *ei*) and ⟨ei⟩ (< MHG *ī*), but usually spelt ⟨au⟩ for both MHG *ou* (but also ⟨a⟩) and MHG *ū*, and ⟨eu⟩ for MHG *öu, iu*.

(v) In Bavarian and many other areas of Upper German (e.g. Alsace, Swabia) and Central German the rounded front vowels /ü, iu, ö, œ, üe, öu/ were unrounded to *i, e, ie, ei*, and occasional spellings such as *ibel, glick, vreide* for MHG *übel, glück, vreude*, testify to this widespread phenomenon. But increasing standardization counteracted it in the written language.

There were, of course, numerous other vocalic changes in MHG such as palatalizations (*guot > güet*); rounding of *ā > ō* (*slāfen > slōfen*); labialization of *e > ö* (*vremede > vrömde*); lowering of *i, u > e, o* (*vrum > vrom*); shortening of long vowels before consonantal clusters (*lieht > liht, Licht; brāhte > brahte, brachte*); and so on. Most of these were regionally restricted and in the end of little or only sporadic importance for the further development of the German standard language.

5.4.3 | The unstressed vowels

(i) In classical MHG all unstressed vowels in inflectional or word morphs had become *e*, a 'neutral' central vowel, which was sometimes spelt ⟨i⟩, especially in Central German texts. Cf. OHG *biotan – biutu – biutis – boto*: MHG *bieten – biute – biutest – bote*. One exception was the ending *-iu* of the nom. sg. fem. and nom. acc. pl. n. of the strong declension of adjectives. This was the only OHG diphthongal ending. In Central German, where OHG had *-u*, the ending was *-e*. In Alemannic non-literary texts vowel signs other than ⟨e⟩ indicate that the former long vowels (e.g. *ō, ā*) still had distinct reflexes.

Conditioned loss of this unstressed neutral *-e* through apocope or syncope began in Bavarian and was widespread if not very regular by the thirteenth century. Especially liquids and nasals favoured this development, e.g. OHG *sālida* – MHG *sælde*; OHG *garo* – MHG *gar*; OHG *tiufales* – MHG *tiufels*; OHG *wirsiro* – MHG *wirser*; OHG *anderemo* – MHG *anderme, anderem*. For reasons of morphological interference, rhythm, and divergent regional developments this phenomenon shows a bewildering and motley picture in the various texts. Most widespread are apocope and syncope in former dissyllabics with short stems ending in *-l, -r* or in former polysyllabics with long stems ending in *-el, -er, -em, -en*.

Syncope of *-e-* between like or similar consonants was also frequent, e.g. OHG *tiuriro* – MHG *tiurre*; *rette* for *redete*; *wirt* for *wirdet*; *bœste* for *bœseste*. The prefixes *be-* and *ge-* tended to be reduced before liquids and nasals, e.g. *genuoc* – *gnuoc*; *gelīch* – *glīch*; *belīben* – *blīben*.

On the whole Upper German favoured syncope and apocope while Central German tended to retain unstressed *e*. Towards the end of MHG a new wave of apocope began in Upper German which led to the loss of final *-e* in all other conditions, e.g. *bote* > *bot*; *klage* > *klag*; *schœne* > *schön*. It is usually known as the ENHG apocope (see 6.5.3).

(ii) In derivational suffixes, which had a secondary stress, full vowels were preserved, e.g. *wīgant* 'fighter', *leichære* 'minstrel', *lengelëht* 'longish', *leitlīch* 'painful', *lērunge* 'instruction'. The suffix *-lich* was generally short in Alem. and Rh. Franc. but long (*-līch*) in Bav. (> *-leich*) and EFranc. Variations occurred also in the case of *-in, -īn, -inne* (*künegīn* or *küneginne*), and *-ic, -ec*, where the reflexes of OHG *-ag* and *-ig* had become confused. In the case of *-ære* there were also regional differences: Upper Gm. had *-ære* (< OHG *-āri*), Central Gm. *-er* (< OHG *-eri*) but the distinction was lost in the course of the thirteenth century.

5.4.4 | The consonant system

In classical MHG the OHG consonant system of the Upper German region of the middle of the ninth century was still in existence (see Stage VIII p. 174). It was a complicated system, complicated above all because it was so much dependent upon the position within the word. If anything, positional restrictions had increased by the twelfth century. They did, however, in the end lead to a simplification.

The system of plosives and fricatives rested on a contrast of lenis and fortis oppositions:

Stage IX:

/v/		/s/	/h/	lenis
/ff-f/	/zz-z/	/ss/	/ʃ/	/xx-x/	fortis
/b/	/d/		/g/	lenis
/pp-p/	/t/	/tt/	/kk-k/	fortis
/pf/	/ts/		/kx/	

Examples:

	Initial		*Medial*		*Final*	
/v/	*varen*	'to travel'	*grāve*	'count'	} *hof*	'court'
/ff-f/	—		*schaffen*	'to work'/	*schif*	'ship'
			slāfen	'to sleep'		
/b/	*bin*	'(I) am'	*lībes*	'body' gen.	} *līp*	'body'
/pp-p/	*palas*	'palace'	*rippe*	'rib'/	*schuop*	'scale'
			rūpe	'caterpillar'		
/pf/	*phal*	'pole'	*apfel*	'apple'	*kroph*	'crop'
/s/	*sun*	'son'	*lesen*	'to read'	} *las*	'read'
/ss/	—		*küssen*	'to kiss'	*kus*	'kiss'
/zz-z/	—		*nüzzelin*	'nut' dim./	*nuz*	'nut'
			niezen	'to use'		
/ʃ/	*schif*	'ship'	*eischen*	'to ask'	*visch*	'fish'
/d/	*durch*	'through'	*līden*	'to suffer'	} *leit*	'pain'
/t/	*teil*	'part'	*geriten*	'ridden'	*leit*	'rope'
					(-seil)	
/tt/	—		*bitter*	'bitter'	—	
/ts/	*zwīc*	'twig'	*witze*	'wits'	*schuz*	'protec-tion'
/h/	*hān*	'to have'	*sehen*	'to see'	} *sach*	'saw'
	—		*ma(c)chen*	'to make'/	*dach*	'roof'
			rāche	'revenge'		
/g/	*gar*	'wholly'	*regen*	'rain'	} *lac*	'lay'
/kk-k/	*kar*	'care'	*ecke, egge*	'edge'/	*ruck(e)*	'back'
			sweig(g)en	'to silence'	*rugg(e)*	
/kx/	*kar*	'care'	*seckel*	'purse'	*sac*	'sack'
					sack	

The lenis fricatives had originally been voiceless, but the lenis plosives had been voiced and probably lost the feature of voice when the system had become based on a contrast of length (Stage VI). In OHG the system had come to rest on a contrast of intensity (lenis – fortis) but this was only fully operative in medial and final position in voiced surroundings. The fortis fricatives did not occur initially, which left /f, s, h/ indeterminate as to voice and intensity. In the same position the fortis plosive /p/ only occurred where it had been reintroduced through foreign words and /k/ only regionally, where initial Gmc. *k* had remained unshifted. Velar fortis plosive and affricate were only kept apart in those dialects which had separate reflexes of Gmc. *gg* (> fortis /kk-k/) and Gmc. *k, kk* (> affricate /kx/) (see p. 175 and W. Kleiber in Maurer, *Vorarbeiten*, pp. 207–24). In classical MHG they may be assumed to have coalesced.

In final position the contrast between lenis and fortis was eliminated in late OHG and the spellings ⟨f, s, z, ch (occasionally h), p, t, k (c)⟩ testified to this phenomenon known as *Auslautsverhärtung*, i.e. neutralization in word final and syllable final position with possible semi-fortis realization. It was thus only in medial postvocalic position where the contrast was fully developed, but in such a manner that most fortis consonants had long or geminate allophones after short vowels and short allophones after long vowels or diphthongs. Exceptions existed among the dental fricatives where /zz-z/ had no lenis counterpart except /s/ and where /ss/ had no allophonic distribution analogous to the others but contrasted with /s/ only after short vowels. Here lay undoubtedly the structural reason for the coalescence of /s/ and the allophone *z* and of /ss/ and the allophone *zz* in the thirteenth century, and for the emergence of /ʃ/ from previous *sk* and from initial *s* before consonants, cf. NHG *schön, Stein, springen, schwimmen, schlimm Schnee*, MHG *scœne, stein, springen, swimmen, slim, snē*. Early MHG /s/ and /ss/ were *sh*-type fricatives. Through the losos f /k/ and its reflexes in the cluster /sk/ a new phoneme /ʃ/ arose in contrast with /s/ which through coalescence with /zz-z/ became more *s*-like: *scīn – sīn* > *schīn – sīn*. At what stage this phonemicization occurred is extremely difficult to say, for ⟨sc⟩ remained as an archaic spelling and the new ⟨sch⟩ or ⟨sh⟩ were not unambiguous. Only when these spellings were introduced into position which never had a *k*, e.g. *snē* > *schnē*, can we be certain.

Among the velar fricatives the allophonic distribution of geminate fortis and simple fortis is well attested in some modern South German dialects, although it is not usually in evidence in MHG orthography.

The anomalous contrast /t/ – /tt/ was an early victim of levelling in most areas, but modern Bavarian dialects show clear reflexes, e.g. *bittn* 'to beg' – *grīdn* 'ridden', MHG *bitten – geriten*, NHG *bitten – geritten*.

The lenis fricatives tended to become voiced, e.g. *s* > [z] though probably not in the south; *h* had a subsequent history similar to that of *w* and *j*, and /v/ eventually coalesced with the reflexes of /ff-f/ although again many dialects have kept the ancient distinctions.

Modern South German dialects (HAlem., South Bav.) have retained systems based on a contrast of intensity. Elsewhere in the Upper German and Central German dialects a change of far-reaching consequences led to a restructuring: the so-called *binnenhochdeutsche Konsonantenschwächung*. It implied lenition of all former fortis (incl. geminate) consonants except initial *p-*, *k-* before vowels, and some coalescence with the former lenis consonants. But Bavarian (except South Bav.) former intervocalic geminates (*-pp-*, *-tt-*, *-kk-*, *-ff-*, *-ss-*, *-zz-*) and clusters (*-pf-*, *-ts-*, *-st-*, *-sp-*, *-ks-*, *-ft-*, *-cht-*) remained fortis. In both the western area of consonantal weakening and in Bavarian, coalescence with the former lenis consonants was, however, reduced because they in their turn were in many dialects also subject to weakening, e.g. *-b-*, *-d-*, *-g-* > *-w-*, *-γ-*, *j*, *w-*, *-ð-* or even to complete loss. Homophony was also a small danger since prior lengthening of originally short vowels before lenis consonants (5.4.2 (iii)) had moved differentiation from the consonants to the vowels, e.g. MHG *rīse(n)* 'giants' – *gerizzen* 'torn' > dialectal *rīsen – gerīsen*, NHG *Riesen, gerissen*.

This fundamental sound change was responsible for much of the orthographic wavering in the expression of the manner of articulation among consonants. But in the end the German orthographic consonantal system retained its old-established East Franconian-Alemannic basis and with it a direct link with classical MHG and even OHG in its East Franconian form.

The late MHG system of plosives, affricates and fricatives in the Upper German dialects unaffected by the *binnenhochdeutsche*

Konsonantenschwächung may be assumed to have been: Stage X:

/f/	/s/			lenis
/ff/	/ss/	/ʃ/	/x/	fortis
/b/	/d/		/g/	lenis
/pp/	/tt/		/kk/	fortis
/pf/	/ts/		/kx/	

The lenis sounds were probably voiceless like the fortis. They occurred in all positions (except clusters of fricatives and plosives); with the disappearance of *Auslautsverhärtung* in some areas, perhaps in consequence of the late medieval apocope, also in final position. In the case of the fortis sounds the former allophonic distribution was still valid. (It is not repeated in the above chart, where the fortis sounds are represented by geminates to indicate their length, and the voiceless lenis fricatives by the corresponding single letters.) The fortis fricatives did not occur initially: /ʃ/, and in HAlem. /x/, developed lenis allophones in this position. The affricates were found in all positions, but the fortis velar plosive did not occur initially. The incidence of /d/ was increased through assimilatory weakening of OHG *t* after *n*, and less frequently after *l*, cf. OHG *bintan* – MHG *binden*, OHG *milti* – MHG *milde*, or OHG *haltan* – MHG *halden* and *halten*.

Liquids and nasals also had a contrast of single and geminate in medial position:

/l/	*bole*	'bowl'	/r/	*hēre*	'honour', 'esteem'
/ll/	*bolle*	'bud'	/rr/	*hērre*	'lord'
/m/	*hame*	'cover'	/n/	*hane*	'cockerel'
/mm/	*hamme*	'ham'	/nn/	*henne*	'hen'

Some *mm* were arising through assimilation of former *mb*, e.g. *lammes* < *lambes* 'lamb' gen. And *m* in the unstressed syllable *-em* tended to become *-n*, e.g. *buosem* > *buosen* cf. E *bosom*, Gm. *Busen*.

The semi-vowels, *w*, *j*, and also *h*, were in the process of becoming restricted to initial position:

	/w/			/j/
MHG	NHG		MHG	NHG
wîp	*Weib*		*jār*	*Jahr*
swalwe > *swalbe*	*Schwalbe*		*verje* > *verge*	*Ferge*
houwen > *houen*	*hauen*		*blüejen* > *blüen*, > *blūwen*	*blühen*

/h/

MHG	NHG
hœren	*hören*
schilhen > *schiln*	*schielen*
stahel > *stāl*	*Stahl*

It is perhaps for this reason that it is advisable to regard *h* as a separate phoneme, rather than as an allophone of /x/.

5·5 | Morphology: Inflection

5·5·1 | Noun inflection

The inherited system (see 4.5.1) was profoundly affected by three processes: a) the neutralization (> *e*) of all vowels in inflectional endings; b) the completion of the phonemicization of the vowels resulting from *i*-mutation and the functionalization of mutation; c) the apocope of final -*e* in certain circumstances (see 5.4.3(i)).

Neutralization affected above all the case system. German now had only four inflectional endings: -*e*, -(*e*)*s*, -(*e*)*n*, -*er*, (*e* in brackets means it was subject to syncope). Of these only -(*e*)*s* was a clear case marker: gen. sg. of many masc. and neuter nouns, while -*er* was only a plural marker. Although -(*e*)*n* had many functions, the dat. pl. of all nouns was always marked by -(*e*)*n* without exception. In the plural, case distinction, if it existed at all, centred on the opposition of a common nom. acc. gen. *vs.* a dat. case. There was only one exception to this pattern: the fem. of the IV declensional class (the so-called unmarked pl. class, see below).

Mutation was now a morphological device and, as it happened, it was a plural marker in the case of all three genders (⸚*e* m., f.; ⸚*er* n.) and a case marker in the sg. only with fem. nouns. Retraction on number distinction was one of the changes within the MHG period.

Apocope (OHG *zala* > MHG *zal*) increased the number of nouns with a deficient number distinction (nom. acc. sg. = nom. acc. pl.). While neutralization of the vowels in inflectional endings wrought havoc among the case distinctions and thus enhanced number distinction as the chief inflectional category, apocope had results which were contrary to and in conflict with this general tendency. We thus get in MHG as a temporary and transitory phenomenon a fairly large class with unmarked plural. The later ENHG and Upper Gm. apocope (e.g. MHG *tac – tage* > ENHG *tag – tag*) also temporarily swelled this declensional class. With number distinction as the chief inflectional category it is not surprising that this anomalous declensional class was most subject to fluctuation and change. Moreover, the MHG apocope (and syncope) rules were regional and hardly ever applied with the rigour laid down in normalized classical MHG (see von Kienle §65).

The MHG declensional system was a complex one. In OHG it is possible to predict the declension of a noun on the basis of the two co-ordinates of nom. acc. pl. and gender, e.g. nom. acc. pl. *taga* m., *barn* n., *zalā* f., *slegi* m., *betti* n., *hūti* f. etc., and only relatively few nouns have to be listed lexically as otherwise anomalous, e.g. nom. acc. pl. *hirta* m. (*hirti*, not like *taga – tag*). It is therefore possible to base the OHG declensional system on the plural. This is also advisable for MHG. Many important declensional distinctions are not predictable on the basis of the sg., e.g. m. *tac – tage* but *gast – geste, slite – sliten* but *hirte – hirte*; n. *wort – wort* but *kalp – kelber, herze – herzen* but *bette – bette*; f. *zunge – zungen* but *klage – klage*. Many more alternations are predictable from the plural, but a few are not, e.g. m. pl. *geste – gast* but *erbe – erbe*; f. pl. *krefte – kraft* but *rede – rede*. All neuters, however, are predictable on the basis of the plural. For a strictly synchronic and formal analysis it is therefore advisable to base the declensional classes on the plural.

I. *e-plural*

		M	F	M	F
Pl.	Nom. acc. gen.	-*e*		steine	pflichte
	Dat.		-*en*	steinen	pflichten
Sg.	Nom. acc.	-ø	-ø	stein	pflicht
	Gen.	-*es*	-*e*/-ø	steines	pflicht(e)
	Dat.	-*e*	-*e*/-ø	steine	pflicht(e)

Notes:

(1) Where the root ends in -*w* before the ending, *w* is deleted before zero endings, e.g. *sēwe* – *sē* 'lake'.

(2) Where the root ends in *b, d, g, v* or *h*, these change to *p, t, k(c), f* or *ch* before zero ending, e.g. *tage* – *tac, hove* – *hof, schuohe* – *schuoch*, and geminates are reduced to simple consonants: *stalle* – *stal* 'stable', *stocke* – *stoc* 'stick'.

(3) Beside the pl. *manne* 'men' and *vriunde* 'friends' there was also the pl. *man, vriunt*, otherwise these words followed this declensional class.

(4) Dissyllabic words ending in other than nasal or liquid consonants generally lost their unstressed medial -*e*-, e.g. *dienest* but *dienste*.

(5) In the gen. and dat. sg. f. -*e* and -*ø* may be regarded as free variants.

Historically this declension continued the masc. *a*-stem class and had absorbed some masc. and those fem. *i*- (and *u*-) stem nouns incapable of *i*-mutation, e.g. *scrit* 'step'. Most fem. had a stem ending in -*t*.

II. *Plural with mutation*

		M	F	M	F
Pl.	Nom. acc.	⸚*e*		slege	hiute
	gen.				
	Dat.	⸚*en*		slegen	hiuten
Sg.	Nom. acc.	-*ø*	-*ø*	slac	hūt
	Gen.	-*es*	⸚*e*/-*ø*	slages	hiute/hūt
	Dat.	-*e*	⸚*e*/-*ø*	slage	hiute/hūt

(⸚ indicates mutation)

Notes:

(1) For consonantal alternations see Notes (1) and (2) in I.

(2) Apocope and syncope where applicable (see 5.4.3(i)) produce phonologically determined variants (e.g. *epfel* – *apfel*), which leave the primary distinctive feature of this declension, mutation, untouched.

(3) A number of nouns waver between declension I and II, e.g. pl. m. *satele* – *sätele* 'saddles'.

(4) *Hand* and *naht* usually follow this declension, with occasional anomalous forms (dat. pl. *handen*), so do *vater, bruoder* (gen. sg. often without -*s*) and *muoter, tohter*. In fem. nouns the zero form and ⸚*e* in gen. dat. sg. must be regarded as free variants.

Historically this declension is based on m. and f. *i*-stems where mutation took place.

III. *er-plural*

		N	N
Pl.	Nom. acc. gen.	˜er	kelber
	Dat.	˜ern	kelbern
Sg.	Nom. acc.	-ø	kalp
	Gen.	-es	kalbes
	Dat.	-e	kalbe

Notes:

(1) Some neuters, incapable of showing mutation, e.g. *ei* 'egg', *rint* 'heifer', *rīs* 'twig', are nevertheless unmistakably marked as members of this class by *-er*. In other words, *-er* is the primary marker and mutation is only subsidiary. This is why it is not advisable to regard this class as the neuter variant of the preceding mutation class.

(2) The original stock of about fifteen neuters is gradually increased in the course of the MHG period by the accession of *buoch* 'book', *gras* 'grass', *holz* 'wood', *horn* 'horn', *hūs* 'house', *kint* 'child', *kleit* 'dress', *tuoch* 'cloth' and others, with considerable regional differences.

(3) Texts of a strongly dialectal character tend to have many more *-er-* forms than the works of classical MHG literature.

(4) Some masc. nouns, the earliest being *got* and *geist*, begin to adopt this plural form in the thirteenth century.

Historically this declension derives from the OHG neuter *-ir-* formations and as a stem class from PGmc. *s*-stems.

IV. *The unmarked plural*

		M	N	F	M	N	N	F
Pl.	Nom. acc.	-E	-E	-ø	-E	hirte	bette	wort	sünde
	Gen.	-E	-E	-e	-En	hirte	bette	worte	sünder
	Dat.	-En	-En	-en	-En	hirten	betten	worten	sünder
Sg.	Nom. acc.	-E	-E	-ø	-E	hirte	bette	wort	sünde
	Gen.	-Es	-Es	-es	-E	hirtes	bettes	wortes	sünde
	Dat.	-E	-E	-e	-E	hirte	bette	worte	sünde

Notes:

(1) The capital -E indicates the word final, which characterizes this class of nouns. The lower case letters are the inflectional endings.

(2) Apocope and syncope apply according to the rule set out in 5.4.3(i) and in fact are responsible for the presence of a large number of nouns in

this class, e.g. m. *esel* 'ass', *engel* 'angel', *zügel* 'bridle', *stil* 'stem', *vischer* or *vischære* 'fisherman'; n. *her* 'army', *gewæfen* 'weapon', *spil* 'game', *gewezzer* 'water'; f. *zal* 'number', *nādel* 'needle', *gabel(e)* 'fork', *versen* 'heel'.

(3) For -*w*- in the root see I Note (1).

(4) A number of fem. nouns have the gen. pl. in -*e* according to declensions I and II, e.g. *āventiure* 'adventure', *krōne* 'crown', *ünde* 'wave'. Fem. nouns ending in -*inne* in the pl. have beside -*inne* in the sg. a regional and sometimes free variant in -*īn*, e.g. *künegīn* – *küneginne*.

Historically this declension is made up of former m. and n. *ja*-stems, f. *jō*-stems, f. *i*-stems, and f. *ō*-stems, and neuter *a*-stems, and additional words which were subject to apocope. What unites them all is that certain cases are marked, notably gen. sg. and dat. pl. and that no distinction is made between nom. acc. sg. and nom. acc. pl. It is this distinctive feature, the lack of number distinction, which eventually led to the virtual elimination of this class, cf. NHG *Hirt – Hirten, Bett – Betten, Wort – Worte, Wörter, Sünde – Sünden, Stiel – Stiele, Spiel – Spiele, Zahl – Zahlen, Nadel – Nadeln, Gabel – Gabeln, Höhe – Höhen*, but still *Fischer – Fischer, Gewässer – Gewässer* etc.

It is of course possible, on the basis of complementary distribution, to regard words of the type *stil, spil, tür*, i.e. where apocope occurred, and the n. type *wort*, as variants of declensional class I. However, formal dissimilarity leading to a subsequent different development, makes this inadvisable. Formal similarity is a postulate parallel to that of phonetic similarity in phonology, on the basis of which English [h] and [ŋ] are not assigned to the same phoneme despite the complementary nature of their distribution.

V. *n-plural*

		M	F	N	M	F	N
Pl. Nom. acc. gen. dat.			-*En*		garten	zungen	herzen
	Nom.		-*E*		garte	zunge	herze
Sg.	Acc.	-*En*		-*E*	garten	zungen	herze
	Gen. dat.		-*En*		garten	zungen	herzen

Notes:

(1) All nouns in this declension end in -*e* in the nom. sg., hence -*E*, and have the declensional ending -*n* in the plural. Where apocope or syncope

applies -*E* disappears (except in -*n* after *n*), e.g. m. *van – vanen* 'flag', f. *bir – birn* 'pear'.

(2) There were only four neuters *herze, ouge, ōre, wange*.

(3) Many masc. nouns wavered between I and V, e.g. *helm – helme* 'helmet', *storch – storche* 'stork'.

5.5.2 | Adjective inflection

The MHG adjectival system is formally a direct continuation of the OHG system having been affected only by neutralization of vowels in inflectional endings (except -*iu*) and by apocope and syncope (see 5.4.3(i)). The unmarked form ends either in a consonant as in OHG, e.g. *junc, übel, irdīn, diutsch, gesalbet*, or in -*e*, e.g. *schœne, dünne, swære, nemende* (see 4.5.2). Apocope has produced a small anomalous group ending in -*l* or -*r* after a short vowel or in -*ā*, -*ō*. In the marked forms these adjectives have -*w*- before the endings, e.g. *gel* 'yellow', *kal* 'bald', *gar* 'ready', *var* 'coloured', *blā* 'blue', *grā* 'grey' – *gelwe, blāwe* etc.

The weak paradigm was identical with the *n*-pl. declension of nouns (see 5.5.1 Class V).

The strong paradigm

		M	N	F	M	N	F
Sg.	Nom.	-ø, -er	-ø, -ez	-ø, -iu(-e)	junger	jungez	jungiu
	Acc.	-en	-ø, -ez	-e	jungen	jungez	junge
	Gen.		-es	-er(e)		junges	junger(e)
	Dat.		-em(e)	-er(e)		jungem(e)	junger(e)
Pl.	Nom. acc.	-e	-iu(-e)	-e	junge	jungiu	junge
	Gen.		-er(e)			junger(e)	
	Dat.		-en			jungen	

Notes

(1) For -*ø* read -*e* where lexically required; before endings, this -*e* is dropped.

(2) -*iu* was Upper German with mutation in a few adjectives especially *älliu*; Central German had -*e*.

(3) For the use of zero forms and inflectional forms see 5.7.2(ii).

(4) The forms with bracketed -(*e*), e.g. -*em(e)*, -*er(e)*, were generally realized with -*e* in Central German, while Upper German had apocope.

Adjectives in *-el*, *-er*, *-en*, or *-l*, *-r* after short vowels had also undergone apocope and syncope, i.e. *-e* > *-ø*; *-ez*, *-es*, *-en* > *-z*, *-s*, *-n*; *-eme*, *-ere* > *-me*, *-re*.

Comparison had now only one suffix for each degree: *-er* and *-est*, but the presence or absence of mutation was a reflex of the earlier two distinct suffixes. Most monosyllabic adjectives had mutated forms in the comparative and superlative, but many wavered, e.g. *arm* – *armer/ermer*; *junc* – *junger/jünger*. While in OHG only the weak declension occurred in the second and third degree, MHG had both the strong and the weak declension and applied the same syntactical rules as in the positive.

5·5·3 | Verb inflection

Nearly all the changes from the OHG to the MHG verbal system can be put down to the vowel neutralization in inflectional endings and, to a lesser degree, to apocope.

(i) The basic inherited division into three main classes (dental-suffix type, apophonic type, apophonic dental-suffix type) was maintained, but the subdivisions of the dental-suffix or *weak verbs* were profoundly affected by the vocalic developments. Instead of the four classes, Ia, Ib, II and III of OHG (see 4.5.3) there were three different distinct classes in MHG: class I characterized by the preterite suffix *-te* with vowel alternation between inf., pres. and pret., past part. (*Rückumlaut*); class II characterized by the preterite suffix *-ete* and no vowel alternation; class III with the preterite suffix *-te* and no vowel alternation.

I. *-te with vowel alternation*

Inf. Pres.		Pret.	Past Part.
brennen	'to burn'	*brante*	*gebrennet, gebrant*
sezzen	'to set'	*sazte*	*gesetzet, gesazt*
lœsen	'to loosen'	*lōste*	*gelœset, gelōst*
füllen	'to fill'	*fulte*	*gefüllet, gefult*
füeren	'to lead'	*fuorte*	*gefüeret, gefuort*
liuten	'to sound'	*lūte*	*geliut, gelūt*
denken	'to think'	*dāhte*	*gedāht*

This was a large class and particularly characteristic of MHG. It continued historically the OHG class Ia. In the inf. and pres. these verbs had a vowel resulting from mutation. Some further verbs were attracted to this class, e.g. *liuhten* 'to light' – *lūhte*, *kēren* 'to turn' – *kārte*, more usually *kērte*. In the past part. OHG had an inflected form with *Rückumlaut* and an uninflected form with the mutated vowel of the inf. and pres. This functional distinction was no longer made in MHG and the two forms became free variants, which strongly undermined the functional power of vowel alternation. There were anyway a few important verbs with alternative forms such as *zeln* 'to count' – *zelte/zalte*, *sæjen* 'to sow' – *sæte/sāte*, *retten* 'to save' – *rette/ratte*. There were also consonantal alternations, which being 'irregularities' must have attracted levelling, e.g. *merken* 'to notice' – *marhte* but also *markte*, *merkete*; *hengen* 'to hang' – *hancte*; *decken* 'to cover' – *dahte*, *dakte* – *gedechet/gedaht*; *zücken* 'to pull' – *zuhte*, *zucte*; *würken* 'to effect' – *worhte*.

II. -ete

Inf. Pres.		Pret.	Past Part.
denen	'to stretch'	denete	gedenet
baden	'to bathe'	badete	gebadet
lernen	'to learn'	lernete	gelernet

The MHG class continued the OHG classes Ib, II and III, except where syncope occurred. In conservative areas forms with *o* were still found, e.g. *gemarterot* 'martyred'.

III. -te without vowel alternation

Inf. Pres.		Pret.	Past Part.
nern	'to feed'	nerte	genert
weln	'to choose'	welte	gewelt
schamen	'to be ashamed'	schamte	geschamt
wundern	'to wonder'	wunderte	gewundert
vröuwen	'to rejoice'	vröute	gevröut
gelouben	'to believe'	geloupte	geloupt, geloubet
suochen	'to seek'	suohte	gesuoht, gesuochet
teilen	'to divide'	teilte	geteilt

In this class were found those verbs of the OHG classes Ib, II and III which were subject to syncope in MHG (see 5.4.3(i)). All those formerly belonging to class Ia which owing to the phonetic character of their root vowels did not undergo mutation (*gelouben, suochen, teilen*) must also be considered as belonging to this class.

In OHG the primary feature of class distinction may be deemed to have been the medial vowel in the suffix (pret., p.p.): -ø-, -i-, -ō-, -ē-, with vowel alternation in the root as a subsidiary adjunct. In MHG vowel alternation was undoubtedly the primary class marker. The MHG class III which was thus established (as an unmarked class) was a powerful magnet for the verbs of class II, with syncope operating especially in Upper German with increasing force, e.g. *trūrete > trūrte, lebete > lebte*.

Classification of the Middle High German apophonic verbs

Tradi-tional class	MHG stem grades				
	Inf. pl. pres.	3rd sg. pres.	Sg. pret.	Pl. pret.	P.p.
Ia	*ī*	*ī*	*ei*	*i*	*i*
	trīben	trībet	treip	triben	getriben
b	*ī*	*ī*	*ē*	*i*	*i*
	zīhen	zīhet	zēch	zigen	gezigen
IIa	*ie*	*iu*	*ou*	*u*	*o*
	sliefen	sliufet	slouf	sluffen	gesloffen
b	*ie*	*iu*	*ō*	*u*	*o*
	sieden	siudet	sōt	suten	gesoten
IIIa	*e*	*i*	*a*	*u*	*o*
	werfen	wirfet	warf	wurfen	geworfen
b	*i*	*i*	*a*	*u*	*u*
	spinnen	spinnet	span	spunnen	gespunnen
IV	*e*	*i*	*a*	*ā*	*o*
	steln	stilt	stal	stālen	gestoln
V	*e*	*i*	*a*	*ā*	*e*
	geben	gibet	gap	gāben	gegeben
VI	*a*	*e*	*uo*		*a*
	schaben	schebet	schuop(-ben)		geschaben
VII	*ei/ou/a/ ā/uo/ō*	*ei/öu/e/ æ/üe/œ*	*ie*		*ei/ou/a/ ā/uo/ō*
	loufen	löufet	lief(-en)		geloufen
	(heizen, valten, lāzen, ruofen, stōzen)				

The *strong verbs* (apophonic type) had undergone the characteristic phonological changes from OHG to MHG, but the system itself was unchanged except for a coalescence in class VII in consequence of phonological change. Grammatical change and other OHG anomalies were on the whole maintained, but with regional variation.

The *preterite-presents* (apophonic dental-suffix type) are attested with the usual phonological changes. But there are also strong morphological tendencies of levelling, especially in the preterite, e.g. *wizzen – wiste, weste* (beside older *wisse, wesse*) with a new p.p. *gewist, gewest*, and *muosta* (beside older *muosa*). *Unnan* was replaced by *gunnen/günnen*. Mutated inf. and pres. pl. arose also in the case of *kunnen, durfen, turren, suln, mugen*:*künnen, dürfen, türren, süln, mügen*, and *müezen*. The origin of these mutated forms is not entirely clear, but it seems most likely that the forms of the subjunctive penetrated into the indicative and finally the infinitive. Structurally, though not historically, *wellen* 'to want' belongs here as well.

The monosyllabic verbs *tuon* 'to do', *gān/gēn* 'to go', *stān/stēn* 'to stand', *sīn* 'to be', *lān* 'to let', *hān* 'to have' had an irregular stem formation, although their inflectional endings conformed to those of all other verbs.

The MHG preterite-presents

Inf. (=pl.p.)		1st, 3rd sg. pres.	2nd sg. pres.	Pret.	Past Part.
wizzen		weiz	weist	wisse, wiste (-e-)	gewist, -e- 'to know'
tugen,	-ü-	touc (impers.)		tohte	'it is useful'
gunnen,	-ü-	gan	ganst	gunde	gegunnet(-n) 'to grant'
kunnen,	-ü-	kan	kanst	kunde (-o-)	'can'
durfen,	-ü-	darf	darft	dorfte	'may'
turren,	-ü-	tar	tarst	torste	'to dare'
suln,	-ü-	sol (sal)	solt	solde (-t-)	'shall'
mugen,	-ü-	mac	maht	mahte (-o-)	'can'
müezen		muoz	muost	muose, muoste	'must' 'may'
wellen		wil	wilt	wolde (-t-)	'to want'

(ii) The most important change in the *inflectional endings* was the coalescence of the endings of weak and strong verbs in the *present*. There were two positional variants for both classes and certain vocalic changes in strong verbs. Different allomorphs marked the preterite-presents.

Ind. pret.   Subj. pres.

	I	II		*nemen*	*künnen*	*nemen*
1st sg.	–(e)	–ø	–(e)	nime	kan	neme
2nd sg.	–(e)st	–st	–(e)st	nimest	kanst	nemest
3rd sg.	–(e)t	–ø	–(e)	nimet	kan	nemet
1st pl.	–(e)n	–en	–(e)n	nemen	künnen	nemen
2nd pl.	–(e)t	–et	–(e)t	nemet	künnet	nemet
3rd pl.	–(e)nt	–en	–(e)n	nement	künnen	nemen

Notes:

(1) The allomorphs listed under I apply to strong and weak verbs, those under II to the preterite-presents.

(2) All strong verbs with the root vowel -*e*- in the inf. change it to -*i*- in the sg. ind. (except *heben, schepfen, entseben, swern* of class VI); those with -*ie*- change it to -*iu*-.

(3) Strong verbs with the root vowels -*a*-, -*ā*-, -*ō*-, -*u*-, -*ou*- have the corresponding mutated vowels in the 2nd and 3rd pers. sg. ind., e.g., *graben-grebest, rāten-rætest, stōzen-stœzest, kumen-kümest, loufen-löufest*, but there was a good deal of regional variation and only the mutation of *a* was regular.

(4) The bracketed (*e*) is dropped where apocope and syncope apply, e.g. *steln* 'to steal': *stil, stilst, stil, steln, stelt, stelnt*. These short forms also apply in the case of the monosyllabic verbs, except that in the first pers. sg. ind. most retain the -*n* of the inf. (*hān, lān, stān, gān, tuon*, also *stā, gā, tuo*). In the application of apocope and syncope there is much regional variation and in the south especially both phenomena increase considerably in the course of the MHG period.

(5) The preterite-presents, to which scheme II applies, have the vowel alternation between sg. and pl. ind. listed above. They form the subj. on the basis of the stem form of the pl. (with mutation). Beside the more modern analogical forms *darfst, solst, magst* there were also still the historical forms *darft, solt, maht* and of *wellen* usually *wilt*.

In the *preterite* ind. there were separate paradigms for weak and strong verbs; weak verbs did not distinguish indicative and sub-

junctive. As far as the endings were concerned there was altogether no difference between subj. pres. and subj. pret. In the
case of mutable strong verbs the contrast ind. pret. - subj. pret.
was borne by mutation which had thus become morphemically
relevant. Only the 2nd pers. sg. was an exception: here the contrast still rested with the endings, as had generally been the case
in OHG. Where no mood difference existed it was eventually
reintroduced by means of a periphrastic form (*würde* + inf.). MHG
represents an intermediate stage between OHG (modal distinction
by means of suffixes) and NHG (modal distinction by means of
root variants (*nahmen* – *nähmen*) or periphrastic forms (*würden
nehmen*)).

	Ind. pret.		Subj. pret.			
	I	II	I	I	II	I
1st, 3rd sg.	-ø(P₁)	-(e)t-e	-(e)(P₂)	nam	badete	næme
2nd sg.	-e(P₂)	-(e)t-est	-(e)st(P₂)	næme	badetest	næmest
1st, 3rd pl.	-en(P₂)	-(e)t-en	-(e)n(P₂)	nämen	badeten	næmen
2nd pl.	-et(P₂)	-(e)t-et	-(e)t(P₂)	nämet	badetet	næmet

Notes:

(1) I is the paradigm of the strong verbs, II of the weak.

(2) P_1 means stem form 1 of the pret. P_2 stem form 2 of the pret.

(3) Strong verbs with mutable vowels had mutations in 2nd sg. ind.
and throughout the subj. pret.

(4) The endings -en, -et of the strong paradigm were subject to
syncopation in, for instance, *rirn* – *rīsen* 'to rise', *verlurn* – *verliesen* 'to
lose'.

(5) In the case of weak verbs bracketed (e) refers to the three classes
(see (i) above).

Weak and strong verbs were further distinguished in the 2nd
pers. sg. of the imperative where the former had the ending -e
(*bade!* but *hol!* with apocope) and the latter had no ending and
used the stem form of the 1st pers. sg. pres. ind. (*nim!, biut!, grap!*).

(iii) The *periphrastic forms*, developed in OHG, were all still in
use in MHG. It is a moot point to what extent modality was being
superseded by tense (future) in phrases such as *sol, wil, muoz* plus
infinitive. In many cases a future tense can be discerned and
German was undoubtedly in the process of forming a new peri-

phrastic tense analogous in form to the English future. These modal phrases were not the only means of expressing futurity. The mainly durative aspect of phrases such as *sīn* plus the present participle was paralleled by a mainly inchoative durative consisting of *werden* plus present participle, e.g. *er wirt komende*. It could be used to combine tenses and aspect, e.g. *er wart diende, er wil diende sīn.* It was the phrase *werden* plus present participle that was to point the way to the future tense that we know in modern German. In the fourteenth century there was increasing confusion between the form of the present participle *-ende* and the inflected forms of the infinitive, especially the dative *-enne*. When subsequently the inflected infinitive went more and more out of use the ending *-ende* was reduced to *-en* not only in the infinitive but also in the present participle. In the fifteenth century the periphrastic form of the future thus became *werden + infinitive* which in the thirteenth and fourteenth centuries had been predominantly *werden + present participle*. (See 5.7.3 (ii).)

5.6 | Morphology: Word Formation

5.6.1 | Noun derivation

From OHG to MHG significant changes occurred within the inventory of noun suffixes. Several of the most productive suffixes of OHG had ceased being active, and where they were still found in numerous nouns these tended to become fossils. By being lexicalized such formations passed from morphological derivation to the lexicon. Suffixes of relatively modest functional importance in OHG now became fully productive. Sometimes a lexicalized item of derivation was directly supplemented by a new productive derivation such as in the abstracts *milte* and *miltecheit* 'generosity'. Among the OHG suffixes which had ceased to be productive were *-o* (*nomina agentis*), *-ī*, *-ida* (both fem. abstracts from adj.). In MHG they were *-e*, *-ede* (*-de*) and it is not immaterial that they had been affected most by the process of vowel neutralization. Those which had become increasingly productive were: OHG -*ari*, -*heit* and -*unga*, while -*nissi*, -*scaf* and -*tuom* remained more or less static. There was only one completely new suffix: MHG -*īe*.

(i) *Nomina agentis* now depended on the suffix -*ære*(-*er* in CGm.), e.g. in *Iwein*:[1] *geltære* 'he who pays', *volgære* 'follower', in *Luc. leser* 'reader', *vrager* 'questioner', with *e*-formations as lexicalized remnants, e.g. *wissage* (*Luc.*) 'prophet', *torwarte* (*Iwein*) 'guard'.

(ii) -*inne* and -*īn*: designate females. The former suffix derives from the oblique cases of OHG -*in* and is the basis of modern -*in* (*Köchin*). The lengthened form was a MHG innovation and left no echo. It was less frequent than -*inne*, e.g. *Iwein*: *vriundīn* 'friend', *süenerinne* 'conciliator'. Derivations from masc. *nomina agentis* were particularly frequent.

(iii) -*e*: a large number of such fem. abstracts, originally formed from adjectives, survived in MHG, especially in courtly literature, while prose favoured the competing suffix -*heit* (-*keit*). While in *Iwein* the proportion of -*e* : -*heit* (-*keit*) is $1:1\frac{1}{2}$, in *Lucidarius* it is $1:2\frac{1}{2}$. Among the MHG words we have e.g. *schœne* 'beauty', *süeze* 'sweetness' in *Iwein*, and *ungehorsami* 'disobedience' in *Luc.*

(iv) -*ede* (-*de*): such forms are even more lexicalized than the more numerous -*e* abstracts. A few of the words current in MHG are still in existence today, e.g. *gebærde* 'gesture, behaviour', *gelübde* 'promise' (*Iwein*) or *gemeinde* 'community' (*Luc.*), while others have died out: *erbermede* 'compassion', *gehugede* 'memory', *gescóphede* 'creation' in *Luc.*, and the courtly term *sælde* 'happiness'.

(v) -*nisse* (-*nüsse* especially UGm.): the Upper German courtly poets made hardly any use of such words (*Iwein* has only *vancnüsse* 'imprisonment'), but in ECGm. theological and philosophical writings -*nisse*, mainly fem. but also n., was fairly frequent (Johansson, pp. 125f., Henzen, § 114). In *Luc.* we find *gevancnisse*, *verdampnisse* 'damnation', *vinsternisse* 'darkness'. With derivations from adjectives, nouns, and most frequently from verbs, this suffix is relatively ill defined.

(vi) -*unge*: both in gender and derivation this highly productive suffix is clearly defined (see 4.6.1 (vii)). Poetry made little use of such verbal abstracts: *Iwein* has only *handelunge*, *manunge*,

---

[1] The examples are from *Iwein* (G. F. Benecke, *Wörterbuch zu Hartmanns Iwein*, 3rd ed., Leipzig, 1901) and *Lucidarius* (ed. F. Heidlauf, *Deutsche Texte des Mittelalters*, 28, Berlin, 1915).

samnunge, wandelunge. But in learned prose they proliferated: *Luc.* has two dozen e.g. *verendunge* 'completion', *brechunge des brotes* 'the breaking of the bread'. HG had uniformly *-unge*, LG overwhelmingly *-inge*.

(vii) *ge – e*: the older neuter collective formation is well attested in *Iwein*, e.g. *gebeine* 'bones', *gemiure* 'walls', *gevidere* 'plumage'. An extension of function and meaning came about through derivation from verbs: 'repeated or repetitive action', e.g. in *Luc. gekœse* 'chattering', *getœze* 'noise'.

(viii) *-heit*: from modest beginnings this suffix had become the most prolific in MHG. Derivation from nouns designating human beings was relatively static, c.g. *manheit* 'humanity', *kindheit* 'childhood', but derivation from adjectives, including past participles, increased enormously at the expense of other means current in OHG, e.g. in *Iwein*: *karcheit* 'cunning' (cf. *kerge*), *krancheit* 'weakness' (cf. *krenke*), *swacheit* 'insignificance, disgrace' (cf. *sweche*) or in *Luc. unwissentheit* 'ignorance', *unzergancheit* 'immortality'. A fusion between the adjectival suffix *-ec* and the nominal suffix *-heit* produced the new form *-keit* which was then analogically extended to adjectives without *-ec*, e.g. *heilec* > *heilecheit*, *heilekeit* 'sanctity', *vrum* or *vrümec* > *vrümekeit* 'bravery', *snel* > *snelheit* and *snellikeit* 'quickness'. Especially derivative adjectives in *-lich*, *-bære*, *-sam* came to prefer *-keit*.

(ix) *-schaft*: fem. collectives and abstracts are formed mainly with personal nouns, e.g. in *Iwein*: *genōzschaft* 'company', *künneschaft* 'kinship', *rīterschaft* 'chivalry', *wirtschaft* 'hospitality'. Abstracts in *-heit* generally denote a quality while the much less frequent formations in *-schaft* indicate the state or action connected with the basic word. Although *-scaf* predominated in OHG and *-schaft* in MHG it appears that both forms go back to Germanic antiquity.

(x) *-tuom*: both masc. and neuter abstracts denoting mainly 'status' or 'condition', e.g. in *Luc. wistům* 'wisdom', *richtům* 'riches', *magetům* 'virginity', or *Iwein siechtuom* 'sickness'.

(xi) *-līn*: although diminutives were not very frequent in MHG this suffix was productive, e.g. *Iwein hiuselīn* 'little house', *türlīn* 'little door'. In poetic language we even get diminutives of abstracts, e.g. Walther von der Vogelweide *trœstelīn*, *fröudelīn*. It is likely that the ample use of diminution in Latin had some influence on the spread of diminution in German, mainly imitatively in OHG but productively in MHG. In West Central German texts *-chin* is occasionally found and its LG counterpart *-kīn* occurs in some HG texts in loanwords. The suffix *-el*, e.g. *brüstel* 'little breasts', *röckel* 'small frock' tended to be productive in certain regions.

(xii) *-īe*: the only new suffix in MHG came into the language from medieval Latin, e.g. *abbatia* > *abdīe* 'abbey' and from French in such loanwords as *massenīe* 'company' (*Iwein*) or *fogeteige* (*vogetīe*) 'advocacy' (*Luc.*) and was added mainly to *-er* nouns to denote an activity, e.g. *rouberīe* 'robbery', with considerable extension in subsequent centuries.

(xiii) The infinitive, originating as a verbal noun (*nomen actionis*), could be used as a noun in OHG, but it was in MHG that this characteristic usage of German was first extended, e.g. by the use of attributes before the inf.: (*Iwein*) *ein vehten von zwein sō guoten knehten* 'fighting by two such splendid knights'; *sīn ēwigez clagen* 'his everlasting lamenting'; *diu vreude verkērte sich in ein weinen unde ein clagen* 'joy turned into weeping and lamenting'.

5.6.2 | Adjective derivation

Among the adjective derivations which were no longer productive in MHG are OHG *-al* and *-muoti*. By far the most frequent was still the semantically rather vague *-lich* followed by *-ec*, *-ic*, added mainly to abstract nouns. The latter had resulted from the coalescence of OHG *-ag* and *-ig*, but the presence or absence of mutation remained somewhat arbitrary, e.g. *kreftec* but *zornec*, *nōtec* now *nötig*, *einvaltec* now *einfältig*. Even in OHG the two suffixes were occasionally combined. Now in MHG, *-eclich* became a fashionable device, e.g. *snel* > *snelleclich*, *vol* > *volleclich*. The suffix *-esch*, *-isch* still denoted mainly 'belonging to', e.g. the new word *hövesch* 'courtly, appertaining to courtly society', and *-īn* had the significance 'made of' or 'consisting of', e.g. *marmelīn* 'of marble', *hürnīn* 'of horn'. As a replacement of older adjective *bahuvrīhi* compounds the composite forms *ge – et* and *be – et* played a part but never acquired the importance of *-ed* (e.g. *red-handed*) in English, e.g. *gehendet* 'with hands', *beredet* 'with speech' (NHG *beredt*). Similarly fairly well-defined was *-eht* (a) 'being like', e.g. *eseleht* 'asinine', *gabeleht* 'like a fork', or

(b) 'having' e.g. *büheleht* 'hilly' (< *bühel* 'hill'), *horneht* 'having horns'. Dialectal variants of -*eht* were -*oht*, -*aht*, being archaic forms.

The suffixes -*haft*, -*sam*, -*bære*, -*lōs* were joined by -*var* 'coloured' or 'looking like'; although the adjectives with the latter retained more of the flavour of a compound than the former, except possibly -*lōs*; by the test of frequency all these may together be regarded as productive suffixes. E.g. *angesthaft* 'anxious', *lustsam* 'pleasurable', *vreudebære* 'causing pleasure, joyous', *herzelōs* 'heartless', *ruozvar* 'sooty', 'of the colour of soot', *tōtvar* 'deathly white', *zornvar* 'of an angry look'. While -*haft* was particularly popular with UGm. writers, -*sam* was more frequent in ECGm. It was typical of MHG that adjectives were derived almost exclusively from nouns and not from verbs. The latter practice is modern and has led to the creation of whole new semantic niches, giving great popularity to the former relatively infrequently used suffixes -*haft*, -*bar*, -*sam*, e.g. *wohnhaft*, *eßbar*, *wirksam*.

5.6.3 | Adverb formation

MHG possessed a number of fully lexicalized adverbs such as *hier*, *bī* (also a preposition) or *stætes* 'always', *nahtes* 'at night', *wīlen* 'erstwhile'. The last three derive, like many others, from case forms of adjectives or nouns. As far as adverb derivation was concerned an interesting evolutionary stage had been reached in MHG. There was the inherited formation in OHG -*o*, e.g. *lang – lango* > MHG *lanc – lange*; *kuoni–kuono* > MHG *küene – kuone*. While the overworked -*e* with its extensive declensional role was clearly a feeble device, a kind of *Rückumlaut* had thus also become an adverb-forming means, but only with a limited number of adjectives. The *Rückumlaut* phenomenon was regionally and lexically too restricted to become effective, and only a few lexicalized items have survived, e.g. *fest* (< adj.) – *fast* (< adv.), *schön* (< adj.) – *schon* (< adv.). Another possibility offered itself with the enormously productive suffix -*lich* which had adverbial forms in -*liche* and -*lichen* (*i* long or short). These tended to replace the feeble -*e* suffix: *starc – starke* > *starc – stercliche* (*starcliche*). Although this suffix (-*liche*(*n*)) was particularly favoured in forming adverbs it was hardly less popular for forming adjectives (*sterclich*). Hence while it seemed that German might have acquired an adverb-forming suffix analogous to English -*ly* (*strong* – *strongly*), its continuing popularity with adjectives in the end prevented this from happening.

5.6.4 | Verb derivation

Weak verbs formed from adjectives in -*ec*, -*ic* gave rise to a new verbal suffix: -*igen*, e.g. *ledec* > *ledegen* 'to free', *stætec* (< *stæte*) > *stætigen* beside *stæten* 'to confirm, to fasten' and thus in *Luc.*: *gehuldigen* 'to reconcile, to pay homage', *kriuzigen* 'to crucify' beside *kriuzen*. This is a purely formal development without any semantic implication.

As a new suffix MHG adopted – *ieren* from French, first in loanwords such as *punieren* (< *poignier*), *buhurdieren* (< *behorder*). Since in many cases Old French had -*er* verbs rather than -*ier* verbs, it has been suggested that the Old French agent noun suffix -*ier* was influential as well as the inf. -*ier* in spreading -*ieren* in German.

5.6.5 | Nominal composition

(i) By far the most productive type was noun + noun, overwhelmingly of the determinative kind. The two nouns were usually simple, that is not themselves derivatives or compounds. Compounds of the type *Holzkohlenfeuer* were very rare, e.g. *karfrītag* 'Good Friday'. Prefix nouns as second element were, however, usual, e.g. *hantgetāt* 'creature'; derived nouns as second element were not yet frequent, e.g. *heimsuochunge* 'breaking-in, disturbing the peace', and formations of the type *Unabhängigkeitstag* or *Straßenbahnendstation* did not occur. The most usual type of compound was thus: *hūsherre* 'master of the house', *burcmūre* 'castle wall'. Primary composition, that is composition with the first element in the undeclined form of the stem, predominated. Secondary composition is on the whole only identifiable by the declensional endings -(*e*)*s* or -*en*, e.g. *botenbrōt* 'reward for the messenger', *ougenweide* 'spectacle, a sight to behold', *dunrestac* 'Thursday', but *hungernōt* 'starvation', cf. NHG *Hungersnot*, *seitspil* NHG *Saitenspiel*. It is of course difficult to say to what extent genitive phrases, e.g. *gotes sun* 'God's Son' were compounds, but as the great expansion of the -*s* formations, for instance even with feminines (*Liebesdienst*), did not occur until centuries later, it is advisable to regard most genitive phrases as syntactical groups rather than as compounds. In MHG noun composition was thus still predominantly of the primary composition type.

Adjectives + nouns formed a second, though not extensive, class of nominal compounds, e.g. in *Iwein*: *altherre, armwîp, gâchspîse* (cf. NHG *Schnellimbiß*), *hôchzît, kurzwîle*.

Determinative compounds with adjectives as second element could have either a noun or an adjective as the first element, e.g. in *Iwein*: *kampfwîse* 'experienced in fighting', *spannelanc* 'a span wide', *tôtmager*, cf. colloquial E 'dead thin', *tumpræze* 'foolhardy', *wegemüede* 'tired of the journey'. Poets also coined copulative compounds (known as *dvandva*), e.g. *rôtsüeze* 'red and sweet'.

MHG also still had a number of exocentric adjective compounds or *bahuvrîhis* (see 3.7.5 (ii)), e.g. in *Iwein*: *barmherze* 'compassionate', *barschenkel* 'with bare thighs', *barvuoz* 'barefoot', *einvalt* 'simple' and similar constructions with the prefix *ge-*: *gehaz* 'inimical', *gemuot* 'being of a certain mind', *gezan* 'having teeth'.

(ii) Prefix composition can be said to have become almost as widespread, although not nearly as frequent, with nouns as with verbs where it originated. A few forms are old prefix nouns, especially those in *un-* and those in *ant-, ur-*, and *bî-* where the vowels indicate noun accentuation as opposed to the corresponding verbal prefixes *ent-, er-, be-* resulting from verbal accentuation. *Vor-* is ambiguous as it may be the nominal counterpart of verbal *ver-* or the verbal *vor-* in deverbal nouns. The only really productive, exclusively nominal prefix was *un-* negating nouns and especially adjectives.

Investigations have shown that ECGm. writings extended the use of noun prefixation considerably and showed a vitality which was to enrich the German language permanently. In view of the fact that this extension occurred in the wake of the intensification of the old-established verb prefixation the two constructions will be considered together in the next paragraph.

5.6.6 | Verbal composition

Verbal composition other than prefixation continued to play a marginal role (see 4.6.5), but prefixation was one of the major means of increasing the vocabulary. Theological and philosophical writers especially made ample use of it. Two kinds of particles had evolved in OHG: a group of bound morphemes (prefixes, in the narrow sense of the word) and a much larger group of free morphemes (often called particles; grammatically they were prepositions and adverbs).

Although prefixation was much more frequent and extensive with verbs than with nouns, the following list of prefixes contains parallel examples for nouns as well as verbs, thus demonstrating prefixation as the highly characteristic feature of the German language that it is.

(i) Bound prefix morphemes:

be-	begern	'to desire'	beger	'request'
en-/ent-	engelten	'to pay'	engelt	'costs'
er-	erkennen	'to acknowledge'	erkennunge	'recognition'
ge-	geleiten	'to lead'	geleite	'escort'
ver-	verbergen	'to hide'	verberc	'hiding place'
zer-	zergān	'to part'	zerganc	'dissolution'
un-	unprīsen	'to disgrace'	unprīs	'disgrace'.

In the last case there are a few denominal verbs, in the other cases there are innumerable verbs and a few deverbal nouns and adjectives. *Ge-* was equally frequent with verbs and nominals thus reflecting the fact that it was an ancient verbal and nominal prefix.

(ii) Free prefix morphemes:

abe (ab/ap)	abegān	'to desist'	abeganc	'descent'
after	afterkōsen	'to slander'	afterkōser	'slanderer'
ane (an)	anegān	'to begin'	aneganc	'beginning'
bī	bīgān	'to approach'	bīganc	'digression'
durch	durchgān	'to penetrate'	durchganc	'diarrhoea'
gegen	gegenloufen	'to run towards'	gegenlouf	'running towards'
hin	hingān	'to depart'	hinganc	'departure'
in (inne)	ingān	'to enter'	inganc	'entry'
īn	īnvliezen	'to pour'	īnvluz	'influence'
misse	missegān	'to go wrong'	misserāt	'bad advice'
mite	mitegān	'to follow'	mitegengel	'fellow traveller'
nāch	nāchgān	'to succeed'	nāchganc	'succession'
nider	nidergān	'to decline'	niderganc	'decline'

über	*übergān*	'to cross'	*überganc*	'transition'
ūf	*ūfgān*	'to rise'	*ūfganc*	'rise'
umbe	*umbegān*	'to go around'	*umbeganc*	'round walk'
under	*undergān*	'to go down'	*underganc*	'decline'
ūz	*ūzgān*	'to go out'	*ūzganc*	'exit'
vor	*vorgān*	'to precede'	*vorganc*	'precedence'
vür	*vürgān*	'to precede'	*vürganc*	'introduction'
wider	*widergān*	'to go against'	*widerganc*	'encounter'
zuo	*zuogān*	'to approach'	*zuoganc*	'entry'

Of the above particles *after* was rare with verbs which proves that it was no longer productive. The fairly numerous nouns with this adverb may therefore be regarded as lexicalized rather than as prefix compounds. The demise of *after* in German was thus already clearly foreshadowed in MHG. Choosing mainly the extremely frequent verb *gān* it is possible to demonstrate the parallelism between verbal and nominal prefixation. The predominance of verbal prefixation was however great; with *durch*, for instance, Lexer (*Mittelhochdeutsches Handwörterbuch*, Leipzig, 1872–8) lists over two hundred verbs but only twenty-five nouns and fifty-one adjectives.

5·7 | Syntax

5.7.1 | Sentence structure

On the basis of the position of the finite verb three major clause-types can be distinguished in MHG:

(i) *Initial position* of the finite verb is found in:

(a) Yes-or-no questions: *mugint /sie getûn waz si wellent?* (*Luc.*) 'can they do as they wish?'

(b) Commands and exclamations: *lāt /bœse rede und tuot diu werc* (*Iwein*, 5009) 'abandon evil talk and do what is expected of you'. Particles such as *nu*, *sō* may precede.

(c) Conditional clauses without conjunction: *wil /dū danne niht verzagen* (*Iwein*, 592) 'if you do not want to give up'.

Head position of the finite verb in main clauses, which was still

found in OHG, was no longer current in MHG. The construction
with the grammatical subject *ez* (see below) now permits the verb
to be moved into prominent position.

(ii) *Second position* of the finite verb prevails in:

(a) Independent statements with the subject, an object, an
adverbial complement or a dependent clause in first position:

Subj.   *dise lant alle |ligent| in Europa* (*Luc.*) 'all these countries
        are in Europe'.

        ez|hanget|von eim aste von golde ein becke her abe (*Iwein*, 586)
        'a golden bowl hangs down from a branch'.

Obj.   *den |reichet| der munt von eime oren unz an daz andere* (*Luc.*)
        'the mouths of these (beasts) extend from one ear to the
        other'.

Adver- *Andem wildem berge| springt| der Rin* (*Luc.*) 'the Rhine
bial   rises in the wild mountain'.

Subord. *dō slāfennes zīt wart, |do gedāht| ich an mīne vart* (*Iwein*,
clause   383) 'when it was bedtime I thought of departing'.

Where a subordinate clause precedes a main clause the subordinating conjunction is almost regularly repeated as an anaphoric pronoun or adverb. This is a characteristic feature of MHG. See also:

   so sie sprechin wellint, |so bellent| sie alse die hunde (*Luc.*) 'when
they want to speak they bark like dogs'.

   daz ich sī alle nenne die ich dā erkenne |daz ist| alsō guot vermiten
(*Iwein*, 4709) 'that I should name them all whom I recognize
there, had better be avoided'.

   swar sich ein ouge keret, |dar keret| sich daz ander nach (*Luc.*)
'where one eye turns there turns the other'.

   Reference back to the subordinate clause may also be more
oblique:

   *dō wir mit vreuden gāzen und dā nāch gesāzen und ich im hāte geseit
daz ich nāch aventiure reit |des wundert| in vil sēre* (*Iwein*, 369)
'when we had pleasantly concluded our meal and had settled down
and I had told him that I was in search of adventure he was very
astonished'.

   unz er den schilt vor im treit, |sō ist| er ein sicher man (*Iwein*,
7136) 'as long as he carries his shield before him he will be safe'.

   If however there is no anaphoric particle the main clause follows
paratactically, also of course, with the finite verb in second
position, e.g.

dō daz diu juncvrouwe ersach, /sī zōch/ in wider unde sprach (*Iwein*, 1483) 'when the young lady noticed this she drew him near and said—'.

(b) In independent clauses expressing a wish the finite verb has the subjunctive mood:

got /müez/ iuch bewarn und /gebe/ iu sælde und ēre (*Iwein*, 5530) 'may God protect you and give you happiness and honour'.

(c) In independent clauses after *und* the verb may take up the second position as if *und* was an adverb rather than a co-ordinating conjunction:

so willet sich denne der luft under den nebel, /unde bluwet/ sie der wint zesamene (*Luc.*) 'thus the air mingles with the mist, and the wind blows them together'.

(d) In independent sentences without an introductory conjunction the finite verb is also in second position. Subordination is expressed by the subjunctive in such cases:

er scribet /er/ sehe/ ein wip (*Luc.*) 'he writes that he sees a woman'.

dō zēch mich vrou Minne, /ich/ wære/ kranker sinne (*Iwein*, 3011) 'Lady Minne accused me of being weak in determination'.

mīn vrouwe sol iuch niht erlān /irn/ saget/ iuwer mære (*Iwein*, 226) 'my lady will not release you from telling your story'.

This order is particularly common with the negative particle *ne*.

(e) The finite verb is again in second position in questions introduced by an interrogative pronoun or phrase:

wa von /kument/ die winde? (*Luc.*) 'from where do the winds come?'

weler hande /ist/ der regenbogen? (*Luc*). 'of what kind is the rainbow?'

(iii) *Retarded position* of the finite verb is found in:

(a) Dependent clauses introduced by a subordinating particle. According to the particles one can distinguish four kinds of subordinate clauses: relative clauses, indirect interrogatory clauses, *daz*-clauses, and conjunctional clauses expressing several kinds of relations (temporal, spatial, conditional, modal etc.).

Rel. clause	*nu sulen wir sagen von den inseln /die/ in dem mer /sint/* (*Luc.*) 'now we are going to tell about the islands which are in the sea'.

Apart from the relative pronouns *der, diu, daz* MHG had generalizing pronouns *swer, swaz, swelch, sweder* etc.:

nū hān ich dir vil gar geseit /swes/ dū/ geruochtest/ vrāgen (Iwein,
518) 'now I have told you what you deigned to ask'.

Indirect ichn weiz /wem/ liebe dran /geschach/ (Iwein, 907) 'I do
interr.   not know who felt pleasure'.

clauses und [sī] vrāget in mære /ob/ im iht kunt /wære/ umb in den
          sī dā suochte (Iwein, 5937) 'and she asked him whether
          he knew him for whom she was looking'.

The most important particles were *wer, waz, welch, weder, wā,
war, wannen, wie* and *ob.*

daz-clauses   ŏch die dritte sache waz, /daz/ der tivel von dem
               ubermûte /viel/ (Luc.) 'and the third thing was
               that the devil fell on account of arrogance'.

Conjunctional und vil schiere sach ich komen, /dō/ ich in die burc
clauses   /gienc,/ eine juncvrowen diu mich enpfienc (Iwein,
               312) 'and I soon saw a girl coming to receive me
               when I entered the castle'.
               doch verlant sie die engele niemer /e/ si verteilet /wirt/
               (Luc.) 'yet the angels never leave it (the soul)
               until it has been judged'.

There were a large number of conjunctions, the semantic range
of which has much to do with the difficulty the learner experiences
when reading MHG. In contrast to OHG the causal conjunction
wande, wan 'for, because' was now also subordinating as well as
co-ordinating, perhaps because of confusion with the new conjunction *wan* 'unless, failing that': /wand/ ez an in /was/ verlān,
sō wart ez wol verendet (Iwein, 7717) 'because it was given to them
it was well completed'. In many cases it is impossible to say whether
wande functions as a subordinating conjunction or not, for the
finite verb is in retarded not in final position, e.g. *do was dez
tivels schulde merer dan dez menschen, /wan/ der tivel /viel/ von
sins selbes schulde (Luc.)* 'the devil's guilt was greater than man's
because the devil fell through his own fault'. Retarded position
simply means that more than one element precedes the finite verb.
Final position was not the rule until centuries later, and several
kinds of complements regularly followed the finite verb.

(b) The finite verb is found in final position in the parallel comparative clauses corresponding to E *the – the: sō er ie sērer ranc,*

sō minne ie vaster wider twanc (*Tristan*, 903) 'the more strongly he fought the more powerfully love compelled him'.

(c) In poetic language the finite verb may also occur in final or retarded position in main clauses: *diu vrouwe jæmerlichen sprach* (*Iwein*, 1889) 'the lady spoke full of sorrow'.

5.7.2 | The noun phrase

(i) In the three-way opposition of *definite article – indefinite article – zero article* some significant changes had occurred since OHG. The main function of the definite article had been specification or anaphoric reference back to something already mentioned or generally known. It now indicated primarily something definite as opposed to something indefinite. Its use was therefore much more expanded compared with OHG. After prepositions, in many formulaic expressions, it was, however, still lacking, e.g. *zů himel* 'to heaven', cf. NHG *in den Himmel*.

The MHG version of John, 4, 6–9, in the *Evangelienbuch* translated for Matthias von Beheim in 1343, compared to the version of the OHG *Tatian* (see p. 206) shows some of the changes:

Abir dā was der born Jācobis, und Jhēsus was mūde ūz dem wege und saz alsō ūf dem borne. Abir di stunde was alse sexte. Dō quam ein wīp von Samārien zů schepfine wazzir ... Und sīne jungern wāren inwec gegangen in di stat, daz si spīse kouften. Und darumme sprach zů ime daz wīp jene Samāritāna...

The indefinite article was now used regularly as an indication of indefiniteness. But as *ein* functioned also as an attributive indefinite pronoun ('a certain, some'), as well as being a numeral, MHG usage differed somewhat from modern usage, see for instance: *[er] tranc... eines wazzers* (*Iwein*, 3311) 'he drank some water'; *[daz mer] wirt dicke unde alse ein salz* (*Luc.*) 'the sea becomes thick and like salt'; and in the pl. *zeinen pfingesten* (*Iwein*, 33) 'at some Whitsuntide'; *ein diu schœniste maget* 'a certain most beautiful girl'. Both articles could occur together with the possessive pronoun: *ein mīn wange* 'one of my cheeks'; *die mīne vröude* 'my joy'.

(ii) The use of the *adjectives* confronts us with three problems: the occurrence of the weak and of the strong declensions, and in the latter, inflected *vs.* uninflected forms in the masc. and fem. nom.

sg. and neuter nom./acc. sg. (see 5.5.2). The weak declension contained historically the semantic element of definiteness and the strong declension expressed indefiniteness. Both semantic elements had now more and more been transferred to the definite and indefinite articles so that the adjectival declensions gradually became mere conventions devoid of semantic value in themselves. In MHG, by and large, the unaccompanied attributive adjective and that preceded by the indefinite article had the strong declension, and the adjective following a definite article had the weak forms. But where a possessive adjective preceded or where more than one attributive adjective was involved both kinds of declensions were used. A new principle gradually supplemented or replaced the old principle which was breaking down: the declensional category was to be expressed once and once only by a strong form. The uninflected strong forms frequently infringed this newly emerging principle and thus receded gradually throughout our period although they were still frequent. In *Iwein* we find: *disiu grōze clage* (4011): def. wk.; *ein alsō armiu magt* (4024): indef. str. decl.; *mīn senediu nōt* (4236): poss. adj. str. decl.; *ein alsō vrumer man* (4063): indef. str. decl.; *daz smæhlīche ungemach* (3207): def. wk.; *ir starkez ungemüete* (1601): poss. adj. str. decl.; but also uninflected strong forms: *ein sælic man* (3970); *ein tägelich herzeleit* (4407); *guot rāt* (4629).

The predicative adjective was usually undeclined, but predicative attributes were declined, e.g. *und wær dā tōter gesehn* (6358) 'would have been seen dead'. Attributive adjectives only followed their nouns in poetry, where this position was an archaism. They were usually uninflected, but inflected forms occur as well, e.g. *sehs knappen wætliche* (*Iwein*, 4375).

(iii) In the use of the *nominal cases* MHG differed greatly from the modern language. The genitive, above all, was of great and varied functional importance. Its use after nouns, then as now its most important function, was more extended, e.g. *daz ich des lībes sī ein zage* (*Iwein*, 4913) 'that I was a coward concerning my life'. The genitive of time was also more widespread than now: *dez winters loufet si [die sunne] aller hohist* (*Luc.*) 'in the winter the sun climbs highest'; *des ābents do ich dā reit* (*Iwein*, 787) 'in the evening when I arrived'; *ein burne, der ist dages so calt, daz in nieman vor kelte mac getrinken* (*Luc.*) 'a spring so cold during the day that nobody can drink from it on account of its coldness'.

A large number of verbs governed the genitive, the use of which was in some cases purely syntactical, in others of some semantic significance, for instance as partitive genitive. E.g. *ichn möhte niht geniezen iwers lobes und iuwer vriuntschaft* (*Iwein*, 210) 'I would not wish to have your praise and your friendship'; *doch sol man... mīnes sagennes enbern* (*Iwein*, 217) 'yet they will have to do without my story'; *Wulcanus, der der helle porten phliget* (*Luc.*) 'Vulcan who looks after the gates of hell'; *swel sieche dez burnen getrinket, der wirt gesunt* (*Luc.*) 'whatever sick man drinks from the spring will be cured'; *swez du mich fragist, dez berithe* (=*ht*) *ich dich gerne* (*Luc.*) 'whatever you ask me, I will gladly explain to you'; *ich wil im mīnes brōtes gebn* (*Iwein*, 3301) 'I will give him some of my bread'. The verb *sīn* 'to be' governed the genitive if it expressed 'belonging to' and 'having a certain quality', e.g. *vil juncvrouwen, die ir gesindes wāren* (*Iwein*, 5200) 'many girls belonging to her retinue'; *suueler ist heizer unde nazer nature* (*Luc.*) 'which [star] is of a hot and wet nature'.

The modern language has retained a certain number of such constructions. They are often archaic, poetic or fossilized, e.g. *er ist des Teufels, Vergißmeinnicht*.

A large number of adjectives also governed the genitive, especially where participation or its opposite was implied, e.g. *die insula ist vol fúrez* (*Luc.*) 'the island is full of fire'; *des trōstes wurden sī vrō* (*Iwein*, 4803) 'they were happy with this comfort'; *boum...loubes alsō lære* (*Iwein*, 661) 'a tree completely defoliated'. Characteristically, indefinite and interrogative pronouns such as *iht, niht, ieman, nieman, wer, swer, waz*, also governed the genitive: *iht gelīches* (*Iwein*, 2662) 'something alike'. And numerals: *der strazen sin zwelfe an dem himele* (*Luc.*) 'there are twelve paths across the sky'.

Compared with the genitive with its extensive range in MHG and its greatly reduced role in the modern language, the other cases, notably the accusative and the dative, have changed little in their functions, although both have given ground to prepositional constructions and there have been some changes in the government of individual verbs.

(iv) Among the salient features of the use of the *pronouns* were:
(a) the non-occurrence of the personal pronoun. Although the subject pronoun was now regular, there were residual cases where it did not usually occur, for instance, where the subject had

already been given as a noun or as a pronoun, e.g. *in der insulen stat ein burc heizet Syne (Luc.)* 'on the island there was a castle called Syne'.

(b) With personal names the impersonal *ez* was used as an additional predicate, e.g. *ich bin ez Iwein* (2611) 'I am Iwein'.

(c) The reflexive pronoun *sich* was only accusative. For the dative the personal pronouns were used, e.g. *niene vürhte dir (Iwein,* 516) 'do not be frightened'.

(d) The possessive pronouns *mīn, dīn* etc. were used both as attributive adjectives and as nouns, cf. E *my – mine,* Gm. *mein – der meinige.* E.g. *daz ist dīn site (Iwein,* 137) 'this is your habit'; *alle ir sper: daz sīn behielt aber er (Iwein,* 5321) 'all their spears: but he kept his'.

(e) MHG had two parallel sets of relative pronouns: the more specific *der, diu, daz,* which was basically the demonstrative, and the generalizing *swer* ('whosoever'), *swaz, swelch, sweder,* which had evolved from interrogatives and the particle *sō (swer < sō wer (sō)).*

(f) Among the indefinite pronouns *dehein (kein)* was both negative and positive ('any, no-one'): *daz du den iemer hazzen muost deme dehein ēre geschiht (Iwein,* 141) 'that you always have to hate him whom the world respects'; *des ist zwīvel dehein (Iwein,* 915) 'there is no doubt about it'. The negative *niht* 'nothing' was matched by the positive form *iht* 'something', beside which, with subtle semantic differences, there was *etewaz >* modern *etwas* which in MHG was more definite and concrete than the more indefinite, hypothetical *iht.*

5.7.3 | The verb phrase

(i) The *order of the finite and non-finite parts* of the verbal phrase is in German determined by the so-called principle of incapsulation. According to this principle the non-finite parts have retarded position in the independent clause and the finite part has retarded position in the dependent clause. But how many elements and which elements are actually included in the incapsulation has varied in the history of the language. In MHG incapsulation is more moderate in extent than in the later classical written language. In the independent clause the non-finite parts (infinitive, participles) are rarely separated from the finite verb by more than one or two elements, and adverbial complements are usually placed after the non-finite part, e.g. in *Luc. dem |ist| das houbet |geschafen| nach eines menschen houbet* 'its head is formed in the shape of a human head'; *die | werdent| bede von dem endecriste |erslagen|* 'both are slain by the Antichrist'; *nu |hestu| mir genûc |geseit| von disen dingen* 'now you have told me enough of these things'. In the dependent clause it became the general rule within the MHG period that the finite verbs (*sīn, hān, werden* and the modal auxiliaries) followed the non-finite parts, e.g. in *Luc. daz wir daz ware lieht |enpfangin| hant|* 'that we have received the true light'; *(der mensche), der so groze not |liden|mûz|* 'the man who has to bear such great pain'; *wen so die schuldigen mit rehtem urteile |verdament| werdent|* 'when the guilty are condemned by a fair judgment'. However, examples where the finite verb precedes the non-finite elements are not infrequent and the new order prevailed only gradually and with regional variations. E.g. in *Luc.*: *do die planeten wurden geschafen* 'when the planets were created'; *wen sie zuht niht wolten lernen* 'because they would not learn discipline'.

(ii) The two simple *tense* forms of MHG were generally used in such a way that the present indicated non-past time and the preterite undifferentiated past time. That is, although there were the periphrastic tense forms of the future on the one hand, and of the perfect and pluperfect on the other, these were not employed for a systematic differentiation of either present and future time or completed, incompleted and distant past events. The narrative form for past time was the preterite. It could be supplemented by the verbal forms with the prefix *ge-* to indicate a perfective, resultative action. In many such cases the modern language would employ the pluperfect. In the same way the durative aspect could be expressed by means of *sīn* 'to be' plus the present participle, and the inchoative aspect by means of *werden* 'to become' plus the present participle. The latter form was ultimately to lead to the future tense form of German (see 5.5.3 (iii)). The construction *werden* plus infinitive, generally an expression of the modality of supposition and probability, was also, though not frequently, attested, and may also have contributed to the emergence of the forms of the German future. In MHG these aspectual possibilities were not fully systematized. They remained in the realm of style, that is in the realm of free grammatical choice and finally vanished again from the language or developed into tense forms.

(iii) With regard to the *moods* of MHG two essential facts must be noted. First, the modern periphrastic construction with *würde* did not yet exist, and secondly, the semantic aspect of the moods was more important than later. There was thus greater freedom of use and much more widespread use of the subjunctive than later, when it became more grammaticalized (as mood of indirect speech or of condition). Semantically the subjunctive expressed volition, request, potentiality, irreality, supposition or expectation, and its employment was to a great extent determined by the attitude of the speaker (or writer) towards the action. Within the composite sentence the sequence of tenses was generally observed, although the widespread formal coalescence of the indicative and the subjunctive in MHG (see 5.5.3(ii)) eventually led to changes such as the abandonment of the sequence of tenses where the expression of mood demanded it and the increased use of the modal auxiliaries. A further feature of the use of the subjunctive in MHG was attraction, that is where a main clause had a subjunctive verbal form, this was very frequently repeated in the subordinate clause. Highly characteristic of the MHG use of the subjunctive were further the subordinate negative clauses without conjunction, where *ne*+subj. had the meaning of 'unless, except, if not, without', e.g. *Iwein*, 2829 *sone wart ich nie... des über... /ichn müese/ koufen das korn* 'I was never relieved of having to buy corn'; 1920 *wer wær der sich sō grōz arbeit iemer genæme durch iuch an, /erne wære/ iuwer man?* 'who would take upon himself for your sake such trouble unless he were your husband?' (see also p. 301). After a comparative with *danne* 'than' in a positive main clause, the verb of the subordinate clause was usually in the subjunctive: 536 *sō hāt man mich vür einen man, und wirde werder danne ich sī* 'I shall be regarded as a man and I shall be more worthy'.

(iv) In the field of *voice* an important distinction between English and German gradually developed in OHG and MHG. OHG possessed, in contrast to the North Sea group of Germanic languages, a special reflexive pronoun in the accusative, *sih*. This was increasingly used with transitive verbs to indicate and to distinguish formally a 'middle' voice from the active voice, cf. OHG *Tatian* 211, 4 *Oh ein thero kemphono mit speru sina sita giofanota* 'and one of the soldiers opened [pierced] his side with a spear' (active) – 4, 12 *gioffonota sih thō sliumo sīn mund* 'his mouth opened quickly' (middle voice – reflexive). This category of impersonal reflexives expanded further when in MHG the former formal distinction between inchoative (OHG *-ēn*) and causative verbs (OHG *-en* < *-jan*) had vanished (see pp. 314f). E.g. in MHG *dem glīchet sich daz leben mīn* (Hartmann, 'my life is (made) similar'); *ouch begunde liuhten sich der walt* (Wolfram, *Parzival* 'the forest began to lighten'); *daz mer lit...under der sunnen unde sudet sich tegelich* (*Luc.* 'the sea lies under the sun and boils daily'). Neither the primitive feature of personalization of such impersonal processes nor foreign influence can be successfully adduced to explain the growth of the reflexive verbs in German. Only the desire to distinguish certain features of voice and the ready means of so doing by the use of the reflexive construction, of which the personal-objective form (*er wusch sich /he washed himself*) afforded an ancient model, appears to explain what has become such a characteristic feature of German.

5.7.4 | Negation

In MHG negation consisted typically of a double form: *ne* (*en*, *n*)+*niht. Ne*, or its alternative realizations, was used proclitically immediately before the finite verb, that is fused with the verb, or sometimes enclitically attached to the preceding word, e.g. *Iwein*, 882 *unde /enlac/ niht langer dā* 'and did not lie there longer'; 560 *dā /ne zwīvel/ ich niht an* 'of this I have no doubt'.

The place of *niht* could be taken by other negative adverbs or pronouns, for instance, *nie* 'never', *niemer* 'no more', *dehein* 'no', *nieman* 'nobody' and others, e.g. 1743 *ich/n gewan/ liebern tac /nie/* 'I never experienced a happier day'; 258 *ich/n wil/ iu /keine/ lüge sagen* 'I shall not tell you a lie'. In all such cases the force of negation was borne mainly by the second element and *ne* gradually became redundant and was finally lost in the course of the MHG period. It survived longest in Central Franconian. On the other hand, there were still cases where *ne* could stand alone, in particular before the modal auxiliaries and the verbs *wizzen* and *ruochen*, e.g. in *Iwein*, 7542 *nu/ne mac/ ich anders wan alsō* 'now I cannot (do) otherwise than...'; 127 *ir/ne wizzet/...waz* 'you do not know what'.

Double negation did not make the sentence positive: *Iwein*, 547 *ich/n gehört/.../nie/ selhes /niht/ gesagen* 'I have never heard anything like this'. So-called strengthened negative expressions, combining the negative particle with a noun such as *ein hār* 'a hair', *ein bast* 'bast, something worthless', thrived for a time.

The decline of *ne* as a negative particle was paralleled by the decline of the construction *ne* plus subjunctive in dependent clauses (see p. 308).

5.8 | Lexicon

5.8.1 | The native stock

(i) In the restructuring of the closed part of the vocabulary MHG is very much a transition period between OHG and NHG. In the personal pronouns, for instance, the modern common dat. and acc. pl. *uns* was already established, the older acc. *unsich* having become practically defunct. But in the second person pl. there was much wavering between *iu* (the continuation of the older dat.) and *iuch* (the continuation of the older acc.). Although there was coalescence of the two cases, the establishment of *iuch* (> *euch*) as the common form was not yet achieved. There was also widespread confusion in the case of the *s*-forms, where *sie* and the reduced forms *sī, si* tended gradually to prevail over *siu* (originally fem. nom. sg. and n. nom. acc. pl.). The same was true of the demonstrative and def. article *die* – *diu*. In the masc. gen. sg. of the personal pronoun the older *es* was being ousted by *sīn* in analogy to the gen. of the first and second persons (*mīn, dīn*), in view of the threatening coalescence with the neuter nom. acc. *ez*. The neuter gen. sg. *es* survived longer and is still current in phrases like *ich bin es satt, ich werde es gewahr* (although interpreted as an acc.) where a noun construction is in the genitive (*einer Sache, des Wartens*). The common dat. pl. form *in* gradually acquired the powerful nominal dat. pl. marker -*en* (> *inen*, NHG *ihnen*), first in thirteenth-century Alemannic. The genitive fem. form of the personal pronoun, *ir*, now joined the possessive adjectives and began to be inflected.

Among the indefinite pronouns *sum* is last recorded in MHG, and modern *kein* 'no' or 'not a', gradually takes shape. Earlier *dech* + *ein* 'any' developed forms like *dehein* and *kein* just as *nech* + *ein* 'no-one' or *ne* – *dehein* 'not any' also yielded *kein* in consequence of the demise of the negative particle *ne* (see 5.7.4).

The old numeral *zehenzec* 'hundred' was already rare in MHG and the future belonged to the newer *hundert*.

As far as the stock of strong verbs and preterite-presents is concerned MHG was conservative. The majority of the losses which were to occur belong to later phases of the language. There were something like forty to fifty strong verbs still in existence which were subsequently to die out. Most already showed signs of being rare and probably regional.

Among the open-ended part of the lexicon we again note the relatively high degree of discontinuity among compounds. If we compare for instance the nominal compounds with MHG *hirn* as the first element with those of NHG *Hirn* we get the following lists:

Lexer: *Mittelhochdeutsches Taschenwörterbuch* (33rd ed., Stuttgart 1969)	Mackensen: *Deutsches Wörterbuch* (3rd ed., Laupheim, 1955)
hirn-bein 'Stirnknochen'	Hirnanhang
hirn-bolle 'Hirnschädel'	Hirnbrecher
hirn-gupfe 'Bedeckung des Hirns'	Hirngespinst
hirn-hūbe 'kriegerische Kopfbedeckung'	*Hirnhaube*
hirn-ribe/-rebe 'Hirnschale'	Hirnholz
hirn-schal '*Hirnschale*'	Hirnkappe
hirn-schedel '*Hirnschädel*'	Hirnkasten
hirn-schībe 'Hirnschädel'	Hirnleiste
hirn-schiel 'Hirnschale'	(*Hirnschädel*)
hirn-stal 'Stirn, Schädel'	*Hirnschale*
hirn-suht 'Hirnkrankheit'	Hirnschmalz
hirn-vel 'Hirnhaut'	Hirnspuk
	Hirnwurst

(Corresponding words are italicized. Mackensen has, of course, nothing like a complete list of the modern compounds, cf. Trevor Jones, *Harrap's Standard German and English Dictionary*.)

On the other hand a number of modern compounds do derive formally from MHG formations and reflect the importance they had in the world of chivalry, for instance, *Augenblick* < MHG *ougenblic* 'a glance'; *Augenweide* < MHG *ougenweide* 'a feast for the eyes, a sight'; *Herzeleid* < MHG *herzeleit* 'great pain, injury'; *Hoffart* < MHG *hôchvart* 'pride, arrogance'; *Hochmut* < MHG *hôchmuot* 'pride, self-confidence, high spirits' also *hôher muot*; *Hochzeit* < MHG *hôchzît, hôchgezît* 'ceremony, festivity', e.g. *Iwein* 35 *Ez het der künec Artûs ze Karidôl in sîn hûs zeinen pfingesten geleit...ein alsô schæne hôchzît*; *Kurzweil* < MHG *kurz(e)wîle* 'pastime, entertainment'; *Schwertleite* < MHG *swertleite* 'knighting ceremony'.

In the field of derivation discontinuity is no less marked, as the following lists show (for the OHG forms see p. 215):

Lexer: *Taschenwörterbuch*	Mackensen: *Deutsches Wörterbuch*
trüebe adj.	*trübe*
trüebe noun	—
trüebec adj.	—
trüebekeit noun	—
trüebeclich adj.	—
trüebecliche adv.	—
trüebede noun	—
trüebehaft adj.	—
trüebeheit noun	*Trübheit*
trüebelich adj.	*(betrüblich)*
trüebeliche adv.	—
trüeben verb	*trüben*
trüebenisse noun	*Trübnis*
trüebesal noun	*Trübsal*
trüebesalunge noun	—
trüebesam adj.	—
truobe adv.	—
truoben verb	—
—	trübselig
—	Trübseligkeit
—	Trübung

In the case of simple words as lexical elements it is interesting above all to identify the structural types where the greatest number of losses have occurred.

Among nouns great losses occurred especially in the oldest layers of derivations from ancient verbal roots, e.g. masc. *biet* 'command', *bil* 'barking voice', *bint* 'ribbon', *blāst* 'blowing', *gelinc* 'luck', *glit* 'fall, glide'; fem. *becke* 'bakery, baking', *bediute* 'interpretation', *ber* 'fruit', *bewege* 'movement', *biege* 'inclination', *bāte* 'request', *bræche* 'breaking', *diube* 'theft', *gebe* 'gift', *ger* 'desire', *grift* 'gripping'; n. *bit* 'prayer', *gelach* 'laughter', *heiz* 'command'. Derivations which were no longer productive in MHG but still existed lexicalized, also suffered numerous losses in the subsequent centuries, e.g. fem. *-e* abstracts from adjectives: *arme* 'poverty', *benge* 'fear', *bitter(e)* 'bitterness', *bleiche* 'bleaching', *blenke* 'whiteness', *dünne* 'thinness', *geile* 'exuberance', *genze* 'completeness'. The decline of the alternative abstract formations in *-ede* may have been accelerated by the predominance of the south where it was never as popular as in the northern regions. Among the losses are, for instance: *bewegede* 'movement', *dünnede* 'thinness', *gesehede* 'face, vision', *grimmede* 'grimness', *hæhede* 'height'. *Nomina agentis* in *-e* (see 5.6.1) were still frequent in MHG although they had already greatly diminished in numbers since OHG. Of 118 OHG *-o*-formations paralleled by *-ari*-formations only 36 *-o*-formations were still current in MHG, while 78 *-ari*-formations survived (Weinreich, pp. 175–205; see p. 193). Among the later losses are MHG *becke* 'baker', *bierbriuwe* 'beer-brewer', *gebe* 'giver', *gerwe* 'tanner', *hinke* 'one who limps'. The other old *nomen agentis* formant, MHG *-el*, was equally exposed to erosion, e.g. *bitel* 'wooer', *briuwel* 'brewer'.

Among adjectives there were still many which had the same form as nouns, e.g. *arc* 'evil', *gerwe* 'ready, tanned' and fem. 'preparation, tannery', *glanz* 'bright' and masc. 'brightness', *grim* 'grim' and masc. 'grimness', *ungemach* 'disturbing' and masc. or n. 'disturbance, discomfort', *zorn* 'angry' and masc. 'anger'. It has already been shown that there was a powerful tendency in the German language to separate formally the originally identical Indo-European parts of speech of noun and adjective. Where the forms were still identical in MHG either the noun or the adjective tended to be doomed. Only a few cases still survive in modern German, for instance, *der Gram* and *er ist mir gram*. Existing or developing semantic difference often ensured the survival, e.g. *guot* 'good' and n. noun 'property', NHG *gut*, *das Gut*. Great losses occurred also among the MHG structural type *-e* (former *-ja* stems). It has been shown that of 125 MHG adjectives of this type only 45 survive in modern German (Hotzenköcherle, pp. 324–5). The others either died out or were replaced by newer formations, e.g. *æze* 'edible' > *eßbar*, *bræde* 'fragile', *dræte* 'quick', *heim-lege* > *zu Hause liegend*, *gæbe* 'welcome', but see the idiom *gang und gäbe*, *gelenke* > *gelenkig*. Among the older suffix types which were greatly reduced or altogether eliminated in subsequent centuries were: *-īn*, *-eht*, *-var*, *ge – et*, while *-bære* with many meanings was completely replaced by the new suffix *-bar* with the meaning 'feasible', e.g. *gangbar* 'can be walked on'. The suffix *-īn* was very frequent, e.g. *beinīn* 'of bone', *birkīn* 'of birch-wood', *blüemīn* 'of flowers'; *-eht* and the others were replaced by analytical constructions, e.g. *blesseht* > *mit einer Blesse versehen*, *eseleht* > *eselhaft*, *gabeleht* > *gabelförmig*; *bleich-var* > *bleich von Farbe*, *grīs-var* > *von grauer Farbe*, *grau aussehend*; *geslozzet* > *ein Schloß besitzend*, *gebartet* > *bärtig* cf. E *bearded*, *genaset* > *mit einer Nase versehen*. Examples for the replacement of *-bære* formations are: *herzebære* > *das Herz betreffend*, *im Herzen getragen*, *hovebære* > *dem Hofe angemessen*, *jāmerbære* > *Herzeleid tragend* or *erweckend*, *kampfbære* > *zum Zweikampf tüchtig*.

An example of the restructuring of a word field is afforded by the words for 'big' and 'little' where the MHG surfeit of synonyms, e.g. *michel* and *grōz*, *lützel* and *klein(e)*, was in each case resolved by the concentration on *groß* and *klein*.

Many MHG adverbs were formed on the basis of cases of nouns or adjectives, e.g. *baldes* 'quickly', *drabes* 'at a trot', *gāhes* 'at once', *ēwen* 'eternally', *heimen* 'home'. Very few such forms survived. Nor did the adjective – adverb distinction by means of *-lich/-liche* last (see 5.6.3). An important medieval distinction which later vanished was that between temporal *dō* 'then' and spatial *dā* 'there'. Many synthetic forms gave way to analytical expressions, for instance, *hīnaht* 'tonight', *hiure* 'this year', although *hiute* has survived as *heute*, and the others are found in dialects.

Losses among verbs can also be shown to involve a transition from a more synthetic to a more analytical construction. MHG inherited large numbers of pairs of weak verbs, one of which was inchoative ('becoming') or static ('being') and the other of which was causative ('causing to' or 'making'). These semantic distinctions had originally rested, in the infinitive, on a formal distinction between the suffixes *-ēn* and *-jan* (see 4.5.3). By MHG times this formal distinction had vanished from the ending, both original forms having become -*en*. Where the root allowed mutation the distinction was now borne by a vowel difference in the root, e.g. *kelten* 'to make cold' or 'to chill', *kalten* 'to become cold', *gelwen* 'to become yellow', *gilwen* 'to make yellow'. With large numbers of verbs such root distinction was impossible, e.g. *geilen* 'to be exuberant', 'to become exuberant', and 'to make exuberant'; *rīchen* 'to be', 'to become' or 'to make rich or powerful'. Such polysemy rendered large numbers of verbs indeterminate. Owing to much wavering in the incidence of mutation the number of such indeterminate verbs was further swelled. Mutation, in fact, never became a proper substitute for the former meaning distinction expressed by the suffixes. Hundreds of such verbs subsequently vanished from the language.

A similar semantic distinction existed between strong verbs and derivative weak verbs, e.g. *springen* 'to run' and *sprengen* 'to make run'; *brinnen* 'to be burning' and *brennen* 'to cause to burn'. Although formally some such verb pairs have survived, the semantic connection has generally been broken, for instance, *schwimmen – schwemmen, trinken – tränken, winden – wenden*. German has on the whole preserved a formal distinction between intransitive verbs and transitive verbs but the distinction is now borne by different means, either by prefixation or by syntactic-group constructions. In either case the modern language is both much more explicit, having resolved the MHG ambiguity, and much more analytical than MHG.

MHG also made a semantic or aspectual distinction, ill-defined though it frequently was, between a verb with the prefix *ge-* and the simple verb (see 4.5.3), e.g. *stōzen* 'to push' – *gestōzen* 'to push, to come across'; *rīten* 'to ride on horseback', 'to travel' – *geriten* 'to ride on horseback', 'to travel through'. Where such pairs have survived they have gone separate ways semantically, e.g. *raten – geraten, loben – geloben*. Most have been eliminated.

(ii) In turning to the semantic aspect of the lexicon it has to be remembered that the writings of the thirteenth century present a very much wider spectrum of cultural activities than the documents of former centuries. Not only was the vocabulary of many trades and occupations registered for the first time, literary culture itself had taken a decisive turn. The rich and sophisticated world of medieval chivalry, depicted so splendidly and exuberantly in epic literature and lyric poetry, spreads before us a whole new world of terminology and contents. In most cases the natural polysemy of words led either to the stressing of one particular semantic component of the word or to the extension of the former range of meanings by the addition of new components. Where a word survived it may have retained a particular emphasis given it at that time, or more likely, it may have lost it again and received a new semantic structuring conditioned by later cultural circumstances. The semantic history of only very few words can be given, or rather, be hinted at. As it was the literature of chivalry which achieved lasting merit and was characteristic of the age just as religious writing was the hallmark of the Carolingian era, examples will be drawn from the field of courtly chivalry.

In the second half of the twelfth century the agent noun *rīter* or *rītære* began to designate the mounted warrior serving a noble lord. An alternative form *ritter* arose almost at the same time. As vowel length was normally not indicated in spelling and even the doubling of consonants was far from being consistent, the origin of the form with the short vowel is still in doubt. The assumption that the Middle Dutch or Flemish form *riddere* called MHG *ritter* into being is no longer undisputed and internal German developments may well have led to the alternative form. What is, however, not in dispute is that both forms were filled with the ethical content of French *chevalier*. *Rīter* or *ritter* became the fashionable term for the heavily-armed mounted warrior of the late twelfth and first half of the thirteenth centuries, while the older warrior words like *wīgant*, *degen*, *helt*, *recke* were shunned by the courtly writers of the period. It is interesting to note that *ritter* is attested only four times in the early *Rolandslied* but *helt* 184 times, *degen* (including compounds) 27 times, and *recke* 19 times. In Hartmann's great epics *Erec* and *Iwein* together, *ritter* occurs 217 times, *helt* but 5 times and *degen* only 15 times, of which 11 instances are in the earlier *Erec*. The heroic epics, *Nibelungenlied* and *Kudrun*, combine a liking for *ritter* with a distinct preference for the older terms *helt*, *degen*, and *wīgant* (Bumke, pp. 32–4). Attributes of praise and admiration also changed in a similar way. Words such as *balt*, *biderbe*, *ellenhaft*, *mære*, *snel*, *wæhe*, *wætlich*, *ziere* went out of fashion, while adjectives such as *edel*, *guot*, *küene*, *wert* were viewed with favour.

Adjectives denoting beauty underwent a significant shift between the early works, the great chivalric epics, and finally the post-classical writings. The early epics, the so-called *Spielmannsepen*, favour *hērlich* beside *schœne* and use words like *mære, tiure, lussam, ziere, zierlich*, with *lobesam* in some later *Spielmannsepen*. In the classical phase of chivalry and in *Minnesang, schœne* still ranks as the first adjective of beauty, but *hērlich* is completely shunned by the classical *Minnesingers*, avoided by Wolfram, and used by Hartmann only in *Erec*, his earliest work (3198 of the garments of knights: *ir kleider sint herlich* is the last occurrence). Gottfried used it sparingly, referring to noblemen and things belonging to them exclusively. Adjectives of beauty most characteristic of the classical writers are *lieht* (also *lieht gemal, lieht gevar* in Wolfram), *clār* (especially Wolfram and his imitators), *wünneclich, minneclich, süeze*. In the later heroic epics *hērlich* is again important. In *Kudrun* it is used widely even as an attribute of women, to the exclusion of men. The *Nibelungenlied* affords an example of a blend between the old and the new. In the group of MSS to which B belongs *wætlich* occurs much more frequently than in the group to which C belongs. When referring to women this version prefers *minneclich*, when referring to men *küene*. *Wætlich* is an adjective of the so-called *Spielmannsepen* of the twelfth century. It is not found in Wolfram's *Parzival*. But it is common in *Kudrun*, alongside *minneclich*. The MS group of the Nibelungenlied to which C belongs has a significantly larger occurrence of *minneclich* than the other group, including such phrases as *der minnecliche recke* (241, 3–B: *der wætliche recke*). In late MHG epics, e.g. *Der Rosengarten von Worms*, a whole number of new adjectives denote beauty, for instance *fin, hübsch, lieplich, zart*. When Brünhild and *helden* came to be called *zart*, a different age had indeed arrived.

Perhaps the greatest difficulty which the modern reader of MHG has to contend with is that he recognizes so many lexical items yet is frustrated by their semantic content. To illustrate the semantic restructuring which has affected some of the most usual adjectives some examples are listed on the following page.

All the great ideas of chivalry were expressed by means of established native words, but in most cases we have to reckon with some *semantic borrowing*. The specific chivalric meaning generally derives from French or Provençal. Such is the case, for instance, with *hövisch, hovelich, hovebære, hövescheit* which had all absorbed the meaning of French *courtois* (OF *cortois*), *courtoisie*. That *rīter*

MHG	NHG
bescheiden: sensible, informed, knowing what is befitting	'modest'
bœse: evil, worthless, ignoble, of low social estate	'bad, wicked, angry'
hovelich: befitting the court, courtly, educated	'polite'
hübesch, hövesch: courtly, well-mannered	'pretty'
kleine: neat, fine, delicate, small	'small'
kluoc: fine, elegant, smart	'clever'
kranc: weak, powerless, slight, worthless	'sick'
rīche: powerful, noble, splendid, having plenty	'rich'
swach: worthless, bad, inferior, powerless	'weak'
tump: inexperienced, lacking in understanding, foolish	'stupid'
vrum: skilled, brave, honourable, helpful	'pious, devout'
wert: valuable, worthy, splendid, noble	'worth, deserving'
wīse: learned, experienced, knowledgeable	'wise'

owed its contemporary semantic content to *chevalier* has already been stated. *Süeze* was used of people of sensitive, courtly disposition in imitation of the use of French *doux*. The German words *geselleschaft* and *ingesinde* were given the same significance as the loanwords *massenīe* which derived from OF *masnie, maisnie* and designated the courtly company or household. 'The giving of surety', that is the solemn promise of the defeated knight to serve his victor, was expressed by the German word *sicherheit*, although in many epics of chivalry the loanword *fīanze* is preferred. *Māze*, 'the right measure or proportion', derived its specific chivalric meaning of 'moderation' and 'self-restraint' from Provençal *mezura* or Old French *mesure*. *Vröude* 'joie de vivre', 'gaiety' echoed French *joie* and its opposite *swære* 'sadness, heartache' derived its specific courtly meaning from OF *pesance, grevance*. *Lōn* 'reward' had the same refined meaning as *merci, merce*. *Minne*, an old polysemous word for 'love' with many aspects (*caritas, amor, eros* etc.), was given the component 'courtly love' like OF *amor*, and *vriundinne* the meaning of *amie*, which also occurred as a loanword, *amīe*. The new word *werdekeit* and the older abstracts *werde, wirde* 'excellence, nobility' absorbed the meaning of *valor*. Among the new adjectives denoting beauty was *keiserlich* which was no doubt influenced semantically by OF *emperial* 'splendid, beautiful'. The verb *unēren, geunēren* 'to disgrace' became a characteristic courtly term in imitation of the Old French verb *honnir* (*Honi soit qui mal y pense*); *genāden*, in OHG 'to be merciful', 'to show compassion', now meant also 'to thank' from OF *mercier*, which was borrowed directly by Gottfried von Strassburg (*merzīen*).

A kind of semantic loan, too, is the MHG use of *ir*, the second person plural, as the new form of polite address modelled on French practice.

(iii) *Loan translation* in the widest sense of the word, that is, including loan rendition and loan creation, in order to render foreign concepts by means of native words, is not a particularly highly developed phenomenon in the medieval French-German contact. In lyric poetry it was only the themes of French and Provençal poetry which inspired the German *Minnesingers*. The French epics of chivalry were adapted rather than translated, and adaptation did not require the sort of close patterning of German expressions in imitation of the original foreign terminology which was so characteristic of the German-Latin cultural encounter during OHG times.

Loan translations are, however, *ritterschaft tuon* 'to perform deeds of chivalry' from French *faire chevalerie*; *iuwer genāde* 'thank you' from *vostre merci*; *sunder væl(e)* or *āne væl(e)* 'without fail' from OF *senz faille*, where *væl(e)* itself was a loanword (< *faille*); *kriechisch viur* 'Greek fire' OF < *feu gregeois*; *ein spil teilen* 'to offer two choices' < *partir un jeu* or medieval Latin *partiri iocum*, cf. E *jeopardy* < OF *jeu parti* 'a game in which the chances are equal', i.e. 'a risk'; *mīn her Iwein* (etc.) for Chrétien de Troyes' *mes sire Yvains*; *über mer* 'the Holy Land' < OF *d'outre mer* or Latin *ultra mare*; *mīn līp* 'I', *sīn līp* 'he' etc. were greatly popularized by OF *mon cors* etc., although the phrase may also have been of native origin; *wolgetān* 'beautiful, elegant' < *bien fait*; *grōzmuoter, grōzvater* < OF *grandmere, grandpere*; *perilmuoter* 'mother of pearl' < OF *mere perle* or medieval Latin *mater perlarum*.

In the thirteenth century many Latin terms of scholasticism were rendered into German. Mystics were no less inspired by Latin theological terminology. Large numbers of words in *-ung* were modelled on Latin abstracts in *-tio*, and nouns in *-heit*, *-keit* on Latin *-tas* forms, e.g. *unitas*: *einicheit*; *intellectualitas*: *fornuftikeit*; *temporalitas*: *zītheit*; *imaginatio*: *inbildunge*. Other loan translations are: *īndruc* (*īmpressio*); *īnblic* (*intuitus*); *īnganc* (*introi-*

tus); *învluz* (*influxus*); *zuoval* (*accidentia*); *umbestant* (*circumstantia*); *vürwurf* (*objectum*); *samewizzecheit* (*conscientia*); *wesen* (*esse, ens*). Hundreds of such words were introduced into the German language by scholars, priests and preachers whose first language of learning was after all Latin.

5.8.2 | Borrowed vocabulary

While German never ceased during the Middle Ages to draw on Latin for borrowing words, it was French that was the characteristic foreign source for MHG from the twelfth to the fourteenth centuries. Compared with these two languages others contributed very little loan vocabulary. Towards the end of the period and in the subsequent century, after the sharp decline of French influence, Italian became of some importance. It was the world of commerce and banking that was enriched with Italian words just as formerly the world of chivalry, to a much greater extent, had relied on French. Not only the most fashionable part of narrative literature derived from France, but also material goods, manners of behaviour, and many features of contemporary cultural life came to the Germans from their western neighbours, often through the Low Countries, in particular Flanders, Brabant, and Limburg. Knowledge of French ways and of the French language must have been common, at least in noble households.

(i) *French influence*

It has been estimated by E. Öhmann that, in the twelfth century something like 300, in the thirteenth century about 700, and in the fourteenth century perhaps another 300 French loanwords were imported into German. With the numerous derivations and compounds the total stock of vocabulary derived from French amounted to no less than 2,000 items. Much of this vocabulary was purely literary and remained a decorative element of the epic literature of chivalry. Wolfram and Gottfried, in particular, were given to using foreign words. Such words and many others which were technical terms of chivalric life vanished with the culture to which they belonged. A large number of words, however, became incorporated into the general language and thus permanently enriched German. It is such words which will be quoted.

It is often difficult to decide whether a particular word was of French or medieval Latin origin. Especially in the case of scholarly or learned words, Latin, if not actually the source, exercised an influence. Words which might have been borrowed from French were refashioned by reference to the Latin form. For instance *creatiure* with its *iu* derived from French, but the later and modern word *Kreatur* was influenced by Latin *creatura*. The medieval name for *Beryll* was *berille, barille* from OF *beril, berille*. Later it was replaced by the Latin form. In many cases the subsequent phonological development is proof of the word's continued presence in German, e.g. *Abenteuer* < MHG *āventiure* < OF *aventure*; in other cases one must reckon with later reborrowing. Thus it is doubtful whether modern *galoppieren* uninterruptedly continues MHG *walopieren, galopieren* < OF *waloper, galoper* 'to gallop'. Modern *blond* derives from a seventeenth-century loan from French which replaced the MHG *blunt* < OF *blond*. Some loans from French derive in fact from an eastern, Arabic or Persian, source, but as they reached German from French they testify to French influence, whatever their ultimate source may have been. In the following thematic arrangement the modern word is given first.

Chivalry and its life:

Abenteuer < *āventiure* < OF *aventure* 'strange event, dangerous chivalric undertaking'; *Admiral* < *amiral, admirāt* etc. < OF *amiral, emiral* 'oriental commander or prince', cf. Arabic *Emir*; *Baron*, MHG *barūn* < OF *baron*, reborrowed in the 16th/17th cent.; *Bastard* < *bastart, basthart* < OF *bastard* 'illegitimate child'; *birschen* < *birsen, pirsen* 'to hunt with dogs', 'to track' < OF *berser* 'to shoot an arrow', 'to hunt'; *falsch* < *vals, valsch* 'disloyal, dishonourable' < OF *fals, falske*, probably via Middle Dutch *falsc*; *Fasan* < *fasān, vasant* < OF *faisan*; *fein* < *fīn* < OF *fin* 'fine, tender'; *Firnis* < *virnīs* 'lacquer, varnish' < OF *vernis*; *Koppel* < *koppel, kuppel* < OF *cople, couple* 'leash, dogs leashed together', hence *kuppeln, koppeln*; *Kummer* < *kumber* 'need, distress' < OF *encombrier* 'rubble, load, heavy weight, sorrow', cf. E *encumber*; *Kumpan* < *kumpān, kompān* < OF *compain* 'companion, fellow', in MHG also *kumpānīe*, reborrowed from Italian in the fourteenth and from French in the seventeenth centuries > *Kompanie* in the commercial and military sense; *logieren*, MHG *loschieren* < OF *logier* 'to accommodate, to billet', reborrowed in the 17th cent.; *Palast* < *palas* < OF *palais* 'living quarters in the castle, ceremonial hall'; *Plan* < *plān* 'flat surface, square' < OF *plain*, also

perhaps < Lat. *planum*, also MHG *plānen* 'to smooth', the modern
words *Plan*, *planieren* were reborrowed; *Parlament*, MHG *parlement*
(<OF) 'meeting, disputation', reborrowed with the modern meaning
of 'assembly'; *Preis* < *prīs* 'praise, fame, reward', later > 'price', <
OF *pris*, also MHG *prīsen* 'to praise' > *preisen*; *Prinz* < *prinze* < OF
prince; *prüfen* < *prüeven* 'to consider, to assess, to probe' < OF
prover, *pruef*, *prueve*, attested first in the twelfth century, but earlier
borrowing of Vulgar Latin *provare* (*probare*) cannot be ruled out,
proben, *Probe*, *probieren* are borrowed later directly from Latin *probare*,
proba; *Rotte* < *rot(t)e* 'group, gang', < OF *rote*; *rund* < *runt* < OF
reont, *ront*; *Tafelrunde*, MHG *tavelrunde* < OF *table ronde* 'King
Arthur's round table', resuscitated in the 18th cent.; *Tresor*, MHG
trisor 'treasure' < OF *tresor*, reintroduced in the last century; *Thron* <
trōn < OF *tron*; *Turm* < *turn*, *torn* < OF **torn*, *tournelle*; *Vasall* <
vassal < OF *vassal*.

Warfare and equipment:

Banner < *banier* < OF *baniere*; *Buhurt*, *buhurdieren* < *behurt*,
behurten < OF *behort*, *behorder* 'cavalry game, attack', renewed in the
19th cent.; *Erker* < *erker(e)* < OF *arquiere* 'embrasure'; *fehlen* <
vælen 'to miss the aim with lance or arrow' < OF *faillir* 'to miss';
galoppieren, MHG *walopieren*, *galopieren* < OF *waloper*, *galoper*, perhaps reborrowed from Italian *galoppare*; *Harnisch* < *harnas*, *harnasch*
< OF *harnais* 'armour'; *Hast*, *hasten* < MLG *hast*, Middle Dutch
haast < OF *haste* 'hurry'; *hurtig* < *hurtec*, *hurt(e)* 'attack, thrust',
hurten 'to thrust, to attack' < OF *hurter* 'to dash against', cf. E *to
hurt*, *to hurtle*; *Koller* < *kollier*, *gollier* 'neckpiece of armour' < OF
collier; *Lanze* < *lanze* < OF *lance*; *Panzer* < *pancier* 'breast-plate of
armour' < OF *pancier*; *Platte* < *blate*, *plate* 'breast-plate' < OF
plate, also borrowed from Latin *platta* 'sheet of metal'; *Platz* < *plaz* <
OF *place*; *Sold* < *solt* 'pay for military service' < OF *solde* 'gold
coin, pay', hence *Söldner* < *soldenære*, *soldier*; *Spital* < *spital*, *spitel* <
OF *hospital*, perhaps Latin *hospitale*; *tasten* < *tasten* < OF *taster* 'to
touch'; *Tjost* < *juste*, *justieren* 'to joust' < OF *joste* reintroduced in
modern times; *Turnier* < *turnei*, *tornei*, later *turnier*, cf. *turnieren* <
OF *tornei*, *tournei* 'tournament' < OF *tornier*, *tourn(o)ier* 'to turn, to
ride horses', *turnen* is a 19th-cent. reintroduction of OHG *turnēn* <
Latin *tornare*.

Entertainment:

Fee, MHG *fei* < OF *feie*, *fee*, cf. E *fay*; *Fest* < *fest*, *veste* < OF *feste*;
Flöte < *floite* < OF *flaüte* 'flute'; *-lei* (*mancherlei*, *keinerlei*) < *lei(e)*
'manner' < OF *ley* 'manner'; *Melodie* < *melodīe* < OF *melodie*, added
borrowing of Latin *melodia* is more than likely; *Pinsel* < *bensel*, *pinsel*

< OF *pincel* 'paint-brush'; *Posaune* < *pusūne, busūne* 'trombone' < OF *buisine*; *Reim* < *rīm* < OF *rime*; *Schach* < *schāch* 'chess' < OF *eschac, eschiec* from Persian *shah* 'king', MHG *ch* for OF *c* may result from the analogical correspondence of HG *ch* = Middle Dutch *k*; *Schachmatt* < *schāch unde mat* 'check-mate' from Persian *shah māt* 'the king is dead'; *Schalmei* < *schal(e)mīe* < OF *chalemie* 'shawm'; *Tambour, Tamburin* < *tambūr* 'drum, tamburin' < OF *tabor, tambor*, ultimately from Arabic; *Tanz, tanzen* < *tanz, tanzen* < OF *danse, dancier*. The twelfth-century appearance and the cultural implications suggest this to be a loanword, but it is not impossible that the etymon existed in German (OHG UGm. *tanzōn, Rhenish *danzōn). Such an assumption (see Brosman) would explain the MHG *t-*, and the Rhenish form would yield a satisfactory etymology for OF *dancier*. In that case MHG *tanzen* would be a semantic loan.

Luxury goods:

Alabaster < *alabaster* < OF *alabastre* or Lat. *alabastrum*; *Baldachin*, MHG *baldekīn* 'fine silk of Bagdad' < OF *baldekin, baudequin*, the modern form was later borrowed from Italian *balducchino*; *Brosche*, MHG *brosche* < OF *broche*, the modern word was reborrowed in the 19th cent.; *Ingwer* < *ingeber, ingewer* < OF *gingebre*, of Indian origin; *Korduan(leder)* < *kurdewān, korrūn* < OF *cordouan* 'sheepskin leather from Cordova' cf. E *cordwain, cordwainer*; *Lampe* < *lampe* < OF *lampe*; *Muskat(nuß)* < *muscāt* < OF *muscate*; *Papagei*, MHG *papegān* < OF *papegai*; *Rosine* < *rosīn* < OF *raisin*; *Safran* < *saffrān* < OF *safran* (<Arabic); *Samt* < *samīt* < OF *samit*; *Scharlach* < *scharlach-(en), scharlāt* < OF *escarlate* (cf. E *scarlet*) 'red cloth', adapted to MHG *lachen* 'cloth, sheet', cf. *Laken* (<LG); *Teller* < *teller, telier* < OF *tailleor* or Italian *tagliere* 'chopping-board, plate'; *Zinnober* < *zinober* < OF *cenobre, cinabre*. The names of jewels first entered German at this time. In most cases French may have been the intermediary, but the Latin (Greek) forms were finally to prove decisive, e.g. *Amethyst* but MHG *ametiste* < OF *ametiste*. Only *Karfunkel* < MHG *karbunkel, karfunkel* < OF *carboncle*, seems to have escaped subsequent Latin influence.

(ii) *Middle Dutch influence*

No part of the Empire was more open to French influence than the western Low Countries. Indeed, the county of Flanders belonged to the Kingdom of France. Thus the new civilization of chivalry was first taken up in Flanders and Brabant before it spread to more eastern regions. It was no accident that it was Heinrich von Veldeke from the region of Maastricht, who, as

Gottfried von Strassburg said 'inpfete daz erste ris in tiutischer zungen', that is, first wrote courtly poetry in German. Many new ideas and new words reached Germany through Middle Dutch. The new meaning of *rīter*, and even the form *ritter*, may have been inspired by Middle Dutch *riddere* (but see p. 316). Its opposite concept, expressed by French *vilain*, *vilenie* was infused into Middle Dutch *dorper*, *dorperīe*, *dorperheit* (a semantic loan) and these words were among the earliest German loanwords from Dutch: *dörper*, *dörperīe*, *dörperheit*, *dörperlich*. No attempt was made to render the idea by the native word *dorf* and its derivatives. NHG *Tölpel* is a last reflex of this borrowing. Other words which show Middle Dutch origin in their phonology are *ors* 'horse' (MHG *ros*); *wāpen* 'arms' (MHG *wāfen*) now *Wappen*; and diminutives in *-kīn*, e.g. *kindekīn* – MHG *kindelīn*. To speak Flemish or *vlæmen* counted as being fashionable and this is very skilfully parodied in *Meier Helmbrecht* by Wernher der Gartenære:

717	*'vil liebe soete kindekīn,*
	got lāt' iuch immer sælec sīn.'
764	*'Ey waz sakent ir gebūrekīn*
	und jenez gunērte wīf?
	mīn parit, mīnen klāren līf,
	sol dehein gebūric man
	zwāre nimmer grīpen an.'

Not only the obviously northern dialect forms (*soete* for *süeze*, *kindekīn* for *kindelīn*, *lāt'* for *lāz*, the spurious *sakent* for *sagent*, *gebūrekīn* for *gebiurlīn*, *wīf*, *līf* for *wīp*, *līp*, *grīpen* for *grīfen*) show young Helmbrecht's wish to be taken for a man from the Low Countries. In the choice of words, too, the Flemish fashionable terms stand out, e.g. the use of *soete*, *gunērt*, *parit* related to *Pferd* (for MHG *ros*), and *klār*.

A number of epithets, apart from *klār*, betray their earlier popularity in the north-west, for example *blīde* 'happy', *kluoc* 'elegant', *wert* 'distinguished', *fīn* and *gehiure* 'fine'. Some French loanwords reveal that they passed through Flemish. Many more probably followed the same way without this being linguistically obvious. Among the former are *schach* (see p. 323); *falsch* (see p. 321); *kabel* < OF *chable*, Picardic *cable* via Flanders; *kapūn* < OF *chapon*, Picardic *c-* > Middle Dutch *cap(p)oen*, NHG *Kapaun*; *begīne* 'lay sister' < Middle Dutch *beghīne* < OF *beguine*.

(iii) *Latin influence*

To discover the continuing, powerful stream of Latin loanwords we have to leave the literature of chivalry and turn to the didactic, religious, and scholarly prose writings and the poetry of the Mastersingers. Here we find a whole new class of verbs, those in *-ieren* with a Latin base, for example: *absolvieren, appellieren, clarificieren, compilieren, contemplieren, dispensieren, disputieren, interpretieren, jubilieren, meditieren, ordinieren, polieren, regieren, regulieren, speculieren, studieren, temperieren, visieren, visitieren.* No other foreign influence has ever resulted in the adoption of so many verbs. The earliest German verbs with this suffix are *halbieren* and *hovieren* 'to live a courtly life' or 'to serve at court', now *hofieren* with typical semantic deterioration 'to toady to, to flatter'.

Among the large number of nouns the following may show the Latin impact in the various fields of learning (the words are given in their modern forms):

Absolution, Abstinenz, Advokat, Alaun, Albe, Apotheke, Appellation, Argument, Artikel, Arznei, Astrologie, Astronomie, Baptist, Bulle, Chronik, Dekret, Differenz, Dissonanz, Disziplin, Element, Exempel, Figur, Firmament, Geometrie, Glorie, Glosse, Grad, Grammatik, Gummi, Häresie, Historie, Hostie, Instrument, Jurist, Kapuze, Konfirmation, Konzil, Magnet, Majestät, Materie, Metall, Oktave, Pastor, Patron, Person, Phantasie, Planet, Praktik, Prälat, Privileg, Prophet, Provinz, Prozeß, Pulver, Quinte, Regiment, Register, Sakrament, Sakristei, Salpeter, Senat, Session, Statut, Student, Substanz, Text, Universität, Zirkel.

(iv) *Italian influence*

The supremacy in commerce and banking which Italian, in particular Lombard, cities gained, resulted in an influx of Italian loanwords in the second half of the thirteenth and in the fourteenth centuries. For example: *Barke* < MHG *barke* < It. *barca*, cf. OF *barge*, E *barge*; *Bastei* < It. *bastia* 'bulwark'; *Groschen* < It. *grosso* or Lat. *denarius grossus*; *Golf* probably < It. *golfo*, a Mediterranean nautical term; *Kamel* < MHG *kemel, kamel* < It. *cammello*, or Greek *kámēlos*; *Kapitän*, MHG *kapitān* from OF *capitaine* or It. *capitano*; *Ketzer* < *ketzer* < It. *gazaro*, Lat. *Cathari* 'Cathars'; *Kompaß* < It. *compasso* 'the needle of the compass'; *Lavendel* < *lavendel(e)* < It. *lavendola*; *Pirat* < It. *pirata* (from Greek); *Reis* < *rīs* < It. *riso*, ultimately of Indian origin;

Scharmützel < *scharmutzel, scharmützel* < It. *scaramuza, scara-muccia* 'fight'; *spazieren* < *spacziren* < It. *spaziare* 'to perambulate'; *Spezerei* < *specerīe* < It. *spezieria* 'spices'; *Zucker* < *cuccer, zuccer* < It. *zucchero*, ultimately of Indian origin.

In the fifteenth and sixteenth centuries many more Italian words were added to the few MHG loans.

5.8.3 | Onomastics

(i) The period between the eleventh and the fourteenth centurie brought about two momentous events which had consequences for German *toponyms*. First, internal colonization pushed back the primeval forests everywhere and led to the establishment of settlements in hitherto afforested and usually higher-lying regions. Although most of the urban developments affected already existing places, some new towns were established even in the old territories. Secondly, the eastward expansion across the Elbe and Saale rivers into Slav lands brought with it the absorption of many Slav place-names and necessitated the naming of new foundations.

The forest clearings produced new naming fashions. Name elements referring to clearings are: *-reut, -rode* (LG), from MHG *riute* 'plot of cleared land', *riuten* 'to clear', e.g. *Bayreuth* 'the Bavarian clearing', *Güntersrod, Wernigerode, Rüti* (with Swiss preservation of MHG *iu*); *-schwand, -schwendi* or *-brand* for clearing by fire, e.g. *Altenschwand*; *-hagen, -hain,* related to E *haw(thorn)*, shedged-in compound', e.g. *Falkenhain, Meinerzhagen* (< *Meginhardes-hagen*); *-scheid* 'boundary', especially in western Germany in the Ruhr-Main-Nahe region, e.g. *Remscheid, Lüdenscheid*. Existing nature names now often became habitation names, e.g. those in *-wald, -holt* or *-holz, -horst, -hard, -bach, -ach* (either the river element OHG *-aha* or the collective suffix *-ahi*). Many of the new villages and hamlets in forest clearings lay on unfavourable soil and later became deserted again.

The growth of old-established villages often led to differentiation by means of attributes like *Neu-, Alt-, Ober-, Unter-, Nieder-, Groß-, Klein-*.

Some old naming elements continued to be used, notably *-dorf*, while *-stadt*, as an appellative, underwent the semantic change from former 'place' to the modern meaning 'town'. At the same time *burg* became restricted to the 'fortified stronghold' of a nobleman or *ministerialis*, i.e. the modern *Burg*. The hundreds and thousands of *Burgen* which were built at that time, usually on hilltops, were designated by *-burg* (*Marksburg, Habsburg, Wartburg*), *-stein* (*Rheinstein, Liechtenstein, Falkenstein*), *-fels* (*Stolzenfels, Rheinfels, Drachenfels*) or *-eck*, cf. E *edge*, (*Lahneck, Sooneck*). The new towns were often given a propagandistic boost by names with *Frei-* such as *Freiburg im Breisgau* and *Freiburg im Üchtland* (i.e. *Fribourg* in Switzerland). A fashionable French name was coined by Archbishop Philipp of Cologne for his new foundation A.D. 1182: *Pirremont* 'Peter's Mount', now *Pyrmont*.

Colonization in the east only rarely meant a transfer of an old place-name to the new homeland. The best-known example is *Frankfurt an der Oder* from *Frankfurt am Main*, another is *Kaufungen* (near *Kassel*) which was twice transferred to Upper Saxony and once to Silesia. Also attested are *Aachen, Köln*, and *Niemegk* from *Nijmegen, Tornau* from *Doornik*, carried east by Dutch settlers. On the whole the settlers preferred to coin new names, not with the most characteristic name elements of their old homelands, e.g. *-ingen, -heim, -leben, -büttel, -weiler, -hausen, -hofen*, but with the new, then fashionable and current elements: *-wald(e)*, *-hagen/-hain, -reut/-rode* and above all the perennial *-dorf*, the most widespread name element in the east (*Heinersdorf, Kunersdorf*), occasionally *-stetten*. Hope and satisfaction were expressed in names like *Reichenbach, Schönau, Freiberg* (where silver mining was free or unrestricted), *Neudorf, Neustadt, Neumarkt*. A few regionally restricted clearings names such as *-grün*, (e.g. *Wolfersgrün < Wolframsgrün*, from Upper Palatinate and East Franconia), spread to some new lands (Bohemia, Vogtland). Many natural features were used for forming names, e.g. *-berg, -born/-brunn*, *-feld*, as well as *-bach* and *-au*.

Slavonic names were often retained and the modern map is a fair reflection of original Slavonic settlement. Where German names abound and Slavonic names are absent, the Germans were the first settlers and the land had been uninhabited before they arrived. Slavonic names which were retained are, for instance, *Graz* (Slav. for *Burg*), *Dresden* (< Sorbian 'forest dwellers'), *Leipzig* (< Sorbian 'place of lime trees'), *Lübeck* (< Slav. *ljubu* 'dear'), *Breslau, Chemnitz, Görlitz, Berlin, Rostock, Stettin, Schwerin* etc. The Slavonic languages had a suffix denoting 'the descendants of a man' or 'a group of settlers' analogous to the Germanic *-ing-* suffix: *-ici* or *-ovici*. These as well as the appellative suffix *-ica* are the basis of most of the frequent eastern names in *-itz* (*Löbnitz*). The name *Klagenfurt* is assumed to be a translation of a Slovene word meaning 'ford of the lamenting women'.

As usual, the names of the large rivers were borrowed from the original inhabitants. But as the east which was now being occupied by Germans had been in Slav hands only for something like six hundred years and had been Germanic before the Age of Migrations, many of the large rivers had Slavicized Germanic names, or even earlier names, for instance *Moldau* from *Vltava* < **wilthaahwō* 'wild water', or *Weichsel* from **Wistula* with the same first element as in *Weser*. The present names, of course, derive from Slavonic forms, e.g. also *Drau, Neiße, Drina, Mulde, Netze, Mur, Steyr, Raab, Rabnitz*.

For many foreign places MHG had native words which were later replaced by foreign borrowed names, for example *Pfāt* (*Po*), *Raben* (*Ravenna*), *Berne* (*Verona*), *Antorf* (*Antwerpen*), *Pülle* (*Apulia*), *Waskenwalt* (Gm. *Vogesen*), *Lamparten* (Lombardy, Italy).

(ii) In the field of *personal names* there were two changes of great significance in this period. First, the inherited Germanic system of name-giving finally collapsed and there was a substantial influx of foreign names. Secondly, a two-name system came to supplant the previous one-name system by the gradual introduction of hereditary surnames.

In late OHG times there were many signs of a decline in the inherited system of nomenclature (see pp. 231–3). More and more Germanic names were dying out. There were few new combinations of the old dithematic type and where new combinations were made they often contained such untraditional elements as *-man* and *-wif*. Fewer and fewer names were borne by more and more people. Among the special favourites were: *Friedrich, Heinrich, Hermann, Konrad, Ludwig, Otto, Ulrich, Wilhelm, Adelheid, Gertrud, Hedwig, Mathilde*, but with considerable local variation. There were far more short forms, or at least far more short forms were now recorded, that is, were used for more formal occasions. A name tended to be abbreviated in many different ways, e.g. *Dietrich* > *Dieto, Dietel, Dieteken, Dietze, Dietzmann, Dirk, Thilo, Tileko, Tymme*, again with much local variation. In

the area of Magdeburg the dithematic name *Conrad* was recorded
105 times in the thirteenth century and the short form *Cone* only
nine times, but in the fourteenth century the relation was *Cone*
(106) – *Conrad* (76) (A. Bach, I. §304).

This impoverished and now largely unmotivated system of
nomenclature began to be increasingly supplemented in the
thirteenth century by an influx of saints' names. The cult of saints
had received a powerful impulse by ecclesiastical movements
since the late twelfth century. The new mendicant orders had
brought saints' names to everybody's attention. The saints'
calendar gained more and more importance. Pilgrimages to saints'
shrines were a feature of the time. While a vital native system of
nomenclature had left little room for foreign Biblical names in
Carolingian times, saints' names now provided a new motivation
and meaning to name-giving. They did not enrich the stock of
names greatly, for only relatively few were first absorbed, for
example, *Johannes* (< John the Baptist, mainly), *Nicolaus, Petrus,
Martinus, Georgius, Gregorius, Michaelis, Antonius, Augustinus.*
Nor did they affect the current typology of naming. They were
soon Germanized and they, too, were shortened, e.g. *Nicolaus >
Nicol, Nikel* or *Claus*; *Andreas > Drees*; *Antonius > Toni,
Tönnies, Dönges*; *Johannes > John, Jan, Hannes, Hans*; *Michaelis >
Michel*. Again there were distinct regional differences. On the
whole, women's saints' names were even more popular than men's
and among the favourites were: *Agnes, Catherina, Elisabeth, Mar-
garetha, Sophia.*

The new nomenclature was not confined to Germany. It was a
common European phenomenon which spread through the German territories from the west and south, that is the regions border-
ing the Romance countries, towards the east and north. The city
patricians were the first to take to the new fashion. Among peasants and artisans in the west foreign names were not particularly
frequent before the end of the thirteenth century. On the whole,
the east and the north lagged a century behind the west. In twelfth-
century Cologne, by far the largest city in Germany, 14 per cent
of all names were of foreign origin. In Berne the proportion of
native to foreign names was seven to one in 1200, but one to two
in 1375, which clearly shows the swing in MHG. But an overwhelming predominance of the names of foreign origin was only
reached in the fifteenth and sixteenth centuries (in Berne twelve

to one in 1550). In fourteenth-century Dresden, forty-nine city councillors had a native name and fifty-nine a foreign name. Among those who had a foreign saint's name, 30·5 per cent were called *Johannes*, 23·7 per cent *Nikolaus* and 15·2 per cent *Petrus* (see Fleischer).

Some native names benefited from being saints' names and retained their popularity, for example *Albert, Bernhard, Erhard, Heinrich, Konrad, Oswald,* and *Wolfgang.* There appears to have been no official direction in the choice of names at that time, and the new nomenclature was an expression of a genuine feeling prevalent at that period. It was not until the Council of Trent (1545–63) that the Roman Catholic Church required the use of saints' names.

The advent of hereditary surnames falls in the same centuries and was concurrent with the introduction of saints' names. The first step was the increased use of a *cognomen.* Patronymics and nicknames were used in Germanic antiquity and in OHG times, whenever closer identification was required: *Hiltibrant Heribrantes sunu, Guntchramnus Boso, Charles the Bald.* But they did not become usual before the twelfth century. Again there was considerable local variation. In Cologne only 18 per cent of recorded names had a *cognomen* in 1150, but by 1250 already 70–90 per cent appeared in this form. In Strasbourg all personal names were accompanied by a *cognomen* or surname by the end of the thirteenth century and in Vienna no name was without a second element after 1288. But in Frankfurt am Main 34 per cent of all recorded names were still single names as late as 1351, and in the east, in Lübeck and Rostock, *cognomina* or surnames were not yet firmly established in the fourteenth century. In other words, a two-name system first appeared in the large western cities at the beginning of the twelfth century and was more or less completed in all major areas by the end of the fourteenth and the beginning of the fifteenth centuries. As with the saints' names, there was a clear pattern of diffusion from the west and the south to the east and the north. Some areas, notably Friesland, were extremely conservative and in these, surnames did not become usual till the eighteenth century, by that time normally by official action. Everywhere peasants and servile persons lagged behind other classes. The lead was given by the nobility of the south-west, to whose personal names the names of their forts or fiefs, made hereditary in the middle of the eleventh century, were generally attached: A.D. 1141 *Wernherus comes de Habisburc*; A.D. 1189 *Hermannus comes de Froburg*; *Gotefrit de Eptingen*, probably a knight. The example of the nobility was soon followed by the class of the *ministeriales*, the unfree knights, and then by the burghers. One of the earliest such names may be A.D. 1004 *Wolferat de Alshusa*, where *Alshusin* remained in the family over the next few generations.

There are three questions which demand investigation. First, where did this new system originate? Secondly, why did it spread at that time? Thirdly, how were these new surnames formed?

The pattern of dissemination from the vicinity of Romance-speaking countries suggests that, as with the saints' names, Romance practice must have been exemplary. In Italian cities *cognomina* and surnames are known from as early as the eighth century. Provence and France followed. The new feudal nobility must have found hereditary local designations useful in their claims to hereditary fiefs. The great expansion of cities and the increase in population, expanding commerce and travel, the establishment of literate city administrations with record-keeping – all this, coupled with a diminishingly effective naming system, called for more detailed designation and appellation. *Cognomina* and nicknames had long been in existence. They now increased substantially. But a *cognomen* is not a surname or family name. It is given to one individual and may change within the lifetime of that individual. A surname is hereditary and no longer motivated or meaningful. If John or Hereward is named 'baker' or '*pistor*' because he is a baker, he has a *cognomen*. He may later be styled 'pastrycook', when he changes his trade. But if he is called 'Baker' even if he is a butcher, we know that 'Baker' is a surname and no longer a *cognomen*; see, for instance, *Chûnradus dictus Murer sutor*, i.e. 'Conrad, called Mason, a shoemaker'. Medieval evidence is often exceedingly difficult to interpret. Expressions such as *dictus, cognomento, cognomine, dicitur* or in German *ze nanamen geheizen, geheizzen, der da heizzet, genant* generally indicate the existence of a hereditary surname but the absence of such phrases does not prove the contrary. We can only really be sure if a name cannot possibly be an indication of the place from which the bearer comes, of an occupation the bearer actually has, or of a quality that characterizes him in reality. Proof that a name is passed on from generation to generation is also conclusive evidence that we have a genuine surname and not just a *cognomen* or an ad hoc designation.

Surnames arose and were formed on the basis of (a) local names, (b) relationships, (c) occupations, (d) nicknames.

(a) Local or territorial names were first given with *de* or German *von*, e.g. *Grave Otto von Liningen, Her Walther von Klingen, Walther von der Vogelweide*. At this stage the preposition *von* was in no way a sign of nobility, only in the seventeenth century did *von* become a privilege of noble names. Even then there were regions where this was not the case, for instance, in the north-west and the Netherlands (*van Beethoven*) and in Switzerland (*von Allmen, von Arx, von Moos, von Wartburg*). Later *de* or *von* was usually dispensed with: *von Homburg* > *Homburg*. Often other morphological means replaced *von*, notably -*er*, -*ing*, -*isch*, -*mann*, usually with clear regional preferences. Thus -*er* formations were frequent in the south while unmarked place-names were usual in the centre and the north (*Homburger – Homburg*). Frequently there was interchange. *Hartman von Ouwe* was also known as *der Ouwære, Walther von der Vogelweide* as *Vogelweider, Oswald von Wolkenstein* as *Wolkensteiner*. Apart from actual place-names, other local designations such as geographical features (*Bachmann* < 'somebody living by a brook', *Brühlmann* < MHG *brüel* 'watermeadow', *Vogelsanger* < a spot known as 'Vogelsang') or names of houses (*Rosenberg, Schönau, Steiger*) could form the basis of a surname. Again north-western and Swiss names frequently incorporate a preposition: *ten Brink* or *Tenbrink, Imhof, Zurbriggen*. The suffix -*er* is, of course, the usual means of indicating the place of origin in modern German, for instance, *Frankfurter, Wiener, Londoner*.

(b) Names based on relationships were predominantly patronymics. First mention is usually in the form of *Fridericus filius Hiltimari, Albertus filius Ortliebi, Burchardus filius Witonis* or *Johans Heinrichs sun, Ruodolf Kuonrats sun*. In southern Germany the frequent mention of *her*, e.g. *Heinrich hern Philippes sun* shows that *sun* rarely became an integral part of a surname. Gradually *filius* or *sun* was left out and the surname was a genitive form, e.g. *Hugo Eberhardi, Conradus Hermanni, Heinci Richartz*, or modern *Conradi, Lorenzen, Brahms* (< *Abraham*), *Lutz*, or it lost its genitive ending: *Cûnradus Diether, Cûnradus Eckehart*, or modern *Arnold, Ernst, Konrad, Kuhn* (< a short form), *Lorenz, Thomas*. Patronymics with *-sen* (< *sun*) have survived in Schleswig-Holstein (*Detlevsen, Jansen, Andersen, Thießen* (< *Matthias*)), while genitive forms in *-s* are especially frequent in the lower Rhinelands, e.g. *Heinrichs, Frings* (< *Severinus*). Relationship could also be expressed by means of suffixes such as *-er* (*Kuhner, Kuhnert, Klauser*), *-ing* (*Humperdinck* < *Hunbrecht*), *-mann* (*Peter-mann, Hanselmann*) or diminutive suffixes: *-i* (*Rüedi, Fritschi*), *-li, -lin, -el* (*Niggli, Henslin, Nickel, Helmbrechtel*), *-ke(n)* (*Beneke, Heinke, Künecke*) and by means of attributes: *Kleinpeter, Jungan-dreas*. It is thanks to these patronymics that many old Germanic names which have died out as first names have survived as sur-names, e.g. *Hunbrecht*. The fact that saints' names, even in shortened forms, have contributed many surnames shows that saints' names were already thoroughly Germanized by the time that surnames came into being. Metronymics, that is names which derive from the mother's name, occur as well although they are not very frequent: *Heinricus Gerdrudis filius, Heinrich Katerinun*, or modern *Gretler* (< *Grete*), *Juttensen* (< *Jutta*) or cf. E *Widdowson*.

(c) Surnames that derive from occupations, trades or offices were rather later than names of relationship or origin. They belonged characteristically to the urban artisan class. At first they generally had an article: *Ulrich der Murer, Hans der Schmid*, cf. Dutch *De Smet, De Jong*. Apart from occupations that exist today (*Müller, Schneider, Fischer, Wagner, Koch, Hirt*) such names often recall medieval trades which have long vanished, e.g. *Heinricus Strichære* ('rope-maker') or *Faßbind* (a barrel-maker or cooper), *Kugler* (maker of a *cuculla* or hood), *Fechner* (a furrier). Occupation names, too, could have derivative suffixes, e.g. *-ing* (*Vögting*), genitive *-s* (*Chûnrad Suters, Pferdemenges* 'horse dealer') or diminutive endings (*Sütterlin* < *sutor* 'shoemaker').

(d) In many regions nicknames stand out as a numerically particularly strong class. Here we have names such as *Henricus qui dicitur Angist, Chûnrat Trost, Arnoldus qui Vulpis dicitur, Arnold der Fuhs, Guntherus Fuhs, Heinrich Rehpoch* ('roebuck'), *Jacobus Stegereif* ('stirrup'), *Cunradus Rufus* ('red') or modern *Angst, Trost, Lang, Kurz, Schwarz, Bock, Kopf, Pfefferkorn, Hasenbein*. Among nicknames we also find so-called phrase-names, cf. E *Drinkwater, Goodenough, Shakespeare*. Medieval German examples are *Suchenwirt, Rumezlant, Frauenlob, Rütelschrīn, Scheißind-*

pluomen (parodistically in Wittenwiler's *Ring*). Such names flourished especially in the coarser climate of the late Middle Ages. The oldest types of names are the relationship names, forming about 16–20 per cent of all surnames between the twelfth and sixteenth centuries, and the local names, originally constituting about half of all surnames in many places, e.g. in Hamburg 40 per cent, in Lübeck 53 per cent, and in Rostock 48 per cent (Fleischer, *Personennamen*, p. 158). But the percentage of the local names tended to decrease as the occupation names increased, finally to form the biggest German name group. Naturally there were big local differences. In the Rhenish cities surnames from house names tended to make up a large contingent. In Bavaria they played practically no part at all. Both typologically and phonologically the German surnames frequently betray the ultimate home of their bearers' ancestors: *Herr Witte* (from North Germany), *Herr Weiß* (from South Germany), *Herr Wyß* (from Switzerland or Alsace), although levelling out in favour of the standard German form (*Weiß*) may in many cases have obliterated the original regional provenance. As a cultural feature the German surnames are the heritage of the latter half of the Middle Ages.

Select Bibliography

H. Bach, *Die thüringisch-sächsische Kanzleisprache bis 1325*, 2 vols., Copenhagen, 1937, 1943; B. Boesch, *Untersuchungen zur alemannischen Urkundensprache des 13. Jahrhunderts*, Berne, 1946; H. Brinkmann, 'Das deutsche Adjektiv in synchronischer und diachronischer Sicht', *WW*, 14 (1964) 94–104; P. W. Brosman, 'Old French *dancier*, German *tanzen*', *Romance Notes*, 2 (1961) 141–6; J. Bumke, *Studien zum Ritterbegriff im 12. und 13. Jahrhundert*, Heidelberg, 1964; G. Eis, *Mittelalterliche Fachliteratur*, Stuttgart, 1962; W. Fleischer, 'Die Namen der Dresdener Ratsmitglieder bis 1500', *BNF*, 12 (1961) 44–87; R. Hotzenköcherle, 'Entwicklungsgeschichtliche Grundzüge des Nhd.', *WW*, 12 (1962) 321–31; E. Johansson, *Die Deutschordenschronik des Nicolaus von Jeroschin*, Lund, 1964; G. Korlén, *Die mittelniederdeutschen Texte des 13. Jahrhunderts*, Lund, 1945; K. J. Küpper,

Studien zur Verbstellung in den Kölner Jahrbüchern des 14./15. Jahrhunderts, Bonn, 1971; P. Lessiak, *Beiträge zur Geschichte des deutschen Konsonantismus*, Prague, 1933; K. B. Lindgren, *Die Ausbreitung der nhd. Diphthongierung bis 1500*, Helsinki, 1961; id., *Die Apokope des mhd. e in seinen verschiedenen Funktionen*, Helsinki, 1953; F. Maurer, *Vorarbeiten und Studien zur Vertiefung der südwestdeutschen Sprachgeschichte*, Stuttgart, 1965; E. Öhmann, 'Die mhd. Suffixe *-ie* und *-eie*', *Neuphil. Mitt.*, 67 (1966) 225–34; id., 'Das deutsche Verbaluffix *-ieren*', ibid., 71 (1970) 337–57; id., *Die mittelhochdeutsche Lehnprägung nach altfranz. Vorbild*, Helsinki, 1951; id., 'Der romanische Einfluß auf das Deutsche bis zum Ausgang des Mittelalters', in F. Maurer, H. Rupp, *Deutsche Wortgeschichte*, 3rd ed., Berlin, 1974, pp. 323–96; H. Paul, H. Moser, I. Schröbler, *Mittelhochdeutsche Grammatik*, 21st ed., Tübingen, 1975; L. Saltveit, *Studien zum dt. Futur*, Bergen, Oslo, 1962; G. Schieb, 'Mittelhochdeutsch' in L. E. Schmitt (ed.), *Kurzer Grundriß der germanischen Philologie bis 1500*, vol. I, Berlin, 1970, pp. 347–85; R. Schützeichel, *Mundart, Urkundensprache und Schriftsprache. Studien zur Sprachgeschichte am Mittelrhein*, Bonn, 1960; A. Socin, *Mittelhochdeutsches Namenbuch*, Basle, 1903; E. Wiessner, H. Burger, 'Die höfische Blütezeit' in F. Maurer, H. Rupp, *Deutsche Wortgeschichte*, 3rd ed., Berlin, 1974, pp. 189–253; F. Wilhelm et al., *Corpus der Altdeutschen Originalurkunden bis zum Jahre 1300*, 5 vols., Lahr, 1932–68, vol. VI, 1970– .

The Sixteenth-century Achievement

6.1 | The period and the linguistic territory

6.1.1 | The period

The next stage in the evolution of the German language at which a synchronic cross-section must be made is the sixteenth century. The designation traditionally given to this linguistic phase is Early New High German. How far back in time the period is considered to extend and how far forward, depends on many factors. In consequence, scholars tend to give various dates. Many of the factors are extralinguistic, for linguistically, of course, there are no sharp lines of demarcation. But one linguistic factor at least speaks firmly in favour of the view that the middle of the fourteenth century is an important landmark. It is at that time that the remarkable blend of Upper German and Central German features which was to become so characteristic of New High German and which distinguishes it so sharply from Middle High German was in evidence for the first time. And what is more: it was the language of the imperial chancery itself which showed these characteristics.

In many other ways the middle of the fourteenth century proved to be a landmark in the history of German society. The Black Death of 1348 and the many subsequent epidemics during the next hundred years amounted to a demographic catastrophe of immense consequence. It is estimated that Germany's population was reduced by about a quarter. Recovery was long prevented by recurring waves of pestilence and plague. The population figure of about fifteen million in the first half of the fourteenth century was only reached again by about 1500. The feudal society of chivalry, already seriously weakened by a hundred years of fluctuating monarchical power following the fall of the Hohenstaufen, did not survive the economic consequences of the demographic decline. The military role of the feudal levies of knights was coming to an end and fighting was increasingly done by mercenary forces. Power and wealth had decidedly shifted to the towns and the territorial princes.

The beginning of a new period was also marked by the establishment of a new dynasty in 1347 with the election of Charles of Luxemburg, king of Bohemia, as German king. For nearly a century, under Charles IV, Wenceslas and Sigismund, the centre of the empire, in so far as one can speak of a centre in this diffuse realm, lay in Bohemia with Prague as the imperial city. This move of the political centre to the east forms a sharp contrast to the Middle High German period when the power base had been in the south-west. The MHG period has therefore quite correctly been called the *Schwäbisches Zeitalter*. This lay now in the past and the fate of the empire rested from now on in the hands of eastern dynasties. Constitutionally, too, the middle of the fourteenth century is significant. In 1356 the Golden Bull set the seal on a long process of political evolution of monarchical and princely power. German kings were henceforth to be elected by a majority decision of seven electoral princes whose position, if they were secular princes, was guaranteed by the rule of primogeniture. Three electors were princes of the church: the archbishops of Mainz (the arch-chancellor), Cologne and Trier. The four secular electors were: the count palatine of the Rhine, the margrave of Brandenburg, the duke of Saxony and the king of Bohemia. Although the empire was extremely loosely organized and lacked centralized institutions, there was plenty of supra-regional activity. The king was to be elected in Frankfurt, crowned in Aachen, and was to hold his first imperial diet in Nuremberg. Diets were otherwise convened in a number of cities, for instance Worms, Speyer, Mainz, Cologne, Augsburg, Constance, Lindau, but Nuremberg became the favoured venue. They were attended not only by the electors, but also by numerous princes of the empire, counts and knights, prelates and bishops, and representatives of the towns. If these potentates prevented the growth of a powerful, centralizing, hereditary monarchy, they at least met, negotiated and talked, and thus kept alive and fostered a degree of unity in their common medium of communication, the German language. However useful Latin was, it did not impede the awareness of the existence of a common mother tongue.

One further important innovation helps us to recognize the middle of the fourteenth century as a watershed: the establishment of German universities, beginning with the foundation of the Caroline University of Prague in 1348. Eight more universities were to be established during the reign of the Luxemburg kings and another eight before the Reformation. The character and cultural climate of the next three hundred years was to be powerfully influenced by these institutions.

There can thus be little doubt that for both linguistic and extralinguistic reasons (which, of course, also made an impact on the German language) there is sound justification for dating the Early New High German period from 1350.

The end of the period is demarcated equally clearly by both linguistic criteria and extralinguistic events. In the first half of the seventeenth century Germany was plunged into a catastrophic succession of savage and extremely destructive wars, collectively known as the Thirty Years War (1618–48). The population which had prospered and increased throughout the sixteenth century and may well have reached a figure of twenty million by 1600 suffered tremendous losses. These varied greatly from region to region: Mecklenburg and Pomerania in the north, Thuringia in the centre, and Württemberg and the Palatinate in the south-west are estimated to have lost over fifty per cent of their inhabitants. The total decrease of the German population may well have amounted to between one third and two fifths. Politically the outcome of the Thirty Years War only confirmed the existence of a large number, in fact about three hundred and fifty, large, medium and small, autonomous, practically sovereign secular and ecclesiastical states and lordships, constituting together the Holy Roman Empire of the German Nation.

Linguistically, the middle of the seventeenth century also marked a turning point. The existence of a uniform standard language or at least the desire for one, with its fixed norm, was for the first time explicitly proclaimed. North Germany had abandoned its own written medium (Middle Low German) and had generally adopted the evolving High German standard language. What is more, leading circles of North German society had even begun to speak this new standard language which otherwise existed merely as a written language. Regional deviations from the normalized written standard language, still rife in the south, were now recognized as such and became anachronistic. Latin was now on the wane. In the second half of the seventeenth century, for the first time, more books were printed in German than in Latin. Societies with the aim of cultivating the German language (*Sprach-*

gesellschaften) were active from the first half of the seventeenth century. Daily newspapers, the oldest being established in 1636, were to add a new dimension to the use of German from now on.

The Early New High German period may therefore be dated from 1350 to 1650. Its central core is formed by the reigns of the Habsburg emperors Maximilian I (1493–1519) and his grandson Charles V (1519–56), and includes, of course, the momentous decades of the Reformation (1520–55). The Reformation had the greatest impact on the German language. Not only did it produce a book which found its way into German homes in north and south, east and west, as no book had ever done before, but it opened up whole new fields for the German language. A flood of printed literature made the public aware for the first time of the existence of a common, if still diverse, written language. In education and learning, too, the first half of the sixteenth century with its efficient and effective printing presses, marked a break with the past and opened up a new world of which the German language was the medium. This advance of written German in the very decades of victorious humanism with its purified Ciceronian Latin may sound paradoxical. Yet there was now actually room for both, for a time at least. German had arrived as a written medium and stood now, albeit on a lower cultural level, beside Latin. It was the national language just as Latin was the international language. Where choice was available it was the intended readership which decided which language was to be used. If a book was aimed at a wider German public it was the national language which was now used.

The century and a half which led up to this middle period was a century of reconstruction and reform, filled with despair and despondency at the failure to achieve the longed-for improvements in church and state. It was in Huizinga's phrase the *Herbst des Mittelalters*. It was also a period when those momentous discoveries were made that were to come to fruition in the next and subsequent centuries: the invention of gunpowder and firearms; the discovery of the American continent and of the sea routes to Asia; the invention of paper and of the printing press; the rediscovery of the pagan world of classical Greece and Rome; the rediscovery of the spherical nature of the earth, and, later, the discovery of the heliocentricity of the planetary system.

The papacy was rent by schism, and there was a general feeling

that the church needed a thorough reform. The conciliar movement, at the two great church councils of Constance and Basle,
failed to give the church a new constitution and organization, and
was unable to solve the problem of the first great modern heresy,
the Hussite movement, although it achieved the ending of the
Great Schism. The grievances of the German nation against the
church of Rome, the *Gravamina nationis Germanicae*, which were
brought before every imperial diet after 1456, were allowed to
fester. If the reform of the church failed, so that eventually there
was the Reformation, the reform of the empire failed equally.

During Maximilian's reign, it is true, certain institutions were
introduced: the *Ewiger Landfrieden*, which greatly reduced feuding;
a highest court of law, the *Reichskammergericht*; an (abortive)
imperial governing council, the *Reichsregiment*; a new organization
of the empire consisting of ten *Kreise*; a renovated *Reichstag*;
and for a time even an imperial tax, the Common Penny. In so
far as these innovations endured, they were confirmations of
existing practices rather than far-reaching reforms. However, it
was with these institutions that the empire lived till its dissolution
in 1806. Monarchy as a centralizing power had to accept defeat
and abdication in favour of the princes. Germany remained a
polyfocal realm with numerous thriving, and some languishing,
principalities and prosperous, culturally active towns. If great
power eluded these political units, to the deep chagrin of generations of German historians, if the cultural splendour of a great
metropolitan centre was lacking, it should never be overlooked
that Germany thereby also escaped the blight of having culturally
deprived and sterile provinces. The German language, too, was
polycentric in this age. Its use or form was not determined by the
Habsburg dynasty in the way that the Carolingian inspiration had
moulded Old High German or that in Middle High German the
Hohenstaufen cultural impact had made itself felt. Hence, attractive though it would have been to call this chapter 'The Habsburg
Achievement', to do so would have provoked objections much
more powerful than any that can be levied against 'The Carolingian
Beginning' or 'The Hohenstaufen Flowering'. The phrase
Kaiser and *Reich* now epitomized the duality of the political
regime. Basically, the emperor was little more than a symbolic
head of the empire and otherwise simply a prince among princes.
The Habsburgs were particularly successful princes, and when in

1526 Charles V's brother Ferdinand succeeded to the crowns of Bohemia and Hungary, the basis for the future separate Habsburg monarchy was laid. Although the rise of autonomous, virtually sovereign principalities and states could have meant linguistic separation and incapsulation, this was in fact not so. The high nobility themselves were supra-regional. The Bavarian dynasty of the Wittelsbachs also had a foothold in the Upper Palatinate and the Rhenish Palatinate and members of their family frequently held one or other of the Rhenish archbishoprics. The Hohenzollern interests embraced southern territories as well as Brandenburg in the north-east. The Luxemburg dynasty held territories in the west and in the east. The Habsburg lands included the Netherlands, *Vorderösterreich*, i.e. the Sundgau in southern Alsace and the Breisgau, as well as their eastern duchies in Austria. Members of the house of Wettin from Saxony and of the Hohenzollern family held the archbishopric of Mainz at important and decisive times in the fifteenth and sixteenth centuries. Switzerland, although it no longer recognized the decisions of the *Reichstag* after 1495 and refused to accept the jurisdiction of the *Reichskammergericht*, and further asserted its *de facto* independence in the Swabian War of 1499, nevertheless continued to regard itself as a country of the German tongue.

The centrifugal tendencies not only benefited the princes. They allowed a large number of towns to achieve self-government and great prosperity. Unlike Italian city states they did not acquire a great military potential. The cities in the north, linked in the Hanseatic league, controlled the exchange of goods in the Baltic and the North Sea. The cities of the south were themselves great manufacturing centres and traded in the produce of the booming mining industry of Bohemia, Hungary, the Tyrol and Saxony. The banking and trading firms of Nuremberg and Augsburg were wealthy enough to supply even Charles V, the monarch over whose empire the sun never set. To buy the necessary electoral votes, or, put more delicately, to recompense the noble electors for their trouble, Charles borrowed over half a million guilders, or two thirds of the total sum required, from the Augsburg banker Jakob Fugger. Maximilian needed Fugger's financial help regularly whenever political or military demands arose. The management of the money economy, characteristic of the age, was largely in the hands of the towns. The political achievements of the towns were, however, small and by 1500 their power was on the wane. Lübeck, the leader of the Hansa, was seriously weakened by 1535. Mainz lost its independence to the archbishop as early as 1462. The city leagues, such as the Rhenish and the Swabian, failed. Perhaps the towns' last hour of glory came when at the diet of Speyer in 1529 fourteen towns joined the Lutheran princes in the famous Protestation: Strasbourg, Ulm, Nuremberg, Wissembourg, Windsheim, Constance, Lindau, Memmingen, Kempten, Nördlingen, Heilbronn, Reutlingen, Isny and St Gall, or in 1530 when at the diet of Augsburg four reforming cities (Strasbourg, Constance, Lindau, Memmingen), wishing to follow neither Luther (*Confessio Augustana*) nor Zwingli, submitted their own declaration of faith, the *Confessio Tetrapolitana*. The Schmalkaldic War and the defeat of the Protestant League put an end to the proud position of most south German towns. Not only were many recatholicized by force, some also lost their independence. Constance, for instance, became an insignificant Habsburg provincial city. Although of the total population of the empire not more than ten per cent lived in towns and although of the three thousand towns no more than about fifteen to twenty had populations of over ten thousand inhabitants and only a hundred and fifty had over a thousand inhabitants, the cultural significance of the towns was and remained great throughout this period.

It was in the towns, often princely towns rather than free towns, that the new universities were situated. They were the places where the administrators of the new states were educated, mainly in law. It was from the law faculties that Roman law gradually found its way into the German juridical system. This new class of administrators was highly mobile. They tended to study at several universities, usually including Italian ones, such as Pavia, Padua or Bologna, and entered the service of any prince or city that needed them. In the universities, and city and state administrations, educated men from all parts of the German-speaking lands met. This was not without importance for the German language. The universities also became the centres of the new humanist learning, and the men of letters in both Latin and German were generally university men. Martin Luther was nearly all his adult life a professor of Biblical exegesis at the university of Wittenberg. Between 1520 and 1560 some sixteen thousand students attended the university of Wittenberg and became familiar with the Lutheran message. The university-educated man was typically the writer and leading cultural figure of the age, just as the knight, a Wolfram von Eschenbach or a Hartmann von Aue, had been in the Hohenstaufen age. Alongside the educated nobleman like the humanist Ulrich von Hutten, or the cleric like Thomas Murner, we now find especially the educated layman and burgher, a Willibald Pirckheimer or a Johannes Aventinus. Many scholars were closely associated with the early printing houses which were all established in towns, such as Mainz, Strasbourg, Basle, Augsburg, Nuremberg, Cologne, or Wittenberg. The printing presses also often had connections with the universities. Besides Latin schools the towns now also had German elementary schools. The urban artisans, organized in their guilds, as well as the educated patrician burghers, were a literate public to whom the publications and pamphlets, pouring from the printing presses during the Reformation, were addressed. Apart from the servile classes most people in towns were able to read. That literacy was no longer confined to the highly educated is attested by the flood of artistically and intellectually unassuming *Volksbücher*. Arno Schirokauer used a telling expression when he referred to the language of the age as *Städterdeutsch* in contrast to the *Ritterdeutsch* and *Mönchsdeutsch* of earlier periods.

The third part of the Early New High German period began promisingly with the Peace of Augsburg in 1555. The two great denominations, Catholicism and Lutheranism, appeared to declare that they would tolerate each other on the basis of the principle of *cuius regio, eius religio*; that is, although freedom of religion was denied to the individual it was granted to the rulers, who were free to force their own religion on their subjects. But many problems were left unsolved, and Calvinism was not covered by the agreement. The Counter-Reformation was in its early stages and the consolidation and incapsulation of the denominational states was gradually leading to a hardening of attitudes and greater militancy. The age of dogmatic uncertainty, of the search for reforms, was giving way to an age of dogmatic certainty, of faiths claiming universal validity. As an age of orthodoxy and authoritarianism it resorted to brutal force with appalling ease and the opposing camps of true believers finally plunged the empire into the holocaust of the Thirty Years War.

6.1.2 | The linguistic territory

The German linguistic territory, by and large, remained
the same as it had been at the end of the Middle High German
period. In the west, the Franco-German linguistic boundary,
although not the Franco-Flemish boundary, was static. In the
south, Rheto-Romance lost its foothold in Vorarlberg and the
Rhine valley up to Chur. In 1538 Chur was reported to be German-
speaking, although it had been Rheto-Romance only a few
generations before. The abandonment of Rheto-Romance by the
one significant town in its territory, Chur, which was also the seat
of its bishop, meant that Rheto-Romance would have no chance
of developing a standard language and would henceforth consist
only of disparate dialects, cut off from each other. This is the
sort of linguistic situation which usually, and in the long run,
at least under modern conditions, means a fatally weakened
language.

In the east the developments were more far-reaching. The age
of settlement (see pp. 238–40) had led to much intermingling of
populations. By 1500 a linguistic boundary had become consolidated which in many areas remained until the Second World War.
Such was the case, for instance, in Carinthia and Styria. Klagenfurt, however, was still a German enclave in Slovene territory and
remained so until the end of the eighteenth century, when it was
joined to the solid German settlement area. The modern German-
Hungarian boundary was also established in this period, with
considerable regression of German north of the Danube in Slovakia. In central Bohemia the Hussite wars between 1420 and 1436
virtually eliminated the stray German urban and rural settlements.
In 1458 a Czech nobleman, George Podiebrad, was elected king of
Bohemia. Even when in 1526 a German dynasty, the Habsburgs,
became once more established in Bohemia, the Czech nobility
retained its ascendancy in the Bohemian estates. It was only after
the battle of the White Mountain in 1620, which spelt the ruin of
the Czech nobility and the Bohemian estates, that the golden age of
Czech supremacy was terminated and German again began to gain
ground. Even then, however, central Bohemia remained safely
Czech.

The Polish-German boundary also became more clearly defined. Many German enclaves in Polish surroundings became
Polish-speaking, notably the former German towns of Posen (now

Poznań) and Cracow. Slav enclaves behind the linguistic frontier dwindled, although the larger ones, for instance that of the Sorbs in Lusatia, survived to the present day, and the Wends in the Hanover Wendland near Dannenberg maintained their language until the eighteenth century.

In the north-east, political events put an end to further German advances except against the Baltic language of the Prussians. In 1545 it was still spoken by enough people for it to be worthwhile to translate the Lutheran Catechism from German into Prussian. But towards the end of the seventeenth century it died out. The territories of the Teutonic Order came under Polish sovereignty in consequence of its defeat at Tannenberg in 1410. The settlements in the Baltic countries, in Estonia and Latvia, passed under Swedish and later Russian domination, and those in Lithuania were incorporated in the Polish-Lithuanian kingdom. In 1460 Schleswig-Holstein was united with Denmark, but no important consequences ensued for the position of the German language.

Two linguistically interesting settlements in the east resulted from the Reformation. A sect, the Anabaptists, split into many sub-groups, were cruelly persecuted by both the Catholics and the Protestants. From the Netherlands and North Germany many followers of Menno Simons escaped to the region of the lower Vistula. There Mennonite Low German speaking communities survived and after further repression eventually settled, first in Russia and later in parts of Canada and the United States, where some prospering communities have survived to the present day. South German Anabaptists, among them many Swiss and Tyroleans, following Jakob Huter, and hence known as Hutterer or Hutterites, found a refuge in southern Moravia where they founded flourishing, communistically organized brotherhoods. At the time of the Thirty Years War further persecutions drove them to Hungary, and later to Russia. Some communities are now found in North America.

To some extent these migrations to the east, caused by the religious upheavals of the period, formed part of the German movement eastward which was generally resumed after 1500. The large increase in population in the sixteenth century again led to colonization, but this time it was confined almost exclusively to territory already settled by Germans. The new colonists now mainly filled the gaps caused by the great epidemics. Deserted and depopulated farms, hamlets, villages and towns were once more occupied and expanded. The linguistic territory as such was hardly affected by this renewed colonization.

6.1.3 | The growth of Yiddish

One wave of migration, that of German Jews, led ultimately to the formation of a new language, *Yiddish*. In the early Middle Ages prospering colonies of Jews had grown up in many cities of western and central Germany, especially those along the Rhine, Moselle and Danube. As these Jewish communities formed close-knit groups their German contained many dialectal features of its own, deriving in part from their earlier languages such as French, in part from their religious languages, Hebrew and Aramaic. However, these particularist features would seem to have been slight until the greater restrictions imposed on the Jews in the thirteenth century. It was mainly the Black Death and the other epidemics of the fourteenth century which evoked the cruel waves of pogroms and persecutions which drove great masses of Jews out of Germany. The earlier persecutions in the wake of the Crusades had already led to Jewish emigration to the east. Now, between 1350 and 1500, the kingdom of Lithuania and Poland offered a new and safe haven. In the towns of the east the emigrants met oriental Jews and German settlers, who also contributed to the language of the Jewish communities. Although they retained their German language in their new environment, they naturally also absorbed linguistic elements from Slavonic and Baltic languages. Owing to the great mobility of this urban merchant and artisan population their speech forms remained remarkably uniform. In the west the Jewish ghetto population also retained their specific language, West Yiddish, at least until the eighteenth century when a more liberal climate encouraged rapid integration in the general German linguistic scene.

But in the east where contact with German was greatly reduced, Yiddish gradually acquired its specific characteristics. Its Hebrew and Aramaic components grew considerably. The Slav host languages influenced grammar, lexicon and phonology (e.g. the introduction of a series of palatalized consonants). In morphology and syntax it departed considerably from German. Its lexicon remained about seventy-five per cent German, although with many semantic innovations. Many of its phonological features reflect German urban dialects of the west and the centre during the late MHG period and the fifteenth century. For instance diphthongization of MHG *ī, ū, iu* (*mayn* – MHG *mīn, hoyz* – MHG *hūs, layt* – MHG *liute*); monophthongization of MHG *ie, uo, üe* (*rimen* – MHG *rieme, gut* – MHG *guot, grin* – MHG *grüene*); unrounding (*taitsh* – MHG *tiutsch*, *Yid* – MHG *jüde, greser* – MHG *græzer*); coalescence of MHG *ei, ou*, and *ē, ō* (*shteyn* – MHG *stein, shney* – MHG *snē, boym* – MHG *boum, shoyn* – MHG *schōn*); rounding and lowering of MHG *ā* (*hor* – MHG *hār*); early lengthening of short vowels in open syllables and subsequent identical development with the long vowels (*zogn* – MHG *sagen, beysm* – MHG *besem, koyl* – MHG *kol*); apocope (*zayt* – MHG *sīte*); preservation of prefix *ge-*; *-p(-)* for MHG *-pf(-)* (*kop* – MHG *kopf*). Two German dialectal areas are thus clearly excluded as possible home bases: Low German and High Alemannic. The Rhine-Main town dialects on the other hand would appear to form the basic German element.

From the beginning Yiddish was written in Hebrew characters. The earliest Yiddish text is *Dukus Horant*, an adaptation of the *Kudrun* legend, of 1382. From the fifteenth and sixteenth centuries there are texts of various kinds and in the seventeenth century there were a number of renderings of German *Volksbücher*, e.g *Fortunatus* (1699), *Die schöne Magelone* and *Till Eulenspiegel* (see p. 353). In the nineteenth century Yiddish acquired the full status of a literary language. Its home base was at that time the vast stretch of eastern Europe extending from a line west of present-day Leningrad to west of Rostov in the south and reaching to the western boundary of Russian Poland and of Hungary. Many sizeable towns, for instance, Minsk, Pinsk, Berdichev and Odessa, were predominantly inhabited by Yiddish-speaking Jews. Others such as Vilna and Warsaw had large Yiddish-speaking minorities. Before the Second World War it was spoken by about eight million people. Emigration had already carried it to America and some cities of western Europe. The holocaust of the Second World War led to the almost complete Jewish depopulation of its home base. Yiddish speakers in Israel, America, and western Europe are now in the process of abandoning their ancestral tongue in favour of Hebrew or their new host languages.

6.2 | The range of the literary language

When Charles of Habsburg, the king of Spain, wrote to the German electors in connection with his election to the German kingship, he did so, from Barcelona, in German in his own hand, claiming, for instance in his letter to Elector Frederick of Saxony, of 3rd June 1519 'das wir ain Teutscher von gebluet und gemuet, von gepurt und zungen sein.' This French-speaking Burgundian, having been brought up in what is now Belgium, had obviously been made aware of the importance and position of the German language at that time. His fellow contender for the German crown, Francis I, the king of France, on the other hand, wrote his letters soliciting support in French. In paragraph 16 of the 'electoral capitulation' or promissory declaration which Charles V issued after his election (the so-called *Wahlverschreibung* of 3rd July 1519) and which is also in German, he undertook:

Darzue in schriften und handlungen des reichs kain ander zunge oder sprach gebrauchen lassen, wann die Teutsch oder Lateinisch zung; es wer dann an orten, da gemeinlich ein ander sprach in ubung und gebrauch stuend, alsdann mugen wir und die unsern uns derselbigen daselbs auch behelfen.

The status of the German language was thus for the first time officially recognized. This recognition was, however, only a confirmation of what had been the practice for a long time. German princes now corresponded with each other in German. The acts and decisions of the imperial diet were published in German. While fifty per cent of the documents issuing from the chancery of Charles IV had still been in Latin, and German had only become predominant in the time of Wenceslas, it was now the regular medium except in correspondence with the Pope and some foreign powers. Even the imperial code of criminal law, the *Carolina* or *Peinliche Halsgerichtsordnung* of 1531, was in German. The important social and political document embodying so many of the hopes and aspirations of the previous era, the anonymous *Reformatio Sigismundi*, of c. 1439 printed in 1476 and 1497, had also been in German. The Emperor Frederick III, who had kept a private book of notes or diary since he was twenty-two, did so in German. That the Twelve Articles, the mildly revolutionary demands of the peasants of 1525, were in German is self-evident. Jakob Fugger's invoice to Charles V for his election expenses was also drawn up in German. The historian Sebastian Franck, who wrote the first universal history in German (*Chronica, Zeytbuch und geschycht-bibel*, Strasbourg 1531), described the boundaries of Germany in terms of the linguistic boundaries. The Protestant princes, who in 1552 concluded the Treaty of Chambord with the king of France against their emperor and purchased the support of France with the surrender of the bishoprics of Metz, Toul and Verdun, justified their action with the argument that it was a good thing that the king of France should take possession of and keep as 'vicar' on behalf of the Holy Roman Empire 'die stett, so zum reich von alters her gehöret und nit Teutscher sprach sein'. At the decisive diet of 1530 at Augsburg the Lutheran Confession (*Confessio Augustana*) and Martin Bucer's *Confessio Tetrapolitana* were submitted, on the emperor's instructions, each in a German and a Latin version. Zwingli sent in his *Fidei ratio* and the German version *Zů Karoln Römischen Keyser jetzund vff dem Rychstag zů Ougsburg Bekentnuß des Gloubens*. Both versions were published by Froschauer in Zürich in the same year. That the most important political document of the age, the Religious Peace of Augsburg, dated 25th September 1555, should also be in German, only confirms the position of German in the national and political sphere.

The bilingualism, clearly confirmed in Charles V's *Wahlverschreibung*, was now no longer the functional bilingualism of earlier centuries, but a bilingualism of the educated. German was fit to be used, could be used and was used for all purposes. Even one of the most highly cultured of the scholars and humanists of the age, Willibald Pirckheimer, asserted the dignity and suitability of German. Equally, Rudolf Agricola, who died in 1485, demanded that the Roman historians should be translated into German so that the people could know them and so that German would be 'perfected'. Wimpheling agreed with him. Indeed many German humanists, although not Erasmus, held views not dissimilar to those held by many Italians, such as Pietro Bembo (*Prose della volgar lingua*, 1525) or Iacopo Sannazaro, concerning the Italian vernacular. Of course, many others made disparaging remarks about the 'vulgar vernacular'. If the humanists wrote mostly, and in some cases exclusively, in Latin (e.g. Erasmus), it was because they venerated and loved the polished and refined Latin of Cicero and Seneca as the vehicle of the culture to the rediscovery and study of which they dedicated their lives.

Many of them, incidentally, were happy to contribute to the wider dissemination of the literature of classical antiquity by translating Latin and Greek works into German. Thomas Murner translated the *Institutions of Roman Law* (1519) and Virgil's *Aeneid*, published in 1515 as *Vergilij maronis dryzehen Aeneadische Bücher*. The first direct translations from the Greek were Johannes Reuchlin's *Demosthenes' First Olynthian Oration* and *The Twelfth of Lucian's Dialogues of the Dead*. Reuchlin is said to have also translated part of Homer's *Iliad* into German verse, although it is not preserved. Simon Schaidenreisser translated the *Odyssey* from the original Greek into German prose in 1537. Willibald Pirckheimer translated not only from Greek into Latin, but also from both languages into German. His friend Albrecht Dürer wrote his letters to him in German. We do not know in what language Pirckheimer replied since his part of the correspondence is lost. Another humanist, Matthias Ringmann Philesius, translated Caesar's *De Bello Gallico* (1507): *Julius der erst Römisch Kaiser von seinen kriegen*.

Some humanists also demonstrated their personal bilingualism by writing some of their own original works in German, notably Reuchlin in his controversy with Pfefferkorn. Reuchlin, the most famous Hebraist of his day, reacted to four German publications by a converted Jew, Johannes Pfefferkorn, who demanded the destruction of Hebrew writings other than the Old Testament (1507–09), by two well-reasoned pamphlets: *Augenspiegel* (1511) and *Ain clare verstentnus in tütsch* (1512). As early as 1505 had appeared *Doctor iohanns Reuchlins tütsch missive, warumb die Judē so lang im ellend sind* (Pforzheim). Ulrich von Hutten, who had only written in Latin up to the end of 1520, turned afterwards to German and also translated some of his own earlier Latin works. Thomas Murner wrote in Latin and in German. The latter he used especially in his more satirical works. Theophrastus von Hohenheim, known as Paracelsus, did more than most to raise German to the level of a language of science. He wrote nearly all his scientific, medical and theological-philosophical works in German, and in 1527, as a professor at the university of Basle, was the first to lecture in German.

A considerable number of the contemporary Latin works of the humanists appeared in German almost simultaneously or only slightly later. Johannes Aventinus also wrote a German version of his own *Annales ducum Boiariae* (1521): *Bairische Chronik* (1522–33). Erasmus' famous *Stultitiae Laus* (1509) appeared in 1534 in a translation by Sebastian Franck. The German best-seller of the age, Sebastian Brant's *Narrenschiff* (1494), on the other hand, was translated into Latin by Jakob Locher under the title *Stultifera navis* (1497), from which translations were made into nearly all European languages. Especially works of historiography seem to have found eager translators and an avid reading public. Georg Alt translated Konrad Celtis' famous description of Nuremberg, the *Norimberga*, in 1495, in the very year of its appearance in Latin. In 1497 he brought out a translation of Hart-mann Schedel's *Liber Chronicarum* (1493). Ladislaus Suntheim of Ravensburg translated Enea Silvio's description of Austria. Johannes Trithemius' *Annales de origine Francorum* (1515) appeared at Speyer in 1522 in a translation by J. Schenk. The political chronicle of the Reformation and the age of Charles V published in Strasbourg in 1555 by Johannes Sleidanus (*De statu religionis et reipublicae Carolo Quinto Caesare commentarii*) came out in Basle in 1556 in a German translation by Heinrich Pantaleon and in Strasbourg in another translation by Marcus Stamler. Many contemporary travel books and descriptions of foreign countries appeared in German and Latin versions more or less at the same time.

Among contemporary Latin plays rendered into German were Johannes Reuchlin's *Henno*, translated by Hans Sachs, *Sergius*, translated by M. Roet and Thomas Naogeorgus' *Pammachius*. The Latin moral satire *Grobianus* (1549) by Friedrich Dedekind was translated by Kaspar Scheidt in 1551. Writings of the Refor-mation which were in Latin and therefore primarily addressed to a learned, theological public were nevertheless often translated into German, for instance Luther's *De captivitate babylonica ecclesiae* by his adversary Thomas Murner.

Translations from contemporary Latin were not confined to books which had appeared in Germany. Savonarola's *Meditations* appeared in German at Nuremberg in 1499/1500 and at Augsburg in 1501. Marsilio Ficino's *De vita triplici* followed in 1505 in a translation by the Strasbourg physician Johann Adelphus Muling, which introduced Florentine platonism to the German reading public. Sir Thomas More's *Utopia* (1516) was translated into German as early as 1524, that is before it was translated into any other vernacular: Italian 1548, French 1550, English 1551.

Such translations of the works of contemporary humanists or of the works of classical antiquity continued a tradition of the fifteenth century. The prolific translators of the previous century were Niklas von Wyle, whose eighteen *Translatzen* appeared between 1461 and 1478; Heinrich Schlüsselfelder (Arigo) who translated Boccaccio's *Decamerone c.* 1460; Heinrich Steinhöwel, among whose many translations were the fables of Aesop; Albrecht von Eyb; Dietrich von Pleningen; and many more. Cicero, Terence, Seneca and Livy were the most frequently translated Latin authors. It is not surprising that Tacitus' *Germania*, which was rediscovered in the middle of the fifteenth century, edited by Beatus Rhenanus and others, and lectured on by the foremost German humanist poet and scholar, Konrad Celtis, was also translated and published (by Johann Eberlin von Günzburg in 1526 and by J. Micyllus; only the latter's version was published, Mainz, 1535). After all, it inspired the national pride which welled up at that time and was a stimulus to much of the historiography of the time. It lay behind Celtis' plan to write a great descriptive work on Germany, its culture and achievements, the *Germania illustrata*, and Jakob Wimpheling's patriotic treatise *Germania* (1501) and history *Epitome rerum Germanicarum usque ad nostra tempora* (1505). Ulrich von Hutten, too, derived his high opinion of the Germanic past and his national hero Arminius from the works of Tacitus.

Latin and Italian were not the only sources. French tales of chivalry and adventure were translated by Elizabeth von Nassau-Saarbrücken and Eleonore of Austria. These forerunners of the prose novel linked up with numerous prose versions which were made of earlier verse epics and led to one of the most popular *genres* of the time, the *Volksbuch*.

Substantial as the link was between the international Latin literary world and the national vernacular German sphere, nobody can of course overlook the fact that Latin was the language of high culture and that German remained essentially the medium of popular culture. However much was written in German, much more was written in Latin. And both German literature in translation and German original writings were characterized by a general lack of the highest achievement. Compared with the refined elegance and polished form of the literature of the Hohenstaufen age or the highly developed prose and poetry of the German Classical Age the works of the sixteenth century lack formal perfection and do not fully compensate by earthy vigour and punch. The writer who perhaps more than any other epitomizes the literature of the age, Hans Sachs, also characteristically represents its modest literary achievements. But lack of literary excellence, especially in comparison with contemporary Italy, France or Spain, must not lead us to assume that the German language as such languished or was not a fully emancipated national vernacular. The literary historian and the linguistic purist have been severe critics of the linguistic scene of sixteenth-century Germany, excepting always and only Luther's Bible translation. The student of the German language as a means of communication can only record that the German language of the time was fully capable of fulfilling its function and in fact did so.

The range of writings in German was complete. Original production was especially prolific in religious and political pamphleteering, in verse and prose satires, and in rudimentary forms of the novel, and derived its material from the heroic epic, classical and Arthurian romances and contemporary German and foreign narrative. Four literary works perhaps, apart from Sebastian Brant's *Narrenschiff*, which has already been mentioned, stand out among this large mass of writings: the first bourgeois prose tale, the *Geschichte von Fortunatus und seinen Söhnen*, written in the last quarter of the fifteenth century by an unknown Augsburg citizen, first printed in 1509 and subsequently translated into many languages; a collection of comic tales *Ein Kurtzweilig Lesen von Dyl Ulenspiegel*, adapted from a Low German version of probably 1478, first printed in High German in 1515 and also much translated and later known as *Till Eulenspiegel*; the Low German verse epic *Reynke de Vos* printed at Lübeck in 1498, a successful satirical verse epic version of the ancient animal fable of Reynard the Fox; and the *Historia von D. Johann Fausten, dem weitbeschreyten Zauberer und Schwartzkünstler*, first printed in 1587, which inspired both Marlowe's drama (through the English translation: *The historie of the damnable life and deserved death of Dr. John Faustus*, London, 1592) and Goethe's *Faust*. The Emperor Maximilian I himself contributed to the literature of the age in many ways including his own verse epic of chivalry and romance, *Theuerdank* (1505–12, first printed 1517) and his prose novel of chivalry, *Weißkunig* (about 1514, not printed until 1775).

In drama, Biblical themes and popular farcical topics found form in a multitude of religious plays and Shrovetide playlets (*Fastnachtspiele*), of which over a hundred and fifty have been preserved. If lyric poetry included much sterile versifying produced by the mastersingers, it also included the German *Kirchenlied*, a moving creation of the age, the *Volkslied*, and the historical ballad. Chronicle writing was, of course, not new. It began in late Middle High German times, but it thrived quite particularly during the heyday of the towns. More and more the medieval mixture of legend and history, often going back to the Creation, gave way to more factual and even documented historiography. A new branch arose in the topographical and biographical reports, giving descriptions of far-away places, especially the Holy Land and other oriental countries, and relating factual and fictional experiences.

The voyages of discovery were also made known to the German reading public. Christopher Columbus' famous letter of 1493 relating his first voyage, published simultaneously at Barcelona, Rome, Paris and Basle, appeared in a German translation at Strasbourg in 1497. And there was, for example, Balthasar Springer's *Die Meerfart vun erfarung nüwer Schiffung vnd Wege zu viln onerkannten Inseln vnd Kunigreichen*, 1509. The new picture of the world was introduced, for instance, by Johann Adelphus Muling's *Der Welt Kugel. Beschrybung der Welt vnd des gantzen Ertreichs hie angezögt vnd vergleicht einer rotunden kuglen*, 1509. Old and modern science existed side by side. The medieval *Lucidarius* appeared in no fewer than thirty-nine editions between 1479–1518. On the other hand there were new German treatises on astronomy, geometry, algebra, warfare, agriculture, architecture, mining, pharmacy and medicine, as well as on the less reputable branches such as astrology, chiromancy and alchemy. Germany in fact had a great contemporary reputation for its advanced 'mechanical arts', that is the sciences. The main works on the science of fortification, on geometry and proportion were written in German by Germany's greatest artist of the age, Albrecht Dürer (1471–1528): *Vnderweysung der Messung mit dem zirckel vnd richtscheyt in Linien, ebenen vnnd gantzen corporen durch Albrecht Dürer zů samen getzogen*, Nuremberg, 1525; *Etliche vnderricht zu befestigung der Stett, Schloß vnd flecken*, Nuremberg, 1527; *Vier bücher von menschlicher Proportion*, Nuremberg, 1528.

Language itself was the subject of the first books on spelling and grammar. There were also dictionaries. In every branch of secular learning specialist literature (*Fachliteratur*) in German grew immensely. In the field of jurisprudence the gradual introduction of Roman law towards the end of the fifteenth and in the early sixteenth centuries produced many popular writings. If seventy per cent of all extant German manuscripts date from the fifteenth century this groundswell of specialist writings contributed considerably. Some scriptoria were organized as industrial workshops with many scribes at work simultaneously. After the invention of printing, by wood blocks or movable metal types, this kind of industrial organization spread rapidly.

In one respect the age was linked firmly with the Middle Ages. It was still religion which was responsible for the greatest amount of writing. Compilations of saints' lives, manuals of spiritual consolation, and other edificatory and devotional tracts were as much in demand as ever. There were no fewer than fifty editions of the *Passional* between 1500 and 1521 alone. Thomas à Kempis' *Imitatio Christi* was as popular in its German version as in the many other vernacular translations. The pericopes were printed fifty-seven times in High German and twenty-one times in Low German editions before 1522. In 1516 and 1518 Luther edited the *Theologia deutsch.* Sermons by the famous Alsatian preacher Johann Geiler von Kaisersberg appeared in many prints, e.g. *Predigten teutsch* (1508).

The first German Bible, based on a possibly Nuremberg translation of the Vulgate of about a hundred years earlier, was printed in Strasbourg by Johann Mentelin about 1466. Up to 1518 this was reprinted, with some later emendations, thirteen times and there were also four Low German pre-Lutheran printings. Martin Luther, beginning his translation of the New Testament in December 1521, used Erasmus' edition of the Greek New Testament as well as the Latin Vulgate and the German Bible. It appeared in September 1522. For the Old Testament he went back to the Hebrew and all other evangelical translators did likewise. Luther's complete Bible appeared first in 1534. The Catholics then brought out their version by Johann Eck in 1537. Luther's writings achieved a dissemination beyond anything that had ever happened before. His ninety-five theses in Latin, nailed to the famous door of the *Schloßkirche* at Wittenberg in 1517, also appeared, to his annoyance, in an unauthorized German translation. In 1520 his famous treatises *An den christlichen Adel deutscher Nation* and *Von der Freiheit eines Christenmenschen* started a flood of German theological writing. Tracts, treatises, sermons, missives, dialogues, pamphlets of abuse and condemnation, and of exhortation, poured from the printing presses. And there was above all else: the German Bible. The history of the German language took a new turn: the printed German written language reached every corner of the German-speaking countries and influenced and shaped even the political destiny of the entire nation.

6.3 | The invention of printing

In the year 1439 there took place a trial before the Strasbourg magistrates, in the course of which one of the witnesses, a goldsmith called Hans Dünne, stated that three years earlier Johannes Gutenberg had paid him about a hundred guilders just for 'daz zu dem trucken gehöret'. This is the first time that the Upper German verb *drucken* was recorded in connection with printing. From other evidence we know that the Mainz patrician Johannes Gensfleisch, known as Gutenberg after the family residence in Mainz, *zum Gutenberg*, had been engaged in secret experiments in a new process of 'artificial writing', involving movable metal types and a press. Gutenberg was at that time in exile in Strasbourg (perhaps from 1428 to 1444). Towards the end of 1455 he was again involved in a law suit, this time in Mainz, when his creditor Johannes Fust sued him for the repayment of the then large sum of about 1600 guilders with interest. It was this sum, in all probability, which had financed the completion of the invention and development of printing and had enabled Gutenberg to produce the first masterpiece of the new art, the 42-line Latin Bible, probably completed in 1455. At the same time his workshop had more than likely produced various editions of the much demanded Latin primer by Donatus and some ephemera. The first datable German publication is the *Türkenkalender* (a calendar with monthly exhortations for the fight against the Turks) for the year 1455, presumably finished in 1454.

German was thus used in printing right from the beginning. It is a fact worth remembering that the first Bible printed in German, and in any modern vernacular, appeared only eleven years after the first substantial printed work, the 42-line Latin so-called Gutenberg Bible. It was published at Strasbourg by Johann Mentelin in 1466. Even before that, had appeared *Der Ackermann aus Böhmen*, printed at Bamberg probably in 1460. This first edition was followed in the fifteenth century alone by a further twelve editions: one other at Bamberg, four at Basle, two at Strasbourg and one each at Augsburg, Ulm, Esslingen, Leipzig and Heidelberg. The first dated, as opposed to datable, German book, Ulrich Boner's *Edelstein* (14th February 1461) had no such success. While *Der Ackermann aus Böhmen* of around 1400 was in a form of German that soon became the most favoured kind of printed German, the much older *Edelstein* was in Middle High German. The great classic of Middle High German, Wolfram von Eschenbach's *Parzival*, printed by Mentelin at Strasbourg in 1477, also remained an isolated example of the older German literature to be printed. Printers learnt that the antiquated and obsolete language was an obstacle to the printing of older German literary works.

No such impediment attached to Latin. The first half-century of printing up to 1500, the era of the *incunabula*, was thus dedicated to the recording in print of practically the whole treasury of Latin writing, above all the patristic and scholastic works of theology, the liturgical books of daily church life, the primers of schools and universities, and increasingly the works of Christian and classical antiquity in Latin and Greek. Church and humanism together thus first reaped the immense benefits of this great invention. The manuscript on papyrus, parchment and latterly paper, which had moulded European cultural life for two thousand years, now rapidly gave way to the mechanically reproduced printed book. By 1500 there had appeared in over two hundred and fifty places about thirty-five thousand different editions representing perhaps about fifteen thousand different texts. It is estimated that of the *incunabula* seventy-seven per cent were in Latin and about twenty-two per cent in the vernacular languages: seven per cent in Italian and five to six per cent in German, the two most important vernacular languages in the field of early printing. Nearly half the production may be classified as religious, about a third as literary (classical, medieval and contemporary) and about a tenth each as legal and scientific. Of the fables of Aesop, for example, there were eighty-five editions in Latin, fifteen in German, seven in French and three in English. Nearly everywhere the majority of the vernacular works were translations. One can indeed say that up to 1500 printing served the past above all. In the sixteenth century there was first a shift from religious writings to secular. It has been estimated that in the fifteenth century at Strasbourg, one of the most important early printing centres, over fifty per cent of the production was religious and less than ten per cent classical, secular literature. From 1500 to 1520, however, about a third falls into the category of classical Latin, Greek and humanist writings and only twenty-seven per cent is religious. The Reformation brought a further fundamental swing, this time in favour of the vernacular. A veritable press campaign, overwhelmingly in German, was launched for the first time.

Publication in German, unlike in Latin as we have already seen, depended on contemporary writings. These were provided at first primarily by translators. Thus we find the German works of the translators of the fifteenth century, Heinrich Steinhöwel, Albrecht von Eyb, Niklas von Wyle, among the early printed books. The first contemporary book composed in German which was also a success was Sebastian Brant's *Narrenschiff*. The translators were not idle and it is remarkable that by 1500 there were already about six hundred editions of German books. Many of the German books were furnished with woodcuts. The *leyenbuch*, as a book in German was called, was typically a picture book. This fact was, of course, a reflection of the cultural situation. So was also the fact that the far greater part of German printing consisted of ephemera: broadsheets and pamphlets consisting of one or a few leaves concerning contemporary events, calendars and notifications of the authorities to the general public. The Emperor Maximilian, for instance, made much use of the printing press to inform the German nation of dynastic or national events. German culture was the popular culture alongside the high culture in Latin, and what was printed reflected this fact accurately. But as a vernacular culture it was very much alive and compared favourably with all others except Italian. The reception of the account of

Marco Polo's journeys may demonstrate this. The Old French text was translated into German and printed at Nuremberg as early as 1477 with the title *Das puch des edelñ Ritters vñ landtfarers Marcho polo*. It was reprinted at Augsburg in 1481. A Latin translation appeared at Antwerp probably in 1485, an Italian one in 1496, a Spanish one in 1503, a French one (not the original Old French version) in 1556 and an English version in 1579. German was very much a reading language by the end of the fifteenth century as opposed to being a language in which people were mainly read to, which it had been in earlier centuries.

But this was only a modest beginning compared to what happened from 1518 onwards. The *Sermon von Ablaß und Gnade*, i.e. the gist of Luther's ninety-five theses in German, appeared in twenty-two editions in the space of two years. In August 1520 the Wittenberg printer Melchior Lotther brought out Luther's *An den christlichen Adel* in an edition of four thousand copies, probably the biggest of any up to then. (By comparison the first Latin Bible of 1455 had probably come out in an edition of about one hundred and eighty copies.) Within a week a reprint was needed and in a short while no fewer than fifteen editions and reprints were in circulation. *Von der Freiheit eines Christenmenschen*, also of 1520, ran to eighteen editions by 1526. By 1525 there were no fewer than two thousand editions of writings by Luther. Between 1522 and 1534 there were eighty-five editions of his New Testament and up to the death of Luther (1546), including part editions, altogether over four hundred. Unauthorized reprints had appeared everywhere. As early as December 1522 Adam Petri in Basle brought out the September Testament and reprinted it in March 1523 with a glossary for South German readers. Within two years there were sixty-six unauthorized reprints. All included certain linguistic changes. The Zürich Bible was printed by Froschauer in Zürich twenty-eight times between 1524 and 1564. The 1524 edition was in fact an unauthorized edition of Luther's New Testament rendered into the locally current Swiss German written language. Later editions with translations by the Zürich reformers also included numerous linguistic alterations.

Between 1500 and 1526 over four thousand publications in German appeared in print. Hundreds of pamphlets spread or fought against the new teaching. Between 1518 and 1525 Luther's writings amounted to more than a third of all German publications. Never again was one man so to dominate the market. Hans Lufft of Wittenberg alone published thirty-seven editions of the whole Bible and is said to have sold a hundred thousand copies between 1534 and 1584. What this surge of publications in German, mainly in Lutheran German, meant for the German language, can easily be guessed, but has not yet been exhaustively examined. That it was possible at all was, of course, entirely due to the printing press.

The role that Latin still played did little to diminish the importance of printing for German. If at the most important book fair in Germany, that of Frankfurt, there were on offer in 1566 to 1570 226 books in Latin as against 118 in German, and in 1601 to 1605 out of 1334 books for sale 813 in Latin but only 422 in German, it must not be forgotten that we are comparing the international market with the national market. The Frankfurt book fair was the most important market place for books in Europe from the second half of the sixteenth century to the first half of the seventeenth. Of the over twenty thousand titles offered between 1564 and 1600 nearly a third came from outside Germany. Frankfurt was the international market of the Latin book as well as the national market of the German book. With the decline of the Frankfurt book fair during the Thirty Years War the international market became fragmented and divided into national markets, to the detriment of Latin and the benefit of the national vernaculars. Leipzig became the German book market, having become a serious competitor of Frankfurt as early as 1600. Throughout the Early New High German period, it is true, Latin remained the language of high culture and German the language of popular culture. In contrast to later centuries this period still possessed a genuinely neutral international language. From the second half of the seventeenth century onwards, more and more, there were only national languages in Europe.

Two events contributed to the rapid spread of the new art of printing. First, the rupture of the partnership of Johannes Gutenberg and Johannes Fust in 1455, in consequence of which the secret of the new process must have leaked, and secondly the sack of Mainz in 1462 which seems to have caused the dispersal of many of the printers of the original Gutenberg workshop. From about 1460 printing presses existed at Strasbourg and Bamberg. By 1470 there were establishments in Cologne, Eltville,

Augsburg, Nuremberg, Basle, Constance and Beromünster. German printers had also spread the art abroad, first to Italy, where Venice was soon to rise to pre-eminence, to Paris and the Netherlands. By 1500 printing had been carried out at some sixty centres in the German-speaking territories, although in that year only at twenty-one places were a total of about sixty presses in operation. The trade was speculative and highly competitive. Many early printers went bankrupt. The most prosperous printing centres were Cologne, Strasbourg, Basle, Augsburg and Nuremberg. In each of these over a thousand editions had appeared by 1500. Together with Leipzig these five towns had produced nearly two thirds of the output of all the German presses. The German output itself amounted perhaps to not quite one third of all *incunabula* in Europe. In 1500 about one sixth of the books, but two-thirds of the broadsheets, were in German, the rest in Latin. During the Reformation Wittenberg and Zürich rose to eminence as printing centres. After the middle of the sixteenth century Frankfurt became predominant and Ingolstadt and Tübingen also became important. In the early period it was thus above all the west and the south which predominated. But after 1520 there was to be an enormous rise of production in the east and the north. The Frankfurt–Leipzig axis was to supplement the older Strasbourg–Nuremberg axis. Basle, and later Zürich, did much to join Switzerland to the 'Common German' to which the printers were now making such a significant contribution.

In the actual appearance of the book the advent of printing meant little change. The early printers aimed at producing books as close as possible to the manuscript books. It is a remarkable fact that the early printers created and printed allographs not graphemes. Imitating the innumerable manuscript ligatures and abbreviations of the scribes Gutenberg had employed two hundred and ninety types instead of the twenty-six or so letters of the alphabet which would have enabled him to reap the full reward for the mechanization he had invented. Only gradually did the new art emancipate itself from the world of the scribe and the scriptorium. In the actual handling of language there was equally no sharp rupture with the previous practice. Spelling in German was allowed to remain irregular and often arbitrary. In a Strasbourg text practically any percentage of spellings with ⟨o⟩ for MHG *ā* might occur. When Basle printers started using the graphs ⟨ei, au, eu⟩

for dialectal and MHG *ī*, *ū*, *iu* in imitation of eastern, for example Augsburg or Nuremberg, practice, the same kaleidoscopic mixture tended to prevail for several decades. Nor was change rectilinear. After a print with a predominance of the new digraph forms there might suddenly again be a reversion to the older spellings. The reader of manuscripts was used to a multiplicity of dialectal forms and irregularity of spelling. The reader of printed books expected nothing else and accepted the same orthographic abundance. As an age it was insensitive to and inured to dialectal and orthographic variation. Printing made no difference, or at least not initially and then only very gradually. Printers were a highly mobile class of artisans. In most printing places both the masters and the journeymen came from all parts of Germany. They were used to adapting themselves to local conditions and local linguistic conventions. Printers and readers alike accepted that, say, 'to do' could be spelt *dun, tůn, tun, thůn* etc. or that 'shine' could be *schyn, schin, scheyn, schein* etc. For 'king' they were familiar with such spellings as *kůnig, kunig, khunig, konnig, kônig* etc. Although printers and booksellers were no doubt interested in nationwide sales, linguistic uniformity was not a precondition. When Froschauer printed the 1527 edition of the Zürich Bible with the new diphthongs, against the local tradition and dialect, it is more than likely that he had sales in Germany in mind. But he also continued printing the dialectal monophthongs for a long time still, and anyway was no more consistent in his practice than any of the other printers. We know that Luther himself was only really interested in the preservation of the *sense* of what he had written but hardly in the *form* in which it was presented. In the end printing did help to bring about greater uniformity in language, but it is an exaggeration to say that it was the major factor in the eventual emergence of a uniform standard language. This, anyway, did not occur in the Early New High German period.

The printers, of whom the most important were found in perhaps a dozen or two dozen towns, thus at first largely conformed to the local linguistic traditions. In the early sixteenth century one can therefore speak of several regional printers' languages, always remembering that each one was itself basically lacking in a norm and characterized by wide latitude and tendencies rather than uniformity. One can thus distinguish an Upper Rhenish printers' language (Strasbourg, Basle), a Swabian (Augsburg, Tübingen,

Ulm), an Austro-Bavarian (Ingolstadt, Munich, Vienna), a West Central German (Mainz, Frankfurt, Worms, and more and more also Cologne), an East Franconian (Nuremberg, Bamberg), an East Central German (Leipzig, Wittenberg). Both the Upper German and the Central German groups were already moving nearer to each other when the Swiss printers' language (Zürich) was still considerably distinct. Even more removed from the converging Common German were the Low German printing presses (Lübeck, Hamburg, Münster, Rostock). Here the development was to be abrupt: the Low German centres eventually simply went over to printing in High German (mainly East Central German). In the same way in which certain chanceries, for instance, the Saxon chancery and the Imperial chancery, had proved more and more exemplary, so the important printing centres acted as preceptors and had thus a unifying influence.

The same casual attitude which the age showed with regard to linguistic form manifested itself in the relation of printer and author. Printers handled manuscripts submitted to them extremely freely and authors did not seem to object. The private language of writers, especially in terms of spelling, and the public language of the printers therefore often differed considerably. For instance, Dürer's private language looks much more archaic than the language of his printed works. Printers and above all their proof readers played an important role in reducing the possible spelling variants by eliminating archaic and regionally too restricted forms. In many places they were more 'modern' than the local chanceries. But universities and schools in general were also encouraging the tendency to greater uniformity. The printing press was only one of the several innovating factors of the time. It was in this way that the printers' language was influential and helped to mould the further evolution of the language. In studying the language of the age it is therefore the public language of the printers which is important and must be primarily considered.

Fig. 12

The Empire in the early sixteenth century.

6.4 | The written language, standardization and regional forms

6.4.1 | The written language

In the early sixteenth century the state and condition of the German language as a written medium were both extraordinarily complicated and very much in flux. The complications were the result of the enormous increase in writing and printing in many more centres than ever before. The accelerated rate of change was caused by the revolution in linguistic contact and communication. The spread of the written language over the whole territory and over a much wider range of cultural activities than in earlier times, is responsible for the impression of the greatest divergence and extreme diversification which the German language makes in the fourteenth century and until towards the last decades of the fifteenth. In the second half of the fifteenth century however, forces making for gradually increasing convergence became more and more evident.

These showed themselves first in the documentary language (*Kanzleisprache*) of the imperial chancery and of the larger principalities. While under Ludwig the Bavarian (1313–47) the language of the imperial chancery had been broadly Bavarian, under the Habsburgs Frederick III and Maximilian I it was much less so. In between, it is true, it had been centred on Prague and had acquired a Central German appearance. What was, however, a significant new feature was that even after its return to the Bavarian dialectal region the imperial chancery did not also return to a narrowly Bavarian linguistic form. Thus, for instance, the Bavarian diphthongs in unstressed syllables (-*leich*, -*ein*) were largely avoided (-*lich*, -*in*); ⟨o, u⟩ often served for both mutated and unmutated sounds in the Central German fashion but against the prevalent Bavarian practice, e.g. frequently *Wir Maximilian von gots gnaden Romischer Kunig*; ⟨e⟩ for MHG *ä*, *æ* was widespread while Bavarian normally used ⟨å⟩; for MHG *uo* and *u* the same sign ⟨u⟩ was sometimes used in contrast to the clear distinction normally observed in Bavarian; where the reflex of MHG *uo* was indicated the sign was generally ⟨ue⟩ rather than ⟨ů⟩. If in most other respects the language of the imperial chancery was indeed Bavarian this was less remarkable than that it did reveal a degree of retraction from pure regionalism. The reason is probably that the personnel of the chancery was recruited from a less regionally restricted background than the personnel in ducal and other minor offices.

It used to be assumed that the language of the imperial chancery had a great influence on other writing centres. In particular, the relatively modern looking Prague *Kanzleisprache* under Charles IV was at one time claimed to constitute the earliest stage from which, in direct line, the NHG standard language evolved. While direct influence as such cannot be proved and is unlikely, what remains important is the growing detachment of the written languages from their regional and thus dialectal backgrounds. In all the most important cultural centres linguistic features of limited validity were gradually pushed back and finally eliminated. In this development the printers from the early decades of the sixteenth century onwards were usually the leaders. From about 1520 the *Druckersprachen* became generally more important than the *Kanzleisprachen* in the movement away from the spoken dialects and in the growing trend towards standardization. In Augsburg the typically Swabian spelling ⟨au⟩ for MHG *ā* (*schlauffen* for *schlafen*) tended to disappear from printed works, while it lingered very much longer in private documents as in less important centres. In Strasbourg originally fairly widespread unrounding, e.g. *ibel* for *übel*, became more and more rare. In Nuremberg dialectal ⟨a⟩ for MHG *ou, ei* was gradually eliminated. What was to become of the greatest consequence was the gradual detachment from the dialectal base which occurred in one of the most extensive and prosperous of all German principalities, that of the electorate and duchy of Saxony.

Here the written language of the electoral chancery, of municipal administrations and of prose in general, the *Geschäftssprache*, as it is usually called, underwent fairly far-reaching changes in the fifteenth century. A relatively homogeneous linguistic type had evolved early extending from Eisenach and Erfurt in Thuringia to Wittenberg and Dresden in Saxony. This type was also to be found in the Prussian territories under the dominance of the Teutonic Knights and, with more variations, in Lusatia and Silesia. Even in the fourteenth and fifteenth centuries the written language had incorporated many southern and western features characteristic of Middle High German, but the then extremely wide range of variations had nevertheless accommodated many dialectal features (see pp. 253–4, 265–6). The tendency to regional standardization which made itself felt towards the end of the fifteenth century and during the sixteenth led both to a reduction of the number of variants and to an elimination of the specifically dialectal variants. Some of the features which were now recessive were purely orthographic, e.g. ⟨i⟩ instead of ⟨e⟩ in unstressed syllables, or ⟨cz, zc⟩ for ⟨z, tz⟩. A regional spelling peculiarity was thus recognized as such and gradually abandoned in favour of forms generally current elsewhere. Some of the features were based in the local dialects, such as MHG *i* > *e* (*wese* 'meadow'), MHG *u* > *o* (*korcz* 'short'),

MHG *ā* > *o* (*jor* 'year'), MHG *iuw* > *au/aw* (*nau* 'new'), MHG *ei* > *e* (*kled* 'garment'), MHG *ou* > *o* (*bom* 'tree') and many more. Such traits, generally in a minority from the beginning of German writing, were progressively eliminated, first in the written language of the electoral chancery, while at the same time lingering on in other chanceries and even more so in private writings. Further features which characterized ECGm. about a generation before Luther were: former *he, her* > *er*; former *wie* > *wir*; *unse* > *unser*; infinitives without -*n*, formerly widespread in Thuringian, had disappeared; ⟨o⟩ for MHG *u, ü* especially before *r* and some other consonants was now generally restricted to individual words such as *sonst, fromm, komen, sontagk, sonnabend, konig, son, sommer*; ⟨ie⟩ for MHG *ie* was general despite dialectal monophthongization and there was a gradual increase of ⟨ie⟩ for lengthened MHG *i* in open syllables; *sal* gave way to *sol*, and *ob, oder, gegen* prevailed against earlier *ab, adir, kegin*; forms such as *greve, fregen, sente* were replaced by *grave, fragen, sant*. A firm and characteristic feature of ECGm. was the non-indication of mutation in the case of *o* and *u*. The graphs ⟨o⟩ for MHG *o, ö, ō, œ* and ⟨u⟩ for MHG *u, ü, uo, üe* persisted as long as ECGm. was a regional written language. When the distinction ⟨o/ö⟩, ⟨u/ü⟩ was introduced, generally towards the end of the sixteenth century and ⟨ä⟩ was also adopted, ECGm. can be said to have evolved and merged into NHG.

Of course, no changes were quick or neat. Much depended on the individual scribe, his place of origin and education. Variety in language, even if being reduced, was still the hallmark of the period. The development was often not straight: the direction was sometimes reversed. The history of the ECGm. chancery spelling *vor*- for the usual *ver*- is particularly illustrative (Kettmann pp. 133–5): in the first half of the fourteenth century *vor*- replaced *ver*- almost completely; in the fifteenth century *ver*- gained ground but remained a minority form; from the end of the fifteenth century up to 1520 *ver*- predominated with *vor*- amounting to no more than a quarter of all cases; between 1520 and 1530 they drew nearly equal; between 1530 and 1540 *ver*- fell back to a mere third of all cases; and in 1540 to 1546 *vor*- had become the rule.

The reduction in the number of variants by the gradual elimination of dialectal features, which anyway had only constituted a minority of forms, meant of course no change in the system. But one innovation was adopted in the fifteenth century which affected the system. From about 1440 the spellings ⟨ei, au, eu⟩ for MHG *ī*, *ū*, *iu* gradually increased and became the majority in the electoral chancery between 1485 and 1490. After 1500 there were only sporadic ⟨i⟩ and ⟨u⟩ spellings. The spoken dialects over most of the area had undergone a diphthongization and the question is: was this orthographic change the consequence of the prior diphthongization in the spoken language? The answer is almost certainly negative. At a time when already established dialectal spellings were eliminated, when innumerable other dialectal features such as the unrounding of the MHG rounded front vowels (*ü* > *i*, *ö* > *e*), the coalescence of the voiced and voiceless or lenis and fortis series of plosives and fricatives (*binnenhochdeutsche Konsonantenschwächung*, e.g. the coalescence of *d* and *t* in *leiden* – *leiten*), the monophthongization of MHG *ei*, *ou* > *e*, *o* were not adopted into the spelling system, it is highly unlikely that the dialectal diphthongization would have been reflected in spelling. What is much more likely is that these spellings were adopted from the area to the south-west, from East Franconia, in particular Nuremberg. And beyond East Franconia there was, of course, the extensive Bavarian dialectal area with the same diphthongal spellings. In Bohemia, too, for instance in Prague and Eger, the new diphthongs were spelt. That the adoption of these spellings undoubtedly eased the spelling of the long high-tongue vowels is a fact. But that the strain on the graphemic system alone could have led to the innovation is difficult to accept in the light of the fact that throughout the fourteenth and fifteenth centuries the changes in the ECGm. written language had taken place in consequence of a most powerful south-western influence. This influence continued in the sixteenth century when even Bavarianisms, such as ⟨ai⟩ for MHG *ei*, ⟨å⟩ for mutated *a*, ⟨ue⟩ for usual ⟨u⟩ (MHG *uo*, *üe*), ⟨kh⟩ for usual ⟨k⟩, the first and third person pl. pres. ind. of 'to be' *seind* for *sind*, or the western form *nit* for *nicht* were to be found. After 1520 the spelling ⟨ai⟩ became as frequent as ⟨ei⟩ for MHG *ei* in the electoral chancery, although it hardly occurred outside chancery practice. Early in the sixteenth century the diphthongal graphs ⟨ei, au, eu⟩ were also adopted in WCGm. where the dialectal diphthongization had undoubtedly occurred considerably earlier. In the Low Alemannic written language, especially that of the printers, the diphthongs spread from the early sixteenth century onward.

despite the continued existence of monophthongs in the dialect. The same was true, only much later, in Switzerland. In all these cases it was the spelling practice of the eastern Upper German regions which proved exemplary, whatever might have or might not have changed in the spoken dialects.

The most characteristic phenomena of the written language of the time, then, are the marked development away from the dialects and the tendency to regional levelling and increased standardization. What must now also be emphasized is that basically the written language was still idiolectal. Every manuscript and every print is its own version of written German on the one hand and of the still somewhat abstract regional or local variant of it on the other. The factors which determined an idiolect were, as in Middle High German, the provenance and educational background of every writer, copyist or printer, the character of the text (original, copy, reprint, adaptation), the register of the linguistic text (private letters, documentary language, popular or elevated literature, Biblical language and so on), the place of composition and the time of composition. Contamination was still the general condition of a piece of writing. For valid comparisons which would yield neat results one would require 'pure' texts, i.e. original texts written at the same time by local writers in the 'average' local form, being also texts in the same register. However, since such texts were highly unusual they would be unrepresentative of the German language in this period.

An author's texts were often printed far from where he lived. Ulrich von Hutten from Hesse had his German works printed in Leipzig and Strasbourg. When Johann Mentelin printed the first German Bible in Strasbourg in 1466 he did not print it in the local Low Alemannic but retained the Central Upper German form of the text. Printers in Basle and Strasbourg frequently retained the Augsburg form of what they printed. Froschauer in Zürich often printed simultaneously one format of the Bible in Swiss and another in general Upper German. Where his text of the Bible was general Upper German the preface, either that by Zwingli or the other by Jud, was much nearer Swiss. The famous dialogue *Karsthans*, printed at Strasbourg, is in a form of language which suggests that the text originated farther south, in High Alemannic territory. Successful works tended to be reprinted in many places with all possible shades of adaptation. Brant's

Narrenschiff, originally Alemannic, was reprinted in Nuremberg and Augsburg in the local printers' languages.

The German written language of the time was contaminated, but nevertheless in the process of achieving greater detachment from the dialects and greater homogeneity albeit at first within regional units. Regions, of course, were not sharply defined but tended to be differently delimited for different phenomena. But the regional written languages were moving nearer to each other. The written language on the one hand and the spoken language, that is the dialects, on the other, were, in contrast, moving farther apart.

6.4.2 | The origin of the standard language

There can be no doubt that the New High German standard language, at least as a written medium, had begun to evolve in this period. Generations of scholars have therefore asked themselves: where was the cradle and who was the father?

Both questions suffer from excessive naïvety. There was no 'cradle' and there was no 'father'. The first time a type of language appeared which approximated to the New High German standard language, was at Prague in the middle of the fourteenth century. The second time a similar type emerged was around 1500 in East Central Germany. But no direct link between the two can be established. There was only the fortuitous link forged by similar conditions: the same sort of dialectal background of a mixture of Upper German and Central German with the same strong dependence on the earlier written language of Upper Franconia and the south. When Burdach's and Bernt's theory of the Bohemian or Prague origin had been disproved, for there had been no continuity or influence of Prague on Meissen, it was replaced by the persuasively argued theory of the dialectal base. Theodor Frings claimed that 'ein übersehbarer Weg führt von der Sprache der Siedler zur Sprache der Schreiber, zu Luther und zur neuhochdeutschen Schriftsprache' (p. 5). Elsewhere he stated that in his view New High German was

das neue Deutsch im Munde der Ostsiedler vorgeformt und [es] wurd gesprochen, lange bevor es seit dem 13. Jahrhundert in die Schreib stube einzog. Es ist ein Gewächs des neudeutschen Volksbodens, ein Schöpfung des Volks, nicht des Papiers und des Humanismus.

He and his Leipzig followers specified the *Volkssprache* as meaning a *koloniale Ausgleichssprache* from which was to develop the written *Geschäftssprache*. However, the whole development of the ECGm. written language, in the fourteenth century as shown by H. Bach, in the fifteenth and early sixteenth centuries as investigated by L. E. Schmitt, E. Skála, W. Fleischer and G. Kettmann, reveals an increasing detachment from the dialects and an extremely powerful influence from the written languages of the neighbouring south-western regions. In addition to the features mentioned above (pp. 366–8) one could further adduce the absence in the written language of reflexes of the dialectal changes of MHG *ē* > *ī* (*snē* > *schnī*), MHG *ō* > *ū* (*hōch* > *hūch*), MHG *ë* > *a* (*wëter* > *watter*), or of MHG -*b*-, -*g*- to fricatives, or the adoption of the UGm. spelling *pf*- instead of dialectal *f*-, or of -*mpf*- for dialectal -*mp*-, the retention of -*nd*- for dialectal -*ng*- (*gefunden* instead of *gefungen*), the adoption of UGm. spellings like *Churfurst* with *ch* or the frequent occurrence of the UGm. apocope (*nam* 'name').

It is, of course, true that *Meissnisch*, on the other hand, contains a number of dialectal features which also appear as characteristic features of the NHG standard language. Frings has listed: the personal pronouns with -*r* and -*ch* (*mir, mich, dir, dich, er, wir, euch*); the diminutive in -*chen*; the noun phrase of the type *mein liebes Kind*; the word *nur*; *Rückumlaut* in the pret. and past part. of verbs like *brennen*; the verbs for 'to go, to stand' with the root vowel -*e*-; monophthongs *i, u* in *lieb, Bruder*; diphthongs *au, ei* in *Haus, Zeit*; [ks] in *sechs, Ochsen, wachsen*; the dative ending -*e*, e.g. *im Hause*; the unsyncopated prefixes *ge*-, *be*- and the endings -*en*, -*es* (*gestohlen, bestellt, gebrochen, liebes*). That regional dialectal features should occur in the regional written language is, of course, to be expected, especially if these also had the support of the written language of the areas which exercised the strongest influence on Meissen, such as East Franconia and other areas to the south and west. This is largely the case with the above characteristics.

In the light of such overwhelming evidence one is bound to conclude that what was happening was happening primarily on paper. Exactly because it was relatively non-dialectal and had become a well-levelled written medium the *Meissnisch* of the time received wide acclaim. It is, of course, likely that this written language also had a spoken counterpart in court, administrative, ecclesiastical, and university circles. By having been open to southern influences for so long the written medium had enabled that compromise to come about to which Luther alluded when he said:

Ich habe keine gewisse, sonderliche, eigene Sprache im Deutschen, sondern brauche der gemeinen deutschen Sprache, daß mich beide, Ober- und Niederländer verstehen mögen. Ich rede nach der sächsischen Canzeley, welcher nachfolgen alle Fürsten und Könige in Deutschland; alle Reichsstädte, Fürsten-Höfe schreiben nach der sächsischen und unsers Fürsten Canzeley, darum ists auch die gemeinste deutsche Sprache. Kaiser Maximilian und Kurf. Friedrich, H. zu Sachsen ec. haben im römischen Reich die deutschen Sprachen also in eine gewisse Sprache gezogen. (*Weimar Ausgabe, Tischreden*, 1, p. 524.)

Lacking hindsight and the knowledge of what a normalized standard vernacular language is like, he no doubt exaggerated.

A unified, normalized standard language did not exist yet. But the process of its formation had started. It was clearly recognizable to contemporaries and can be confirmed by the modern observer. But it took at least another hundred and fifty years to reach completion. Many factors, most of all the historical significance of Martin Luther himself, contributed to making the ECGm. written variant of Common German the most direct base of New High German. That it was able to provide such a base is undoubtedly the result of its having absorbed so many southern and western features over a long time. That the German standard emerged not from the spoken and written language of *one* area (like French from Paris and the Île de France) is the result of German history. It originated more as a written language and remained one longer than say French or English, again for historical reasons. And as a written language it was a receptacle of contributions from many regions, even if one proved more important than others. When Wittenberg ceased to be the great centre for the dissemination of the ECGm. written language, Luther's Bible was distributed from the great printing houses of Frankfurt am Main. WCGm. influence thus became important from about 1560. The Frankfurt printers were largely responsible for introducing and generalizing the Upper German graphs ⟨å, ỏ, ủ⟩ or ⟨ä, ö, ü⟩. On the levels of grammar and lexis, however, the ECGm. strand continued to be decisive right into the period of the Classical language, around 1800.

Many contemporaries of Luther held the view that a kind of common High German, although with variants, existed. The Silesian Fabian Frangk writing in 1531 on German usage said that *Oberlendisch* (i.e. High German), though orderly and clear, was in many respects not uniform for in no region was it used quite properly and correctly. He who wanted to avoid abuses and write correctly was advised not to follow the practice of any one particular region but to get to know many regional *Landsprachen* and their shortcomings so that he might avoid what was not correct. Frangk also thought that it was particularly helpful to know good German books or documents and to follow their example, and he recommended especially the writings of Emperor Maximilian's chancery, of Martin Luther and the books printed by Johann Schönsperger in Augsburg. In other words, for him, as for Luther, Common German was not to be found in any particular region – Meissen or Augsburg – but in the 'best' language of both East Central Germany and Upper Germany. For him standardization was clearly a desirable postulate, and he realized that much progress had already been made.

Sebastian Helber (*Teutsches Syllabierbüchlein*, Freiburg i.U.), writing admittedly late in the century (1593), stated that *das Gemeine Hoch Teütsche*, from which he excluded Dutch, Low German, and *Cölnisch*, was printed in three different variants: *die Mitter Teütsche, die Donawische* and *die Höchst Reinische*. He thus distinguished within Common High German: Central German (in which he included the following printing centres: Mainz, Speyer, Frankfurt, Würzburg, Heidelberg, Nuremberg, Strasbourg, Leipzig, Erfurt and the Cologne printers 'wan si das Ober Teütsch verfertigen'), Swabian-Bavarian and Swiss (printed Swiss having by then moved nearer to common Upper German).

Gemeines Deutsch is a designation used by many authorities for Upper German, excluding in the early sixteenth century Swiss, i.e. South or High Alemannic. It is, however, doubtful whether the opposition ECGm. *vs. Gemeines Deutsch* is really justified, and in the light of Luther's and Frangk's comments made almost in the same year, it is unlikely that contemporaries saw their language situation in this way. Furthermore, although *gemein* could mean 'common' then as now, in most of the occurrences of *Gemeines Deutsch* at that time it meant 'simple, ordinary, straightforward German' as opposed to the involved, artificial, latinizing style of much contemporary writing. It seems therefore more correct to see the linguistic situation in the early decades of the sixteenth century as follows:

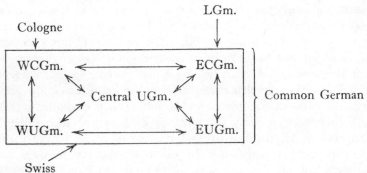

WCGm.: Mainz, Worms (Rhen. Franc.)

ECGm.: Erfurt, Wittenberg, Leipzig (Thuringian, Upper Saxon)

Central UGm.: Nuremberg, Bamberg, Würzburg (East Franc.)

WUGm.: Strasbourg, Basle (Low Alem.)

EUGm.: Augsburg, Ingolstadt, Vienna (Swabian, Bavarian, Austrian)

Within Common German the arrows with two heads are meant to symbolize the give and take, adaptation, selection and levelling taking place. Basle, which joined the Swiss Confederation in 1501, was in some ways already in the process of adaptation to the rest of Upper German. The three areas still outside the Common German were Cologne (Ripuarian), Switzerland (High or South Alemannic), and Low Germany. Here the arrows with one head indicate the *Anschluss* which was later, in the sixteenth and seventeenth centuries, to occur and its direction. Any of the three might have gone separate ways: Cologne might have been absorbed in Dutch or Netherlands if the political preconditions had existed, but they did not and by 1575 Cologne had to all intents and purposes joined the WCGm. form of Common German; North Germany had its own highly developed, levelled-out written language, Hanseatic Low German, which gave way to the ECGm. variant of Common German on the decline of the Hansa; Switzerland, detaching itself from the empire after 1499, possessed a written language which was the most immediate heir to Middle High German and remained therewith strongly hinged to Common German.

In the case of Low Germany and of Switzerland one can indeed speak of the adoption and reception of New High German. Of the two areas one would perhaps expect Low Germany to resist the intrusion of the new Common German more. It was not so, despite the fact that a written language existed and flourished which was almost as well regulated and detached from its dialectal sources as the ECGm. written language. It had, however, been very much the medium of the Hanseatic league and was thus tied to its fortune. The decline of the economic strength of this primarily Baltic league coincided with the rise of the Atlantic trade based on Antwerp and the rise of Leipzig as a trading centre in the interior, joining the already important southern manufacturing and trading cities of Nuremberg and Augsburg. North German princes, after Latin had ceased to function as the first language of administration, often favoured High German. In Brandenburg the ruling dynasties, first the Bavarian Wittelsbach and then the Franconian Hohenzollern, employed many High German officials. The reputation of High German as a language of chivalric culture had been high throughout the Middle Ages. South Germany had gone ahead in the adoption of German as the language of administration. Other new fashions such as saints' names as first names and the adoption of surnames had also reached North Germany from the south and west. Although North Germany did not lack universities these were not found in the leading Hanseatic cities. And of course there were many more in the High German regions. It was above all there that the new learning of Humanism flourished which, although Latin was its language, nevertheless fertilized and encouraged German letters. The new legal system based on Roman Law and promoted by Emperor Maximilian developed in the south and was cultivated at High German universities. Lawyers, doctors, scholars, either from North Germany or from High Germany, educated at universities such as Erfurt, Leipzig, Heidelberg or even farther south, occupied leading positions in the north. The political reforms introduced under Maximilian and the unending succession of imperial diets, wrestling with the problems of the reform of church and state and all being held in the south, further enhanced the cultural supremacy of the south. The literature of the age, with very few exceptions, was produced in High German. The printing press was an invention of the south and had its leading houses there, although Lübeck was also an early printing centre. Books in High German were available in large numbers and, given the perennial respect for High German, easily penetrated into northern educated circles. Schools are known to have taught High German in the early sixteenth century. Then came the Reformation which spread from Wittenberg and won most of North Germany in a short time. North German cities had early formed the habit of corresponding in High German with cities in the south, for example Danzig with Leipzig or Lübeck with Mainz. Gradually they also adopted High German as their official language for internal use, Königsberg as early as 1530, Brunswick and Stettin around 1550, and Magdeburg, Dortmund, Bielefeld, and Rostock in the course of the next two decades. The last large cities to make the change in internal use and communications were Hamburg and Lübeck: both shortly after 1600. The spoken language, however, at least for the time being, remained Low German. The situation of diglossia, where one form of the language serves for one set of purposes and another form for a different but clearly defined set of purposes, lasted perhaps for up to a century. Afterwards the bourgeoisie adopted the New High German standard language also as its spoken medium.

Especially in the eastern areas High German had long advanced against Low German. Cities like Halle, Eisleben, Merseburg, Wittenberg and Frankfurt on Oder had gone over to High German as early as the fourteenth or fifteenth centuries. Berlin and surroundings followed shortly after 1500. In Magdeburg a mixture of *Meissnisch* and Low German was spoken as early as 1530. High German, known as *Misnisch* (< *Meissen*), was thus in competition with the native *Sassisch* even on the level of the spoken language. In the written language, too, High and Low German came to be mixed. The word *Missingsch* with its connotation of *Messing*, i.e. brass rather than pure gold, became the derogatory name for this form of language. But while in Brandenburg and elsewhere in regions adjacent to ECGm. High German was advancing even on the level of the spoken language, and while

some princely and urban administrations adopted High German
as their documentary language, Hanseatic Low German flourished
especially in Lübeck and along the coast till after the first decades
of the sixteenth century.

Before the Reformation four Low German Bibles had appeared
in print. In about 1478 Heinrich Quentell in Cologne had brought
out a Low German Bible in two versions, one in the language of
the Lower Rhine region and another in a more eastern variant.
In 1494 Steffen Arndes in Lübeck printed a beautifully illustrated
Bible in North Saxon Low German, that is in Hanseatic Middle
Low German, and a fourth pre-Lutheran Bible appeared at
Halberstadt in 1522. Luther's own New Testament was immediately translated into Low German, probably by Low German
students at Wittenberg under the guidance of Luther's associate
Johannes Bugenhagen, and appeared at Wittenberg in 1525.
In 1534 there followed the complete Bible. Up to 1621, when the
last edition was printed at Goslar, there were altogether twenty-
nine editions of the Bible in Low German. If demand then
petered out it was despite Luther's encouragement of the use of
people's native language. The general tendency of the age was, as
we have seen, to move away from regionally restricted forms of the
written language. From the last quarter of the sixteenth century
onwards literature was almost exclusively in High German. In
dramas, only peasants and servants were shown to be Low German
speaking, which clearly indicates the then social standing of Low
German.

Luther's writings and the Reformation, whose spiritual centre
was sited in ECGm. territory, were bound to strengthen the
already powerful and respected position of High German. Many
High German pastors, recommended by Luther and his associa-
tes, filled posts in Low Germany. Many Low German theologians
received their training in Wittenberg. The organization of the
Lutheran church in Low Germany also favoured the use of High
German in church ordinances, theological publications and even
sermons. By 1600 there was very little preaching in Low German.
Even the little town of Husum, for instance, heard its sermons
in High German from 1617 onwards. Thus the Reformation, in
the end, became another reason for the supplanting of Low German. Within hardly more than a century, i.e. by 1600, the thriving
Low German written language, which had exercised such a power-

ful influence on the Scandinavian languages in the fourteenth and fifteenth centuries, had ceased to exist. North Germany's adoption of the ECGm. variant of Common German gave the latter the strength which helped to tip the balance within Common German decidedly in its favour. More than ever it was now a supra-regional *Schriftsprache.*

In Switzerland the adoption of the New High German standard language took at least twice as long, although the step was much less great. Perhaps for this reason it could be taken more leisurely. That it would be taken could never be in doubt. Switzerland's High Alemannic dialect formed part of High German. Its contribution to cultural life in the age of chivalric literature had been considerable. Its insistence on complete political autonomy at first amounted to hardly more than the German princes' insistence on their *Libertät.* That it was to result in political independence and sovereignty, as known in the age of nationalism, could not be foreseen in the sixteenth century. Switzerland's economic position was incomparably weaker than that of the Low Countries, which were developing their own standard language. Its largest city, Basle, with its only university, had started making linguistic concessions, at least in its printed language, even before joining the Confederation in 1501. Zwingli attached very great importance to the links of his Reformation with that of south German cities, above all Strasbourg, Constance, Memmingen and Augsburg. He even entered into an alliance with the Landgrave of Hesse. His Zürich Bible, far from being a cornerstone of the Swiss written language, was in fact a Trojan horse. It was the first notable Swiss printed work which made concessions to common Upper German, for instance in its adoption of the Bavarian diphthongs. While all the important cities, with the exception of Lucerne, joined the Zwinglian Reformation, the rural and Alpine heartland of Switzerland did not. And most of the Reformed cities and cantons eventually preferred Luther's Bible to the Zürich Bible. In an extremely slow process, the printing presses, chanceries, schools and writers gradually moved away from the dialectally-based Swiss written language and adopted first the common Upper German and finally, by 1800, the Classical New High German standard language.

The process of adoption happened in stages, linguistic feature by linguistic feature. Thus the first step in the history of the

Zürich Bible was taken in the 1527–9 edition with the introduction of ⟨ei/ey⟩, ⟨au⟩ and ⟨eü⟩ for the Alemannic *ī, ū, ṻ*. In this and the next few editions ⟨ei⟩ was used mainly in *mein, dein, sein*, with otherwise increasing preference for ⟨ey⟩. For MHG *ī*, except in the pronouns, ⟨ey⟩ was preferred, while for MHG *ei* there were still numerous ⟨ei⟩ spellings, although ⟨ey⟩ already predominated. For MHG *iu* and *öu* the graphic distinction after the adoption of EUGm. ⟨eu⟩ was ⟨eü⟩ (MHG *iu*) and ⟨o̊u⟩ (MHG *öu*). Thus the Zürich printers managed to approach the EUGm. orthography without entirely sacrificing structural distinctions, except in the case of ⟨au⟩ for both MHG *ū* and *ou*. The UGm. distinction of the reflexes of lengthened MHG *i, u, ü* and MHG *ie, uo, üe* by the spellings ⟨i, u, ü⟩ and ⟨ie, ů, ů⟩ was retained up to the 1665/67 editions. The Zürich Bible thus remained purely Alemannic (written, of course, not dialectal), except for some stray ECGm. Lutherisms, only until 1525. From 1527/29 it was general UGm. with local features till 1665/67, when it made the transition from the UGm. type to the ECGm. type, with an accelerated rate of adoption in individual features from the beginning of the seventeenth century.

But the Swiss publishers, with an eye to the export market, were not representative of the way people actually wrote in Switzerland. The written language of the council offices and law courts remained Alemannic very much longer. Here, too, the transition was extremely slow and gradual, feature by feature, extending in St Gall from 1545 to 1800, in Schaffhausen from 1580 to 1800, in Zürich from 1600 to 1800, in Lucerne from 1620 to 1800. In all places the personality and education of individual clerks tended to be important. But if they were too much ahead of their time a reaction would usually follow. Thus for every individual NHG feature to become finally predominant we must generally reckon with its taking over a hundred years. The following selective chart (see Sager) giving the final predominance of a particular NHG feature shows just how late the process of the adoption of the NHG standard language in official use actually ended.

This whole process was, of course, entirely confined to the written medium. As a spoken medium the NHG standard language is even today restricted to very few functions. The present diglossia situation has thus been in existence for over three centuries.

Final predominance of a NHG feature	Basle	St Gall	Schaff-hausen	Zürich	Berne	Lucerne
NHG diphthongs	1590–1600	1605	1610	1650–80	1670	1700–
NHG monophthongs	1620	1750–1620	1710	1730	1740*	1750–
3rd pers. pl. *-end* > *-en*		1620	1650	1700	1740	1710

* No exact date for ⟨ů, ǚ⟩ > ⟨u, ü⟩ is available. Date refers to ⟨ie⟩ for lengthened MHG *i*.

6.4.3 | The role of Martin Luther

The role of Martin Luther in the rise of the German standard language has been debated ever since he was first declared its father or creator. Erasmus Alberus, a contemporary of Luther, stated: *Lutherus linguae Germanicae parens, sicut Cicero Latinae*. Fabian Frangk, as we have seen (p. 373), listed him among the preceptors to be followed. One of the first serious grammars of German was based on his works: Johannes Clajus, *Grammatica Germanicae linguae ex bibliis Lutheri Germanicis et aliis eius libris collecta*, Leipzig, 1578. By the immense, dominating output of his writings alone (see pp. 359–60) he was bound to have a profound impact. But was it a lasting one, and was his language something new, something he created that did not exist before? He himself claimed that he had no special language, but was writing in the common form of the Saxon chancery. The written forms of German were in fact in the process of being levelled and adapted to each other. Luther himself joined in this movement. Words which he learnt to identify as dialectal and regionally too restricted, he often replaced by more widely current ones. Spellings and linguistic forms which differed from those in use in Central or South-east Upper German he sometimes abandoned in favour of the southern forms, for example when his earlier *borg* became later *Burg*, or *kegen* became *gegen*, *gewest* gave way to *gewesen*, *nach*, *dach* to *noch*, *doch*, *widder* to *weder*. Where he wavered in his early writings he often gradually settled for one form, for instance, *sun/sohn* > *Sohn*, *nit/nicht* > *nicht*, *brengen/bringen* > *bringen*. In other cases, however, e.g. *ane/one* for *ohne*, *sunder/sonder*, *künnen/können*, *Münch/Mönch* he never finally resolved the question himself. His proof-readers were even more responsible than Luther himself for ever-increasing standardization and the elimination of variants.

The early Luther was more tied to his regional background. Especially between 1522 and 1531 he consciously worked at his language to widen its impact. The written languages of Nuremberg and of the imperial chancery frequently provided the example he then followed. The lexicon presented him with particularly great problems. Although the common lexical stock of German was even then considerable, there was a tenacious residue of regionalism (see 6.9.1). It is this which, for instance, caused the publisher Adam Petri in Basle to add a glossary of about two hundred words to his 1522 reprint of Luther's New Testament for the benefit of his Upper German readers. The South German Catholic Bible of Johann Eck replaced many ECGm. words with southern words, e.g. *grentze* > *landmark, hügel* > *bühel, töpfer* > *hafner, ziege* > *gaiss, heuchler* > *gleissner*. Nevertheless, there remains the fact that by the success of the Reformation and of his writings, in particular his Bible, the ECGm. written language received a boost which put it ahead of its competitors and familiarized the whole of Germany with this form of language or elements of it, above all its vocabulary.

Luther found himself, by accident of birth and career, using the already well-developed written language of Meissen which, with other regional written languages, was in a process of mutual adaptation and greater standardization. If he usually moved with the current of the time, indeed often accelerated it himself, he also sometimes used archaic forms which were later swept aside, e.g. his *wilch* for *welch, hirschen* for *herrschen, erbeit* for *Arbeit, gleuben* (beside *glauben*) for *glauben*, or *er schreib* for *er schrieb*. In all this he was very much a man of his time, even if he was usually in the vanguard.

In one respect, however, he was truly an innovator and creator. Not for him the latinizing stilted German of so much of contemporary writing. He was to fuse the written German with the spoken German of the man in the street. He was to create a truly popular German style, which the people would really understand. This is what *dolmetschen*, as he called it, meant to him. He used the written language of his region only as a mould into which he cast a new form of popular language. It was not an easy task. He took weeks and years over it. As far as his Bible translation was concerned his search ended only with his death. He worked at his language all his life always bearing in mind the famous principle he had laid down in his own memorable *Sendbrief von Dolmetschen*, written at Coburg in 1530:

/ den man mus nicht die buchstaben inn der lateinischen sprachen fragen / wie man sol Deutsch reden / wie diese esel thun / sondern /man mus die mutter jhm hause / die kinder auff der gassen / den gemeinen man auff dem marckt drumb fragen / vnd den selbigen auff das maul sehen / wie sie reden / vnd darnach dolmetzschen so verstehen sie es den / vnd mercken / das man Deutsch mit jn redet.

His language is thus full of homely sayings, idioms and proverbs, for instance, in the same *Sendbrief*:

ihr ycka ycka ist zu schwach 'their ee-aw, ee-aw is too weak'.

Es heist | Wer am wege bawet | der hat viel meister. 'He who builds in public has many masters who tell him how to do it.'

so hette yhr keiner gewist gack dazu zu sagen 'none of them would have been capable of saying boo to a goose'.

das sie ym die schuch hetten sollen wischen 'not fit to clean his boots'.

die wellt wil meister klüglin bleiben 'all want to be knowalls'.

Ich habs fur siben jaren gewist | das hüffnegel eysen sind 'I have known for seven years that horseshoe nails are of iron'.

Zwar es durfft ein Esel nicht viel singen | man kennet yn sonst wol bey den ohren 'a donkey does not have to sing, he can be recognized straightaway by his ears'.

Es ist gut pflugen | wenn der acker gereinigt ist 'it is easy to plough when the field is cleared of stones'.

Welche buchstaben die Eselsköpff ansehen | wie die kue ein new thor 'words at which the fools gape like a cow at a new gate'.

Other writers, such as his adversary the Franciscan Thomas Murner, Hans Sachs, the mastersinger and popular writer, and many of the pamphleteers of the age used a similar down-to-earth language. But times were to change. There followed an aristocratic reaction which shunned Luther's style and syntax. The religious split hardened. *Meissnisch* became a 'Protestant dialect' and the Upper German written language was supported by the Jesuits. Further unification and standardization were arrested and when the movement was finally resumed in the second half of the eighteenth century it received its impetus from different sources and owed little to Luther.

In one way, however, Luther's work was enduring. It was he who gave the Germans their Bible. Looking at a passage from the 1546 edition, regarded by the editors of the *Weimarer Ausgabe* as the *Ausgabe letzter Hand*, we realize how close to Classical German his language already was. When we remember that this was half a century before Shakespeare, we might hesitate to repeat the frequently heard plaintive observation that German became a standard language much later than English or French. There can be little doubt, when we compare the 1546 text with a modern version (e.g. that of 1905), that we must conclude that in one register at least, that of the language of the Bible, German approached the level of the modern standard as early as the sixteenth century. That was Martin Luther's achievement.

Matthew 14, 23–33 from the 1546 edition, published at Wittenberg by Hans Lufft. (For comparison see 4.9, 5.3.3(vi) and 6.4.4 (i), (ii), (vi), (viii).)

Vnd da er das Volck von sich gelassen hatte, steig er auff eynen Berg alleine das er betet. Vnd am abend war er alleine daselbs. Vnd das Schiff war schon mitten auff dem Meer vnd leid not von den Wellen, Denn der wind war jnen wider. Aber in der vierden Nachtwache kam Jhesus zu jnen, vnd gieng auff dem Meer. Vnd da jn die Jünger sahen auff dem Meer gehen, erschracken sie, vnd sprachen, Es ist ein Gespenst vnd schrien fur furcht. Aber als bald redete Jhesus mit jnen, vnd sprach, Seid getrost, Ich bins, Fürchtet euch nicht.

PEtrus aber antwortet jm, vnd sprach, HErr bistu es, so heis mich zu dir komen auff dem Wasser. Vnd er sprach, Kom her. Vnd Petrus trat aus dem Schiff, vnd gieng auff dem Wasser, das er zu Jhesu keme. Er sahe aber einen starcken Wind, da erschrack er, vnd hub an zu sincken, schrey vnd sprach, HErr, hilff mir. Jhesus aber recket bald die Hand aus vnd ergreiff jn, vnd sprach zu jm, O du Kleingleubiger, warumb zweiffeltestu? Vnd sie tratten in das Schiff, vnd der Wind leget sich. Die aber im Schiff waren, kamen vnd fielen fur jn nider, vnd sprachen, Du bist warlich Gottes son.

The same text in a modern edition (Berlin, 1905):

Und da er das Volk von sich gelassen hatte, stieg er auf einen Berg allein, daß er betete. Und am Abend war er allein daselbst. Und das Schiff war schon mitten auf dem Meer, und litt Not von den Wellen;

denn der Wind war ihnen zuwider. Aber in der vierten Nachtwache
kam Jesus zu ihnen, und ging auf dem Meer. Und da ihn die Jünger
sahen auf dem Meer gehen, erschraken sie, und sprachen: Es ist ein
Gespenst! und schrieen vor Furcht. Aber alsbald redete Jesus mit
ihnen und sprach: Seid getrost, Ich bin's; fürchtet euch nicht! Petrus
aber antwortete ihm und sprach: Herr, bist du es, so heiß mich zu dir
kommen auf dem Wasser. Und er sprach: Komm her! Und Petrus trat
aus dem Schiff, und ging auf dem Wasser, daß er zu Jesu käme. Er sah
aber einen starken Wind; da erschrak er, und hub an zu sinken, schrie
und sprach: Herr, hilf mir! Jesus aber reckte alsbald die Hand aus, und
ergriff ihn, und sprach zu ihm: O du Kleingläubiger, warum zweifeltest
du? Und sie traten in das Schiff, und der Wind legte sich. Die aber im
Schiff waren, kamen, und fielen vor ihm nieder, und sprachen: Du bist
wahrlich Gottes Sohn.

Luther's greatest archaism was the preservation of two stem
forms in the preterite of many strong verbs (*er schrey – sie schrien*),
and the different apocope/syncope rule in the preterite of weak
verbs (*leget* – modern *legte*). For the rest, the difference is mainly
orthographic: the distribution of single and double consonants
(*f/ff*, *t/tt*, *k/ck*), of *e* and *ä*, the use of *h* in the pronouns, the
distinction between *das/daß* and the use of capitals. The revised
text of 1956 (Stuttgart) contains the following changes: *zuwider* >
entgegen; *daß er zu Jesu käme* > *und kam auf Jesu zu*; *Er sah
aber einen starken Wind*; *da erschrak er und hub an zu sinken* > *Als
er aber den Wind sah, erschrak er und hob an zu sinken*; *kamen, und
fielen* > *fielen*. Such changes are a matter of style and taste rather
than language.

6.4.4 | Regional variants

Since the German written language in the sixteenth
century remained diverse and differed regionally, the most important regional variants need to be briefly illustrated.

The following linguistic comments are based on each selected
text, though not all features may be illustrated in the short passage
actually given. Reference may also be made to other characteristics
of the regional written language concerned. For ease of comparison with the samples given in 5.3.3, MHG is used as the base.

For the location and designation of the regional variants see
p. 374.

(i) *Central Upper German*

(a) Matthew 14, 23–33 (cf. 4.9, 5.3.3(vi), 6.4.3, and (ii), (vi), (viii) in this section.)

Vnd do er hett gelassen die geselschaffte . er staig auf allein bettent an dem berg. Wann do der abent wart gemacht er was allein do Wann das schifflein wart geworffen von den vnden in mitzt des meres. Wann der wint der was in widerwertig. Wann vmb die vierden wach der nacht . er kam zů in gend auff dem mere . sy wurden betrůbt sagent: wann es ist ein trúgniß. Vnd rieffen vor vorchten. Vnd zehant jhesus redt zů ine sagent. Habt zůuersicht: jch bins: nichten wǒlt euch fúrchten. Wann peter antwurt er sprach . o herr ob dus bist so gebeut mir zekumen zů dir auf den wassern Vnd er sprach. Kum. Vnd peter steig ab von dem schifflein er ging auff den wassern daz er kem zů jhesus Wann do er sach ein starcken winde er vorcht sich. Vnd do er begund zesincken: er rief sagent. O herr mach mich behalten. Vnd zehant jhesus strackt die hant vnd begreiff in: vnd sprach zů im. Lútzels glauben worumb hastu gezweifelt? Vnd do er was auf gestigen in das schifflein: der wint hort auf. Wann die do warn in dem schifflein: die kament vnd anbetent in sagent. Gewerlich du bist der sun gotz.

From the first German Bible ever printed, the so-called Mentelin Bible of 1466, printed by Johann Mentelin at Strasbourg from a translation made considerably earlier, probably in the region of Nuremberg. The language is Central Upper German and not Alsatian, although the book was printed at Strasbourg. From the copy in the John Rylands University Library of Manchester. The abbreviations are expanded.

MHG *ie, uo, üe*: generally ⟨ie, ů, ů⟩, but often *ging* for *gieng*, ⟨u⟩ and ⟨ú⟩ occasionally for *uo* and *üe*.

MHG *ei, ou, öu*: ⟨ai⟩ and ⟨ei⟩ perhaps equally frequent, but ⟨au⟩ and ⟨eú/eu⟩ are general.

MHG *ī, ū, iu*: generally ⟨ei, au, eú/eu⟩ with occasional ⟨ey⟩ for MHG *ī*.

MHG *ü, ö, œ*: generally ⟨ú, ǒ⟩.

MHG *ë, e, ē, ä, æ*: ⟨e⟩, with very rare ⟨ae⟩.

MHG *a, ā*: ⟨a⟩.

The consonantism is general East Franconian. There are no EUGm. spellings of ⟨p-⟩ for MHG *b* or ⟨kh-⟩ for MHG *k*. MHG *s* before consonants is ⟨sch⟩ except in *st, sp*. The text has *gen, sten, sun, kumen, kúnig, nit* rather than *nicht*, the full forms *haben* and *lassen* not *han, lan*, the 3rd pers. pl. pres. ind. of 'to be' is *seint*, the 3rd sg. pret. ind. *was/waz* and the pret. ind. of 'to have' *hett(e)*. The prefix *ge-* has not lost its vowel. Frequent unhistorical -*e* testifies to the apocope, which the text, however, tries to avoid, hence the 'hypercorrect' -*e* spellings. The diminutive suffix is -*lein*; instead of the prefix *er-* the text often has *der-*.

The text is in unlocalizable UGm. In its distinction of the reflexes of MHG *ie* and *i, uo* and *u, üe* and *ü* and of mutated and unmutated vowels it differs from the usual written language of Nuremberg at this time. In having occasionally ⟨o⟩ for MHG *u* or with *ging* for *gieng* and ⟨u⟩ for MHG *uo* it has links with CGm. The ending -*ent* in the 3rd pers. pl. pret. *kament* is probably an error rather than an Alemannism. The lack of a strict distinction between the reflexes of MHG *ī* and *ei* by means of ⟨ei⟩ and ⟨ai⟩ suggests a location outside EUGm.

(b) Jtem welicher einem trunckenboltz auf sein begrebnuß ein gedechtnus wolt aufrichten der mȯcht sich einer solichen nachfolgeten aufgerisnen maynung gebrauchen. Erstlich sein grab daran ein epitauium machen das den wollust mit gespȯt lobet / v̄n auf das grab ein pier tunnen aufrecht stellen / v̄n oben mit einem bretspil zȗdecken / darauf zwo schȗssel vber einander stȗrtzen / darin wirt fresserey sey / darnach auf der ȯberen schȗssel boden gestelt ein weyt nidertrechdigen pierkrug mit zweyen hand haben / das deck mit einem teller zȗ v̄n stȗrtz darauf ein hochs vmgekertes bierglas / v̄n setz auf des glas boden ein kȯrblein mit brot / kes v̄n butteren. Der gleychen von anderen dingen mȯcht man gar manicherley nach eines yetlichen leben sein begrebnus zieren / solichs hab jch von abenteuer wegen wȯllen anzeygen vnnd zȗ sambt den anderen seulen aufgerissen.

From Albrecht Dürer's *Vnderweysung der messung / mit dem zirckel v̄n rechtscheyt / in Linien ebenen vnnd gantzen corporen*, printed by Hieronymus Andreae at Nuremberg in 1525 (p. J of the copy in the John Rylands University Library of Manchester). The few abbreviations except *v̄n* are spelt out.

MHG *ie*: ⟨ie⟩, which is occasionally also used for lengthened MHG *i*; MHG *uo, üe*: these and MHG *ü* are most frequently spelt ⟨ȗ⟩. There are also some ⟨ủ⟩ and ⟨u⟩ spellings.

MHG *ei, ou, öu* and MHG *ī, ū, iu* have coalesced and are spelt ⟨ei, ey⟩ (with only a sporadic ⟨ay⟩), ⟨au⟩, ⟨eu⟩.

MHG *ö, œ*: ⟨ȯ⟩.

MHG *ë, e, ē, ä, æ*: ⟨e⟩ with an occasional etymological ⟨á⟩ or ⟨å⟩.

MHG *a, ā*: ⟨a⟩, but *gethon* 'done'. Dürer generally used ⟨o⟩ for MHG *ā* in his private letters.

The consonantism is characterized by frequent ⟨p-⟩ for MHG *b-*. The text has *geen, steen, sonne* and *sunn, sonders* and *sunderlich, nit*, the full forms *lassen* and *haben*, the 1st and 3rd pret. sg. of 'to be' is *was*, the 3rd pers. pl. pres. has *-en*. Apocope and syncope occur: *zierd, gsims*. The diminutive suffix is *-lein*.

(ii) *East Central German*

Matthew 14, 23–33 (for comparison see 4.9; 5.3.3 (vi); 6.4.3 and (i), (vi) and (viii) in this section).

vnd da er das volck von sich gelassen hatte / steyg er auff eynen berg alleyne / das er bette / vnd am abent / war er alleyn daselbs / vnnd das schiff war schon mitten auff dem meer / vnd leyd nodt von den wellen / denn der wind war yhn widder. Aber ynn der vierden nachtwache / kam Jhesus zu yhn vnd gieng auff dem meer / vnd da yhn die iunger sahen auf dem meer gehen / erschracken sie / vnd sprachen / Es ist eyn spugnisz / vnd schryen fur furcht / Aber als bald redte Jhesus mit yhn / vnd sprach / seyd getrost / ich byns / furcht euch nicht.

Petrus aber antwort yhm vnnd sprach / Herre / bistu es / so heysz mich zu dyr komen auf dem wasser / vnnd er sprach / kom her / vnd Petrus trat aus dem schiff / vnnd gieng auff dem wasser / das er zu Jhesu keme. Er sahe aber eynen starcken wind / da erschrack er / vnd hub an zu sincken / schrey vnnd sprach / Herr hilff mir / Jhesus aber recket seyne hand aus / vnnd erwisscht yhn / vnnd sprach zu yhm / o du kleyn glewbiger / warumb zweyfeltistu? vnd traten yn das schiff / vnd der wind leget sich. Die aber im schiff waren / kamen vnd fielen fur yhn nyder / vnnd sprachen du bist warlich gottis son.

From Luther's *Septembertestament*, his first edition of the New Testament, printed by Melchior Lotther at Wittenberg in September 1522. From the copy in the John Rylands University Library of Manchester. Punctuation is retained, abbreviations are expanded.

MHG *ie, uo, üe*: ⟨ie/i, u⟩, ⟨ie⟩ may also stand for the reflex of MHG *i*, which is otherwise spelt ⟨i⟩ or ⟨y⟩.

MHG *ei, ou, öu*: ⟨ey, au, eu⟩. Other ECGm. texts have ⟨ei⟩. Beside ⟨au, eu⟩ there are usually the variants ⟨aw, ew⟩. The most significant fact is the coalescence with the following:

MHG *ī, ū, iu*: ⟨ey, au, eu⟩, with ⟨ei, aw, ew⟩ as variants in many ECGm. texts.

MHG *ü*, *ö*, *œ*: no indication of mutation. But after 1523 there is gradually an increase of ⟨ü, ö⟩.

MHG *ë*, *e*, *ē*, *ä*, *æ*: ⟨e⟩.

MHG *a*, *ā*: ⟨a⟩.

MHG *u*: ⟨o⟩ in a number of words, e.g. *son, sonst, from* etc. but also *frum* as a variant.

In unstressed inflectional syllables ⟨e⟩ is common, but there are still some ⟨i⟩, e.g. *gottis*. Indication of vowel length through doubling is on the increase, e.g. *meer*, and ⟨h⟩ is also used for the same purpose. There is little trace of apocope, but some forms are due to South German influence.

The consonantism has the general EFranc. basis common in the regional written language with deviations in individual words. After *ge-*: *b* > *p*, e.g. *geporn*. The dental affricate is usually spelt ⟨z⟩ initially and ⟨tz⟩ medially and finally, but we also get occasionally initial ⟨tz⟩, and in other texts ⟨cz⟩. Initial ⟨k-⟩ varies with final and medial ⟨ck⟩. Doubling of consonants, fashionable at the time, is responsible for spellings such as *teufell* beside *tewfel* or *weynenn* beside *weynen*.

This text has *gehen, stehen, son, komen, konig, nit* and *nicht, haben, lassen, sie sind* and *seynd, war, hatte*. The diminutive suffix is generally *-lin*.

In comparing the 1522 and 1546 versions (see p. 383) we note the general replacement of ⟨ey⟩ by ⟨ei⟩, of ⟨y⟩ by ⟨i⟩ or, in the pronouns, by ⟨j⟩, ⟨i⟩ in unstressed syllables by ⟨e⟩, the introduction of ⟨ů⟩ and ⟨ô⟩, and the replacement of the ECGm. *spugnisz* as the translation of *fantasma* by UGm. *Gespenst*. In replacing *erwisscht* by *ergreiff* in the sentence *Jhesus aber recket seyne hand aus / vnnd erwisscht yhn* Luther would seem to have toned down his colloquial style.

(iii) *West Central German*

Historia ist nichts anders dann eyn gezeug der zeyt / eyn liecht der warheyt / eyn leben der gedåchtnuß / eyn vnderweiserin oder meysterin des lebens / vnd der vergangen welt verkünderin / deren lesen dem menschen nit alleyn vast nutz / sonder ergetzlich vnd kurtzweilig pflegt zů sein. Vnd so aller kunst wissenheyt dem menschlichen geschlecht nutzbar vnd ergetzlichen / ist on zweiuel erkantnuß der historien aller nutzbarst vnd aller ergetzlichst. Da durch wir aller exempel vnd beispeil leer / gleich wie inn eynem scheinbaren spiegel besichtigen /

auch welchen geschichten nach zů volgen / vn̄ was zů fliehen sei / erkunden mőgen. Es schaffen die schreiber der Historien / das wir alle gedanck / wort vnd werck der vorigen vnd langst abgestorbenen welt / die do nützlich seind / vnnd menschlichem leben dienen / besichtigen / lernen vnd jnen nachuolgen / auch auß irrungen vn̄ mißhandeln anderer menschen vnser leben formlicher vnnd rechter anlassen mőgen.

From Bernhart Schöfferlin's *Titi Liuij deß aller redtsprechsten vn̄ hochberümpsten geschichtschreibers: Rőmische Historien*, printed by Ivo Schöffer at Mainz in 1538 (p. ii of the copy in the John Rylands University Library of Manchester).

MHG *ie, uo, üe*: generally ⟨ie, ů, ü⟩, but ⟨ie⟩ also for lengthened MHG *i*.

MHG *ei, ou, öu*: ⟨ey, au, eu⟩.

MHG *ī, ū, iu*: ⟨ei, au, eu⟩. The contrast between ⟨ey⟩ and ⟨ei⟩ is very much a feature of Schöffer's printing establishment. Although there are some slips, the distinction is remarkably regular.

MHG *ü, ö, œ*: ⟨ü⟩ (see above MHG *üe*), ⟨ő⟩.

MHG *ë, e, ē, ä, æ*: generally ⟨e⟩ but with a fair number of etymological spellings with ⟨å⟩, e.g. *trågt, våtter, tåglich*.

MHG *a, ā*: generally ⟨a⟩, but with some ⟨o⟩, especially *on* 'without'.

The consonantism is non-dialectal, although some Rhenish Franconian *d*- spellings for MHG *t* still occur, e.g. *dochter*. The text has *son, kommen, kőnig, sonder, gehn, stehn, gewesen*, the full forms *haben* and *lassen*, the negative *nit*, and the diminutive suffix *-lin*. The 3rd pers. pl. pres. ends in *-en*, of 'to be' it is *seind* or *sind*, and the pret. of 'to have' is *hett(e)*. Apocope is found, e.g. in *gebirg*.

The text is a good example of the advanced character of the language of the Schöffer establishment. Many earlier CGm. features, e.g. ⟨i⟩ as a length sign (*roit*), ⟨u⟩ for MHG *uo* and *u*, ⟨o⟩ for MHG *u*, frequent ⟨d⟩ for MHG *t*, ⟨p-⟩ for MHG *pf-*, have been abandoned. As the printer of the acts of the imperial diets, Schöffer had by the third decade of the sixteenth century reached a remarkable compromise between CGm. and UGm.

(iv) *East Upper German*

> Eins mals der Kung an seim pet lag
> Gedacht nun ist khomen der tag

Das Jch sol ordenen mein sach
Dann Jch bin worden alt vnd schwach
Das empfindt Jch an mir ganntz wol
Doch hoff Jch nicht ersterben sol
Auff federen in einem pet
Dann wenig wurd als dann geredt
Von meinem todt in künfftig zeit
Jch ways ein schóngarten nit weit
Von hynn . der ist lustig umbfangen
Mit eim graben . dainn verlangen
Hab Jch zů schliessen mein letzt teg
In solhen dannckhen reyt Er weg
Als Er nun in den garten kam
Empfand vnd das Er seer ab nam
An seinem leib vnnd auch leben
Darumb wolt Er zůuersteen geben
Zuuor sein Råtten wen Er wolt
Den sein kynd zůman haben solt

From *Die geuerlicheiten vnd einsteils der geschichten des loblichen streytparen vnd hochberúmbten helds vnd ritters herr Teẁrdannckhs*, by Melchior Pfinzing and Emperor Maximilian I, printed in Nuremberg, 1517, by the Augsburg printer Hanns Schónsperger (p. a ix of the copy in the John Rylands University Library of Manchester).

MHG *ie, uo, üe*: ⟨ie, ů, üe⟩.

MHG *ei, ou, öu*: ⟨ai/ay, au, eu/ew⟩, instead of ⟨ai⟩ there is also occasionally ⟨ei⟩, e.g. *zeigen, klein, khein, ein*, but in *geist* the spelling may reflect a genuine Austrian-Bavarian phoneme switch.

MHG *ī, ū, iu*: ⟨ei/ey, au/aw, eu/ew⟩.

MHG *ü, ö, œ*: ⟨ü, ó⟩.

MHG *ë, e, ē, ä, æ*: ⟨e⟩ and ⟨å⟩.

MHG *a, ā*: ⟨a⟩ with some ⟨o⟩ for the long vowel.

Characteristic of the consonantism are ⟨p-⟩ and ⟨kh-⟩: *pet* for *bet*, *khomen* for *komen*, and a certain exuberance in the use of double consonants, e.g. *gedannckhen, khenndt*. Inverse spellings like ⟨b⟩ for *w* (*lóben* for *lówen*) or *póst* for *best* and *-und* in the present participle (*eylunds*) also reveal features typical of EUGm. Apocope is general. This text has the forms: *frumb, sun*, generally *künig, khomen, sonnder, sunne, gehn, stehn* with *gan/stan* or *gon/ston* in rhymes, and the full forms *haben, lassen, nit* and *seind* in the 3rd pers. pl. pres. of 'to be'; *-lein* in the diminutive.

Although this text was printed at Nuremberg it is an example of the Augsburg printers' language, with some features (e.g. ⟨kh-⟩) deriving from the spelling practice of the imperial chancery.

(v) *West Upper German*

> Got wil es keim menschen hie erlauben,
>   Das sein zů stelen vnd zů rauben.
> Warumb woltestu mir nemen das,
>   Das ich mit gůtem recht besaß
>   Vnd mit rechtem titel was?
> Ein deckmantel sie erdichtet hond,
>   Vff das die gemein das nit verstond;
> So můß es sein ein cristlich ler,
>   Ob es schon als erlogen wer.
> Wan sie die güter alle nemen
>   Vnd vff ein huffen legten zůsemen,
> So würd dem armen das daruon,
>   Als sie in Bôhem haben gethon.
> Da auch der arm meint, das im würd
>   Von geraubtem gůt ein zimlich bürd;
> Da nam es der reich vnd ließ den armen
>   Sich im ellend gon erbarmen.

From Thomas Murner's (1475–1537) *Von dem grossen Lutherischen Narren* (ll. 743–59), printed by Johannes Grienninger (Grüninger) at Strasbourg, 19 December 1522, ed. A. E. Berger, *Satirische Feldzüge wider die Reformation*, (Deutsche Literatur in Entwicklungsreihen, Reformation, 3), Leipzig, 1933; also ed. P. Merker, vol. 9, Strasbourg, 1918, of *Thomas Murners Deutsche Schriften*.

MHG *ie, uo, üe*: regularly ⟨ie, ů⟩, but for *üe*: either ⟨ü⟩ or, as a reflex of unrounding, ⟨ie⟩. MHG *ie* and *i* are kept apart.

MHG *ei, ou, öu*: regularly ⟨ei, au⟩; as well as the usual ⟨eu⟩ there is also to be found ⟨ei⟩ as a reflex of unrounding. Other Strasbourg texts retain ⟨ou⟩.

MHG *ī, ū, iu*: almost always ⟨ei⟩ with a few ⟨i⟩ spellings; predominantly ⟨u⟩ with a fair number of ⟨au⟩ spellings; predominantly ⟨ü⟩ with a few ⟨eu⟩ especially in the pronominal forms *euch, euwer*, and ⟨ôw⟩. Other Murner texts have a predominance of ⟨i/y⟩.

MHG *ü, ö, œ*: predominantly ⟨ü⟩ and ⟨ô⟩, with ⟨i⟩ for unrounding.

MHG *ë, e, ē, ä, æ*: generally ⟨e⟩, with very few etymological ⟨ä⟩

spellings, e.g. *närrisch*, and also for MHG *a* before *sch*: *weschen*. MHG *a*, *ā*: ⟨a⟩ for the short vowel, but for *ā* there are at least an equal number of ⟨o⟩ spellings.

In labial surroundings we find evidence of labialization, e.g. *würd* for *wird*. MHG *u*, *ü* before nasals are preserved, hence *frum*, *sun*, *künig*, *kumen*, *sunder*. Apocope is common, e.g. *die sach*, but *be-* and *ge-* usually contain a vowel.

The consonantism shows the following deviations from the general MHG features: occasional ⟨d⟩ initially for MHG *t*, e.g. *dochter*; occasional coalescence of lenis and fortis fricatives, e.g. *grosen*, *müsen* but *bewissen* for NHG *großen*, *müssen*, *bewiesen*. Both might testify to the dialectal *binnenhochdeutsche Konsonanten-schwächung*. M. Philipp has, however, discovered that Murner did not rhyme words with fortis and lenis *s*, or *d* and *t*.

The pl. pres. ind. of verbs has the uniform ending *-en* or *-nd* in contracted forms. Beside *lassen* and *haben* there are the contracted forms *lon/lan*, *hon/han* and the 1st and 3rd pers. sg. pret. of 'to be' is *was*. 'To go' is *gon/gan*. The negatives are *nit* and *nüt* although for the latter *nichtz* also occurs. The diminutive suffix is *-lin*.

(vi) *Swiss*

Matthew 14, 23–33 (for comparison see 4.9; 5.3.3 (vi); 6.4.3 and (i), (ii) and (viii) in this section).

Vnd do er das volck von jm gelassen hat / steig er vff einen berg allein / das er bettete: vnd am abend was er allein da selbs / vnd das schiff was schon mitten vff dem meer / vnd leid not von den wellen / denn der wind was jnen wider. Aber in der vierten nacht wach / kam Jesus zů jnen / vnd gieng vff dem meer. Vnd do in die iünger sahend vff dem meer gon / erschrackend sy / vnnd sprachend: Es ist ein gspenst / vnd schrüwend vor forcht. Aber als bald redt Jesus mit jnen / vnd sprach: Sind getrõst / ich bins / fõrcht üch nit.

Petrus aber antwort im vnd sprach: Herr / bistu es / so heiss mich zů dir kommen vff dem wasser. Vnd er sprach: Komm her. Vnd petrus tratt uß dem schiff / vnd gieng vff dem wasser das er zů Jesu kåme. Er sach aber einen starcken wind / do erschrack er / vnd hůb an zů sincken / schrey vnd sprach: Herr / hilff mir. Jesus aber streckt sin hand vß / vnd erwüst in / vnd sprach zů im: O du kleingleubiger / warumb zwifelstu? vnd trattend in das schiff / vnd der wind leget sich. Die aber im schiff warend / kamend vnnd fielen for im nider / vnd sprachend: Du bist warlich gottes sun.

From *Das gantz Nüw Testament recht grüntlich vertütscht*, printed by Christopher Froschauer in Zürich, 1524, which is a transposition into Swiss of Luther's text. From the copy in the John Rylands University Library of Manchester. The punctuation is retained, but the abbreviations are expanded.

MHG *ie, uo, üe*: ⟨ie, ů, ů⟩.
MHG *ei, ou, öu*: ⟨ei, ou, ŏu⟩, also ⟨ey⟩ and ⟨eü⟩.
MHG *ī, ū, iu*: ⟨y, u, ü⟩, instead of ⟨y⟩ also ⟨i⟩.
MHG *ü, ö, œ*: ⟨ü, ŏ⟩, but before ⟨ck⟩ no mutation: *stuck*.
MHG *ë, e, ē*: generally ⟨e⟩, but for *ë* also ⟨å⟩.
MHG *ä, æ*: generally ⟨å⟩, also for *a* before *sch*, e.g. *wåschen*.
MHG *a, ā*: ⟨a⟩, but beside *gat, gan* also *gon*.

In labial surroundings rounding is general, e.g. *frŏmd, zwŏlf, erwüst*, i.e. *erwischt* with ⟨st⟩ for Alem. *scht*, or *schrüwend*, i.e. *schrien*. MHG *u, ü* before *n*: *sun, künig*, and usually also *kumen*. Apocope and syncope are general, e.g. *wach, gspenst*, but *ge-* in the past participle is often preserved.

The consonantism shows the general MHG features, including initial ⟨k-⟩ rather than dialectal ⟨ch-⟩.

For the reflexive in the dat. the pers. pronoun is still used, cf. *von im* with Luther's *von sich*. *Was* is still current and in the whole pl. pres. and pret. ind. the ending *-end* has been generalized. The contracted verbal forms *han* and *lan* are general in HAlem., with *håt* for *hat* and *het* for *hatte*. The uniform pl. pres. ind. of 'to be' is *sind*. The negatives are *nit* for *nicht* and *nüt* for *nichts*. Diminutives are specially frequent, e.g. *hündlin, brŏsamlin, fischlin*.

Although the 1531 edition of the whole Bible had the diphthongs ⟨ei/ey, au, eu⟩ for MHG *ī, ū, iu* it was more Alemannic in containing the following alterations: *bettete > battete, wellen > wållen, komm her > kumm hår, zů sincken > zesincken, kleingleubiger > kleinglŏubiger, fielen > fielend*.

(vii) Cologne (Ripuarian)

Mer der eyrste vynder der druckerye is gewest eyn Burger tzo Mentz. ind was geboren van Straißburch. ind hiesch joncker Johan Gudenburch Item van Mentz is die vurß kunst komen alre eyrst tzo Coellen. Dairnae tzo Straisburch / ind dairnae tzo Venedige. Dat begynne ind vortganck der vurß kunst hait myr muntlich vertzelt der Eirsame man Meyster Vlrich tzell van Hanauwe. Boichdrucker zo Coellen noch zertzijt.

anno MCCCCXCIX. durch den die kunst vurß is zo Coellen komen. Item idt syn ouch eyndeill vurwitziger man. vnd die sagen. men haue ouch vurmails boicher gedruckt / mer dat is niet wair. want men vynt in geynen landen der boicher die tzo den seluen tzijden gedruckt syn.

[vurß = vursteinde 'aforementioned']

From *Die Cronica van der hilliger Stat van Coellen,* printed by Johann Koelhoff, Cologne, 1499 (p. 312 of the copy in the John Rylands University Library of Manchester).

MHG *ie, uo, üe*: ⟨ie⟩ (⟨ye⟩) and ⟨oi/oy/oe⟩, the latter spellings stand also for the reflex of MHG *ō*.

MHG *ei, ou, öu*: mainly ⟨ey/ei⟩ which also stand for MHG *ē*; ⟨ou⟩; ⟨eu⟩.

MHG *ī, ū, iu*: mainly ⟨ij⟩; ⟨u/uy⟩.

MHG *ü, ö, œ*: no indication of mutation.

MHG *ë, e, ē, ä, æ*: ⟨e⟩ and ⟨ei/ey⟩.

Where a MHG *i* is in an open syllable we get ⟨e⟩, e.g. *vrede*; for a MHG *o* before *l* we often find ⟨ou⟩, e.g. *houltz*; for MHG *u* mainly ⟨o⟩. The most noteworthy vocalic feature is the much more consistent indication of vowel length, by means of ⟨i, y⟩ or ⟨e⟩, than is usual in any other form of written German at that time.

The consonantism is broadly Central Franconian. It thus differs from other High German written forms in having ⟨-v-⟩ or ⟨-f⟩ for *b*, e.g. *geven, schreif*; ⟨-ch⟩ for *-g*, e.g. *genoich*; ⟨d⟩ for *t*: *deil, vader*; ⟨p-⟩, ⟨-pp-⟩ for *pf* (*dapper*), ⟨lp⟩, ⟨rp⟩ for *lf, rf*: *helpen, werpen*; further *dat, dit, wat, it, allit.* Before consonants *s* is retained, e.g. *sniden, sloss, snee*.

In this text we find further: *koning* or *konynck, komen, sonder, gewest, of* 'or', *minschen, niet* for the negative, *van, tusschen* 'between', *he* 'he', *gain* 'to go', *laissen* 'to let', *ind* 'and', the diminutive *boichelgin* 'little book'.

(viii) *Low German*

Matthew 14, 23–33 (for comparison see 4.9; 5.3.3 (vi); 6.4.3 and (i), (ii) and (vi) in this section).

vn̄ do he hadde vorlaten de schare . he ghink vp allenen bedende an enen berghe. Vn̄ do dat auent ward he was allenen dar. Auer dat schepeken ward ghewor pen in den middel des meres. vormiddelst den bulghen wente de wynt was en enteghen. Vn̄ vp de verden wachte.

quam he to en ghande vp dem mere. v̄n also se ene segen vp dem mere wanderende. vorschrecket worden se sprekende. dat is ene spôkenisse. v̄n van vruchten repen se v̄n to handes sprak ihūs [Jesus] to en. hebbet louen ick bin id. nicht en willet iuw vruchten. Sunder petrus antwerde v̄n sprak. O here efte du dat bist. So bede mi kamente to di vp dat water. v̄n he sprak. kum v̄n petrus ghink vt dem schepe v̄n ghink vp dat water vp dat he queme to ihū [Jesu]. also he do sach enen starken wynd. he vruchtede sik. v̄n do he beghunde vnder to ghan. reep he segghende. O here help mi v̄n make mi sund. v̄n tohand ihūs [Jesus] vtstreckede sine hand v̄n begrep ene v̄n sprak to eme. van klenen louen worum me hefstu ghetwyuelt: v̄n do he was vpghesteghen vn dat schip. de wind horde vp. v̄n de weren in dem schepe de quemen v̄n ambededen ene. v̄n spreken. vorwar du bist de sone gades.

From the Low German Bible printed by Steffen Arndes at Lübeck in 1494, in the John Rylands University Library of Manchester. The punctuation is retained but all abbreviations, of which there are many, except *v̄n* 'and', are expanded.

Where MHG has *ie, uo*, MLG has ⟨e, o⟩, also for MHG *ei, ou*, except that ⟨ei⟩ is found where mutation may be assumed. For MHG *üe* we find ⟨ô⟩. ⟨i, u⟩ occur where MHG has *ī, ū, iu*. The correspondence of MHG *ë, e, ē, ä, æ* is ⟨e⟩, and of MHG *a, ā* it is ⟨a⟩. Where MHG had *i* and this occurs in an open syllable in MLG, the dialectal lowering (and lengthening) is indicated by ⟨e⟩ (⟨ee⟩), e.g. *seede*, MHG *site*, *schepeken* but *schip*, and likewise for MHG *o, u* we find ⟨a⟩, e.g. *gades* MHG *gotes*, *kamen* 'to come'. The mutation of *u* is not marked, but that of *o* is: *koerve*, NHG *Körbe*, also *hôret, soene, ôvel* (NHG *übel*). In early MLG texts mutations other than of *a > e* were not spelt.

The consonantism is, of course, marked by the absence of the Second Sound Shift. Among the further many characteristic features we note: ⟨gh⟩; the *r*-metathesis in *vrucht* cf. E *fright* but Gm. *Furcht*; the diminutive suffix *-ken*; *quam* for pret. of 'to come'; the mutated form in the pret. pl. ind. of strong verbs deriving from a generalized subjunctive, e.g. *segen* NHG *sahen*, *quemen* NHG *kamen*; 'to go' is *ghan*, 'to have' is *hebben* with 3rd pers. sg. pres. *hefft*, the 1st and 3rd pers. sg. pret. of 'to be' is *was*, the negative is *nicht*; the forms *minsch* NHG *Mensch*, *weinig* NHG *wenig*; many lexical differences, e.g. *bulghen* for 'waves'; note also *spôkenisse* as a translation of *fantasma* and compare with *spôck* in the next text and *spugnisz* in the 1522 Luther text, all related to E *spook*, but see the HG translations: *trúgniß, Gespenst*. Nevertheless, by far the larger part of the vocabulary is identical with that of other forms of written German.

Martin Luther's *New Testament* was also translated into Low German as it was into Swiss. Here is the same passage from *Dat Nye Testament duedesch. Wittemberch*, 1525, from the copy in the John Rylands University Library of Manchester:

Vnde do he dat volck van sich gelaten hadde steech he up eynen berch allene / dat he bedede. Vnde an dem auende was he dar súluest allene / vnde dat schip was rede midden vp dem meere / vn̄ lĕdt nodt van den búlgen / wente de wint was en entyegen. Ouerst in der veerden nacht-wake / quam Jhesus tho en / vn̄ ginck vp dem meere. Vnde do en de júngeren segen vp dem meere ghande / vorscrocken se vnde sprecken / Jdt ys ein spŏck / vnde scryeden van fruchten. Ouerst also balde redete Jhesus mit en vnde sprack / Weset frẙmŏdich jck bint /frúchtet iuw nicht.
    Petrus ŏuerst antwerde eme vnde sprack / Here bistu ydt / so hete my tho dy kamen vp dem water. Vnde he sprack / Kum hĕr. Vnde Petrus trat vth dem schepe / vnde ginck vp dem water / dat he tho Jhesu queme. He sach ŏuerst eynen starcken wint do vorscrack he / vnde hŏff an tho sinckende / scryede vnde sprack / Here help my. Jhesus ŏuerst recke de syne handt vth / vn̄ begrep en / vnde sprack tho eme / O du klĕn lŏuige / worumme twyuelstu? Vn̄ treden in dat schyp / vnde de windt lede sick. De ŏuerst in dem schepe weren / quemen vnde vellen vor en nedder vn̄ spreken / Du bist warliken Gades sŏne.

We note that the indication of mutation has made progress and now includes that of *u*.

6.5 | Phonology

6.5.1 | Letters and sounds

The inherited medieval spelling traditions of German included the non-indication of vowel length and the indication of gemination of consonants. These traditions were powerfully affected when in the late medieval centuries, over most of the territory, the short vowels in open syllables were lengthened and the consonantal geminates were reduced to simple consonants. Diphthongization of MHG *ī, ū, iu* and, in CGm., monophthongization of MHG *ie, uo, üe* posed further problems for German spelling. Other sound changes, especially the unrounding of MHG *ü, iu, ö, œ, öu*, and the rounding of MHG *i, e, ë* in labial surroundings, though generally shunned by the written language, nevertheless made themselves evident in an age when normalization was incipient rather than established. Commentators have often stated that spelling was chaotic in the ENHG phase. If we accept that variation was indeed a feature of the spelling of the time we can, however, hope to discover the underlying principles which any spelling must possess. Basically, in an age of idiolects, every writer or printer and every text has his or its own spelling system. Investigations are therefore most successfully based on one author or text. However, people were able to read one another's writings. It is *their* problem and *their* approach which therefore interests us most. Philologists have not set up a standardized spelling system for ENHG, as they have for MHG. It is the whole range of the spelling with which the contemporaries were confronted, from which we must therefore abstract the system which the written language possessed and which ensured its communicative function.

To simplify the problem we shall confine ourselves to the graphemic system of the Common German of the early sixteenth century, as defined in 6.4.2. This Common German can be said, in contrast to MHG, to have incorporated the diphthongization of MHG *ī, ū, iu*, but in contrast to NHG, to have embraced forms with monophthongization of MHG *ie, uo, üe* as well as forms which retained diphthongs for MHG *ie, uo, üe*. This Common German furthermore can be said to have rejected as dialectal the extremely widespread unrounding and to have been indifferent as to the also widespread labialization.

The graphemic system of ENHG was characterized by very great allographic variation, both within the sub-system of a given text and the overall system of the written language. Allographic variation was based on the following factors:

(a) Position within the word. In many cases a grapheme, say ⟨ei⟩ or ⟨k⟩, was represented by different allographs according to word initial, medial or final, prevocalic or preconsonantal position, e.g. ⟨ei⟩ in medial, but ⟨ey⟩ in final position: *sein, sey*; or ⟨k⟩

in initial, but ⌐ck⌐ in medial and final position: *kranck*. The grapheme ⟨u⟩ had ⌐u⌐ generally medially, but ⌐v⌐ initially.

(b) Dependence on the lexical item. The grapheme might be represented fairly regularly by one particular allograph in certain lexical items, e.g. ⟨ai⟩ as a representation of MHG *ei* was often ⌐ei⌐ in the words *ein*, *kein*, or ⟨u⟩ might be ⌐ue⌐ in the word *stuel*. Lexical spellings tended to be highly idiosyncratic, but some were fairly general, e.g. ⟨k⟩ was often represented by ⌐ch⌐ in the word *churfürst*.

(c) Aesthetic or calligraphic reasons. Short words were often filled out to look less insignificant, e.g. *vnnd* 'and'; ⟨i⟩ might be spelt ⌐j⌐ before nasals to provide variation in length of the letters, or might be spelt ⌐jh⌐ to give more body to a short word or to distinguish it from its homophone, e.g. *jhn:jn*. Sometimes it would appear that the writer simply varied the spelling of a word to avoid the boredom of identical repetition.

(d) Etymological reasons. The grapheme ⟨e⟩ might occasionally be spelt ⌐å⌐, e.g. *ast – åste* rather than *este*, where the etymology made it seem desirable. Or ⟨d⟩ might be spelt ⌐dt⌐ to indicate the phonetic character, but also the etymological connection: *scheiden, schiedt*.

(e) Assimilation. This often showed the greater responsiveness of ENHG spelling than of NHG spelling to the phonetic realities, e.g. *haben, gehapt*.

(i) *Vowels*

Much variation was the result of the use of different diacritics. A ring on top of a vowel letter might vary with a triangle, with one or two dots, which might be level or rising or falling, with a crescent with the opening to the left or to the right, upwards or downwards. In order not to overburden the lists of allographs such variation will be left out of account in the following table, where letters with superscript *e* and two dots, perhaps the most frequent variants, serve as representative allographs. Where an allograph is very often a positional variant, this is indicated by a hyphen. The allographs appear roughly in a descending order of frequency. Where the graphemes or allographs of Common German are predominantly regionally distributed this is indicated by the global identifications CGm. or UGm. Nowhere is it more true than in ENHG graphemics: there is no rule without exception.

Grapheme	Allographs	Corresponding phoneme(s) (see 6.5.2)	Reflex of MHG phoneme(s)
⟨i⟩	⟨i, y, j; CGm. ie, ih⟩	/i/ /i:/	/i/ CGm. /ie/
⟨e⟩	⟨e, ee, eh, å⟩	/e/ /ɛ/ /e:/ /ɛ:/	/ē/ /e/ /ä/ /ē/ /æ/
UGm. ⟨å⟩	⟨å, ä, e, ee⟩	/ɛ/ /ɛ:/	/ē/ /ä/ /æ/
⟨a⟩	⟨ā, rare: aa, ah⟩	/a/ /a:/	/a/ /ā/
⟨o⟩	⟨o, rare: oo, oh⟩	/o/ /o:/ CGm. /ö/ /ö:/	/o/ /ō/ CGm. /ö/ /œ/
⟨u⟩	⟨u, v-, w; CGm. ů, û, ue⟩	/u/ /u:/ UGm. /uə/	/u/ /uo/ CGm. /ü/ /üe/
UGm. ⟨ü⟩	⟨ü, u, v-, û, ue⟩	/ü/ /ü:/	/ü/
UGm. ⟨ổ⟩	⟨ổ, ö, œ, o⟩	/ö/ /ö:/	/ö/ /œ/
⟨ie⟩	⟨ie; CGm. i, y, ih⟩	UGm. /iə/ CGm. /i:/	/ie/ /i/
UGm. ⟨û⟩	⟨û, uo, ů, u, w⟩	UGm. /uə/	/uo/
UGm. ⟨û⟩	⟨û, ue, üe, u⟩	UGm. /üə/	/üe/
⟨ei⟩	⟨ei, ej, ey, ai, ay⟩	/ɛi/ /ai/	/ī/ /ei/
⟨au⟩	⟨au, aw, ou, ow⟩	/au/ (/åu/)	/ū/ /ou/
UGm. ⟨ai⟩	⟨ai, ay, ei, ey⟩	/ai/ /ɛi/	/ei/ /ī/
⟨eu⟩	⟨eu, ew, eü, äu⟩	/öü/ (/öu/)	/iu/ /öu/

From the above lists we see that vowel quantity was not expressed graphemically, but quality was, with the exception of the
rounded front vowels, the two mid unrounded front vowels and
the two *ei*-diphthongs in CGm., especially ECGm. Rarely was any
difference made between a possible contrast /au/ – /åu/ or /öü/ – /öu/.
We also note that some letters or graphs were graphemes in UGm.,
e.g. ⟨å, ů, ai⟩, but allographs or grapheme variants where they
occurred in CGm.

(ii) *Consonants*

The graphemic system shows that Common German maintained
the historical opposition of lenis/fortis plosives and, to a lesser
extent, fricatives. In other words, it rejected the *binnenhochdeutsche Konsonantenschwächung* which affected, in one form or
another, the whole territory of Common German, although we
do not know when. The 'Third Sound Shift' thus remained dialectal. The graphemic system, however, does not reveal whether
the inherited opposition of simple and geminate nasals and liquids
was still in existence or not. We know from NHG and the modern
dialects in the relevant areas that it was abandoned, but again we

do not know when. The spelling was conservative in this respect and still distinguished, for instance, *stelen – stellen*. It is probably correct to assume that the opposition was now in ENHG one of vowel quantity and that the consonantal quantity distinction had been abandoned. The historical spelling yielded thus the basis for an important spelling principle of NHG: double consonants indicate the shortness of the preceding vowel.

It is possible that the exuberance in the use of double consonant graphs, which is characteristic of certain texts of this time, was based on the availability of these graphs. Once all consonant phonemes were simple, the doubling of graphs was no longer functionally required and became merely a matter of aesthetics, at least until the new principle of the indication of vowel shortness again gave some functional use to this device. Generally the indication of neutralization in final position (*Auslautsverhärtung*), which had been an important feature of many good MHG manuscripts, was no longer in evidence in ENHG.

Grapheme	Allographs	Corresponding phoneme(s) (see 6.5.4)	Reflex of MHG phoneme(s)
⟨b⟩	⊏b; CGm.-bb-; p, pp; EUGm.p-, w-⊐	/b/	/b/
⟨p⟩	⊏p, pp, b-⊐	/p/	/pp-p/
⟨d⟩	⊏d, t-; CGm. dd; -dt⊐	/d/	/d/
⟨t⟩	⊏t-, -tt(-), th, d, -dt, dtt⊐	/t/	/t/ /tt/
⟨g⟩	⊏g, -gg-, k, -gk⊐	/g/	/g/
⟨k⟩	⊏k-, -ck(-); EUGm.kh, ckh, ch; c-+l, r, q(u)⊐	/k/	/kk–k/
⟨f⟩	⊏f-, -ff-, v-, -u-⊐	/f/	/ff-f/ /v/
⟨s⟩	⊏s-, -ß(-), -s(-)⊐	/z/	/s/
⟨ss⟩	⊏-ss(-), -ß(-), -s⊐	/s/	/zz-z/ /ss/
⟨ch⟩	⊏-ch-, h(+cons.), g⊐	/x/	/x/
⟨sch⟩	⊏sch, sh, s+cons.⊐	/ʃ/	/sch/
⟨l⟩	⊏l, -ll-⊐	/l/	/l/ /ll/
⟨r⟩	⊏r, -rr-⊐	/r/	/r/ /rr/
⟨n⟩	⊏n, -nn-⊐	/n/	/n/ /nn/
⟨m⟩	⊏m, -mm-⊐	/m/	/m/ /mm/
⟨j⟩	⊏j, i, y⊐	/j/	/j/
⟨w⟩	⊏w; EUGm.b⊐	/w/	/w/
⟨h⟩	⊏h⊐	/h/	/h/
⟨z⟩	⊏z-, zc-, tz(-)⊐	/ts/	/ts/
⟨pf⟩	⊏pf-, -pff-, ph⊐	/pf/	/pf/

6.5.2 | The stressed vowel system

The graphemic system established for the written language proves to be an unsatisfactory guide to the phonemic system of the spoken language. If it was difficult to arrive at an overall graphemic system, it is practically impossible to set up a phonemic system for more than individual idiolects or local forms. Even this has to rely on comparative linguistics, i.e. on comparison with preceding and subsequent stages of the language, in conjunction with graphemics. We know from rhyme studies that writers spoke their local dialects and pronounced the written language correspondingly. Even if there were educated circles which began to practise the new principle: speak as you write, they must have been the exception rather than the rule. Yet it was a most important and, for the future development of the German standard language, even decisive principle. It first found wide and no doubt necessary acceptance in North Germany.

Assuming then that there were speakers of Common German who followed the pattern of the written language, while retaining those salient features of their home dialects which were not too much in conflict with the graphemics of the written language, we get the following phonemic system:

Stage IX

/i/	/ü/	/u/	/i:/	/ü:/	/u:/	(/iə/ /üə/ /uə/)
	/e/	/ö/	/o/	/e:/	/ö:/	/o:/	/ɛi/ /öü/ (/öu/)
	/ɛ/	/a/		/ɛ:/	/a:/	/ai/ /au/ (/åu/)

The notation may seem contradictory since some signs derive from phonetic script, e.g. [ɛ, :], while others are the ordinary letters of the alphabet. To use phonetic script would imply that we knew the phonetic values, which is not the case. On the other hand, a departure from the alphabetic convention is necessary to indicate that we are concerned with hypothetical phonemic units. For the examples below a spelling has been chosen which indicates that the principle: double consonant signs indicate vowel shortness, was not yet in operation. It also reflects the frequent spelling feature of ⟨t⟩ having the allograph ⟨tt⟩ medially and finally. All examples could equally well be spelt with ⟨t⟩. In reality there would be variation, which is at least hinted at by the use of ⟨th⟩ in the word *rathen*, which was particularly common.

Examples:

/i/	ritten '(they) rode'	/i:/	rietten '(they) advised'	(/iə/	rietten '(they) advised')
/e/	retten 'to save'	/e:/	wethum 'pain'	/ɛi/	reitten 'to ride'
/ɛ/	wetter 'weather'	/ɛ:/	båtten '(they) would pray'	/ai/	leitten 'to lead'
/ü/	bütten 'tubs'	/ü:/	hutten 'to protect'	(/üə/	håtten 'to protect')
/ö/	götter 'gods'	/ö:/	lötten 'to solder'	/öü/	leutten 'people' (dat. pl.)
/u/	kutten 'cassocks'	/u:/	'rods' rutten	/au/	lautter 'pure'
/o/	rotten 'gangs'	/o:/	rotten 'red' (decl.)	(/uə/	růtten 'rods')
/a/	schatten 'shade'	/a:/	rathen 'to advise'	(/åu/	lauffen 'to run')
				(/öu/	leuffig 'current')

Whether the systems of the short and long vowels ought to be drawn up as triangles or quadrilaterals is a moot point. The fact that long and short *a* are back vowels in the modern dialects of much of the area of the then Common German makes the quadrilateral the more likely solution. This is, of course, also tied up with the supposition about the mid front vowels. It must be presumed that the number of the three MHG vowels /e/ /ë/ /ä/ was reduced nearly everywhere either through coalescence of /ë/ and /ä/ or through coalescence of /e/ and /ë/. Both solutions are found in large areas. The crucial question is: had all three coalesced? The spelling in most of CGm. would seem to suggest it for CGm. Yet, many modern dialects retain two reflexes, e.g. Rhen. Fr. *besser* but *äsoe*, or *läwe*, NHG *leben* (MHG *ë*), *hewe*, NHG *heben* (MHG *e*). Upper Saxon too, has two reflexes, so has the *Ostvogtland*: /besər/ NHG *besser*, /wädər/ NHG *Wetter*. We therefore assume that Common German was pronounced with two short mid front phonemes. It was presumably North German speakers who, following the principle of spelling pronunciation, effected the eventual merger of the *e*-type phonemes. The same assumption must also be made for the long vowels: there was a more open and a more close mid front vowel. In incidence they no doubt differed, but in general we can postulate the following diachronic development:

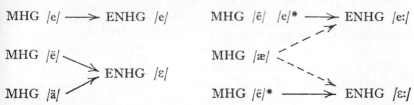

* Under conditions of lengthening; the dotted arrows indicate that both developments are widely attested. In Bavarian MHG/ĕ/ coalesced under most conditions with MHG/e/.

The long phonemes /i:/ /ü:/ /u:/ existed everywhere where lengthening had occurred (< MHG /i, ü, u/). But in CGm. they also derived from the MHG diphthongs /ie, üe, uo/, while in UGm. this merger had not taken place. The bracketed diphthongs in the diagram refer to these UGm. phonemes.

Among the remaining diphthongs three derive from MHG diphthongs (MHG *ei, ou, öu*) and three arose through diphthongization of the MHG long high-tongue vowels *ī, ū, iu*. Eventually the two series were to merge in one on the basis of spelling pronunciation. Most modern dialects have kept them apart, with some exceptions, e.g. the widespread Bavarian merger of the reflexes of MHG *ū* and *ou*. It is probably safe to assume that UGm. and CGm. speakers of ENHG still kept the two series apart, but that LG speakers of ENHG merged them. Diagrammatically the merger may be illustrated as follows:

MHG	ENHG	CGm.	EUGm.	later	NHG
/ī/ ⟶	/ɛi/	⟨ei⟩	⟨ei⟩	⟨ei⟩ ⟶	/ae/
/ei/ ⟶	/ai/	⟨ei⟩	⟨ai⟩		
/ū/ ⟶	/au/	⟨au⟩		⟶	/ao/
/ou/ ⟶	/åu/				
/iu/ ⟶	/öü/	⟨eu⟩		⟶	/ɔø/
/öu/ ⟶	/öu/				

The notations ENHG /ɛi/ and /ai/ are, of course, only symbolic and express the suggestion that the reflex of MHG /ī/ was higher, the reflex of MHG /ei/ lower. The phonetic realizations of these ENHG phonemes depended on the dialectal background of the speakers. No suggestions with regard to the phonetic character of /au/ and /åu/, /öü/ and /öu/ are intended. Phonemically these reflexes of MHG phonemes were probably still apart.
Examples:

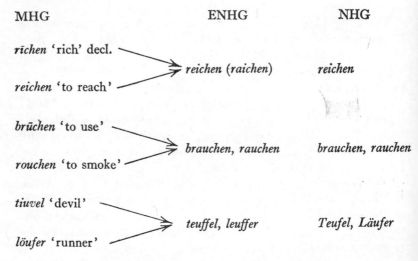

MHG	ENHG	NHG
rīchen 'rich' decl.	*reichen (raichen)*	*reichen*
reichen 'to reach'		
brūchen 'to use'	*brauchen, rauchen*	*brauchen, rauchen*
rouchen 'to smoke'		
tiuvel 'devil'	*teuffel, leuffer*	*Teufel, Läufer*
löufer 'runner'		

Other diachronic changes affected only the incidence of the phonemes. The most important was the lengthening of all short medial vowels before single lenis consonants and the concomitant but rarer shortening of long vowels before consonantal clusters, e.g. *săgen > sāgen, lĕben > lēben; dāhte > dăchte*. The general principle admitted, however, regional variation, and vowel length before single *r* or *r*-clusters, *m* and also *t* reflects special developments. Especially before the final syllables *-er* and *-el* former /m/ would appear to have become /mm/, which then prevented the lengthening: MHG *hamer* NHG *Hammer*, MHG *himel* NHG *Himmel*, but MHG *name* is NHG *Name*. The dental fortis plosive MHG /t/ was the only fortis plosive forming an opposition with a geminate /tt/ (see 5.4.4) and early absorption in /tt/ can be assumed, hence the preceding short vowel is generally preserved: *bitten, Bretter, Vetter* but not in *treten, beten, Vater*.

The following diachronic changes were dialectal, but have left traces in the standard language, e.g. MHG /u/ /ü/ > ENHG /o/ /ö/ before *n, m* in some lexical items (*vrum* > *fromm, münch* > *mönch*); MHG /e/ > ENHG /ö/ in labial surroundings (*leffel* > *löffel*); MHG /ü/ > ENHG /i/, i.e. unrounding (*küssen* > *kissen*); MHG /ā/ > ENHG /o:/ mainly before *n* (*āne* > *ohne*) but also *kāt* > *Kot* 'dirt'.

6.5.3 | The unstressed vowels

In MHG innumerable word forms ended in *-e*, a neutral central vowel. Under certain conditions this *-e* was dropped. This phenomenon is known as the MHG apocope (see 5.4.3). In Bavarian territory these conditions became much wider and apocope became general even before the end of the MHG period. Elsewhere in Upper German this second phase of apocope became dominant in texts by the end of the fourteenth or the first quarter of the fifteenth century. It is therefore known as the ENHG apocope. In the west it also affected CGm. but in the east it appears at best to have spread as another southern influence. Basically it remained an UGm. phenomenon and later resistance on the part of ECGm. writers and grammarians largely eliminated it again from the written language. Only if non-inflectional *-e* followed upon a derivational element did apocope become regularly accepted by the written language of subsequent centuries, e.g. MHG *-ære, -unge, -nisse, -inne* > *-er, -ung, -nis, -in*. Its incidence is, however, very much a feature of ENHG, see in 6.4.4 Luther's *nachtwache* but *wach* in the Mentelin and Swiss Bibles, further 6.4.4 (iv) *mein sach* (NHG *meine Sache*), 6.4.4 (v) *ein cristlich ler, wer* (NHG *eine christliche Lehre, wäre*). Since apocope had far-reaching consequences for the inflectional system, it cannot be seen only as a phonological phenomenon. While it affected in principle every final unstressed MHG *-e* and led to its loss, the adjectival inflectional system was affected much less. The result was first of all much confusion, and perhaps in no other respect was the language as idiolectal as in the incidence of apocope and its complement syncope.

Syncope affected unstressed prefinal *-e-* in inflectional endings, e.g. in the preterite of one class of weak verbs (see 5.5.3) the ending *-ete* underwent either syncope > *-te* or apocope > *-et* or, more rarely, both > *-t*. In Luther *-et* is the most frequent form (see 6.4.3 and 6.4.4 (ii) *antwortet, recket, leget,* but also *erwisscht*). Owing to coalescence with the 3rd pers. sg. pres. this form, characteristic of many ENHG texts, was gradually more and more replaced by *-te*. The unstressed elements *-ele, -ere, -ene-* lost either the first or the second *-e-* with much regional variation (*wandeln* or *wandlen, hindern* or *hindren, eigen(e)* or *eigne*). On the whole UGm. preferred *-le*, CGm. *-el*, while *-er* was more frequent than *-re*, *-ne* than *-en*. And in the case of *-ene* both *e* were more readily preserved than in the other two endings (e.g. *eigene*).

In final syllables, e.g. MHG *-es, -et, -est*, syncope occurred as well (*tages* or *tags, hilfet* or *hilft*).

In UGm. syncope also occurred in the prefixes *ge-* and *be-*, but the written language, on the whole, tended to avoid it. The morphophonemic consequences of this syncope brought about too great a phonetic change. Some modern words do, however, testify to this dialectal syncope, e.g. *bleiben* (< MHG *belīben*), *Glück, gleich, Glaube, Gnade, Glied* or *Gleis – Geleise*.

As there was such very great variation regionally, within one text, and according to morphological classes, we also get the phenomenon of epithesis, that is the addition of an unhistorical *-e*, especially in the 1st and 3rd pers. sg. pret. of strong verbs, e.g. *er sahe*, or in the imperative of strong verbs.

In the course of the ENHG period the convention became gradually established that the unstressed prefixes and inflectional suffixes were to be spelt with ⟨e⟩ rather than ⟨i⟩ as had been common, for instance, in ECGm. On the other hand, derivational suffixes, probably always bearing a secondary stress, came to favour ⟨i⟩ where ⟨e⟩ had before also been current, e.g. *torecht* > *töricht, machtec* > *mächtig*. Thus *-lich, -ig, -isch, -icht, -in* (in nouns) but *-en*, against the rule, in adjectives (*seiden*) became established. In other suffixes other 'full' vowels were restored or retained, e.g. *-bar* (*achtbar*), *-at* (*Heimat*), *-ung(e)*, *-niss(e)*.

In monosyllabic words where diphthongization had occurred before *-r* an excrescent unstressed vowel *-e-* tended to appear, e.g. MHG *sūr, fiur* > ENHG *saur* or *sauer, feur* or *feuer*. It eventually became the norm, hence NHG *sauer, Feuer*.

6.5.4 | The consonant system

The whole territory of Common German was at some stage affected by the *binnenhochdeutsche Konsonantenschwächung* (see 5.4.4). Only areas outside the range of the Common German of the early sixteenth century, e.g. Central Franconian or High Alemannic, remained untouched. Yet Common German, by and large, retained in its spelling a reflection of the earlier, that is MHG consonantal system. It is therefore extremely difficult to establish a phonological system of consonants, given the fact that people spoke largely dialectally. It was only when the written standard language was supplemented by a spoken counterpart that we can posit a phonological as opposed to a graphemic system of ENHG. At some stage, we must assume, the MHG system consisting of an opposition of short lenis and long (geminate) fortis plosives, fricatives, liquids, and nasals changed to a simpler opposition of lenis and fortis plosives and fricatives, realized as voiced and voiceless plosives and fricatives in Central Franconian and other northern forms of High German. When High German became the standard medium of North Germany the spoken language also rested in its consonantism on an opposition of voiced and voiceless plosives and fricatives.

The elimination of the feature of quantity in the consonantism was undoubtedly somehow concatenated with the new principle of vowel length: short medial vowels were lengthened before single lenis consonants and long vowels were shortened before consonantal clusters. Only after diphthongs did the contrast rest entirely on the consonants.

Although the principle of neutralization in final position in the word or syllable (*Auslautsverhärtung*) was abandoned on the graphemic level in ENHG, it is to be assumed that it was retained in phonology over much of the territory. The North German pronunciation of NHG would, of course, also have reinforced this feature.

Among the fricatives the opposition lenis/fortis was abandoned for the velars when the lenis /h/ disappeared intervocalically in late MHG. In some ENHG variants the opposition /f/ – /ff/ was also abandoned medially although it was introduced initially when MHG *w-* became a voiced (or lenis) labiodental fricative. Only the dentals preserved the medial opposition [z] – [s], *reisen – reißen.*

For ENHG we may therefore posit:

Stage XI:

/v/	/z/			lenis (voiced)	⎫ fricatives
/f/	/s/	/ʃ/	/x/	fortis (voiceless)	⎭
/b/	/d/	/g/		lenis (voiced)	⎫ plosives
/p/	/t/	/k/		fortis (voiceless)	⎭
/pf/	/ts/			affricates (could be regarded as clusters)	
/m/	/n/	(/ŋ/)		nasals	
/l/				⎫ liquids	
/r/				⎭	
	/j/	/h/		semi-consonants.	

Examples:

Initial position

/v/	*war*	'true'	/z/	*sarg*	'coffin'				
/f/	*far*	'danger'	/s/	—			/ʃ/	*schar*	'group'
							/x/	—	
/b/	*bar*	'bare'	/d/	*dar*	'there'	/g/	*gar*	'quite'	
/p/	*par*	'pair'	/t/	*tar*	'(I) dare'	/k/	*kar*	'vessel'	
/pf/	*pfarre*	'parish'	/ts/	*zart*	'tender'				
/m/	*mark*	'marrow'	/n/	*narr*	'fool'	(/ŋ/)	—		
	/l/	*lar*	'study'						
	/r/	*rar*	'rare'						
			/j/	*jar*	'year'	/h/	*har*	'hair'	

Medial position

/v/	—		/z/	*hasen*	'hares'		
/f/	*hafen*	'pots'	/s/	*hassen*	'to hate'	/x/	*hacher*
			/ʃ/	*haschen*	'to catch'		'hangman'
/b/	*haben*	'to have'	/d/	*hader*	'quarrel'	/g/	*hagen* 'to fence'
/p/	*rappen*	'ravens'	/t/	*hatten*	'had'	/k/	*haken* 'hooks'
/pf/	*stapfen*	'to step'	/ts/	*hetzen*	'to chase'		—
/m/	*hamme*	'ham'	/n/	*hanen*	'cocks'	(/ŋ/)	*hangen* 'to hang')
	/l/	*hallen*	'to echo'				
	/r/	*harren*	'to wait'				
			/j/	—		/h/	—

Where the occurrence is positionally limited the gaps tend to be filled with foreign loans. We have little information on when [v] might have been introduced medially (*Slawen*) or [x, ç] initially (*Chirurgie*). The semi-consonants retained their limited distribution but we must reckon with a good deal of local variation and /j/ in particular occurred medially in some areas such as parts of Alemannia. In other areas it had become *g*, e.g. in *Scherge*. A new, third nasal phoneme appeared when [ŋ] ceased being a positional variant of /n/ before velars, that is when *hangen* was no longer pronounced [haŋgən] but became [haŋən]. The brackets are intended to indicate our ignorance about the exact date when this occurred.

As far as incidence is concerned, the labial plosives increased owing to the change of MHG *rw, lw* > *rb, lb* (*gelw, farwe* > *gelb, farbe*) and owing to frequent insertion as a glide between *m + d, t*, e.g. *frembd, gesampt*. The dentals were also added for phonetic reasons, e.g. *d* between *n* and liquids (*spindel, gewöndlich*) and many forms have remained (*öffentlich, wöchentlich, meinetwegen* < *meinentwegen*). The incidence of /ts/ increased when *t* in the initial cluster MHG *tw-* changed to *z-*, e.g. MHG *twingen* > ENHG *zwingen*. In some areas, especially ECGm., MHG *tw-* developed to *kw-* (⟨*qu*⟩). *Quer* from MHG *twerch* is a present-day attestation of this change while the same root in *Zwerchfell* shows the UGm. development. At the end of a word ending in *-s, -ch,* or *-f* an excrescent *t* became added, for instance, in *Saft* (MHG *saf* E *sap*), *Hüfte* (MHG *huf* E *hip*), *Papst* (MHG *bābes*), *Palast* (MHG *palas*), *Obst* (MHG *obez*), *selbst* (< *selbes*), *Habicht* (MHG *habech* E *hawk*), and after *n* in *Mond* (< *mon, man*), *jemand, niemand* (< *ieman, nieman*). In many cases the incidence differs from NHG because dialectal developments found a way into the written language. For instance, the widespread coalescence of UGm. *d-* and *t-* gave rise to forms such as *toppel* (*doppel*), *teutsch, tausend*, of which only the last example has survived. In other cases the CGm. regional form prevailed, e.g. in *dumm* (MHG *tump* E *dumb*) or *dunkel* (MHG *tunkel*).

6.6 | Morphology: Inflection

6.6.1 | Noun inflection

Two features of ENHG led to a profound restructuring of the inflectional system of nouns and to an even greater reassignment of nouns within the system. First, the phonological feature of apocope caused, or would have caused, an enormous increase in the number of nouns with an unmarked plural. Secondly, the growth of a written standard language spread regional features to other areas and by making them supra-regional increased variation and thus morphological confusion. Eventually, it led however to a regularization which, towards the end of the ENHG period, re-established regionally extinct morphological types, accepted new compromise or mixed form classes, and fixed the lexical membership of individual inflectional classes. It is in the latter respect that the greatest changes are to be noted when we compare modern German with medieval German.

In Upper German, for example, apocope wiped out the *e*-plural class. MHG *stein – steine* became unmarked, but MHG *tac – tage* escaped homophony by joining the mutated plural class: *tag – täg*; MHG *geist – geiste* by adopting -*er*: *geist – geister*; MHG *sē – sēwe* by joining the *n*-class: *see – seen*. In ECGm. the *e*-pl. class stayed alive and it was its *tag – tage* which was finally adopted into the standard language. In ENHG it was characteristic that the plural of *tag* could be *tag*, *täg* or *tage*. Of *dorn* all possible plurals (*dorn, dorne, dörn, dörner, dornen*) are recorded. While it is true that variants usually had a regional basis the general levelling trend of the written language tended to spread forms.

The inclination to mark plurality was not the only agent. The case system, too, was in flux and a strongly marked case such as the genitive singular in -(*e*)*s* was spreading. Gender and semantic categories such as animate and inanimate tended also to be instrumental in the formation of new inflectional classes, in the preservation of existing ones, or in the assignment of individual words to form classes.

MHG had a uniform dative plural marker, -(*e*)*n*, in all classes (indistinguishable from the other plural cases in the *n*-plural class). Although at the time of the greatest confusion this form was occasionally threatened, it proved too strongly entrenched and thus survived to the present day. In the case of the genitive singular there was a two-way opposition: masc. and neuter nouns had a marked ending, fem. nouns had not. Masc. and neuter nouns had either -(e)s or -en as markers. However, only -(e)s was an unambiguous marker; -en marked the oblique cases vs. the nominative in the masculines, and marked the genitive and dative in the neuters. There were only four such neuter nouns against hundreds with -(e)s. Little wonder then that they fell in line. NHG has *Herz – Herzens*, but *Auge – Auges, Ohr – Ohrs*, while MHG *wange* has become feminine, no doubt via the plural. All neuters now have a genitive singular in -(e)s. The two masc. genitive markers were more evenly distributed, but -(e)s was an unambiguous form while -en was not. The unambiguous sign -s thus encroached on the *n*-class and a compromise form -ens arose. Wavering between -en and -ens, apart from the outright adoption of -(e)s by many individual words, was eventually settled on the basis of animate vs. inanimate, thus *Knabe – Knaben* but *Gedanke – Gedankens*. The large number of substantivized adjectives denoting persons and ending in -en in the genitive singular may have proved the decisive influence (*der Gerechte, des Gerechten; der Heilige, des Heiligen*). Some nouns took the *s*-genitive although they had the *n*-plural. This led to the formation of a further new declensional class, e.g. *Mast – Masts – Masten, Schmerz – Schmerzes – Schmerzen*.

Case distinction in feminines was not unambiguous and was already much weakened in MHG. Its only means both in the plural and singular was -en, but since it was much more frequent in the plural, it was eventually ousted from the singular. In ENHG there was much wavering.

Compared with the relatively simple restructuring of the case system, the reorganization of the plural system was more involved and produced a mass of reassignments of nouns to classes.

As long as the lack of indication of plurality was primarily a hallmark of the neuters (MHG *wort – wort, bette – bette*), with only four nouns in the *n*-pl. class and about an original dozen in the -er sub-class, this unmarked class maintained itself quite well. Characteristically it stayed longest preserved in ECGm. where apocope had not destroyed the primarily masc. *e*-pl. class. But once this gender barrier was breached and vast numbers of masculines lost their former plural markers (-e) analogy had free play: most neuters adopted the one existing unambiguous plural marker among neuters, -er. The collapse of the gender barrier between masc. and neuter, of course, not only opened the way for masc. nouns to adopt the *er*-pl. marker, it also led to the adoption of the *e*-pl. by many neuters (*Wort – Worte, Heer – Heere*) and even to the introduction of mutation (only *Floß – Flöße, Kloster – Klöster, Wasser – Wässer*). The *e*-pl. was, of course, only available in areas where apocope was not dominant. From there these forms entered the standard language in the seventeenth and subsequent centuries.

Mutation was by late MHG times a clear plural marker among feminines (*hūt – hiute, kraft – krefte*) and remained intact after the occurrence of apocope (ENHG *haut – heut, kraft – kreft*). It was, however, a relatively small class among feminines, where *-en* was much more widely represented and remained also unaffected by apocope. All feminine nouns which were not marked by mutation had *-en* both in some cases in the sg. (perhaps about half the total number of fem.) and in some cases in the plural (most nouns in gen. and all in dat. pl. and about half in nom. acc. pl. as well). As there was one clear unmarked form, the nom. sg. (*pflicht, sünd(e), zung(e)*), the feeling must have become established that the sg. was unmarked and the plural had the plus form (*pflichten, sünden, zungen*). Throughout the ENHG phase the *en*-ending was, however, also found in the oblique cases of the singular, and in some dialects, notably Bavarian, also in the nominative (*Brucken, Gassen*). The *en*-pl. class eventually became the typical fem. class. Some few feminines in *-nis*, however, adopted the *e*-type plural (*Kenntnis – Kenntnisse*) because the more numerous neuters in *-nis* had adopted *-nisse* in the plural. This is a clear case where similarity of form proved stronger than gender.

A great number of reassignments occurred in the masculine classes where there were the fewest typological changes. The *e*-pl. type was restored through ECGm. influence, but many nouns had in the meantime gone over to the stronger mutation class (*Stall – Ställe, Baum – Bäume, Stuhl – Stühle*), which thus became the most typical masc. class. The oldest stratum of the unmarked class, the old *ja*-stems, joined other classes (*Hirte – Hirten*). A large number of the former *n*-pl. nouns joined the *e*-pl. or mutation classes (*Greis – Greise, Garten – Gärten, Hahn – Hähne*). Others became unmarked (*Balken – Balken, Daumen – Daumen*). Especially abstracts and words denoting things tended to lose the nominative – accusative distinction which was the characteristic feature of the old *n*-pl. class and of this class alone. The syntactic predominance of the objective case, the prior intrusion of -*s* into the genitive (-*en* > -*ens*) must have suggested that the type acc. *samen*, gen. *samens* was the same as the type acc. *wagen*, gen. *wagens*, leading to a new nom. *samen* for earlier *same* in analogy to *wagen*. Some old *e*-pl. nouns, denoting animates, characteristically changed to the *n*-pl. class, e.g. *Held – Helden*. The only new masc. plural class, the *er*-class, established itself in ENHG (*gott – götter* etc.) but is still relatively thinly represented.

The unmarked-plural class, so very typical of ENHG and greatly swollen at one time yet constantly under attack, was eventually restricted to the following groups of nouns:

(a) most masc. nouns in -*er*, -*el*, -*en* irrespective of the original class to which they belonged (*Finger, Bäcker, Maler*; *Schatten, Wagen, Rücken, Haufen*; *Ärmel, Deckel*) though some have mutation (*Vater – Väter, Nagel – Nägel, Vogel – Vögel, Boden – Böden, Hafen – Häfen*) and very few the *n*-pl. (*Stachel – Stacheln, Vetter – Vettern*);

(b) one isolated survivor of the old *ja*-class (*Käse*);

(c) neuter nouns in -*er*, -*el*, -*en*, -*chen*, and -*lein* (*Messer, Ruder, Bündel, Mädchen*) although two have mutation (*Kloster – Klöster, Wasser – Wässer* in the sense of 'mineral water');

(d) some neuter nouns in *Ge*-(root)-*e* (*Gebirge, Gebäude*). Characteristically this class has been enormously reduced and now contains no feminines, perhaps because in the fem. gender alone there is no number distinction in the definite article (cf. m. *der – die*, n. *das – die*, but f. *die – die*).

There were not only numerous changes in the lexical membership of the declensional classes, gender, too, was affected by the process of restructuring which was taking place in the noun system. Both semantic and formal reasons were operative in gender change. The most important single factor was no doubt that the genders were not distinguished in the plural of the gender-markers, i.e. articles, pronouns, adjectives. Nouns which were used predominantly in the plural could thus easily be affected by semantic or formal analogy and change gender accordingly. Thus some originally masculine plant names and names for small animals which had the *n*-pl. declension changed gender from masc. to fem., e.g. *Blume, Traube, Heuschrecke, Schnecke, Schlange*. Many originally masc. abstract nouns in -*t* became fem., e.g. *Last, List, Luft, Lust, Angst, Gewalt* (perhaps by semantic association with

Kraft, Macht, Stärke). Some neuters also became fem.: *Ähre, Beere, Rippe, Ecke, Wange*. Although fem. gained perhaps more than the other genders, many nouns also changed to masc., e.g. some nouns in *-el* (from n.: *Beutel*, from f.: *Frevel, Gürtel, Scheitel*) or in *-er* (from n.: *Acker, Jammer, Wucher*), and to neuter, e.g. from fem. *Begehr, Gelübde, Geschöpf, Gesicht, Gespenst, Gewissen* in analogy to other n. *Ge-* words. In MHG many nouns were recorded with more than one gender and, no doubt, there were often ancient dialectal differences behind such gender differences. The NHG standard language favoured in general the gender found in ECGm. It has been found that in Luther's 1545 Bible there were two hundred and seventy nouns with gender change compared with MHG and in nearly all cases NHG has followed Luther.

Where everything was in the melting-pot it is hazardous to set up paradigms. If this is nevertheless attempted it is because declensional types, however blurred the outlines and confused the lexical membership, did exist and were the fixed points which influenced the development. Since predictability, in so far as it existed, depended on the plural form to a much greater extent than on the singular, the classes will again be based on the plural.

I. *e-plural* (only ECGm.)

		M		
Pl.	Nom. acc.	*-(e)*	stein(e)	
	Gen.			
	Dat.	*-en*	steinen	
Sg.	Nom. acc.	*-ø*	stein	
	Gen.	*-(e)s*	stein(e)s	
	Dat.	*-(e)*	stein(e)	

Notes:

(1) As *-en* spread early throughout the system of the feminines except those with mutated plural, no feminines are included here. Those in *-nis* which later joined this class belonged to the unmarked class in ENHG (*-nis* or *-nisse, -nüs*).

(2) Since the unmarked neuters (*wort – wort*) remained unmarked longest in ECGm., the only area where the *e*-plural class survived, neuters are not yet included. Many began to model their plural formation on this class (*bein – beine*).

(3) In ECGm. texts, where apocope affected the dissyllabic words, forms like *jünger – jüngere* are nevertheless attested in the fifteenth and sixteenth centuries.

(4) Bracketed forms indicate the incidence of the apocope which had to some extent spread everywhere.

II. *Plural with mutation*

		M.		F.	
Pl.	Nom. acc.	⸚(e)		schleg(e)	heut(e)
	Gen.				
	Dat.	⸚en		schlegen	heuten
Sg.	Nom. acc.	-ø		schlag	haut
	Gen.	-(e)s	-ø	schlag(e)s	haut
	Dat.	-(e)	-ø	schlag(e)	haut

Notes:

(1) This type is particularly extensive in UGm. among masculines: *ärm, täg.*

(2) Neuters adopted mutation to a very minor extent to escape from the lack of the indication of plurality. But individual examples are met with throughout the ENHG period: *maul – mäul, band – bende, schaf – schäf.* Although there are some survivors of this innovation (*Floß – Flöße, Kloster – Klöster*) the mutated plural cannot be said to have become a type among neuters.

III. *er-plural*

		N.	M.		
Pl.	Nom. acc.	⸚er	kelber	geister	
	Gen.				
	Dat.	⸚ern	kelbern	geistern	
Sg.	Nom. acc.	-ø	kalb	geist	
	Gen.	-(e)s	kalb(e)s	geistes	
	Dat.	-(e)	kalb(e)	geist(e)	

Notes:

(1) This type proved itself to be the most productive among neuters, more so in UGm. than in CGm. (e.g. UGm. also *rösser*). Its extension was halted by the spread of the CGm. *e*-plural class. Foreign words have seldom adopted this plural, cf. *Interesse, Atom, Elektron* etc., but see *Regiment(er), Spital – Spitäler.*

(2) Among masculines *männer* was formed early perhaps in analogy to *weiber, kinder.* Other early ones are *geister, götter, leiber, wälder.*

IV. *n-plural*

	M. (a)	M. (b)	M. (c)	F.	N. (b)	N. (c)
Pl. Nom. acc. Gen. dat.				*-(E)n*		
Sg. Nom.				*-(E)*		*-(E)*
Acc.	*-En*	*-En*	*-ø*	*-(En)*	*-(E)*	*-(E)*
Gen.	*-En*	*-Ens*	*-(E)s*	*-(En)*	*-Ens*	*-s(E)*
Dat.	*-En*	*-En*	*-ø*	*-(En)*	*-En*	*-(E)*

	M. (a)		M. (b)	M. (c)	F.	N. (b)	N. (c)
Pl.	menschen	boten	namen	masten	zungen	hertzen	augen
Sg. Nom.	mensch	bot(e)	nam(e)	mast	zung(e)	hertz(e)	aug(e)
Acc.	menschen	boten	namen	mast	zung(en)	hertz(e)	aug(e)
Gen.	menschen	boten	namens	mast(e)s	zung(en)	hertzens	aug(e)s
Dat.	menschen	boten	namen	mast	zung(en)	hertzen	aug(e)

Notes:

(1) Apocope removed the final -*e* in the nom. sg. where all nouns in MHG had -*e*. The rule which reintroduced -*e* in some words (*Bote, Gatte, Beichte*) but not in others (*Mensch, Narr, Acht*) was only established in the seventeenth century. If we assume that -*e* is normal and predictable we have to list the less numerous nouns without -*e* as exceptions.

(2) In the gen. of masculines and neuters -*en*/-*ens* competed with each other until they sorted themselves out on the basis of animate (a) and inanimate (b). A relatively small group (c) dropped -*en* from the singular altogether. Lexical membership of these sub-classes was established centuries after the types as such had arisen and were in competition with one another.

V. *The unmarked plural*

		M.	N.	
		M.	**N.**	
Pl.	Nom. acc.	-ø	hirt	bett
	Gen.			
	Dat.	-*en*	hirten	betten
Sg.	Nom. acc.	-ø	hirt	bett
	Dat.			
	Gen.	-(*e*)*s*	hirt(e)s	bett(e)s

Notes:

(1) The masc. class was very large with the temporary accession of the former *e*-plural type (*tage* > *tag*), but was rapidly reduced by recourse to vital types (*tag* > *tage*, *hirt* > *hirten*, *baum* > *bäum(e)*). Of the masculines only those mentioned on p. 413 remained.

(2) The neuter type *bett* (former *ja*-stem) represents also *wort* (former *a*-stem). The neuter class was reduced to those given on p. 413.

(3) It is assumed in the above diagram that the early diffusion of -*en* in the feminines (*sünde* > *sünden*) had removed the feminines as a type from this class in ENHG times.

6.6.2 | Adjective inflection

The only adjectival endings of MHG which had a vowel other than the neutral vowel -*e*, Upper German nom. sg. fem. and nom. acc. pl. neuter of the strong declension with -*iu*, changed this -*iu* to -*e* in late medieval times. This -*e* was not subject to the Upper German apocope. Spellings with ⟨-i-⟩ in Alemannic texts and with ⟨-eu-⟩ in Bavarian texts in fact show that the vowel did not merge with the older unstressed -*e*. Modern Upper German dialects have also reflexes which differ from that of MHG -*e*. Apocope in ENHG texts, including Luther, may have resulted from the general confusion concerning apocope.

Apocope had a different effect on the stem-final -*e* and the inflectional -*e* of MHG. Most of the adjectives with stem-final -*e* lost it, e.g. *schön, dünn, schwer, nemend*, so that these former *ja*-stems now had the same appearance as the old *a/ō*-stems. A few, especially those ending in a voiced or lenis consonant, preserved the final -*e* under ECGm. influence, e.g. *trübe, mürbe, feige, träge, blöde, öde, müde, böse, leise, weise, irre*.

The nom. acc. pl. masc. and fem. of the strong paradigm (MHG *junge*) escaped apocope in many texts perhaps under the influence of the neuter form (*junge < jungiu*) or to prevent the plural from becoming unmarked. Hans Sachs has, for instance, *grosse schetz, reiche bürger, andere arme krancke Christen*. The MHG ending -*e* in the acc. sg. fem. also survived, perhaps through merger with the reflex of the nom. -*iu*.

The weak paradigm ceased being identical with the *n*-pl. declension of nouns when the acc. sg. fem. became identical with the nom. and when the gen. and dat. sg. of fem. nouns became endingless while the weak adjective preserved the ending -*en*. Compare:

	MHG	NHG
nom.	*diu lange zunge*	*die lange Zunge*
acc.	*die langen zungen*	*die lange Zunge*
gen. dat.	*der langen zungen*	*der langen Zunge*

ENHG showed much wavering. Hans Sachs has, for instance, *in die ganze welt* (=NHG) but *die geistlichen tröstung* (acc., adj. = MHG). Luther generally followed the MHG practice.

Apocope was most in evidence in the nom. sg. of all genders in the weak declension, e.g. Hans Sachs *der erst fisch, das hailig almusen, die gantz regel*.

Syncope in the ending -*es* was quite usual in ENHG, e.g. *jungs*; it was later removed (>*junges*).

In the strong paradigm the ending -*es* of the gen. sg. masc. and neuter began to make way for the weak ending -*en* (*frohes Mutes > frohen Mutes*) only in the seventeenth century, but both forms continued side by side into the nineteenth, when -*en* finally became the accepted norm.

In the vocative, however, nouns in the plural regularly had their adjectival attributes with the weak ending where NHG now uses the strong form, e.g. ENHG *lieben brüder!* – NHG *liebe Brüder!*

6.6.3 Verb inflection

(i) In the *stem formation* the historical tripartition (dental-suffix or weak type, apophonic or strong type, apophonic dental-suffix type or preterite-presents) remained basically unaltered.

The three MHG classes of the dental-suffix type rested on secondary features (vowel alternation or *Rückumlaut*, presence or absence of -*e*- before the dental suffix). Syncope then affected medial -*e*-, while at the same time apocope threatened final -*e* in the first and third persons singular. The resultant wavering concerning the dental suffixes (pret. -*ete*, -*et*, -*te*, -*t*; past part. -*et* or -*t*) meant the merger of the MHG classes II and III, that is the MHG -*te* and -*ete* classes without vowel alternation. In some writers and some areas the phonetic environment seems to have weighed in favour of the presence or absence of syncope. Luther often preferred -*e*- after vowels, liquids and nasals (*bawete, horet, dieneten*) and syncope after *ch, g, tz, pf* (*machte* or *macht, legten*). His practice varied slightly in the course of his career and the issue remained unsettled. Variation was the most characteristic feature in this respect, although in the first and third persons singular of the preterite -*et* was the most frequent form. In the past participle -*et* and -*t* were more or less evenly distributed.

The other secondary feature, *Rückumlaut*, on which the MHG class I rested (see 5.5.3 (i)), was already shaken in the past participle, and a number of MHG verbs had stem forms with or without *Rückumlaut* in the preterite. This uncertainty increased greatly in the fourteenth and fifteenth centuries. In Luther there are only a few verbs in addition to the six of NHG (*kennen, brennen, wenden, senden, nennen, rennen*) and the anomalous *bringen, denken* and ENHG *dünken*, which still showed *Rückumlaut*. For instance: *setzen* – *er satzt* (pret.), *mercken* – *marckte, keren* – *kart*, *keuffen – kauffte.* Hans Sachs had only *gekant, nant, sant* with some frequency. Upper German writers tended to have many more verbs with *Rückumlaut.* In the chronicle of the Zürich city councillor Gerold Edlibach (1454–1530) there are still fifty-five verbs in the weak class I with *Rückumlaut.*

For ENHG we may therefore posit the following two dental-suffix classes:

I *-t/-te* with vowel alternation:
  setzen – satzt(e) – gesetzt (Rückumlaut in the past part. was almost only found before *-nn, -nd).*

II *-ete/-et/-te/-t* without vowel alternation:
  schicken – schickte/schicket/schickt – geschickt/geschicket.

The forms with syncope and apocope (*schickt*) or with apocope only (*schicket*) are particularly characteristic of ENHG. The NHG type *schickte* later prevailed because it restored the difference between the 3rd pers. sg. pret. and pres.

The stem formation of the apophonic or strong verbs was greatly affected by levelling and, to some extent, by the vocalic developments. Levelling removed the differences in the pret. sg. of the MHG classes I (Ia *-ei-, treib* /Ib *-ē-, zēch*) and II (IIa *-ou-, slouf* /IIb *-ō-, sōt*), in the present of class II (sg. *-iu-, er sliufet* /pl. *-ie-, wir sliefen*), and the stem alternation in the preterite throughout the system. Vocalic developments created new sub-classes in class I, e.g. p.p. *gegriffen / getrieben* /i/ – /i:/, and class II, e.g. p.p. *gegossen / geboten* /o/ – /o:/, in classes IV and V, e.g. p.p. *genommen / gestohlen* /o/ – /o :/; *gesessen / gebeten* /e/ – /e:/. The vocalic developments were mainly regular within the framework of the lengthening of short vowels in open syllables, but some created new types, e.g. MHG *u* before *nn, mm > o* (*gesponnen, geschwommen*), and the lexical adherence to certain types was altered.

The big issue was obviously the levelling of the two stem forms in the preterite in favour of either the singular (1st, 3rd pers.) or the plural form. Several reasons have been adduced for this process. In Upper German the preterite indicative fell gradually into disuse and the perfect was used more and more as the tense of the past. Although this happened only in the spoken language, it must have weakened the two preterite forms. The verbs of classes VI and VII were already uniform in the preterite. After the lengthening of short vowels before certain lenis consonants in monosyllabics, many verbs of classes IV and V also had a uniform preterite, e.g. *stal – stālen* > *stāl – stālen*. The many weak verbs with vowel alternation (*Rückumlaut*) also had only one form in the preterite (*setzen – satzt(e) – satzten*). In class II the ECGm. change of *u* (pl.) > *o* must have added to the levelling (sg. had -*o*-). Finally, the whole distinction in the pret. was irrational. In so far as vowel gradation was functional it served tense distinction (see p. 96), while number distinction was expressed by inflectional endings. However, the process took a very long time. It started in Swabian in the fifteenth century and had become quite general in the Swabian printers' language early in the sixteenth century in all classes of apophonic verbs. Hans Sachs of Nuremberg had the new levelled-out forms in class I (except that he still preferred *reyt* and *schrey*), wavered in class II between -*u*- and -*o*- in the plural, although -*o*- in both sg., where only few -*u*- forms occurred, and pl. was already more frequent than -*u*-. He still had the old -*a*- / -*u*- contrast before *n*+consonant in class III. The Swiss Gerold Edlibach, on the other hand, still kept the MHG forms more or less intact. Luther maintained the distinction in the first and third classes, but had levelled -*o*- (-*ou*-) / -*u*- in the second class in favour of the *o*-form. The NHG levelled classes thus do not derive from Luther's language. In fact his archaic use probably delayed the adoption of the South German levelling by the rising standard language and prolonged the state of confusion. In some classes the confusion was not resolved until the rules of Gottsched and Adelung were universally adopted in the eighteenth century.

The solution which was eventually adopted by the written language is shown in the table overleaf.

The *preterite-presents* (apophonic dental-suffix type) lost some further characteristic but anomalous forms. *Darft* and *maht* were replaced by *darfst* and *magst*. The other old forms of the 2nd pers. sg. *solt* and *wilt* were in competition with the newer analogical forms *sollst* and *willst* but survived into the eighteenth century. There was much contamination between the MHG verbs *durfen/ dürfen* and *türren*. Luther still used forms of the latter verb but by the eighteenth century it had died out. In the pl. pres. and inf. competing forms with or without mutation generally continued throughout the ENHG period. The impersonal *es taug* and *gonnen / gönnen* became regular weak verbs. *Wissen* developed a new pret.

	Inf. pres.	Pret.	Past part.	Levelling in pret. in favour of:
I	treiben greifen	trieb /i:/ griff /i/	getrieben ⎫ gegriffen ⎰	pl. and p.p.
II	sieden bieten	sott /o/ bot /o:/	gesotten ⎫ geboten ⎰	sg. and p.p.
III	werfen binden	warf band	geworfen ⎫ gebunden ⎰	sg.
IV	stehlen sprechen	stahl sprach	gestohlen /o:/ ⎫ gesprochen /o/ ⎰	pl.
V	geben messen	gab maß	gegeben /e:/ ⎫ gemessen /ɛ/ ⎰	pl.
VI	graben wachsen	grub /u:/ wuchs /u/	gegraben /a:/ ⎫ gewachsen /a/ ⎰	already uniform
VII	laufen (heißen, halten, rufen, stoßen)	lief	gelaufen	already uniform already uniform

Notes:

(1) To set up stem form paradigms for ENHG is impossible. It can only be done for individuals.

(2) Grammatical change was also levelled out except in *leiden – litten, schneiden – schnitten, ziehen – zogen, sieden – sotten,* and in *waren – gewesen* where it has survived. Levelling in different directions accounts for the differences now between E *to freeze, to lose, to choose* and Gm. *frieren, verlieren, küren* (*erkiesen* being archaic).

(3) In the second class the difference between the sg. and pl. of the pres. (UGm.) *ich beut, du beutst, er beut – wir bieten, ihr bietet, sie bieten* (CGm. had *ich biete* in the 1st pers. sg.) endured into the eighteenth century. Elsewhere the vowel change *e – i* (*geben – gibt*) and mutation (*graben – gräbt, stoßen – stößt, laufen – läuft*) have remained in most verbs.

(4) Some verbs of the third class adopted -*o*- in the pret., e.g. *glimmen, klimmen, schmelzen, schwellen,* and one took -*u*- (*schinden*). Only one verb still has four stem forms, although the pret. sg. belongs to elevated style only: *werden – ward – wurden – geworden.*

(5) The subj. pret. was originally based on the stem of the pret. pl. After the levelling, mutation became its primary distinctive feature and it was generally derived from whichever stem had prevailed in the indicative. But as the subj. had retained its original stem vowel for a considerable time beyond the levelling in the indicative, much confusion prevailed for a long time and is still not entirely resolved. The subj. pret. of some verbs of the third class retained its original stem, hence we also get four stem forms in that class, e.g. *bot – böte* but *starb – stürbe.*

(6) As the classes in general suffered considerable losses through verbs

becoming weak or dying out, the more isolated verbs with anomalous forms, e.g. *sitzen, saufen, saugen, lügen, schwören* and others, increased the already existing uncertainty and finally gave the whole apophonic type the character of irregularity. For a synchronic description of NHG a large number of classes, only loosely connected with the historical classes, have to be set up (see 7.6.3(i)). In modern German the strong class based on the historical apophonic type comprises about a hundred and sixty-five verbs. The losses since German was first recorded, most of which occurred in the ENHG centuries, amount to nearly ninety verbs. Relatively few verbs now waver between the two types (e.g. *backen – buk* or *backte*) but it was typical of ENHG that a large number of verbs did so.

and p.p. form *wuste, gewust*, the origin of which is not entirely clear. In the pret. the general rule became established: indicative without mutation, subjunctive with mutation. As there was a great deal of variation throughout the period, the forms of Luther will be given.

The ENHG preterite-presents (Luther)

Inf. pl. pres.	1st, 3rd sg. pres.	Pret.	Past part.
wissen	weis	wuste(wiste)	gewust(gewist)
tügen	(es)taug	(es)tuchte/-o-	—
künnen/können	kan	kundte/-o-	kund
dürffen/dorffen	darff	durffte	(be)durfft(-o-)
thüren	thar	thurste	—
sollen	sal/sol	solte	solt
magen/-ü/ö-	mag	mochte	mocht
müssen	muss	muste	must
wollen/wöllen	wil	wolte	wolt

(ii) Very great variety is also to be found in the *inflectional paradigms*. The main reason for it lies in the interpenetration of different regional patterns. Apocope and syncope, which were of UGm. origin, nevertheless made themselves felt everywhere in Common German. Among the strong verbs UGm. resistance to mutation before certain consonantal clusters with analogical extension to other forms, was responsible for unmutated forms like *wachst, halt(et), laufft, schlafft*, where CGm. had *wechst, helt(et), leufft, schlefft* etc. In classes II, III, IV and V where vowel alternations also occurred, UGm. had a contrast sg. *vs.* pl., e.g. *zeuch – zeuchst – zeucht vs. ziehen, gib – gibst – gibt vs. geben*, while CGm. had a contrast 2nd/3rd sg. *vs.* 1st sg. and pl., e.g. *ziehe – zeuchst – zeucht, gebe – gibst – gibt*.

In the course of the ENHG period different types and different patterns of levelling gained the upper hand at different times. The solutions which we now know were not finally achieved until well into the eighteenth century. In the case of the *e–i* alternation in strong verbs, the CGm. pattern which conformed to the mutation pattern in other classes prevailed. But some verbs notably *schaffen, kommen, saugen, rufen* established themselves with unmutated forms. In the case of the *eu–ie* alternation, UGm. abandoned the *eu*-forms altogether and it was this clean sweep which eventually recommended itself to the grammarians of NHG.

The endings of the present, leaving aside the preterite-presents and the anomalous verbs *sein, tun, stehen, gehen* tended to fall into the following two typological patterns:

	Ind. pres.		Subj. pres.			
	UGm.	*CGm.*			*nemen*	
1st sg.	*-ø*	*-(e)*	*-e*	nim	neme	neme
2nd sg.	*-st*	*-est*	*-est*	nimst	nimest	nemest
3rd sg.	*-t*	*-(e)t*	*-e*	nimt	nimet	neme
1st pl.	*-en*	*-en*	*-en*	nemen	nemen	nemen
2nd pl.	*-(e)t*	*-et*	*-et*	nemet	nemet	nemet
3rd pl.	*-end*	*-en*	*-en*	nemend	nemen	nemen

Notes:

(1) In the 1st pers. sg. ind. Luther had apocope frequently only in early texts, later he preferred *-e*. In the 3rd pers. sg. ind. syncopated and un-syncopated forms were both frequent, even after *t*. The NHG rule which adopted syncope except after *d* and *t* did not yet apply.

(2) In the subjunctive apocope and syncope were much less frequent than in the indicative even in UGm.

(3) In the pl. Luther had the same forms as NHG except for the un-syncopated 2nd pers. Swiss had a uniform pl. ind. in *-end* or *-ent* and Alsatian generally in *-en*. Both in Swabian and WCGm. *-end* is also found in the 2nd pres. pl. ind. alongside the modern forms *-en*, *-(e)t*, *-en*. With the change of *-end > -en* the suffixes of all persons in the plural were the same in both tenses and moods. In inversion it was common to leave out the ending: *nem wir*.

In the preterite levelling undermined and finally removed all anomalies which were additional to the main function, i.e. the expression of tense by means of gradation or a *t*-suffix and the indication of person by means of a standard personal marker. The inherited personal inflections differed in the first and third persons sg. (-*ø* against -*e*:*nam* – *sagete*) and in the second person sg. (-*e* against -*est*:*næme* – *sagetest*) while the plural was already uniform for each person and furthermore corresponded to the endings of the present, at least in many regions (ECGm. -*en*, -*et*, -*en*). The second pers. sg. ind. pret. of apophonic verbs was the most anomalous. The ending -*st* was the hallmark of the second pers. sg. everywhere else and was now introduced into the ind. pret. as well. With the disappearance of the stem vowel difference the form became entirely regular: MHG *du næme* > ENHG *du nam(e)st*.

In the first and third pers. sg., levelling produced two solutions – both abortive in the end – which removed the difference between weak and strong verbs:

nam > *name*	*nam* > *nam*
or	
sagete > *sagte*	*sagete* > *saget, sagt*
(pers. ending: -*e*)	(pers. ending: -*ø*)

The second solution which is especially frequent in Luther implied homophony of the weak verbs in the third pers. sg. pres. and pret., in other words, confusion between the tense function and the personal inflection function of -*t*. Hence it did not win acceptance. The first solution conflicted with the tendency to apocope and arose out of the confusion caused by an only partially successful apocope. The aversion of ECGm. to apocope seems to have given the 'Lutheran -*e*' a certain stylistic distinction. Thus these *e*-forms became a feature of the rising standard language especially of the south. Some spread also into ECGm. although in Luther only *sahe* was at all frequent. The highest point in the history of this unhistorical -*e* was reached between 1650 and 1675. Afterwards there was rapid decline. Gottsched pronounced himself against it. The only remnant of this once quite widespread fashion is *wurde*.

The ENHG pret. paradigms were:

	Ind. pret.	Subj. pret.		
1st, 3rd sg.	*-ø, -e*	*-e*	nam(e)	nåme
2nd sg.	*-(e)st*	*-est*	nam(e)st	nåmest
1st, 3rd pl.	*-en*	*-en*	namen	nåmen
2nd pl.	*-(e)t*	*-et*	nam(e)t	nåmen

Notes:

(1) Weak verbs had either apocope (*saget*) or syncope (*sagte*) or both (*sagt*). The MHG form (*sagete*) was only found in ECGm.

(2) In UGm. apocope also occurred in the subjunctive but was less frequent than in the indicative.

In the imperative where there was also a difference between strong and weak verbs (*nim! sage!*) an epithetic *-e* was also added to strong verbs (*neme!* or *nime!*). In UGm. apocope in the weak verbs was general (*sag!*). In the end the old forms received the sanction of the grammarians.

6.7 | Morphology: Word Formation

6.7.1 | Noun derivation

Among the most productive suffixes were *-er*, *-ung* and *-heit/-keit*. The diminutive suffix *-lin/-lein* and the feminine *-in* were also employed quite freely. Some writers also made fairly free use of *-nis/-nus*. Most of the words formed with *-schaft* and *-tum* were lexicalized and little use was made of the suffixes in the word-forming process. This was even more true of *-de* (e.g. *zierde, gelübd(e)*). But *liebde* in the princely address *ewer liebden* was frequent at the time. To a lesser extent this restriction also applied to the composite element *ge*-(root)-*(e)*. The most highly productive new suffix was undoubtedly *-erei(-erey)*. As there were a large number of foreign words in the language, those linked by a common foreign suffix began to form patterns which were analogically extended. The most productive at this stage was -*ist*.

(i) Most new *nomina agentis* were formed in -*er*, e.g. Luther:[1] *eyfferer, wircker, sudeler, handthierer, buchstaber* 'one who is excessively true to the letter', or with pejorative meaning: -*ler*, *fasteler* 'one who believes in fasting', *geistler* 'sectarian', or -*ling*: *gleubling, freßling*. Hans Sachs has *einnemer* and *außgeber* 'collector' and 'spender', *observantzer* 'one who is excessively given to observance'.

(ii) -*in* designating females was occasionally used beyond what is current in the modern language, e.g. Luther *blindyn, glewbiginne, lesterinne*. It was also added to the foreign suffix -*isse* in *ebtissin*.

(iii) The diminutive suffix used by Luther was -*lin*, e.g. *klůglin* 'one who thinks himself clever', *wortlin, gloßlin*, very rarely -*el* (*kindeln*). Thomas Murner also used -*lin*, e.g. *kleidlin, liedlin*, while H. Sachs had generally -*lein* (*hütlein* but *mendlin* 'little man'). Diminution had now become fully productive and was much used.

(iv) The one foreign suffix designating human beings which was also used with native words was -*ist*, e.g. *sophist, romanist* 'a follower of Rome' not as now 'a student of Romance languages', *papist, ewangelist* and in Luther: *buchstabilist, eselist*.

(v) -*ung* indicated as a productive suffix the action or result of an action and formed verbal abstracts, e.g. Luther *erwelung* 'election', *verdolmetzschung* 'translation', H. Sachs *zuthuung*, but some had acquired a concrete meaning: *kleydung, narung, rechnung*. Derivations with this suffix were often in competition with the substantivized infinitive, e.g. H. Sachs *ein spigelfechten*, Luther *lesterung – ir lestern, mein dolmetschung – mein verdolmetschen*.

(vi) -*erei*(-*erey*) also formed verbal abstracts indicating the process or the result of an action with the connotation 'irksome, undesirable, despicable'. It had evolved from the MHG suffix -*īe* (see 5.6.1 (xii)) added to -*er* nouns with a possible influence of French -*erie*, e.g. H. Sachs *heüchlerey, ketzerey*, Murner *lutherei* 'the movement of Luther', *abgôterey*, and with extension to nouns without -*er*, e.g. Luther: *buberey, geytzerey, pfafferey, muncherey*

---

[1] Most examples in this section are from Luther, *Ein Sendbrief von Dolmetschen, An den christlichen Adel*; H. Sachs, prose dialogues (Bibl. d. Litt. Ver. Stuttgart, 201); T. Murner, *Von dem grossen Lutherischen Narren*.

We get pairs like *vorfurung* 'seduction, seducing' and *vorfurerey* 'abominable seducing'.

(vii) *-heit/-keit* was now the only productive suffix forming abstracts denoting state from adjectives and past participles, e.g. *kranckheit, vermessenheit, eygensinnickeit* 'stubbornness'. Those derived from nouns designating persons, which were among the oldest of such formations, were now generally concrete, e.g. *geistlicheit* and *pfaffheit* 'clergy', *oberkeit* 'authority'.

(viii) *-nis/-nus*: many of the examples are lexicalized and are also found today, e.g. in Luther *gefencknus, ergernis, finsternis, hynderniß, gedechnis*, but also *vfferstentniß* now *Auferstehung*.

(ix) *-schaft*: most words designate collectives and are formed with personal nouns, e.g. *priesterschafft, gefatterschafft, kauffmanschafft*, but some are abstract, e.g. *feintschafft*, or concrete: *rechenschafft* 'account'.

(x) *-tum*: this suffix is found mainly in designations of offices, e.g. *priesterthum, bistumb, keyßertumb, furstenthum, bapstum*, but some lexicalized abstracts have also survived: *irrthumb, heyltumb* (H. Sachs).

(xi) *ge-*(root)(*-e*): most of the older denominal collective derivations were lexicalized, e.g. Luther *gesind*. Deverbal derivations expressing an action were productive, e.g. *geschwetz*. Many indicated a repeated, irksome action.

(xii) *-ei*: the unextended suffix in contrast to *-erei* was not very productive. Luther had, for instance, *probstey, wusteney, tyrraney*.

(xiii) *-tet*: this suffix corresponded to French *-té* and Latin *-tatem* and it is most likely that contamination gave rise to the German form. An alternative view sees it as borrowed from eastern French dialects where final *t* was still preserved in the fourteenth century. An etymologizing tendency changed it gradually to *-tåt*. At first it was only found in loanwords, e.g. *universitet* (middle of the fifteenth century), *dignitet*, but *grobität* (< *grob*) was coined as early as 1551. Other foreign derivations are: *-ant* (H. Sachs *bachant* 'vagrant, scholar'); *-ian* (H. Sachs *gardian*) also in some foreign names. With this suffix the hybrid *Grobianus, Grobian* (< *grob*) 'coarse fellow, boor' was formed towards the end of the fifteenth century.

Some second elements of compounds have the appearance of suffixes on account of the frequency of their occurrence, the loss of their original semantic definition, and by being in competition with genuine suffixes, e.g. *-man* (*handtwercksman* – *handtwerker*, *werckman – wircker*), *-werk* (*münchwerck – muncherey, larvenwerck, narrenwerck, lumpenwerck, menschenwerck, holhüppelwerck* 'knavery', *zauberwerck – zauberey*) with a similar pejorative connotation to that of *-erey*, or with a collective meaning in *laubwerk* 'decorations', 'foliage'.

A rather fashionable prefix was *Erz-* (OHG *erzi-* < Greek *archi-* mainly in ecclesiastical titles and words), now *Erzherzog* (a fifteenth-century loan translation of *archidux*), *Erzbube, Erzbösewicht, Erzesel, Erzhure*. Luther favoured this prefix.

6.7.2 | Adjective derivation

It was characteristic of the derivative suffixes forming adjectives in MHG that they were nearly all semantically ill-defined and therefore to a high degree synonymous, e.g. *lobebære, lobehaft, lobelich, löbic, lobeclich, lobesam*. Only *-īn* and *-isch* had somewhat restricted meanings.

Most derivations had as their base a noun or, rather superfluously, an adjective. Some bases could, however, also be interpreted as being verbal and in consequence of the general weak definition of adjective derivation, new formations from verbal stems were on the increase. This new trend became particularly marked in the sixteenth century in the case of the suffix *-bar*. Over half of all the new derivations were from verbal bases. The total occurrence of *-bar* formations included, of course, many ancient and by now lexicalized items such as *sonderbar, offenbar, scheinbar*. These were the denominal derivations while the really productive ones were the passive deverbal formations such as *glaubbar, unbiegbar* with the meaning 'what can be done'. In the total number of such adjectives the static denominal and the productive deverbal formations were nearly equal, thus confirming the high degree of suffix variability which was still typical of the ENHG phase; compare, for instance, the words for 'foolish': *torlich, törisch, töricht, torhaft, torhafftig*. The trend towards deverbal derivation was supported by the Latin *-bilis* adjectives, e.g. *valtbære* as a translation of *plicabilis* or *unneigebære* for *indeclinabilis*.

While in the case of *-bar* a functional concentration was forming, which was to be achieved in the eighteenth century, the *-ig* and *-lich* forms remained vague. But they were by far the most frequent derivations. The former gained further ground as it encroached on -*icht*, e.g. *steinicht* > *steinig*. It could also be added to adverbs turning them into adjectives, e.g. *hieig* (later *hiesig*, e.g. U.v. Hutten *die hiygen feldthůner*), *daig, jetzig, dortig*. Others such as -*sam* and -*haft* were static. Luther had many adjectives with combined suffixes such as *schalckhafftig, ganghafftig*.

The suffix -*en* (< MHG -*īn*) had the meaning 'consisting of' or 'made of', e.g. Luther *hultzen, steinen*. It was the one adjectival derivative suffix which had formally become homophonous with inflectional endings. Perhaps for this reason the extended form -*ern* began to spread in ENHG. Deriving from the fusion of a base in -*er*, e.g. *silber + en*, i.e. *silbern*, it was often added to bases without -*er*. Luther had, for instance, *diße stroeren vnd papyren mauren* 'these walls of straw and paper'.

The suffix -*isch* had not yet acquired the pejorative connotation which it now has in many cases, e.g. Luther *kindisch, weibisch*. The numerous derivations with abusive and pejorative intent, however, began to affect the connotation of the suffix, e.g. Luther *affenschmaltzisch, bösewichtisch, hurisch*. It still was mainly applied to personal nouns, thus *ketzrisch, Lutherisch, bepstisch* (also *bepstlich*). As a suffix forming adjectives from proper names (*böhmisch*), it received competition from nominal -*er* derivations used attributively (*Böhmer*), e.g. *die Lunenburger Heyd, schweitzer lant* (Thomas Murner). It was very often added to foreign roots to turn them into German adjectives, e.g. *animalisch, electrisch, empirisch, mineralisch*.

The new MHG suffix -*var* 'coloured' had become -*farb(en)* on the basis of the oblique cases (< -*varwe*-), e.g. *ascherfarb*.

Substantivization of adjectives was very common and some derivative adjectival suffixes thus competed with nominal ones, see *ir lutherische, Rômische* 'followers of Rome' (= *Romanisten*).

A MHG genitival or prepositional group with the loanword *leie* 'manner', e.g. *maneger leie, in jeder ley*, becomes fused, e.g. *mancherlei, vielerlei*, and is used as an indeclinable adjective, for example, *allerley stendt*. The origin of the word *leie* is not entirely clear. It first turns up in MHG and appears to be borrowed from OF *lei, loi* 'law, manner'. As it is not found in the courtly literature it would not seem to form part of the courtly French loan vocabulary. For this reason borrowing from medieval Latin *lege* (< *lex* 'law') cannot be ruled out.

6.7.3 | Adverb formation

With regard to the adjective – adverb distinction ENHG stands nearer MHG than NHG. The distinction by means of vowel alternation (*spet* – *spat*) was, however, greatly weakened and the distinction by means of *-e* (*lang* – *lange*) was removed in UGm. by the apocope. Luther still marked many adj. – adv. distinctions by *-e*, e.g. *still* – *stille, lang* – *lange* etc. In the case of adjectives in *-ig* he regularly formed the adverbs in *-iglich*. But he added *-lich* also in a large number of other cases, e.g. *bitter* – *bitterlich, klar* – *klerlich* (*klerlich schreyben*), *strenglich vorpieten, behendiglich vorhyndert, weißlich geredt, groblich genarret*; or Murner: *schwechlich frum* (< *schwach*). Some adverbial forms have survived the demise of this practice, e.g. *elendiglich, lediglich, inniglich*. The MHG practice of forming adverbs from adjectives in *-lich* by means of the case form *-en* was much extended by analogy, e.g. *wunderlich* (adj.) – *wunderlichen* (adv.).

The genitival group of the type MHG *gelīcher wīse, maniger wīse* used adverbially, developed into a new type of compound adverb in *-weise*, e.g. *möglicherweise*. Prepositional groups, e.g. MHG *in kriuzes wīse*, also became adverbs in the sixteenth century through the loss of the preposition. In analogy to nominal compounds the indication of the genitival relationship could be lacking. In this way arose forms like *kreuzweise, gastweise, hauffenweise, stückweise*. Hans Sachs had *erzweis* 'in the manner of ore'. Later the nominal compounds (e.g. *schrittweise, stufenweise*) but not the adjectival compounds (e.g. *glücklicherweise*) began to be used also as adjectives.

6.7.4 | Verb derivation

The highly restricted nature of derivation in this word class is underlined by the fact that the total number of suffixes, or better, extensions of the verbal suffixes, that is *-l-, -r-, -ier-, -ig-*, remained practically static. In the seventeenth century the many foreign words in French *-iser* and corresponding Latin words introduced the further extension *-is-ier-*, e.g. *kritisieren, autorisieren*. The number of verbs in *-ieren* was greatly increased through loans from Latin.

6.7.5 | Nominal composition

The most frequent type was the noun plus noun determinative compound with the first element in undeclined form. For instance, in Thomas Murner we find *iartag, buntgenoß, sawtrog*, in Hans Sachs *eselkopf, seelmess, tagzeyt*. Secondary composition, where the first element is declined, was also frequent but not yet as frequent as later and now. The declensional endings were -*s* or -(*e*)*n* in masculine and neuter nouns and -(*e*)*n* in feminines. The ending -*s* in feminine nouns, and -*er* were still very rare. Luther had, for example, *geburtsbrief, geburtstag, fastnachtslarve* and *kindertauffe*. This -*s* with feminines appears to have spread from Middle Low German. Among Hans Sachs's inflectional compounds with -*s* are: *gotzdienst, todtsnöten, gerichßhendel, wirtzhawß*. The genitive -*en* is particularly widespread with weak nouns (or *n*-pl. nouns), e.g. Thomas Murner *affenspil, schelmenstück, kuttenkleidt, nunnenkleidt*; Hans Sachs has *menschenleer, narrenwerk, fürstenhewßer, ornbeicht*.

As it was still quite usual to leave the elements separate, e.g. *blut vorgissen, priester stand* (Luther), it is, of course, difficult to decide whether combinations consisting of a genitive plus a noun (*gottes wort, leyen standt, kuniges kinder, hurn kinder*) are to be regarded as compounds or syntactical groups. Since in the majority of cases the elements were joined together, we must assume that this was caused by these combinations having the stress pattern of compounds rather than that of genitival groups. One consequence of this development was that the inflectional endings, -*s*, -*en*, -*er*, lost their original syntactic function and became a formal juncture feature of composition. They then spread more and more and -*s* with feminine nouns is to be seen primarily as an indication of this restructuring of the inflectional endings. This development also points to the fact that composition as such was becoming increasingly popular.

Compounds consisting of a compound as one of the two elements were now common although not particularly frequent. But compounds where both elements were themselves compounds, or conglomerates of several members, were not yet usual. Luther has, for example, *todstocknar, helgrundsuppe*; H. Sachs: *kauffmanschatz, handtwerckßleüt*. Schottelius, in 1663, was proud of German compounds consisting of four elements such as *Oberberghauptmann, Erbküchenmeisterambt*.

Adjectival compounds were also mainly of the determinative kind with either an adjective or a noun as the first element: H. Sachs *haußarm, wurmstichig*; Luther *christglaubig, geltsuchtig, boßwillig, armgeystig*. Superlatives were often compounded with *aller-*, e.g. H. Sachs *allerheyligist, allernöttigst*; Luther *allertorlichst, allerdurchleuchtigist. Aller* was originally the gen. pl. of *all*.

6.7.6 | Verbal composition

There was an apparent increase in verbal compounds with a noun or an adjective as the first element. Luther had, for instance, *ehescheiden, ehrbieten, ehrwirdigen, heimstellen, spiegelfechten* (*was spiegelficht er denn?*); Hans Sachs and Luther had *frolocken* 'to jump for joy', *heymsuchen* 'to visit at home' or 'to attack somebody in his home', *stilschweygen, weklagen* and with an adverb *wolsprechen, vbel-reden*. From such verbal compounds are to be distinguished verbs like *handhaben*, a verb derived from the nominal compound *handhabe*, and syntactic groups such as *haim tragen, zu boden stossen, herauf faren*. The boundary is, however, ill-defined and some syntactic groups developed later into compounds, for example, *heimführen*. Many of the new compounds arose on the basis of the infinitive used as a noun. It is, of course, characteristic that composition, which is essentially a feature of the nominals, should enter the range of the verb where the verb itself becomes substantivized. Among the frequent noun plus infinitive compounds there are, for instance, in Hans Sachs: *alles kirchengeen, fleyschessen, flaischmeyden, gotzlestern, pfaffenschenden*, and it is likely that the verb *spiegelfechten* arose via the substantivized infinitive. Genuine compound verbs remain separable, but some are more or less confined to the infinitive and the present participle, e.g. *hohnlachen*. Verbs derived from nominal compounds are never separable, e.g. *handhaben, frühstücken, wetteifern*, and few of the substantivized infinitive compounds are used as finite verbs, but see *spiegelficht* above.

The most characteristic form of composition among verbs was, of course, prefix composition. In this field no new developments occurred in the ENHG period. It remained as vital and productive as ever.

6.7.7 | Phrase composition

The earliest nominal compounds resulting from the contraction of a verb plus a complement are found in MHG, e.g. *hebestrīt* 'quarrelsome woman'. Many are nicknames such as *Suochentrunk, Rūmelant* or *Rūmezlant*. The verb is often in the imperative form. In the fifteenth century such formations became more numerous and this type of composition can be regarded as first having become productive in ENHG. To what extent analogous French compositions (e.g. *vaurien, fainéant*) were influential is not known. This type is also found in English, for example, *turncoat, telltale, ne'er-do-well, good-for-nothing*. Many of the German phrase compounds were first recorded at this time, e.g. 1548 *tügenichts* > *Taugenichts*. Further examples are *Störenfried, Habenichts, Springinsfeld, Tunichtgut, Wagehals*.

6.8 | Syntax

6.8.1 | Sentence structure

(i) *Initial position* of the finite verb in independent clauses other than yes-or-no questions, commands, or conditional clauses without a conjunction is frequently found in ENHG and appears to be quite popular between about 1450 and 1600. For example, in Luther: *Spricht zu im einer seiner Jünger*; *Sende das alles ewr wirde*. Such cases were, however, not survivals of a possibly ancient type of initial position of the verb but had newly arisen through ellipsis of a subject pronoun (*es, ich*) or an adverb (*da*). The initial position was thus occupied by a zero form, which was illuminated by the context. As a stylistic device this practice belonged to a popular or oral style. After *und* such omission was very frequent; for instance, in Luther's *Sendbrief von Dolmetschen* we find: *Das sey auff eur erste Frag geantwortet | vñ bitte euch |* ; *Mir ist ynn des gnug | vnd bin fro; So kan ichs doch wol leiden | vnnd schadet mir sonderlich nichts.*

(ii) *Retarded position* or even *final position* of the finite verb in main clauses was very much the exception, but writers who wished to imitate Latin syntax in German, such as Niclas von Wyle, did sometimes construct such sentences. While the finite verb was normally in second position in the main clause, the position of the non-finite part was still relatively free. It is true, the principle of incapsulation prevailed in a majority of cases, but rhythm and emphasis were still allowed to determine the placing. In other words, the final position of the non-finite elements was not yet absolute or grammaticalized. The freedom of positioning was such that some complements might be incapsulated while others followed the non-finite part of the verb.

Final position of the non-finite elements (H. Sachs):

> *Er hat uns nit auß seinem aigen kopff gelert. So muß ich mit meinen knechten den gantzen tag arbaiten.*

Non-final position of the non-finite elements (H. Sachs):

> *wir haben nicht umbsunst das brot genommen von yemant.*
> *ir sölt euch nit lassen mayster nennen.*

Or Luther:

> *Sie sein auch die heubter geweßen dißes iamers zu Costnitz.*

The finite verb is found in final position in the parallel comparative clauses, which were introduced by *sō – sō* in MHG (see 5.7.1 (iii) b) and by *je – je* in ENHG (NHG *je – desto*).

In dependent clauses the finite verb enjoyed a similar stylistic freedom, although the final position was now becoming more frequent and more general than in MHG. In MHG at least a quarter, often a third of all dependent clauses had complements after the finite verb. Non-finite elements such as infinitives and participles continued to be frequently placed after the finite verb right through the sixteenth century, but from the seventeenth onwards this became more and more rare. It appears that the rules existing in the modern language were first successfully imposed by the grammarians and the schoolmen of the seventeenth century. The most rigorous application of the rule of the final position of the finite verb in the dependent clause (except where two non-finite verbal elements are present) prevailed in the eighteenth century. But adverbial and prepositional complements have at all times been allowed to escape incapsulation as a concession to stylistic freedom and to colloquial usage. In H. Sachs we find, for instance: *ob wir etwas zu vil hart wider euch hetten geredt*;

darumb köndt ir got nit dienen, weil ir dem mammon dient mit dem hertzen. Even objects could still follow the verb if they were to be emphasized: H. Sachs *Weyter regirt der geytz gewaltigklich unter den kauffherren und verlegern, die da drucken ire arbeyter und stückwercker.* An infinitive dependent on the verb followed the non-finite part quite regularly at this period, unlike in NHG, e.g. U. von Hutten *er hab in vier Monaten sein gelust nit künnen büssen*; Luther *Vnd wenn ich sie hette sollen fragen.*

A new fashion was the omission of the finite verb in dependent clauses mainly if a participle was present: Luther *diesen sendt-brieff | der mir durch einen guten freundt zu handen kommen* (NHG *gekommen ist*); *Hab ich drinnen etwa gefeilet (das mir doch nicht bewůst | vnd...*).

(iii) In the order and number of clauses constituting sentences there were also significant changes at this time. In scholarly prose the number of clauses increased greatly mainly by means of addition rather than incapsulation. In this way rambling sentences of considerable length came to be construed. See Luther:

Vnd das nicht yemand hie dencke / ich liege / So nym beide Testament fur dich / des Luthers vnd des Sudelers / halt sie gegen ein ander / so wirstu sehē / wer yn allen beidē der dolmetzscher sey / Denn was er yn wenig orten geflickt vnd geendert hat (wie wol mirs nicht alles gefellet) So kan ichs doch wol leiden / vnnd schadet mir sonderlich nichts / so viel es den text betrifft / darumb ich auch nie da wider hab wǒllen schreiben / sondern hab der grossen weißheit mǔssen lachen / das man mein New Testament so grewlich gelestert / verdampt / verboten hat / weil es vnter meinē namen ist außgangen / Aber doch mǔssen lesen / weil es vnter eines andern namen ist außgangen.

German originally preferred the order main clause – subordinate clause. Under Latin influence the head position of the subordinate clause increased at times and medial position (incapsulation) also had a modest range. It has been calculated that in medieval German about seventy-five per cent of complex sentences had the main clause in initial position, about twenty per cent the subordinate clause, while in about five per cent of all cases the subordinate clause was incapsulated. In the course of the sixteenth century the incidence of the medial position of the subordinate clause increased considerably and became numerically equal to that of the initial position.

The main clause which was preceded by a subordinate clause had usually the link word *so* which is a further development of the anaphoric use of pronouns or adverbs current in MHG. In the above complex sentence we have, for instance:... *das nicht yemand hie dencke ... So nym. So* functioned, however, also as a conjunction and as a relative connective.

The greater freedom of sentence structure in ENHG in contrast to NHG is also shown by the not infrequent occurrence of anacoluthon, the so-called ungrammatical continuation of, or linking between, clauses. Considerations of meaning had usually greater weight than those of logical grammar in the application of congruence, as the following example from H. Sachs shows: *Nachmalß aber ist der römisch hauf verzweyfelt an der überwindung mit disputieren und schreyben und wöllen die Christlich gemayn under dem römischen joch behalten.* ENHG is in this respect nearer to English than to NHG which applies the rule of congruence very strictly.

(iv) The number and the use of conjunctions was greatly expanded in ENHG in connection with the growth of the complexity of sentence structure. Latin no doubt frequently inspired the development of clause subordination by means of conjunctions, just as it inspired the occasional imitation of accusative cum infinitive constructions. Such constructions were not unheard of in German, but they were restricted to the use after the verbs *lassen, heißen, sehen,* and *hören.* But in ENHG there were also such expressions after verbs of speaking, e.g. in Theuerdank *ich red on spot*; *mich gewesen sein in groszer not*; U. von Hutten *sagt das brot vnschmackhafft sein.* The use of conjunctions also increased as subordination by means of the subjunctive mood decreased.

Perhaps the most significant development in the field of conjunctions was the rise of *denn* and *weil* as conjunctions introducing causal clauses. Up to the first half of the fifteenth century *wan* (*wande*) was almost the only causal conjunction (see p. 302). In the second half of the fifteenth century *denn* and *weil* competed strongly with it and shortly after 1500 the older *wan* died out over most of the territory. The Nuremberg writers Sachs and Dürer still wrote the obsolescent *wan* when Alemannia, Bavaria, ECGm. and WCGm. had already abandoned it. LG continued to use *wente.* The weakness of *wan* (*wande*) was that, owing to the earlier coalescence of two forms, it functioned both as a subordinating and a coordinating conjunction. The trend of the age was, however, to separate the two clause types, dependent and independent, more sharply from each other. *Wan* in the sense of 'except, only' was in competition with the comparative particle *dann/denn*, which first replaced *wan* in this field and subsequently also in the causal field as the conjunction serving mainly in independent clauses. *Weil* developed from the temporal adverbial expression *die wīle so, die wīle, wīle*. In ENHG it was both temporal and causal, e.g. Luther [*Jhr fragt*] *ob auch die verstorbenen Heiligen fur vns bitten | weil wir lesen | das ja die Engel fur vns bitten*. Latin also had a conjunction (*cum*) which was both temporal and causal. *Weil* or, somewhat earlier, *die weil*, introduced subordinate clauses. When it eventually became entirely causal the originally temporal *dō*, later also *da*, took its place towards the end of the seventeenth century. Other competitors of *weil* in ENHG were among others *seit, seitemal, sintemal, so*.

There were also significant changes in the relative pronouns. The MHG generalizing pronouns with *s-* (*swer* etc.) lost their *s-* in the fourteenth century which introduced the interrogative pronouns into the relative construction. Sometimes the demonstrative particle was used to reinforce the old established relative pronouns *der, die, das*, which had themselves developed from demonstrative pronouns: *der da, die da*, etc. The interrogative adjective *welch* was also drawn into the field of the relative pronouns, first through the development of MHG *swelich > welch* and then also in imitation of Latin usage. Finally the field was further enriched by the use of the particle *so* in relative constructions. ENHG thus had a rich field of relative connectives. The modern usage was finally the result of the rulings of the seventeenth- and eighteenth-century grammarians.

Some ENHG examples from H. Sachs are:

der, die, das:	*den geist in eure hertzen, der schreyt.*
	ander leüt, die den geist gottes haben.
	des wercks, das Christus fodern wird.
der da etc.:	*Jhesus, der da heißt Christus.* (Luther N. T.)
welch:	*das biechlein..., welches er dem bapst... zugeschickt hat.*
was:	*Ir sagt, was ir welt.*
da (rinn):	*die menschlichen lugen, darinn wir gewandert haben.*

so: *den, so die göttlich warheit vor erkant haben.*

leyen, so die feintschafft dieser welt auf sich laden.

(Luther) *Aber segē kompt vber den | so es verkaufft [das korn].*

The relative particles with *da* (*darin, damit, darauf, daraus, davon*) also functioned as demonstrative connectives, hence the finite verb could take up either a main-clause position or a subordinate-clause position. In NHG these functions are divided between *worin* and *darin* etc.

6.8.2 | The noun phrase

(i) The system of *articles*, as it was established in MHG, made further advances in the direction in which it had evolved. Although there were still many formulaic expressions without articles after prepositions, e.g. *vor augen sehen, zu dienst tun, zu richter leiden* (all these in Luther), *zů man haben* (Theuerdank), *das fewr von hymel* (Sachs), we now find *zur zeit, am wege, ym hymel, in der hell, ym finsternis*. Latin words were often used without articles, e.g. H. Sachs *das die vätter in conciliis beschlossen ... haben*; Luther *das widerspiel in Apocalypsi*.

The short contracted forms which were now general for *zu, an, in, von* and some others + *dem, der* had first spread in the fourteenth century. ENHG also tolerated contractions with *den* (*in* = *in den, von* = *von den*), e.g. Luther *in druck geben, zun Römern*; H. Sachs *ich wil in chor. So gee du an marckt*.

The definite article was also used with personal names. This practice started with foreign names where inflection was not possible (*den Adam*), first in oblique cases and then also in the nominative, e.g. *des Luthers New Testament*; *das der Luther gemacht hat*; *vnd des Luthers bůch on Luthers namen*.

In many individual cases ENHG practice still differed from modern German. A noun with an attributive adjective if it formed a unitary notion could dispense with the article, see for instance Luther's *An den christlichen Adel deutscher Nation* (NHG *der deutschen Nation*); *der verdolmetzschunge halben | altes vnnd newes testaments |*. On the other hand some idiosyncratic MHG uses, e.g. *ein mīn* or *ein diu*, were dying out in this period.

(ii) In the use of the *adjectives* within the noun phrase there were also some changes. The postpositional attribute (*der degen rīche*) was no longer acceptable. Although Latin influence maintained for a while the postpositional participial apposition, this too began to become rarer in the second half of the sixteenth century; H. Sachs *wir als verirrte schäflein, solcher, haylsamen leer unbedacht und schier gantz vergessen, seynd gangen....* In learned prose the post-positional participial apposition or attribute has never completely disappeared in German, but its role has always been modest and uneasy. As this device is very common in English there thus arose an important syntactic difference between the two languages. In German it is a basic syntactic principle that the syntactically sub-ordinate element precedes the element to which it is subordinate. German thus has a so-called centripetal word order, that is every-thing builds up to a final semantic and functional climax. Post-positional adjectival and participial attributes are obviously in conflict with this principle and their elimination thus followed the already established principle. The phenomenon of incapsulation, which was discussed in connection with the development of the rule of the absolute final position of the non-finite parts of the verb in the main clause, and of the absolute final position of the finite verb in the subordinate clause, is of course an expression of the same principle.

Two additional developments in ENHG further consolidated this basic principle of German syntax: the growth of a gerundive and the emergence of a pre-positional expanded adjectival or participial attribute. Both are quite alien to English syntax.

The gerundive is an attributive infinitive:

Gm. *ein Buch, das zu lesen ist* > *ein zu lesendes Buch*
E *a book which must be read* or *a book to be read.*

The expanded attribute uses the same principle of incapsula-tion between article and noun. Medieval German like English had adjectival attributes which were expanded by an adverb, especially an adverb of degree: *eine alsō schœne hōchzīt, ir vil starken segelseil.* Now that the expanded postpositional participial apposition, despite support from Latin, was on the wane, the pre-positional adjectival and participial attribute was built up. Some of the earliest examples are to be found in *Der Ackermann aus Böhmen,* e.g. *die...allerlei meisterschaft wol vermugenden leut,* as an expres-sion of an individual author's style.

In the second half of the sixteenth century it became possible to turn a whole sentence into an adjectival or participial attribute. Here, too, Latin influence may have played a part, but in this case it worked in harmony with the basic principle of German syntax, unlike in the case of the participial apposition. The expanded adjectival or participial attribute, embedded between the article and the noun it determined, became a characteristic stylistic feature of seventeenth-century South German chancery language, but soon spread into the registers of science and literature. As a stylistic device it achieved the climax of its popularity in the nineteenth century. Somewhat reduced in length, it is still a feature of the modern written language.

Typologically we can distinguish the following expansions:

(a) accusative expansion: *eine sehr viel Wasser aufnehmende Pflanze*;
(b) dative expansion: *das der Mannschaft gegebene Versprechen*;
(c) genitive expansion (rare): *der seiner Sache unsicher gewordene Anwalt*;
(d) prepositional expansion: *die von den Gewerkschaftea erhobenen Lohnforderungen*;
(e) adverbial expansion: *das heute abend stattfindende Konzert.*

All five types of expansion can be combined if the resulting length of the attribute is not too much of a deterrent to the stylistic sensibility of the writer: *eine im Frühling der Erde durch kräftige Wurzeln viel Wasser entziehende Pflanze.*

(iii) In the use of the *nominal cases* we note in this period the beginning of the decline of the genitive especially as a verbal complement. Instead of saying *wañ er dieses weyns trinckt* one could also say *wann er diesen wein trinckt*; *viel* could govern the genitive (*viel iamers*) or be used as an attributive adjective (*viel gelt*). A number of verbs which had originally governed the genitive could now take the accusative, e.g. *verlangen, verschmähen, begeren.* Only proper names in the genitive now preceded the governing noun, other nouns followed. Where names followed, Latin influence is likely. E.g. Luther *des Luthers teutsch*; *solchen fluch des herren*; *die feinde der warheit.*

6.8.3 | The verb phrase

The ordering of the finite and non-finite parts of the verb phrase was discussed as part of the structure of sentences (see 6.8.1). As far as the grammatical and semantic categories of the verb are concerned we note in this period a positive trend to build up and complete the tense, mood, and voice systems. Latin, no doubt, was an example in this respect too.

(i) In the *tense* system the establishment of a future tense by means of a periphrastic form consisting of *werden* plus infinitive was now completed. Although the present could still be used where events in the future were concerned, greater use was now made of the periphrastic tense. Even a second future (future perfect) was being introduced to parallel the Latin *futurum exactum*: *er wird helfen – er wird geholfen haben*.

A similar extension occurred in the past tense. A pluperfect was being formed more and more regularly to differentiate between different levels of past time: *er half* or *er hat geholfen – er hatte geholfen* or rarely, with the perfect of the auxiliary, *er hat geholfen gehabt*. To some extent this development was also encouraged by the decline of the *ge-* construction which is a further example of the progress of analytical forms at the expense of synthetic forms. In Upper German texts, especially those of a more popular kind, a decline in the use of the simple preterite and an increase in the use of the perfect have been noted. This is connected with the decline of the simple preterite in the spoken language of southern Germany in the early sixteenth century. The written language was affected only to a limited extent and the preterite continued to be employed as the tense of the narration of past events and facts, while the perfect expressed the relevance of past events and facts to the writer in the present. South German writers adhered to this rule less strictly and thus showed that the preterite was a form with which they were less familiar.

The periphrastic form *sein* plus present participle: *er ist helfende* gave way to *sein* plus infinitive > *er ist helfen* on account of the contamination of the forms of the present participle and of the infinitive. As this construction was heavily dependent upon identical Latin models, it was most often found in older translations. In chancery language it became rather formulaic. More popular writings shunned it and in the language of the Bible it was one of those latinizing constructions with which Luther had no patience. Syntactically *er ist helfen* had become synonymous with *er hilft*, which made it redundant. It died out towards the end of the ENHG period.

Werden could originally be similarly combined with the present participle to indicate the beginning of an action. After the rise of the future tense, forms with *ward* and the infinitive (*er ward helfen*) lingered for a while as a remnant of the earlier construction, no longer meaningfully distinguished from the usual preterite.

A paraphrase, characteristic of popular language, is that with *tun*, e.g. H. Sachs *Lucas...thut sagen*: *ich hab dich thun erhaschen*. Unlike in English this device was never properly functionalized, although it can be found from the fourteenth century onwards.

(ii) A new periphrastic form replacing the unmarked preterite *subjunctive* of the weak verbs began to be formed in the fifteenth century. It consisted of the preterite subjunctive of *werden* (*würde*) plus the infinitive. For instance, H. Sachs *die euch yetzund ketzer nennen, würden euch Christen haissen*; *die euch yetzt fluchen, würden euch loben*. Eventually it was to encroach upon the marked preterite subjunctive forms of the strong verbs.

(iii) In the *passive*, medieval German distinguished between a process and a state with *wirdet/ward* or *ist/was* plus the past participle, but did not form a perfect. In the fourteenth and fifteenth centuries perfect and pluperfect forms with *worden* and *gewesen* began to be added to the system. The process was, however, not completed till the end of the ENHG period and a form like *ist geschlagen* often stands for what was later regularly given as *ist geschlagen worden*. A future tense of the passive (*er wird geschlagen werden*) also makes its first appearance in this period.

6.9 | Lexicon

6.9.1 | The native stock

(i) In the closed part of the vocabulary many of the changes were formal. In the fifteenth century the genitive of the personal pronouns was still *mein, dein, sein, ir* (*si spotten sein*, H. Sachs *ich hab ir nye keins gelesen*), but in the sixteenth, adjectival endings appeared (*meiner* etc.) and in the seventeenth they were already quite general (*ich achte deiner*). In the genitive plural similar extensions occurred in the seventeenth century (*unser* > *unserer*) but were later rejected. In the dative plural *in* and *inen* were in competition for most of the period. The texts given in 6.4.4 show *in* in the Mentelin Bible of 1466, Luther's September Testament of 1522, the Lübeck Bible of 1494, but *jnen* in the Zürich NT of 1524 and in Luther's 1546 Bible. Luther thus finally decided in favour of a form which had first spread in Alemannic. In the dative sg. fem. and genitive pl. the quasi archaic form *iro* enjoyed some popularity in ENHG, e.g. in the address *Ihro Gnaden*.

The forms of the demonstrative and relative *der*, *des*, *den* in pronominal use tended to become extended to *derer*, *deren*, *dessen*, *denen*, but the distribution of the short and long forms was not regulated until NHG times. See, for instance, U.v. Hutten *meinst du das du denen gůtthåt beweisest, bey den du herbergst?* We must also note that there was no distinction between the demonstrative *das* and the conjunction. Only towards the end of the seventeenth century did the distinction *das/daß* become general. The demonstrative forms *dirre* and *ditz* died out in ENHG and were replaced by the regular forms *dieser* and *dieses*. The interrogative *wes* was also extended to *wessen* and *was* occasionally to *waser*, also *waserley*. On the other hand the phrase *was für ein* replaced the older construction of *was* plus genitive. The indefinite pronouns *ieman*, *nieman* acquired an excrescent -*d*, sometimes even -*ds*, and adjectival endings began to be added in the dative and accusative in the seventeenth century, thus: *niemandem*, *niemanden*.

Among the alterations made by the Zürich 1524 transcription of Luther's September Testament was the replacement of *von sich gelassen* by *von jm gelassen*. CGm. already employed the accusative reflexive *sich* for the dative where older German had originally used the forms of the personal pronouns. UGm. still adhered to the older practice, although *sich* had begun to encroach on the pers. pron. forms of the dative. Luther's choice became the choice of the standard language and the use of the personal pronouns as the dative of the reflexive is now a dialectal feature of South German.

Among the particles we observe the coalescence of MHG *dā* (spatial) and *dō* (temporal) with both forms being used indiscriminately. Eventually *da* was generalized. As the particle of comparison *als* was still used (*rot als blut*) and in the comparative construction the inherited *dann/denn* (H. Sachs *mechtiger dann der keyser*) prevailed till the second half of the sixteenth century when it was replaced by the modern *als*. For 'until' the older *unz* was replaced by *bis* in the course of the fifteenth century.

That the tendency to regularize was very much in the air can be seen in the gradual elimination of some isolated anomalous words, e.g. the comparative and superlative of *übel*: *wirser, wirste*, and the comparatives of the adverbs *wirs* and *bas* (> *besser*) and in the emergence of the analogous ordinal numeral *zweite* competing with the still prevalent *ander*.

For the verbs 'to go' and 'to stand' the forms with -*e*- (*gen, sten*) became the standard forms and those with -*a*- (-*o*-) dialectal. Luther abandoned his early *a*-forms in favour of *e*-forms, which ensured the victory of the originally only Bavarian and East Franconian *e*-forms. The south-east also provided the standard form for the past participle of 'to be'. In ENHG there were three competing forms: *gesin* (Alem.), *gewesen* (Bav. and parts of East Franc.), *gewest* (CGm. and LG). ECGm. had originally only *gewest*, but Luther used both *gewest* and *gewesen* with some preponderance of *gewesen*.

With the last two examples we have broached the greatest issue of the age in the lexical field: the gradual formation of a standard lexicon. It is not easy to assess the extent to which German already possessed a common vocabulary around 1500. If we compare the three texts given in 6.4.4 which, while being parallel versions of the same Latin original, are more or less independent of one another, we must conclude that over ninety per cent of the vocabulary was already common. The texts are the CUGm. Mentelin Bible (1466), the Lübeck LG Bible (1494), and the ECGm. Luther version (1522). The Zürich Bible of 1524, based on Luther's text, made lexical alterations only where there were strong Alem. objections. The greatest difficulty is to differentiate between the literary-stylistic reasons for a certain choice of words and the lexically, dialectally enforced reasons. Genuine regional lexical differences we have undoubtedly in the following cases: *er* (HG) – *he* (LG). *Wellen* (Luther) – *vnden* (Mentelin) – *bulghen* (LG): the contrast of *wellen* (HG) and *bulghen* (LG) is genuinely synchronic and regional, that between *wellen* – *vnden* is basically diachronic (modern – archaic, obsolete). The Augsburg 1475 reprint by Zainer replaced *vnden* by *wellen*. *Denn* (Luther) – *wann* (Mentelin)– *wente* (LG): with the same synchronic-diachronic pattern as in the previous example. *Gehen* (Luther) – *gon* (Zürich) – *ghan* (LG); *spugnisz* (Luther) – *trúgniß* (Mentelin) – *gspenst* (Zürich) – *spŏkenisse* (LG): Luther replaced the ECGm. dialectism akin to LG by the UGm. *gespenst* in later editions which thus became the standard German word. *Als bald* (Luther) – *zehant* (Mentelin) – *to handes* (LG): Luther's modern expression prevailed over the more archaic forms. *Ob* (HG) – *efte* (LG); *recket* (Luther) – *strackt* (Mentelin) – *streckt vß* (Zürich) – *vtstreckede* (LG): although both are Gmc. words, the latter is much more common in German and Luther's choice did not endanger it. *Vnd* (Luther) – *wann* (Mentelin) – *aver* (LG) as translations of *autem*: again Mentelin had an archaism which the Zainer reprint (Augsburg, 1475) regularly replaced by *vnd*. *Mitten* (Luther) – *mitzt* (Mentelin) – *middel* (LG): the Mentelin form was replaced by Zainer (> *mitt*), for the rest we have a HG – LG contrast. *Warlich* (Luther) – *gewerlich* (Mentelin) > *fúrwar* (Zainer) – *vorwar* (LG): shows how forms often differed in their derivation and how Luther's form became standard. Other differences seem to result from different choices among possible variants: Luther *heysz mich* – Mentelin *gebeut mir* – LG *bede mi* for 'bid me'; *seyd getrost* – Mentelin *habt zůuersicht* – LG *hebbet louen*; Luther *volck* – Mentelin *gesel-schaffte* (> *schare* in Zainer) – LG *schare*; Luther *schryen* – Mentelin *rieffen* – LG *repen* and several other cases. Luther, the skilful translator, is seen at work when he translates *veni* by *kom her*, where the others had only *kom*; *modice fidei* by *du kleyn glewbiger* where Mentelin had *lútzels glauben* and the Lübeck Bible *van klenen louen*, both Emser (1527) and the Zürich Bible copied Luther's creation; or *cessauit ventus* by *der wint leget sich* for the pale Mentelin version *der wint hort auf* or the LG *de wind horde vp*.

It is easy to exaggerate the lexical differences in the various regional forms of incipient Common German. Of the two hundred words which the Basle editor and printer Adam Petri included in a glossary in his New Testament edition of 1523 and which many other UGm. editions also contained, some were also current in Upper Germany although in a slightly different meaning or with different stylistic connotations. The few hundred different renderings in Johann Eck's Catholic Bible, printed at Ingolstadt, 1537, were to a considerable extent inspired by a different interpretation of the original text. Nevertheless there were many genuine regional differences. They have often been listed. Only a few examples can be given. They are in the modern form and where one of the variants is now only dialectal this is indicated by an asterisk. Where different variants are incorporated in the standard language there are now generally semantic or stylistic differences.

CGm., Luther	UGm.		
Abend	Niedergang der Sonne	*Hülfe	Hilfe
alber(n)	unweis, einfältig	Kahn	Nachen
Antlitz	Angesicht	Küchlein	*Hünklen, junges Hühnlein
bang	Angst haben, betrübt	Lappen	*Bletz, Fleck
beben	*bidmen	Lippe	Lefze
bersten	brechen	Meuchel- mörder	heimlicher Mörder
Beule	*Mase	mieten	*dingen, bestellen
Blüte	Blume, *Blust		
brausen	rauschen	Morgen	Aufgang der Sonne
bunt	gescheckt, *gespreckelt	Motte	*Schabe
Ekel	Greuel, Abscheu	Neffe	Enkel, Kindes- kind
entbehren	mangeln	Otter	Natter, Schlange
ernten	schneiden	Qual	Pein
fett	feist	Scheune	*Scheuer
Fliege	Mucke	schlummern	*naffezen, schläfrig sein
flugs	bald		
freien	zur Ehe nehmen	Seuche	Siechtum
fühlen	empfinden, spüren	sichten	*reitern, sieben
		Sperling	Spatz
Gefäß	Geschirr	Splitter	*Spleiß, *Spieße
gehorchen	gehorsam sein	steupen	mit Ruten schlagen
Gerücht	Geschrei, *Gerüft	täuschen	betrügen
Grenze	Gegend, March	tauchen	eintunken
Hälfte	Halbteil, Halb	Topf	*Hafen
Halle	Vorschopf	Töpfer	*Hafner
harren	warten	Ufer	Gestade
Heuchler	Gleißner	zermalmen	zerreiben
horchen	*losen	Ziege	*Geiß
Hügel	Gipfel, *Bühel		

The establishment of a standard lexicon operated in two ways. One of the regional or social variants would become the general standard term, e.g. northern *Pferd*. The southern and western variants also entered the German standard language, the former (*Roß*) in the poetic register, the latter (*Gaul*) as a pejorative term. Regional variability was in this case changed to a stylistic variability within the standard. The second possibility is that one of the regional variants is accepted as standard and the others are relegated to the dialectal level or condemned to obsolescence, e.g. *Motte* and dialectal *Schabe, horchen* and dialectal *losen, Knöchel* and dialectal *Knoden*. Originally horizontal variability was thus changed into a vertical variability.

Mainly through ECGm. and Luther a fair number of LG words found acceptance into the standard language. Even more were adopted directly in the seventeenth and eighteenth centuries when NHG had become the standard language of North Germany. They often reinforced the link with English, being etymological correspondences of English words: *fühlen* (*to feel*) for *empfinden* etc.; *gleiten* (*to glide*) for *schlipfern* etc.; *Halle* (*hall*) for *Vorschopf* etc.; *hoffen* (*to hope*) for *gedingen*; *horchen* (*to hark*) for *losen*; *Krippe* (*crib*) for *Barn* etc.; *Krume* (*crumb*) for *Brosame*; *Lippe* (*lip*) for *Lefze*; *Mettwurst* (*meat*); *pflügen* (*to plough*) for *ackern* etc.; *schal* (*shallow*) for *seiger*; *Schicht* (*shift*) as a technical ECGm. mining term 'shift working'; *schlummern* (*to slumber*) for *naffezen*; *sichten* (*to sift*) for *reitern*; *stottern* (*to stutter*) for *staggeln* etc.; *Teer* (*tar*); *Torf* 'peat' (*turf*); *Zwist* (*twist*) High Germanized for LG *twist*, with different meanings in E and Gm.

On the other hand a large number of Germanic words which happen to be preserved in English became obsolete in German, thus weakening the lexical-etymological connection between the two languages. Some such etyma which died out in this period are: *bald* (*bold*) > (i.e. supplanted by) *kühn*; *beiten* (*to bide, abide*) > *warten*; *boßen* (*to beat*) > *stoßen, schlagen*; *bridel, brittel* (*bridle*) > *Zügel*; *diech* (*thigh*) > *Oberschenkel*; *enkel* (*ankle*) > *Knöchel*; *feim* (*foam*) > *Schaum*; *hiefe* (rose*hip*) > *Hagebutte*; *molte* (*mould*) > *Erde*; *sele* (*seal*) > *Seelhund* at first, then by popular etymology *Seehund*; *ser* (*sore*) > *Schmerz*; *siech* (*sick*) > *krank*; *siuwen* (*to sew*) > *nähen*; *smieren* (*to smirk*) and *smielen* (*to smile*) > *lächeln*; *töuwen* (*to die*) > *sterben*; *wat* (widow's *weeds*) > *Kleid*; *wieche* (*wick*) > *Docht*; *wite* (*wood*) > *Holz*; *wuofen* (*to weep*) > *schreien, weinen*; *zagel* (*tail*) > *Schwanz*; *Zäher, Zähre* (*tear*) > *Träne*; *zeisen* (*to tease*) > *zupfen*.

A further notable loss was *minne*, now completely replaced by *Liebe*.

Luther's Bible translation, on which were also based the Catholic translations by Hieronymus Emser, Johann Eck and Johann Dietenberger, did more than any other single literary work to determine the lexicon of the literary standard language. Many of Luther's own personal word creations have become part of the standard vocabulary, for instance, *Bubenstück, Dachrinne, Fallstrick, Feuereifer, Fleischtopf, gastfrei, geistreich, kleingläubig, lebenssatt, Linsengericht, Lückenbüßer, Machtwort, Schwarmgeist*. Many memorable expressions and idioms originated in the same way, e.g. *der Mensch lebt nicht allein vom Brot*; *Perlen vor die Schweine werfen*; *den ersten Stein werfen*; *welches Geistes Kinder sein*; *mit Feuer und Schwert*; *der Stein des Anstoßes*; *sein Licht unter den Scheffel stellen*; *im Schweiße seines Angesichts*.

New or relatively uncommon words were often coupled with a synonym which helped to spread knowledge of the new words, e.g. *Gleißner und Heuchler*; *Hoffnung und Zuversicht*; *fett und feist*; *bekümmern und vexieren*; *angst und bange*.

Although Luther's influence and the position of ECGm. were very important, it is now evident that all regions contributed to the vocabulary of the standard language. There was many a word which Luther himself abandoned when he learnt that another word had already wide currency. Some of his words, e.g. *glum* 'dreary, dirty', did not find acceptance. If Luther's ECGm., CUGm. and EUGm. were in agreement no other regional term could compete. But where all Upper German regions were united it was often the Upper German word which prevailed – sometimes the decision was delayed for several hundred years as happened in the case of *Hülfe – Hilfe*.

The following three maps by Gerhard Ising may illustrate the process of the formation of the standard German vocabulary. They are based on an examination of fourteenth- and fifteenth-century Bible translations (circles) and glossaries (squares). The forms in Luther's last Bible edition are given in the right-hand corner, and the total number of occurrences on which the maps are based in the centre at the bottom. 1 is the translation made for Matthias von Beheim in 1343 (see 5.3.3 (vi)), 2 is the Lübeck Bible of 1494, 3 the Mentelin Bible of 1466, 4 the Zainer reprint, Augsburg 1475. The first map giving the translation of *figulus*

'potter' shows how Luther's choice led to the adoption of an
ECGm. word as the standard term; the second map illustrates the
German synonyms for *arare* 'to plough' and shows Luther's
preference for a North German/CGm. word; the third map, that
for *placere* 'to like', shows Luther's preference for an EFr. and
South German term, *gefallen*, alongside which the LG and CGm.
behagen also entered the standard lexicon.

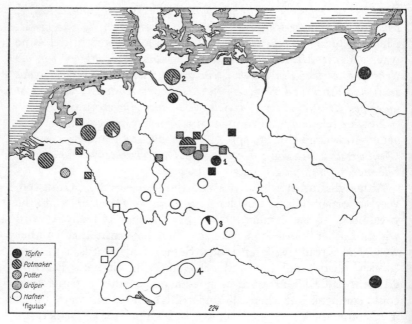

Fig. 13

An interesting example of the restructuring of a whole word
field is afforded by the designations for the in-law relationships.
Medieval German possessed simple roots: MHG *swiger* 'mother-
in-law', *swëher* 'father-in-law', *snur* or *snuor* 'daughter-in-law',
eidem 'son-in-law', with *swäger* 'brother-in-law' or 'father-in-
law' and *geschwei* 'brother-in-law' or 'sister-in-law' in etymological
and semantic competition with some of the former group. Phonetic
developments undermined the distinction between the forms
beginning with *sw-*. The non-transparency of these words per-

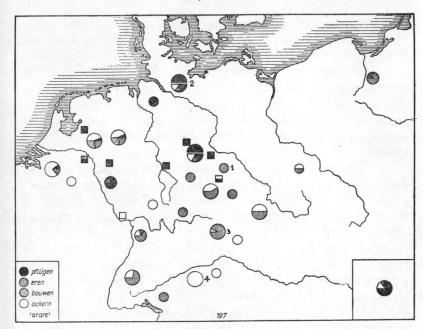

Fig. 14

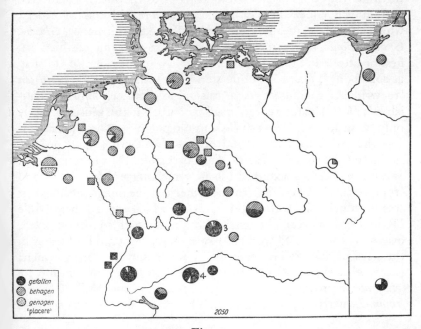

Fig. 15

mitted many semantic crossings and contaminations, and the homophony of *snur* 'daughter-in-law' and *snur* 'string' further weakened one partner. Gradually, spreading from the north, new telling and classificatory compounds with *Schwieger-*, perhaps the most important among the designations for in-laws, began to replace the obscure, inherited words: *Schwiegermutter*, *Schwiegervater*, *Schwiegertochter* and *Schwiegersohn*, although *Schwager* and the new derivation *Schwägerin* retain the connection with the old lexical system.

(ii) The *semantic* aspect of the lexicon tends to reflect the great cultural and spiritual movements of an age as well as internal structural changes on the plane of meaning. The word *Beruf* first rendered the idea of 'vocation' as experienced by monks and clerics. With the Lutheran concept of the general priesthood of all true believers, the meaning widened to permit reference to all ranks of society and, when finally secularized, it became the general German term for 'occupation'. The medieval meaning of *Arbeit* stressed the components 'trouble, toil' which those had to bear who were not dedicated to a contemplative life. Luther's concept of justification by faith alone removed this barrier and dignified the 'toil' of all by elevating it to the idea of dedicated and dutiful endeavour. Other key concepts of the reformers, which shaped the meaning of words, affected, for instance, *Glaube*, *Gnade*, *Sünde*, *Buße*, *fromm*, *evangelisch*. New meanings which can first be attested at this time are: *anfahren* in the sense of 'to snap at somebody'; *fassen* 'to understand'; *entrüstet* 'angry'; *verfassen* 'to write, to compose'; *elend* 'miserable', formerly 'abroad, banished'; *Hort* 'shelter, refuge' used by Luther in this sense, formerly only 'treasure', cf. E *hoard*; *Bube* in the pejorative sense of 'rascal' was thus used by Luther and other CGm. writers and became standard German while UGm. dialects retained the meaning 'boy'; *drucken* and *setzen* acquired the new meanings of 'printing' and 'type-setting' in addition to the inherited meanings, although it was eventually the CGm. form *drücken* which carried these while UGm. *drucken* became specialized in the sense of 'to print'; *Braut*, originally 'newly-wed woman' like E *bride*, was used by Luther in the sense of 'fiancée', the meaning it now has in standard German; *queck*, *keck* changed from 'lively, alive' to 'arrogant, cheeky'; *e* (*ehe*) was narrowed to 'marriage', losing the meaning of 'law'; *fromm* formerly 'capable, excellent' changed to 'devout'; *evangelisch*,

Konfession, Reformation, all pre-ENHG loanwords, received their modern specialized meanings in consequence of the Reformation. While MHG *kriec* corresponds more or less to NHG *Streit,* i.e. 'quarrel', MHG *strīt* was used in the sense of 'war' in the literature of chivalry. A re-ordering of this semantic field with the inclusion of *Zank* and *Zwist* occurred after the decline of the civilization of chivalry.

The old German word for body was *Leichnam* (OHG *lichenamo*) alongside which as a hyponym there was *Leib* (MHG *līp*) with the meaning 'live body, life'. As *līp* was more and more used for *corpus, Leichnam* was deprived of its component 'live body' and the modern distribution of *Leib* and *Leichnam* gradually evolved.

In MHG the antonym of *gesund* was *siech,* that of *stark* was *krank,* while *schwach* had the meaning 'miserable, ignoble'. Again there was a built-in element of hyponymy to the extent that whoever was 'sick' was also *krank* and he who was 'weak' was also *schwach.* In the north *krank* thus impinged more and more upon LG *seke.* Perhaps the fact that Latin *infirmus* included both 'sick' and 'weak' helped *krank* against *seke* which was more precise. Luther introduced the antonyms *krank* and *gesund* into the emerging standard language, condemning *siech* to obsolescence. For 'weak' he no longer used *krank* but preferred *schwach.*

There can be no doubt that in an age when foreign influence was so strong many existing German words took on meanings from their foreign counterparts, such as *geselleschafft* the meaning of 'commercial organization' from Italian *compagnia. Semantic borrowing* was particularly extensive in the evolving German specialist languages. There has, however, been little research into the problem of semantic loans in this period. The process can be illustrated, for instance, in the language of mathematics where we have, among others, the following examples of an existing German word taking on an additional technical meaning from a corresponding Latin technical term: *ähnlich (similis); Aufgabe (problema); berühren (tangere); beweisen, Beweis (demonstrare, demonstratio); Bruch (fractio); Ebene (planum); Fläche (superficies); gegeben (datum); gerade, ungerade (par, impar, linea recta); gleich, Gleichung (aequalis, aequatio); Kegel (conus); Kugel (sphaera); Sehne (chorda); Seite (latus); teilen (dividere); Winkel (angulus); Würfel (cubus); Wurzel (radix).* Semantic borrowing must, of course, be seen in conjunction with loan translation and borrowing of foreign words. Together they were the processes which enabled German to become a fully competent medium of communication.

(iii) There was also much *loan translation* in the wider sense of the word, that is including part-for-part translation, the freer loan rendition, and much completely free loan creation. The study of the world of classical antiquity by the humanists, the rapid advancement of science and the adoption of Roman Law, all coincidental with the rise in the use of German as a vehicle of writing, produced both large-scale borrowing of foreign vocabulary and translation into the native lexicon. Among the loan translations of this period we find (the words are given in their modern form where possible): *abwesend* (*absens*); *Eigenname*, 1530 by Kolroß as *eygene name* < *nomen proprium*; *Gegenbild* (*antitypus*); *Gegensatz* (*oppositio*); *Gesichtskreis* (*Horizont*); *Gesprächsbüchlein*, U. von Hutten for *dialogus*; *gleichmütig*, 1528 Luther < *aequanimus*; *Irrgarten*, 1547 < *Labyrinth*; *Jahrbuch*, 1537 < *annales*; *Menschenfeind*, 1540 < *misanthropus*; *Mitlaut(er)*, Fabian Frangk (1531) for 'consonant' also *Selbstlaut(er)* for 'vowel'; *Mitschüler*, 1521 < *condiscipulus*; *Muttersprache* < *lingua materna*, a medieval Latin expression first recorded in the twelfth century in northern France with reference to the vanishing Frankish then still the language of the home and learnt from the mothers; *mueterstat* < *metropolis*, an abortive translation by Aventinus (1528); *myßhoffnung* < *desperatio*; *obliegen* < *incumbere*; *Säugling* < *lactens*, introduced into the written standard by Luther; *Schauplatz*, Luther (1522) < *theatron*; *Seltenheit* < *raritas* for older *seltsæne*; *tachmeister*, an abortive translation of *architectus*; *Unterredner*, by U. von Hutten for *interlocutor*; *Vollmacht* < *plenipotentia*; *Wohlwollen* < *benevolentia*; *Zeitgenosse* < *synchronus* by Sebastian Franck (1531).

Some Italian commercial terms were similarly translated: *lettera di cambio* > *Wechselbrief*; *tenere i libri* > *büecher halten* > *Buch halten, Buchhalter* etc.; *chiudere i conti* > *Rechnung schließen* (*abschließen*).

The technical languages, where German was only just becoming emancipated from Latin, again offer the largest number of examples. From the language of mathematics we may quote: *abziehen* (< *subtrahere*), often at first used in the double formula *subtrahieren oder abzien*; for 'parallel lines' Dürer used *Barlinien*, for 'parabola' *Brennlinie*, for 'ellipse/-is' *Eierlinie*; *einschreiben* (< *inscribere*); *Mittelpunkt* a loan rendition of *centrum*; *Nenner* (< *denominator*); *Rechenkunst*, a loan creation for *arithmetica*; *rechter Winkel* (< *angulus rectus*), *spitzer Winkel* (< *angulus acutus*), *stumpfer Winkel* (< *angulus obtusus*); *Teiler* (< *divisor*); *umschreiben* (< *circumscribere*); *vielfältigen*, later *vervielfältigen* for *multiplicare*; *Zähler* (< *numerator*); and for *quadrangulum, sexangulum, octangulum* we have *Viereck, Sechseck, Achteck*.

(iv) Humanist interest in philology led to the first works of lexicography. They were the Latin-German dictionaries of the Swiss Petrus Dasypodius whose *Dictionarium Latino-germanicum vice versa Germanico-latinum*, first published at Strasbourg in 1535, ran to many editions over the next two centuries, and of the Hessian Erasmus Alberus entitled *Novum dictionarii genus*, Frankfurt on Main, 1540. In contrast to the glossaries, extending from the eighth to the fifteenth centuries, these new works of lexicography accorded German a much more than ancillary role and showed an awareness of the Common German written language split, as it still was, into regional variants.

6.9.2 | Borrowed vocabulary

The establishment of German as a fully emancipated vernacular medium occurred at a time when the humanists were opening up the immensely rich storehouse of classical antiquity. Rather than having to rely on word derivation and composition, on semantic loans and loan translation in the wider meaning of the word, German was thus enabled to take a short cut by gaining direct access to the learned vocabulary of Latin. The bilingual educated community thus hinged German to the common European patrimony and created that international part of the German vocabulary which the evolving sciences required. Although a gulf was thus created between the educated and the uneducated, centuries of schooling were to reduce it and to transform it from a division between native and foreign into one between general and technical vocabulary. Every member of a modern European speech community is ignorant of a vast part of the lexicon of his language, not because it is of foreign origin but because he is ignorant in the specialisms of which that part of the lexicon is the technical linguistic medium. That contemporaries were aware of the problem posed by large-scale borrowing is shown by many comments such as Dürer's in his *Vnderweysung der Messung*: 'Den ersten [Kegel-] schnyt heysen die gelerten Elipsis ... Die Elipsis will jch ein eyer lini nennen.' His reference to *die gelerten* points to the educational gap which he tried to bridge by his loan creation *eyer lini* for foreign *ellipsis*. It was, however, large-scale borrowing which became a characteristic feature of the age. In 1571 the first dictionary of foreign words appeared at Augsburg (Simon Roth, *Ein Teutscher Dictionarius daz ist ein außleger schwerer vnbekanter Teutscher, Griechischer, Lateinischer, Hebräischer, Welscher vnd Französischer etc. Wörter*) listing about two thousand mainly Latin loanwords. Although there were some humanists who pronounced themselves against foreign words in German, purism as such did not become a feature of the German linguistic scene until the early seventeenth century. Luther's attitude was probably widely characteristic of the creative phase of borrowing in the fifteenth and early sixteenth centuries as opposed to the manneristic phase in the age of the Thirty Years War. He was not troubled about the origin of a word, but was passionately concerned to convey the correct sense and to be comprehensible to his fellow countrymen. Thus he preferred the foreign words *Apostel* and *Prophet* to the native *bote*, *zwelfbote* and *weissage(r)* because they conveyed a more precise technical meaning. At one of his table talks he explained: 'Apostoli, Epistel, Euangelistae, Engel sind als geste gewesen in germanica lingua ante Ecclesiam Christianam, iam habent burgerrecht gewonnen.' Thus what mattered to him was that the words should have a function and through use should have become native and thus intelligible.

The quotation also shows how learned discourse among the bilingual educated made use of the resources of both languages. On the whole it was mainly Latin nouns which were borrowed, as in the following Luther sentence: 'In den *casibus* sihet man, das das liebe *coniugium* einer guten *benedictio* bedarff' (B. Stolt, p. 120). At first they tended to be used without an article and inflected in the Latin manner. Then the German article crept in and the nominative singular would be used in all cases of the singular. Finally, the Latin plural formation was abandoned too, and the Latin ending replaced by a generalized German ending, e.g. *-tio* by *-tion*, *-atio* by *-atz*, *-tas* by *-tät*, *-entia/-antia* by *-enz/-anz* and the adjectival suffix -*alis* by -*alisch*. The incorporation of verbs was facilitated by the ending -*ieren* which dates from MHG (see 5.6.4), and was sometimes extended to -*isieren*. Over three hundred such verbs have been counted from this period. The following sentence from Luther's *An den christlichen Adel* shows the various stages of assimilation: 'Drumb wo es sein mocht, zuscheyden die hedder vnd krieg, das der primat in Germanien ein gemein Consistorium hielte, mit auditoribus, Cantzelern, der, wie zu Rom, signaturas gratiae vnnd iustitiae regiret, zu wilchem durch Appellation die sachen in deutschen landen wurden ordenlich bracht vnd trieben.'

The amount of borrowing from Latin was so great that it is, of course, impossible to list more than a few examples from representative semantic fields.

(i) *Latin influence*

As Latin never ceased to supply loanwords, and continuity is difficult to establish, it is often impossible to say at what period a particular loanword entered the language and maintained itself uninterruptedly. The following examples date with a fair degree of certainty from the ENHG period (the words are given in their modern forms). Words of Greek origin are included in the following lists since most reached German via Latin.

Church and religion
Bibel, Blasphemie, Doktrin, Kapitel, Kaplan, Kardinal, Legat, Minister, Ministerium, Mirakel, Observanz, Patriarch, Prädestination, Predikant, Religion, Sekte, Skandal, Symbol, Testament, Theologe, Theologie, Zeremonie.

Education and scholarship
Absenz, Akademie, Alphabet, Argument, Artist (member of the faculty of arts, as well as 'artist'), *Assistent, Auditorium, Autor, Bibliothek* (earlier *Liberey*), *Definition, Dekan, Dialektik, Dialog, Direktor, Disputant, Disputation, (Disputatz), Doktor, Eloquenz, Epistel, Examen, Exemplar, Fakultät, Ferien, Fraktur, Geographie, Gymnasium, Humanität, Kalender, Kandidat, Katheder, Klasse, Kollegium, Kommentar, Kompendium, Konsequenz, Korrektur, Logik, Manuskript, Pensum, Philosoph(ie), Primaner (Sekundaner* etc.), *Professor, Qualität, Realist, Rektor, Revision, Rhetorik, Scholar, Skribent, Sophist, Spekulation, Stipendium, Summa, Talar, Tradition, Tyrannei, Vikar.* Among the many verbs in -*ieren* there were: *artikulieren, deklamieren, demonstrieren, gratulieren, korrigieren, präparieren, repetieren, rezitieren.*

Students began to have their own slang. Some words have been in the language ever since then: *burschikos, fidel, Gaudium, Jux, Karzer, Kommers, Moneten, Pfiffikus, Prosit, Silentium.*

Philology
Akzent, Diphthong, Etymologie, Konjugation, Konsonant, Orthographie, Parenthese, Punkt, Verbum, Vokabel, Vokal.

Law and administration
Administration, Akte, Alimente, Amnestie, Archiv, Arrest, Assessor, Audienz, Auktion, authentisch, Delinquent, Deportation, Deputation, Disposition, Exekution, Familie, Fiskus, Formular, Hypothek, Immunität, Instanz, Instruktion, Inventar, juristisch, Justiz, Kanzlei, Kaution, Klausel, Konferenz, Kontrakt, legal, Legalität, Legation, Magistrat, Mandat, Monarch, Nation in the sense of 'nation', synonymous with *teutsche zunge,* replacing the medieval meaning of 'regional grouping of students at a university', *Patent, Polizei* (ENHG 'order' < L *policia), Prärogativ, Protestation, Regent, Residenz, Skrupel, Termin, Tribut.* Among the verbs are: *adoptieren, annektieren, annullieren, approbieren, disponieren, instruieren, kompromieren, konfiszieren, korrumpieren, protestieren, ratifizieren, rebellieren, subskribieren, suspendieren, transferieren, transponieren.* Many of these are now rather archaic.

General science
Words which are claimed to have been introduced by Paracelsus are marked by (P). *Absolut* (P), *aktiv, alchimistisch* (P), *animalisch* (P), *aromatisch, Arsenik* (P), *Asphalt, Astrologie, Äther* (P), *Atlas, Bestie, chirurgisch* (P), *Distanz, Effekt, elektrisch* (P), *Elevation, Elixier* (P), *Embryo* (P), *Epilepsie* (P), *Essenz, Extrakt, Ferment* (P), *Fixstern, hermaphroditisch* (P), *Horizont, Infektion* (P), *Insekt, Inspiration* (P), *Irregularität, Klima, Koagulation* (P), *Kolik, Kuriosität, Laboratorium* (P), *Medizin, Mikrokosmos* (P), *Operation, Opium, orientalisch, Ozean, passiv, Pest, Pestilenz, Petroleum, Phlegma, physikalisch* (P), *Position, Prinzip(ium), Psychologie, Quintessenz* (P), *Region, Spiritus, Sterilität* (P), *subtil* (also MHG), *Subtilität, Temperament* (P), *Temperatur, Zentrum.* Among the verbs are: *determinieren, experimentieren, imaginieren, purgieren, reduzieren.*

Mathematics
Algebra, Algorismus, Algorithmus, Arithmetik, Basis, Diagonale, Differenz, Dimension, Ellipsis(-e), Fazit, Hyperbel, Hypotenuse, Corpus > Körper, Mathematik, minus, Minute, Null, oval, Parabel, parallel, plus, Polygon, Primzahl (<*numerus primus*), *Probe* (<*proba, probatio), Produkt, Proportion, Pyramide, Quadrat, Quantität, Quotient, Rhomboid, Rhombus, Sektor, Sinus, Stereometrie, Trapez, Ziffer* (< Lat. *cifera*

'nought' < Arabic), *Zylinder*. And the verbs: *addieren, dividieren, multiplizieren, probieren, subtrahieren*.

The arts
Allegorie, Aphorismus, Architektur, Dekoration, Komödie (*comedi*), *Komponist, Perspektive, Poet, Prolog, Symphonie, Tragödie* (*tragedi*), and the verbs: *florieren,* 'to decorate', *inkorporieren, stenzilieren, temperieren* 'to mix colours in the right proportions'.

It was also customary in the sixteenth century to name the months by their Latin designations, e.g. *Januarius, Februarius* etc. Gradually they lost their Latin endings. Older Germanized forms such as *Jänner*, or German words such as *Hornung* became dialectal or obsolete.

(ii) *French influence*

This reached its peak in the seventeenth and eighteenth centuries. Even in the fifteenth and sixteenth centuries French supremacy in the art of comfortable and luxurious living and in military affairs led to the importation of hundreds of loanwords. Many denoted fashionable objects of the age such as fabrics and materials and have vanished again. Of those that have survived the following lists may provide a sample.

General cultural loans
Appetit, Autorität, Bankier, Barbier (perhaps from It.), *Barett, Biskuit, Boi* 'woollen cloth' < OF *baie* (>E *bay, baize*), *Bordell, Bordüre, Büffel, doppelt* (ENHG *doppel* < F *double*), *Fabrik, Faktorei, Fasson, fatal, favorisieren, Finanz* (ENHG 'cheating' < F *finance* or L *financia*), *Firlefanz, frank, Franse, Frikassee, Garderobe, Gardine, Herold* (< OF *heralt*, F *héraut*, ENHG by popular etymology > *Erenhold*), *Jacke, Juwel* (OF *joël* > Middle Dutch *juweel*), *Kandis*(*zucker*), *Klavier, Koffer, Konterfei,* 'picture' < F *contrefait, Kordel, Kurtisane* (in ENHG also masc. for 'courtier', originally from It. *cortigiano*), *Lakai, Letter, liefern, liquidieren, Manier, Marzipan* (perhaps from It.), *Medaille, Melone* (perhaps from It. *mellone*), *Morast, Muff* (ENHG *Muffel* < F *moufle*), *Mummerei, nett, Orange, Partie, Paß, passen, passieren, Pinte, pissen, Planke, Polier, Pomp, Pott, Profit, Puder, Pumpe, pur, quittieren, Quittung* (ENHG *quitantz* < OF *quitance*), *Reputation, Revier* (OF *riviere* 'river', 'area' originally along a river), *Sauce* (now *Soße*), *Sekt* (F *vin sec*, also > E *sack*), *Serviette, Sorte* (or from It. *sorta*), (*aus*)*staffieren* (OF *estofer* 'to equip'), *Taille, Tapisserie, Tasse, Uhr*.

Military terms
Armee, Artillerie, Attacke, Bagage, Barrikade, Batterie, blockieren, Bresche, defensiv, exerzieren, Flanke, Front, Furage, Furier, galoppieren,

Garde, Garnison, General, Infanterie (originally from Spanish), *Ingenieur, Kaliber, Kamerad, Kanaille, Karabiner, Kartusche, Kavallerie, Kommandeur, kommandieren, Kommiß, Kompanie, Korporal, Kürassier, Lafette, Leutnant, Marschall, marschieren, massakrieren, Meute, Meuterei* (<OF *muete, meute* 'rebellion'), *Mine, Munition, neutral, offensiv, Offizier, Palisade, Parade, Partisan* (originally from It. *partigiano*), *Patrone, Pike, Pistole, Rapier, Rapport, Regiment, rekognoszieren, Rekrut, Runde, Salve, Spion, Troß, Truppe.*

These are just some examples of the military vocabulary of the time which have survived. There were many more loanwords such as for weapons which became obsolete, and many were later rejected as, for instance, *armieren, bataille, combat, occasion* 'battle', *parlamentieren* 'to parley', *ranzon* 'ransom', *retirieren* 'to retreat', *salvieren* 'to save', *trenchee* 'trench'.

The *à la mode* period of the seventeenth century saw a polite society completely under the spell of France. The use of French words and of whole sentences in French became an affectation of many members of court society while in some circles and courts French became even the normal medium of conversation. Of the innumerable loanwords of the time the following are survivors: *adieu, Allee, Bagatelle, Charge, Dame, Diskurs, dissimilieren, Etage, express, Exzellenz* (perhaps from Latin), *Favorit, Finesse, Finte, frisieren, Galanterie, Gavotte, Kavalier, Kompliment, Konversation, Mätresse, Miene, Mode, nobel, Offerte, Page, Parfüm, Perücke, pikant, rar, scharmant, Serviteur, tranchieren, Trubel.*

(iii) *Italian influence*

Marjatta Wis, whose study of Italian loanwords in German covers the period from 1350 to 1600, lists nearly nine hundred Italianisms. The majority are ephemeral loans which crop up in translations from the Italian or in travel books concerned with Italy. But the commercial and cultural relations between Italy and Germany were very close in this period. Italian cities, above all Venice, were leading centres of commerce where Germans learned modern methods of trading and were themselves engaged in commerce. Italian universities attracted many students from Germany. Artists sat at the feet of Italian masters. Finally, the Italian wars of Maximilian I and Charles V brought German armies to Italy and acquainted them with Italian methods of warfare. Of the nearly nine hundred Italianisms only 2·7 per cent were recorded in the fourteenth century. This increased to 39 per cent in the fifteenth century and the bulk (58·3 per cent) entered German in the sixteenth. It is often extremely difficult to say whether Italian or French was the source. Thus German *Rest* could either be borrowed from F *reste* or It. *resto*. Sometimes the earliest recorded form shows an Italian origin, e.g. *bischoten* (< *biscotto*), but the later form *Biskuit* points to a reborrowing from French or remodelling under French influence. Many of the Italian words were of Oriental origin, especially those connected with Mediterranean trade.

Thematically the largest group are the commercial terms, being made up of words for produce, fabrics, wines, weights, measures and coins. A second large category are the maritime expressions for navigation, ships, parts of ships, equipment, winds, coastlines and so on. Words from the field of music and other cultural pursuits entered German in great masses only from the second half of the seventeenth century when the Italian influence on south German courts was at its strongest.

Among the ENHG loans which have permanently enriched the German language we find:

Alarm (< *all'arme* 'to arms', developed also to *Lärm*), *Alefanz, Alt, Armada, Arsenal* (originally < Arabic), *Artischocke, Bandit, Bank, Bankett, Bankrott, Baß, Bilanz, brutto, Damast* (ENHG *damasch* < *damasco*), *Dattel, Diskont, dito, Dukaten, Fagott, Fratze, Galeasse, Galeere, Galerie, Galopp, Gant, Gazelle, Giro, Gondel, Granate, Grotte, Havarie, Kamin, Kanal, Kanone, Kap, Kapriole, Kapuze, Karawane, Kartoffel* (< It. *tartufoli*, early seventeenth century with unexplained later change of *t-* > *k-*), *Kasse, Kommando, Konto, Konzert, Kornett, kredenzen, Kredit, Kuppel, kurant, Lagune, Lazarett, Levante, Madrigal, Magazin, Mameluck, Marketender, Maske, Matratze, Million, Mosaik, Moschee, Motette, Muskete, Muster, netto, Olive, Pantoffel, parieren, Pasquill, Passagier, Pilot, Pokal, Pomade, Pomeranze, Porzellan, Post, Postillion, Proviant, Punzen, Rakete, Rest, Rhabarber, Salat, Sardelle, Sardine, Schachtel, Scharlatan, Schwadron, Soldat, Soldateska, Sonett, Spachtel, Spagat, Spargel, Spaß, spedieren, Spinat, Stafette, Stiefel, Strapaze, Tapete, Tenor, Tratte, Wirsing, Zitadelle, Zitrone.*

(iv) *Spanish influence*

This shows itself above all in a number of exotic words which the Spaniards brought back to Europe from their sea voyages and conquests in the New World. It is difficult to trace the exact route these words took to reach German. In some cases French or Dutch were the intermediaries. But as these loanwords owe their importation to Europe ultimately to Spanish they must be listed as testifying to Spanish influence in this period: *Alligator* (perhaps via F), *Alpaca* (in ENHG *Paco*), *Armada* (or < It.), *Eldorado, Fregatte* (probably via F), *Guano, Hängematte* (Spanish *hamaca*, F *hamac* entered Dutch as *hangmak, hangmat* owing to popular etymology and became *Hängematte* 'hammock' in German), *Jasmin* (from Persian), *Kakao, Kannibale, Kokain* (ENHG *Coca*), *Kondor, Lama, Mais, Mestize, Moskito, Neger* (perhaps also < F), *Schokolade* (via Dutch), *Tabak, Tomate* (perhaps also via other languages).

(v) *Dutch influence*

In the sixteenth century the Dutch rose rapidly to great commercial and maritime importance. A number of German words reveal by their linguistic forms that they were borrowed from Dutch. Not a few came from further afield and were themselves loanwords in Dutch. Among the imports from Dutch in ENHG there are:

Aktie, Almanach, Boje, Börse, bugsieren, Büse, Dose, Düne, Flinte (perhaps from Swedish), *Hai, Harpune, Kajüte, Kante, Kaper, Karotte, Klippe, Koje, lavieren, Lotse, Lotterie, Matrose, Niete* 'blank', *Reuter, Staat, Stellage, Stüber, Süden, Tulpe.*

(vi) *Eastern European influence*

The earliest Slavonic loanwords resulted from the fur trade. German migration to the east led to a good deal of intermingling of populations and a certain amount of borrowing of foreign vocabulary. Most of these words did not travel beyond the eastern local dialects but some entered the standard language. The Hussite wars and the Thirty Years War brought further borrowing from the various Slavonic languages. Some of the words originated in Turkish and other non-Slavonic languages. Among the imports from the east which reached the standard language we have:

Dolch (uncertain), *Dolmetsch* (<Hungarian < Turkish), *Graupe, Grenze, Grippe, Gurke, Halunke, Haubitze, Horde* (<Tartar), *Husar, Jauche, Jause* (an Austrianism), *Kalesche, Kren* 'horseradish' (eastern South Gm.), *Kürschner* (borrowed in OHG and MHG times), *Kutsche, Nerz, Peitsche, Petschaft, Popanz, Preisel(beere), Quark, Quarz, Reizker, Säbel, Scharwenzel, Schmetten* (ECGm. dialect word for 'cream', but

its derivative *Schmetterling* 'butterfly' has become standard), *Stieglitz,*
Tolpatsch, Tornister, Trabant, Trafik, Wallach, Zeisig (first in MHG),
Zobel (first in OHG).

6.9.3 | Onomastics

(i) In the field of *place-names* the age of Humanism and of
the Reformation was rather unimportant. German seemed to have
lost the impulse and the ability to create new types of toponyms.
New settlements generally took existing nature names. Where
settlements were deserted, former habitation names frequently
became nature names. The growth of the towns, the devastation of
the wars and the uneconomic nature of some settlements on in-
fertile soils produced a good deal of internal migration and resettlement, however, without a concomitant echo in toponymics.

The two linguistically important movements of the age had,
however, an impact on place-names. First, the rise of the standard
language brought about a gradual standardization of many formerly
dialectally determined place-names. Low German forms like
Dusseldorp, Ossendorp, Holthusen, Gripswolde became High German
Düsseldorf, Ochsendorf, Holzhausen, Greifswald, and Alemannic
place-names like *Schaffhusen, Wildhus* came to be spelt *Schaffhausen, Wildhaus*. The place and canton of *Schwyz* in its EUGm.
form *Schweiz* yielded the German name for Switzerland, while its
native form *Schwyz* was retained for the old locality. The language
of the chanceries fixed the place-names in their modern forms
choosing among variants often archaic or quasi archaic forms, e.g.
Veltheim rather than *Velten, Jena, Vechta, Fulda* with -*a* rather
than -*e*.

Secondly, Humanism restored many old names, such as *Italia*,
later *Italie, Italien* for what was formerly known as *Lamparten,*
Walholand or *Wälisch land*. *Germania* and *Germani*, both eventually becoming the English names of Germany and the Germans,
were borrowed from the writings of classical antiquity at the same
time as the name *Deutschland* became gradually established as a
compound replacing earlier attributive phrases, MHG *daz tiutsche
lant* or pl. *tiutsche lant*. Most names of countries were written in
their Latin forms, e.g. *Hispania, Hungaria*, but both in analogy to
names of German regions such as *Franken, Hessen, Sachsen* and

from their oblique forms when Germanized to *-ie* (*Hispanie*, obl. cases *Hispanien*), the modern ending *-ien* (*Italien*, *Kroatien*, *Spanien* etc.) became gradually established.

New kinds of toponyms frequently recorded in this age are the street names and house names in the cities. These and names of inns sometimes retain ENHG linguistic forms, e.g. *Zum Schwanen*, *Zum Rechberg* (now *Reh-* 'roe-deer'), *Kuglergasse* (from the former trade of cowl-makers).

(ii) In this period Germans had as now two *personal names*, a Christian name and a surname: *Thomas Müntzer*, *Felix Manz*, *Balthasar Hubmaier*, *Albrecht Dürer*, *Willibald Pirckheimer*. Generally they had only one Christian name, which was nearly always the name of a saint. In the sixteenth century a new custom of giving children two Christian names (*Johann Sebastian*, *Maria Susanna*) spread from France into the western regions. In this way the father's or godfather's name could be handed on or perhaps it was hoped that the child would command the support of two patron saints rather than of only one. Under the influence of Humanism some names of pagan antiquity began to be used such as *Hektor*, *Agrippa*, *Claudius*, *Julius*, *Augustus*. Hohenzollern princes of this period bore names such as *Albrecht Achilles*, *Albrecht Alcibiades*, *Johann Cicero*. The first German emperor with a non-German name was Maximilian I, although it is not certain whether this was meant as a saint's name or as a name deriving from classical antiquity. Established Christian names of educated people were usually latinized, e.g. *Henricus*, *Martinus*, *Joachimus*.

The Reformation brought a slow decline in the use of saints' names and instead introduced Old Testament names such as *Benjamin*, *Jonas*, *Daniel*, *David*, *Rebekka*, *Martha*. The Calvinistic predilection for Biblical names did not, however, last beyond the eighteenth century, which explains why such names as *David*, *Enoch*, *Elias* are very rare in Germany. In the eighteenth century German Protestants favoured German names with a moral flavour, for instance, *Gottfried*, *Gotthold*, *Gotthelf*, *Fürchtegott*, *Liebfried*. On the whole, Protestantism prepared a return to Germanic names.

Humanists were also interested in Germanic antiquity and in consequence in Germanic names. Johann Fischart favoured names such as *Hildebrand*, *Hartmann*, *Reinhold*, etc. The Catholics on the other hand clung tenaciously to saints' names. Certain names became characteristically Catholic such as *Ignaz, Xaver, Franz, Josef* and *Maria*. Female Christian names were basically of the same kind as male names. Willibald Pirckheimer's sisters were called *Charitas, Felicitas, Eufemia, Sabina, Katherina,* and *Walburg*; his daughters: *Charitas, Crescentia* and *Katherina,* his wife *Crescentia* and his mother *Barbara*.

Christian names were still more important than surnames. Although these were hereditary and common in most areas of Germany they could still be changed relatively easily. The family name of Gutenberg was *Gensfleisch* but the name by which the inventor of printing became known was the name of their family residence in Mainz, *zum Gutenberg*. Townspeople often changed their surnames according to their trades or place of residence. Scholars, in particular, were often called after their place of origin: Luther's famous Catholic opponent *Johann Eck* was really called *Maier* but took his name from his birthplace *Egg an der Günz*. His fellow reformer *Andreas Bodenstein* is better known as *Karlstadt,* after the place where he was born. His Pomeranian associate Johannes Bugenhagen was often referred to as *Dr. Pommer* or *Pomeranus*. Surnames in *-ing* or *-son* easily changed into those in *-er*, as did those using *von* with a place-name. In Austria *von* had already become an attribute of nobility. In North Germany many names exchanged *von/van* for the suffix *-mann* (*von Brügge* > *Brüggemann,* cf. UGm. *von Brugg* > *Brugger*). In the sixteenth century phrase-names (e.g. *Gibunsgenug, Schlagdenhauffen*) enjoyed a certain popularity.

It was only in modern times that a change of surname was prohibited, e.g. in Bavaria in 1677, in Austria in 1776, and in Prussia in 1794. There were some regions, e.g. Friesland, where surnames were not even common in this period. The fact that new words such as *Kutscher, Dragoner, Kornett* could still become surnames, of course, also testifies to the relative fluidity in surname usage.

Again the great cultural trends of the age made themselves felt in nomenclature. Many surnames were High-Germanized, e.g. Low German *Schulte* > *Schulz, Witt* > *Weiß, Scheper* > *Schäfer, Holthusen* > *Holzhausen* or hybrid *Holthausen*; Bavarian *Holzamer* > *Holzheimer*; Swiss *Wyss* > *Weiß, Huser* > *Hauser*. Of course, many remained untouched such as *Kriesi* or *Rüegg* in Switzerland or *Lempke, Niekerken* in North Germany.

Humanism favoured the adoption of Latin and in some cases even Greek names. Geert Geerts of Rotterdam is known in history as *Desiderius* (*desiderare = begehren*) *Erasmus Roterodamus*. The scholar of the age had typically a tripartite name like a Roman: *Conradus Mutianus Rufus*, *Conradus Celtis Protucius* (Konrad Bickel), *Helius Eobanus Hessius*, *Joannes Crotus Rubianus* (Johann Jäger from Dornheim); others translated their surnames into Latin or Greek: *Johannes von Sommerfeld* > *Aesticampianus*, *Rudolf Hausmann* > *Rudolfus Agricola*, *Johannes Hausschein* > *Oecolampadius*, *Philipp Schwarzert* > *Melanchthon*; others at least added Latin endings to their names: *Lutherus*, *Matthesius*, (< *Matthes*), *Schottelius* (< *Schottel*), *Bilibaldus Pirckheimerus*. Not a few such humanistic creations have lasted, e.g. *Pistorius* (*Bäcker*), *Curtius* (*Kurz*), *Venator* (*Jäger*), *Faber* (*Schmid*), *Mercator* (*Kaufmann*), *Piscator* (*Fischer*), *Textor* (*Weber*), *Viëtor* (*Faßbinder*), *Minor* (*Klein*), *Vulpius* (*Wolf*).

The age of Humanism thus left a permanent, if slight, trace in the evolution of German name-giving.

Select Bibliography

V. G. Admoni, 'Der Umfang und die Gestaltungsmittel des Satzes in der dt. Literatursprache bis zum Ende des 18. Jahrhunderts', *Beitr.* (Halle), 89 (1967) 144–99; H. P. Althaus, 'Die Erforschung der jiddischen Sprache' in L. E. Schmitt (ed.), *Germanische Dialektologie*, Wiesbaden, 1968, vol. 1, 224–63; E. Arndt, 'Luther im Lichte der Sprachgeschichte', *Beitr.* (Halle), 92 (1970) 1–20; id., 'Das Aufkommen des begründenden *weil*', *Beitr.* (Halle), 81 (1959) 388–415; H. Bach, *Laut- und Formenlehre der Sprache Luthers*, Copenhagen, 1934; id., 'Die Entstehung der dt. Hochsprache im Frühneuhochdeutschen', *ZMF*, 23 (1955) 193–201; K. von Bahder, *Grundlagen des nhd. Lautsystems*, Strasbourg, 1890; id., *Zur Wortwahl in der frühnhd. Schriftsprache*, Heidelberg, 1925; W. Besch, *Sprachlandschaften und Sprachausgleich im 15. Jahrhundert*, Munich, 1967; id., 'Zur Entstehung der nhd. Schriftsprache', *ZDP*, 87 (1968) 405–26; F. Debus, 'Die deutschen Bezeichnungen für die Heiratsverwandtschaft', in *Deutsche*

Wortforschung in europ. Bezügen, vol. 1, Giessen, 1958, pp. 1–116; I. Eichler, G. Bergmann, 'Zum Meißnischen Deutsch', *Beitr.* (Halle), 89 (1967) 1–57; J. Erben, 'Frühneuhochdeutsch' in L. E. Schmitt (ed.), *Kurzer Grundriß der germanischen Philologie bis 1500*, vol. 1, Berlin, 1970, pp. 386–440; id., *Grundzüge einer Syntax der Sprache Luthers*, Berlin, 1954; id., 'Luther und die nhd. Schriftsprache' in F. Maurer, H. Rupp, *Deutsche Wortgeschichte*, vol. 1, 3rd ed., Berlin, 1974, pp. 509–81; id., 'Deutsche Wortbildung in synchronischer und diachronischer Sicht', *WW*, 14 (1964) 83–93; L. Fèbvre, H. J. Martin, *L'apparition du livre*, Paris, 1958; W. Fleischer, *Strukturelle Untersuchungen zur Geschichte des Neuhochdeutschen*, Berlin, 1966; id., *Untersuchungen zur Geschäftssprache des 16. Jahrhunderts in Dresden*, Berlin, 1970; W. W. Florer, 'Gender-Change from MHG to Luther', *PMLA*, 15 (1900) 442–91; R. Flury, *Struktur- und Bedeutungsgeschichte des Adjektivsuffixes '-bar'*, Winterthur, 1964; C. Franke, *Grundzüge der Schriftsprache Luthers*, 3 vols., 2nd ed., Halle, 1913–22; T. Frings, *Sprache und Geschichte*, vol. 3, Halle, 1956; G. Ising, *Zur Wortgeographie spätmittelalterlicher deutscher Schriftdialekte*, 2 vols., Berlin, 1968; M. H. Jellinek, *Geschichte der nhd. Grammatik von den Anfängen bis auf Adelung*, 2 vols., Heidelberg, 1913–14; A. Keller, *Zur Sprache des Chronisten Gerold Edlibach*, Zürich, 1965; G. Kettmann, *Die kursächsische Kanzleisprache zwischen 1486 und 1546*, 2nd ed., Berlin, 1969; F. Kluge, *Von Luther bis Lessing*, 5th ed., *Leipzig*, 1918; K. B. Lindgren, *Über den oberdeutschen Präteritumschwund*, Helsinki, 1957; D. F. Malherbe, *Das Fremdwort im Reformationszeitalter*, Freiburg i. Br., 1906; H. Moser, H. Stopp, *Grammatik des Frühneuhochdeutschen*, 2 vols., Heidelberg, 1970/73; V. Moser, *Historisch-grammatische Einführung in die frühnhd. Schriftdialekte*, Halle, 1909; id., *Frühnhd. Grammatik*, 2 vols., Heidelberg, 1929/51; J. Müller, *Quellenschriften und Geschichte des deutschsprachlichen Unterrichtes bis zur Mitte des 16. Jahrhunderts*, Gotha, 1882; E. Öhmann, 'Das deutsche Suffix -(i)tät', *Neuphil. Mitt.*, 68 (1967) 242–9; id., 'Das deutsche Suffix -lei', ibid., 70 (1969) 441–8; M. Philipp, *Phonologie des graphies et des rimes. L'Alsacien de Thomas Murner*, Paris, 1968; E. Sager, *Die Aufnahme der nhd. Schriftsprache in der Kanzlei St. Gallen*, Zürich, 1949; H.-J. Schädlich, *Phonologie des Ostvogtländischen*, Berlin, 1966; J. Schildt, 'Zur Ausbildung des Satzrahmens in Aussagesätzen der Bibelsprache, 1350–1550', *Beitr.* (Halle), 90 (1968) 174–97; A. Schirmer, 'Der Wortschatz der Mathematik nach Alter und Herkunft untersucht', *ZfdWf.*, 14 (1912/13) Beiheft, 1–80; L. E. Schmitt, *Untersuchungen zu Entstehung und Struktur der «nhd. Schriftsprache»*, vol. I, Cologne, Graz, 1966; E. Skála, 'Süddeutschland in der Entstehung der deutschen Schriftsprache', *Beitr.* (Halle), 92 (1970) 93–110; B. Stolt, *Die Sprachmischung in Luthers Tischreden*, Stockholm, 1964; L. S. Thompson, 'German Translations of the Classics between

1450 and 1550', *JEGP*, 42 (1943) 343–62; H. Weber, *Das erweiterte Adjektiv- und Partizipialattribut im Deutschen*, Munich, 1971; K.-H. Weimann, 'Paracelsus und der dt. Wortschatz', in *Dt. Wortforschung in europäischen Bezügen*, vol. 2, Giessen, 1963, pp. 359–408; S. N. Werbow, '«Die gemeine teutsch» – Ausdruck und Begriff', *ZDP*, 82 (1963) 44–63; O. Werner, 'Das deutsche Pluralsystem', in *Sprache der Gegenwart*, 5, Düsseldorf, 1969, pp. 92–128; M. Wis, 'Ricerche sopra gli italianismi nella lingua tedesca dalla metà del secolo XIV alla fine del secolo XVI', *Mémoires de la société néophilologique de Helsinki*, 17, Helsinki, 1955, pp. 1–310.

The Classical Literary Language and Modern German

7.1 | The period and the linguistic territory

7.1.1 | The period

Over four and a half centuries have passed since Luther stirred the Germans by his early reforming tracts and by his Gospel translation, or since Maximilian's and Pfinzing's *Theuerdank* delighted book lovers, or again since Thomas Murner entertained the German reading public with his satires. If this, the next and last linguistic cross-section, has nevertheless to embrace both the Classical Literary Language of around 1800 and contemporary Modern German, the reason is partly that there are not enough chronological isoglosses to enable us further to subdivide the New High German phase of the language and partly that we lack the benefit of distance and hindsight. Stylistically and sociolinguistically the contemporary modern language may be a far cry from the language of Goethe and Schiller. But there is no gainsaying that the latter is still part of the contemporary linguistic scene. It constitutes a register of the modern language in a sense in which no form of the Early New High German phase does. Observers in a couple of hundred years may well wish to separate the New High German of around 1800 from what they may call the Late New High German of the twenty-first century. In that case the first half of the twentieth century will probably be seen as the period in which many of the decisive and divisive processes took place. The present-day observer can try to identify many of these trends, but their consequences and the evolution which they are likely to engender are yet beyond our certain comprehension.

The New High German linguistic period may thus perforce be said to fall into three phases: the preparatory phase of the century and a half after the end of the Thirty Years War during which the Classical Literary Language emerged and matured (1650–1800); the century and a half during which the Classical Literary Language evolved into Modern Standard German with its written and spoken forms, in other words, the phase when a select written medium of a cultured elite in all German-speaking lands evolved into a 'vulgarized' written and spoken medium of the majority of the German-speaking peoples (1800–1950); and finally a third phase in which many of the seminal changes of the twentieth century crystallize in such a manner that future generations may see in this phase the beginning of a new linguistic period.

In the political and cultural history of the German-speaking peoples there are many events which point to a similar division. As always, these external factors helped to determine the development of the language.

In the first phase the German-speaking territory was still, by and large, held together by the gentle if feeble hand of the Holy Roman Empire. The outcome of the Thirty Years War had ensured that the empire would not become a centralized power. The peace treaties had confirmed the independence of the United Provinces of the Netherlands and of Switzerland. In the former case, this put the seal on the already well-established independence of the Dutch language. In the latter case, this had no linguistic consequence, although the subsequent persistence of diglossia (the use of two fairly distinct forms of the same language, German, for different purposes) was no doubt encouraged by a separate nationhood. In many places in the east, German-speaking populations lived outside the confines of the Holy Roman Empire, notably in the Polish duchy of Prussia (later known as East Prussia). For the first time in history this was now also the case in the west: German-speaking Alsace, although not the ten Alsatian imperial free cities, passed into French sovereignty under the provisions of the Treaty of Münster (1648). The cities followed in the subsequent decades, Strasbourg (1681) being the last. With this one, as history was to prove, tragically important exception, the western boundary of the empire gradually began to coincide with the linguistic and cultural boundary between France and Germany: French-speaking Franche Comté (1674/78) and Lorraine (1735/66) were detached from the empire and joined to the French monarchy.

Although in the north, Sweden and Denmark held territories belonging to the empire, sovereignty itself was not in dispute. The empire was a loose association of about three hundred and fifty principalities and lordships owing nominal allegiance to the emperor, who, although still elective, was now (with one brief exception) always the Habsburg king of Bohemia and Hungary and the ruler of the hereditary Austrian duchies. Real power lay in the hands of the princes, who made themselves more and more into absolutist rulers. It may seem surprising that under such conditions there were no further secessions from the empire. The main reason was that both people and princes felt themselves to be Germans, held together by strong linguistic, cultural and historical ties. The princes had all the power they wanted without secession. The heyday of the free imperial cities was now over. Commerce had withered in the turmoil of the religious wars. The autocratically ruled absolutist principalities were commercially incapsulated. Inspiration for economic expansion came from the princes and their mercantilistic bureaucracies bent only upon promoting the cohesion, wealth and, in some cases, military power of their states. The towns which acquired fame as centres of cultural distinction in the eighteenth century were, therefore, princely residences: Dresden, Mannheim, Berlin, Munich, Karlsruhe, Kassel, Hanover, Weimar, Stuttgart and, of course, Vienna, the largest German city. The greatest of the free cities was now Hamburg. In the age of absolutism culture was everywhere dominated by the courts. Hamburg in the north and Zürich in republican Switzerland were almost the only exceptions. Universities were encouraged to serve the absolutist states and new ones were founded for this purpose, e.g. Halle (1694) by Prussia and Göttingen (1737) by Hanover. The new ideas of rationalism and the movement of enlightenment permeated both many universities and the livelier courts.

The western territories of the empire were completely dominated by French power and dazzled by French cultural achievements. The eastern principalities had more elbow-room for independent power politics. Austria continued its policy of eastward expansion. With Bohemia already firmly in the Habsburg grip it succeeded in finally wresting its dynasty's Hungarian legacy from the empire of the Ottoman Turks. Thus the slow decline of the Ottoman Empire after the last Turkish siege of Vienna in 1683, began to shape the history of Austria, ultimately to lead to a new confrontation with a new power in the east, Russia.

Saxony's eastern adventure was purely dynastic. Its rulers became kings of Poland (1697–1763), but Saxony itself did not become involved in Poland's history. It was Brandenburg under its Hohenzollern electors which brought about the greatest political change in the empire after the Thirty Years War. Having acquired the Polish duchy of Prussia in 1618 its princes eventually succeeded in gaining sovereignty for Prussia (1656), then in making themselves kings in Prussia (1701), and finally in closing the territorial gap between Brandenburg and Pomerania in the west and Prussia in the east. The shameful partitions of Poland between Prussia and Russia, with Austria as a relatively unwilling third partner, led to the tragic entanglement of Germany with Poland, the consequences of which have extended into our own generation. In the First Polish Partition (1772) Prussia acquired Ermland, Pomerelia and West Prussia; in the Second (1792) Danzig and 'South Prussia' or the province of Posen (Poznań), and in the Third (1795) so much purely Polish territory that in 1795 almost a quarter of all Prussian subjects were Polish-speaking. Although at the Congress of Vienna in 1815 Prussia surrendered a large part of its purely Polish territory, the entanglement was to last. In the age of absolutism these dynastic expansions of Austria and Prussia into the east had no 'national' consequences. The subsequent age of nationalism, however, regarded Prussia and Austria as 'colonial' powers and the ensuing conflict finally led to that cataclysmic clash between Teuton and Slav which has resulted in the present European division between East and West.

Eastward expansion was only one aspect of the rise of Brandenburg-Prussia. Of more immediate significance was its emergence as a highly organized, centralized, autocratic state with a powerful, ever-increasing standing army. In the course of the eighteenth century Prussia became the foremost military power in the empire. The final north German aspect of the German standard language is a direct result of this shift of power to the north. Another north German state, Hanover, rose in the same period. In 1692 a ninth electorate was created for the Welf dynasty of Hanover, Bavaria having been raised to the same position during the Thirty Years War. The Holy Roman Empire was such a loose and strange organization that it could accommodate both these momentous external expansions on the part of Austria and Prussia and the powerful internal shifts including the wars between the emperor and his most important 'subject', the king of Prussia. Nevertheless, it was moribund.

Its eclipse was brought about by the French Revolution, which thus marks the turning point between the first and the second phase of our period. After the first successful assault of revolutionary France had led to the French occupation of the imperial territories on the left bank of the Rhine (1792), the princes of the empire themselves carved up the old order in their *Reichsdeputations-hauptschluss* (1803). The emperor, Francis II, anticipating the final dissolution made himself Emperor of Austria as Francis I (1804) and on 6th August 1806 he issued the proclamation dissolving the Holy Roman Empire. The over three hundred and fifty principalities were reduced to over thirty large and medium-sized states. In a way Germany had split into three parts: the Austrian empire, most of which was non-German; the kingdom of Prussia; and the rest, the middle-sized states which Napoleon organized in the Confederation of the Rhine, handing out royal crowns to Saxony, Bavaria and Württemberg in the process. In 1815 the electorate of Hanover also became a kingdom.

The more than twenty years between the outbreak of the French Revolution and the fall of Napoleon left an indelible mark on the Germans. The age of absolutism and of dynastic states was over; the new ideas of liberalism and nationalism filled many Germans with an enthusiasm for something new: a liberal, powerful nation state of their own. But the past would not die and the future could not be born. The painful age of nationalism was ushered in amongst the ruins of Napoleon's empire but at first appeared to be stillborn. The two old dynastic great powers of the Holy Roman Empire survived and the new middle-sized kingdoms and grand-duchies were equally happy to continue the old system. The restoration in 1815 produced the German Confederation as a mirror image of the old empire without an emperor. It survived the great liberal and national revolution of 1848–9 but ceased to exist when Prussia became willing to assume the supremacy in Germany after the exclusion of the Danubian Monarchy of the Habsburgs (1866). The earlier customs union of most states of Germany except Austria (1834) and the North German Confederation (1866–71) were milestones on the way to the creation of the Prussian-dominated Second Reich, proclaimed at Versailles on 18th January 1871. Prussia had become the foremost German state in 1815 when it gave up the larger part of its purely Polish territory and received the Rhine Province and Westphalia. After acquiring Schleswig-

Holstein, Hanover, Hesse-Kassel, Nassau and Frankfurt in 1866 it had become considerably more than half of Germany. The four south German states of Hesse-Darmstadt, Baden, Württemberg and Bavaria were militarily closely allied to Prussia. Prussia's advance did, however, lead to a secession of one of the territories of the German Confederation and of the former Holy Roman Empire. In 1867 the Grand Duchy of Luxemburg, since 1815 part of the Kingdom of the Netherlands although remaining in the German Confederation, was neutralized by an agreement between the powers, and its Prussian garrison was withdrawn. In this way Luxemburg became one of the independent states of Europe.

Unlike Prussia, Austria could not grow into a 'national' role. The Habsburg Monarchy was the very antithesis of a national state. If the national empire, dreamed-of and hoped-for by the German nationalists, was to be founded on a basis which they called *grossdeutsch*, the Habsburg Monarchy had to be destroyed. Prussia, under Bismarck, chose the *kleindeutsch* solution and preferred to preserve and support the Danubian Monarchy. Both the principle of German nationalism, embodied in the Second Empire, and of German (Austrian) domination over the smaller central European nations (Czechs, Slovaks, Poles, Slovenes, Croats, Serbs, Rumanians) appeared to be satisfied – even if the domination had to be shared with the Hungarians. The Bismarckian solution proved untenable in the long run. It meant that the nationalistic strivings of some were pandered to but those of others frustrated. In 1910 Austria-Hungary had a population of 48·8 million. Only 23·5 per cent were Germans and 19·5 per cent were Hungarians, the majority were subject races, mainly Slavs. The German Austrians as Germans looked to Germany and never became a nation of their own which could have dealt on equal terms with the other nationalities in the Monarchy. They regarded themselves at the same time both as the leading nationality and as a threatened minority. When the Bismarckian solution broke down and the Austro-Hungarian Monarchy collapsed in 1918 the Germans hoped for the delayed *grossdeutsch* solution. It was denied them in 1918 but they got it in 1938. Nationalism and domination had by then entered the most nakedly brutal alliance of all times. The deliberately launched attack on the Slav world ended in 1945 in conditions which are reminiscent neither of the *grossdeutsch* nor of the *kleindeutsch* solutions. The territory of the Holy Roman Empire is now split into three German states all of which may eventually develop a sense of separate nationhood. Austria has probably already done so. A large part of the former territory is no longer German. Territorial losses, the like of which the feeble Holy Roman Empire never remotely endured, thus resulted from the policy of the most powerful *Machtstaat* the Germans ever developed in their history.

The age of the absolutism of the old Holy Roman Empire and the age of the nationalism of the Second Empire and of the infamous Third Empire are also profoundly different from each other in other respects: the former was predominantly a world of peasants and artisans moving at best at the pace of a horse with an overwhelming proportion of the population living on the land; the latter became a world of factory workers and scientists moving by train, steamer, motor car and aeroplane, living predominantly in conurbations. Whereas the wars of the old empire had been fought by mercenary armies, the French Revolution called into being citizen armies based on general conscription. While the first great efflorescence of German literature and philosophy straddled the last decades of the Holy Roman Empire and the first decades after 1800, the greatest creative phase of the German universities in humanist scholarship and scientific research alike, filled the first half of the nineteenth century. Prussia was the first country to introduce universal state education (1809). The first half of the nineteenth century saw the elimination of illiteracy in Germany. After about 1870 the gradual mechanization of every aspect of life and the industrialization of production brought about changes in society compared with which the great social upheavals of past centuries appear insignificant. Whereas an educated man of former centuries could be familiar with most of the vocabulary of his language, modern man can know only a fragment. In every great modern European language the lexicon of technical registers comprises hundreds of thousands of words. That of the general language with which every educated individual can be deemed to be conversant is to be measured in tens of thousands of words. Whereas in former ages linguistic dissemination depended on speech from man to man or on the written or printed rendering of language, the modern age can electronically reproduce, transmit and store the spoken word. Language in its regional and social manifestations dates from before these inventions. Their full impact cannot possibly be gauged yet.

In size of population, too, the two phases are markedly different. In 1800 the Germans numbered about twenty-seven million. This is not significantly greater than the population figure for the years immediately before the Thirty Years War. But by 1848 there were already forty million Germans, at the time of the foundation of the Second Empire (1871) over fifty million and in 1939 there were eighty million. At the end of 1971 there were over ninety million native speakers of German in the five states in which German is the national language or one of the official state languages: the Federal Republic of Germany (61·5m.), the German Democratic Republic (17m.), Austria (7·4m.), Switzerland and Liechtenstein (4·1m.), Luxemburg (300,000). In Alsace and Lorraine, where standard German has no official recognition, about 1½ million inhabitants speak German dialects. In Italy where German is recognized as a minority language in South Tyrol there are a quarter of a million German speakers. In Belgium German is also recognized as a minority language in the region of Eupen and Malmédy and there are about 75,000 speakers of German. There are also a small number in Denmark (25,000). By far the largest eastern German enclaves are in Rumania (Banat: 173,000, Transylvania: 195,000, Bukarest, Sathmar, Bukovina, etc.) totalling about 400,000 German speakers. In Rumania, too, German enjoys an officially recognized status. There are perhaps about 300,000 native German speakers in Hungary. In other eastern countries, such as Poland, Czechoslovakia, Yugoslavia and the Soviet Union, speakers of German must be assumed to be a rapidly dwindling population, although for the Soviet Union estimates of as many as two million German speakers have been made. In overseas countries, e.g. Brazil, Argentina, the United States, Canada and Australia, German immigrants have often maintained their mother tongue for many generations, although most are also speakers of the respective national language. On the whole assimilation is more rapid in English-speaking countries than elsewhere.

Perhaps, the history of the last hundred years has at last swept away the dreadful confusion between language and nationality. Nationhood is primarily an historical, political and cultural entity. Language is basically a means of communication. Of course, in so far as communication is likely to be liveliest within the confines of a nation and in so far as a feeling of common nationality is most likely to grow up within an area of intense communication, the two concepts do to some extent overlap. But to attempt a forceful merger of the two is tantamount to succumbing to the fallacy of the identity of the two concepts. Not even in the case of France, the oldest nation-state in Europe, are nation and language identical. French is spoken also in Belgium, Switzerland and Italy in territories adjacent to France. English is the native medium of communication of at least seven sovereign independent nations. There is no reason to think that German as a language will not continue to flourish after it is at last liberated from the unholy confusion between the concepts of nation and language.

7.1.2 | The linguistic territory

The western and southern linguistic boundaries of German have remained virtually static throughout the New High German period down to the present day. The political changes have, however, affected the standing of German, especially the position of the standard language which is, after all, rather distinct and remote from the dialects spoken along the border regions. When the Second or Hohenzollern Empire annexed Alsace and a part of Lorraine in 1871, its main justification was historical and linguistic. But although the linguistic boundary had not altered since the middle of the seventeenth century when these territories had become part of France, the national sentiment had. The stirring events of the French Revolution and of the Napoleonic era had made the population, at least the educated and vocal classes, French in spirit. Forty years of *Reichsland* status did not change this. The second, if brief, German annexation during the Second World War, caused a reaction which has led to the anomalous position that the German standard language has no status except that of a foreign language even in the German-dialect-speaking regions. The only official language tolerated throughout Alsace-Lorraine is French. Although the immigration of French-speaking workers into some industrialized districts, e.g. Mulhouse, has created areas of mixed populations with different mother tongues, the linguistic boundary as such has remained unaffected.

When the old Grand Duchy of Luxemburg was divided between the German-speaking part (*quartier allemand*) and the predominantly French-speaking part (*quartier wallon*) which was given to

Belgium, a small strip of German-speaking territory around Arel (German) or Arlon (French) found itself incorporated in the French-speaking Belgian province of Luxembourg. Its official language is French, and German has on the whole declined in the last century. In the formerly German territory of Eupen and Malmédy, ceded to Belgium after the First World War, German is recognized as one of the official languages. The independent Grand Duchy of Luxemburg accords to both French and German the status of official languages. Although by outward appearance (public and commercial signs) the country gives the impression of being French-speaking, the population is still completely German-dialect-speaking.

In Switzerland the Franco-German linguistic boundary has altered only in minor details. The biggest change is perhaps that the formerly German-speaking border town of *Biel* (German) or *Bienne* (French) is now bilingual chiefly on account of the immigration of French-speaking watchmakers and other industrial workers. In general, however, the permanence and inviolability of the linguistic territory became accepted as the principles of Swiss national life and this has ensured complete linguistic peace. In Switzerland language thus adheres to territory and not to people, which is the very opposite of what was the case in eastern Europe with such unhappy consequences (see pp. 481–3). Rheto-Romance in the Swiss canton of Grisons has, however, been under great pressure chiefly for social and economic reasons. Practically the whole population of nearly 50,000 is now bilingual (Rheto-Romance and German); along the boundary some villages have changed to German; German enclaves have formed on account of tourism (e.g. St Moritz, Flims), and many villages especially those with industry now have a mixed population. In 1938 Rheto-Romance was declared Switzerland's fourth national language and many Germanized place-names were again given their ancient Romance forms, e.g. *Samaden > Samedan, Schuls > Scuol*. This step together with the activity of the cultural leagues for the defence of Rheto-Romance have led to a stabilization of the language situation.

Along the Italian–German boundary many of the isolated German-speaking communities have become Italianized in the last hundred years. After the First World War Italy received the German-speaking South Tyrol. Although the status of German was under attack during the Fascist era and although Italian immigration into the valleys was encouraged, the actual boundary changed little. German now enjoys the status of an official language in the autonomous region of the Trentino.

The Slovene–German boundary in the Austrian provinces of Styria and Carinthia moved slowly and only little southwards during the eighteenth and nineteenth centuries. With the creation of the Yugoslav state, the linguistic boundary has tended to move towards the national frontier.

The northern boundary of German between it and Danish has, in the last thousand years, moved about forty miles northwards from the river Eider to the Flensburg Fjord. In the eighteenth century the city of Schleswig was still mixed and the countryside predominantly Danish. In 1864 the duchies of Schleswig and Holstein were detached from Denmark, but after the First World War the national frontier was moved south, roughly to the linguistic boundary. In western Schleswig German has, over the last century, also gained ground against Frisian, so that Frisian is now almost confined to the islands off the coast.

All these changes along the western, southern and northern boundaries fade into insignificance compared with what happened on the eastern frontier of German. There the events during the New High German period can be divided into three phases. In the first phase, extending to the end of the seventeenth century, the German migration to the east continued largely on an individual basis. The cities of the old territory, hardly increasing between the middle of the sixteenth and the eighteenth centuries, failed to attract the surplus rural population. On the other hand there was much empty and deserted land along the eastern frontier which was attractive to land-hungry peasants. Industrial possibilities in the Bohemian forest and mountain areas drew miners, glass workers and other artisans from the stagnating cities in the west. In two places at least the area of German settlement was pushed eastward: in eastern Brandenburg (Neumark) and Pomerania, and in Bohemia. In Bohemia German had been readmitted as an official language beside Czech by the Habsburg rulers as early as 1627. German immigrants now fanned out from the Bohemian border regions adding considerably to the already existing German settlements. Towns like Pilsen became partly German, while others like Saaz, Neumarkt and Leitmeritz became entirely German. By about

1700 the linguistic boundary as it existed in the nineteenth century was reached.

The second phase was the immediate result of the dynastic and political eastward expansion of Brandenburg and Austria. The former's new acquisition, the Duchy of Prussia (geographically East Prussia), was thinly populated. The rulers of Brandenburg therefore launched a policy of deliberate settlement by attracting immigrants from all parts. After 1685 over twenty thousand French Huguenots settled in Brandenburg and Prussia. German and other refugees from religious persecution and from the devastation of the French wars swelled the waves of immigrants. The Protestant Salzburgers, evicted in 1732 by their bishop, were welcomed in East Prussia. Germanization was not the aim of this state-directed immigration. Enlightened absolutist monarchs simply recognized the financial and military advantages of what was at that time called *Peuplierung*. Between 1713 and 1740 the population of East Prussia rose by a quarter mainly on account of immigration. In Silesia Frederick II promoted drainage schemes, the clearing of woodlands and the establishment of ironworks. Everywhere in this colonization and amelioration not only Germans took part but also Czechs and Poles, in southern East Prussia above all Masurians, who as Lutherans became loyal subjects of Prussia. After the partitions of Poland, West Prussia and the province of Posen or Poznań also received immigrants. The Ermland, surrounded by East Prussian territory, was most extensively Germanized while the other formerly Polish provinces became mixed.

Austria began its eastward march after 1683, the year of the last Turkish siege of Vienna. But while the Prussian effort of colonization had led to a considerable increase of the compact German linguistic territory, even if it was rather scattered in the Polish provinces, Habsburg colonization was more distant. German settlers were directed to depopulated yet strategically important parts of Hungary as it was reconquered from the Turks. The main regions were the area known as Swabian Turkey, i.e. the hilly region between the Danube and the Drava near Fünfkirchen (now Pécs); the Bakony Wald (Hungarian Bakonyerdo) west of Budapest; the Bacska between the Danube and the Theiss (Tisa); further east the region known as Banat with the city of Temesvár (Hungarian), now Timisoara (Rumanian); Sathmar in the north-west of Hungary, now in Rumania (Satu Mare); and Bukovina with its capital Czernowitz in north-eastern Rumania and the south-western Ukraine. The settlers in Hungary were generally called 'Swabians' while the much earlier German immigrants in Transylvania were known as 'Siebenbürger Sachsen'. Habsburg colonization neither attempted to establish nor unintentionally succeeded in establishing large, compact, secure areas of German settlement. In 1784 Emperor Joseph II nevertheless decreed German to be the sole official state language in all his eastern territories.

The third eastern power to embark upon a deliberate policy of colonization and immigration was Russia after 1762, the year of the accession to the throne of Catherine II. She also attracted Germans, especially to the region of Saratov on the Volga and to the vicinity of St Petersburg. These distant settlements only increased the number of isolated German colonies. Just as state-directed colonization had started last in Russia, it also continued longest there. Prussia abandoned its policy in the Napoleonic wars, Austria at the time of the 1848 revolution, and Russia as late as 1870 (South Russia, Volhynia). It was thus the policy of these three multinational dynastic and absolutist states which was responsible for the mixture of populations so characteristic of the eastern Europe of before the Second World War and which appeared such an affront and a nightmare to the nationalists of the nineteenth and twentieth centuries.

We thus reach the third phase of the history of the eastern boundary of German within the New High German period. After the spontaneous eastward drift of German settlers and the state-directed colonization came the reaction of the age of nationalism in the nineteenth and twentieth centuries. The first eastern Germans to come under pressure were the German Balts. The Russian government pursued a policy of Russianization in the second half of the nineteenth century, which many Germans countered by emigrating. Riga, where in 1867 43 per cent of the citizens spoke German, had only 13·8 per cent German-speaking inhabitants in 1913. Where Germany and Austria held sway the conflict of nationalities was influenced in favour of German. Even so, in 1882 the oldest university of the old empire, the Caroline University of Prague, had to be divided into German and Czech universities. In many linguistically mixed parts of Bohemia Czech was again advancing. Under Bismarck the Prussian government pursued a policy of Germanization in the Polish provinces. In 1872/73 German became the sole language of state education and after 1876 the only official language. In 1886 a deliberate policy of attracting German peasant settlers was inaugurated; but although about 130,000 were given land and farms, emigration to the west far exceeded this gain. The policy of the nationalistic *Deutscher Ostmarkenverein* was countered by Polish aspirations. Repression only incited resistance and instilled hatred in the oppressed nationality. A higher birthrate of the Slavs and the large-scale emigration of German agricultural labourers to the industrialized regions of western Germany from 1850 onwards enhanced the national apprehensions of the Germans. America, too, appeared a haven to all nationalities in the eastern lands riven by national conflicts and oppressed by Prussian Junkers and bureaucrats or Czarist rulers. National self-determination finally became the slogan in an atmosphere where nationality and language tended to become identified. In some areas old-fashioned state loyalty resisted this new polarization. The Kashubs in Pomerelia and the Masurians in southern East Prussia did not easily identify with their fellow Slavs, the Poles.

After the First World War, which arose to a large extent from the fear and antagonism felt by Germans and Slavs for each other, the principle of national self-determination was meant to bring a solution to the national entanglements and a rectification of the injustice of the Polish partitions. It was, however, not easy to apply, as it conflicted with too many geographical and historical factors, and as it ran counter to many national emotions and aspirations. The master and servant of yesterday were not able just to settle down in harmony as equals.

In Pomerelia Kashubs and Poles together had a slight majority, hence Pomerelia was given to Poland under the Versailles Treaty. Most of the province of West Prussia and of the province of Posen (Poznań), where the Poles were in the majority, was also allotted to Poland, but German Danzig was made into a Free City under the League of Nations. The Memelland with a predominantly German population came under Lithuanian sovereignty. In parts of East Prussia and West Prussia and in Upper Silesia plebiscites were held. In East and West Prussia the population voted for Germany with many Slavs confounding the theory of the identity of nationality and language. The eastern part of Upper Silesia with a slight Polish majority was given to Poland. Nearly three-quarters of a million Germans left their homelands ceded to Poland and Lithuania. Whereas before the war large numbers of Poles were under German domination, the reverse was true after the war although to a lesser extent. In 1939 there would appear to have been nearly a million monolingual German-speakers in Poland.

In the case of Bohemia the geographical principle prevailed. The historical frontiers along the mountain ranges remained and in consequence three and a half million German-speaking Bohemians were included in the Czechoslovak Republic.

Nationalism became even more virulent when the principle of self-determination had not really brought about a satisfactory solution. Where populations were intermingled as they were in many parts of eastern Europe, no nationalistic solution was in fact possible. Finally, the Second World War came, which was the most brutal aggression against the Slav peoples. At its conclusion German eastern colonization was reversed and territories which had been German-speaking for six hundred years passed into Slav hands. Even during the war the Nazis resettled nearly 900,000 so-called *Volksdeutsche* or ethnic Germans from distant enclaves (Ukraine, Dobruja, Bessarabia, Bukovina, Volhynia, the Gottschee in Yugoslavia and the Baltic States) mainly in western Poland in an attempt to Germanize it. At the end of the war the boundary between Poland and Germany was drawn along the Oder–Neisse line and the old Bohemian frontier was restored. All Germans living east of this new line were evicted if they had not already fled. East Germany west of the 1937 frontiers and east of the Oder-Neisse line had about nine million inhabitants, and Bohemia and Moravia about three and a half million Germans. Nearly all German enclaves in eastern countries, except for those in Rumania, had also been eliminated, either on account of Hitler's resettlement policy or through expulsion. The international standing of German was no less severely affected. For several hundred years throughout eastern Europe German had served as a kind of *lingua franca* and latterly as the first foreign language of education and science. Of this status German was deprived after 1945, having already been weakened in 1918. It is too early to speculate on any likely recovery in present conditions.

German emigration overseas has nowhere led to a firm and secure enlargement of the German linguistic territory. The longest estab-

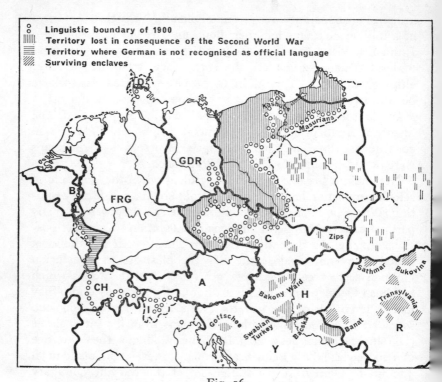

Fig. 16

The territory of the Modern German Language

B	Belgium (area of Eupen)	FRG	Federal Republic of
L	Luxemburg		Germany
F	France (Alsace and parts	GDR	German Democratic
	of Lorraine)		Republic
CH	Switzerland	D	Denmark (part of North
I	Italy (South Tyrol)		Schleswig)
A	Austria	R	Rumania (Banat, Transylvania,
			Sathmar, Bukovina, etc.)

lished linguistic colony is that formed by the emigration to Pennsylvania of people from the Palatinate and other south-western regions after 1683. Although Pennsylvania German or Pennsylvania Dutch, as the German dialect of the colonists is often called, flourished for over two centuries, the speakers have more and more changed to English which functions as the written standard language, and its territory has shrunk. Other isolated, Mennonite and Hutterite settlements in North America (see p. 345), tend to

be small. In the former German colony of South West Africa a few
thousand settlers still use their mother tongue.

As we have seen, the number of the native speakers of German
has continued to rise so that German has still by far the largest
community of speakers in Europe apart from Russian. The
territory of the German language, however, has suffered a contraction which surpasses anything that has happened to other major
European languages.

7.2 | The creation of the Classical Literary Language

7.2.1 | The language problem

The advances in use and in esteem which the German
language experienced in the decades of the Reformation gradually
came to a halt before the swelling tide of the Counter-Reformation.
In Catholic Germany education returned to Latin with renewed
zeal and in Protestant Germany the grammar schools and the
universities also maintained Latin as the chief medium of learning.
In book production German books for the first time outnumbered
Latin books in 1681, but it was not till after 1692 that German was
finally dominant. In 1740 over one quarter of all books published
in Germany were still in Latin. Only in the second half of the
eighteenth century did the Latin book enter the phase of its rapid
decline: 1754 one quarter, 1759 one fifth, 1781 one eighth, 1787
one tenth,1799 one twentieth. The advance of German was tied to
the various disciplines and individual writers. In philosophy, jurisprudence and theology Latin maintained a particularly strong position. The universities had lost much of the vigour that they had
displayed in the sixteenth century and it was not until new universities were founded (Halle in 1694, Göttingen in 1737) that
universities were once more in the vanguard of cultural development. When, for the autumn term 1687, the philosopher Christian
Thomasius announced in German a lecture course in German at

the University of Leipzig he caused such a stir that his own position became untenable in the long run. It was the new university of Halle which offered him scope for his promotion of German. By 1711, we are told, most Halle professors lectured in German, and Latin was practically ousted. At about the same time another Halle philosopher, Christian Wolff, began to write in German and it was he who did more than anybody else to equip German with a philosophical and mathematical terminology. In many cases it was more a matter of confirmation by use and sharper definition of terms which had been used earlier (see pp. 453, 455), than of actual invention of completely new expressions.

It was not only the position of Latin which caused German to stagnate in the seventeenth century. In south German courts, above all at the imperial court in Vienna, Spanish and Italian influences became very strong. This happened at a time when the most widely current form of Common German, its East Central variant, was suspect as a 'Protestant dialect'. The Protestant principalities, often relying on French support, were open to French cultural penetration like the rest of Germany. As early as 1663 the elector of Brandenburg had a treaty drawn up in French as well as in Latin. International conventions which had universally been composed in Latin, began more and more, during the reign of Louis XIV, to be in French. At the negotiations for the Treaty of Utrecht in 1714 the diplomats of the Holy Roman Empire employed the French language in their agreement with France, and from then on French was established as the language of diplomacy. The cultural ascendancy of France was at its zenith. As the vehicle of a much admired classical literature French became the medium of German princes and courtiers and finally even of the urban patriciate. The *A la mode* period even captivated the austere, anti-French soldier king Frederick William I of Prussia who generally conversed in French with his wife. His son, Frederick II, the enlightened despot and philosopher, was even more completely Frenchified. He not only wrote all his own works (*Histoire de mon temps*; *Histoire de la guerre de sept ans*; etc.) in French, but also turned the Prussian Academy of Sciences, among whose original aims had been the cultivation of the German language, into the *Académie des sciences et belles lettres* with the French philosopher Maupertuis as its president. Naturally its publications were in French. Frederick II's association with Voltaire is well known, as is Voltaire's comment on the Prussian court: 'Je me trouve ici en France. On ne parle que notre langue. L'allemand est pour les soldats et pour les chevaux; il n'est nécessaire que pour la route' (1750, in a letter to the Marquis de Thibouville). In such a cultural climate it is not surprising that ten per cent of all books published in Germany between 1750 and 1780 were in French. Nor is it surprising that the further unification of German into a written standard language was retarded compared with other major European languages. As long as culture was predominantly aristocratic and concentrated in the courts, too many members of the influential *élite* were lost to German. Although German was used in most of the creative writing of the time, it failed to win wide acclaim. And when taste changed from the convoluted Baroque of the seventeenth century to the sober classicism of the Enlightenment, it was France once more and French literature which set the pace. German writing lagged behind, and thus acquired the reputation among the cultured of being barbarous. Frederick II's harsh and negative judgment in his *De la littérature allemande*, of 1780, was a late and, in fact, already outdated expression of that prejudice.

The linguistic situation of Germany in the seventeenth century and the first half of the eighteenth century was by and large that Latin functioned as the language of learning, French as the language of society and German as the language of literature. It is symptomatic that Germany's greatest thinker of the age, Gottfried Wilhelm Leibniz (1646–1716), wrote nearly all his works in Latin or French. That he nevertheless advocated the use of German by German scholars for works of scholarship may seem paradoxical. But this fact reflects both the prevailing cultural situation and the aspirations of many thinking men. The position of French in French culture, of Dutch in the Netherlands, and of English, Spanish and Italian in their respective countries was envied. Many voices expressed anguish at the sad state in which German found itself. It suffered in their opinion both from the cultural dominance of Latin and the Romance languages and from what appeared to many purists as iniquitous linguistic penetration. The profound internal divisions of German society and its body politic prevented advance in the direction of greater standardization. For a century and a half German writers, educationalists and grammarians, as well as well-meaning patriots and lovers of their mother tongue, felt themselves to be on the defensive. Many wrote plaintively and often at the same time assertively about what appeared to them to be the sorry and undeserved state of the German language. Their *uralte Haupt- und Heldensprache*, they claimed stridently, merited a better fate. It was an 'original' language descended in direct line from the language confusion of Babel. Although the greater antiquity and priority of Hebrew as the language of God was generally conceded, it was German which came next in venerability. Stemming from Japheth himself, it was the direct development out of the original European language called *Celtisch*. Unlike German, which was a pure descendant of this original language, Greek and Latin, so it was claimed, were not unadulterated. In nearly all European languages roots deriving from German were to be seen, hence precedence belonged to German.

Justus Georgius Schottelius (1612–76), the most important German grammarian and linguist of the seventeenth century, begins his *Ausführliche Arbeit von der Teutschen HaubtSprache*, Brunswick, 1663, with ten eulogies (*Lobreden von der Uhralten Teutschen HauptSprache*) in which he quotes many of the apposite assertions of his predecessors to paint a grandiloquent picture of the eminence of German. Likewise, the unknown author of the first English grammar of German offers his readers such an anthology: 'The Prolegomena doe here comprehend (in lieu of a Preface) some Testimonies of several great and learned Men concerning the Knowledge of Languages in general, and particularly of the Excellency of the Highdutch most Copious and Significant, Majestick and Sweet, Perfect and Pure, Easie and Usefull, Antient and Universal Toung.' In all probability the author of *The Highdutch Minerva A-la-Mode or A Perfect Grammar never extant before, whereby the English may both easily and exactly learne the Neatest Dialect of the German Mother-Language used throughout all Europe*, London, 1680, was inspired by Schottelius. These are Schottelius' own words with which he describes the proud position of German among languages:

Es haben unsere uhralte Teutsche Vorfahren eiferig in acht genommen jhre Muttersprache / dieselbe frey und reinlich gebraucht / behalten / und jhre Kinder gelehrt / mit nichten (wie etzliche *Critici* treumen und alfentzen) von jhren Feinden jhre Rede erbettelt: Sondern vielmehr haben alle Europeische Sprachen viele Wůrtzelen / Wŏrter / Saft / Kraft und Geist aus dieser reinen uhralten Haubtsprache der Teutschen. (p. 123)

... die Teutsche Sprache, welche die *Teutones*, so lange her-
nach *Germani* genant / gebrauchet / als der vornemste *Dialectus* von der
alten Celtischen oder Japhetischen Sprache / und also eine rechte /
echte / wolsprechende Tochter der Ertzmutter, die jhren Anfang und
Geburt von Gott selbst bey dem Babilonischen Turme ůberkommen
... (p. 151/2)

Such protestations were often born of frustration and dis-
appointment with the reality of the situation. Individuals and
learned societies which came into being in the seventeenth century
strove to create a better climate for German and to achieve that
degree of standardization which they believed their language
needed. As early as 1617 the *Fruchtbringende Gesellschaft* was
founded at Weimar. Its aim was the preservation and furtherance
of the German language, as well as the cultivation of 'virtue', or as
Prince Ludwig von Anhalt-Köthen, one of its founder members
and its first president, expressed it in his *Kurtzer Bericht der
Fruchtbringenden Gesellschaft Zweck und Vorhaben*, Köthen, 1622:

... daß man die Hochdeutsche Sprache in jhren rechten wesen und
standt / ohne einmischung frembder außlåndischer wort / auffs mög-
lichste und thunlichste erhalte / und sich so wohl der besten auß-
sprache im reden / alß der reinesten art im schreiben und Reimen-
dichten befleißigen.

Sprachgesellschaften, mainly in imitation of the *Fruchtbringende
Gesellschaft*, sprang up in a number of places: the *Aufrichtige
Tannengesellschaft*, 1633, in Strasbourg was concerned mainly with
the problem of spelling; the *Deutschgesinnete Genossenschaft*, 1642,
in Hamburg was founded by Philipp von Zesen, who was given to
an exaggerated purism; the *Pegnesischer Blumenorden* was set up
by Georg Philipp Harsdörffer and Johann Klaj in Nuremberg in
1644; the *Elbschwanenorden* in Lübeck followed in 1658. There
were several others, some of which were more interested in poetics
and rhetoric than in language. Many were shortlived. Their importance should not be exaggerated. Throughout the seventeenth
century writers paid tribute, however, to the *Fruchtbringende
Gesellschaft*, including the unknown author of the *Highdutch
Minerva*, mentioned above, who referred to a list of foreign words
to be shunned which had been assembled by 'the fructifying
Society, whose most illustrious Head and Patron resides in High-
Saxony at Hall the very Athens of the most refined Wits and

language' (p. 35). It was modelled on the Florentine *Accademia della Crusca*, founded in 1582, of which Prince Ludwig von Anhalt-Köthen became a member in 1600. Although it never achieved the great German dictionary in imitation of the Italian academy's *Vocabulario degli Accademii della Crusca*, Venice, 1612, one of its eminent members, Justus Georgius Schottelius, produced the first grammar of German, unsurpassed for almost a century. Christian Gueintz's *Deutsche Rechtschreibung*, 1645, emerged from discussions in the society: 'Von der Fruchtbringenden Gesellschaft übersehen', as the title page indicates. Many translations were inspired or encouraged by the activities of the *Sprachgesellschaften*. Apart from several eminent aristocratic members the *Fruchtbringende Gesellschaft* included many of the leading writers of the age, for example, Andreas Gryphius, Georg Philipp Harsdörffer, Friedrich von Logau, Sigmund von Birken, Johann Michael Moscherosch, Martin Opitz and Philipp von Zesen.

Their sentiments are effectively summarized by Sigmund von Birken (1669):

Jeztbenannte helden und Edle Geister / haben / nach dem vorsatze allerlöblichst- gedachter Fruchtbringenden Gesellschaft / ihre Schriften in unserer Teutschen Haupt = und Helden-Sprache / verfasset: hierinn dem fürbilde / nicht allein der alten Griechen und Römer / sondern auch der heutigen Italiäner / Franzosen und anderer Nationen nachahmend / welche ihren Kunstfleiß zu ausübung und aufname ihrer Muttersprache / und nicht frömder sprachen / anzuwenden pflegen. Es ist an sich selbst lächerlich / daß wir Teutsche mit grossem unkosten / frömde Sprachen zu erlernen / ausreisen / und unsere eigene edle Sprache zu haus verunachtsamen: da doch die Frömden uns diese Ehre hinwiederum nicht anthun / und wird man nicht allein keinen Wälschen oder Franzosen / an stat seiner Muttersprache / teutsch reden hören / sondern auch ihrer keiner wird mit sich anderst / als in selbiger seiner Sprache / reden lassen / oder eher eine dritte Sprache / wie in Gesandschaften zu geschehen pfleget / hierzu erwehlen. Thun nun diß die Frömden / mit ihren unvollkommenen Strümpel-Sprachen: was hat dann unsere Teutsche Sprache / die doch eine Welthaupt=Sprache ist / und von Babel mit ausgegangen / verschuldet / daß wir sie zum Pöbel verbannen / und lieber den Frömden nachparlen? Und wird dannenhero auch billich dem Irrwahn etlicher Schul-gelehrten in Teutschland widersprochen / die dem Teutschen Sprach=fleiß / und auch-gute Teutsche Schrifften / allein darum verachten / weil sie nicht in Latein geschrieben sind.

We have already seen how the efforts of men like Thomasius, Wolff and Schottelius, and of influential members of *Sprachgesellschaften* advanced the cause of German during the seventeenth and in the early decades of the eighteenth century. In the middle of the eighteenth century the indefatigable activities of Gottsched not only helped to spread the newly-fashioned elegant medium of standard German itself, but thus also provided the patriotic, again self-confident bourgeoisie with an alternative to French. He maintained that German was superior to French, Italian or English because it was not the result of the mingling of the languages of several peoples, thus echoing the nationalistic claims of Schottelius and his seventeenth-century contemporaries. Both bourgeoisie and aristocracy had learnt to appreciate the ideal of a normalized standard language albeit in a foreign language. Gottsched now offered them the same in German. In the 1780s, we are told by the *Berlinische Monatsschrift*, German had won the upper hand in Berlin society. *Der alte Fritz* had become an anachronism in his own lifetime. The establishment of German at the expense of the foreign languages, Latin and French, was however only one of the problems. It was purely external. There were also very serious internal problems.

Let us now examine in greater detail the internal problems confronting those concerned with the German language. For this purpose we may well start with an assessment of the situation given by Martin Opitz in his *Buch von der Deutschen Poeterey*, Breslau, 1624 (Chapter VI, p. E^r):

Die ziehrligkeit erfodert das die worte reine vnd deutlich sein. Damit wir aber reine reden mögen / sollen wir vns befleissen deme welches wir Hochdeutsch nennen besten vermögens nach zue kommen / vnd nicht derer örter sprache / wo falsch geredet wird / in vnsere schrifften vermischen: als da sind / *es geschach* / für / *es geschahe* / *er sach* / für / *er sahe*; *sie han* / für *sie haben* vnd anderes mehr: welches dem reime auch bißweilen außhelffen sol; als:

> *Der darff nicht sorgen für den spot /*
> *Der einen schaden krieget hot.*

So stehet es auch zum hefftigsten vnsauber / wenn allerley Lateinische / Frantzösische / Spanische vnnd Welsche wörter in den text vnserer rede geflickt werden; als wenn ich wolte sagen:

> Nemt an die *courtoisie*, vnd die *deuotion*,
> Die euch ein *cheualier*, *madonna* / thut erzeigen;

Ein handvol von *fauor petirt* er nur zue lohn /
Vnd bleibet ewer Knecht vnd *seruiteur* gantz eigen.

Wie seltzam dieses nun klinget / so ist nichts desto weniger die
thorheit innerhalb kurtzen Jharen so eingeriessen / das ein jeder / der
nur drey oder vier außländische wörter / die er zum öffteren nicht
verstehet / erwuscht hat / bey aller gelegenheit sich bemühet dieselben
herauß zue werffen / . . .

We note that there are two problems which occupy Opitz. First,
there is the problem of a norm or the question of what is standard
German; secondly, there is the problem of undigested foreign
intrusions in the German of the time, or the question of 'purity'
of language.

7.2.2 | What is High German?

The Common German of the early sixteenth century was
a convergent, yet unstandardized written language realized in
regional variants. This state of affairs became more and more unacceptable in the seventeenth and eighteenth centuries. For one
thing, French was much more normalized and thus offered an
example to be imitated. In fact, German had to achieve a similar
standardization if it was effectively to compete with French as the
medium of polite society in Germany. Deliberate attempts at
standardization in the Netherlands were also known to German
linguists and writers. Christian Thomasius pointed to the French
model in his pamphlet: *Welcher Gestalt man denen Frantzosen in
gemeinem Leben und Wandel nachahmen solle?* (1687). He admired
the way the French used their vernacular as the language of
scholarship, but he thought German was as yet deficient. Later he
and Wolff did much to correct this deficiency.

Leibniz had even earlier (probably in 1683) written his un-
published *Ermahnung an die Teutsche, ihren verstand und sprache
besser zu üben* and followed it about 1697 with his essay *Unvorgreiff-
liche Gedancken, betreffend die Ausübung und Verbesserung der
Teutschen Sprache*, which was published in 1717 by J. G. Eccard.
We note that the plea for the use of German is coupled with the
demand for improvement. Language was for Leibniz *ein Spiegel
des Verstandes*. Clear thinking presupposed a clear language. The
German language, he thought, was already highly developed in all

matters concerned with the five senses, also in the fields of crafts, mining, hunting and seafaring. But in emotional and speculative matters, in morality and the art of government German was still to be developed. This development he did not want to see pursued by fanatical purism but by a sensible compromise. He thought there was great need for a comprehensive dictionary which would include also useful words from the dialects and the related Germanic languages. Of a language he demanded three qualities: *Reichthum*, *Reinigkeit*, and *Glantz*. By the first quality he meant that a language must be self-sufficient in its lexicon, and must possess an abundance of terms so that speakers do not have to resort to paraphrases. French appears deficient to him as it does not possess a single word for German *reiten* or Latin *equitare*. If necessary, words may be introduced from dialects; old words may be resuscitated and foreign terms may be naturalized, and finally neologisms through derivation and composition may be used 'so vermittelst des Urteils und Ansehens wackerer Leute in Schwang gebracht werden müsten' (§ 64). As to naturalization he refers to English, among other relevant cases:

die Englische Sprache hat alles angenommen, und wann jedermann das Seinige abfodern wolte, würde es den Engländern gehen, wie der Esopischen Krähe, da andere Vögel ihre Federn wieder gehohlet. Wir Teutschen haben es weniger vonnöthen als andere, müssen uns aber dieses nützlichen Rechts nicht gäntzlich begeben (§ 68).

We notice that his first principle in nursing German to health and vigour is reasonableness. Language is subject to correction and improvement. Schottelius, too, was of the opinion that German could be developed through effort and instruction. The age of rationalism was optimistic in its search for order, general validity, and clarity.

By the postulate of *Reinigkeit* Leibniz wished to ensure that the language should be 'good German', decent and intelligible. '*Verba obsoleta*', such as Luther's *Schächer* or 'unzeitig angebrachte Verba Provincialia', such as *schmecken* instead of *riechen*, were to be avoided. Foreign words are objected to, as being in many cases unintelligible to many. A further aspect of *Reinigkeit* is regularity and correctness. A grammar should be established to set up rules; too many grammatical features are still unregulated. He mentions the gender of *Urteil*, which is feminine in the imperial Chamber Court but neuter in the Upper Saxon courts.

And finally he defines *Glantz* and *Zierde*. By this he means a cultivated, elegant style, in which respect he highly praises the French. His unified, regularized, decent, intelligible, pleasing (*zierlich*) and clear German was thus also to be written in a new, elegant style. If Leibniz's ideas have been dealt with at some length, it is because his rationalism is so characteristic of the spirit of the age – the spirit that created the linguistic tool which in the hands of writers like Klopstock and Lessing, Goethe and Schiller was to become a truly great literary language.

If grammarians and writers were generally in agreement about the qualities of *Hochdeutsch*, as their ideal was called at that time, there was no such agreement about where *Hochdeutsch* was to be found. Many commentators of the time, especially those from North Germany, claimed that it existed in the language of the best writers. This was, for instance, the opinion of Schottelius and of Johann Bödiker, a Berlin headmaster. In Bödiker's own words: 'Die Hochdeutsche Sprache ist keine Mund-Art eines einigen Volcks oder Nation der Deutschen, sondern auß allen durch Fleiß der Gelahrten zu solcher Zierde erwachsen, und in gantz Deutschland üblich.' Schottelius, too, held that High German was not a dialect, but itself was divided into dialects, such as Meissnisch, Thuringian, Hessian, Franconian, Swabian, Bavarian, Austrian, Silesian, Swiss, etc. (p. 162). It was *Lingua ipsa Germanica* (p. 174). Perhaps the order in which he mentions the dialects is of some significance, for although he rejects any claims of precedence and priority made by people from Meissen, he concedes:

Die rechte Meißnische Ausrede / wie sie zu Leipzig / Merseburg / Wittenberg / Dresden üblich / ist lieblich und wollautend / und hat in vielen Wôrteren das Hochteutsche sich wol daraufgezogen / wie breit und verzogen aber der Meisnische *Dialectus* auf dem Lande und unter den Bauren sey / ist nicht unbewust (p. 159).

He thus makes a clear distinction between Meissen dialect and High German which is supra-regional although its pronunciationis said to be particularly attractive and euphonious in the Upper Saxon cities. The Mecklenburg grammarian Daniel Georg Morhof also said 'die Meissner Außrede ist die zierlichste.'

A similar ambiguity, stressing both the supra-regional and supra-dialectal character of High German and the exemplariness of *Meissnisch*, is also found in the writings of Johann Christoph

Gottsched (1700–66). An East Prussian by birth, his centre of activity was Leipzig. In his *Deutsche Sprachkunst, Nach den Mustern der besten Schriftsteller des vorigen und itzigen Jahrhunderts*, Leipzig, 1748, he declared:

Ganz Ober=und Niederdeutschland hat bereits den Ausspruch gethan: daß das mittellåndische, oder obersåchsische Deutsch, die beste hochdeutsche Mundart sey; indem es dasselbe ûberall, von Bern in der Schweiz, bis nach Reval in Liefland, und von Schleswig bis nach Trident im Tyrol, ja von Brüssel bis Ungarn und Siebenbûrgen, auch im Schreiben nachzuahmen und zu erreichen suchet (5th ed., 1762, p. 69).

To some extent this was propaganda. What he was aiming at was above all the unification and standardization of German. For this purpose High German had to be made free from archaisms and regionalisms. Uniformity, regularity and clarity were to be its characteristics. In so far as High German was supra-regional it was the product of the best writers in the land, in so far as some regional basis was still needed for unification and standardization, Upper Saxony was to provide it. Upper Saxony was the region where a fairly uniform chancery language had emerged relatively early; the Reformation and Luther had enhanced the status of its language; Low Germany when it abandoned its own written medium had adopted the Upper Saxon written variant of Common German; in the seventeenth and eighteenth centuries nearly all the poets and writers hailed from this part of Germany: Opitz, Fleming, Logau, Hofmannswaldau, Lohenstein, Gryphius, Gerhardt, Zesen, Gellert, Weise; so did the philosophers Thomasius and Wolff, and the North German grammarians Schottelius, Bödiker and Morhof wrote in this form of German, the eminence of which was of long standing. It only remained for the East Prussian Gottsched and the Pomeranian Adelung to complete the standardization on this basis.

The Zürich literary critics Bodmer and Breitinger and the Bernese poet Albrecht von Haller acknowledged the supremacy of Meissen when they modelled their language on East Central German and corrected their own form of German on suggestions of East German friends. Bodmer's later rejection of the supremacy of Meissen was occasioned more by questions of style and poetic diction than by the overriding language question. Basically the Enlightenment of the eighteenth century demanded a unified standard language as much as did the Rationalism of the seventeenth.

Other South German writers stressed the supra-regional character of High German. C. F. Aichinger from the Palatinate who often favoured southern forms had to concede that most of the writers employed the eastern variant. The Catholic priest Augustin Dornblüth was anachronistic when he upheld the claims of the South German chancery language of the end of the seventeenth century in his *Observationes* of 1755. The Swabians K. F. Fulda and J. Nast advocated the principles of correctness and purity, which were also Gottsched's principles, while they expressed a forlorn hope when they claimed 'das Hochteütsche ist eigentlich im südlichen Teütschland zu Haus.'

As long as the North Germans regarded High German as an acquired, more or less foreign, language which they had to learn, they found it to be realized in speech nearest to its written form in Upper Saxony. The colloquial speech of upper class society in the Upper Saxon cities was no doubt based, to a large extent, on spelling pronunciation inculcated by the schools. But even so, dialectal features, such as the coalescence of *b/p*, *d/t*, *g/k* and of *i/ü*, *e/ö*, *ei/äu*, *eu* were noticed. The North Germans, too, pronounced High German according to the spelling, but their dialectal background let them avoid those coalescences and they soon began to claim that they had the better pronunciation. In this way it was finally a North German form of pronunciation which became exemplary in the eighteenth century. The German standard language became thus as synthetic in its phonetic form as in phonology, grammar and lexis. Most of the abstract terminology of science and scholarship was formed in the supra-regional written language, although in more homely fields the contribution of East Central Germany remained dominant.

If the move towards uniformity and towards a standard form of High German owed much to Gottsched's activity in the middle of the eighteenth century, the final stage of completion was reached through the efforts of Johann Christoph Adelung (1732–1806) towards the end of the century. He was also the last and most outspoken defender of the supremacy of *Meissnisch*. In volume 1 of his *Umständliches Lehrgebäude der Deutschen Sprache* of 1782 he claimed uncompromisingly that there was no general German language based on the usage of the best writers of all provinces, that there were only dialects and that the dialect of the southern electoral Saxon lands, as spoken by the upper classes, was good and correct High German. In this, of course, he confused the spoken colloquial language with the written literary language. In his opinion High German as a literary medium flourished in the period between 1740 and 1760. His real importance lies, however, in the fact that his works became widely spread and were declared obligatory in the schools of nearly all German regions. The phonology and morphology of Classical Literary German can be said to be based largely on his norms. His dictionary *Versuch eines vollständigen grammatisch-kritischen Wörterbuches der Hochdeutschen Mundart, mit beständiger Vergleichung der übrigen Mundarten, besonders aber der oberdeutschen*, Leipzig, 1774–86, was the first really comprehensive scholarly lexicon of the German language. In his approach he was strictly synchronic and normative, eschewing obsolete or dialectal words. He excluded, for instance, words such as *Abenteuer, Buhle, Degen, Recke, Minne, Wonne.*

What Gottsched and Adelung had achieved was the standardization of written German. In laying down norms also for style and vocabulary they fashioned a harness which their successors cast away again. Their critics gave greater scope to the individual creative writer and left him the freedom to choose or make up words as he wished, be they archaic or dialectal, or his own inventions. Expressiveness became the postulate once unity and standardization had been achieved and were no longer in danger. The standard language was now definitely and definitively supraregional and uniform – uniform in the sense which applies to natural languages, of course, not in the sense of absolute validity which languages of mathematics and logic possess.

7.2.3 | The problem of spelling

Those who claimed that the best pronunciation was that which was based on spelling or that High German should be pronounced as it was spelt, immediately ran into the problem of which was the best spelling. That question was often answered by the advice that people should spell as they speak. The vicious circle was complete. Pronunciation according to spelling presupposed a 'correct spelling' and spelling was to be normalized on the basis of pronunciation. In practice, advance on one front went hand in hand with advance on the other. One was to pro-

nounce *Glück* and not *Glick* because one spelt ⟨Glück⟩ and was not
to spell ⟨Glick⟩. And one spelt ⟨Glück⟩ because of tradition and
because ⟨Glick⟩ was declared to be dialectal and therefore erron-
eous. The principle of phonetic spelling or spelling based on
pronunciation was supplemented by the principle of etymological
or morphological spelling (*Pferd* not *Pferdt, Pfert* because of
Pferdes, Pferde); by the principle of economy; by the tendency to
differentiate between homophones (*Waise – Weise*); and by what
was called *usus scribendi*. It was on this basis that radical spelling
reformers like Philipp von Zesen and Klopstock were rejected.

Philipp von Zesen's spelling was regular but certainly did not
conform to the *usus scribendi*:

Dan der geiz hat alhihr so sehr ůber=hand-genommen / daß auch
ofter=mahls di alten buklichten låute noch bis in ihre gruben hin=ein
dåm gålde tahg' und nacht nahch=trachten / und nicht aufhören / si
fahren dan dahrmit ganz und gahr zur höllen hin=unter (*Adriatische
Rosemund*, Amsterdam, 1645, p. 287)

Klopstock's principles were:

Kein Laut darf mẹr als Ein Zeichen; und kein Zeichen mẹr als Einen
Laut haben. . . . Wir müssen weder ferschwenden, noch geizen. . . .
Bei der Rechtschreibung kan nụr in so fern fon Andeütung der Eti-
mologi di Rede sein, als dise mit der Aus*sprạche* übereinstimt.

It was Adelung's *Vollständige Anweisung zur Deutschen Orthographie* of 1788, being based on the reforms which had evolved
over the previous century and a half and following the moderate
principles mentioned above, which provided the spelling for the
Classical Literary Language. The major reforms of ENHG spelling
which had gradually come about were: the replacement of ⟨aw, ew⟩
by ⟨au, eu⟩; the distribution of ⟨e⟩ and ⟨å⟩ and ⟨eu⟩ and ⟨äu⟩
according to etymological principles; the general indication of
mutation; the almost complete elimination of ⟨ai⟩; ⟨ie⟩ for long *i*,
except in words like *ihn, ihm, ihr*; the use of ⟨i⟩ and ⟨j⟩, ⟨u⟩ and ⟨v⟩
as vowels and consonants respectively; the indication of vowel
length both by means of ⟨h⟩ and doubling (*Kehle, Seele*) in an
usus scribendi fashion; the reduction of postconsonantal ⟨th⟩, ⟨ck⟩,
⟨tz⟩ to ⟨t⟩ ,⟨k⟩ and ⟨z⟩ (*Ort, Dank, Herz*); the simplification of
⟨pff⟩ to ⟨pf⟩, of ⟨ff⟩ to ⟨f⟩ after long vowels and diphthongs and
before or after consonants (*Heft, helfen*); the elimination of 'silent'
⟨b⟩ or ⟨p⟩ after ⟨m⟩ and of other 'superfluous' letters (*vmb* > *um*,

vnndt > *und*); the doubling of consonants to indicate the shortness of the preceding vowel, hence the distinction of ⟨ß⟩ and ⟨ss⟩ (*Füße* but *müssen*); the gradual restriction of initial capitals to nouns, proper names and the sentence beginning; the abolition of the hyphenation of compound nouns.

7·2·4 | The problem of purism

The admittedly considerable admixture of foreign words came under attack in this period for two main reasons. First, the entrenched position of Latin and French and the neglect of German and its inferior position were resented and the intruding foreign words were seen as symbols of this sorry state of affairs. Patriotic or nationalistic reasons were certainly uttered very frequently. More serious critics also objected on other grounds; Opitz thought the foreign words were stylistically objectionable; Leibniz opposed them because they were frequently not or not properly understood. Secondly, linguists believed in the 'purity' of language and claimed a quite particular eminence for German on account of its unblemished descent. Foreign words were thus bound to appear as a fly in the ointment. The *Sprachgesellschaften* were dedicated to the purification of German. Many individual members of these societies wrote satires against the *A la mode* use of foreign words. There were also opponents who poked fun at the activities of the purists. The most radical standard-bearer of purism was Philipp von Zesen (1619–89). He suggested and used hundreds of *Verdeutschungen*. Some of them have permanently enriched the language as they exist alongside their foreign counterparts, e.g. *Anschrift/Adresse, Zeughaus/Arsenal, Freistatt/Asyl, Bücherei/Bibliothek, Blumenstrauß/Bouquet, Rechtschreibung/Orthographie, Hochschule/Universität, Tagebuch/Journal, Trauerspiel/ Tragödie, Glückspiel/Lotterie, Handschrift/Manuskript*. Many have mercifully vanished again, such as the grammatical terms *Klagendung* 'accusative', *Gebendung* 'dative' or *Geburtsendung* 'genitive'. Few will lament the loss of *Buschgötze* for *Faun, Entgliederkunst* for *Anatomie, Krautbeschreiber* for *Botaniker, Scheidekunst* for *Chemie, Meuchelpuffer* for *Pistole*.

The writing of grammar flourished in this period, as we have already seen. The grammarians naturally had the 'purity' of

FGL

German at heart and it is not surprising that they on the whole used a German terminology. Between using the Latin terminology with its Latin morphology, as was customary, and using puristic German inventions there was, however, a third way. The Latin terms could be used as German words with German endings, e.g. *Verb – Verben* instead of *verbum – verba*. By the middle of the eighteenth century there existed in fact the Germanized Latin terminology as we know it today alongside German loan translations or loan creations. A language is indeed strained when a foreign morphological system is superimposed. Even Schottelius could write

Bey den Stammletteren ist wol zumerken / daß dieselbe so wol in den *Verbis Anomalis*, als auch in den *Nominibus, quo ad Casus, Numeros* und sonst unterweilen geendert werden / welches aber *investigationi radicis* nichts benehmen muß / (p. 194), or 'Auch ist dieses zumerken / daß viele *Nomina* den *Genitivum formir*en *apponendo litteram* s' (p. 195).

That such a practice is unacceptable in the long run is clear, for it presupposes the knowledge of two languages for what one language can normally perform perfectly well. Though it was widely current in scholarly and scientific writing of all kinds, it gradually ceased in the course of our period. If foreign loans are successfully incorporated in the native phonology and morphology and are not socially divisive, there is much to be said in their favour. Unmotivated or non-transparent words like *Substantiv* or *Genetiv* are more obviously precise technical terms than motivated words like *Hauptwort* or Zesen's *Geburtsendung* with their suggestive transparency. On account of its history German still practises both naturalization of foreign words and loan translation.

7.2.5 | Phonological and grammatical problems

It is clear that the grammarians, such as Schottelius, Gottsched and Adelung and the many others who were active in the seventeenth and eighteenth centuries, played a very big part in the creation of the Classical Literary Language. Yet it is noticeable that there is often a great discrepancy between the recommendations or prescriptive rules of the grammarians and the practical use of language by writers. The grammarians' rules are well known, but their application or non-application in the writings of the time has been little studied. Therefore only a few salient and crucial phonological and grammatical points can here be examined.[1]

(i) Initial ⟨d/t⟩

The written language had continued to distinguish the reflexes of WGmc. þ and d since OHG (EFr.) and MHG, but in nearly all dialects they had coalesced, either in a voiced d as in LG and CFr. or in a voiceless lenis d as in Rh. Fr. and in much of ECGm., or in a semifortis d or a fortis t as in UGm. This had led to a great deal of variability in the written language. Schottelius (p. 207) gives *drŭkken/trŭkken, Deutsch/Teutsch, dichten/tichten, Dunkel/ tunkel* etc. and states 'Der Gebrauch ist hierunter sehr variabel, und muß es nohtwendig oft auf Muhtmassungen hinaus lauffen'. Gottsched was of the opinion that in such cases only a list of examples would help, as none of his eight spelling rules would provide an unambiguous answer. In his article 'Ob man Deutsch oder Teutsch schreiben solle', printed in the appendix (pp. 673ff), he comes very sensibly down in favour of ⟨d-⟩ because the initial is here a reflex of former þ, which is normally spelt with ⟨d⟩ in German. English examples, e.g. *thine – dein*m show this correspondence. Such a rational argument did, however, not oust *teutsch* immediately. For emotional reasons the more forceful initial was preferred by many people right to the end of the nineteenth century.

(ii) Apocope of final ⟨e⟩

This UGm. dialectal phenomenon (see 6.5.3) had spread into the UGm. written language and to some extent also into the ECGm. written language at the time of Luther. It had, however, no backing in the ECGm. dialects and was therefore constantly under attack. The confusion was very great. Was it to be *der Hirt* or *der Hirte*, *das Stück* or *das Stücke, die Seel* or *die Seele*? The grammarians

---

[1] In this section reference is made to J. G. Schottelius, *Ausführliche Arbeit Von der Teutschen HaubtSprache*, Brunswick, 1663; J. C. Gottsched, *Deutsche Sprachkunst*, 5th ed., Leipzig, 1762; J. C. Adelung, *Umständliches Lehrgebäude der Deutschen Sprache*, 2 vols., Leipzig, 1782; *The Highdutch Minerva* (see p. 488); J. J. Wagner, *Mercurius Helveticus*, 3rd ed., Zürich, 1701 (1st ed. 1684).

wrestled with the problem, without much success. The *Highdutch Minerva* had this to say to English learners:

> but note well, that there is never a letter more abused both in the meetre and here in the gender, than the vowel E, which abuse crept in by a bad custom and by the variety of dialects. for some of them as the Thuringian, Misnian, Silesian etc. add it, when they should not, e.g. in the masculine and neuter substantives: *der fürste, der hake* . . ., *das gesihte, das herze* etc. when they should say and write: *der fürst*, prince, *hak*, hook . . . *das gesiht* sight, *herz* heart; whereas some others as the Frankonian, the Oster- or Voghtlandish, and that of the Palatinate, omitte it both in writing and speaking feminin substantivs . . . *ein stub, een kaz* . . . when they ought to add it thus: . . . *eine stube* stove, *kaze* cat . . . (pp. 48–9).

This was certainly a neat rationalization. In an age when grammarians believed in the *Grundrichtigkeit* (Schottelius' term) of every language, which was there to be discovered by grammarians, such a solution seemed commendable. But German was not to be tamed in this way. Gottsched recommended *der Aff, Bub, Fürst, Herr, Knab, Pfaff* etc. (p. 235). Adelung regarded the question as a matter of euphony and carped 'Gottsched war harthörig genug, alle diese Substantive mit dem mildernden e zu verdammen und die harte Oberdeutsche Form vorzuziehen . . .' (p. 312). Thus he used *Bube, Knabe, Gatte* etc. and condemned the earlier rule: 'Selbst das so genannte weibliche e ist im Grunde nichts anders, als dieses e euphonicum, weil kein Grund vorhanden ist, warum man es gerade nur einigen weiblichen Hauptwörtern sollte angehångt haben . . .' (pp. 311, 319). Eventually it was usage which decided in favour of *Mensch, Graf* and *Affe, Knabe*, and eliminated the -*e* in *Herre, Stücke, Bette* etc. Adelung lists the forms as they are still valid today (p. 437).

Believing that nouns needed an inflectional ending in the plural Schottelius had ruled that the nouns in -*er* and -*el* should form their plural in -*ere*, -*ele*: *die Bürgere, die Himmele* (p. 307). In Alem. such plurals were for a time not infrequent, e.g. *Brüdere* in *Mercurius Helveticus*. Gottsched and Adelung gave only the endingless plural. Adelung remarked 'Einige alte Oberdeutsche Mundarten hängen den Wörtern auf er besonders den männlichen dieser Art im Nominativ des Plurals noch ein e an . . . *Bürgermeistere*' and added that it was 'im Hochdeutschen ein Fehler' (p. 419).

(iii) *Syncope of -e- in verbal forms*
While this was general in UGm. writings CGm. grammarians
recommended *-est*, *-et* for the endings of the sg. of verbs, e.g.
Gottsched *du lobest, er lobet*, in the preterite *lobetest, lobete* and in
the past part. *gelobet*. But for *sehen* the endings were *-st*, *-t*.
Adelung has both *lobest, lobet* and *lobst, lobt*, but refers to the
necessity of a euphonic form. In the preterite he distinguishes
between the ind. *lobtest, lobte* and the subj. *lobetest, lobete* (p. 780).
Semenjuk (pp. 106–13) noted the relatively early increase of syncopated forms in strong verbs and weak verbs ending in a voiced
consonant, while in other weak verbs the two forms remained as
free variants with a gradual swing towards the syncopated forms.
The same was true in the past part. forms (*gelobet/gelobt*). She
made the interesting discovery that the transition to syncopated
forms occurred earlier in literary journals than in political newspapers, while scholarly and scientific periodicals came in between.

(iv) *Mutation*
There was variability in the roots of many words (*Stuck/Stück*,
Burger/Bürger), in plural formation (*Tag(e)/Täg(e)*), and in the
second and third persons sg. of strong verbs with the root vowels
a and *au* (*fallt/fällt, lauft/läuft*) and in some other cases, e.g.
kommt/kömmt. Here it was mainly a difference between UGm.
(without mutation) and CGm. (with mutation). But even in the
ECGm. written language *Wägen, Läden, Täge* were used alongside
the more frequent *Wagen, Laden, Tage* (Semenjuk, p. 96).
Gottsched and Adelung supported the forms which have become
valid, Adelung remarking that *Böden* and *Bögen* were also used
without mutation by many and that *kömmst, kömmt* were current
'in den gemeinen Sprecharten' (p. 818).

(v) *Other dialectal features in vocalism or consonantism*
Labialization of *i* and *e* was quite widespread, especially in Alem.,
e.g. in *Mercurius Helveticus* we find *Gebürg, Wüssenschaften,
Frömbder*, and there are many overcompensations in Bav. texts,
e.g. *Sütz* (for *Sitz*), *Bewögungen*, mixed with unroundings, e.g.
freidenreich, zertrimmern (Kaiser, pp. 129–31). Long and short
vowels were often differently distributed in the dialects, and spellings like *Vatter, Botten, getretten*, e.g. in *Mercurius Helveticus*, are
indications of this. Rhymes like *Fuß* and *muß* in the works of

Silesian poets derive also from the dialectal background. Upper Saxon spellings like *Jabe, Jott* for *Gabe, Gott* were condemned by Gottsched. Consonantal spellings like *Befelch* (*Befehl*), *Viech* (*Vieh*), *du sichst, er sicht* for *siehst, sieht*, explicitly condemned by Gottsched, are found in UGm. texts.

(vi) In the *inflection of nouns* there were a number of competing forms. Schottelius still gave the fem. gen. and dat. sg. endings *-en, die Lade, der Laden* (p. 310) except for derivatives which were to be endingless in the sg. (*Eitelkeit*). Semenjuk noticed the rapid decline of such forms which she still found in *Frau, Sonne, Zunge, Straße, Gasse, Wiege* etc. and most frequently in *Kirche* and *Erde* (pp. 92–3). In the conservative areas of UGm. they lingered. Gottsched explained 'daß diejenigen unrecht thun, die bei dem Worte *Frau* in der 2. (=gen.) 3. (=dat.) und 6. (=ablative) Endung ein en anflicken' (p. 235).

In the weak masc. inflection there was competition between *-en* and *-ens*, but Gottsched ruled 'daß die 2. Endung kein s annimmt, wie einige aus böser Gewohnheit bey Menschens, Herrns, Grafens, Fürstens u.d.gl. zu sprechen pflegen' (p. 234). In the gen. pl. of masc. and neuter nouns UGm. had *-en* but CGm. had *-e*, e.g. *Mercurius Helveticus*: *deren Bischoffen* (= *der Bischöfe*), *deren Orthen* (= *der Orte*); Dornblüth advocated this form (*Übersetzeren*), but Albrecht von Haller and Bodmer corrected these gen. pl. forms when their Leipzig colleagues pointed them out as errors.

Among the masc. and neuter pl. types that in *-er* was least settled. Semenjuk found that only *Orte/Örter* and *Lande/Länder* varied. But Gottsched adduced *Dörner* (also *Dornen*), *Flecker, Hälmer* (also *Hälme*), *Klößer, Klötzer, Klumpfer, Örter, Pflöcker, Sträußer* (p. 241). Adelung (p. 414) introduced the distinction between what he called 'collective' and 'distributive'. Thus *Dörner, Örter, Wörter* and *Bänder* he said were 'distributive', but *Dorne, Orte, Worte, Bande* 'collective'. Prescriptive grammarians of modern German still teach this distinction for *Worte/Wörter* – without much success. In UGm., especially Bavarian texts, there were many more *er*-pl. forms, e.g. *Beiner, Better*; and *Rösser* can still be seen in modern Bav. provincial newspapers.

(vii) *Noun genders*
All grammarians agreed that there were many cases of gender

differences. Kaiser has some 170 examples, Adelung lists over 230. Gottsched gives the gender current in *Meissnisch* first, the deviation second. Most examples show that the gender of these words in modern German has followed Meissen, e.g. *der Bach* (UGm. *die*), *die Butter* (UGm. *der*), *die Ecke* (UGm. *das*), *die Gewalt* (UGm. *der*), *die Luft* (UGm. *der*); but in the case of *die Duft, die Dunst* (UGm. *der*) Adelung reverses the order: *der Duft, der Dunst* (Meissen *die*). Nerius concluded his study with the observation 'daß sich gegen Ende des 18. Jahrhunderts im Genus der Substantive eine für das gesamte deutsche Sprachgebiet weitgehend einheitliche literatursprachliche Norm entwickelt hat' (p. 128).

CGm. words in *-niß* were predominantly neuter, their UGm. counterparts in *-nuß, -nüß* or *-niß* generally fem., e.g. UGm. *die Begräbnuß, Bildnuß, Finsternuß*, but in the early eighteenth century there was also much wavering. Adelung (p. 352) listed them with the genders that now prevail: f.: *Bedrängniß, Besorgniß, Bewandtniß, Erlaubniß, Finsterniß*, but neuter: *Ärgerniß, Bedürfniß, Begräbniß, Bildniß, Gedächtniß*, etc. He also rejected the older rule whereby such nouns had the fem. gender if they were abstracts but were neuter if they had a concrete meaning.

(viii) *Diminutives*

Schottelius only mentions *-lein* (p. 245). Gottsched (pp. 187–8) gives *-lein* and adds that certain regions use *-el* or *-le* and the Swiss *-lin*, but comments that 'mit besserem Rechte gehört *-chen* hieher', thus *Männlein* or *Männchen*, but *Männgen* he calls 'fälschlich geschrieben'. The latter form was the only one that the *Highdutch Minerva* taught its English readers. The reason why Gottsched preferred *-lein* was that it was the form occurring in the Bible and religious songs, although he admitted that *-chen* was current in a large part of Germany. He rejected the spelling with ⟨g⟩ with the interesting argument that LG had *-ken* and that in fact *k* and *ch* were related to each other (*Saken – Sachen*). Again it was Adelung (p. 317) who stated the modern rule: *-chen* (*Bildchen, Söhnchen*) in all cases except after *ch, k, g* where for euphonic reasons *-lein* was to be preferred (*Bächlein, Berglein*).

(ix) *Gen. and dat. pl. of the definite article*

The older language (ENHG) had developed the forms *derer, denen* (cf. 6.9.1(i)), e.g. *Mercurius Helveticus: von denen Bauren.*

Schottelius still had these forms in his paradigm (p. 226) although he added (p. 229) 'Man schreibt / und sagt oftmals / durch den gemeinen bestetigten Gebrauch den / fûr denen: der / fûr derer'. Gottsched rejected the extended forms for the article but pointed to their use as pronouns, e.g. *den Fischen; denen, die sich gelagert hatten* (p. 164). Adelung condemned the UGm. usage: 'Im Oberdeutschen hat man aus der dieser Mundart eigenen Liebe zur Weitschweifigkeit und Vielsylbigkeit die zweysylbige Form des Pronominis für den Plural des Artikels von Alters her behalten' (p. 549), but, according to him, it was an error in HG.

(x) *The ending of the attributive adjective after articles etc. in the plural*
UGm. texts generally had *-e*, e.g. *die heutige Eidgnossen* (*Mercurius Helveticus*). Gottsched gives *-en* (*die armen Männer*) and comments 'Viele . . . beißen hier sehr unrecht das n ab' (p. 252). In ECGm. writings there was much wavering. Adelung (p. 620) demanded *-en* but added that after *einige* and *etliche -e* was often used, and commonly after *viel, mehr, wenig, alle*, e.g. *etliche große Bäume, viele neue Thaler, alle übrige Gäste*. We know that the problem has continued to plague German grammarians. After *alle* the *-en* form is now demanded, after the others the *-e* form, but usage is still not uniform.

(xi) *Adverb formation*
Schottelius states that all derivative adverbs as opposed to the root adverbs (e.g. *bisher*) are formed by means of the addition of *-lich*, e.g. *heilsam – heilsamlich, gut – gûtlich*. But those adjectives in *-lich* (e.g. *freundlich*) can also function as adverbs or can be marked by the ending *-en*, e.g. *gewißlichen vertrôsten* (pp. 256–63). Adelung (vol. II, p. 52) noted that many words in *-lich* were adjectives while some were only adverbs, e.g. *höchlich, kürzlich, säuberlich* and therefore were comparable to the adverbs in English like *highly* and *greatly*. And he adds perceptively

Im Oberdeutschen scheint man diese Zweydeutigkeit der Ableitungsilbe lich dunkel empfunden zu haben, daher man ihr, wenn sie wirklich ein Umstandswort bilden soll, noch gern die vorige Ableitungsylbe en anhängt: bittlichen, sich kläglichen geberden, grausamlichen. Im Hochdeutschen, wo man die Häufung der Ableitungsylben gern vermeidet, ist dieser Anhang ungewöhnlich, weil die Deutlichkeit hier nichts dabey gewinnet oder verlieret . . .

Thus any attempt to mark adverbs in German was discontinued.

(xii) *First person sg. of strong verbs with* -e- *root vowel*
UGm. texts here often had -*i*-, e.g. *ich wird, gib*, but these never impinged upon the ECGm. written language, and although Dornblüth defended these forms, the CGm. grammarians saw no need to oppose them. They were clearly southern.

(xiii) *Imperative singular*
Schottelius (p. 548) concluded that the *Grundrichtigkeit* demanded that the imperative be monosyllabic since it was identical with the stem. Hence he gave *gib, trag, lauff, sih, werd, brich* and also *hör, lieb*. Gottsched, however, gave the weak verbs the ending -*e*, e.g. *lebe, liebe, lobe, lache*, and ruled that *siehe, gebe, stehe, schreibe* were wrong. Adelung (p.768) permitted *fliehe, gehe, bitte* for euphonic reasons alongside *flieh, geh*, but otherwise gave -*e* only to the weak verbs (*liebe, lobe, bringe, rede* but *brich, gib, hilf, sieh, komm*). In the modern language strong verbs with -*i*- (*e* in the infinitive root) have no -*e*, except that Luther's *siehe* has survived in a special sense. All other verbs (including *werden*) have -*e* in elevated standard (*trage*) but are usually endingless in colloquial usage (*trag*).

(xiv) *Second and third person sg. of strong verbs with* -ie- *root vowel*
Schottelius' paradigm (p. 580) was *ich betriege, du betreugst, er betreugt* and he kept the alternation *ie/eu* in all relevant verbs. Gottsched (p. 332), too, demanded this alternation, because this was the usage of the ancients as attested by the Bible and religious songs. But he added: 'Allein die Unbeständigkeit der Aussprache hat hier in Meißen gemachet, daß man zwar diese alte und gute Art noch kennet, und nicht verwirft; aber doch im gemeinen Gebrauche nicht mehr beobachtet.' Adelung called forms like *treugst, beugst* poetical (p. 810).

(xv) *The preterite of strong verbs*
Schottelius still had many of the older forms, e.g. *ich, er band, du bundest, wir bunden* (p. 580); *ich, er drang, du drungest, wir drungen*, and of all other verbs of this type; *ich, er schwall, du*

schwollest, wir schwollen; ich, er verdarb, du verdurbest or *verdorbest,
wir verdurben* or *verdorben* and of the other verbs of this type. The
-e is found only with *sahe*, an alternative of *sah*. Semenjuk recorded
the *-e* also in the case of *versahe, geschahe, stunde, hielte, wurde*
(p. 114). Gottsched ruled against the added *-e*, and recorded the
modern apophonic variations. Adelung only tolerated *ich ward* or
wurde.

(xvi) *Rückumlaut*

This occurred in the six verbs *brennen, kennen, nennen, rennen,
senden, wenden*. The *-e-* forms in the pret. and past part. were
originally UGm. (*brennete*) while ECGm. had *-a-* (*brannte*). But in
the seventeenth and eighteenth centuries both forms spread in both
variants of the written language. The grammarians recorded the
variability and on the whole preferred the 'regular' form, e.g.
Schottelius (p. 575): 'die gleichfliessende sey die richtigste und
gebräuchlichste'; Gottsched wished to ban the *-a-* forms: 'allein
ist dieses nur eine Verkürzung aus wendete, kennete, nennete,
welche auch noch gewöhnlich geblieben sind' (p. 347); Adelung
rejected Gottsched's surmise but wrote: 'viele brauchen schon die
reguläre Form, aber im Hochdeutschen ist die irreguläre noch die
üblichste' (p. 795).

(xvii) *Sind or seynd*

The former was the ECGm. form, the latter had originated in
EUGm., but had spread everywhere in the written language.
Schottelius' paradigm is *wir seyn | ihr seyd | sie sind | oder seyn*
(p. 553); Gottsched's *wir sind, ihr seyd, sie sind (nicht seyn!)*
(p. 302); Adelung's *wir sind* (UGm. *seyn, seynd*, LG *sunt*), *ihr seyd*
(UGm. *seindt*, LG *sunt*), *sie sind* (UGm. *seindt*, LG *sunt*) which, in
view of his general forceful deprecation of UGm., amounted to
a recommendation of *sind*.

Variability and inconsistency were characteristics of German
which were very much under attack in this age of reason and
enlightenment. The elegance and regularity of French were to be
emulated, German was to become a standard language at last.
Scholars like Thomasius, Leibniz and Wolff had pointed the way;
grammarians like Schottelius, Gottsched and Adelung had set up
the signposts; the flourishing moral and literary journals and
eighteenth-century writers and poets completed the long march.

The German Enlightenment, whatever subsequent generations were to think of it, had achieved the goal of a literary standard language.

To assess the change which had come about we need only to compare the following passage written by Gottsched in 1748 with what Sigmund von Birken had written in 1669 (see p. 490), less than eighty years earlier.

Was kostet es nicht für Mühe, nur alle die größern und kleinen grammatischen Schriften, unserer Vorfahren kennen zu lernen? Wie viel schwerer ist es, nur die meisten und besten davon aufzutreiben? Wie viel Zeit endlich brauchet es nicht, sie zu lesen, zu prüfen, und theils unter sich, theils mit der heutigen besten Mundart zu vergleichen? Und wenn man nun dieses alles gethan hat: so geht nunmehr erst die rechte Schwierigkeit an. Man soll alles Gute, das man darinn angetroffen hat, zusammen nehmen, ohne seine Vorgånger zu bestehlen. Man soll alles in gute Verbindung und Ordnung bringen, ohne jemanden gar zu sclavisch zu folgen. Man soll aber auch manche Lücken, die unsre lieben Alten noch übrig gelassen, ergänzen; manches veraltete weglassen; manches das heute zu Tage anstößig ist, erneueren; und alles nach dem heutigen, weit feinern Geschmacke der Deutschen einrichten. Mit einem Worte, man soll es auch besser machen, als es unsre Vorgånger gemachet haben; ja ohne sie abzuschreiben, soll man sie auch weit, weit übertreffen! Dieses, dieses alles fodern unsre heutigen kritischen Zeiten: und ich überlasse einem jeden das Urtheil, ob es so leicht ist, solche Foderungen zu erfüllen? (*Vorrede*, 5th ed. p. a4v.)

7.3 | Modern German: uses and users

7.3.1 | Stratification

The modern German language is in use over a large and varied territory. It serves a population engaged in the most modern technologies as well as in ancient crafts. It is spoken by sailors and mountain peasants, by highly educated scholars and scientists and by urban and rural labourers of very limited education. It is written in a professional capacity by administrators, journalists, poets and many others and it is written by all for occasional purposes. It is spoken on formal and informal occasions, in highly technical or philosophical discussions, as well as in banal conversations. Its written form has given expression to philosophies and ideologies from Idealism to Existentialism, from Marxism to Liberalism and National Socialism. Poetry and prose of lasting fascination have been written in German no less than texts of the most ephemeral and trivial kind. The range and variety of contemporary German in all its realizations and manifestations is thus vast. To identify, define, and classify the innumerable varieties of the language, various models have been set up. They tend to be controversial and contradictory. For there are no fixed points, no sharp contours.

Users have many roles. One man may be a computer scientist or a motor mechanic and at the same time a football fan, a father, an amateur photographer or a lay preacher. He will use different modes of language in his different roles and in different situations.

Uses of language shade into one another. A freely spoken, unscripted, unrehearsed lecture may be nearer to written German in its linguistic form than to spoken German, despite being 'spoken German'. A written text may imitate the spoken language. A technical or specialist language may be extremely precise in a textbook, contaminated by colloquialisms in the oral instruction of apprentices and very diluted when used across the counter between the technical expert, acting as a salesman, and an uninformed purchaser. General language may be larded with terms deriving from specialist languages, e.g. *anvisieren, anpeilen, Komplex.*

Industrialization and urbanization have increased social mobility both horizontally and vertically. They have also compartmentalized the lives of individuals. Along the spatial dimension, language has become more convergent, but along the social dimension it has become much more distended. The growth of specialist disciplines has immensely increased the field of the specialist languages and widened the difference between general language and technical language. The spread of education, the evolution of political democracy and the coming of the mass media (popular press, radio, film, television) have narrowed the once greater gap between standard and non-standard. The Classical Literary Language which was practically the sole standard form around 1800 has been demoted from this position of uniqueness. It is now just one (slightly archaic) register of the standard language. Its academic, elevated,

aristocratic background and its excessively written-language character have made it outdated and inadequate in the age of democracy, mass education and mass participation in the linguistic processes. Other forms of standard have evolved: a written standard
more attuned to the less classical and academic nature of education
and a spoken standard which has taken the place of the earlier
pattern of general dialect-speaking with some standard-speaking
by the upper classes. But as the notion of standard has become
more varied, so has its opposite pole. Local, historically evolved,
relatively 'pure' dialects have given way over most of the territory
to regional, much contaminated intermediate forms between dialects and the standard. In sloughing off dialects and in aiming at a
standard form speakers have evolved colloquial forms of the standard or semi-standard *Umgangssprachen*. But owing to the fact that
the individual has many social roles he may also have at his command more than one linguistic form: dialect or something ap-
proaching it with his parents or his rural relatives, the regional
semi-standard at work and in his home, standard, or what he
intends to be standard, in committee meetings or on public plat-
forms and generally in writing. In most of Germany and Austria
the relation between standard and non-standard has become fluid
and blurred. The very concepts of standard and non-standard have
become somewhat questionable as the norms, once rigid, are now
loosened and sliding.

We have seen that it is difficult to retain the uses or dimensions
of the medium (standard/non-standard; written/spoken; general/
specialist) as fixed points, or the registers which I would define as
subtypes of uses (e.g. advertising, sports commentary, sermon,
popular journalism, learned articles and so on, covering the whole
range of language activity). The users have many roles and belong
to several circles or social groups participating accordingly in
various sociolects or group languages. Where language is still
strongly determined by the geographical dimension, dialects enter
into the picture as well. Personal style, that is personal predilection
for and choice of verbal means, may be left out as not belonging to
the sociolinguistic dimensions but to the field of taste. Even so, to
identify fixed points along the axis of the user or the dimensions
determined by the user (formal/informal; educated/uneducated) is
just as difficult and problematic as along the axis of use. Nor is it
always easy to distinguish between forms of language (dialect;

Umgangssprache; written language, etc.) and functions of language (informal conversational 'style'; formal 'style' of lecturing, etc.). The modern language is infinitely varied in its realizations and multi-dimensional in its determining factors. It is perhaps most appropriate and simplest to think of these factors or dimensions in terms of oppositions rather than in terms of clearly defined and delimited phenomena. By so doing we may visualize the oppositions determining the use or the forms of language as corners of a hexagon:

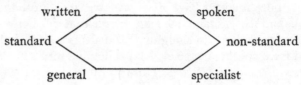

The central axis is here seen as that constituted by the opposition standard/non-standard. Each manifestation of language along this axis is also inevitably determined by the other two oppositions (written/spoken; general/specialist). The socio-stylistic dimensions of the user (e.g. formal/informal; educated/uneducated), while never absent, impinge to a lesser extent on the actualization of language. As subsidiary dimensions they are not included in the diagram.

Many of the various combinations are well-known language forms, such as general written standard (formal or informal; generally presupposing a measure of education) and specialist written standard (formal; educated user), or general spoken standard and specialist spoken standard. Equally well known are the general spoken non-standard forms (say dialect or semi-standard *Umgangssprache*). But we also have spoken specialist non-standard, for instance, the language of Moselle-Franconian dialect-speaking viticulturalists or the language of Alemannic dialect-speaking cattle-breeders. The general written non-standard is represented by dialect writing, while specialist written non-standard is, almost by definition, excluded. The dividing line between dialect and language is always difficult to draw, but one of the most useful criteria to apply is, in fact, the existence or non-existence of specialist written prose.

Some registers are by their nature confined. Those of headlines and of advertising occur only in the written form. Spoken radio or television advertising is, of course, carefully scripted. On the other hand a sports commentary can be in written or spoken form. In a diglossic situation, such as prevails in German-speaking Switzerland (see p. 516), it can even be in dialect. The social standing of dialect in general decides whether this non-standard form is acceptable in advertising, as does the nature of the product to be advertised. In Switzerland cheese and bread might well be advertised in dialect, but almost certainly not gold watches or high-class jewellery. Other registers, such as that of auctioneering, are restricted to spoken language.

By seeing language varieties in terms of oppositions we are no longer forced to identify forms which by the very nature of the situation are impossible to define. Forms are illimitable because they are open-ended and sliding. Thinking in terms of oppositions helps us to appreciate the features which the various forms possess. These dimensional oppositions have now to be examined in greater detail.

7.3.2 | Standard and non-standard

Standard is perhaps easiest to define and to describe. In its written form, standard German has a fixed orthography as laid down by the *Duden Rechtschreibung* and a grammar as described in the *Duden Grammatik* (or by Jung or Erben). Its spoken form has at least a regulated pronunciation (*Siebs, Duden Aussprachewörterbuch, Wörterbuch der deutschen Aussprache*) although it only applies to the declamatory register of the classical stage, and the *gemäßigte Hochlautung* has not the same precise definition. But its grammar, in particular its syntax, is the subject of much controversy and endeavour. Many scholars would deny the existence of a conversational standard, instead they would speak of *Alltagssprache* or *Umgangssprache*. The reasons are both historical and terminological. Standard German arose primarily as a written standard language. The common terms for the German standard language, *Schriftsprache* or *Schriftdeutsch*, are in fact a reflection of this origin. Yet in some cities and court circles spoken forms other than dialects are attested as having existed as early as the sixteenth century. The term *Hochsprache* which is often applied to spoken standard is pegged to definite cultural, literary and social values and excludes ordinary conversation. The term 'standard' which is now also in use in German stresses the most essential feature: the existence of a norm in the form of a codified grammar and phonology. This norm is what the foreigner learning German is taught. Standard is thus most conveniently found in general prose, in textbooks and in quality journals. It is archetypally written language. It has supra-regional validity and its norm is the subject of instruction in schools. Yet, there can be no doubt that standard German also has a spoken variant. If in phonology it does not follow the *Bühnenaussprache*, originally laid down by Siebs in 1898, this does not mean that there is no spoken standard. The *gemäßigte Hochlautung* of the most recent editions of Siebs and of Duden and the revised spoken norms of the East German *Wörterbuch der deutschen Aussprache* (Leipzig, 1964) recognize the existence of a spoken standard. The meaning of 'norm' is, however, we must not forget, also determined by the medium; it cannot be the same in spoken and in written language. We already know that the syntax of the spoken standard differs from that of the written standard, although it has not yet been elaborated in the same sort of normative code as that of the written standard. The orthography of the written language can be and is normalized to an extent to which the phonology of the spoken language outside the artificial ambience of the professional stage cannot possibly be. The spoken standard must accommodate the feature known as 'accent'. An educated speaker from Württemberg, Bavaria, Hanover or Upper Saxony as well as from Austria or Switzerland, may well have an accent, but this does not mean that he speaks non-standard, let alone dialect. In its mildest form an accent may consist only of characteristic prosodic features such as intonation, stress and speed. Substantial phonetic departures from the norm of the *gemäßigte Hochlautung* may be based on incidence ([x] in *sagte*) or on phonetic realization ([i] rather than [ɪ] for stressed short *i*). The dividing line between an accent and a non-standard form is naturally not easy to draw, but it may perhaps be tentatively suggested that where phonemic contrasts of the standard (e.g. /i/ – /ü/, /d/ – /t/) are not maintained or where phonemic contrasts are made which are not found in standard (e.g. /e/ < MHG *e* – /ɛ/ < MHG *ë*, or /ai/ < MHG *ei* – /ɛi/ < MHG *î*) we are no longer confronted with an accent of standard German but with a non-standard form.

There are fields where standardization, originally based mainly on the written medium, has by nature hardly occurred at all or has not been completed. This is mainly the case in the field of domestic life. Here we can either say that there are no standard terms (*Schnur – Bindfaden*; *Klempner – Spengler*; *Metzger – Fleischer – Schlächter – Fleischhauer*) but only regional words, or more realistically, that the standard language tolerates regional synonyms. One term may be the national norm (e.g. *Tischler*), but another one may be accepted as regionally also standard (e.g. *Schreiner*). Modern mobility sees to it that such regionalisms become known at least passively by the population as a whole.

The archetypally non-standard forms of German are the *dialects*. By dialects I mean the historically developed local forms only minimally or not at all influenced by the movement of standardization. Under the conditions now prevailing in Germany and Austria dialects are used primarily by the rural population and the lowest social strata (though not everywhere). Dialects are typically spoken language. That is why the contrast between standard language and dialect is not straightforward. We are not only concerned with a principally normalized supra-regional form and a principally non-standardized local form but also with two forms principally distinguished by the formal criteria of written/spoken and by the social criteria of educated/non-educated. When one says that a dialect has no fixed norm one means, of course, that there is no normative grammar to which speakers deliberately adhere. In standard the speakers aim at achieving the norm set by others and by former generations. A standard language is relatively more detached from the dimensions of space and time. A dialect is particularly strongly determined by these dimensions. Its grammar commands no special respect. It is a free-and-easy, expressionistic form of speech without prescription by authorities and without an effort on the part of speakers to conform to principles of correctness. Dialect lacks what Henzen called 'die Absicht auf Überbrückung verschiedener horizontaler oder vertikaler Sprachschichten' (p. 18). Its basic principle is local or regional autarchy. Borrowing means the loss of its self-sufficiency. It is not enriched by outside influences but threatened in its existence. Social and geographical mobility have undermined dialects everywhere. Mobility leads to the rise of supra-regional speech forms.

Dialect can also be written, although the absence of spelling conventions makes this difficult both for writers and readers. In being written, dialect naturally assumes some of the characteristics of that medium and sheds some of those of the spoken medium normally associated with dialects. It is for this reason that some scholars have asserted that dialects cannot be written or that dialect literature is not genuine dialect. Such contentions are, however, based on too narrow a view of what dialect is.

Although dialect is now in many areas restricted to the speech of the lowest strata of society it should nevertheless not be identified with *Volksprache*, which is seen by F. Maurer as characterized by such extra-linguistic features as exaggeration, illogicality, lack of abstraction, emotivity, vulgarity, associative thinking, etc., amounting therefore to a psycholinguistic attitude rather than a form of language. There are still areas where dialect is spoken by the whole spectrum of society, for instance in Switzerland and Luxemburg, or by nearly the whole social range, for instance in parts of Bavaria, Württemberg, Austria and Hesse. In such societies dialect therefore also embraces the socio-stylistic criteria of formal/informal and educated/uneducated, as well as slang and specialist languages. In areas where dialect has survived as a language form, people are generally 'bilingual' (dialect and standard). The 'bilinguality' may be informal or institutionalized. In the latter case we speak of diglossia.

Diglossia prevails, for instance, in German-speaking Switzerland. There the two divergent forms of the language, standard German and dialect, are employed by all classes of the native population for different, clearly defined purposes. The Swiss dialects, collectively known as *Schwyzertüütsch*, are always used in ordinary conversation and also in some public speaking. There is a certain amount of dialect literature which, irrespective of its quality, is of moderate importance, being generally written by the few for the few. Standard German is confined to writing, lecturing, teaching and preaching of a formal kind. It is also used in conversation with foreigners and, of course, generally in the theatre. It predominates in radio and television. This situation of diglossia where there is a functionalized dichotomy of two language varieties is rather exceptional. What is much more common in southern and central Germany and in Austria is an extremely complicated gradualism in which the dialects are losing more and more ground.

The transition from dialect to standard or semi-standard is the typical event in the present-day evolutionary stage of German. It is not directly education, the ubiquitous presence of the mass media or the mobility of the population which are responsible for this change. It is rather the psychological predisposition to this change that they engender which causes the abandonment of dialect. Both sociolinguistic and statistical studies have shown that it is the individual's will to adapt and his wish for his own advancement or for that of his children which is basically responsible for the flight from dialect. K. Spangenberg has shown how a small village in western Thuringia where the population in the 1930s was almost completely dialect-speaking was affected by the resettlements in consequence of the war. By 1950 only 74 per cent of the inhabitants still spoke dialect. After 1945 some dialect-speaking parents had begun to speak standard with their children. However, the position of dialect among schoolchildren remained fairly strong. But between 1950 and 1960 a decisive change occurred. Although many of the refugee families had departed, only 61 per cent of the population still used dialect. Of the 167 households of the village only 47 spoke exclusively dialect; most consisted of elderly people. In 87 households parents spoke standard with their children although dialect with each other. Of 81 schoolchildren only 15 had learnt dialect as their first language; altogether only 33 per cent could still speak dialect properly, although they did so only in certain cases and only with certain partners. Especially girls had turned their backs on dialect: 84 per cent now spoke standard. In other words, within one decade the use of standard among schoolchildren increased from 23 per cent to 67 per cent. It was the psychological attitude of the parents which brought about this rapid change. According to K. Spangenberg his results for Unterellen are representative of the language situation in many parts of Thuringia.

Where dialect has been abandoned by a substantial part of the population and where this state has lasted for some time, a form of *semi-standard* has generally arisen. This language form is usually called *Umgangssprache*, although the term has many meanings and is notably also used in the sense of *Sprache des Umgangs*, thus indicating a function of language rather than a form. By *Umgangssprache* or semi-standard I refer to the linguistic form between dialect and standard. Between these two poles (themselves by no means wholly stable) there is a vast amount of linguistic fluidity. It is first of all determined by the fact that this linguistic stratum is basically only spoken language. It is further determined by the spatial factor from which it derives a dialect colouring in phonology; by the social factor from which it derives its largely urban character and its different social registers; and by the interlocutory situation which causes the individual speaker to modify his speech according to the status of his interlocutor. This language form therefore tends to be extraordinarily open, although it is generally delimited from standard and from dialect. The forms of the latter may be deliberately avoided by the speakers as being too coarse and rustic while the forms of the former may be aimed at but not reached or may be deliberately avoided as being too 'high' or 'posh'. Speakers of *Umgangssprache* may speak this form by conscious departure from the standard or by conscious or unconscious abandonment of dialect. The resultant speech form may thus be either very close to standard or very close to dialect. On the other hand, in many urban areas, e.g. the Ruhr or Upper Saxony, where there are no dialects, it may simply be the everyday medium of the less well-educated, their new 'dialect' so to speak. In this case it is *Umgangssprache* only from the point of view of the language historian.

Semi-standard forms are above all found in towns and in industrial areas. In areas where dialect is only now being given up, e.g. in western Thuringia, people strive to attain the standard, and an *Umgangssprache* has not yet evolved. In Switzerland and Luxemburg where dialect speaking is still universal no semi-standard forms exist. Where the situation demands the use of dialect in functions for which it is ill-suited, diglossia often reaches breaking point and semi-standard sentences may arise on an ad hoc basis. The deviant forms of standard German which the foreigner is likely to hear in conversation in these two countries, are not *Umgangssprache* but accents of standard German. Where these are very marked, they are perhaps on a par with a 'foreign accent'.

It must be clear that such a heterogeneous phenomenon as German semi-standard is extremely elusive. While the standard language (in its written form) has been exhaustively investigated and while the dialects (as spoken forms) have received no less attention, the semi-standard, or better still, the several semi-standards, are largely unexamined. Although dialects have been mapped for a hundred years, the first atlas of *Umgangssprachen* has only just appeared. Although elements of phonology and syntax have been described, we have no full description of any regionally delimited *Umgangssprache*. Perhaps the social and idiolectal aspects are too obtrusive to permit a comprehensive yet unitary description.

But since semi-standard is such an important aspect of the contemporary German linguistic scene and since it seems to exercise such a powerful influence on certain registers of the written standard, an attempt must be made to examine some at least of its supra-regional characteristics. Although *Umgangssprache* is regionally determined, many features seem to be widespread and general. They derive, however, from various component factors.

General linguistic characteristics of *Umgangssprachen* are for instance:

(i) Certain systematic phonological differences from the standard. This is the most regionally determined feature, e.g. the coalescence of *b/p, d/t, g/k, s/ss* for instance in East Franconia, Upper Saxony and other parts of southern and central Germany, e.g. in *bar – Paar, leiden – leiten, gleiten – kleiden, rauben – Raupen, Greis – Kreis, reisen – reißen*; the coalescence of [ç] and [ʃ] in the Upper Saxon urban centres, in Frankfurt am Main and other Rhine Franconian cities ([dɪʃ] i.e. *Tisch* and *dich*, [ʃ] in *richtig, städtisch, lächerlich*); fricative values for standard *g* in many central and north German areas (*fliegen* with [ʃ] or [ç], *ganz* with [j] etc.); standard *pf* initially replaced by *f*, medially and finally by *p/b* (*Pfund > Fund, klopfen > klopm*); unrounding of *ü > i, ö > e*, especially in Upper Saxony; the suffix *-ung* realized as *-unk* in much of North Germany; for standard [aː] there are rounded values such as [ɔː] or [ɒː] in many areas; for standard /eː/ and /ɛː/ there is one correspondence /eː/ (e.g. in *Beeren* and *Bären*); rounding of *i > ü* in words like *immer, bin, frisch* etc. in Hamburg and other North German areas; vocalizations of *r* after vowels [meː ɒ] *mehr, schwaz* for *schwarz* mainly in northern Germany, or of *l* in Bavaria and Austria: [kɒet] *kalt*; monophthongs of *ē* and *ō* quality as reflexes of MHG *ei* and *ou* respectively, for instance in Upper Saxony; the existence of /ɒ/ (or /ɔ/) and /a/, e.g. in *ganz*[ɒ] but *praktisch* [a] where standard has only /a/, in many of the Austro-Bavarian regions. Only if the phonological differences from the standard are structural and combined with other features, e.g. grammatical ones, need we speak of semi-standard. If they are predominantly phonetic and isolated it may be preferable to regard the language form as an

accent of standard German. It is characteristic of the phonology
of an *Umgangssprache* that it is based on regional dialectal features,
but that its features do not necessarily lie half-way between
dialect and standard. When a Darmstadt dialect speaker aban-
dons his form [dɒːg] 'day' he is more likely to adopt the Rhenish
semi-standard form [daːx] than an approximation to the standard
[thaːk].

(ii) All kinds of assimilations and consonant reductions, e.g. *nich*
or *net* for *nicht*, *nix* for *nichts*, *krich* for *kriegt*, *kom̥* for *kommen*, *is*
for *ist*, *hallen* for *halten*, *Schanne* for *Schande*, *ham* for *haben*.

(iii) Similar assimilatory processes lead to fusions of function
words, e.g. *inne* for *in die*, *mitte* for *mit die*, *son* for *so ein*, *sin* for
sie ein, *vonne* for *von der* or *von einer*, *mitner* for *mit einer*. Beyond
the fusions of prepositions and articles tolerated by the standard
language (*beim, am, im, zur* etc.) there are many more, e.g.
überm, ausm, umn, vorm, vors, zun, fürs, fürn etc.

(iv) Articles may be shortened: *e* (*ein*), *ne* (*eine*), *ner* (*einer*), *s* (*das*).

(v) Verb and personal pronoun in inversion are fused: *hammer*
(*haben wir*), *hast* or *haste* (*hast du*), *bist* or *biste* (*bist du*), *hanse*
(*haben sie*).

(vi) Verbal forms in -*e* lose the ending: *ich hab, ich sag, ich hol*;
ich konnt, ich wollt; *leg! setz!*

(vii) Adverbs with *her* and *hin* are shortened and the distinction
between the two is often obliterated: *ran, raus* (also *nan, naus*
and other *n*-forms), *rein, rüber, runter* etc. Other shortenings are
etwas > *was*, *einmal* > *mal*, *heute* > *heut*.

(viii) The ending -*en* is generally assimilated to [m] after labials,
[ŋ] after velars, [n] after dentals, e.g. *lebm* (*leben*), *hackng* (*hacken*),
redn (*reden*).

(ix) Weak masc. nouns are frequently used without the ending -*en*
in the oblique cases of the sg.: *n Mensch* (*einen Menschen*). The
dat. sg. of strong masc. and neuter nouns lacks -*e*: *zu Haus, am
Tag*.

(x) The *s*-pl. is much more frequent especially in northern
Germany: *Kerls, Jungens, Mädels, Kumpels, Krans* (for *Krane* or
Kräne), *Loks* (*Lokomotiven*).

(xi) For the possessive genitive (*die Pfeife meines Vaters*) a construction with *von* is general (*die Pfeife von meinem Vater*) or in
the lowest stratum of semi-standard the dialectal dative paraphrase is heard (*meinem Vater seine Pfeife*). The genitive has

generally only survived in formulas: *in Gotts Namn, um Himmels willen, ich bin der Meinung, kurzer Hand*. But it is also typical of many speakers of semi-standard that they use quotations from the standard, e.g. *nach Fertigstellung der Arbeit, beim Einschalten des Motors*. It is a sign of the heterogeneity of this form of language that otherwise such abstract phrases are normally avoided. *Bei der Abfahrt des Zuges* becomes *wenn der Zug abfährt, die Gründe seiner Tat: warum er das gemacht hat*.

(xii) In many areas of northern Germany the distinction between acc. and dat. is obliterated; in Rhenish areas the distinction between nom. and acc.

(xiii) Adjectival phrases with the dative are often replaced by prepositional phrases: *uns gefährlich > gefährlich für uns*. On the other hand the ethic dative is popular: *du bist mir ein Frecher*.

(xiv) Ellipsis of the subject pronoun or a grammatical subject: *weiß nich (ich)*; *kannst mal gehen (du)*; *müßt das lassen endlich (ihr)*; *gibts nich (das)*; *kommt nich in Frage (das)*.

(xv) Replacement of the personal pronouns by the demonstrative pronoun: *der bleibt nich lang (er)*; *jetzt stell dir vor, die lesen das (sie)*; *die hat mir ne Karte geschickt (sie)*.

(xvi) The demonstrative pronoun is usually *der, die, das* not *dieser, jener*, often extended to *der da*: *die da hats schon gewußt*; *mit dem Mensch da*. The relative pronoun is also *der, die, das* not *welcher*; often it is expanded to *der wo* etc. or replaced by *wo* or *was*. In northern Germany the compounds of demonstrative and preposition are replaced by separate forms, e.g. standard *davon*: *da weiß ich nichts von*.

(xvii) The definite article is general with names: *die Hildegard, der Fritz, der Barzel, der Strauß*. In northern Germany words denoting members of the family are used without the def. art.: *bei Großmutter*; *Vater hat gesagt*.

(xviii) Some prepositions governing the genitive are construed with the dative: *wegen dem Kind*; *statt dem gelben*. Many prepositions are altogether confined to standard, e.g. *anläßlich, anstelle, diesseits, innerhalb, kraft, vermöge, mittels* and many more.

(xix) The comparative particle is *wie* or *als wie* rather than *als* as in standard (*jünger wie ich*).

(xx) Expanded forms with *tun* as an auxiliary: *und riechen tun sie alle wie Hasen*; *sie tut kochen*; *da tut er mal nachschauen*; in the subjunctive II: *ich tät sagen*; *er täts bringen*. Otherwise the conditional is formed with *würd* (*würd bringen, würd kommen* not *brächte, käme*). But *hätt(e), wär(e), könnt(e)* and the other modals are frequent in hypothetical sentences.

(xxi) In southern and much of central Germany the perfect is used as the tense of narration. Past tense forms are usually only: *war, hatt*, and the modal auxiliaries (*konnt', mußt'* etc.). Beside *wir hatten nix gesehen* there is also the pluperfect *wir haben nix gesehen gehabt*.

(xxii) The subjunctive I (present subjunctive) has practically vanished: *ich habe gehört, er sei dabei eingeschlafen* > *du! ich hab gehört, der is dabei eingeschlafen.*

(xxiii) Sentence types: (a) Questions are often put in the form of a statement: *Du hast ihn schon gesehen? Woher das bloß kommt?* Sometimes *ja* and *nich* function as interrogative particles: *kommst doch schon, ja? hast ihn getroffen, nich?* (b) Parataxis is often preferred to subordination: *ich geh nich ins Kino, ich hab kein Geld* (i.e. *weil ich kein Geld habe*); *ich versprech, ich lauf nich weg* (*daß*).

(xxiv) Pronominal repetition of the subject: *die Mutter, die ist einkaufen gegangen*; *mein Chef, der hat* . . .

(xxv) The principle of incapsulation is very often not adhered to (extrapolation) especially in the case of adverbial complements of time and place: *der hat mir n neuen Fußball gebracht gestern abend* (main clause); *der mir n neuen Fußball gebracht hat gestern abend* (subordinate clause); *der hat Post bekommen von zu Haus*. Extrapolation, parenthesis (interruption of the sentence by the insertion of another sentence), anacoluthon (grammatically incorrect continuation of the sentence), ellipsis (omission of grammatically and semantically necessary parts usually supplied by the context or the situation) and aposiopesis (sudden breaking-off in speech) are characteristics of spontaneous spoken language and thus also of semi-standard. Where the standard (written) uses extended attributes, the semi-standard as speech and as speech of the less well-educated prefers the so-called enumerative manner: new ideas are added as they occur to the speaker. The result is often a loosely connected chain of associated ideas expressed in a grammatically incorrectly connected sequence.

(xxvi) In lexis we notice the frequent avoidance of abstract terms, e.g. *trinkbar* > *was man trinken kann*; *kinderlos* > *keine Kinder haben*; *Unterricht* > *Schule haben*; *Ungläubiger* > *e Mensch, was nix glaubt*; *sich vergewissern* > *nachgucken, obs stimmt*. If the speaker cannot remember the correct term he replaces it by meaningless substitutes: *Dings da, Zeug, Sache,* or words like *Zauber, Zirkus, Spaß, soundso.* He also pads out his utterance with time-gaining stop-gap words: *wie sagt man, sagen wir bloß mal, wer weiß, Gott weiß, weiß der Teufel, na ja, nich* or *nicht wahr, so, eben, halt, gell, eh, nun.* Many interjections occur: *hoppla, hossa, he, ach so, bumms* and so on. Certain words are especially frequent: *kriegen, kucken, ne* or largely confined to semi-standard: *schlacksig, dämlich, mies, prima, mollig, speckig, dufte, kullern, stänkern* and, of course, many more. Dialect words are also taken up into semi-standard, e.g. *doof* 'stupid', the LG form for HG *taub; dat, wat* in the northern Rhinelands and elsewhere in the north, *Gören* 'children', *lütt* 'little', *snacken* 'to talk' in the north. As far as lexical usage is concerned semi-standard shares many of its characteristics with *Volkssprache.* Emotionalism often means that matter-of-fact, neutral terms are regularly replaced by loaded expressions, either positive or negative ones. 'A young chap' is either *ein toller Kerl* or *ein dummer Aff.* For 'to beat' and 'to throw' the affective terms *hauen* and *schmeißen* are used, not the neutral *schlagen, werfen.* The coarse terms *fressen* and *saufen* replace *essen* and *trinken;* or *abgesoffen* stands for *ertrunken; krepieren, verrecken* for *sterben; Maul* for *Mund.* Vulgarisms abound at the lower end of the sociolinguistic spectrum (*Fresse, Scheiße,* determinative elements like *Sau-, Schwein-, Dreck-, Huren-*). Concrete idioms are favoured: *auf Stottern kaufen (auf Abzahlung); der Bart ist ab (die Sache ist erledigt); sich die Beine in den Leib stehen (lange warten); er hat einen Besenstiel verschluckt (er ist steif, verbeugt sich nicht); am Ball bleiben (die Sache nicht aus den Augen lassen);* there are many humorous expressions: *Bauplatz (Glatze); Lumpensammler (Spätzug); er hat die Baumschule besucht (nichts gelernt); Begatterich (Ehemann);* there are exaggerations like *wahnsinnig, stierisch ernst, stinkbesoffen, Affenhitze, Biereifer, Blitzkerl, Bombengeschäft, Teufelskerl, Heidendurst, Höllenlärm;* all kinds of expressions from slang and specialist languages are also found in *Umgangssprache: Biene* 'a girl of light virtue', with the attributes *dufte, kesse* or *schräge; Bluse (pars pro toto:* 'young girl'); *jemandem etwas andrehen; Betriebskurven (dunkle Ringe unter den Augen); Dauerbrenner (langer Kuß); Dachschaden (geistig beschränkt);* and from thieves' slang: *beschummeln* (for *betrügen*), *betucht* (for *wohlhabend*).

The following parody in a form of the semi-standard of the Ruhr district may serve as a sample of written *Umgangssprache*:

Der Betriebsrat is inne Ohren gekommen, daß es einige von uns gibt, die noch nich richtig aufgeklärt sind mitte Entwicklungshilfe, vor allem seit dat amtlich is, daß wir nächsten Donnerstag acht schwatte Praktikanten kriegen, von Negeria. Und darüber wollt' ich jetzt hier mal ein paar Wörter verlieren!

Herrschaften! Die erste Sache is, dat manche von euch, wenn die ein Neger sehen, dann kriegen die gleich so'n feudalen Grinsen im Gesicht und glaubense, bloß weil sie 'n bißken weißer sind wie der, da wären sie schon wer weiß wat! – Wat is? – Ja komm, bitte schön, hier die Kollegen vonne Fahrbereitschaft, die können das nämlich bescheinigen, wie ihr euch benehmen tut, wenn einer von euch schon mal mit 'ne Verletzung im Unfallkrankenhaus kommt und soll da von diesen Doktor Uwamba behandelt werden, der da is – auf einmal wollense nich oder sagen, wär schon alles wieder heil und tät auch gar nich mehr wehtun ... lauter so Sachen! Dabei is dieser Mann ein richtig gelernten Arzt und is bloß hier für seinen Facharzt zu machen, und da will ich euch mal wat zu erzählen:

Ein alten Kumpel von mir, der Jupp Koschinski, ne, der war nämlich genauso; wenn der ein'n Neger gewahr wurde, dann war er auch immer gleich dran mit „Bananbieger", „Entwicklungsgorilla" und so häßliche Schimpfwörter. Jetzt, letzten März, schickt ihm seine Firma unten nach Afrika für Trafo-Stationen zum Montieren, und kaum daß er da is, fängt er auch schon mit Bauchschmerzen an. Wat is gewesen?? – Hier, die weiße Kollegen von Gelsenkirchen, die mit bei waren, die ham gesagt: „Komm, stech'n Finger im Hals!" oder „Hier, haste Rhinzinus!" – aber seine schwatten Hiwis, die ham ihm auf'm Buckel genommen und im nächsten Krankenhaus geschleppt, und da war auch so'n Neger, der hier in Deutschland, in München, glaub ich, hatte der sein Facharzt gemacht, und der hat ihm dann vielleicht einen Blinddarm 'rausgeholt, mein lieber Scholli! – da hat die Beerdigungsfirma schon mit'n Sarg vor de Tür gestanden, so ein Kawenzmann war dat!

Und seitdem sagt der Jupp: Wenn er noch mal ein'n Blinddarm kriegen sollte, da würde er direkt bis inne Wüste mit fahren, bloß für daß er ein Schwatten hätte, der ihm dat Dingen 'rausmontieren könnte – so schön und angenehm hat ihm dieser Doktor damals dat Leben gerettet! So, und nu seid ihr dran, könnt ihr selber urteilen, wer eigentlich diese Entwicklungshilfe am meisten von gehabt hat.

Ich meine, ich hab' die Tage mal persönlich mit den Minister gesprochen, der in Bonn diese ganze Neger und Araber und Entwicklungssachen alles unter sich hat, der Herr Wischnewski, der muß dat ja schließlich wissen, der Mann, und der sagt: Es war doch ein Blödsinn, wenn't immer heißt, dat wir die ganze Entwicklungsmillionen nur verschenken täten! Nix! Die Herrschaften kriegen de Mäuse nur geborgt und müssense jeden einzigen Pfennig wieder zurückzahlen mit Zins und Zinsenzins mit bei, da wären die in Bonn ganz pingelig für. Dat is genauso, als wenn ihr ein Farbfernseher auf Stottern kauft: wenn ihr da mal nich pünktlich seid mit de Raten, bumms, is der Bart ab!

Jürgen von Manger in
'Der Spiegel', 23 October 1967.

7·3·3 | Written and spoken language

These two opposite poles, too, are abstractions. Not everything that is written is 'written language' and not everything that is spoken is 'spoken language'. The transitions are manifold. In the nineteenth century the German standard language was, by and large, 'written language'. Only in the *Sturm und Drang* period in the eighteenth century and in the Naturalism of the late nineteenth century was an attempt made to catch the real 'spoken language'. Otherwise what purported to be 'spoken', for instance in classical drama, was nothing but an offshoot of that rarefied medium, the written language of the time. This written language was above all characterized by an elaborate construction of involved sentence periods. Subordination in all kinds of ways, including much subordination within subordination held together by the principle of incapsulation, was meant to reflect careful, logical, organized thinking and required deliberate, precise formulation. A large part of the weight of such constructions was carried by verbs. Of course, this style of writing can still be found today. The classical literary register is indeed one of the modes of expression of written German. But most ordinary everyday prose of textbooks or quality journals follows a different style. The period has given way to a main-clause type of construction. Subordination is rarer. Sentence length has been generally reduced. Much of the information is carried in nominal expansions, such as expanded attributes, appositions, and genitival and prepositional groups. This packed, concise style conveys as much information as possible in an economic, word-saving way. Much use is made of ad hoc compounds and substantivizations and finite verbs play a numerically less important part. Hans Eggers (p. 61) gives as illustrative examples a sentence by Goethe (a) and one which a modern author (b) might write:

(a) Es scheint nicht überflüssig zu sein, genau anzuzeigen, was wir uns bei diesen Worten denken, welche wir öfters brauchen werden.

(b) Die genaue Angabe des bei diesen öfters zu brauchenden Wörtern Gedachten scheint nicht überflüssig.

As an example of the older type of literary and scholarly prose there follows a passage from Wilhelm von Humboldt's *Ideen zu einem Versuch, die Grenzen der Wirksamkeit des Staats zu bestimmen* (written 1792, published 1851, *Werke*, Berlin, 1903, vol. 1, p. 179):

Diejenigen, deren Sicherheit erhalten werden muß, sind auf der einen Seite alle Bürger, in völliger Gleichheit, auf der andren der Staat selbst. Die Sicherheit des Staats selbst hat ein Objekt von größerem oder geringerem Umfange, je weiter man seine Rechte ausdehnt, oder je enger man sie beschränkt, und daher hängt hier die Bestimmung von der Bestimmung des Zwecks derselben ab. Wie ich nun diese hier bis jetzt versucht habe, dürfte er für nichts andres Sicherheit fordern können, als für die Gewalt, welche ihm eingeräumt, und das Vermögen, welches ihm zugestanden worden. Hingegen Handlungen in Hinsicht auf diese Sicherheit einschränken, wodurch ein Bürger, ohne eigentliches Recht zu kränken – und folglich vorausgesetzt, daß er nicht in einem besondren persönlichen, oder temporellen Verhältnisse mit dem Staat stehe, wie z. B. zur Zeit eines Krieges – sich oder sein Eigentum ihm entzieht, könnte er nicht. Denn die Staatsvereinigung ist bloß ein untergeordnetes Mittel, welchem der wahre Zweck, der Mensch, nicht aufgeopfert werden darf, es müßte denn der Fall einer solchen Kollision eintreten, daß, wenn auch der Einzelne nicht verbunden wäre, sich zum Opfer zu geben, doch die Menge das Recht hätte, ihn als Opfer zu nehmen. Ueberdies aber darf, den entwickelten Grundsätzen nach, der Staat nicht für das Wohl der Bürger sorgen, und um ihre Sicherheit zu erhalten, kann das nicht notwendig sein, was gerade die Freiheit und mithin auch die Sicherheit aufhebt.

The following passage on a similar topic from an article by Hans Schueler in *Die Zeit*, 29 March 1974, illustrates the more modern type of prose:

Zur Zeit der Entstehung des Grundgesetzes standen sich die Sozialstaatsmodelle der Union und der SPD annähernd chancengleich gegenüber; heute erlebt das Modell der Sozialdemokraten eine gewisse

Renaissance, nachdem es in den fünfziger Jahren unter dem Eindruck des Siegeszuges der Marktwirtschaft von seinen Verfechtern weitgehend aufgegeben worden war. Während das marktwirtschaftliche Modell im Grundsatz auf die selbstregulierende Kraft des Marktes vertraut und den Staat auf die Festlegung der Rahmenbedingungen für den im übrigen autonomen Ablauf der Wirtschaftsprozesse beschränkt, forderte die SPD mit ihrem damals schon so bezeichneten Programm des „demokratischen Sozialismus" die staatliche Planung des Wirtschaftsablaufs, die Überführung wichtiger Industriezweige in Gemeineigentum und die Demokratisierung des Wirtschaftslebens durch Mitbestimmung der Arbeitnehmer.

If we have a less complicated construction of periods, we have several examples of 'nominal blocks', as Hans Eggers calls them (*unter dem Eindruck des Siegeszuges der Marktwirtschaft*), of expanded attributes (*mit ihrem damals schon so bezeichneten Programm*), of substantivization (*Überführung, Demokratisierung* and other nouns in *-ung*), and of new compounds (*Sozialstaatsmodelle, chancengleich, selbstregulierend, Wirtschaftsablauf*) and abbreviations (*SPD*).

Both kinds of the literary written language are equally far removed from the spoken language. But it is characteristic of the written language of today that there are now registers strongly influenced by the spoken language and by semi-standard forms. Many contemporary authors cultivate such a style. Naturally the personal style predominates in such cases. More immediately representative of this 'vulgar' contemporary style is the depersonalized language of mass-circulation daily newspapers and weekly magazines. These deliberately go in for the most undemanding kind of writing. The most notable among these is the *Bild-Zeitung*, which has the highest circulation figure of any newspaper in the German language. The following passage (*Bild-Zeitung*, 12 June 1974) may illustrate this:

Was waren wir froh, als unsere Steckdosen während der Ölkrise Strom spuckten. Nachtspeicher-Heizungen liefen, Straßenbahnen fuhren, Kaffee kochte. Die Scheichs mit ihrem Öl – ganz hatten sie uns also nicht in der Hand.

Gestern – die Ölkrise ist fast vergessen – verriet Algeriens Energieminister Abdesselam der "Welt": Eine Kapitalanlage in der deutschen Elektrizitätswirtschaft sei für die Ölländer viel reizvoller als der Kauf von Gold oder Grundstücken.

Das heißt: Mit dem Riesengeld aus den Ölverkäufen wollen die Scheichs jetzt nicht mehr an unsere Grundstücke heran, sondern an unsere Kraftwerke. Dann können sie uns bei der nächsten Krise nicht nur die Ölhähne zudrehen, sondern auch die Stromkabel kappen.
Allah ist groß.
Passen wir auf – sonst wird er allzu mächtig.

A slangy, racy style is meant to entertain the readers (*Strom spucken*; *heran wollen*); concrete expressions rather than abstract terms are to ease comprehension (*Ölhähne zudrehen*; *Stromkabel kappen*; *in der Hand haben*); short sentences, e.g. in a series of parallel clauses (*Nachtspeicher liefen*, etc.) or paratactical constructions (*Das heißt:*), or the use of parenthesis (*–die Ölkrise ist fast vergessen* –), or anacoluthon (*Die Scheichs mit ihrem Öl – ganz hatten sie...*) suggest haste and encourage rapid absorption; the possessive genitive with a proper name (*Algeriens* – rather than *von Algerien*) is a modern journalistic device; the use of *wir* and colloquialisms (*was waren wir froh*; *Riesengeld*) create an atmosphere of matiness; the use of the *s*-pl. (*Scheichs*) rather than the *e*-pl. (*Scheiche*) is a further indication of the popular level deliberately aimed at by the journalists of this newspaper. Mittelberg (pp. 185–9), found that over 60 per cent of all sentences are simple sentences and that the largest number contain only five to nine words.

Of the many different registers of the written language that of administration and that of advertising play a particularly significant role in modern life. It has been shown of the former that it, too, prefers the relatively short, predominantly main-clause type of sentence, not at all the convoluted long period, of which it used to be accused. Indeed, over half of all sentences contain no more than eighteen words and about half of all sentences consist of a main clause only. However, where subordination occurs, the kind of general prose examined by Hans Eggers (see p. 526) prefers relative clauses, but the language of administration has a preponderance of adverbial clauses and puts elements, which could be expressed in relative clauses, into expanded attributes: *in einem Brief, der gestern abgesandt wurde | in einem gestern abgesandten Brief*; *finanzielle Hilfe, die ausbezahlt werden muß | die auszubezahlende finanzielle Hilfe*. Like modern prose generally it favours nominal paraphrases (*einen Antrag stellen*) which often have a special technical meaning (*Klage einreichen, Einspruch erheben*), substantivizations and nominal blocks. A clause like 'dem dort vorliegenden Antrag auf Durchführung des Verfahrens auf Untersagung der Ausübung des selbständigen Gewerbes' is difficult to grasp because of the packed density of the nominal constructions. Prepositional formulas are often regarded as typical bureaucratic German: *aus Zweckmäßigkeitsgründen, im Verhinderungsfall, bei Arbeitsunfähigkeitsmeldung*. Replacing subordinate clauses, as they often do, they are however economic. Many compounds have a similar effect and are therefore favoured: *dienstplanmäßig, ausländerbehördlich*. A special feature of this register is further the extensive use made of the passive. Hildegard Wagner found that not only over a quarter of all sentences were in the passive, but that in addition many other constructions were passive in content, e.g. *es empfiehlt sich*; *etwas ist zu tun* rather than *jemand hat etwas zu tun*.

The register of advertising is equally characterized by special features of syntax and word formation. It often uses incomplete comparisons: *X ist größer*. It favours ad hoc compounds which are meant to surprise the reader, e.g. *hautkosmetisch, formschön, fußgesund, Mehrzweckmantel, Tiefformkoffer*. Frequently such compounds have a technical ring about them and are meant to flatter the reader's intelligence and expertise. Many coalescent compounds also give the impression of being technical and hence precise terms, e.g. *Frischmilch* rather than *frische Milch*. Exaggeration is naturally the stock-in-trade of advertising: *hochmodern, super-aktiv, erfüllt die verwöhntesten Forderungen*. This register is also recognizable by the innumerable word creations of the commercial world: *Wella* (*Haarpflegemittel*), *Sinalco* (< *sine alcohole*, a soft drink), *Persil* (< *Perborat + Silicium*) and by many foreign loans (*Twinset, Slip*), including bilingual puns (*wer beatet mehr?*).

The spoken language is much less well known than the written language. Any detailed scientific investigation has in fact only been possible since the invention of magnetic recording. It is now evident that spoken language is a many-faceted, complicated phenomenon. It is determined by such factors as speaker, listener, subject and situation. The term situation is here used in a wide sense including not only the material surroundings but also the experience and knowledge of speaker(s) and listener(s) and their recourse to gestures and mimicry. The relation between speaker and listener marks a spoken text as a monologue or a dialogue, the two basic types of spoken language. In forms like lectures, sermons, live commentaries and narratives we have pure monologues with captive listeners and a given subject. The extra-linguistic situation, except in the live commentary, has only a weak influence. Monologues occur, of course, also in more evenly balanced speaker/listener relations, such as in discussions (set theme with equal participation), interviews (set theme but unequal participation) or in conversation (no set theme with equal participation). Again, the extra-linguistic situation varies in importance. It tends to be of least significance in discussions, may or may not be of significance in interviews (compare a medical consultation with an interview concerned with a distant past event), or may be of overpowering significance, for instance, in free conversations. In fact, in many free conversations the role of the situation may be so great as to reduce language to a mere ancillary role or to make it almost unnecessary. If such conversations are deprived of their circumstantial background, as they are in a tape recording, they are practically incomprehensible to a listener who was not an original participant. Such spoken language is, of course, an extreme case and the extreme opposite of written language, where the situation has always to be filled in in detail by verbal means. It is, however, a mistake to claim this form of the spoken language as the only genuine and representative form. Statements which stress the extreme difference of spoken from written language are based on such a fallacy. A register of the spoken language where the extra-linguistic factor of the situation impinges to such an extreme degree on the linguistic performance cannot possibly reflect the typical linguistic characteristics of spoken language.

The spoken language thus embraces many registers, and the extra-linguistic criteria determining them vary in their impact in each register. Within the major forms or registers (conversation, narrative, discussion, etc.) the linguistic types of monologue and dialogue may vary no less. What a definition of spoken language must include, however, are the following points set up by Hugo Steger (pp. 262–4): (a) the text must be spoken without having been previously written down; (b) it must not have been thought out and formulated beforehand (some scholars would, however, admit this form as spoken language); (c) it must not be in verse or rhymed; (d) it must be in a form regarded as 'normal', i.e.

'correct' in the given context. This last point was amended by Barbara Wackernagel-Jolles to: it must be in a form which is understood by the listener without any need for asking for further elucidation. This seems an improvement since it deals with the problem of norm, error and incorrectness in a way more appropriate to the linguistic medium with which we are concerned. That is, we are not referred to norms possibly valid in a different medium, i.e. the written language.

The problem of segmentation into units, i.e. sentences, is crucial in spoken language. Of the three possible criteria: content, intonation and grammatical patterning, only the last two are germane to language. Intonation seems an attractive criterion but investigations have shown that listeners seem unable to distinguish intonational segments with any marked degree of unanimity. In a study where the segmentation was based on intonation, the informants were unanimous only in a minority of cases excluding terminations of utterances (Wackernagel-Jolles pp. 147, 150). It would therefore appear that segmentation must be based on grammatical criteria. In the following sample text of spoken standard German – a monologue passage from a discussion – the following punctuation marks are used: full stop to mark the end of an independent main clause; comma to mark a dependent subordinate clause; colon to indicate a dependent main clause; dash indicates a broken-off construction; dots indicate non-lexical elements. (The original text as given in *Texte gesprochener deutscher Standardsprache*, vol. 1, 1971, p. 236, a discussion among students on marriage, uses a somewhat different system of notation.) The alphabetic spelling of the written language is used. It would, of course, be desirable that spoken language should be *heard*, but as sound reproduction is obviously impossible here a transposition into the medium of letters must be accepted.

Ich ich meine. Ich vertrete . . . meinen Standpunkt nicht . . . bezüglich der Konventionen, weil ich einfach meine: der Mensch kommt in – is einfach zu schwach. Oder manchmal ist der Mensch zu schlecht. Oder er schafft es nicht. Er liebt seine Frau. Aber es gibt Momente, . . . wo die Frau oder wo der Mann . . . einfach dessen überdrüssig is und . . . meint: sie wolle nicht mehr, und daß in solchen Momenten einfach die die Konvention . . . oder dieses Bewußtsein vor der Gesellschaft einfach wieder eine Hilfe ist, und daß keiner so stark ist, das so ein Leben lang auszuführen. Denn in n meisten Fällen is ja so n bißchen Müde-Sein von der Ehe – wird in jedem Fall auftreten. Und, wenn die jetzt nich so stark schon von außen her zusammengekettet sind, so sind sie ja viel eher… bereit, in einem solchen Augenblick nun alles aufzugeben. Und das halt ich für zu gefährlich.

Taking into account that spoken language comprises many registers with different characteristics the following points may be claimed to have some general validity:

(i) The basic syntactic laws and sentential structures are the same in written and in spoken German (see Jecklin, pp. 51, 150; Wackernagel-Jolles, p. 202).

(ii) The greater the importance of the situation the more truncated is the language. More complicated sentence patterns and increased filling-out with non-obligatory complements are found in reflective monologues (see Jecklin, pp. 54–5).

(iii) Sentence length and the proportion of simple sentences vary according to the register. C. Leska (p. 444) found that over 65 per cent of the sentences in her material were simple sentences, but in B. Wackernagel-Jolles's interpretation only 25 per cent were of this type. Many sentences are paratactical and the question of linking obviously affects the interpretation. B. Wackernagel-Jolles (p. 177) found that the greatest number of sentences fell within the bracket of 5–14 word sentences; C. Leska noted that nearly half of all the sentences in her spoken material were within the 5–10 word bracket, while in Hans Eggers' written material the peak was in the 16–18 word bracket. Spoken parliamentary language seems to be hypotactical to a considerable degree (Uhlig, pp. 98–136).

(iv) Extrapolation is frequent. Uhlig (pp. 145–51) makes the useful distinction of extrapolation based on (a) associative thinking (what was forgotten is added): 'Ich sehe, daß ich mich ein wenig vergallopiert [sic] habe in der Redezeit…'; (b) stylistic reasons (important elements are placed outside the verbal bracket for reasons of stress): 'Sie treten Ihr Amt an bei Vollbeschäftigung, bei stabilem Geld und wohlgeordneten Finanzen'; (c) the tendency to form nominal blocks: 'Die Überlegenheit auf dem nuklearen Gebiet ist gekennzeichnet durch über 850 sowjetische Mittelstreckenraketen, wo eine gleichwertige Waffe in Mitteleuropa bei der Nato nicht zur Verfügung steht.'

(v) Sentences are often broken off (aposiopesis, ellipsis) or continued with a switch to a different construction (anacoluthon).

The possibility of instant correction is frequently used, either because of error or *lapsus linguae*, dissatisfaction with the lack of precision, or because additions are desired. Nominal elements (nouns, adjectives, articles, pronouns) can be more easily improved upon than verbal elements (Wackernagel-Jolles, p. 166).

(vi) Sentences are often interrupted by parenthesis.

(vii) Repetitions are frequent either because the thread has been momentarily lost or because the speaker wishes to be emphatic. There is thus a high degree of redundance in spoken language counteracting the fleeting nature of the medium and facilitating comprehension. Anaphoric constructions (see *Oder . . . , Oder . . .* in the text) also serve to emphasize and further save the speaker the effort of finding new constructions.

(viii) Non-lexical sound sequences and pauses permit reflection. Stuttering may be caused by the need to gain time. Clichés (*wie sagt man, sagen wir mal*) and filler words (*ja, mal, eh, ach* etc.) also retard the flow of speech. Similar elements (*nich, gell, na, so, da*) seem also to act as effective sentence boundary markers and as function words establishing contact, enlivening the utterance or commenting on it.

(ix) After verbs or nouns of speaking or denoting the expression of an opinion an asyndetic main clause is usual in spoken language where written German would use direct speech or subordinate clauses introduced by a conjunction (see the colon notations in the text, and Wackernagel-Jolles, pp. 185–203). Subordinate clauses may occur with the main clause being understood (ellipsis).

(x) There are many pronominal and demonstrative elements often loosely employed and making imprecise reference to antecedent events (see *dessen*; *das so ein Leben lang auszuführen* in the text).

(xi) The most frequent conjunctions are *und*, sometimes expanded to *und da, und dann*, and *daß*, followed by *wenn* and at some distance by *weil* (Wackernagel-Jolles, pp. 203–15). A much greater proportion of the subordinate clauses of spoken German are introduced by conjunctions (*daß, wenn*) than by relative pronouns (*der, die, das*): nearly 62 per cent as against just over 38 per cent (C. Leska, p. 445). In written German the two types are more evenly balanced (53 per cent to 47 per cent).

(xii) While written German favours expanded attributes and nominal blocks, the spoken variant avoids them to a large extent.

(xiii) The subjunctive is practically confined to auxiliaries and modal verbs. The passive occurs very rarely (see Wackernagel-Jolles, pp. 231–6).

(xiv) In North German speech preterite and perfect are interchangeable as narrative tenses of the past. The pret. of auxiliaries and modals is more frequent than of other verbs, where it appears more formal (Wackernagel-Jolles, pp. 215–29, 236).

In conclusion it must be stressed that while the difference in medium produces significant differences between spoken and written languages the constant use of both forms by socially and culturally important users also forms an important bridge. In the past it was in the written language that the German standard language was forged; subsequently it was the written language which directed the trends of standardization in the spoken language. At the present time the bridge is continually being reinforced and crossed in both directions. There are, as we have seen, written registers modelled on the spoken language and there are spoken registers modelled on the written language. This fact is a characteristic feature of contemporary German.

7.3.4 | General and specialist language

These two opposites exist only on the level of lexis and to some extent on the level of grammar (morphology and syntax), but not on the level of phonology. From the angle of lexis we can say that German has three strata of words. First there are those words which are common to all healthy native adult speakers (*Tag, Nacht, essen, trinken*); secondly, there are those words the passive understanding and active use of which presuppose some knowledge derived from education or experience (*Tagundnachtgleiche, Säugetier, Stickstoff, hobeln, löten*); and thirdly, there are words which mean nothing to the average speaker and which presuppose a specialist knowledge of some science, a branch of scholarship, a craft or a trade (*Flansch, Zeigerfahne, Pfeilrad, honen, kuppen*). Everybody would agree that the first set of words belongs to general language and the third set to specialist or technical language. The middle field is constituted by words which derive from some specialist discipline but which have entered the general language of nearly all or a large number of speakers. It is naturally almost impossible to delimit this middle ground. In newspapers and journals which have many grammar-school educated people among their readers, words like *Minne, Tagelied, Hypothenuse, Molekül, Chlorophyll,* are assumed to be part of the general vocabulary of the readership. In publications addressed to readers of a lower educational standard different assumptions would be made about what constitutes a general vocabulary.

The definition of general language must therefore include the parameter of education and experience. It is a characteristic feature of modern German that its lexicon includes innumerable words created in or influenced by specialist languages (*ausloten, Gas geben, ankurbeln, entgleisen, abreagieren, sterilisieren*). If modern technologies and sciences are now the breeding ground of the modern vocabulary, older disciplines played an important part in former periods of the language. Many words of general language reflect, for instance, the influence in the past of hunting, e.g. *Lockvogel* and *Pechvogel* from fowling, *naseweis, pfiffig, vorlaut, unbändig* from descriptions of the behaviour of hunting dogs, *sich drücken* from the reaction of hunted game.

Specialist language also includes several layers of words. Quite obviously, words belonging to group three above form the core of a specialist language. The words of group two must also be included, although they form its outer mantle. To these must be added words belonging to general language (*Wurzel, schlichten*) which have a special meaning in a specialist language (*Wurzel* in mathematics, botany, linguistics; *schlichten* in law or metal-processing) or which are used metaphorically (*Gabel, Kopf, Bauch*). *Betrug* in general language refers to all kinds of deception, trickery and cheating, but in legal language it refers to a particular crime closely defined in the criminal code. *Hund* is known to everybody as the word for 'dog'; in the mining industry it designates a small truck. Literary scholars will use *dramatisch, romantisch, tragisch* in a technical sense while the general public use them loosely. We meet here the important difference between technical terms and general words.

A technical term has a specified, defined value in a particular discipline which may derive from tradition and informed usage, an individual professional act of definition, or from the ruling of some authoritative body. Many sciences, e.g. botany, anatomy, chemistry, have a standardized nomenclature. The word 'nomenclature' is often reserved for the standard names of objects, while 'terminology' is used with reference to defined concepts, processes and objects. In nomenclature definition is most precise, while much conceptual terminology may be open to various definitions. *Schienbein* has an undisputed technical meaning, while some names of illnesses, such as *Asthma* and *chronische Bronchitis*, are not uniquely defined. All linguists know that the term *phoneme* has various definitions. A technical term can nevertheless be clearly distinguished from a general word. It is characterized not only by having a definition but also by being, in consequence, less dependent upon the context for its meaning than the general word and by being relatively free from emotive and stylistic connotation. Its uniqueness may be an ideal rather than an inevitable achievement, but by being a part of a terminological system it carries more semantic freight than the average general word. The term H_2O is a term of chemical nomenclature; *Wasser* as a technical term carries a specific definition of a particular liquid derived from a knowledge of chemistry and physics and is stylistically neutral; *Wasser* as a word of general language carries no such technical information and receives the connotation of 'miserable beverage' in *bei Wasser und Brot* and the connotation of a most desirable drink in *ach, ein Glas Wasser!* if uttered by a sick or thirsty person.

A specialist language is thus above all characterized by possessing technical terms while general language consists of general words. Of course, the bulk of any text in a specialist language, spoken or written, will also contain general words (*und, in, zwei, kalt, Frage*). Especially verbs tend to be only weakly terminologized, if at all: *sich unterscheiden, bestehen, sich eignen, ergänzen*, and so on. But a specialist language often makes a particular use of these general elements, either lexically or syntactically, which thus also adds to its specific nature.

The concept of specialist language has, up to now in this discussion, been used as an undivided whole. It is possible to distinguish certain sub-types of specialist language. German scholars usually use the term *Sondersprache* in this comprehensive sense and distinguish between specialist languages which derive from an extension of knowledge and are conditioned by specialization in a particular branch leading to the creation of much new vocabulary (sub-type *Fachsprache*), and group dialects which are conditioned by social exclusiveness and generally vary only the general vocabulary but do not significantly increase it (sub-type *Standessprache*). Group dialects create linguistic cohesion among social groups. Their prime function is thus social. Very often they use words of general language in an unusual, esoteric way. German huntsmen, for instance, use *Löffel* – 'spoon' in general language – to designate the ear of a hare or a rabbit. The skin of a fox is called *Balg*, of a deer it is *Decke* or *Haut*, of a wild pig it is *Schwarte*. For tails of various animals both German and English huntsmen use a special terminology:

tail of	German	English
red deer	*Wedel*	*single*
fox	*Lunte/Standarte*	*brush*
hare	*Blume*	*scut*
otter	*Rute*	*rudder*
pheasant	*Stoß Spiel*	*train*

While there is a strong tendency in group dialects to individualize, to name the varieties rather than the genus, scientific specialist languages tend to systematize and to use generic terms. In the language of trades the two tendencies often overlap as we can see, for instance, in some terms for tools:

Designation	German	English	Designation
	Bohrer	*drill*	
	Spiralbohrer	*twist drill*	generic term
generic terms	*Holzbohrer*	*auger, wood bit*	variety
	Gewindebohrer	*tap*	variety
variety (metaphor)	*Krauskopf*	*countersink drill*	generic term
	Feile	*file*	
generic term	*Grobfeile*	*roughnut file*	generic term
generic term	*Riffelfeile*	*riffler*	variety
variety	*Raspel*	*rasp, grater*	variety
variety (metaphor)	*Vogelzunge*	*oval file*	generic term

Social exclusiveness tends to play some part in all specialist languages. But it is useful to remember the differences between group dialects and specialist languages in the narrow sense of the word. One kind of group dialect is *slang*. It is a playful, humorous use of the vocabulary of general language, either by elevating or depreciating words or by some other semantic shift. It is usually highly emotive and has a strong social role, either to defuse or heal tensions, fears, anger, feelings of insecurity by a reaction based on humour or mockery. Antagonism to other groups seems to express itself in an exclusive, esoteric vocabulary. In the contemporary slang of juveniles one finds, for instance, the semantic shifts: *steil* > 'pretty', *sauer* > 'bad', *krank* > 'stupid' or the use of *Mäuse* for 'money', *Biene* for 'girl'; *ein dufter Zahn* is 'a pretty girl', *eine steile Haut* 'an elegant young lady', *klamme Leute* are 'boring people', 'squares'.

The specialist languages of technology can usefully be divided into three different realizations: the scientific language, the works language, and the sales language. These terms are based on H. Ischreyt's expressions *Wissenschaftssprache*, *Werkstattsprache* (modified by R. Pelka to *Betriebssprache*), and *Verkäufersprache*. It is in scientific specialist language that we have a standardized nomenclature and well defined, if variable, technical terms. These are often more descriptive than terms in works language, cf. *Überschallgeschwindigkeitsflugzeug – Überschaller*, *Widerstandspunktschweißen – Punktschweißen*. This kind of specialist language is most often met with in written language and is invariably in standard German. Works language, on the other hand, is – though a specialist language – no more precise than it has to be for efficient communication. Since it is most often spoken language it may veer towards semi-standard. The context is fully brought into play. A tool does not have to be called *Spitzbohrer*, *Löffelbohrer* or *Zapfenbohrer* if *Bohrer* will do and the situation supplies the rest. Pejorative and other emotive words may well be used, e.g. *Hundeschwanz* for 'a blunt chisel', *Raspel* for 'a blunt file or saw'. Slangy terms such as *morksen*, *pfuschen*, for 'to work badly', *losrammeln* for 'to start working' are frequently heard in this sphere. Where slang and specialist language overlap Germans usually speak of *Jargon*, while English *jargon* more often denotes simply an excess of technical terminology in circumstances where readers or listeners resent its use. It is in sales language or wherever expert and layman meet to do business that specialist language and general language flow into each other or clash as the case may be, and where technical terminology must make way for general vocabulary.

An interesting case of a clash can be illustrated in the case of the German words for 'lamp' and 'light bulb', as described by H. Ischreyt (pp. 231–53). In the relevant industry the terms *Leuchte* 'lamp' and *(Glüh)lampe* 'light bulb' have been standardized for a long time. Especially for modern appliances the standardized words have become fairly commonly known (*Deckenleuchte, Wandleuchte*), but as general generic terms the standardized nomenclature has not been accepted by German speakers. We thus get the following tension between the two forms of German:

	'light bulb'	'lamp'
Specialist language: technical terms	*(Glüh)lampe*	*Leuchte*
General language: general words	*(Glüh)birne*	*Lampe*

One might be inclined to say that specialist languages are simply registers of written or spoken standard or non-standard German. However, although they have so far been too little investigated, it seems clear that the typical technical and scientific specialist languages of modern German do together constitute a special kind of German. Although it may be premature to give a comprehensive characterization of German specialist language, a tentative list of features of general validity in technological prose must include, for instance:

(i) Mass words, which in general language rarely form plurals, do so frequently in specialist language, e.g. *Bleie, Harze, Salze, Sände, Stähle, Stäube*, or for abstracts *Drücke, Hübe*.

(ii) Derivation of *nomina instrumenti* by means of *-er*, indicating the purpose for which the appliance is used, e.g. *Abstreifer, Auswerfer, Entstauber, Händetrockner, Heizölbrenner, Trennstemmer*.

(iii) Derivation of new fem. nouns in *-e*, e.g. *Kippe, Schließe, Spüle*.

(iv) Derivation of *nomina facti* in *-ung* often designating units composed of several parts, e.g. *Abdeckung, Entlüftung, Kupplung, Umschaltung*. Apart from such collectives there are also many *nomina actionis*, indicating the result, e.g. *Bohrung, Härtung, Verpackung*.

(v) Substantivization of infinitives as *nomina actionis* is very frequent, e.g. *das Bohren, Kühlen, Abdichten*.

(vi) New compound infinitives used as verbs or nouns: *das*

Fließpressen, Eintauchschleifen, Einsatzhärten, Gasschweißen, Hartlöten.

(vii) Nouns are converted into verbs: *blechen, drahten, panzern, punkten, ausbauchen, verachsen.*

(viii) The most usual way of forming new technical terms is by means of composition, e.g. *Drehschalter, Lochabdeckvorrichtung, Blechbiegemaschine, Schmierölpumpenmotor, Schleifstaubsammelbehälter.* The typical nominal compound is a determinative compound consisting of two elements, although both may themselves be compounds. Especially typical are the compounds where the determinative element is verbal, e.g. *Drehscheibe, Schmiertasche, Schalthebel.* R. Pelka (p. 203) found 27 per cent of all determinative compounds to be of this type while in Jacob Grimm's day this type was very rare (about 2 per cent of all determinative compounds). Syntactical groups consisting of an adj. and a noun are 'terminologized' by being turned into compounds: *buntes Metall > Buntmetall.*

(ix) There are many adjective derivations in *-bar*, e.g. *spaltbar, schweißbar.*

(x) Among the numerous adjective compounds there are many with verbal determinative elements, e.g. *drehnachgiebig, einfriersicher, biegefest, störanfällig.* Others have nominal elements: *wartungsarm, zinkhaltig, verdrehungssteif.*

(xi) There are also many adjectival compounds with participles as second element, e.g. *batteriegespeist, druckknopfbetätigt, glasfaserverstärkt, handentrostet.*

(xii) Verbal composition with particles as well as prefix derivation play a very big part, e.g. with *schleifen: ab-, an-, auf-, aus-, ein-, durch-, hinter-, nach-,* etc. *Be-, ver-, ent-* etc. are also very frequently used.

(xiii) Verbs in *-ieren: armieren, gummieren, zentrieren.*

(xiv) Apart from derivation and composition as means of augmenting the lexicon the use of metaphors is characteristic, especially of the less scientifically determined specialist languages. A comparison with the shape or function usually forms the starting point, e.g. *Arm, Auge, Korb, Kranz, Bürste, Finger, Galgen.* Most derive from the human body or the human sphere generally (*Mantel, Schuh, Bett, Kissen*). Animal metaphors are relatively rare (*Igel, Schnecke, Fuchsschwanz, Vogelzunge*). Most occur in compounds. There are also verbal metaphors: *altern, ermüden, fressen, abschrecken.*

(xv) Abbreviations: *S-Haken, V-Rad, kg., UKW, Moped, Farad* (*<Faraday*), *Volt*.

(xvi) Compounds with personal names or place-names: *Thomasstahl, Bessemerstahl, Dieselmotor, Röntgenstrahlen, Derbyschuhe, Manchesterhosen*.

(xvii) Much but varying use, according to the discipline, is made of foreign words, particularly of Greek and Latin origin: *tertiär, thermisch, Torsion*, etc.

(xviii) In the lexicon the process of 'technical grading', *technische Graduation* as L. Mackensen (p. 302) calls it, is typical, e.g. *ein – mehr*: *Einzweckvorrichtung, Mehr-*; *voll – halb – nicht* (say with *automatisch*); *kalt – warm – heiß* (with -*walzwerk*).

(xix) With regard to the syntax of specialist language it has been noted that the simple sentence with expanded attributes and parentheses is typical: 'der hierbei zu untersuchende Fragenkomplex, vielschichtig wie er ist, stellt uns vor folgende Aufgaben'. E. Beneš found verbs to comprise only 9·4 per cent of all words while in general prose they amounted to 14 per cent. This is an indication of the heavily nominal style of specialist prose. The nominal paraphrases (*eine Beobachtung anstellen* rather than *beobachten, zum Abschluß bringen* rather than *abschließen*) add to this tendency. In its preference for expanded attributes and nominal blocks of all kinds scientific specialist language echoes tendencies in general modern German prose and may indeed have reinforced them. Specialist prose also shows a high frequency of passive constructions.

Many of these features may be observed in the following specimen passage of scientific specialist prose, chosen at random (*Stahl und Eisen*, 94 (1974) 12, p. 540):

Die in dieser Arbeit mitgeteilten Ergebnisse wurden mit „Oxytip"-Zellen an unberuhigten, halbberuhigten und beruhigten Stahlschmelzen erhalten. Bei diesen Meßzellen wird ein unten geschlossenes mit MgO teilstabiliertes ZrO_2-Rohr als sauerstoffionenleitender Festelektrolyt und ein $Mo-MoO_2$-Gemisch als Bezugspotential verwendet. Es wurden jeweils drei Messungen in schneller Folge hintereinander in der Pfanne und anschließend drei bis fünf weitere Messungen in verschiedenen Kokillen nach Abguß derselben Schmelze vorgenommen. Nur bei unberuhigten Schmelzen waren auch aufeinanderfolgende Messungen in derselben Kokille über einen längeren Zeitabschnitt möglich. Bei den Messungen stellte es sich sehr bald heraus, daß die Kontaminie-

rung der Meßzelle und des Zellenschaftes mit oxidierter Schlacke die
Reproduzierbarkeit der Pfannenmessungen ungünstig beeinflußt.
Deshalb wurden die Zellen mit einem zusätzlichen Schlackenabweiser
aus dünnem Stahlblech versehen.

7.4 | Spelling and punctuation

7.4.1 | Modern German spelling

The efforts of Gottsched and Adelung provided German
with the spelling system of its classical literature. Their role was
decisive because they acted with circumspection and moderation.
What they achieved had no official status and there was still a
certain amount of variation. But their basic principles, forming
a criss-cross pattern of practical solutions rather than a logical
system, proved acceptable to the whole language community (see
7.2.3). It was in the application of these principles that variation
still occurred. In Prussia headmasters were instructed to introduce uniformity at least within their schools. Individual federal
states, e.g. Saxony and later Bavaria, set up official rule books.
After the establishment of the Second Empire renewed efforts
were made to achieve officially recognized uniformity. One of the
leading figures was a headmaster, Konrad Duden, who published
his first programmatic spelling book in 1872: *Die deutsche Rechtschreibung, Abhandlung, Regeln und Wörterverzeichnis*. In 1876 a
spelling conference, convened by the Prussian minister of education, made suggestions which were fairly radical. Both Duden and
Rudolf von Raumer, a leading Germanist of the day, while recog-
nizing that the existing orthography was deficient in many ways,
concluded that it was better to move slowly and step by step, so
preserving the high degree of unity already achieved. When
Wilhelm Wilmanns was asked to draw up a rule book for Prussia
modelled as closely as possible on that for Bavaria, based on von
Raumer's ideas, the conservative, cautious approach had won.
These rules were declared the norm for Prussian schools in 1880.
Konrad Duden applied them in his first authoritative work:

Vollständiges orthographisches Wörterbuch der deutschen Sprache (Leipzig, 1880). In 1892 a Swiss spelling conference recommended the adoption of the Duden canon.

To eliminate variation and to introduce further improvements representatives of the states of the Second Empire and of Austria met in Berlin in 1901. This turned out to have been the last German orthographic conference to achieve reforms. Among its recommendations were the elimination of variants (*Hülfe/Hilfe* > *Hilfe, ergetzen/ergötzen* > *ergötzen*), of ⟨ey⟩ spellings (*sey, bey* > *sei, bei*), the replacement of -*niß* by -*nis* (*Ergebnis*) and of ⟨c⟩ in foreign words by ⟨z⟩ and ⟨k⟩ (*Circus* > *Zirkus*), and the abolition of the spelling ⟨th⟩ in native words (*Thal* > *Tal, -thum* > -*tum*). In 1902 these new rules were declared obligatory in the Second Empire; Austria and Switzerland concurred. In the same year they were adopted and applied in the seventh edition of Duden's book. Since then Duden has been the prescriptive, authoritative source for German spelling. The editorial staff of the Duden is not authorized to alter any rules, but it can and does interpret them in the light of new developments in the language. Every new edition thus tends to contain some amendments.

The principles underlying the spelling system of modern German are the result of the historical development of the language. Like all principles of such ancestry they are in many respects contradictory. On the one hand they lead to under-representation, on the other to redundancy. In many cases *words* are spelt rather than *sounds*, that is, logographic spelling has replaced alphabetic spelling. Although compared with French and English, this has not happened in German to a critical extent, many German pedagogues are nevertheless unhappy with the 'unphonetic' spelling, thus keeping perennially alive the question of spelling reform.

(i) The oldest principle of any alphabetic script is the phonetic, or better, phonemic principle: every sound (phoneme) is rendered by one and the same letter (grapheme) and every letter (grapheme) renders only one and always the same sound (phoneme). Since German has evolved the practice of indicating vowel shortness by double consonants or clusters, the consonant phonemes tend to be rendered by two different spellings, e.g. /t/ by ⟨t⟩ and ⟨tt⟩, *Liter, bitter*. Purely on an *usus scribendi* basis /f/ is spelt both ⟨v⟩ (*vor*) and ⟨f⟩ (*für*) in initial position. The phoneme /k/ has not only ⟨k⟩ and ⟨ck⟩, where ⟨ck⟩ is an aberrant rendering of doubling paralleled by ⟨tz⟩ for ⟨zz⟩, but also ⟨ch⟩ before /s/ (*Fuchs*) and ⟨q⟩ before ⟨u⟩ (*Quelle*). The cluster /ks/ may alternatively also be spelt ⟨x⟩ (*Hexe*). Since in three cases two or three letters render one consonant phoneme (⟨ch⟩ for /x/, ⟨ng⟩ for /ŋ/ and ⟨sch⟩ for /ʃ/) and since doubling of these spellings is rejected for aesthetic reasons, the indication of vowel quantity is made impossible in these cases. Generally the vowels before these consonants are short but there are some exceptions. This also applies to some extent to the spelling of /s/. When fractura or Gothic type was abandoned in the forties of this century the letter ⟨ß⟩ was carried over into roman type, being now used intervocalically to mark the length of the preceding vowel (*Füße, Flüsse*). Unfortunately the adoption was slavishly based on fractura practice which means this functional use was thrown away in preconsonantal and final positions (*stößt, müßt; Fuß, muß*). Where long vowels occur before clusters alternative means of indicating vowel length are required, but rarely provided (long: *Art, Fahrt*; short: *hart*).

(ii) The second principle is the historical and etymological principle. According to this the letters ⟨e⟩ and ⟨ä⟩, ⟨eu⟩ ⟨äu⟩, and ⟨ie⟩, are retained for /ɛ/, /ɔø/ and /iː/: *Ende, Länge*; *Leute, Bräute*; *Liebe*. It is on an historical and *usus scribendi* basis, too, that the spellings with initial ⟨v⟩ (*Vater*) are retained. When [h] disappeared in medial position its spelling ⟨h⟩ was nevertheless continued. On the one hand ⟨h⟩ now functions as syllable marker (*sehen, ziehen, Ehe*), on the other hand it has become a length sign (*Stuhl*), in which capacity it is generally redundant.

(iii) The third principle is the systematic-morphological principle that the spelling remain the same for the same morph even if morphophonemic rules alter the pronunciation, thus *Liebe – lieb – lieblich* not *Liebe – *liep – *lieplich*. It is according to this principle, linked to the etymological principle, that /ɛ/ and /ɔø/ are spelt ⟨ä⟩ and ⟨äu⟩ in cases of morphological mutation (*alt – älter, Haut – Häute*).

(iv) The fourth principle is the avoidance of homography in cases of homophony: *Moor – Mohr, Weise – Waise*.

(v) The fifth principle relates to short function words which are spelt as economically as possible and to which the doubling of consonants to indicate the shortness of the preceding vowel therefore does not apply: *ab, an, hat, man, das, was, bin, in, mit, von,* etc., equally where such words end in a vowel there is no additional indication of length, e.g. *da, je, so, zu,* see (vi).

(vi) There seems to be also an aesthetic principle which has led to the 'filling-up' of what would otherwise be short triliteral words by doubling of the vowel or by the insertion of an ⟨h⟩ especially before *m, n, l, r: Hahn, Saal, mehr, Meer, Lohn, Moos,* and in final position: *Klee, Schuh, früh, Floh,* except again in function words, e.g. *wo, du, je, ja.* Both for this reason and in order to distinguish them from *in, im* the pronouns *ihn, ihm, ihr, ihnen* have the otherwise unusual spelling ⟨ih⟩.

(vii) German follows the principle that foreign words retain their spelling except in cases where they have become thoroughly integrated and belong to the vocabulary of everyday use rather than the learned part of the lexicon, cf. *System, Drainage – Soße, Büro, Streik.*

(viii) Finally, German orthography carries grammatical information by spelling nouns with an initial capital. Up to the age of Luther only the beginning of texts, pages, paragraphs or verse lines tended to be marked by majuscules. Proper names and the name of the deity were also frequently so indicated. Gradually initial capitalization came to be used to emphasize certain words. In the work of Luther capitalization played a small part up to 1520, but increased gradually up to 1540 when it was quite usual with nouns not so much because they were nouns but because Luther wished to stress these words. In the 1546 edition of his Bible translation (see p. 383) most nouns are spelt with an initial capital but if they are not stressed, e.g. in adverbial phrases, they begin with a minuscule. The seventeenth and eighteenth centuries attached special importance to the *Hauptwort* and thus formalized the practice.

It is easy to see that a spelling system based on such conflicting principles must contain many inconsistencies. They are most serious with regard to the indication of vowel length where we get such cases as *Wal – Wahl – Waal, her – hehr – Heer, Tor – Mohr – Moor, Schere – Lehre – Beere, Bise – Wiese, höre – Föhre, Schnur – fuhr, Bühne – Düne* with multiple representation or, *Bruch – Buch, Haß – Spaß, Rost – Trost, Büsche – Rüsche* with under-representation.

7.4.2 | Vowel and consonant letters

When we attempt to draw up a list of correspondences between letters and sounds we must first ask ourselves what is 'German' spelling. The lexicon embraces the native stock and thousands of foreign words deriving from all over the world. To base our comparison on the total vocabulary would be meaningless since it would yield just about every sound–letter correspondence in the major languages and would thus completely swamp the native German system. To do justice to the latter it is sufficient, for instance, to state that ⟨sch⟩ and in specific cases ⟨s⟩ render the German phoneme /ʃ/. To state that /ʃ/ in German can be spelt ⟨sch⟩ (*Schnee*) or ⟨s⟩ (*Stein*), ⟨ch⟩ (*Chance*), ⟨sh⟩ (*Shorts*), ⟨sk⟩ (*Ski*) or ⟨sc⟩ (*Dekrescendo*) overlooks the fact that only the first two spellings are 'German' spellings. The following table thus only applies to the native and naturalized lexicon.

Vowel Letters and Sounds in Stressed Syllables

Graphemes	Allographs	Corresponding phonemes	Examples	Other cases
⟨i⟩+⟨CC⟩	⊂i (ie)⊃	/ɪ/	*List*	*bin, mit* (v), *Viertel*
⟨e, ä⟩+⟨CC⟩	⊂e, ä⊃	/ɛ/	*Stelle, Ställe*	*es, des, weg* (v)
⟨a⟩+⟨CC⟩	⊂a⊃	/a/	*Stadt*	*an, das, was* (v) ⟨-ß⟩ *Faß, Haß, naß*
⟨o⟩+⟨CC⟩	⊂o⊃	/ɔ/	*Mord*	*ob* (v) ⟨-ß⟩ *floß, goß, Roß, Schloß*
⟨u⟩+⟨CC⟩	⊂u⊃	/ʊ/	*Schuft*	⟨-ß⟩ *Fluß, Genuß, muß*
⟨ü⟩+⟨CC⟩	⊂ü, y⊃	/ʏ/	*Stück, Mystik*	
⟨ö⟩+⟨CC⟩	⊂ö⊃	/œ/	*Götter*	
⟨ie⟩+⟨C/Ø⟩	⊂ie,i,ih,ieh⊃	/i:/	*Tier, dir, ihn, die, Vieh*	*Nische, Dienst* (+CC) (y in Swiss words: *Seldwyla*)
⟨e⟩+⟨C/Ø⟩	⊂e, eh, ee⊃	/e:/	*her, hehr, Heer, See, Reh*	*nebst, Krebs, stets* ⟨-r+dent.⟩ *Erde, erst, Erz, Pferd, werden*

Graphemes	Allographs	Corresponding phonemes	Examples	Other cases
⟨ä⟩+⟨C/∅⟩	⟨ä, äh⟩	/ɛː/	*Bär, wählen*	*Gemälde, Städte, Rätsel* ⟨-ch⟩*bräche, spräche* ⟨-ß⟩ *Gefäß, Gesäß* ⟨-r+dent.⟩ *Gebärde, zärtlich*
⟨a⟩+⟨C/∅⟩	⟨a, ah, aa⟩	/aː/	*Tat, Draht, Saat, da*	*Magd, Papst* ⟨-ch⟩ *Sprache, Gemach* ⟨-ß⟩ *Fraß, saß, Spaß* ⟨-r+dent.⟩ *Art, Arzt, Bart*
⟨o⟩+⟨C/∅⟩	⟨o, oh, oo⟩	/oː/	*Los, Lohn, Moos, wo*	*Mond, Obst, Vogt, Ostern, Kloster, Trost* ⟨-ch⟩ *hoch* ⟨-ß⟩ *bloß, Floß, groß*
⟨u⟩+⟨C/∅⟩	⟨u, uh⟩	/uː/	*tun, Huhn, du, Kuh*	*Husten, Schuster, Wuchs* ⟨-ch⟩ *Buch, Fluch, Tuch, Buche, Kuchen, suchen* ⟨-ß⟩ *Fuß, Gruß, Ruß* ⟨r+dent.⟩ *Geburt*
⟨ü⟩+⟨C/∅⟩	⟨ü, üh, y⟩	/yː/	*schüren, führen, Mythus*	⟨-ß⟩ *süß*
⟨ö⟩+⟨C/∅⟩	⟨ö, öh⟩	/øː/	*schön, Söhne*	*Gehöft, Österreich* ⟨-r+dent.⟩ *Behörde*
⟨ei⟩	⟨ei, ai, eih⟩	/ae/	*Leib, Laib, Reihe*	
⟨au⟩	⟨au, auh⟩	/ao/	*Rauch, rauh*	
⟨eu, äu⟩	⟨eu, äu⟩	/ɔø/	*Beute, Bräute*	

Notes:

(1) CC means 'followed by more than one consonant letter in the same morpheme'; C/∅ means 'followed by one consonant letter' or 'in final position'. ⟨x⟩ counts as two letters. Words ending in *-el, -en, -er* (*edel,*

Regen, über) may lose the unstressed *e* before inflectional endings or derivational suffixes, but they retain the vowel quantity of their base forms (*edle, regnen, übrig*).

(2) The most frequent allographs are posited as graphemes. Otherwise they are given in descending order of frequency. No rules can be given for their occurrence.

(3) The sign (v) refers to the spelling principle given on p. 544.

(4) Only a few examples can be given of cases not conforming to the rules.

(5) Vowel length before ⟨-ß⟩ becomes clear in intervocalic position, e.g. *Roß – Rosse* but *Floß – Flöße*.

(6) The mutated vowels *ä, ü, ö* retain the quantity of the base vowels, e.g. *Bach – Bäche* (short), *Buch – Bücher* (long). They are never doubled, hence *Saal – Sälchen, Boot – Bötchen*.

(7) Of all vowel letters in foreign words only the relatively frequent ⟨y⟩ is included. Most words of Greek and Latin origin conform to the above rules, ⟨ph, th⟩ counting as one letter. Vowel letters before letters for plosive plus liquid count as being in an open syllable and are thus long, e.g. *Metrik, Kobra*.

In syllables not bearing the primary stress the sign ⟨e⟩ in words of German origin generally renders /ə/ except in the prefixes with a secondary stress: *emp-, ent-, er-, her-, ver-, zer-*, where it corresponds to /ɛ/, but for the allophones of /r/ see p. 558. In the native derivational suffixes with secondary stress, ⟨a⟩ in *-bar, -sal* and *-sam* represents /aː/, ⟨o⟩ in *-los* /oː/, ⟨u⟩ in *-tum* /uː/; all other letters stand for short vowels. Words with the stressed suffix *-e'rei*, having also a secondary stress on the root vowel, retain the rules of vowel quantity indication, e.g. *Weberei, Käserei* ([eː], [ɛː]).

7.4.3 | Punctuation

Another feature in which the seventeenth and eighteenth centuries brought about a fundamental change is punctuation. In early medieval manuscripts stops and commas were mainly used to mark parts of texts, such as verse lines. Later they came to indicate syntactical units such as sentences and clauses. The stroke or virgula functioned in the same way and became especially popular between the sixteenth and seventeenth centuries (see pp. 386, 387, 392, 490). It functioned as a marker both of natural pauses and of syntactical units. But the rhythmical principle, still underlying English punctuation today, was gradually giving way to a rationalistic, grammatical approach. More and more, German punctuation was used to indicate the different syntactical elements. Again Gottsched's role was important (see p. 509). Following the practice of Italian printers the Germans had in the meantime also introduced the exclamation mark, colon, semi-colon, and question mark. Modern German punctuation, while not completely eschewing the indication of rhythm and intonation, is basically a system which presupposes the ability to analyse a sentence syntactically. Where the two principles leave doubts, an immensely complicated edifice of rules and exceptions, filling many pages of the Duden, tries to guide the weary writer. He must remember that 'Er ist bereit, zu raten und zu helfen' requires a comma, but that 'Zu raten und zu helfen ist er bereit' does not.

7.4.4 | Spelling reform

After the Second World War dissatisfaction with the existing orthography of German welled up again, encouraged by the chance of a new start in the general reconstruction of state and society. In 1952 the *Arbeitsgemeinschaft für Sprachpflege*, consisting of interested personalities from all four major German-speaking states, set to work and produced, two years later, the so-called *Stuttgarter Empfehlungen*. These proposals amounted to a fairly radical reform since they envisaged the abolition of the initial capitalization of nouns except proper names (*der baum*), the abolition of the spelling ⟨ie⟩ for long *i* (*Liebe* > *libe*) and of *h* as a length sign except after ⟨e⟩ (*wohnen* > *wonen*), the further integration of foreign words (*fair* > *fär*, *Tourist* > *turist*), the replacement of foreign ⟨ph, th, rh⟩ by ⟨f, t, r⟩, of ⟨tz⟩ and ⟨ß⟩ by ⟨z⟩ and ⟨ss⟩, and some new rules concerning the separation of words and punctuation. After much tendentious newspaper reporting and public discussion the education ministers of the states of the Federal Republic finally set up the *Arbeitskreis für Rechtschreibregelung*. Its recommendations, known as the *Wiesbadener Empfehlungen*, were published in 1958. The first point was what came to be called the *gemäßigte Kleinschreibung*. According to this proposal only the sentence beginning, proper names, the name of God, the pronouns of direct address and certain scientific abbreviations were to be spelt with a capital letter. The foreign spellings ⟨ph, th, rh⟩ were to be simplified to ⟨f, t, r⟩, there was to be further naturalization of common foreign words, and there were proposals for reduced use of the comma, and for other minor reforms. Everything now really hinged on capitalization.

Arguments for and against were tossed to and fro. In the Federal Republic of Germany and in the German Democratic Republic the reforms had relatively strong support, but the Austrian commission charged with the examination of the problem was split half for and half against with abstentions in favour of the conservative solution. In 1963 the Swiss Orthography Conference decided overwhelmingly in favour of the retention of capitalization although some easement in the rules was recommended.

The two strongest arguments in favour of the retention of the present practice are: (a) legibility; it is argued that a text with capitals for nouns is easier to read as it appears more plastic. It has, however, been pointed out by L. Weisgerber that it is not fair to give preference to the reader over the writer since reading is anyway a hundred times easier to learn than spelling; (b) the prevalence of expanded nominal attributes gives German a structural character which relies on and benefits from the capitalization of nouns. This argument of R. Hotzenköcherle, the chief Swiss protagonist of the opposition against the reform, would in fact be more cogent if capitalization were used to mark the attributive incapsulation. It is however indiscriminately used for every noun irrespective of its function, as the following sentence of R. Hotzenköcherle shows: 'eine unseres Wissens noch nie beklagte, im tiefsten Sinn sprachgerechte und erprobtermaßen praktische Einrichtung'. The cases of ambiguity which might arise (*der gefangene floh*: *der Gefangene floh* or *der gefangene Floh*) are mainly spurious as the context would resolve the ambiguity. Most examples usually adduced against the reform – there are over fifty in the Swiss commission's report – are contrived.

The argument against the retention of the capitalization of nouns is based on two main weaknesses of the present practice: (a) spelling should not have to convey grammatical information of this kind. The question of what constitutes a noun is intricate and far beyond the capability of a child learning to spell; (b) owing to the difficulty of defining a noun there are innumerable over-subtle rules (*etwas Schönes – etwas anderes*; *in bezug auf – mit Bezug auf*; *angst machen – Angst haben*).

For the time being the spelling reform has failed. The system itself has asserted its venerable right to continue to exist, against all human endeavour to rethink objectively its failings.

7·5 | Phonology

7·5·1 | Standard German pronunciation

With the decline of the reputation of Upper Saxon or Meissen pronunciation the speech of educated North Germans became exemplary, but German still lacked an authoritative canon. Ever since Goethe had demanded a 'pure', non-provincial pronunciation for the theatre the professional stage clamoured for a normalized standard pronunciation. The first pronouncing dictionary was Wilhelm Viëtor's *Die Aussprache des Schriftdeutschen* (1885). Then in the late nineties of the last century a committee of Germanists and theatre people under the direction of Theodor Siebs set themselves the task of establishing an authoritative norm of pronunciation. Basing themselves mainly on the stage practice of North Germans and taking into account also morphological and lexical considerations, they produced a solution which appeared in 1898 as Theodor Siebs' *Deutsche Bühnenaussprache*. Although meant primarily for the stage it was hoped, from the beginning, that the work would provide also a guide to correct pronunciation for all formal occasions. In this Siebs was entirely successful: he did indeed achieve for pronunciation what Duden had done for spelling. In 1922 the title incorporated the term *Hochsprache*, thus indicating the wider function of Siebs' work. In 1957 the expression *Bühnenaussprache* was relegated to the subtitle, the title itself becoming *Deutsche Hochsprache*. Finally, the nineteenth edition of 1969 changed to *Siebs Deutsche Aussprache*, offering for the first time not only a set of rules for the declamatory register but also guide-lines for the so-called *gemäßigte Hochlautung*. In this Siebs followed the example of two other pronouncing dictionaries which had appeared in the intervening years: *Duden Aussprachewörterbuch* (1962), now with the subtitle

Wörterbuch der deutschen Standardaussprache (2nd ed., Mannheim, 1974), and *Wörterbuch der deutschen Aussprache*, edited by a collective of authors, Leipzig, 1964 (fourth ed., 1974).

The rules which have changed or been moderated affect mainly the pronunciation of *r*, unstressed [ə], the glottal stop, the aspiration of voiceless plosives, and the voicing of the voiced plosives and of [z]. Apart from deviations in individual words the three dictionaries are fairly close to each other. Perhaps the greatest differences occur in their treatment of the *a*-sounds and in the transcription of the diphthongs. Duden and Siebs make no quality distinction for short and long *a*, although Duden (1962) remarked that short *a* may be palatal and long *a* velar in some regional versions of colloquial standard, while in others the relation may be reversed. The East German dictionary distinguishes between short front (*helleres*) [a] and long back (*dunkleres*) [ɑ:]. The diphthongs are given as:

Duden: a͜i a͜u ͜ɔy
Siebs: ɑe ɑo ɔø
WDA: a͜e a͜o ɔø

Although in Austria and Switzerland the Siebs rules are accepted for the stage, for other formal speaking certain special rulings have been suggested. The *Österreichisches Beiblatt zu Siebs* by Felix Trojan allows some deviations in individual words, e.g. short vowels in *Behörde, Geburt, Harz, Nische, Städte*, [s] in *Strategie, Struktur* where Siebs permits both [s] and [ʃ], [k] in *Chemie* and [ç] in *Melancholie, Orchester* where Siebs has [ç] and [k] respectively although drawing attention to the different Austrian pronunciation. The Austrian *Beiblatt* also stresses the importance of the preservation of the tongue-tip *r*. *Die Aussprache des Hochdeutschen in der Schweiz. Eine Wegleitung* by Bruno Boesch, Zürich, 1957, encourages more radical departures from Siebs. Again there is variation in the use of long and short vowels. Short vowels are permitted in *Jagd, Magd, Krebs, Obst, Vogt, Liter, Nische, Städte, Art, Arzt, Erde, werden, Pferd, Geburt*, but long ones in: *brachte, Gedächtnis, Hochzeit, Rache, rächen, Rost* 'grill' as opposed to short *o* in *Rost* 'rust'. Differentiation between *Esche/Wäsche, wetten/hätten* ([e–ɛ]) is also accepted. French words like *Buffet, Budget, Filet* are pronounced with the stress on the first syllable and short [ɛ]. For the consonants there are again differences in individual words and the principle that double consonants may be pronounced long (*offen, Wasser*) is adopted. The suffix *-ig* was to contain a plosive; [-ıç] was 'unacceptable' in 1957, although it appears that since then Helvetic susceptibilities have weakened.

7.5.2 | The stressed vowel system

All phonological systems of historical stages of a language are hypothetical. For the modern language we are at last on firmer ground. We may take the phonological material presented by the pronouncing dictionaries as representing modern standard German. We thus arrive at Stage X:

/ɪ/		/ʏ/	/ʊ/	/i:/		/y:/	/u:/	
	/ɛ/	/œ/	/ɔ/	/e:/	/ɛ:/	/ø:/	/o:/	/ɔø/
		/a/		/a:/		/ae/		/ao/

Examples:

/ɪ/ *ritten*	/i:/ *rieten*	/ʏ/ *Hütten*	/y:/ *hüten*
/ɛ/ *retten*	/e/ *beten*	/œ/ *Götter*	/ø:/ *löten*
	/ɛ:/ *bäten*		
/a/ *Ratten*	/a:/ *raten*		/ae/ *reiten*
/ɔ/ *Rotten*	/o:/ *Boten*		/ɔø/ *reuten*
/ʊ/ *Kutten*	/u:/ *Ruten*		/ao/ *Rauten*

All authorities are more or less in agreement that we must reckon with these phonemes in stressed conditions, but their interpretations vary considerably. The phonetic properties are agreed with one exception: some regard the lowest vowels as only marked by the feature of quantity while others state that the short *a* is front (palatal) or higher, and the long *a* back (velar) or lower, in other words, that they are distinguished qualitatively as well as quantitatively (see p. 552). The authorities cannot agree because the speakers make only the quantity distinction clearly but vary with regard to quality, as we may expect, given that there is only one low vowel disposing thus of a great deal of phonological space. It is also agreed that the vowels are distinguished by the properties high – mid – low, front – central – back, and rounded – unrounded. The short stressed vowels are lax, the long stressed vowels tense with the exception of /ɛ:/ and possibly /a, a:/. Scholars are not in agreement about the primary opposition: is it short – long or lax – tense? In unstressed position the opposition tense – lax is maintained in the standard pronunciation prescribed by the pronouncing dictionaries while the opposition of length is suspended. Under secondary stress the quantity distinction persists. Since vowel duration is such a prominent phonetic feature of German, and since the suspension of the opposition long – short is such an obvious corollary of the lack of stress while the opposition lax – tense is not similarly exposed, it seems unwise to make a choice which relegates vowel length to a subsidiary position. The contrasts of /ɛ/ – /ɛ:/ and /a/ – /a:/ further underline the importance of quantity. Hence, to stress the importance of both oppositions, the phonetic notation adopted here expresses them both. The reproach of redundancy can have no validity since language by nature tolerates much redundancy.

The asymmetry between the short and the long systems has often been commented upon. Although /ɛ:/ is prescribed by the pronouncing dictionaries for standard German, the fact is that in northern German it has been generally eliminated by coalescence with /e:/. For this reason, it has often been called marginal or special. The interesting fact about it is that it derives largely from spelling pronunciation: it is the pronunciation of ⟨ä⟩ in conditions of vowel length. Now, many ⟨ä⟩ do derive from MHG æ, the result of the mutation of WGmc. ā, especially as we have the spelling rule that the mutation of a should be spelt ⟨ä⟩, not ⟨e⟩. This is the reason why many MHG e in open syllables are now also represented by ⟨ä⟩ and hence /ɛ:/: Gräser, Räder, zählen, while some others (edel, Beere, Meer) have ⟨e, ee⟩ and consequently /e:/. It is by sheer chance that MHG bër became ⟨Bär⟩ and hence has /ɛ:/, while MHG spër became ⟨Speer⟩ with /e:/ and that MHG dræjen became ⟨drehen⟩ with /e:/ but MHG næjen became ⟨nähen⟩ with /ɛ:/. Where MHG æ is now spelt with ⟨e⟩, as in genehm, bequem, schwer, leer, selig, we have /e:/. Of course, in cases like lägen, wären, gnädig we have an apparent continuity with MHG æ, but it results only from the spelling convention of ⟨ä⟩ as mutation of ⟨a⟩ (lagen, waren, Gnade). Many German speakers coming to the standard language from a dialectal background do, however, make a natural distinction between Seele and *Säle, Beeren* and *Bären*. Nevertheless, if the pronouncing dictionaries were to abandon their present prescription, the coalescence of the two long mid front vowels would spread rapidly in analogy to what happened in the case of the corresponding short vowels (*Esche, Wäsche*).

The diphthongs are sometimes regarded as biphonematic. However, since the combination of a short stressed vowel ([a] or [ɔ]) plus a non-syllabic element is contrary to the overall vowel pattern of German, the interpretation of for instance [ae] as /a/ + /j/ seems inadvisable.

Vowels in initial position in a stressed morpheme are characterized by a glottal stop onset (*am Abend, vereisen*). It is simplest to regard this as a property of a stressed vowel at the morpheme boundary rather than as a consonant.

7·5·3 | Unstressed vowels

Most simple native words have only the distinction between stress and lack of stress. The most frequent unstressed vowel is [ə], which must be assumed to be a phoneme since it may contrast with other unstressed vowels (*Totem* ['toːtɛm], *Atem* ['aːtəm]), which occur however almost only in words of foreign origin. For such words the rule is that the lax vowels [ɪ ɛ ʏ œ ɔ] occur in unstressed closed syllables, but the tense vowels [i e y ø o] in unstressed open syllables. Open syllables end in a vowel, closed ones in a consonant, whereby plosives and fricatives plus liquids are taken to begin the next syllable. In stressed syllables the rules given in 7.4.2 apply. For instance:

de-kli-'nie-ren: [dekli'niːrən]
po-'li-tisch: [po'liːtɪʃ]
Po-li-'tik: [poli'tiːk]
Phi-lo-so-'phie: [filozo'fiː]
Me-ta-mor-'phis-mus: [metamɔr'fɪsmʊs]
Pig-men-ta-ti-'on: [pɪgmɛntati'oːn]
myxö-de-ma-'tös (x = k–s): [mʏksødema'tøːs]

This rule also applies to the few native words with the main stress on a syllable other than the root: *Forelle* [fo'rɛlə], *lebendig* [le-'bɛndɪç].

Native words with derivational suffixes or prefixes and a few dissyllabic ones (*Heimat* [aː], *Heirat* [aː], *Kleinod* [oː], *Armut* [uː]) have a secondary stress apart from a main stress and a possible unstressed element, e.g. *Grabungen* [ˈgraːˌbʊŋən]. Four such suffixes have a long vowel: *-bar*, *-sal*, *-sam*, *-tum*. All others have short vowels: (a) those beginning with a vowel *-ig*, *-in*, *-isch*, *-ung* in front of which consonantal neutralization does not take place (see 7.5.4); (b) those beginning with a consonant in front of which consonantal neutralization does take place (applying also to those with a long vowel): *-haft*, *-heit*, *-lein*, *-lich*, *-ling*, *-nis*, *-schaft*. The following prefixes with [ɛ] also have secondary stress: *er-*, *ent-*, *ver-*, *zer-*, while *ge-* and *be-* are unstressed with [ə], which is also frequently heard in the other prefixes if left unstressed.

The realization of [ə] plays a major role in the differentiation between *reine Hochlautung* and *gemäßigte Hochlautung*. In the endings *-em*, *-en*, [ə] must be preserved after nasals, liquids and vowels (*rennen*, *stehlen*, *nähen*), but may be dropped after all other consonants in the *gemäßigte Hochlautung*. After plosives the syllabic nasal may be assimilated to [m̩] after [p, b] and to [ŋ̍] after [k, g] according to the *Wörterbuch der deutschen Aussprache*, but not according to Siebs who insists on [-bn̩, -gn̩] etc. In the suffix *-chen* [ə] must be preserved.

A new unstressed vowel [ɐ] is now recognized, at least by the *Wörterbuch der deutschen Aussprache* and Duden. It is a vocalic allophone of /ʀ/ after long vowels other than /aː/ where /ʀ/ is a consonant at least in careful speech, e.g. *für* [fyːɐ], *wir* [viːɐ], *hörten* [ˈhøːɐtn̩], *Jahr* [jaːʀ] or [jaːɐ]. In unstressed *-er* it fuses with [ə] > [ɐ], e.g. *meiner* [ˈmaenɐ]– *meine* [ˈmaenə], *Senders* [ˈzɛndɐs], and in *er-*, *ver-*, *zer-* we have [ɛɐ]. In the southern British Received Pronunciation of standard English *mina* and *miner* are completely homophonous. English learners of German must be very careful to preserve the contrast between German unstressed [ə] and [ɐ].

7.5.4 | The consonant system

As the present stage in the evolution of the German consonantism we may posit Stage XII as follows:

/v/	/z/	(/ʒ/)	/j/		voiced	}fricatives
/f/	/s/	/ʃ/	/ç–x/	/h/	voiceless	
/b/	/d/		/g/		voiced	}plosives
/p/	/t/		/k/		voiceless	
/m/	/n/		/ŋ/		nasals	
	/l/			/R/	liquids	

Examples:

Initial position

/v/	*Wahl*	/z/	*Saar*	(/ʒ/	*Jargon*)	/j/	*Jahr*	
/f/	*fahl*	/s/	—	/ʃ/	*Schar*	/ç-/	*China*	/h/ *Haar*
/b/	*bar*	/d/	*der*			/g/	*gar*	
/p/	*Paar*	/t/	*Teer*			/k/	*Kar*	
/m/	*Mal*	/n/	*nah*			/ŋ/	—	
		/l/	*lahm*					/R/ *Rahm*

Medial position

/v/	*Slawen*	/z/	*Hasen*	(/ʒ/	*Gage*)	(/j/	*Boje*)
/f/	*Hafen*	/s/	*hassen*	/ʃ/	*haschen*	/ç-x/	*Sachen*, (/h/ *Uhu*)
							sicher
/b/	*Raben*	/d/	*Schaden*			/g/	*ragen*
/p/	*Rappen*	/t/	*Schatten*			/k/	*Haken*
/m/	*rammen*	/n/	*bannen*			/ŋ/	*bangen*
		/l/	*hallen*				/R/ *harren*

There is much controversy concerning the status of the affricates [pf, ts]. Those who regard them as biphonematic, that is as groups of /p+f/ and /t+s/, point to similar groups such as [tʃ] *Putsch*, [pʃ] *hübsch*, [ps] *Gips*, [ks] *Fuchs* with which [pf] and [ts] can be compared (*hüpf, Putz*) or to cases like *hat's*, phonetically identical with *Hatz*, where the morpheme boundary runs through what some would regard as a unit phoneme. Alternatively, [ts] would have to be differently interpreted according to non-phonological criteria – obviously a dubious procedure. The fact that [ts] is the only cluster which may occur before /v/, e.g. *zwei*, looks like being an argument in favour of a monophonematic solution until it is realized that only two consonants, [k] and [ʃ], can occur before /v/ in native standard German words.

I regard [ç-x], the *ich-* and the *ach-Laut*, as a unit phoneme, [x] being the allophone after /a, a:, ɔ, o:, ʊ, u:, ao/ and [ç] the allophone in all other positions, including the morpheme initial

(*China, Chemie, -chen*). So-called minimal pairs (*Kuchen – Kuhchen*) exist only across a morpheme boundary.

Many phonemes have a very limited distribution: /v/ and /f/ contrast almost only initially; /z/ and /s/ only medially between vowels; /j/ and /h/ occur only in initial position except for loans and onomatopoeic words; /ŋ/ never occurs initially and [ç] only in foreign words. The word-final and morpheme-final positions are marked by a very reduced system of oppositions. The contrast between voiced and voiceless fricatives and plosives is neutralized. Only before the derivational morphemes -*er*, -*in*, -*ig*, -*isch*, -*ung* and the inflectional morphemes beginning with [ə] does neutralization not occur.

It is now traditional to include the loan phoneme /ʒ/ in the German system. It occurs only in loans and is only used by educated speakers who have mastered this French sound. By the same token one might include the nasalized vowels of French in the German vowel system. As a foreign element /ʒ/ is bracketed in Stage XII.

The phoneme which is at the present time most in the throes of allophonic development is /R/. Siebs pressed for the rolled alveolar [r] long after the widespread adoption of the uvular [R]. The present edition now accepts both, although it still prefers [r]. The more realistic *Wörterbuch der deutschen Aussprache* admits the rolled alveolar, the rolled uvular, and the fricative uvular variants in initial, prevocalic and preconsonantal positions after a short vowel (*rot, Grad, Berg*), and a vocalic allophone after long vowels and in prefixes and endings (see 7.5.2). After [aː] it may disappear altogether in colloquial speech while cultured speech uses one of the consonantal allophones of /R/.

7·5·5 | Word stress

Dynamic word stress falls on the root syllable of native or naturalized words if they are simple words ('*Himmel*, '*Fenster*, '*Wagen*) or complex words with the bound prefix morphemes (*be-, er-, ent-, ge-, ver-, zer-*: *Be'such, Ver'zicht*) or with the bound inflectional and derivational morphemes (-*e*, -*er*, -*te*, etc., -*bar*, -*lich*, -*heit*, etc.: '*warme*, '*wärmer*, '*wärmte*, '*tragbar*, *er'träglich*, '*Trägheit*). There are a few exceptions to this rule: some native words with a light first syllable but a heavy second syllable have the stress on the second syllable, e.g. *Fo'relle, Ho'lunder, le'bendig, Wa'cholder*. The bound morphemes *-ei* and *-ieren* betray their foreign origin to this day by still bearing the primary stress (*Par'tei, Bäcke'rei, hal'bieren*).

Compound words have much more complicated rules. Nominal compounds consisting of two elements have the primary stress generally on the first: *'Tischtuch, 'Haustür*. Where inflectional or derivational morphemes occur we have primary stress on the root of the first element, secondary stress on the root of the second element and tertiary stress (or lack of stress) on the bound morphemes (*'Lobge,sang, 'Lobge,sänge*). Compounds of more than two elements are stressed according to the compositional pattern, e.g. *'Sauerstoffbe,hälter* (= *Sauerstoff*+*Behälter*), *'Güter,bahnhof* (= *Güter*+*Bahnhof*). Again there are exceptions: *barm'herzig, unter-'dessen, unter'wegs, über'haupt, Hohe'priester, Jahr'hundert, will-'kommen, durchei'nander, zu'sammen*. Compounds consisting of a particle plus a preposition have the primary stress on the preposition: *da'von, hi naus, vo'raus, wo'ran*. Copulative compounds and abbreviations consisting of letters have the primary stress on the final element: *schwarzrot'gold, Österreich-'Ungarn, Baden-'Württemberg, CD'U, SP'D*.

The real difficulty begins with particle composition. Some particles (*ab-, an-, auf-, aus-, bei-, ein-, mit-, nach-, weg-*) always attract the primary stress: *'Abgang, 'abziehen*. A large number of others do so in some circumstances but not in others. These are: *da-, dar-, durch-, her-, hier-, hin-, hinter-, in-, miß-, ob-, über-, um-, unter-, voll-, vor-, wider-, wieder-, zu-*. The chief criteria are: the kind of composition (nominal/verbal) and separability in the case of verbal composition. Special rules apply to some individual particles. On the whole genuine nominal compounds have the primary stress on the particle: *'Durchfahrt, 'Hinfahrt, 'Inhaber, 'Mißbrauch, 'Obmann, 'Umschwung, 'Unterkunft, 'vollgültig, 'Zukunft*. Inseparable verbs have the primary stress on the verbal root: *durch'dringen* 'to permeate' with the nominal derivation *Durch'dringung*, but separable verbs have the primary stress on the particle: *'durchdringen* 'to penetrate'. In the same way we have *'Überfahrt – 'überführen* 'to transport' but *über'führen* 'to convict, to expose' – *Über'führung*. In the case of nouns and inseparable verbs we therefore have the same alternation of stress between nouns and verbs which is common in English (*'subject – to sub'ject*): *'Überfall – über'fallen, 'Umfang – um'fangen, 'Unterlauf – unter- 'laufen*. Inseparable verbs often have a non-literal meaning.

Verbs with *miß-* are inseparable, but only the simple verbs have root stress (*miß'brauchen*), others have the stress on the prefix (*'mißverstehen*). The most difficult prefix is *un-*. Here there are also differences within the German language community. In general North Germans are more inclined to shift the primary stress away from the head position than are South German speakers. Nouns, and adjectives with *un-* negating the adjective, have the stress on *un-* (*'Untugend, 'unehrlich*), other adjectives have the stress on the adjectival root (*un'säglich*). Where there are heavy suffixes the stress also tends to be retracted (*unauf'haltbar*).

Foreign words deriving from Latin, Greek or French have the primary stress usually on the last heavy syllable (long vowel, or vowel + consonant(s)), excluding native endings: *Bü'ro, Nati'on, Perga'ment, öko'nomisch*. But there are many exceptions.

7.6 | Morphology: Inflection

7.6.1 | Noun inflection

The standardization which led to the emergence of the Classical Literary Language and characterizes modern German affected the lexical membership of the inherited declensional types more than the types themselves. Modern German thus still has a complicated declensional system which, from the synchronic point of view, is highly arbitrary and unpredictable. Nevertheless, there has been much simplification since OHG: among masc. and neuter nouns the unmarked pl. type has been eliminated, unmarkedness now being phonologically (masc. and n.) or morphologically (n.) determined, and there has been a great expansion of the functionally effective classes (mutated pl. among masc., *er-* and *e-*pl. among neuters); the fem. nouns have been realigned to an opposition sg./pl., expressed either by mutation or by *en-*pl. formation, both devices having been eliminated in the sg. The category of number is clearly more dominant than that of case. Most semantically suitable nouns indicate plurality, including the very large number of foreign words. Beside the central, 'German' system we now have an extensive peripheral or foreign system. One originally foreign type (Low German, French and English), the s-pl. class, is now widely used with German words and must therefore be regarded as an accession to the central system. These new developments have further increased the weight of number distinction as against case distinction. The strongly entrenched indication of the dat. pl. is breached: *Antibiotika* or *Kumpels* do not mark the dat. pl. There are also suppletive plural markers, e.g. *Tod – Todesfälle, Streit – Streitigkeiten, Wolle – Wollsorten.* In the very important technical registers mass words also form plurals, e.g. *Stahl – Stähle, Staub – Stäube.* In declensional types with -*e* in the dat. sg. this is largely a free variant. Case indication is now mainly borne by determiners.

Owing to the overlapping of the indications of the categories of case, number and gender (in so far as this is expressed by the noun at all), the declensional patterns are complicated and can be set up in different ways. Since the indication of plurality is without doubt the most important feature and since predictability is greater if the system is based on the mode of plural formation, the system here adopted is based on the indication of plurality.

I. *e-plural*

			M.	N.
Pl.	{ Nom. acc. gen.	-*e*	Steine	Beine
	{ Dat.	-*en*	Steinen	Beinen
Sg.	⌠ Nom. acc.	-ø	Stein	Bein
	⎨ Gen.	-(*e*)*s*	Stein(e)s	Bein(e)s
	⌡ Dat.	-(*e*)	Stein(e)	Bein(e)

Notes:

(1) There are only very few fem. nouns in this class, namely those in -*sal* (*Trübsal*) and -*nis* (*Kenntnis*) which may thus be treated as exceptions. On the other hand, this is one of the major, characteristic classes of masc. and n. nouns.

(2) If we assume that the plural morph -*e* is deleted in masc. and n. nouns ending in -*el*, -*en*, -*er* we may here include all the nouns with unmarked pl.: m. *Schlegel, Wagen, Jäger*; n. *Bündel, Fohlen, Muster.*

Further belong here: all neuters in *-chen, -lein,* and the type *Ge——e: Gebirge, Gefilde,* and in *-er: Gewässer.*

(3) Words with [ə] in the final syllable always delete [ə] in the declensional morphs (*Jäger + en > Jägern*). Words ending in *-n* have *-ø* in the dat. pl.

(4) The gen. ending retains its *-e-* with any regularity only after sibilants (*Hauses, Kusses, Tisches*) and after heavy consonantal clusters (*Kampfes*).

(5) Dat. sg. *-e* is retained mainly with monosyllabic roots ending in a voiced consonant (*Bade, Wege*).

The last three rules apply also to all subsequent classes with the relevant morphs.

II. *Plural with mutation*

			M.	F.	
Pl.	{	Nom. acc. gen.	¨e	Schläge	Häute
		Dat.	¨en	Schlägen	Häuten
Sg.	{	Nom. acc.	-ø	Schlag	Haut
		Gen.	-(e)s -ø	Schlages	Haut
		Dat.	-(e) -ø	Schlage	Haut

Notes:

(1) There are three neuters belonging to this class to be listed as exceptions (*Flöße, Klöster, Wässer*) rather than as a type, since this class is characteristic of a large number of masc. nouns and is the second important class of fem. nouns.

(2) The deletion rule concerning *-e* after *-el, -en, -er* applies here too (see I (2)): *Väter, Mütter, Klöster.* An exception is *Käse* (pl. = sg.)

III. *er-plural*

			N.	M.	
Pl.	{	Nom. acc. gen.	¨er	Kälber	Geister
		Dat.	¨ern	Kälbern	Geistern
Sg.	{	Nom. acc.	-ø	Kalb	Geist
		Gen.	-(e)s	Kalb(e)s	Geistes
		Dat.	-(e)	Kalb(e)	Geist(e)

Notes:

(1) This class contains many more n. than masc. nouns. Mutation shows itself to be a secondary feature by appearing automatically where the root vowel is susceptible to it.

IV. *n-plural*

		M.	F.	N.			
Pl.	Nom. acc. Gen. dat.		*-en*		Menschen	Zungen	Augen
Sg.	Nom.		*-ø*		Mensch	Zunge	Auge
	Acc.	*-en/-ø*	*-ø*	*-ø*	Menschen	Zunge	Auge
	Gen.	*-en/-ens/-(e)s*	*-ø*	*-(e)s*	Menschen Namens Masts	Zunge	Auges
	Dat.	*-en/-ø*	*-ø*	*-ø*	Menschen	Zunge	Auge

Notes:

(1) All nouns in this class have a uniform plural unmarked for case. In the nom. sg. the nouns end either in *-e* (*Knabe, Achse, Auge*) or in a consonant (*Fürst, Bahn, Ohr*). The *e* of the morph *-en* is deleted if the nouns have an [ə] in the last syllable (*Achse, Achsel*).

(2) This is the chief class of feminines.

(3) The masc. nouns divide into three sub-classes according to the formation of the gen. sg.: (a) gen. sg. *-en*, only nouns denoting animate beings; (b) gen. sg. *-ens*, inanimate nouns ending in *-e*, e.g. *Gedanke, Name, Wille*; (c) gen. sg. *-(e)s*, nouns ending in a consonant, e.g. *Mast, Stachel, Muskel, Vetter, Staat*, and the foreign nouns in *-or* (*Direktor*).

(4) There is one exception to the neuter group: *Herz – Herzens*. The normal neuter group is very small (*Bett, Ende, Hemd, Ohr, Auge*, and some foreign ones, e.g. *Insekt, Elektron, Neutron*).

(5) There is some variation among the masc. nouns of group (b), in so far as *-n* is also found in the nom. sg. (*Gedanken, Namen, Willen*) in which case these nouns belong to class I (Note 2). Some nouns waver between classes or have slightly different meanings according to the class they follow (*Worte – Wörter, Bande – Bänder*). There are also anomalous cases such as *Bau – Bauten*.

V. *s-plural*

		M.	F.	N.			
Pl.			*-s*		Kumpels	Kameras	Autos
Sg.	Nom. acc. dat.		*-ø*		Kumpel	Kamera	Auto
	Gen.	*-s*	*-ø*	*-s*	Kumpels	Kamera	Autos

Notes

(1) Words ending in unstressed *-i, -a, -o, -u* (*Nazi, Sofa, Echo, Uhu*), words from LG (*Wrack, Junge*), clause compounds (*Lebewohl*), abbreviations (*Pkw*) and words of foreign origin (*Hotel, Streik*) are found here.

The category of case and, to a lesser extent, that of number is now mainly expressed by the noun phrase as a whole. The determiners (see 7.6.2), of which the def. art. may serve as a representative, function together with the declensional endings of the noun and the endings of the attributive adjective. Thus we can say that the case and number systems are based on the following combinations:

der (+attr. *–e*)+*ø*: masc. nom. sg.
der (+attr. *–en*)+*ø*: fem. gen. dat. sg.
der (+attr. *–en*)+*–e*/*ːe*/*ːer*/*–en–s*: gen. pl.
den (+attr. *–en*)+*ø*/*–en*: masc. acc. sg.
den (+attr. *–en*)+*–en*/*ːen*/*ːern*/*–en*/*–s*: dat. pl.
die (+attr. *–e*)+*ø*: fem. nom. acc. sg.
die (+attr. *–en*)+*–e*/*ːe*/*ːer*/*–en*/*–s*: nom. acc. pl.
das (+attr. *–e*)+*ø*: n. nom. acc. sg.
des (+attr. *–en*)+*–(e)s*/*–en*/*–ens*: masc., n. gen. sg.
dem (+attr. *–en*)+*–(e)*/*–en*: masc., n. dat. sg.

We see, where the combination of determiner+declensional noun morph still leaves ambiguity, the attributive adjective may assume a determinative function and finally even the verb: cf. *den kleinen Knaben* (+*geben*=dat. pl.; +*lieben*=acc. sg.). Despite the great reduction in the inflectional system which has occurred in the history of German, the indication of case and number is preserved. In fact there is far more redundancy than ambiguity. The transition from a synthetic morphology to an analytical one is, however, an unmistakable phenomenon of the history of German.

7.6.2 | Adjective inflection

Of the four grammatical categories of the adjective three (case, number, gender) are inflectional and one (comparison) derivational in character. Inflection is determined by the morphological character of the noun phrase – outside it the German adjective is uninflected. The two inherited inflectional paradigms – once charged with a semantic function – are now entirely dependent on the formal circumstances of the noun phrase. The chief function of the attributive adjective is that of a qualifier of the noun. It is generally preceded by a determiner or quantifier fulfilling an important determinative role in the noun phrase. If there is such a determiner present fulfilling this role, the attributive adjective has always the weak declension which could be called the qualifier declension. If there is no determiner or if the determiner is uninflected the attributive adjective itself assumes this role by means of the strong endings (i.e. the determiner declension). The definite article (*der, die, das*), the demonstratives *dieser, jener,* and the pronominal adjectives *alle, jeglicher, mancher, sämtliche* always act as determiners, but *ein, kein, manch, mein* (and the other possessive adjectives) and *welch* fail to do so when they appear uninflected. In this case the qualifying adjective must itself act as determiner. This is the function of the strong declension.

There are five inflectional morphs: *-e, -em, -en, -er, -es*. Three are strong, i.e. they always act as determining elements (*-em, -er, -es*). Of the other two, *-e* is weak in masc. nom. sg. and in n., fem. nom./acc. sg. but otherwise strong, while *-en* is predominantly weak and only strong in the masc. acc. sg. (cf. *den*) and in the dat. pl. In other words, the strong endings correspond to the determiners, e.g. *der/-er, das/-es, dem/-em, den/-en, die/-e*. One might expect that *-es* would also correspond to *des*. This was indeed the case right into the early nineteenth century (see 6.6.2): *frohes Mutes*. It appears that the strongly determinative function of the noun morph *-es* made the equivalent morph of the adjective redundant, hence it was replaced by the weak ending *-en* (*frohen Mutes*). Pronominal determiners are, however, not so neutralized (*seines Mutes*). We thus have the rule that an adjective in a noun phrase is always weak if a determinative element precedes. Where we have pronominal adjectives in first position modern German usage is still not entirely fixed. If they are regarded primarily as determiners like *alle, keine, sämtliche,* the qualifiers are given weak endings; if they are themselves regarded as qualifiers like *andere, einige, etliche, manche, mehrere, viele, wenige* the following adjective has strong endings. Co-ordinated adjectives (e.g. *schwerer, alter Wein*) always have identical endings.

Substantivized adjectives follow the same pattern: *ein Abgeord-neter, der Abgeordnete.*

7.6.3 | Verb inflection

Probably nowhere in German grammar did standardization mean so much as in the field of verbal inflection. The contrast between ENHG multiplicity and NHG norm is stark.

(i) As far as *stem formation* is concerned the ancient tripartition into a dental-suffix type, an apophonic type and a mixed or apophonic dental-suffix type is preserved, cf. *lachen – lachte – gelacht; trinken – trank – getrunken; können/kann – konnte – gekonnt.*

The dental-suffix type, characterized by the preterite suffix *-(e)te* and by *-(e)t* in the past participle, is now reduced to only two classes: I the regular class, the only productive verbal class of German; II an irregular, closed class with root vowel alternation (*Rückumlaut*) in addition to dental suffixation, containing eight verbs: *brennen, kennen, nennen, rennen, senden, wenden* and *bringen, denken* (with consonantal irregularities). All have *-a-* in the stem of the pret. and past part., although there are also semantically differentiated regular forms of *senden* and *wenden. Haben* is irregular in other respects.

The apophonic verbs, of which there are about 165, are split up into some regular patterns and a very large number of small groups or individual cases. If a classificatory system has to take account of all the verbs it is bound to be extremely complicated. If we accept that 'system' means that at least a small number of cases (say four to five) must follow a particular rule we can set up a classification which covers about three quarters of all apophonic verbs. The rest (nearly forty verbs) have to be regarded as small isolated groups or individual exceptions. This also applies to those verbs which are in the process of moving from one type to another, e.g. *backen – buk* or *backte – gebacken, pflegen – pflog* or *pflegte – gepflogen* or *gepflegt.*

There are three stem forms to be taken into account: the infinitive/present, preterite, and past participle; but not all classes have three different stem alternants. This affords the first classificatory framework. The stem alternants are based on gradation

(3.5.3). Most verbs with a root vowel susceptible to mutation in the inf./pres. stem show a mutated vowel in the 2nd and 3rd pers. sg.

I. Two stem forms (pret. = past part.)

Inf.		Pret.	Past part. Except:
1. -ei-(+vl. C)	*beißen*	-i- *biß*	*heißen,*
(36) (+vd. C)	*bleiben*	-ie- *blieb*	*leiden,*
			schneiden
2. -ie- (+⟨C⟩)	*biegen*	-ō- *bog*	*liegen, sieden*
(18) (+⟨CC⟩)	*riechen*	-o- *roch*	*ziehen*
3. (5) -ē-	*heben* (+*gären*)	-ō- *hob*	
4. (5) -e-	*fechten* (e > i)	-o- *focht*	

II. Two stem forms (inf. = past part.)

5. -a-	*blasen* (a > ä)	-ie- *blies*	
(8) [a/aː]	*geblasen*	(>i+ŋ)	
6. -a-	*fahren* (a > ä)	-ū- *fuhr*	
(8) [a/aː]	*gefahren*		
7. -e-	*geben* (e > i)	-ā- *gab*	
(8) [e/eː]	*gegeben*		

III. Three stem forms

8. (17) -i- (+⟨NC⟩)	*binden*	-a- *band*	-u- *gebunden*	*schinden*
9. (6) -i- (+⟨NN⟩)	*rinnen*	-a- *rann*	-o- *geronnen*	*glimmen,*
				klimmen
10. (9) -e- (+l, r, C)	*helfen* (e > i)	-a- *half*	-o- *geholfen*	*melken,*
				schmelzen
(4) -e- (+ch, ck)	*stechen* (e>i)	-a- *stach*	-o- *gestochen*	
(3) -e- (+r, l)	*stehlen* (e>ie)	-a- *stahl*	-o- *gestohlen*	

Notes:

(1) The figures in parentheses give the number of verbs in each class.

(2) Where there are phonological or graphemic conditioning factors these are indicated, e.g. vl.C. = before voiceless consonant; vd.C. = before voiced consonant; NC = nasal plus consonant.

(3) Phonetic values given in square brackets indicate that the root vowels are long or short according to the rules of German spelling.

(4) The notations (e > i) or (a > ä) indicate the change in the root vowel of the 2nd and 3rd pers. sg.

(5) The subj. pret. is formed by mutation of the ind. pret. base and the addition of the appropriate inflectional suffixes, but one class (10, *helfen*) has a different grade: *ü* or *ö* (*hülfe, gölte*). A few other verbs also have a special base, but all these forms sound rather archaic and are restricted in use.

The apophonic dental-suffix type (preterite-presents) now includes the modal auxiliaries (*dürfen, können, mögen, müssen, sollen, wollen*) and *wissen*. It is characterized morphologically by gradation in the present (with the inflectional endings of the preterite) and by having a regular dental-suffix preterite and past part. with irregular base forms (*durf-, konn-, mocht-, muß-, soll-, woll-, wuß-*).

(ii) In turning to the *inflectional paradigms* we are confronted with the problem of the elision or insertion of -*e*- in certain cases. Some scholars preferring to posit underlying forms with -*e*- speak of elision and point to the historical syncope in support of their argument. But since in ENHG syncope was not prevented in the cases where -*e*- is found now (cf. ENHG *redt* – NHG *redet*), the historical argument is weak. The present rule is the result of rational standardization in the eighteenth century which insisted on the presence of -*e*- where assimilation would otherwise have obliterated the inflectional suffix. One is therefore equally justified in speaking of insertion as of elision. In the following tables I prefer to regard the forms as positional, phonologically conditioned variants.

		Ind. pres.				Subj. pres.		
1st sg.	(ich)	-*e*	lache	rede	(ich)	-*e*	lache	rede
2nd sg.	(du)	-(*e*)*st*	lachst	redest	(du)	-*est*	lachest	redest
3rd sg.	(er)	-(*e*)*t*	lacht	redet	(er)	-*e*	lache	rede
1st pl.	(wir)	-*en*	lachen	reden	(wir)	-*en*	lachen	reden
2nd pl.	(ihr)	-(*e*)*t*	lacht	redet	(ihr)	-*et*	lachet	redet
3rd pl.	(sie)	-*en*	lachen	reden	(sie)	-*en*	lachen	reden

Notes

(1) The bracketed -*e*- occurs if the root ends in -*d*, -*t* or a cluster consisting of a fricative or plosive plus a nasal (*redet, rechnet, atmet*). But in cases of mutation in apophonic verbs where the person appears to be sufficiently marked, -*e*- is not required, hence the distinction between 3rd pers. sg. and 2nd pers. pl.: *tritt* – *tretet*, *brät* – *bratet*. Irregular forms are: *birst* (<*bersten*), *wird* (<*werden*).

(2) In the 2nd pers. sg. ind. pres. -*st* is assimilated after roots in -*s*, e.g. (*du*) *liest, reist, beißt*.

(3) Apophonic verbs with root vowels *a, au, o* have mutation (>*ä, äu, ö*) in 2nd and 3rd pers. sg. ind. except *hauen, kommen, saugen, schaffen, schnauben* and the change of *e* (*ä, ö*) > *i*, except with *bewegen, gären, genesen, pflegen, stecken, weben, gehen, stehen*.

(4) On the realization of *-en* in the spoken language see 7.5.3.

(5) The subjunctive is characterized by an *e*-marker, treated quite differently from the *-(e)* of the ind. The subj. is, however, effectively marked only in the 3rd pers. sg. by the opposition *-e/-t* supplemented by the presence/absence of mutation.

(6) The above paradigms apply to all dental-suffix and apophonic verbs, but to the preterite-presents only in the subjunctive. The irregular verb *sein* has its own paradigm and *haben* has the two special forms (*du*) *hast*, (*er*) *hat*.

The preterite is formed in all types of verbs by means of a tense marker plus inflectional endings. There are two different tense markers: *-(e)te* and the preterite apophonic grade (*G*). The subj. pret. has again the *e*-marker and mutation in apophonic verbs with mutable base vowels. Thus we have the following paradigms:

		Ind. pret.				Subj. pret.	
1st sg.	(ich)	*-(e)te/G+*	*-ø*		(ich)	*-(e)te/G¨ +*	*-e*
2nd sg.	(du)	*-(e)te/G+*	*-(e)st*		(du)	*-(e)te/G¨ +*	*-est*
3rd sg.	(er)	*-(e)te/G+*	*-ø*		(er)	*-(e)te/G¨ +*	*-e*
1st pl.	(wir)	*-(e)te/G+*	*-(e)n*		(wir)	*-(e)te/G¨ +*	*-en*
2nd pl.	(ihr)	*-(e)te/G+*	*-(e)t*		(ihr)	*-(e)te/G¨ +*	*-et*
3rd pl.	(sie)	*-(e)te/G+*	*-(e)n*		(sie)	*-(e)te/G¨ +*	*-en*
1st sg.	lachte	redete	lag	trat		läge	träte
2nd sg.	lachtest	redetest	lagst	tratst		lägest	trätest
3rd sg.	lachte	redete	lag	trat		läge	träte
1st pl.	lachten	redeten	lagen	traten		lägen	träten
2nd pl.	lachtet	redetet	lagt	tratet		läget	trätet
3rd pl.	lachten	redeten	lagen	traten		lägen	träten

Notes:

(1) The bracketed *e* in the tense marker *-(e)te* behaves according to the rule given in Note (1) above.

(2) The bracketed *e* in the inflectional endings is governed by the following rules applying to apophonic verbs only: in the 1st and 3rd pers. pl. it is present in the orthography (in spoken language it is realized according to the rules given in 7.5.3); in the 2nd pers. sg. it occurs after sibilants, e.g. (*du*) *lasest, rissest, wuschest*; in the 2nd pers. pl. it occurs after *d* and *t* (*botet, tratet*).

(3) The preterite-presents follow the above paradigm twice: with *G* in the present and with the tense marker *-te* and the bases given on p. 568 in the preterite.

(4) In the subj. pret. the *e* of the inflectional suffixes fuses, of course,

with the *e* of the tense marker -(*e*)*te*, so that there is no difference between
the ind. and subj. of the regular dental-suffix verbs. But the second,
irregular class marks the subj. pret. by mutation as do most preterite-
presents, e.g. *kennen – kannte* but *kennte* (subj. pret., strictly speaking lack
of *Rückumlaut*), *brächte, dächte, durfte – dürfte*, etc. but *sollte, wollte*
remain unmutated in the subj. pret. The subj. pret. is thus also weakly
determined in most verbs, hence the synthetic construction has been
supplemented by a more efficient analytical one with *würde*.

7.7 | Morphology: Word Formation

7.7.1 | Noun derivation
Derivational morphology, expressing lexical or semantic
categories, is much less systematic than inflectional morphology
expressing grammatical categories. What they have in common is
that the choice of a particular alternative device (derivational
morph or inflectional morph) is dependent to a large degree on the
particular base morph. Thus the denotation of abstract quality is
carried out by -*e* in the case of *stark* (*Stärke*), by -*heit* in the case
of *schön* (*Schönheit*), and by -*igkeit* in the case of *schnell* (*Schnelligkeit*), which is paralleled by the choice of the plural morphs -*e*
(*Tag*), ≟*e* (*Gäste*) or ≟*er* (*Wälder*) being equally dependent on the
base morphs. But in contrast to the function of the inflectional
morphs (say the genitive morph) which is precise, the function
of the derivational morphs is vague and much more dependent
upon context and the content of the base morph. Thus the suffix
-*ler* forming agent nouns from nouns has a different semantic
content in *Künstler* and *Kriegsgewinnler*, or -*er* in *Schreier* and in
Seufzer. The reason is that there are two aspects to word formation: process and result. On the synchronic plane a process takes
place: a device is employed to form a new word. The resultant new
word may enter the lexicon of the speech community and, in the
diachronic dimension, may become lexicalized, that is, leave the
field of active word formation although externally still showing the
signs of word formation. When a composite form is no longer
analysable both formally and semantically, i.e. is no longer moti-

vated, it is lexicalized. *Wohnung* and *Sitzung* may look like *Schaffung* and *Bohrung* but they are completely lexicalized, while the latter two words are still active derivations: *schaff(en)*, *bohr(en)* +*ung* > deverbal abstract noun indicating an action or a result. Sometimes individual words, sometimes whole functional groups become lexicalized. For instance, we can no longer form abstract nouns from adjectives by means of -*e* (**Schöne*, **Schnelle* in analogy to *Stärke*, *Länge*), at least in standard German. All such words are the result of former derivation; the process is closed. But we can still employ this suffix with verbs where we also have a large group of ancient derivations (*Bahre*, *Sprache*) and where analogical new formations are possible (*Trage*, *Schreibe*). What is of interest in a synchronic study is the productive means, the processes which are possible. In this sense, word formation is one of the most vital features of the modern language. Much of the impulse for word formation comes from the scientific and technological specialist languages (see p. 539), from journalism and advertising. The following derivational morphs are productive in modern standard German:

(i) -*er* forms (a) *nomina agentis* from verbal bases (simple, composite or phrasal) (*Leser*, *Einbrecher*, *Nichtstuer*); (b) *nomina instrumenti* (*Schalter*, *Plattenspieler*); this formation is particularly characteristic of technical usage, often replacing such words as -*maschine*, cf. E *washing machine* > *washer*; (c) words designating an action (*Treffer*, *Walzer*), of limited productivity; (d) nouns denoting inhabitants (*Berliner*). Derivation from nouns (except under (d)) is now relatively rare (*Überschaller* < *Überschall(geschwindigkeits)flugzeug*, *Eisenbahner*). To some extent forms with -*ler*, -*ner* from noun bases supplement -*er*: *Fremdsprachler*, *Staatsrechtler*, where the pejorative, affective connotation is absent. Many words, however, retain this connotation (*Provinzler*) which was strong in the eighteenth century (*Vernünftler*).

(ii) -*ling* designates persons with a passive connotation (*Prüfling* cf. *Prüfer*) from verbal bases. Words with a nominal base have mainly a pejorative meaning (*Weichling*, *Dichterling*).

(iii) -*in* designates females and reflects the emancipation of women by its great productivity (*Beamtin*, *Predigerin*, *Maurerin*).

(iv) -*chen/-lein*. In the course of the eighteenth century, which was generally not in favour of diminutives, the Central German suffix -*chen* advanced against the Upper German -*lein*. The distribution of the two suffixes is now partly phonologically determined: roots in *-l* only take *-chen* (*Seelchen*), roots in *-g*, *-ch* only take *-lein* (*Berglein, Bächlein*), partly stylistically: *-chen* is more neutral, *-lein* more poetical.

(v) *-e* forms fem. nouns from verbs by a kind of back-formation: *Halte* (*Haltestelle*), *Absteige, Spüle* (*Spülstein*). Some indicate a thing or the place where an action takes place, others the action itself (*Durchsage, Nachlöse*). It is popular in the slang of juveniles (*die Heule* 'transistor').

(vi) *-ung* is one of the most productive suffixes converting verbs into *nomina actionis*. Many formations from simple nouns are now lexicalized. Specially productive are the derivations from transitive prefix verbs and verbal compounds (*Behandlung, Herausstellung, Grundsteinlegung*).

(vii) *-ei, -elei, -erei*. The first is only slightly productive with the meaning 'place', e.g. *Kartei, Auskunftei*; *-elei* is pejorative (*Frömmelei < frömmeln*); *-erei* expresses 'repeated, irritating action' and first arose mainly on the basis of verbs in *-ern*; it is now very productive: *Angeberei, Lauferei, Kocherei*.

(viii) *-heit, -keit, (-igkeit)*: the chief means of forming abstract nouns indicating a state or a quality from adjectives and past participles (*Dummheit, Entschlossenheit*). The suffix *-keit* is a positional variant after *-ig, -lich, -sam, -bar*, and more frequent than *-heit* after *-el, -er* (*Sicherheit, Sauberkeit*). Although the modern base may lack *-ig* the suffix *-igkeit* may occur, e.g. *schnell – Schnelligkeit*. It is a positional variant after *-haft* and *-los*.

(ix) *-schaft* and *-tum* are productive to a limited extent to form personal collectives (*Partnerschaft, Bauernschaft*) or nouns indicating the rank or character of a group (*Beamtentum, Bauerntum*), both from nouns as bases.

(x) Ge-(root)-e: this composite derivational morpheme forms neuter deverbal nouns indicating an irritating action which gets on people's nerves: *Gefluche, Gepfeife*. The function of *-erei* is very similar but tends to put more stress on the iterative nature of the action (cf. *Flucherei – Gefluche*), but *Ge – e* cannot be used with prefix or compound verbs, hence we have only *Aufschneiderei, Biertrinkerei*.

While the suffixes *-nis* and *-sal* cannot be regarded as still being productive some new elements have begun to move into the orbit of noun derivation: *-gut, -werk, -wesen, -zeug*. The first designates material used for a process (*Saatgut, Versandgut*); -*werk*, already found in ENHG, forms mainly material collectives (*Gangwerk, Gitterwerk*); -*zeug* indicates mainly tools or objects involved in an action or used for a purpose (*Reitzeug, Bettzeug*); -*wesen* added to nouns indicates an 'institution' or a 'branch', e.g. *Bildungswesen, Pressewesen*. The large number of foreign suffixes (-*ant*, -*age*, -*ist*, -(*a*)*tion*, -*tät*, -*ismus*, etc.) are not on the whole used with native bases and are thus not productive in the same sense as the native suffixes, although many are widely and actively used with new foreign words (*Terrorismus, Terrorist*).

The inherited prefixes *Ur-, Un-, Miß-, Erz-* are still productive and are now joined by *Haupt-* (*Hauptfilm*) with the sense 'main'. Through back-formation and conversion of verbs into nouns by means of derivation the verb prefixes and prefix particles are now also completely domesticated in noun formation, e.g. *Bezug, Anzug, Überzug, Hinterziehung*, although this type of formation is still not very widespread with purely nominal bases, e.g. *Aufpreis, Mitmensch* (*mit* is fairly frequent), *Beiblatt, Gegenbeispiel, Vortag*. It is only the relative frequency of their use which makes us consider these prefixes as derivational devices rather than as determinative elements in compounds.

7.7.2 | Adjective derivation

Again an attempt will be made to show the productive means of derivation. It is understood that in each case there are individual words or whole semantic niches now lexicalized, although these will not be discussed.

(i) -*bar* is very productive as a deverbal suffix with the passive meaning 'it can be done', E -*able*/-*ible*: *waschbar, trennbar*. The breakthrough in this functional concentration occurred in the eighteenth century (see 6.7.2).

(ii) -*ig* is also very productive but semantically ill-defined (mainly 'like'). The base is usually a noun (*staubig*). Adverbs can be turned into adjectives as well (*nichtig*). A special group is the phrase derivatives: 'graues Haar habend' > *grauhaarig*; 'zwei Sprachen beherrschend' > *zweisprachig*; 'auf ein Ziel strebend' > *zielstrebig*.

(iii) -*lich* can also express the nature or character (*ländlich*) but many formations have the meaning 'concerning', i.e. they are relational (*verkehrlich, preislich, betrieblich*) and can only be used attributively. This extension seems to have occurred in specialist languages. The base is mainly nominal but can also be verbal (*zerbrechlich*), or from adjectives, mainly with the meaning 'kind of, shade of', e.g. *rötlich*. The incidence of mutation is arbitrary.

(iv) *-isch* is used mainly with nouns. A special group indicates origin (*irisch*) and is derived from names. A characteristic feature is the use of *-isch* with foreign words (*morphologisch*). The pejorative aspect of *-isch* (*kindisch, weibisch*) became established in the eighteenth century.

(v) *en, -ern* have retained their precise definition 'consisting of' and are used only with nouns, e.g. *seiden, stählern*. They are sometimes in opposition to forms in *-ig*: *seidig* 'like silk', *seiden* 'of silk', cf. E *silky – silken*.

(vi) *-haft* with a noun base has mainly the meaning 'of the kind of': *schurkenhaft, löwenhaft* or 'possessing': *schamhaft*.

(vii) *-sam*. Most adjectives are lexicalized. With verb bases the meaning is usually 'inclined to': *empfindsam, fügsam*.

There are also several free forms which are used so frequently that they can be regarded as derivational morphs, e.g. *-arm* (*wasserarm*), *-reich* (*fischreich*), *-voll* (*problemvoll*), *-los* (*gedankenlos*), *-frei* (*verkehrsfrei*). The most popular today seems to be *-mäßig* ('das Ferienhaus ist *lagemäßig* und *ruhemäßig* sehr zu empfehlen') with the meaning 'concerning' or 'according to'. It can be added to all kinds of derivative nouns unlike most of the older suffixes (*überlieferungsmäßig, mannschaftsmäßig*). This formation also increases the stock of relational adjectives with which German is otherwise not well provided, cf. *sorgfältige Betreuung – gesundheitsmäßige Betreuung*.

7.7.3 | Nominal composition

(i) Numerically the most important type is the determinative noun + noun composition. Both the first or determinative element and the base element may be simple nouns, derivatives or compounds: *Regenzeit*; *Staatsbegräbnis, Ansiedlungswünsche*; *Verwaltungsmittelpunkt, Dienstleistungsbetrieb*. The first element may be in the singular or, more rarely, in the plural (*Gottesdienst*,

Götterspeise); it may appear with a juncture element or lack such an element. The distinction between primary and secondary composition which is of historical importance (see 3.7.5; 4.6.4(i); 5.6.5(i); 6.7.5) may be discarded in a synchronic study of the modern period. The masc. and n. genitival *-s*, extended to fem. nouns since the sixteenth century (see 6.7.5), tends to be simply a convention without any function (cf. *Kalbfleisch* but *Kalbsleder*), but it appears generally with determinative elements ending in *-heit, -keit, -schaft, -tum, -ung, -ion, -tät* and occasionally as a glide for phonetic reasons. It does not occur with monosyllabic fem. nouns ending in a consonant or dissyllabic ones in *-e*, except normally *Liebe, Hilfe, Geschichte* (*Liebesdienst, Hilfstruppe, Geschichtsbuch*). Practice varies in most other cases, sometimes with regional differences. The juncture element *-en* is found with present or former *n*-pl. nouns (*Sonnenblume, Schwanenhals, Bubenstreich*) and may go back to a gen. sg. or, less frequently, a pl. form.

Where the two elements are themselves compounds – a form of composition very characteristic of the modern language – the structure is nevertheless generally binary, as the following examples show:

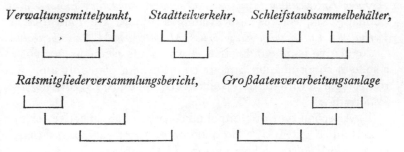

Verwaltungsmittelpunkt, Stadtteilverkehr, Schleifstaubsammelbehälter,

Ratsmitgliederversammlungsbericht, Großdatenverarbeitungsanlage

Compounds of three constituents are now quite common, but compounds of four tend to be restricted to specialist languages. The salient fact about composition in the modern language is the great freedom and readiness to form ad hoc compounds. Syntactically such compounds rest most frequently on a genitive or prepositional construction: *Zeit des Regens, Begräbnis durch den Staat, Wünsche hinsichtlich der Ansiedlung, Mittelpunkt der/für die Verwaltung, Verkehr im Stadtteil, Sammelbehälter für Schleifstaub, Bericht über die Versammlung der Ratsmitglieder*. Other relations may arise through the conversion or omission of a verb, e.g. *Eierfrau* 'eine Frau, die Eier bringt', *Biertrinker* 'einer, der Bier trinkt'. Which relation applies in a particular case is largely determined by the semantic content of the elements and by convention in cases of ambiguity.

There is also a very modern type of compound which can be called a conglomerate. It does not consist of independently existing compounds but is a kind of contraction of a whole phrase or clause: *Unterwasserfernsehgerät* 'ein Fernsehgerät, das unter der Wasseroberfläche benützt werden kann', *Allschneeschnellskier* 'Skier, die bei jedem Schneezustand eine schnelle Fahrt gewährleisten', *Einwegflasche* 'eine Flasche, die vom Verkäufer nicht zurückgenommen wird'.

An old form, on the other hand, is the extrusive compound where one of the elements either of the determinative first compound or of the base is dispensed with, e.g. *Atomkernzertrümmerung > Atomzertrümmerung, Überschallgeschwindigkeitsflugzeug > Überschallflugzeug, Hallenschwimmbad > Hallenbad*.

A new kind of compound, much favoured in modern journals, e.g. *Der Spiegel*, consists of a juxtaposition of a name plus an appellative, for instance: *der Deutschland-Besucher de Gaulle, die Ägypten-Entwicklungshilfe, der Adenauer-Geburtstag, Japan-Autos*. Similar juxtapositions abbreviating a phrase are *Patient-Arzt-Verhältnis, Luft-Boden-Flugkörper, Möchtegern-Mütter, oben-ohne*.

Copulative compounds, that is where the elements are not in a state of subordination but are co-ordinated, play only a modest role compared with the determinative compounds, e.g. *Strumpfhose, Pulloverjacke*.

(ii) A second type of compound consists of an adjective (or to a more limited extent of a pronoun or particle)+a noun: *Schnellrasur, Nurphilologe, Ichbewußtsein*. The contracted or coalescent adj.+noun compounds have increased enormously and are very much a fashion of the modern language. Historically they go back to the attributive phrase in which the strongly declined adjective could be endingless (see 4.5.2, 5.6.5): MHG *junc man, junc vrouwe, junc kind*. On the analogy of old compounds such as *Jungfrau, Frühmesse*, we now have a large number of such contractions: *Schwarzafrikaner, Frischfleisch, Gebrauchtwagen*. In each case the contracted form has the character of a technical term (*Frischfleisch* as opposed to *frisches Fleisch*). Categorization has taken the place of description. To see the world in terms of categories, to pigeon-hole things, is a tendency of modern administrative, commercial and journalistic thinking. Some adjectives are specially favoured in this role, e.g. *klein* (*Kleinfahrzeug*, or in the superlative: *Kleinsthörgerät*), *groß* (*Großwohnung*, *Größtverbraucher*). Many have the appearance of conglomerates, there being no underlying attributive phrase, e.g. *Schnellstraße* 'Straße, auf der man schnell fahren kann', *Vielfachbearbeitungsmaschine.*

On the whole only simple adjectives are permissible in such compounds, but foreign derivative adjectives can be so used, which would seem to prove that these foreign suffixes (-*al*, -*iv*, -*ar*, -*är* though not -*ös*, -*ibel*, -*abel*) do not count as derivational means: *Individualverkehr*, *Idealheim*, *Exklusivbericht.*

Exocentric compounds, especially with names for parts of the human body, are also found: *Dickbauch*, *Dummkopf*, *Bleichgesicht.*

(iii) Very much a modern feature is the nominal compound with a verb as the first element (but see pp. 111, p. 540 (viii)): *Prüfprotokoll*, *Werbeprospekt*, *Drehknopf*, *Reitpferd*, *Frischhaltepakkung*. The verbs always have their root form, -*e* generally occurring only after a voiced plosive or fricative.

The simplest way of converting a verb into a noun is the substantivization of the infinitive. This process can be expanded to include a noun object, a predicative adjective or a reflexive pronoun or a combination of these: *das Kegelschieben*, *Erdgasvorkommen*, *Zurgeltungkommen*, *Sichtbarwerden*, *Sichdurchsetzen*, *Sichnützlichmachen*. Somewhat more concrete, usually indicating the result rather than the process, are the derivatives in -*ung*: *die Herausarbeitung*, *Instandsetzung*. Such derivative compounds may, of course, also be noun plus noun compounds (*die Konferenzbeschickung*) if the elements occur independently as nouns.

(iv) Compounds with adjectives or participles as the base are also extremely popular in modern German. Inventiveness especially among advertisers appears unlimited: *autogerecht*, *kostentreibend*, *verkehrshinderlich*, *erschütterungsfest*, *fußwarm*, *preisgebunden*, *aromafrisch*, *maschinenlesbar*, *erneuerungsfreudig*, *karrierebewußt*, *leistungsbezogen*, *frischbetankt*, *behördenfromm*, *abendfüllend*, *hautschonend*, *straßengängig*, *ölfündig*. In most cases the first element is a noun, but other parts of speech occur as well, e.g. adj. *rotgestrichen*, *schmalspurig*, *dünnflüssig*, *größtgeplant*, pron. *selbstbewußt*, verbs *rutschfest*, *schreibgewandt*. Some adjectives occur rather frequently as bases, e.g. *-frei, -fest, -echt,* especially in advertising. Syntactically such adjective compounds rest on an object or prepositional relation. Nouns as base elements are converted into adjectives by means of an adjective derivational suffix (*Spur* > *spurig*), verbs by *-bar* (*lesen* > *lesbar*) or by conversion into a participle (*füllen* > *füllend, gefüllt*).

(v) No account of word formation in the modern language can leave out abbreviation among nouns. There are three types: first, words are shortened, e.g. *Kombimöbel* (< *Kombination*), *Lok* (< *Lokomotive*), *Labor* (< *Laboratorium*), *Krimi* (<*Kriminalroman*); secondly, initials may be combined to form new words, e.g. *Apo,*

DIN, Vopo; thirdly, the initials are pronounced as letters, e.g. *UKW, EWG, DDR.* There are also compounds with abbreviations: *D-Zug, NS-Belastung, Euro-Gipfel.*

7.7.4 | Verb formation

(i) The terms derivation and composition are of limited use when considering the word formation of verbs. Derivation amounts in practice only to conversion into verbs by means of the one infinitive suffix *-en.* This may be expanded to *-el-n, -er-n, -ig-en, -ier-en, -is-ier-en,* the significance of which was discussed when these expansions arose (see 3.7.4, 4.6.3, 5.6.4, 6.7.4). The latest addition to these is *-ifiz-ier-en* to form transitive, causative verbs from foreign bases, e.g. *klassifizieren.* The model is provided by the Latin suffix *-ficare* (< *facere* 'to make') and its corresponding forms in French (*-ifier*) and English (*-ify*). Conversion from nouns has increased considerably especially in technical languages (*drahten, gummieren, sanden*) and is particularly popular with prefixes (*verlanden, entwässern, ausbauchen*). Causatives (meaning: 'making') from adjectives (*glätten*) can occasionally still be formed, but inchoatives (meaning: 'becoming', *reifen*) and causatives from verbal bases (*senken*) are probably all lexicalized, the types being no longer productive.

Conversion from nominal compounds is also possible: *Leitartikel* > *leitartikeln, Mutmaßung* > *mutmaßen, Ohrfeige* > *ohrfeigen, Strafversetzung* > *strafversetzen.* The process by which they arise is back-formation. Such forms are not to be confused with genuine verbal compounds (see below). They are always inseparable.

(ii) Genuine composition plays a modest part. In specialist languages verb plus verb compounds occur: *fließdrücken, schleifputzen, tauchhärten, mähdreschen*. The last example appears to be a copulative compound. The others are determinative. Some few syntactic groups are now spelt as compounds: *kennenlernen, sitzenbleiben*, but not *stehen lassen*. Such fusions are separable, but the genuine verb plus verb compounds are generally restricted to the nominal forms of the verb, i.e. inf. and participles. They are certainly never separable. Compounds consisting of a noun as a determining element are relatively few. They are separable: *achtgeben, teilnehmen, zugrundegehen, schlittenfahren, maschineschreiben, radfahren*. Where the necessity of separating the parts leads to forms which sound odd, the composition is often dissolved again, e.g. *zähnefletschen* but *er fletscht die Zähne* rather than **er fletscht zähne* or *er zähnefletscht* (Duden, in analogy to the indirectly compounded verbs, see above). Separable compound verbs consisting of an adjective as the first element are more frequent and present fewer problems: *heißlaufen, glattreiben, trockenlegen, fremdgehen*. Pronominal particles as first elements also present no problems: *hinauswerfen, dableiben, herkommen, weiterwursteln, zusammenlöten*.

(iii) The particular form of word formation really characteristic of verbs is prefixation, consisting of two types. The first type is constituted by the six particles which are bound morphemes (*be-, er-, ent-, ver-, zer-, miß-*). In earlier stages of the language there was also *ge-*, but all such verbs are now lexicalized (*fallen – gefallen*) and *ge-* is no longer productive. The second type is the prefixation of adverbs/prepositions all of which are free morphemes (*ab, an, auf* etc.). Most are always separable, but a small special group (*durch, über, um, unter*, more rarely *wider*) can also be inseparable (*'übersetzen – über'setzen*), *hinter* is always inseparable. Many are highly polysemous and form a large number of semantic classes and sub-classes, with many lexicalized individual forms to complicate the patterns further.

Only the inseparable bound morphemes and their main semantic classes can be listed here. Again many individual verbs are lexicalized. The prefixes are given in order of frequency:

ver-   (a) 'to equip with': *verzieren, vergolden*.
      (b) 'to undo or to do wrongly': *verlernen, versteigen*.
      (c) 'to make into or to complete': *verlanden, verwildern*; *ver-*

is especially productive in the formation of de-adjectival verbs.

(d) 'away': *verschenken, verreisen.*

be-   (a) main function: forming trans. verbs: *besingen, besteigen.*
    (b) 'to equip with': *beringen, berasen, bebildern.*
    (c) 'to do something to something': *beschmieren, befriedigen.*

er-   (a) 'transition into another state': *erlahmen, erwachen.*
    (b) 'to complete or achieve': *ersteigen, ersingen.*

ent- (a) 'away from, out of': *entsteigen, entlaufen.*
    (b) 'to remove': *entkeimen, entnazifizieren.*

zer- (a) 'to take apart': *zersetzen, zersingen.*
    (b) 'intensifying the action': *zerschneiden, zerschmettern.*

miß- (a) 'to do wrongly or not at all': *mißbrauchen, mißglücken.*

7.8 | Syntax

7.8.1 | Sentence structure

The earlier sections concerned with syntax have shown how the sentence or clause in German is determined by two elements, the noun phrase and the verb phrase. The noun phrase, organized consecutively and marked by the contiguity of its constituents, is governed within the clause by the verb phrase. The task of the verb phrase is thus the organization of the clause itself. This rests on three important characteristics of the verb phrase: its ability to take up one of three determining positions; its ability to incapsulate other elements, i.e. to act as a discontinuous morph; and its ability to determine the number of complements which must be present (its valency). Of course, it also has other characteristics: the expression of number and person (a morphological feature, see 7.6.3); the expression of mood and tense (a morphological-syntactic feature, see 7.8.3); and the expression of meaning, both inherent and derivational (see 7.7.4). It is the clausal characteristics which concern us here.

Although the positional role of the verb cannot be isolated from other aspects such as intonation, mood and the meaning of the verb, it does offer the most important classificatory framework for the German clause.

(i) *Initial position* of the finite verb is found primarily in the age-old clause types of yes-or-no questions, commands, wishes in the subjunctive, and conditional clauses without a conjunction: *Kommt er wohl noch? Komm schnell! Möge es ihm gelingen! Kommt er heute noch, so können wir gleich anfangen.* In causal second clauses this position also occurs occasionally, especially in literary style: *Er brach zusammen, hatte er doch seit drei Tagen nichts mehr zu trinken bekommen.* On the other hand, in colloquial speech we frequently find this through ellipsis of a pronominal subject: *Weiß nicht. Kommt nicht in Frage*; also as a modern journalistic trick: *Klagt der Minister:...(Bild-Zeitung).* This is reminiscent of ENHG popular style (see 6.8.1(i)).

(ii) *Second position* of the finite verb is the characteristic form of the independent clause. Only one element may precede the finite verb, although through all kinds of accretions it may in fact be quite extensive: *Die Fülle der Lehrbücher über deutsche Sprachlehre mit ihren immer neuen Lösungsversuchen |läßt| es erkennen, daß etwas nicht in Ordnung ist,...*(E. Drach); *den Mann dort drüben |meine| ich.* Independent clause-like elements, of course, do not count: *Ja, gnädige Frau, das |zeige| ich Ihnen gern (das* is the only 'first' element). It is in this position that the ability of the verb to incapsulate complements other than the one in first position is most fully in evidence. The verbal frame can be formed by the following finite plus non-finite verbal parts:

(a) fin. vb. + inf.: *ich |werde| Ihnen morgen den Korb |bringen|.*
　　　　　　　　　　sie |pflegte| ihm jeweils einen Korb |zu geben|.
(b) fin. vb. + past part.: *ich |habe| ihn dir schon gestern |gebracht|.*
(c) fin. vb. + sep. prefix: *ich |nehme| Ihnen den Korb gerne |ab|.*
(d) fin. vb. + verbal compound element: *ich |nehme| morgen mit Freude daran |teil|.*
(e) fin. vb. + noun element: *er |erstattete| dem Chef gleich nach seiner Rückkehr |Bericht|.*

With such nominal paraphrases (*Bericht erstatten*) we are very close to the usual verb + object group, where we also have the principle that what is most closely linked to the verb is found at the greatest distance from the finite verb. Historically the last non-finite elements to be moved to the absolute final position are the infinitives and participles of the modal auxiliaries. We now also have *er hat es nicht gut sehen können* where up to ENHG *können sehen* was as common as it still is in many dialects.

There are, however, certain restrictions on incapsulation. Some are formal or syntactical: subordinate clauses, especially relative clauses and *daß*-clauses, infinitive clauses and comparative clauses with *wie* or *als* are generally not incapsulated, e.g. (a) *Dabei /wurde/ zunächst mit den Begriffen des Lateinischen /gearbeitet/, denen sich, mögen auch einige neue Begriffe hinzugekommen sein, die meisten Lehrbuchverfasser unterordnen* (E. Drach). (b) *Man hat in der Humanistenzeit /begonnen/, die Betrachtungsweise und die Fachbegriffe der griechisch-lateinischen Sprachgelehrsamkeit auf die andern Sprachen zu übertragen* (E. Drach). Some restrictions are rhythmical: the verbal frame must have a certain weight which must not be exceeded by too great a weight of the other elements. Verbal particles are rather weak in this respect and lack the power of enclosing heavy complements. Thus: *aber die Industrie /brachte/ einen neuen Mittelstand /hervor/ : Händler, Agenten, Ingenieure, Industriebeamte, die nicht auf Erlösung durch die Weltrevolution warteten* (R. Rath); *Aber /beziehen/ wir auch gleich den Zuhörer oder Leser /ein/, den Empfänger der Botschaft* (H. Eggers). In many cases the reasons for extrapolations are emotional, stylistic or accentual. Instances are especially frequent in spoken language (see p. 532) and in semi-standard (see p. 522), but fairly free use is nowadays also made in written language, e.g. *Wenn ich /lese/ von einer Jugendgruppe, die am nächsten Sonntag anzelten will* (L. Weisgerber); *Unter Satzlehre /wird/ hier /verstanden/ die Betrachtung des Satzganzen und der in ihm enthaltenen Wortgefüge* (E. Drach); *Nun /wollen/ wir /gehen/ in die Stadt meines Vaters und ansehen, wie sie abgefallen /ist/ von meiner Erinnerung* (Uwe Johnson). Generally, prepositional objects and complements of time, space and manner are most readily found in an unenclosed position. Incapsulation in its most extreme form was practised in the seventeenth and eighteenth centuries.

The second position is also taken up by the finite verb in subordinate sentences where the omission of a subordinating conjunction is permitted: (a) *er sagt, er /habe/ es schon getan (daß)*; (b) *er befahl, es /müsse/ erledigt werden (daß)*; (c) *er wird durchfallen, es /sei/ denn er strenge sich mehr an.* Here subordination is still borne by the subjunctive and not by a conjunction plus the final position of the finite verb.

An independent clause with second position of the finite verb can also be turned into a question by the required intonational pattern alone: *Sie sind schon im Urlaub gewesen?*

(iii) *Final position* of the finite verb is the hallmark of the German subordinate clause. What was originally the retarded position (see 4.7.1 (iii), 5.7.1 (iii)) became increasingly the absolute final position (see 6.8.1(ii)). Eventually even infinitives and participles were enclosed: *Er freute sich, weil er nun endlich einmal Italien besuchen /konnte/.* Behaghel's assertion that it was mainly under Latin influence that this came about is now generally rejected and it is held that the eighteenth-century grammarians were mainly responsible for the stricter rule. The actual verbal frame thus consists of two jambs, one at either end: the subordinating particle (conjunction or relative pronoun) and the finite verb. Only if there are two infinitives is there a departure from the rule. The finite verb precedes these infinitives: *weil er nicht /hat/ warten können* but *weil es nicht gelesen werden /darf/.* Otherwise, extrapolation occurs under conditions similar to those which demand or permit it in independent clauses.

(iv) *Valency* has already been mentioned as the third important clausal characteristic of the verb. All German verbs potentially enforce the presence or absence of certain complements. One can therefore classify them according to their valency. The sentence patterns which exist in the language are basically determined by the valency of the verb. All verbs normally enforce the presence of a subject complement: *Er schläft; es regnet.* If the first place is occupied by a certain personal complement some German verbs can dispense with the impersonal subject: *mich friert < es friert mich, mir wird schlecht < es wird mir schlecht.* A second type of verb demands the presence of a second complement, usually an object in the accusative, dative, genitive (now rare), or with a preposition, an adverbial complement, or a predicative nominal: *er schlägt ihn; er hilft ihm; er wartet auf ihn; sie ist hübsch.* A third type of verb requires three complements for it to be grammatically correctly employed: *er gibt ihm ein Geschenk.* There are various sub-types. The difference between obligatory and optional complements is often not easy to make and the whole field of valency-determined sentence patterns is by no means exhaustively examined and described.

7·8·2 | The noun phrase

The German noun phrase is extraordinarily varied. At one extreme it may consist of just one solitary noun (*Eisen rostet*), at the other it may comprise a couple of dozen or more (up to fifty according to W. Admoni) hierarchically arranged words on either side of the noun nucleus. Prenuclear elements such as articles, demonstrative pronouns, possessives, adjectives, participles, and certain numerals, are linked by congruence. Postnuclear elements such as genitive attributes, prepositional constructions, attributive subordinate clauses lack morphological congruence, except postpositional appositions. It has been observed (by H. Eggers) that as hypotactical constructions have in general become less popular, the noun phrase has tended to swell. Especially scientific and technical prose favours the extended noun phrase. Two constituents carry the main burden of this trend: the expanded participial and adjectival attribute in prenuclear position (see 6.8.2 (ii) on its evolution) and the postnuclear genitive and prepositional attributes. W. Admoni has shown that for the last 150 to 200 years the average length of the noun phrase has, in many scholarly and fictional works, amounted to between four and five words with more than half of all the words of a text occurring in noun phrases (see *Entwicklungstendenzen*, pp. 37–42). The noun phrase can function both as the subject and as any of the complements. Especially as a subject and as an accusative object the noun phrase tends to be at its most extensive.

The structure of the common-noun phrase can be illustrated schematically as follows:

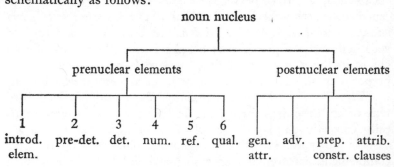

(1) As introductory elements we have phrase adverbs and prepositions. (2) The pre-determiners are *all* and the uninflected forms

all, irgend, manch, solch, welch which can never stand alone before the nucleus but must always be combined with a determiner: *all* with the def. art., *dies-, jen-* or the possessives; the others with *ein-*; *irgend* also with *welch*. (3) The determiners can be divided into definite and potential determiners, the latter being those forms, e.g. *ein, kein* and the possessives, which have uninflected forms unable to fulfil their determining function which is therefore passed on to subsequent elements (see 7.6.2). There are several kinds of determiners: articles, demonstratives, all inflected indefinite pronouns, and the possessive adjectives (which can themselves be preceded by the determiners *dies-* and *jen-*: *diese meine*). *Jed-* and *jeglich-* can be preceded by *ein*. Despite these few exceptions it is characteristic of the noun phrase that we generally have only one single determiner. Determiners form a closed class unlike the qualifiers. Qualifiers can be cumulatively employed. There are certain restrictions imposed on the determiners by the semantic nature of the nucleus, e.g. mass nouns and abstracts can generally not be combined with determiners in the plural. (4) The numerals include indefinite numerals and cardinals. Some can themselves function as determiners (*alle, sämtliche*) while others act in the same way as qualifiers (*andere, einige, viele, wenige,* etc.). (5) The referentials are certain adjectives, acting as qualifiers, but characterized by their position before the genuine qualifiers, referring to textual, temporal or local circumstances, e.g. *vorliegend-, erwähnt-, diesjährig-, ähnlich-, früher-, dortig-, hiesig-*. Ordinals take up the same position. (6) The qualifiers are themselves ordered: general – colour – material – geographical origin – nominal. Nominal qualifiers are those adjectives especially closely linked with the noun, e.g.

die diesjährigen, erfolgreichen, französischen musikalischen Festspiele

det.	referential	general qu.	geogr. qu.	nominal qu.	noun

die zwei engen, grünen, wollenen, französischen Röcke

det.	num.	gen. qu.	col. qu.	mat. qu.	geogr. qu.	noun

A difference can therefore be made between *ein seidenes enganliegendes Kleid* (mat. qu. – nom. qu.) and *ein enganliegendes, seidenes Kleid* (gen. qu. – mat. qu.). Verbal elements which can follow the nucleus as attributive clauses may be converted into prenuclear expanded attributes, e.g. *ein neuer Film, der wiederum in Spanien gedreht wurde > ein neuer, wiederum in Spanien gedrehter Film* (see 6.8.2(ii)).

The postnuclear elements are more freely arranged. While in prenuclear position we find above all pronouns and adjectives and nouns only if they are dependent upon adjectives or participles, the postnuclear field is dominated by nominal elements. The genitive attribute is most closely associated with the nucleus and precedes adverbials and prepositional constructions: *Eine weitere innige Beziehung Zürichs zu Italien war akademischer Art* (F. Ernst). Appositions and attributive clauses appear at the relevant places. Whether attributive clauses are placed in prenuclear or postnuclear position and whether the verbal element is transformed into the nominal element (participle) of a prenuclear expanded attribute is usually a matter of style. Compare the following sentences:

(a) 'gerade in einem Fremdsprachenunterricht, der sich zunehmend an der gesprochenen Sprache orientiert, die nun wieder gekennzeichnet ist durch eine Fülle von Kurzsätzen und Satzabbrüchen, /erscheint/ es uns als gerechtfertigt,...' (L. Götze).

Or: gerade in einem sich zunehmend an der durch eine Fülle von Kurzsätzen und Satzabbrüchen gekennzeichneten gesprochenen Sprache orientierenden Fremdsprachenunterricht, /erscheint/ es uns als gerechtfertigt,...

(b) 'daß Giovanni einen besseren, interessanteren, weil durch autobiographische Erfahrung, polemisch zugespitzte Argumentation und stilistische Vielfalt ebenso authentischen wie widersprüchlichen Film /gemacht hat/,...' (H. G. Blumenberg)....

Or: daß Giovanni einen besseren Film (/gemacht hat/), der auch interessanter ist, weil er durch autobiographische Erfahrung, polemisch zugespitzte Argumentation und stilistische Vielfalt ebenso authentisch wie widersprüchlich ist, (/gemacht hat/),...

In (b) the brackets are meant to indicate that a transfer to the postnuclear field would nowadays make an extrapolation stylistically almost certain, although incapsulation would not be grammatically incorrect.

7·8·3 | The verb phrase

The clausal functions of the verb phrase having been discussed in 7.8.1, attention will here be focused on the grammatical and semantic categories of tense, mood and voice.

(i) The problem of the *tenses* in contemporary German is extremely complicated as is confirmed by recent lively though inconclusive discussions among grammarians. German makes oblique rather than direct reference to real time. The grammatical means for doing so are not obviously systematized but form an intricate web. The tense forms are only one element among these which also include temporal adverbs, the semantic character of the verbs themselves (semantic content; aspects: durative, perfective) and modality (e.g. the speaker's views on the manner or reality of whatever the verb expresses). The formal nature of the tenses (simple *vs.* composite), stylistic considerations, and the *genre* of the text as a whole also play a part in the use of the tenses.

Starting from the tense forms themselves the following major functions may be distinguished:

Present: (a) statements of general, timeless validity – *er raucht*; (b) statements concerning habitual acts – *er raucht Zigaretten*; (c) statements referring to the present time – *schau mal, er raucht seine erste Zigarette*; (d) retrospective statements still valid at the time of speaking – *er raucht (schon) seit fünf Jahren*; (e) statements about the future connected with the present – *ich rauche (zuerst) noch eine Zigarette*; *diese Zigarre rauche ich an meinem Geburtstag* (sometime in the future); (f) statements embedded in a narrative of past events – *sie tanzen, ich rauche, da geht das Licht aus...*; (g) statements about past events of timeless significance – *das Rauchen kommt im 17. Jahrhundert auf.* We see that the present is basically indifferent to time (present, past, future). The connection with present time is made by contrast with other tenses, e.g. the preterite, or by the use of other lexical items (*eben, jetzt*, etc.), or is suggested by the external situation or the linguistic context. By the same token the verbal content can be related to past and future time. The implication is that it is not concluded. Glinz calls the present the *Allgemeinkategorie*.

Preterite: (a) narrative or statement implying the conclusion of the verbal content in the past – *bei der Arbeit rauchte er immer viel.* Important features are that the verbal content is remembered (Brinkmann) and related (Ludwig) by the speaker, there being no continuity into the present, but distance between the present and the verbal content (in the pret.). It is this distance which enables speakers to use the pret. as a kind of polite form in the present: *wer bekam das Bier?* inferring that the verbal content was expressed previously and should really have been remembered by the questioner. The brevity of the form of the pret. is often the reason for its use in headlines: *Zwei kleine Kinder starben.*

Perfect: (a) statements about past events where the verbal content is concluded but still has actuality – *er hat gestern ein neues Auto gekauft*; (b) statements about future events where the verbal content is concluded – *morgen um diese Zeit hat er den Vertrag schon unterzeichnet*; (c) statements of general validity implying conclusion of the verbal content – *das ist schnell passiert*; *sie hat einen Narren gefressen an ihm.* The main problem about the German perfect is that there is much overlapping with the preterite and, to a lesser extent, also with the much rarer future II. Where only past time and conclusion are relevant either the preterite or the perfect may be used by the speaker. By the former he will indicate distance from the present, by the latter actuality: *Goethe sagte einmal – Goethe hat einmal gesagt.* In contrast to the English perfect, which is a retrospective present, the German perfect is primarily a tense relating to past and concluded events actualized by the speaker. This is why Germans can say *Gestern bin ich ins Theater gegangen* as well as *Gestern ging ich ins Theater*, according to the degree of distance or actuality, while English only has *Yesterday I went to the theatre.* In German the past event is isolated and related to the present by the speaker choosing the perfect. The perfect thus expresses a speaker's subjective attitude towards a concluded event; it relates the past to the present while the preterite forms an opposition to the present. The use of the past tenses (pret., perf., pluperf.) may vary considerably between different texts owing to this subjective element. The overall proportion of the three tenses to each other, established for a varied body of material, is nearly 79 per cent pret. to over 12 per cent perf. and nearly 9 per cent pluperfect (Hauser-Suida/Hoppe-Beugel pp. 31–7). There are cases where pret. and perf. are not interchangeable. First, of course, in cases where the perfect is interchangeable with the fut. II (function (b) above); then in certain subordinate clauses: *er sagte es ihr, damit sie die Wahrheit gleich wußte* (not *gewußt hat*); certain idioms and lexical items tolerate only one tense (see (c) above), e.g. *pflegte* in the sense of 'used to'; the auxiliaries *sein*, *haben* and the modal auxiliaries have a definite preference for the pret. and aversion to the perf. (cf. *er hat es ihr gesagt – er wollte es ihr sagen*).

Pluperfect: (a) statements about events anterior to other past events – *er rauchte nicht mehr, aber früher hatte er sehr viel geraucht.* The pluperfect relates completed past events to other past events in the same way that the perfect relates past events to the present.

Future I: (a) in statements stressing the occurrence of the verbal content in the future – *ich werde diese Zigarre an meinem Geburtstag rauchen*; (b) in putative statements about the verbal content in present or future time – *er wird jetzt wohl das Rauchen aufgeben*; (c) in commands and admonitions – *du wirst jetzt aufhören zu rauchen.* Future I, in competition with the present tense in functions (a) and (c), has thus an extremely strong modal aspect. Probably in a majority of occurrences of this tense, a subjective surmise is uppermost. The actual meaning is always dependent upon the situation, the context, and the semantic nature of the verb itself. The characteristic facts are the overlap with the present and the fusion of mood and tense (supposition, expectation and prediction). While the present tense itself implies nothing concerning the beginning of what the verb expresses, future I implies that it has not yet begun at the time of speaking.

Future II: (a) statements with the completion of the verbal content in the future – *er wird die Zigarre geraucht haben*; (b) putative statements, the verbal action having been completed in the past – *er wird die Zigarre bestimmt gestern schon geraucht haben.* Where the modal aspect is not required the more cumbersome future II is usually replaced by the perfect. Basically it has the same relation to fut. I as the pluperfect to the preterite.

(ii) Just as the tenses are only one aspect in the indication of temporality, the *moods* are only one aspect in the indication of modality. The verbal moods together with modal adverbs and the modal auxiliaries form an intricate structure expressing the speaker's subjective attitude. Only brief reference can here be made to the chief functions of the two forms of the German subjunctive. Deriving from and corresponding to the stem forms of the indicative of the present and the preterite, they are often referred to as subj. pres. and subj. pret. Syntactically, however, they are now divorced from the tense system. They are essentially two different moods although they overlap to some extent. The inflectional paradigms (see 7.6.3(ii)) show that only certain verbs and certain persons make a clear distinction between subjunctive and indicative. The distinction is most effective in the auxiliaries *sein* and *haben* and in the modal auxiliaries. Apophonic verbs mark the difference more clearly than dental-suffix verbs. This has importance both for the use of the moods and for the development and use of the suppletive system with *würde*. Unmarked forms can only function as subjunctives in sentences where they are identified by neighbouring marked forms or by other contextual features: *er würde die Prüfung leicht bestehen, wenn er aufhörte zu faulenzen.* Where the subj. I (pres.) is unable to function owing to the non-distinction of subj. and ind. (e.g. *sie haben*) the respective forms of the subj. II are resorted to. In other words, function takes precedence over form. The forms very often receive their meaning only from the context: *sie hätten* can only be interpreted in a context. The vast majority of all subjunctive forms especially of subj. I are in the third person. In the investigation of a large body of material it was found that over 7 per cent of all finite verb forms are in the subjunctive (Jäger, 1971, p. 27). The following functions of the two subjunctives are the most frequent:

Subjunctive I: (a) In statements conveying indirect speech – *er sagt, er habe gelogen*; (*er sagt, sie hätten gelogen*); *sie seien um vier Uhr angekommen.* If such clauses are not introduced by a verb of speaking, the use of the subj. I alone implies that we are concerned with reported speech. In such cases subj. I is obligatory. If the dependent clause is introduced by a verb of speaking and a conjunction, the subjunctive I is often dispensed with, especially in colloquial style and in northern areas. It is more firmly entrenched in the south. Where the form is unmarked for subj. I, the forms of subj. II are chosen (see bracketed example). It is possible to distinguish tenses: *er lüge, werde lügen, habe gelogen, würde gelogen haben.* (b) In clauses expressing a wish, an admonition or a polite command – *Gott sei Dank! Man hüte sich vor dem Hunde! Man nehme drei Eier!* (c) In unreal comparative clauses – *er benahm sich, als ob er ein Türke sei.* (d) In hypothetical idioms – *wie dem auch sei; es sei denn, daß.* (e) In certain subordinate, e.g. final and concessive, clauses – *er arbeitete, damit es seinen Kindern besser gehe; er soll sich anstrengen, sei es auch nutzlos.*

The chief domain of the subj. I is reported speech. It can therefore also be called the quotative subjunctive.

Subjunctive II: (a) In unreal conditional clauses – *wenn er gekommen wäre, hätte er den Preis bekommen; wenn du warten würdest, könnte ich ihn dir gleich geben.* Where conditional clauses appear in indirect speech subj. II is maintained. (b) In hypothetical utterances – *ich hätte es gleich gemacht; er hätte sich geschämt.* (c) In unreal subordinate clauses implying a condition – *der Sack war so schwer, daß Karl fast umgefallen wäre (wenn er ihn nicht rechtzeitig abgestellt hätte).* (d) In clauses expressing a wish, usually with other lexical items (*doch, nur*) – *wäre er nur vorsichtiger gewesen! Hätte er es doch gleich gesagt!* (e) In unreal comparative clauses (rather more usual than the subj. I) – *er benahm sich, als wäre er der Sieger.* (f) In reported speech if the speaker is doubtful about the truth of the statement – *sie behauptete, er hätte gelogen.* However, in many cases where subj. II is used in such sentences this is due to uncertainty about the use of the subjunctive. Subj. II must be used where the forms of the subj. I are not distinguished from those of the indicative (see subj. I (a): *er sagt, sie hätten gelogen*).

The basic function of the subj. II is the expression of unreality in hypothetical, conditional clauses.

Many subj. II forms of apophonic verbs have an archaic flavour (*flöge, hülfe*) and are now often replaced by the paraphrase with *würde* plus infinitive. This has damaged the possible tense distinction (*flöge, würde fliegen, wäre geflogen*). The *würde* construction rather than the synthetic subj. II should be used where futurity is implied: *er sagte, sie kämen – er sagte, sie würden kommen.*

(iii) In respect of the *passive*, grammarians recognize that in German a distinction must be made between a *werden*-passive expressing a process and a *sein*-passive expressing a resultant or immutable state. An investigation (Brinker, p. 107) has shown that whereas the *werden*-passive comprises just over 5 per cent of all finite verb forms in a representative corpus, the *sein*-passive amounts to under 2 per cent. The proportion of the former to the latter form of the passive is therefore about three to one. Most verbs which can form a *sein*-passive can also form a *werden*-passive, but the formation of *sein*-passives is semantically somewhat more restricted than that of *werden*-passives. Both passives have an extensive tense system:

der Brief ist (von ihm) unterschrieben: war, ist gewesen, wird sein.
der Brief wird (von ihm) unterschrieben: wurde, ist worden, wird werden.

(iv) A feature of the modern verb phrase which has recently attracted much attention is what can be called the *nominal paraphrase* or the noun+function verb construction. Expressions like *eine Entscheidung treffen* or *(etwas) zum Abschluß bringen* are often regarded as blown-up phrases for simple *entscheiden* or *abschließen*. But it has been recognized that if used with discrimination such paraphrases fulfil important functions. Structurally we have a division of a synthetic verbal unit into a nominal part conveying the semantic content and a verbal part carrying the syntactical functions (indication of person, number, tense, mood, etc.). But the division nearly always brings with it an enrichment or an alteration of the content: *zur Entscheidung bringen* has a different verbal aspect from *entscheiden*, or *in Angriff nehmen* is different in meaning from *angreifen*. *In Bewegung bringen* suggests the preparation and initiation or causation of some motion, while *bewegen* implies some indefinite durative action; *in Bewegung kommen* on the other hand, suggests the passive beginning of motion. Whereas the finite verb is tied to a given place within the clause, in a nominal paraphrase the semantic component, being placed in a noun, can be shifted to a more favourable position. The formation of nominal paraphrases is an important, ever-growing process comparable to the older processes of inflection, derivation, and composition.

The nominal part is basically a *nomen actionis*. In form we may distinguish between (a) the noun as an accusative object: *eine Frage stellen, Antwort geben, Einwände erheben, Unterricht erteilen*; (b) preposition+noun: *in Ordnung bringen, unter Druck setzen, zum Ausdruck bringen*; (c) the noun in the nominative: *die Schadenmeldung erfolgt, der Besuch findet statt*. The syntactical link between the noun and the verb is usually strongest in the prep. +noun+verb construction. The syntactical function and the meaning of such paraphrases are also often more highly developed than those of the acc. obj.+verb constructions. Many nouns in such constructions lack an article. If they have one it is enclitically joined to the preposition: *zur, zum, ins* (*zum Ausdruck bringen, ins Schleudern geraten*, but *in Gefahr kommen*).

The verbal part is characterized by a definite loss of semantic content, compare *bringen* in *zur Verzweiflung bringen* and *zum Bahnhof bringen*. For this reason such verbs have been called function verbs (P. von Polenz). They are in a way akin to the auxiliaries, although their function is aspectual and not restricted to tense and mood, and their nominal counterpart is a verbal noun not an infinitive or a participle like that of the auxiliaries. Most of the function verbs derive from the field of spatial notions, e.g. *bringen, stellen, stehen, setzen, ziehen, kommen, gelangen, nehmen*. In the paraphrase they lose their concrete, spatial meaning and convert it into designations of aspects. The transfer of meaning from the verb to the noun in these nominal paraphrases contributes, of course, to the tendency towards 'nominalization' which has often been seen as a characteristic feature of modern German.

Nominal paraphrases are to be distinguished from normal syntactical groups on the one hand (*ein Kind tragen, zum Fluß kommen* – *Sorge tragen, zur Ruhe kommen*) and from idiomatic expressions on the other (*aufs Spiel setzen, ins Garn gehen* – *in Gang setzen, zu Werk gehen*). Native speakers can normally rely on their linguistic instinct, but linguists have attempted to formulate the differences in rules. Idiomatic expressions contain an abbreviated image. Their content is non-literal. They are isolated and usually contain a concrete noun. Nominal paraphrases have abstract nouns and occur in paradigms with the same verbs. In syntactic groups the verb retains its lexical meaning (cf. *einen Freund treffen* – *eine Auswahl treffen*; *ins Gericht kommen* – *ins Gespräch kommen*). The noun can be replaced by a pronoun or an adverb (*ihn, hinein*), but not in nominal paraphrases; the question *wozu/wohin* can be asked, but not in nominal paraphrases. In sentences the two constructions play quite different parts.

Compare: *Er brachte ihn* ⎱ different structure,
Er brachte ihn zum Lachen ⎰ different meaning

Er brachte ihn ⎱ same structure,
Er brachte ihn zum Bahnhof ⎰ additional information

Only the paraphrase as a whole, not the individual parts, can be negated by *nicht* (*nicht zur Geltung kommen*). There are, however, many borderline cases.

Nominal paraphrases allow useful semantic variation, e.g. *sich ängstigen, in Angst sein, Angst haben, ängstlich sein*; *hoffen, Hoffnung haben, Hoffnung hegen, (sich) Hoffnung machen.* Certain combinations of a preposition + a particular verb form aspectual patterns, e.g. *in + sein* (or *stehen*) = durative (*in Bewegung sein, in Verbindung stehen*); *in + bringen* (or *setzen*) = inchoative, causative, transitive (*in Gefahr bringen, in Betrieb setzen*); *zu + bringen* = conclusive (*zur Entscheidung bringen*); *in + kommen* = inchoative, perfective, intransitive (*in Bewegung kommen*) or *+ geraten*, unintentional, not desired, sometimes derogatory (*in Gefahr geraten*); *in + halten* = continuative (*in Unruhe halten*); acc. obj. *+ finden* (or *treffen*) = resultative (*Unterstützung finden, Maßnahmen treffen*). Also with an acc. obj. we have *zeigen* (*Gewandtheit*), *haben* (*Ahnung*), *üben* (*Geduld*), *machen* (*Angaben*), *bekleiden* (*Amt*), *treiben* (*Sport*). Such paraphrases also serve as a replacement of the passive, e.g. *in Verdacht kommen* (*verdächtigt werden*), *Förderung erfahren* (*gefördert werden*), or allow a passive construction where otherwise the verb does not form a personal passive (*er bekam Befehl, er erhielt die Erlaubnis*).

Although in bad style excessive use may be made of nominal paraphrases, it cannot be denied that handled carefully they have many semantic and syntactical advantages. Notably, they restore to German the possibility of forming causative constructions which the language lost when the *jan*-formations ceased being productive (OHG *brinnan/brennen* > ENHG *brennen* > NHG *brennen/in Brand stecken*, see pp. 314–5).

7.9 | Lexicon

7.9.1 | The modern development of the vocabulary

Most native speakers of German have at their disposal two kinds of words. One kind, which could be called the personal vocabulary, consists of words regionally or socially restricted. The other, the general vocabulary, embraces all those words which the speaker knows or believes to belong to the standard vocabulary. In this section we shall only be concerned with the general vocabulary of the standard language. If the native speaker is in doubt about a word he can look it up in Duden or one of the other dictionaries where he will be informed of the standing of a particular word. Modern German thus possesses a circumscribed standard lexicon analogous to standard grammar, phonology and orthography, although it is more open and elastic, as is to be expected, than these other aspects of the language.

The general vocabulary of the standard language used today was gradually shaped in the eighteenth and nineteenth centuries. It is, of course, as always, still in a process of evolution. This is true of words both on the plane of expression and on the plane of content. As lexical items words come into use as they are needed or go out of use as they are no longer needed by the language community. They are a reflection of the material condition and spiritual life of the language community. So are the meanings, although here change is more subtle, less tangible, and usually slower. The major part of the lexicon is, of course, little affected by the external changes of society. Here evolution is more of the kind immanent in language in general and subject mainly to forces arising out of the structure of the language itself.

The major lexical developments may be listed under the following headings:

(i) Word formation by means of derivation: *schulisch*, *Unterführung*, *Vergaser*, *bauchlanden*.

(ii) Word formation by means of composition: *Drehbuch*, *Fahrstuhl*, *Fernsehen*, *Klassenkampf*, *Kernzertrümmerung*, *anbrennsicher*, *busensichtig*. Sequences may reflect the external circumstances: *Reichswehr – Wehrmacht – Bundeswehr/Volksarmee*; *Fremdarbeiter – Gastarbeiter*.

These two processes, being by far the most important, were discussed in separate sections (7.6 and 7.7), as was the formation of syntagmatic units (7.8.3(iv)).

(iii) Word creation may come about through onomatopoeic imitation (*Töff* 'motor cycle'). Such words are almost by nature excluded from the standard language. Abbreviation and the invention of commercial designations are now almost the only processes by which words are 'created', e.g. *Agfa*, *Flak* (*Fliegerabwehrkanone*), *Akku*, *Uno*, *Nato*, *Euratom*, *Eternit* (built up on the basis of Latin *aeternus*). *Zug* (< *Eisenbahnzug*), *Kernspaltung* (< *Atomkernspaltung*), *Füller* (< *Füllfeder*) are abbreviations known as extrusive compounds and back-formations. They belong to the field of word formation. The innumerable words in modern European languages built up from Greek and Latin elements are in a way word creations, although they may also fall under the heading of borrowing. Creation often consists of a blend of existing words, e.g. *Telekratie* < *Tele(vision)* + *(Demo)kratie*.

(iv) Semantic shifting. There are many ways in which individual lexical items may change their content. The change may consist in the loss of a former component, e.g. *Magd* losing its former meaning of 'young unmarried woman, work and position unspecified'; or in the gain of a new component in addition to the existing components, e.g. *Welle* 'wave' as a technical term in physics, *drehen* 'to make a film', *bestrahlen* 'to give X-ray treatment', *Wagen* (also 'motor car'), *pendeln* (also 'to commute'), *Strom* (also 'electric current'), *Herd* (also 'gas or electric cooking appliance'), *Presse* (also a collective term for newspapers). Contents may thus become wider or narrower, more elevated or debased. Old meanings may be lost, or the addition of new meanings may strain polysemy to such an extent that we shall have to assume homonymy, i.e. different words having the same phonological form. Is *Herd* in *Kochherd* and *Krankheitsherd* one word with two meanings or are we faced with two homophonous words, i.e. two homonyms? The delimitation of homonymy and polysemy is one of the trickiest problems of semantics and lexicography. Metaphoric use based on similarity of shape or function is perhaps most often responsible for semantic shifting, for instance *Fähre – Mondfähre*; *Quelle – Stromquelle, Rohstoffquelle*; *auftakeln* 'to rig a ship' – *sich auftakeln* 'to tog oneself up'; *ausspannen* 'to unharness (horses)' – 'to relax (of humans)'. Semantic changes often occur through transfer of a lexical item to different spheres, for instance from a specialist language to general language (*Reibungsfläche, Belastungsprobe*) or from general language to a specialist language (*Walzstraße, Elektronenschleuder*). From the world of the theatre German derives: *etwas wird inszeniert, eine Rolle spielen, Szene machen, in der Versenkung verschwinden, Lampenfieber, hinter den Kulissen*. The extension of meaning may come about by a deliberate act. *Funk(e)* 'spark' was thus introduced for wireless telegraphy invented by Marconi in 1897. In 1914 O. Sarrazin suggested the verb *funken* as a new creation in addition to the noun which is now formally different from its source (*Funk – Funke*). Connotations may alter through change of taste or attitude: *gotisch* meant 'crude, barbaric' up to the early eighteenth century, then became a fashionable term of praise for the art style of the High Middle Ages, and finally a neutral technical term of art history. *Brutal, rücksichtslos, fanatisch* have decidedly negative connotations among civilized people. In the ideology of National Socialism they were given a positive value.

(v) Names may occasionally be turned into words, e.g. *röntgen* 'to X-ray', *Dieselmotor, Schillerkragen.*

(vi) Resuscitation of obsolete words. The rediscovery of the poetry of the Middle Ages towards the end of the eighteenth century and Romanticism in the early nineteenth century brought back into circulation: *bieder, Buhle, Ferge, Fehde, Hort, Gau, Held, Degen, Recke, Hüne, Turnier, Aar, Minne, Wonne.* Under English literary influence the words *Halle* and *Heim* came back. More recent reintroductions are *Ampel* (*Verkehrsampel*), *Imbiß* (*Schnell-imbiß*), *Truhe* (*Musiktruhe, Tiefkühltruhe*). *Meiler* was a term of charcoal-burners and as such obsolescent until atomic scientists used it as a translation of 'atomic pile' (*Atommeiler*). *Tarnkappe* was reintroduced into the modern vocabulary around 1800. After the First World War the verb *tarnen* was proposed as a translation of F *camoufler, camouflage*. When the founder of the German gymnastics movement, Friedrich Jahn, used the verb *turnen* (1811, 1816) he believed that he was reintroducing a good old German verb which he found in the works of Notker and which he knew from *Turnier, turnieren* reintroduced from medieval German in his own lifetime. It happened, however, to have been an OHG loan-word from Lat. *tornare*, OF *tourner*.

(vii) Obsolescence occurs most obviously with words for things and notions no longer in use, e.g. *Pferdebahn* and the old terms for measures and coins: *Zoll, Elle, Fuß, Taler, Gulden.* More subtle lexical reasons such as etymological isolation, homophony, ambiguity or the desire for more precise designations also cause obsolescence, e.g. *Bruch* (> *Hose*), *Eidam* (> *Schwiegersohn*), *Näber* (> *Bohrer*), *Quehle* (> *Handtuch*), *Wehtage* (> *Schmerzen*), *englisch* (> *engelhaft*). *Magd, Dienstmädchen* and *Putzfrau* have been generally replaced in active use by *Hausangestellte* and *Raumpflegerin.* Up-grading is an important, psychologically moti-vated process responsible for many changes within the lexicon. Perhaps more usual than complete obsolescence, at least within the relatively short period of NHG, is partial obsolescence, i.e. the obsolescence of one semantic component. Thus *Zeitung* no longer means 'news', *Vorsicht* no longer 'providence', nor *häufig* 'in heaps', *gleichgültig* 'equally valid'.

(viii) Deliberate creation of German words to replace foreign words, e.g. *Fernsprecher* for 'telephone', *Schrifttum* for *Literatur*. This process is called purism (see 7.9.4).

(ix) Borrowing from dialects or regional forms of the language. Words which were regarded as UGm. in the eighteenth century but are now standard are *abhanden, Ahn, Bein, kosen, lugen, vergeuden*. Originally LG words are *Behörde, bersten, beschwichtigen, dicht, sacht, Bucht, binnen, Diele, düster, flau, flink, flott, Hast, stur, Trecker*. Swiss words are: *Stumpen, Heimweh, staunen, tagen, Unbill, Gletscher, Kuhreihen, Putsch, Senne, Firn, Fluh*. Many were introduced by Schiller. *Rodeln* comes from Austria and Bavaria.

(x) Borrowing from foreign languages: *Film, Tunnel, Trend, fair* (see 7.9.5).

The lexicon not only reflects changes in material circumstances (*Zentralheizung* replacing *Kachelofen*), it also is an indicator of spiritual and artistic movements. Thus in the eighteenth century we find the Enlightenment with its key terms *Aufklärung, Verstand, Toleranz, Vernunft, moralisch*, e.g. in *Moralische Wochenschriften* (concerning all things spiritual), *Freiheit, Bildung, Freidenker, Kultur, Menschheit, Menschlichkeit, Humanität*. From the time leading up to the French Revolution come *Menschenrechte, Gleichheit, Brüderlichheit, Gedankenfreiheit, Republik, Revolution, Demokrat, Emigrant, Zivilisation*. Such terms belong to the common European vocabulary and moved freely from one country to another. Pietism in the same century stressed *entzücken, durchdringen, Einkehr, Innigkeit, Geborgenheit* and later irrational movements leading to Romanticism favoured *Begeisterung, Enthusiasmus, empfindsam, Gemüt, Stimmung, Volkslied, Volksgeist, Einfalt, Hochgefühl, Naturgefühl*. In the nineteenth century the technical vocabulary of industry and science was created and social and political concepts such as *Sozialismus, Kommunismus, Kapitalismus, Klassenkampf, Rasse, Reklame, Krankenkasse, Kindergarten* came into being.

7.9.2 | Regionalism in the modern standard language

Within Germany lexical differences in the standard language were very limited up to the end of the Second World War. They were confined almost completely to the domestic sphere where *Umgangssprache* was used rather than the literary standard (see p. 515). Some such well-known differences are *Samstag* (S) – *Sonnabend* (N), *Metzger* (S, W) – *Schlächter/ Schlachter* (N) – *Fleischer* (E), *Böttcher, Töpfer* and *Klempner* (N) – *Küfer, Hafner* and *Spengler* (S). The partition of Germany has meant that differences are now also found in the fields of politics, government, social affairs and ideology (see 7.9.3(ii)). The lexical differences in the standard language found in Germany on the one hand and in Austria and Switzerland on the other, go much deeper and are of long standing. It must be stressed that we are not concerned with the dialects but with the standard language which in the case of Switzerland is almost exclusively a written language. The lexical characteristics have in fact grown up in the written language and have often no support in the local dialects. With regard to the lexicon we must thus distinguish between a German, a Swiss, and an Austrian standard language. Although in certain fields, e.g. in state administration, the differences are very marked and although the differences in general may run to hundreds of words in each case, the fundamental lexical unity of German should not be doubted any more than that of English on account of lexical differences between say British, American, Australian or South African English. Rather it must be accepted that unity in lexis is a different matter from unity in, for instance, grammar. A German reader of even the *Neue Zürcher Zeitung*, the Swiss newspaper with the greatest claim to international standing, will find dozens of words or expressions in each issue which appear unusual to him. This only confirms the existence of *Schweizer Hochdeutsch* as a lexical phenomenon. It does not impede comprehension.

The lexical usage found in Austria or Switzerland differs from that of Germany for five different reasons. (a) Archaism. Neologisms are slower to penetrate to these neighbouring states. (b) Political independence. Designations for state institutions have grown up independently. But also in other fields the standardization in the written language followed to some extent an independent course. (c) Greater openness to the local dialects. Especially in domestic matters where standardization was slow, recourse is had to the dialects. Educated speakers are usually aware of the difference between dialect words and standard words. Their readiness to quote dialect words (e.g. Swiss *Muni, Winde*) does not necessarily mean that they do not know the standard words *Zuchtstier, Dachraum*. A difference must be made between dialect words used in standard and standard words restricted to Austrian or Swiss standard. (d) Resistance to purism. In Germany itself purism was at times very strong, but it had only a moderate influence in Austria and even less in Switzerland. (e) Greater openness to foreign influences from the surrounding languages.

Examples can be found in the following lists. In many individual cases several reasons may be adducible. The words given represent different levels of independence. In some cases they are exclusive to the country for which they are listed and may be hardly known elsewhere and would certainly never be actively used. In some other cases the words are merely the preferred choice or those most likely to be met in that particular country while others are also possible. Many of the Austrian or Swiss words are also current in southern Germany. Semantically, too, the differences are manifold. Sometimes we are concerned with different stylistic levels. Sometimes different connotations, e.g. archaic/neutral/ironic, adhere to the words. On the whole the dictionaries cover this aspect of regionalism rather unsatisfactorily both regarding the underlying theoretical classification and the actual entries.

Germany	Austria	Switzerland
Abendessen, Abendbrot	Nachtmahl	Nachtessen
Abitur, Reifeprüfung	Matura	Maturität
andernfalls, sonst	ansonst(en)	ansonst
Anlieger (Grundstück-nachbar)	Anrainer	Anstößer
Anschrift	Adresse	Adresse
anstiften	anzetteln	anzetteln
Apfelsine, Orange (S)	Orange	Orange
Aprikose	Marille	Aprikose
Arbeitsschicht	Turnus	Turnus
auswringen	auswinden	auswinden
Autofahrer	Automobilist	Automobilist
Bahnsteig	Bahnsteig	Perron m.
Bindfaden	Spagat m.	Schnur
Blumenkohl	Karfiol m.	Blumenkohl
Bürgersteig	Gehsteig	Trottoir n.

Germany	Austria	Switzerland
derzeit	zur Zeit	zur Zeit
dieses Jahr	heuer (heurig)	dieses Jahr
ehrgeizig sein	ambitioniert sein	ehrgeizig sein
Eisbein	Stelze f.	Wädli n.
Erkältung	Verkühlung	Erkältung
Fahrkarte, Rück-	Fahrkarte, Retour-	Billett n., Retour-
Fahrrad	Fahrrad	Velo n.
Februar	Feber	Februar
Friseur	Friseur	Coiffeur
gegebenenfalls	allfällig	allfällig
Gehalt	Gehalt	Salär n.
Geldstrafe, strafen	Geldstrafe	Buße, büßen
Gesellschafts-	Gesellschafts-	Autocar, Car m.
kraftwagen	kraftwagen	
gründlich	einläßlich	einläßlich
Hähnchen	Hendl	Poulet, Güggeli
Hausbesitzer	Hausbesitzer	Hausmeister
Hausmeister	Hausmeister	Abwart
Hörnchen (Gebäck)	Kipfel	Gipfel
hinten einsteigen	rückwärts einsteigen	hinten einsteigen
Januar	Jänner	Januar
Johannisbeere	Ribisel f.	Johannisbeere
jot, qu (ku)	je, que	jot, qu (ku)
Junge	Bub	Bub
Keks	Keks	Biscuit
Kellnerin	Kellnerin	Serviertochter
klingeln	läuten	läuten
Konditorei	Konditorei	Confiserie, Patisserie
Kopfkissen	Polster m.	Kopfkissen
	Pölster pl.	
Krankenhaus	Spital	Spital m.
Krankenwagen	Ambulanz	Ambulanz
Lastkraftwagen	Lastkraftwagen	Camion m.
Lehrstuhl	Lehrkanzel	Lehrstuhl
Marmelade	Marmelade	Konfitüre
mehren	mehren	äufnen
Mittelschule	Hauptschule	Sekundarschule
Oberschule	Mittelschule	Mittelschule
Volksschule	Volksschule	Primarschule
Nachname	Zuname	Geschlechtsname
nicht normal	abnormal	abnormal
parken	parken	parkieren
Postamt	Postamt	Postbureau
Quark	Topfen m.	Quark
räuchern	selchen	räuchern
Rauchwarengeschäft	Tabak-Trafik f.	Tabakladen

Germany	Austria	Switzerland
Rechtsanwalt(schaft)	Advokat(ur)	Advokat(ur)
Regal	Stellage	Gestell
Rosenkohl	Sprossenkohl	Rosenkohl
Rotkohl	Blaukraut	Blaukabis m.
Sahne	Obers n.	Rahm m.
Schaffner	Kondukteur	Kondukteur
schließen	sperren	schließen
	(Mittagssperre)	
Schornstein(feger)	Rauchfang(kehrer)	Kamin n. (-feger)
offener Kamin		Cheminée n.
Schreibwarenhandlung	Papiergeschäft	Papeterie
Schriftleiter	Redakteur	Re'daktor
Speiseeis	Gefrorenes	Glacé f.
Süßspeise	Mehlspeise	Dessert n.m.
Studienassessor, -rat	Professor	Mittelschullehrer
Tag!	Servus!	Salü!
Teig ausrollen	auswalken	auswallen
telephonieren	telephonieren	anläuten
Tomate	Paradeiser	Tomate
	(W Tomate)	
Trecker	Traktor	Traktor
Treppe	Stiege	Treppe
Verkauf (Klein-)	Verschleiß	Verkauf (Detail-)
Vesperbrot, Imbiß	Jause f.	Zvieri m.
Versteigerung	Lizitation	Gant f.
Verzehr	Konsumation	Konsumation
vorkommen	aufscheinen	vorkommen
Waschbecken	Waschbecken	Lavabo n.

These are just a few dozen examples out of many hundreds of different lexical items, meanings and usages. In the terminology of state institutions differences are very far-reaching as the short list on p. 603 may show.

7.9.3 | Ideology and vocabulary

Ideology always has an impact on the use of the vocabulary. Expressions like *Sozialpartner* and *soziale Marktwirtschaft* are just as much ideologically loaded and slanted as *Volksgemeinschaft* and *artecht* or *Arbeiter- und Bauernstaat* and *volkseigen*. In an open society ideological terms can be queried and examined

	FRG	GDR	CH	A
designation of the state	Bundesrepublik	Volksrepublik	Eidgenossenschaft	Bundesrepublik
lower house of parliament	Bundestag	⎱ Volkskammer	Nationalrat	Nationalrat
upper house	Bundesrat	⎰	Ständerat	Bundesrat
central government	Bundesregierung	Ministerrat (Präsidium des)	Bundesrat	Bundesregierung
head of government	Bundeskanzler[1]	Ministerpräsident	Bundespräsident	Bundeskanzler
ministry	Ministerium	Ministerium	Departement	Ressort
federal state	Land	—	Kanton	Land
state parliament	Landtag[2]	—	Kantonsrat/Großrat	Landtag
state government	Landesregierung Staatsregierung (Bavaria) Senat (Berlin, Hamburg, Bremen)	—	Regierungsrat/ Kleiner Rat	Landeshauptmann Landesregierung

[1] In CH the *Bundeskanzler* is the head of the cabinet office and of the civil service and the *Bundespräsident* is the presiding chairman of the collegiate government and acting head of state for one year. In FRG and A the *Bundespräsident* is the elected head of state.

[2] In Hamburg and Bremen: *Bürgerschaft*; in Berlin: *Abgeordnetenhaus*.

and their propagandistic slant can be countered. In an authoritarian society they tend to go unchallenged, which may lead to permanent semantic and lexical changes.

(i) The impact of *National Socialism* on the German lexicon has been studied fairly closely. Three aspects can be distinguished: (1) The formation of new words, mainly as designations of the institutions of the party and the state, e.g. *Sturm*, i.e. a unit of the military party organization known as *SS* (*Schutzstaffel*) with *Sturmführer* 'captain', *Sturmbannführer* 'major'; *Reichspressechef*; *Gauleiter*; *Reichsmarschall*; *Kraft durch Freude*. Such words are now historical terms, their origin being clearly identifiable. (2) The use of key words to propagate the Nazi ideology, e.g. *Führertum, Volksgemeinschaft, arisch*. Many such words are now regarded as 'tainted' and are avoided, others, e.g. *Asphaltpresse, Leistung, Volkswagen*, are regarded as 'harmless' and are therefore still in use. (3) Deliberate semantic shifts in a positive or negative direction, e.g. *brutal, fanatisch* as positive terms or *System* as a negative term for the despised political system of the Weimar republic. The demise of the Nazi ideology has removed the forced revaluation and the connotation is again at the disposal of speakers and writers. It is thus mainly in the second aspect that the impact of Nazi ideology has left some permanent traces in the German lexicon. Directives issued by the authorities concerning the use of words (*Drittes Reich* > *Großdeutsches Reich, das nationalsozialistische Deutschland*; *antisemitisch* > *antijüdisch* to spare Arab susceptibilities; *Katastrophe* > *Großnotstände*) were generally only partially successful.

During the Third *Reich* the impact on the lexicon was particularly marked in a number of semantic-lexical fields, such as in the use of archaic words, the terminology of force and violence, in the use of military terminology, of words of racial mythology, in the use of emotional and idealistic vocabulary, and in the use of metaphors from the fields of religion, biology or medicine. It is mainly in these fields that new words were coined, new slanted meanings propagated, or from which the key words derived. Only a very limited number of examples can be given.

(a) Archaisms: *Bann* (a unit of the *Hitlerjugend*); *Gau* (reintroduced by the gymnastics and youth movements of the nineteenth century and taken up by the *NSDAP*: *Gauleiter, Gauarbeitsführer, Gauwalter*); *Heil* (a supposed Germanic salutation – cf. E *wassail*

< OE *wæs hæil!* – reaching the Nazis via the gymnastics movement and Austrian mountaineers, *Heil Hitler!* being introduced in 1925); *Maid* (*Arbeitsmaid* 'female member of the labour service'); *Mädel* (*Bund Deutscher Mädel, Jungmädel*); *Mark* for frontier regions, e.g. *Nordmark, Ostmark*; *Sippe* for 'family' with a racial connotation (*Sippenbuch, Sippenforschung*); *Thingstätte*; *-wahrer* in *Rechtswahrer* (for *Jurist*), *Sippenwahrer*; *-walter* in *Schulungswalter, Schriftwalter, Amtswalter* (for *Beamter*).

(b) Terminology of violence: *Aufbruch* (*der Nation*); *Blitzkrieg*; *Machtergreifung*; *Sturm* (*-schritt, -abteilung* – *SA* was variably interpreted as *Sturmabteilung, Schutzabteilung* or *Sportabteilung* –). *Brutal, hart/Härte, rücksichtslos, fanatisch, schlagartig, unbändig* were key words with a positive connotation, all stressing the dynamism of the movement.

(c) Militarism: the figurative and frequent use of military terms had a long history in German before the Nazis brought it to a climax. *Einsatz, zum Einsatz bringen, einsetzen* (*Arbeitseinsatz*); *ausrichten*; *Front* (*Arbeitsfront*, the organization replacing trade unions and employers' associations); *Führer* (introduced gradually in the twenties, possibly in imitation of Fascism's *il Duce*, from 1933 official title of Hitler); *Gefolgschaft* (replacing *Belegschaft*); *führen* and *folgen*; *Kamerad* in *Arbeitskamerad* for *Kollege* etc. (*Berufskameradschaft, Kameradschaftsabend*); *Kampf, kämpferisch*, Hitler's *Mein Kampf*; the party's leading journal, the *Völkischer Beobachter*, was called *Kampfblatt*; the years from 1918 to 1933 the *Kampfzeit* and old party members *alte Kämpfer*. The ubiquitous use of *kämpferisch* (*kämpferisches deutsches Blut*) was to underline the party's message that life in all its manifestations (including sport and work) was basically a struggle in which only the strong and the brutal deserve to survive. *Lager* (*Arbeitsdienstlager*); *Marsch, marschieren*; *Schlacht* (*Anbauschlacht, Arbeitsschlacht*, even *Geburtenschlacht*, possibly on the model of the Fascist *battaglia del grano*) also contributed to the militarization of the language.

(d) Racial mythology: *arisch*; *Art* (for 'race' in *artblütig, artecht, artfremd, entartet, artbestimmt* and many more); *Blut* (also for 'race' in *Blutbewußtsein* etc.), *Blutschande* 'incest' became *Rassenschande* 'racial miscegenation', *Blutzeuge* 'martyr' was used for party members killed in street brawls. *Asphalt* was used in contrast to *Boden* for the sterile, cosmopolitan urban environment in terms like *Asphaltliteraten, Asphaltblatt, Asphalt-presse*. The latter has survived as the German word for 'gutter press' even after the disappearance of the *Blut und Boden* ideology. *Mischehe* 'mixed marriage in terms of religion' was reinterpreted as 'racially mixed marriage'. *Rasse*, an eighteenth-century loan-word from French, was used in many new compounds such as *Rassemensch, Rassenseele, Rassenbewußtsein*. Perhaps the greatest role in the field of racial mythology was played by *Volk* and *völkisch* (*Volksboden, Volksgenosse* (now *Staatsbürger*), *Volks-deutscher, Volksgemeinschaft* (dated and tainted), also *Volkswagen* – named, but reference to it was discouraged since the car did not go into production until after the war).

(e) Emotionalism and idealism: fashionable words were *Betreuung, Bewegung*; *Gemeinschaft* for Marxist or bourgeois *Gesellschaft* was supposed to express the unity of all classes of the nation after the abolition of the class struggle (*Arbeitsgemeinschaft, Schicksalsgemeinschaft*). *Geist* was positive, *Intellekt* negative. *Leistung* (*Leistungswille, -volk, -einsatz, -abzeichen, -kampf*) was to replace differences of class and rank and characterize the national and individual effort of the *Volksgemeinschaft* and the *Volksgenos-sen*. It is a key word of the post-war economic miracle (*Leistungs-gesellschaft, -mensch, -bewußt, -bezogen*). *Nationalsozialismus* was to combine the two great aspirations of the nineteenth century, nationalism and socialism, hitherto implacably hostile to each other. It was the height of irony that the word had been coined by the founders of socialist Zionism, Moses Heß and Theodor Herzl. Hitler learned the expression from various extremist groups professing a violent anti-semitism and fanatical nationalism at the same time as opposition to the bourgeois order. Among the frequent emotional terms we find: *Hingabe, Opfer, Schicksal, glühend, zündend, heiß* (*unser heißgeliebter Führer*).

(f) The secularization of religious terms also contributed to an emotional, anti-rational vocabulary: *Ergriffenheit, Glaube, Glaubens-bekenntnis, gottgläubig, ewig, heilig, Vorsehung, Mission, Weihe*.

(g) Hitler himself derived most of his metaphors from biology and medicine: *gesunder Volkskörper, giftige Geschwüre* (his enemies), *Seuche, Pestbeule, Gift, Blut, Spaltpilz, Schädling, Schmarotzer, Zersetzung, Bazillus*.

Manipulation of language was most blatant where euphemisms were used for deliberate concealment, e.g. *Schutzhaft* for imprisonment without due legal proceedings, *Sonderbehandlung* for the killing of Jews.

While Nazi propagandists promoted some purisms such as *Schriftleiter* for *Redakteur* and *Bildberichterstatter* for *Presse-photograph* they nevertheless were not averse to using foreign words of which *Garant, Fanal, Propaganda* (used positively), *Agitation* (used negatively) were favourites.

Perhaps even greater than the impact upon the lexicon was the Nazi influence on style. In many fields other than in party publications the language became hyperbolic, bombastic and antithetical, appealing to emotion rather than reason. German texts written between 1933 and 1945 provide many examples.

(ii) The effect of the *partition of Germany* on the German language is often seen as deleterious to the lexical unity of the language. Complaints are uttered, especially in West Germany, that the lexical divergences are beginning to impede mutual understanding and that the German language is being manipulated in the east. There is no doubt that lexical differences have developed, at least in the official languages of the two German states. Different political systems and different social institutions naturally require different terminologies. The dominant ideologies in east and west fill neutral political terms with different meanings. In the east one ideology, that of Marxism-Leninism, has the monopoly in all official utterances. It naturally tries to put across its views and uses language to this purpose. The lexical differences between east and west can thus be put down to three chief reasons: (1) the independence of the two states with different political and social institutions; (2) the difference in ideology; (3) the different use made of the propagandistic possibilities of language.

Under (1) we find for instance *Bundeswehr* (W) – *Nationale Volksarmee* (E), *Bundesbahn* (W) – *Reichsbahn* (E), *Aktiengesell-schaft* (W) – *volkseigener Betrieb, Kombinat* (E), *Geisteswissen-schaften* (W) – *Gesellschaftswissenschaften* (E) for subjects taught in an arts faculty (see also p. 603). The institutions of the GDR are, of course, ideologically inspired – as are those of the FRG – and their designations reflect the ideas of Marxism-Leninism. A number of words are loanwords from Russian, nearly all internationalisms rather than words of a Russian etymology. Russian are: *die Kolchose* or *der Kolchos, der Kulak, Sowjet*. Loanwords are, for instance: *das Ak'tiv, der Aktivist, das Exponat 'Aus-*

stellungsstück', das Kollektiv (Autorenkollektiv), das Kombinat, der Kursant, das Politbüro, Revanchismus, Tradeunionismus, der Traktorist. Loan formations form a much more significant group, both as loan translations and as semantic loans. It is an important fact that whereas Russian contributed to German practically only loanwords up to the Revolution of 1917, since then and especially after 1945, in the GDR, it has inspired numerous loan translations and semantic loans. According to H. H. Reich just over 30 per cent of all new words or meanings listed in his glossary of the official language of the GDR are Russian influenced. Heidi Lehmann quotes 638 such words in the language of economics. Loan translations are, for instance: *Abenduniversität, Agrostadt, Kulturhaus, Kulturpark, Maschine- und Traktorenstation, Wandzeitung, sozialistischer Wettbewerb.* Semantic loans are, for instance: *Agitator* and *Propagandist* as positive terms, *Akademiker* as 'member of an academy' rather than 'graduate', *Aspirant, Brigade, Diversion* 'subversion of the GDR', *Kader* for new leaders of the party and the economy, *Kandidat* 'person seeking membership of the party', *Lektion* 'lecture', *Norm, Pionier.* Other new terms for institutions are *Direktstudium, Fernstudium, Fünfhunderterbewegung, Jugendweihe, Soll, Volkspolizist.* In the FRG many terms are current which are not found in official use in the east, e.g. *Arbeitgeber, Arbeitnehmer, Sozialpartner, Lastenausgleich, Arbeitslosenversicherung, Volksschule, Volksdeutscher.*

(2) Where ideological terms are concerned we are really faced with a specialist language (a *Fachsprache*). A large number of political terms are technical terms both of Marxism-Leninism and of other ideologies, in the same way as words may serve as technical terms of several disciplines. Ideologists may criticize such use and call it misuse of a term; linguists can only record the use. Such terms are, for instance: *Demokratie, Fortschritt, Formalismus, Freiheit, Gesellschaft, Imperialismus, Kapital(ismus), Klasse, Kommunismus, Masse, Materialismus, Parlamentarismus, Revisionismus.*

(3) The propagandistic use of language is also responsible for many lexical differences between east and west, e.g. if the resettlers after the Second World War are called *Heimatvertriebene* (W) or *Umsiedler, Neubürger* (E). The Berlin Wall is known as *die Schandmauer* in the west and in the east, officially, as *antifaschistischer Schutzwall.* Other propagandistic uses are, for instance: *Aggression, Annexion* (only for actions of the west), *Friedensgrenze*

for the Oder–Neisse frontier, *volkseigen* rather than *verstaatlicht* for state-owned. The official language of the GDR also makes use of key words to give the regime a positive image. Such fashionable terms are, for instance: *Aufbau, Best-(-arbeiter, -student), Bewegung, Errungenschaften, frei (Freie Deutsche Jugend), Friede (Friedensanhänger, -gruß, -kämpfer, -front, -lager,* – the militaristic background is apparently not felt as incongruous), *Jugend, Kampf* and *kämpferisch, national, neu, sozialistisch, Volk, Wissenschaft, wissenschaftlich.*

As there is now a Leipzig Duden as well as a Mannheim Duden both eastern and western words and definitions are recorded. Although there are also linguistic differences (W *Aulas*, E *Aulen* as pl. of *Aula*), most divergences both in listing and in definition are of an ideological rather than a linguistic nature. In lexis and particularly in semantics, language proper and external reality become intertwined and are difficult to separate.

7.9.4 | Purism

German has always borrowed words from other languages. Such words may become widely current and linguistically adapted to the general orthographic, phonological and morphological patterns. Though new they then become an indistinguishable part of the lexicon (*Auto, Streik, Park, Nation, rasieren*). If the linguist calls them *loanwords* he uses a term of diachronic linguistics. He singles them out because they are of cultural and historical interest in the development of the lexicon. Other borrowed words may fit uneasily into the existing patterns, because they present orthographic problems (*fair*), phonological problems (*Bonbon*) or morphological difficulties (*Komma – Kommata*). These difficulties and problems are generally of the borrowers' own making. German speakers, by and large, have not been adaptable borrowers. On account of cultural and educational snobbery they have often kept the borrowed words at arm's length from the speech community as a whole, by insisting on displaying their knowledge of foreign languages. The words have remained *foreign words*. Many critics have therefore held them to be socially divisive.

The historical and cultural developments of the last four

centuries have caused German to become a heavy borrower of foreign words. In the earlier period this foreign influence seemed to impede the growth of a national standard language (see 7.2.1, 7.2.4). Later the *Fremdwörterflut* appeared to be a symbol of the failure to achieve the national aspirations. Political frustration turned to hatred of the foreign lexical intruders. Thus was born the particularly German movement of lexical purism. At its best it was inspired by some ill-thought-out but not ignoble ideas about an integrated lexicon comprehensible to all social classes. At its worst it was motivated by an excessive, racialistic chauvinism arising out of a particularly nasty blend of national self-pity and aggressiveness. Fortunately, as a movement it died during the Second World War.

Another powerful reason for the rise of purism, especially in the nineteenth and early twentieth centuries, was the then preoccupation of philology with the historical evolution of languages. Pristine purity was seen to lie at a point of evolution far back, subsequent to which, processes of corruption and deterioration had set in. Borrowing of foreign words was thus all too easily identified as an act of corruption and linguistic betrayal. From the point of view of the medium itself it is, of course, completely irrelevant where a word comes from. What matters is its function and place in the lexical system and its role in the sociolinguistic stratification of the language. If words erect social barriers, it is not because they are of foreign origin but because particular sections of the speakers lack the knowledge required to understand those words. Words like *Fernsehen*, *Rundfunk* or *einschreiben* are understood not because the speakers know *fern*, *sehen*, *rund*, *Funk(e)*, *ein*, or *schreiben*, but because, though technical terms, they belong to the common everyday vocabulary of the speech community of today. Being motivated words they may well be easier to learn in the first instance than *Television*, *Radio* or *rekommandieren*. But on the other hand the foreign words, being unmotivated, are not misleadingly suggestive like many native motivated technical terms, e.g. *Tätigkeitswort* for 'verb'. It may be aesthetically pleasing to have a largely motivated native vocabulary, but this does not necessarily make for ease of comprehension. *Daseinsbewußtsein* or *Mengenlehre* or *Eierköpfe* are not automatically easy words just because they consist of native elements. Many native words, admittedly, benefit from the transparency of construction, such as

Federballspiel, Frauenarzt, Wochenende for the foreign words *Badminton, Gynäkologe, Weekend.* The tendency of speakers to etymologize when faced with native words they do not fully understand can, however, often be an impediment to proper comprehension. On the whole the German lexicon is difficult and demanding, not because of the borrowed elements but because of the great tolerance of neologisms. Put more positively, one could say that German allows a particularly high degree of lexical creativity. Borrowing is only one aspect of this feature, but it is the one aspect which has often been seized upon by purists for criticism. Perhaps it is the generally high level of permitted creativity which often makes borrowing in addition to native word formation seem just too much.

One positive achievement of the movement has been the enrichment of the German vocabulary which is the result, ironically enough, of partial failure. Where the suggested German term has taken hold without ousting the foreign word we have two terms usually with slight stylistic or semantic differences: *Takt – Feingefühl, Kreislauf – Zirkulation, Richtschnur – Norm, Auto – Kraftwagen.* The movement as a whole has been successful far more often in launching a German word alongside the borrowed word than in totally eliminating the offending word. Attention has already been drawn to the resistance to purism and the greater retention of borrowed words in Austria and Switzerland. The loanword thus has now not only often the component 'archaic', 'recondite', but also 'regional – Austrian or Swiss'.

There have been five periods during which purism thrived and was particularly virulent – all coincided with times of national crisis and nationalistic excitement. The earliest coincided with the Thirty Years War (see 7.2.1 and 7.2.4). The second phase occurred at the time of the French domination during the Revolutionary and Napoleonic wars. The most effective purist was J. H. Campe whose *Wörterbuch zur Erklärung und Verdeutschung der unserer Sprache aufgedrungenen fremden Ausdrücke* appeared in 1801. He translated hundreds of words and was successful in very many cases, e.g. *Stelldichein/Rendezvous, Fallbeil/Guillotine, Tageblatt/Journal, Kreislauf/ Zirkulation, Zerrbild/Karikatur, Eßlust/Appetit, Einzelwesen/Individuum, Bittsteller (Supplikant), Festland/Kontinent.* His contemporary, K. P. Moritz, is responsible for *abscheulich (abominabel), unumgänglich/absolut, Nebeneinkünfte (Akzidentien), belu-*

stigen/amüsieren, Doppelehe/Bigamie, Beschluß/Dekret and many more.

The third phase followed upon the foundation of the Second Empire. Postmaster General H. von Stephan enforced the Germanization of over seven hundred loanwords in the postal service, e.g. *postlagernd* (*poste restante*), *einschreiben* (*rekommandieren*), *Postkarte* (*Korrespondenzkarte*). In 1885 the banner of purism was raised by the *Allgemeiner deutscher Sprachverein*, whose many publications suggested, for instance, among thousands of purisms: *Abteil* (*Coupé*), *Fahrkarte* (*Billet*), *Bahnsteig* (*Perron*), *Gelände* (*Terrain*), *Beförderung* (*Avancement*), *Geschäftsstelle/Büro*, *Warenlager/Magazin*, *Fassungsvermögen/Kapazität*.

The fourth phase flared up at the time of the First World War. The leading publicist was E. Engel, whose books *Sprich Deutsch! Ein Buch zur Entwelschung* (1917), *Deutsche Sprachschöpfer, ein Buch deutschen Trostes* (1919) reached a new level of virulence.

The final climax was reached in the fifth phase at the time of the Nazi take-over of power. A representative is H. L. Stoltenberg, whose books *Deutsche Weisheitssprache* (1933) and *Der eigendeutsche Wortschatz der Weisheitslehre* (1934) attempted the Germanization of scientific language and who suggested, for instance, *Geistgruppwissenschaft* for *Kultursoziologie*, *Seelkunde* for *Psychologie*, *Weibischtum* for *Feminismus*, *Vertragtum* for *Sozialismus*. This was the period when the Duden Grammatik and some historical grammars adopted the German grammatical terminology proposed by Klaudius Bojunga, e.g. *Tätigkeitswort* for *Verb*, *Leideform* for *Passiv*, *Doppellaut* for *Diphthong*. The attitude of the Nazi government was ambivalent. When it suited them they preferred foreign words (*Protektorat Böhmen und Mähren, Generalgouvernement Polen, Konzentrationslager*) and were not going to be taken to task by petty-bourgeois zealots. In 1940 the minister for education decreed that the forced Germanization of loanwords was to discontinue. With this, purism or *Verdeutschung*, not to be confused with the natural process of loan translation, ceased. In the last thirty years German has borrowed extremely freely without this evoking a new wave of purism.

7.9.5 | Foreign influence

There are two reasons why foreign lexical influence on a language is of great interest. First, there is the linguistic problem of the mode of absorption and, secondly, there is the cultural aspect, for we should like to know which semantic fields need or receive foreign infusion at any given time.

(i) The study of the mode of absorption of foreign lexical and semantic elements is much indebted to the work of Werner Betz and Einar Haugen. The following classification further draws on the contributions of E. S. Coleman, B. Carstensen and David Duckworth. Although in many individual cases it may be difficult to assign the words in question with certainty to a particular class, a classification is indispensable if we wish to understand the various processes at work, and provided it does justice to the bulk of the material involved. Borrowing, as has already been shown (see 4.8.1, 4.8.2, 5.8.2(ii) (iii), 6.9.1(ii), 6.9.2) follows two different channels: users import foreign words directly (*loan vocabulary*) or they transform foreign lexical items and meanings by making use of the native lexicon (*loan formations*). On the whole these processes are determined by the behaviour of the individual language

Borrowing

Loan vocabulary	*Loan formations*
(foreign elements adopted)	(foreign elements transformed into native elements)
1. Foreign words unadapted: *Barrister, Ghostwriter, Make-up*	1. Loan forms: (a) loan translation: *Eierköpfe Weißkragenarbeiter* 'eggheads' 'white-collar worker'
2. Foreign words partly adapted: *fighten, Teenagern* (dat. pl.)	(b) loan rendition: *Entwicklungsland Allwetterjäger* 'developing 'all-weather country' fighter'
3. Latin–Greek loan vocabulary: *Option, redundant*	2. Loan creation: *Meinungspflege vollklimatisiert* 'public 'air-conditioned' relations'
4. Loanwords: *Boot, Streik, Partner*	3. Semantic loan: *ausbügeln,* *Papier*
5. Pseudo-loans: *Twen, Sexical*	

Loanblend: *Gehirntrust, Tiefeninterview, Beat-Schuppen*

community and a classification set up for one language cannot automatically be transferred to another. For German the scheme on p. 613 seems most appropriate (with examples from English, the most typical source for borrowing in the twentieth century).

There are several features which make for 'foreignness': the use only for foreign concepts or objects in a foreign context (*exotica*); general unfamiliarity with the word; foreign appearance in orthography, phonology and morphology. Of these features all or only some may be present. Increasing familiarity usually leads to some orthographic or morphological adaptation (*clown* > *Klown*, *gehandikapt*) and often to further native developments (*Babysitter* > *babysitten*). All loans also import a new meaning, but it need not always be the meaning which attaches to the word in the foreign language, e.g. *Keks* (< *cakes*) > 'biscuits', *Smoking* (< *smoking-jacket*) > 'dinner-jacket'. They may also have a slightly different form: *Happy-End* (< *happy ending*), *last not least* (< *last but not least*). Only when all obvious foreign traces have disappeared (*strike* > *Streik*, *testen*) can the word be regarded as fully integrated. Loanwords in this sense are the result of an earlier process of borrowing, recognizable only to the linguist. They are merely of historical and cultural interest. Words of Latin and Greek origin form a special category. Such words have been present in German for hundreds of years. Orthographically and phonologically they constitute a recognizable sub-group of the German lexicon. Morphologically they adapt easily, e.g. nouns in *-tät*, *-tion*, *-ismus*, verbs in *-ieren*, adjectives in native *-isch* as well as foreign but naturalized suffixes. They form an everyday part of the learned and scientific vocabulary and to a minor extent also of the general vocabulary. The reason why so many French words in the seventeenth and eighteenth centuries and English words since then have been borrowed into German is that those of classical origin have fitted in quite easily. German, particularly scientific German, has now been wide open to the classical vocabulary for centuries, like many other European languages. The present English influence has introduced or reintroduced mainly in specialist languages, for instance: *affizieren*, *agieren*, *antizipieren*, *determinieren*, *explizieren*, *implizieren*, *koinzidieren*, *konfrontieren*, *kookkurrieren*, *rezipieren*, *subsumieren*; *praktikabel*, *redundant*, *relevant*, *rigid*, *signifikant*; *Abundanz*, *Consensus*, *Divergenz*, *Effizienz*, *Eskalation*, *Frustration*, *restringierter* or *elaborierter Kode, Kybernetik, Matrix, Nonproliferation, Option, Performanz, Plausibilität, Sozialstatus.*

The pseudo-loans testify to the popularity of English since they are words, unknown in English, which were invented by Germans with English bases, e.g. *Twen c.* 1960 < *twenty* 'young people in their twenties'; *Dressman* 'a male model'; *Greenager* on the model of *teenager* for children not yet in their teens; *Grusical* and *Sexical* on the model of *musical*; *Showmaster* on the analogy of *quiz master.*

Loanblends consist of a native element plus a foreign element: *Pressurgruppe* 'pressure group'; *Testbann* 'test ban' with German *Bann*; *Publicity-bewußt* 'publicity conscious'; *Supermarkt*; *Pilotstudie* 'pilot study' where *-studie* may be regarded as native (loanword) but *Pilot*, although also occurring as a German loanword, is here a semantic loan. Again such hybrids may be German developments without a parallel in English, e.g. *Manager-Krankheit*, *Schuhboy* (*-boy* 'a piece of furniture or equipment of some practical use').

Loan formations present special problems, for how can the foreign inspiration be proved if native lexical elements are employed? Such words betray their origin by occurring first in translations, or in reports about foreign matters, or in juxtaposition with the foreign word, or by being marked as neologisms by quotation marks. If the translation is word for word or part for part we speak of loan translation: *Elfenbein-Turm, Fußball, Mittelklasse, Großwissenschaft, Viersternegeneral, heiße Höschen, Graswurzeln* (*der Partei*), *Rattenrennen, Schneeballeffekt, Familienplanung, Eiserner Vorhang, der Schnelle-Brüter-Reaktor* 'fastbreeder reactor', *Auffindungsprozedur* 'discovery procedure', *Froschmann, Flutlicht, Gehirnwäsche, Gipfelkonferenz.* Whole idioms may be so translated: *Namen fallen lassen*; *im gleichen Boot sitzen* 'to be in the same boat'; *das Beste daraus machen*; *die Schau stehlen*; *in Form sein*; *zur Ordnung rufen*; *eine gute Zeit haben.*

Loan renditions are approximate translations: *Trägerwaffe* or *Beförderungswaffe* for 'means of delivery'; *Atomkopf* 'war head'; *Atommeiler* 'atomic pile'; *Podiumsgespräch* 'panel discussion'; *narrensicher* 'foolproof'; *Erzeugungsgrammatik* 'generative grammar'; *Wolkenkratzer* 'sky-scraper'; *heißer Draht* 'hotline'; *Ausschüttung* 'fall-out'; *Senkrechtstarter* 'vertical take-off aircraft'; *Leitartikel* 'leading article' or 'leader'.

We speak of loan creations where native words are fashioned independently of a foreign form but under the impulse of a foreign notion or object, e.g. *Luftkissenfahrzeug* 'hovercraft ; *Klimaanlage* 'air-conditioning'; *innergewerbliche Beziehungen* 'industrial relations'; *per Anhalter fahren* 'to hitch-hike'; *bügelfrei* 'non-iron'; *Spitzenverkehr* 'rush hour traffic'; *oben ohne* 'topless'. Sometimes several attempts at incorporation are made. Thus for 'public relations' there is also *Öffentlichkeitsarbeit* besides *Meinungspflege*.

If an existing native word acquires an additional meaning in analogy to a foreign word, we have a semantic loan. 'To iron out' has given German *ausbügeln* the figurative meaning in addition to the literal meaning which they both have. This also occurred in the case of *Flaschenhals, Klima, Gipfel. Papier* can now refer both to a written document as well as to the material on the analogy of *paper. Kopie* may be used for *Exemplar*, i.e. with the meaning of E *copy. Resignieren, kontrollieren* and *Suggestion* have taken on the meaning of E *to resign, to control* and *suggestion* in addition to the meanings they already had in German. *Kanäle* in *extraverbale Kanäle* has the meaning of E *channel*.

It has been shown (pp. 607–8) that in the case of Russian influence on the ideologically inspired language of politics and economics of the GDR, loan formation is far more extensive than the borrowing of loan vocabulary. The impact of English on German in the twentieth century appears to be equally strong in loan formation as in loan vocabulary, although we have so far no statistically based exhaustive study. There can, however, be no doubt that the direct borrowing of vocabulary from English is at present much greater than from any other language.

(ii) Borrowing of vocabulary from English began towards the end of the thirteenth century with *Boot*. Probably only *Lotse* (< ME *lodesman*) of about 1400 was also a medieval loan. There were then a few loans in ENHG: *Dogge* (1571), *Lord, Mylord* (1599), *Utopie* and *Gentleman* (1575), reborrowed later. The English Revolution brought in the first significant number, e.g. *Adresse* 'speech' (1689), *Akte* (1649), *Bill* (1683), *Debatte* (1689), *Quäker* (1661), *Rum* (1672). During the Enlightenment and the first wave of the popularity of Shakespeare and the English novel, mainly loan formations testify to the growing English influence, e.g. *popular song* > *Volkslied* later reborrowed into E as *folk song*,

Freidenker, Pantheist, Tatsache, Nationalcharakter, Freimaurer, Elfe, empfindsam, Heißsporn, Blankvers, the modern meaning of *Humor.* Science and politics contributed: *Barometer, Blitzableiter, Pferdekraft, Dampfmaschine, Koalition, Kongreß, Opposition.* In the field of commerce and social life eighteenth-century loans are: *Banknote, Beefsteak, Bowle, boxen, Boxer, Budget, Export, Farmer, fashionable* (*>fesch*), *Flanell, Frack, Gin, Grog, Import, Jobber, Jockei, Klub, Manchester, Panorama, Park, Punsch, puritanisch, Spleen,* and the loan formations *Arbeitsteilung* 'division of labour', *Handelsfreiheit* 'freedom of trade', *Staatsschulden* 'public debts', *Privateigentum* 'private property', spread by the translations of Adam Smith's *The Wealth of Nations.*

Although the growing English influence was commented on before the end of the nineteenth century, it became really significant only in the twentieth century, especially after the Second World War. In many branches of modern science and social life America's great influence is reflected in borrowing. The borrowing of loan vocabulary has always been strongly motivated by fashions. Foreign words are often quoted for effect. It is only when they achieve some widespread and lasting currency that we have to consider them as part of the German language. In studying past periods it is now easy to distinguish between the enduring acquisitions and the ephemeral. Only the former have been considered in earlier sections on the lexicon. The current wave of English imports is more difficult to assess. Journalists, advertising agents and 'with-it' circles pride themselves on their knowledge of English and interlard their texts with English words. The following extract from a parody illustrates the point:

Nach dem Hearing mit anschließendem Roundtable-Gespräch begann das Teach-in zunächst sexy. Ohne jedwedes Understatement bot die First Lady, um up to date zu sein, ihren Striptease im Mini-Bikini neben dem Flower-Power am Rande des Swimming-pools dar, während der Boß mit einer Crew von Provos die Show der High Society eröffnete. Das Meeting, von einem cleveren Entertainer arrangiert, sollte zu einer Open- und Weekend-Party werden. Die Fans der Beat-Band intonierten "Fremde in der Nacht" ("Strangers in the Night"), und die Twens und Teenagers kürten diesen Song zum Hit. Ein Oldtimer probte neben der Musicbox mit einem Starlet einen verjazzten Letkiss, mehr pop als op, wie der Disk-Jockey meinte, aber den Ghostwriter aus Studio A inspirierte gerade dieser Bestseller zur Head-Line für seine Story.

(*Die Zeit,* 8 December 1967)

Many of these direct loans will probably disappear again. The following list, grouped thematically, contains a selection of nineteenth- and twentieth-century loans which have shown some power of persistence (for those of Latin and Greek derivation see pp. 614–15):

Sport
Bob, Butterfly, Caddie, Coach, Doping, dribbeln, fair, fighten, fit, groggy, Handikap, Hockey, kicken, k.o., kontern, kraulen, Match, Odds, Outsider/Außenseiter, Pacemaker/Schrittmacher, Polo, Pony, Racket, Rekord, Reporter, Score, Sport, Sprint, Spurt, Start, stoppen, Surfing, Swimmingpool, Tackling, Tandem, Team, Tennis, Tip, Training, Turf, Volleyball.

Entertainment
Attraktion, Band (f.), *Bar, Blues, Call-girl, Comics, Fan, Feature, Festival, Film, Flirt* (an action, not a person), *Gag, Happening, Happy-End, Hi-Fi, Hitparade, Hosteß, Hot, killen, Limerick, live* (senden), *Mickeymaus, Musical, Op-art, Party, Petting, Pick-up, Pin-up-girl, Poker, Pop-art, Poster, Quiz, Ragtime, Science-fiction, Short story, Show, Song, Star, Striptease, Swing, Thriller, Trip, Twist, Western.*

General cultural and social life
Baby, Babysitter, Background, Beat(nik), *-boy* in the sense of appliance, *Bungalow, Camping, clever, Couch, Covergirl, Dandy, Egghead, Establishment, Folklore, Gangster, Girl, Globetrotter, Hobby, Jamboree, Jeep, Jet-Set, Keep-Smiling, Kidnapper, Komfort, komfortabel, Lift, Lunch, Mob, Motel, Mumps, o.k., Paperback, parken, Penthouse, Playboy, Raid, Ranch, Revolver, Rowdy, Sex*(-appeal), *sexy, shocking, smart, Snackbar, Snob, Steward*(eß), *Store, Streß, Supermarkt, Tank, Teddybär, Teenager, Trick, Tutor, Understatement, up-to-date, Vamp, VIP, WC.*

Commerce and economics
Advertising Agency, Bestseller, Big Business, Boom, Boykott, City, Clearing, Container, Copyright, Design(er), *Discount*(laden), *Dispatcher, Do-it-yourself, Dumping, Expreß, Job, Jute, Kartell, Koks, Lay-out, Leasing, Manager, Marketing, Output, Partner, Pool, Prosperity, Run, Safe, Scheck, Selfmademan, Shop*(ping), *Slogan, Slum*(s), *Standard, Streik* (1844 *strike* with reference to England, 1865 also for German industrial action, after 1880 > *Streik*), *Trend, Trust.*

Politics and public life
Agreement, Appeasement, Come-back (also in sport and generally), *Disengagement, Filibuster, Goodwill, Humbug, Interview, Hearing, Headline, Image, Jury, Komitee* (also < F), *konservativ, Legislatur* (also < F), *Lobby, lynchen, Meeting, Plenar-, Plenum, Votum.*

General science and technology
Air-conditioning, Bulldozer, Cockpit, Computer, Count-down, Dynamo, Fading, Feedback, Hurrikan, Know-how, Laser(strahl), Lokomotive, Nonstop(flug), Photographie, Propeller, Radar, Radio, Service (m.), *Telex, Telstar, Tender, Test, Tram, Transistor, Tunnel, Viadukt, Waggon.*

Cosmetics and fashions
Deodorant, Eyeliner, Jumper, Khaki, Kilt, Kord, Look, Lotion, Make-up, non-iron, Nylon, Overall, Petticoat, Pullover, Schal, Shorts, Slip, Smoking, Spray, Sweater, Tartan, Trenchcoat, Tweed, Twinset, Ulster, Waterproof.

Food and Drink
Chips, Cocktail, Cornflakes, Drink, dry, Flip, Grapefruit, Keks, Ketchup, mixen, on the rocks, Porridge, Pudding, Sandwich, Sherry, soft, Toast, Whisky.

An interesting feature is that borrowed verbs (*killen*) or derived verbs (*babysitten*) generally take the ending *-en*, unlike the verbs from the Romance languages for which *-ieren* is usual.

(iii) Taking the NHG period as a whole the strongest foreign influence has been the French. Most of the borrowing falls in the seventeenth, eighteenth and early nineteenth centuries. A substantial part of the original loan vocabulary has been shed again to some extent as a result of purism. The following selection of words of French origin testify to borrowing within the NHG period:

General cultural and social life
abonnieren, Adresse 'place of living', *Affäre, Akklamation, aktuell, Allüren, Alternative, (sich) amüsieren, Apathie, arrogant, banal, Billard, Blamage, blasiert, borniert, broschieren, brüsk, Chance, dressieren, egal, elegant, Energie, erotisch, eventuell, fad, frappant, Garage, genieren, interessant, Journalist, kompliziert, konstatieren, Kontrolle, Kritik, Lokal, Massage, Migräne, Milieu, modern, naiv, Neger* (see p. 462), *Niveau, Nuance, (sich) orientieren, Panik, Passant, Persiflage, Phantom, Plan, Plateau, plausibel, plazieren, Pointe, populär, Portier, Pose, prekär, Prestige, preziös, primitiv, progressiv, prüde, rasieren, räsonnieren, Redakteur, renommieren, Restaurant, resümieren, rigoros, Rivale, salopp, Sensation, sensibel, seriös, servieren, Sirene, Situation, Skandal, solid, sporadisch, sympathisch, Taxi, Teint, Tirade, Toilette, Tour, vage, vulgär.*

Architecture and the arts
Amateur, Anekdote, antik, Appartement, Arabeske, Atelier, Balance, Balustrade, Baracke (perhaps < It.), *barock, Belletrist, Broschüre, Büfett, Büro, Debüt, Dusche, Email, Fassade, Impressionismus, Kabarett, Karussel, Kino(matograph), Komik, Lektüre, Mansarde, Marionette,*

Memoiren, Nische, Orchester, Ouvertüre, Parkett, Plastik, Polonäse, Pornographie, Portrait, Premiere, Refrain, Renaissance, Repertoire, Revu, Rokoko, Ruine, Salon, Serenade, Silhouette, Souffleur, Szene, Terrasse, Theater, Tribüne, Varieté.

Commerce and economics
Akkord, amortisieren, Baisse, Bon, Defizit, Depesche, Depot, Dividende, Etat, Etikette, Hausse, Hektar, Hotel, Industrie, kolonial, Liter, Marke, Parzelle, Plombe, Plutokratie, Ration, realisieren, Reklame, Tarif (F < It.), *Tendenz, Textil-, transportieren, Volontär.*

Politics
Annexion, Attentat, Bourgeois, Bürokratie, Chauvinismus, Diplomat, Elite, Imperialismus, Initiative, Intrige, Kommunist, liberal, offiziell, offiziös, Polemik, Proletariat, radikal, Reaktionär, Reform, Regime, Repräsentant, Republik, Ressort, Revolution, Sanktion, souverän, sozial, Sozialismus, tolerant.

Military matters
Appell, Aspirant, Bajonett, Bande, Chef, Etappe, Kadett, Kaserne, Manöver, Marine, Militär, Ration, Revanche, Sabotage, Taktik, Uniform.

Science and technology
Automobil, (Luft)ballon, Brikett, Chassis, Chauffeur, desinfizieren, Maschine, Moräne, Omnibus, Panne, Phase, Rasse, Reptil, Sonde, steril, Technik, Telegramm.

Fashions
Agraffe, Bluse, Brillant, Brosche, Dekolleté, Kostüm, Krawatte, Manschette, Negligé, Poplin, Portmonnaie, Revers, Weste.

Food
Bonbon, Bouillon, Kompott, Kotelette, Likör, Limonade, Mayonnaise, Menü, Nougat, Omelett, panieren, Praline, Püree, Ragout, Roulade, Tomate (F < Span. (Mexican)), *Trüffel.*

(iv) It has been said of English that practically any Latin word (or Greek loanword) can be imported. In German this is largely also true, although on the whole such loans and new formations are more strictly confined to the learned and scientific vocabulary. A very large number have nevertheless entered the general language in the NHG period. Most of them are internationalisms and their route of adoption is often difficult to trace. The following are a sample:

Abiturient, abrupt, absorbieren, Abszeß, Affekt, Agrarier, Akustik, Album, Alibi, Allotria, Amphitheater, amputieren, Analphabet, Anarchie, Anomalie, Applaus, Aquarium, Archäologie, Arena, Aroma, Asyl, Athlet, Atom, Autodidakt, Autograph, Bazillus, Biographie, brutal, Despot, diabolisch, Dilemma, Diplom, Dissertation, Dosis, Dozent, drastisch, Dynamit, elastisch, Emanzipation, Epoche, Exil, Existenz, Exkurs, exotisch, Explosion, Faktor, Fanatiker, Floskel, frenetisch, Hegemonie, Hydrant, Impuls, Intellekt, Ironie, Kamera, Komplex, Konjunktur, Konkurs, konsequent, Kontakt, Laborant, Lithographie, Material, Miliz, Mission, Moment, Monogramm, Motor, Muskel, Narkose, Neurose, Oase, obszön, Optimismus, Organ, Pessimismus, Philanthropie, Philatelie, Philister, Plebs, Podium, Präparat, Prognose, Programm, Propaganda, Prothese, Psychoanalyse, quantifizieren, rabiat, reagieren, real, Referat, Referendar, relativ (also < F), *Rheumatismus, Sanatorium, Schema, Sektion, Serum, sezieren, Skepsis, Skulptur, Spektrum, Spekulant, spontan, stabil, Stadium, Stanniol, Symmetrie, Symptom, System, Terror, Thermometer, Torpedo, Tuberkulose, Typ/-us, Urne, Vegetation, Visum, Vitamin, Zone, Zyklus.*

(v) The Italian loan vocabulary is concentrated in the fields of music, the arts, entertainment, commerce and food:

Adagio, allegro, Antenne, Aquarell, Baldachin, bravo, Brokat, Bronze, burlesk, Büste, Cello, Dilettant, Diva, Duett, Fiasko, Finale, Impresario, Influenza, Inkognito, Intermezzo, Kantate, Kasino, Klarinette, Konfetti, Lava, Libretto, Lotto, Makkaroni, Malaria, Mole, Motto, Novelle, Oper, Operette, Primadonna, Putte, Quartett, Rabatt, Razzia, Regatta, Salami, Skala, Skat, Skizze, Solo, Sonate, Sopran, Spaghetti, Spesen, Tempo, Torso, Torte, Transit, Villa, Violine, Virtuose, Zervelat(wurst).

(vi) The Scandinavian languages have contributed only a few words. Some are connected with Norse mythology, e.g. *Norne, Waberlohe, Walhalla, Walküre* and the loan translation *Götterdämmerung.* Others designate Scandinavian features, e.g. *Eider-(ente), Erlkönig, Fjord, Renntier, Schi/Ski, Slalom.*

(vii) For the Russian influence, see 7.9.3(ii).

7.9.6 | Onomastics

(i) *Toponyms* belong to the most archaic strata of the lexicon. There have thus been few developments within the NHG period. The most characteristic innovation would seem to be the introduction of politics into place-name nomenclature. During the heyday of dynastic absolutism some new towns, or castles around which towns grew up, were given names after the founding princes, e.g. *Karlsruhe*, 1715 built by Margrave Karl Wilhelm von Baden-Durlach. Similarly we have *Ludwigsburg, Charlottenburg, Friedrichshafen, Ludwigshafen, Wilhelmshaven, Amalienlust, Wilhelmshöhe. Saarlouis* was named in 1680 after Louis XIV of France. The tradition continued in the Second Empire (*Kaiser-Wilhelm-Kanal*). In the twentieth century the political influence is mainly confined to names for streets and squares, e.g. *Bismarck-Straße, Platz der Republik, Horst-Wessel-Straße, Adolf-Hitler-Platz, Stalinallee, Konrad-Adenauer-Straße, Karl-Marx-Allee.* Where the names honour living politicians they sometimes share the vicissitudes of politics. In the GDR *Chemnitz* has been renamed *Karl-Marx-Stadt.* Names of foreign cities have also been affected by politics. The Nazis introduced the names *Gotenhafen* for *Gdingen* and *Litzmannstadt* for *Łódź*. In the post-war period the pendulum swung the other way. Eastern formerly German cities are only referred to in the GDR by their new Polish or Czech names, e.g. *Gdańsk* (*Danzig*), *Szczecin* (*Stettin*), *Wrocław* (*Breslau*), *Bratislava* (*Preßburg*), *Brno* (*Brünn*). *Straßburg* was for a time given as *Strasbourg* in West German publications. The political upheaval has led to the disappearance of the name *Preußen* from the map and the creation of new names such as *Nordrhein-Westfalen.*

Some towns have been given attributes to help the postal services, e.g. *Halle*(*Saale*), *Marburg*(*Lahn*). In the case of *Rothenburg ob der Tauber* the specification was recorded as early as the fourteenth century and has been firm since the seventeenth. The same desire for clear identification has restored to *München-Gladbach* its northern form *Mönchengladbach*. The vast expansion of towns and the growth of conurbations have led to the formation of hyphenated names, e.g. *Wanne-Eickel, Elberfeld-Barmen* and of new designations of suburbs, e.g. *Berlin-Dahlem, Zürich-Wollishofen.* New towns are generally named after their location, for instance, *Wuppertal, Erfttal.*

(ii) As far as *personal names* are concerned there has been little development in the field of surnames. In a few regions where surnames were not already established at the beginning of the NHG period, such as Friesland, the modern state administrations insisted on their introduction. They have in general been immutable by law. The stock of inherited German surnames has been augmented by many foreign names, for instance, Huguenot names (*Savigny, Fontane*) in the seventeenth century and above all by Slav names (*Nowak, Bielschowski*). In the second half of the nineteenth century the custom of adding the wife's maiden name to her husband's name evolved. It caught on especially in Switzerland. Swiss telephone directories and address-books regularly give hyphenated names: *Hans Meier-Müller*, *Müller* being the wife's maiden name, although they are not used in spoken language and never passed on to the children.

The Christian names, being chosen names, have been much more affected by change. Although many modern first names have been in use for hundreds of years (*Paul, Peter, Hans, Konrad*), some have become obsolete and many more have been added by fashions. On the whole fashions seem to have become more short-lived.

In the sixteenth century the custom arose of giving children two Christian names, e.g. *Johann Philipp, Karl Ludwig, Friedrich Wilhelm. Johann* and *Anna* were by far the most frequent first elements in double names. By 1700 double names were the rule, though with regional variations. The custom had started in the nobility, been taken up by the urban patriciate and finally also been imitated by the artisans and peasants. Between 1800 and the end of the nineteenth century single Christian names were again much more frequent. The German double names have always consisted of the usual Christian names. The English custom of giving the children the mother's maiden name as a middle name has never spread to the German-speaking countries. A distinction must be made between double names (*Karl Heinz*) and compound names (*Karlheinz*). Up to the middle of the nineteenth century genuine double names were the rule, but it is often difficult to say whether they were merely entries on the birth certificates or were actually used. The modern compound names (*Hansjakob, Hansrudolf, Hansjürg(en), Heidemarie, Annamarie*) are regarded as units. Double names very often include the godfather's or godmother's Christian name.

Fashions which have influenced name-giving were for instance: (a) deferential name-giving. Certain names were frequent in dynasties and often given by their subjects, e.g. *Ruprecht, Luitpold* in Bavaria; *Friedrich, Wilhelm* and *Charlotte, Luise* in Prussia;

August, Friedrich in Saxony or *Franz, Josef, Franz-Josef* in Austria. *Karl* became very popular in Catholic areas after the canonization of *CarloBorromeo* in 1610. *Ignaz* and *Xaver* spread in the same way. (b) Name-giving after literary characters, e.g. *Hermann/ Dorothea, Lotte, Minna, Eduard, Emil, Oskar* (< *Ossian*). (c) In the seventeenth and eighteenth centuries French names became fashionable especially for girls: *Charlotte, Henriette, Lisette, Babette, Susette.* (d) English names caught on in the nineteenth century: *Arthur, Edwin, Edgar, Edmund, Alfred, Alice, Fanny, Betty, Edith.* (e) Italian, Slav and Scandinavian names often became known through political or literary personages: *Laura, Guido, Alexander, Wanda, Olga, Helga, Gustav, Hjalmar.* (f) In the late nineteenth century short names became popular: *Klaus, Fritz, Horst, Kurt, Karl, Heinz, Rolf.* (g) Nationalistic and puristic movements encouraged the use of Germanic names: *Günther, Reinhold, Eberhard, Diether, Helmut.* Especially in the thirties such names were favoured, e.g. *Gunhild, Arnhild, Swanhild, Erdmuthe, Heidrun, Hadumot, Ingulf, Diethelm, Volker.* Films and songs now often inspire the popularity of names: *Romy, Kerstin, Ramona.* Among the most popular names today are: *Andreas, Thomas, Matthias, Michael* and among girls *Gabriele, Renate, Karin, Christine.*

As in lexis in general German is at present wide open to the outside world in the field of name-giving. Ponderous dithematic Germanic names like *Hildegard* or *Siegfried* would appear not to conform to contemporary fashion. Language, especially in lexis, shows itself to be both an expression of the needs of the community and an indicator of its tastes and aspirations.

Select Bibliography

W. Admoni, *Der deutsche Sprachbau*, 3rd ed., Munich, 1970; id., *Die Entwicklungstendenzen des deutschen Satzbaus von heute*, Munich, 1973; G. Augst, *Untersuchungen zum Morpheminventar der deutschen Gegenwartssprache*, Tübingen, 1975; id., *Lexikon zur Wortbildung*, 3 vols., Tübingen, 1975; R. Baudusch-Walker, *Klopstock als Sprachwissenschaftler und Orthographiereformer*, Berlin, 1958; G. Bech, 'Zur Morphologie der deutschen Substantive', *Lingua*, 12 (1963) 177–89; E. Beneš,

'Die Fachsprachen', *Deutschunterricht für Ausländer*, 18 (1968) 124–36; id., 'Syntaktische Besonderheiten der deutschen wissenschaftlichen Fachsprache', *Deutsch als Fremdsprache*, 3 (1966) 26–36; C. Berning, *Vom 'Abstammungsnachweis' zum 'Zuchtwart'. Vokabular des National-sozialismus*, Berlin, 1964; U. Bichel, *Problem und Begriff der Umgangs-sprache in der germanistischen Forschung*, Tübingen, 1973; E. A. Blackall, *The Emergence of German as a Literary Language, 1700–1775*, London, 1959; K. Brinker, *Das Passiv im heutigen Deutsch*, Düsseldorf, 1971; H. Brinkmann, *Die deutsche Sprache*, 2nd ed., Düsseldorf, 1971; B. Carstensen, 'Zur Systematik und Terminologie deutsch-englischer Lehnbeziehungen' in *Wortbildung, Syntax und Morphologie. Festschrift H. Marchand*, The Hague, 1968, pp. 32–45; id., *Englische Einflüsse auf die deutsche Sprache nach 1945*, Heidelberg, 1965; K. Daniels, *Substan-tivierungstendenzen in der deutschen Gegenwartssprache*, Düsseldorf, 1963; E. Drach, *Grundgedanken der deutschen Satzlehre*, 4th ed., Darmstadt, 1963; D. Duckworth, 'Der Einfluß des Englischen auf den deutschen Wortschatz seit 1945', *ZDS*, 26 (1970) 9–31; *Duden Gram-matik* by P. Grebe *et al.*, 3rd ed., Mannheim, 1973; H. Eggers, *Deutsche Sprache im 20. Jahrhundert*, Munich, 1973; id., 'Deutsche Sprache der Gegenwath im Wandel der Gesellschaft', in *Sprache der Gegenwart*, 5, Düsseldorf, 1969, pp. 9–29; J. Eichhoff, *Wortatlas der deutschen Umgangs-sprachen*, 2 vols., Berne, Munich, 1977; U. Engel, 'Regeln zur Worts-tellung' in *Forschungsberichte des Instituts für dt. Sprache*, 5 (1970) 3–168; B. Engelen, 'Zum System der Funktionsverbgefüge', *WW*, 18 (1968) 289–303; E. Erämetsä, *Adam Smith als Mittler englisch-deutscher Spracheinflüsse*, Helsinki, 1961; J. Erben, *Deutsche Grammatik. Ein Abriß*, 11th ed., Munich, 1972; H. Fenske, *Schweizerische und öster-reichische Besonderheiten in deutschen Wörterbüchern* (Forschungsberichte des Instituts für dt. Sprache, 10), Tübingen, 1973; W. Fleischer, *Wort-bildung der dt. Gegenwartssprache*, 4th ed., Leipzig, 1976; H.-R. Fluck, *Fachsprachen. Einführung u. Bibliographie*, Munich, 1976; P. F. Ganz, *Der Einfluß des Englischen auf den deutschen Wortschatz 1640–1815*, Berlin, 1957; H. Gelhaus, 'Zum Tempussystem der dt. Hochsprache', *WW*, 16 (1966) 217–30; H. Glinz, *Die innere Form des Deutschen*, 6th ed., Berne, 1972; R. Glunk, 'Erfolg und Mißerfolg der nationalsozialistischen Sprachlenkung' in *ZDS*, 22 (1966)–27 (1971); P. Grebe, 'Geschichte und Leistung des Dudens', *WW*, 12 (1962) 65–73; id., 'Zur Reform der Zeichensetzung', *DU*, 7 (1955) 3, 103–7; S. Grosse, 'Reklamedeutsch', *WW*, 16 (1966) 86–104; E. Haugen, 'The Analysis of Linguistic Bor-rowing', *Lg.*, 26 (1950) 210–31; U. Hauser-Suida, G. Hoppe-Beugel, *Die Vergangenheitstempora der deutschen geschriebenen Sprache der Gegen-wart*, Munich, 1972; R. Hotzenköcherle, 'Großschreibung oder Klein-schreibung?', *DU*, 7 (1955) 3, 30–49; id. 'Gegenwartsprobleme im dt.

Adjektivsystem', *Neuphil. Mitt.*, 69 (1968) 1–28; H. Ischreyt, *Studien zum Verhältnis von Sprache und Technik*, Düsseldorf, 1965; S. Jäger, *Der Konjunktiv in der deutschen Sprache der Gegenwart*, Düsseldorf, 1971; A. Jecklin, *Untersuchungen zu den Satzbauplänen der gesprochenen Sprache*, Berne, 1973; W. Jung, *Grammatik der dt. Sprache*, 5th ed., Leipzig, 1973; K. Kaiser, *Mundart und Schriftsprache – Versuch einer Wesensbestimmung in der Zeit zwischen Leibniz und Gottsched*, Leipzig, 1930; S. Kaiser, *Die Besonderheiten der dt. Schriftsprache in der Schweiz*, 2 vols., Mannheim, 1969–70; A. Kirkness, *Zur Sprachreinigung im Deutschen*, 2 vols., Tübingen, 1975; H. Lehmann, *Russisch-deutsche Lehnbeziehungen im Wortschatz offizieller Wirtschaftstexte der DDR*, Düsseldorf, 1972; W. Lehnemann, 'Vom Einfluß der Weidmannssprache auf das Alltagsdeutsch', *DU*, 15 (1963) 1, 51–62; C. Leska, 'Vergleichende Untersuchungen zur Syntax gesprochener und geschriebener deutscher Gegenwartssprache', *Beitr.* (Halle), 87 (1965) 427–64; K. Lindner, 'Zur Sprache der Jäger', *ZDP*, 85 (1966) 407–31, 86 (1967) 101–25; I. Ljungerud, *Zur Nominalflexion in der dt. Literatursprache nach 1900*, Lund, 1955; O. Ludwig, 'Thesen zu den Tempora im Deutschen', *ZDP*, 91 (1972) 58–81; L. Mackensen, *Die dt. Sprache unserer Zeit*, 2nd ed., Heidelberg, 1971; id., 'Muttersprachliche Leistungen der Technik' in *Sprache – Schlüssel zur Welt. Festschrift L. Weisgerber*, Düsseldorf, 1959, 293–305; F. Maurer, *Volkssprache*, Düsseldorf, 1964; F. Maurer, F. Stroh, *Deutsche Wortgeschichte*, vol. II, 2nd ed., Berlin, 1959 (arts. by Langen, Kainz, Wagner, Moser); E. Mittelberg, *Wortschatz und Syntax der Bildzeitung*, Marburg, 1967; D. Nerius, *Untersuchungen zur Herausbildung einer nationalen Norm der dt. Literatursprache im 18. Jahrhundert*, Halle, 1967; K. F. Otto, *Die Sprachgesellschaften des 17. Jahrhunderts*, Stuttgart, 1972; R. Pelka, *Werkstückbenennungen in der Metallverarbeitung*, Göppingen, 1971; P. von Polenz, *Funktionsverben im heutigen Deutsch*, Düsseldorf, 1963; id., 'Sprachpurismus und Nationalsozialismus' in *Germanistik – eine deutsche Wissenschaft*, 2nd ed., Frankfurt a.M., 1967, pp. 111–65; R. Rath, 'Trennbare Verben und Ausklammerung', *WW*, 15 (1965) 217–32; H. H. Reich, *Sprache und Politik. Untersuchungen zu Wortschatz und Wortwahl des offiziellen Sprachgebrauchs in der DDR*, Munich, 1968; H. Rizzo-Baur, *Die Besonderheiten der dt. Schriftsprache in Österreich*, Mannheim, 1962; N. N. Semenjuk, 'Zustand und Evolution der grammatischen Normen in der ersten Hälfte des 18. Jahrhunderts' in *Studien zur Geschichte des Neuhochdeutschen*, Berlin, 1972, 79–166; K. Spangenberg, 'Tendenzen volkssprachlicher Entwicklung in Thüringen' in H. Rosenkranz, K. Spangenberg, *Sprachsoziologische Studien in Thüringen*, Berlin, 1963, pp. 54–85; H. Steger, 'Gesprochene Sprache. Zu ihrer Typik und Terminologie' in *Sprache der Gegenwart*, I,

Düsseldorf, 1967, pp. 259–91; E. Uhlig, *Studien zu Grammatik u. Syntax der gesprochenen Sprache des Deutschen Bundestages*, Marburg, 1972; B. Wackernagel-Jolles, *Untersuchungen zur gesprochenen Sprache*, Göppingen, 1971; H. Wagner, *Die dt. Verwaltungssprache der Gegenwart*, Düsseldorf, 1970; L. Weisgerber, *Die Verantwortung für die Schrift. Sechzig Jahre Bemühungen um eine Rechtschreibereform*, Mannheim, 1964; A. Weiss, *Syntax spontaner Gespräche*, Düsseldorf, 1975; W. U. Wurzel, *Studien zur deutschen Lautstruktur*, Berlin, 1970.

Select General Bibliography

Bach, A., *Geschichte der deutschen Sprache*, 9th ed., Heidelberg, 1970.

Bach, A., *Deutsche Namenkunde*, 5 vols., 2nd ed., Heidelberg, 1952–6.

Behaghel, O., *Deutsche Syntax*, 4 vols., Heidelberg, 1923–32.

Die deutsche Sprache. Kleine Enzyklopädie. Ed. E. Agricola, W. Fleischer, H. Protze, 2 vols., Leipzig, 1969–70.

Eggers, H., *Deutsche Sprachgeschichte*, 4 vols., Hamburg, 1963–77.

Fleischer, W., *Die deutschen Personennamen*, Berlin, 1964.

Guchmann, M. M., *Der Weg zur deutschen Nationalsprache*, 2 vols., Berlin, 1964–9.

Henzen, W., *Deutsche Wortbildung*, 3rd ed., Tübingen, 1965.

Henzen, W., *Schriftsprache und Mundarten*, 2nd ed., Berne, Munich, 1954.

Keller, R. E., *German Dialects, Phonology and Morphology*, Manchester, 1961.

Kienle, R. von, *Historische Laut- und Formenlehre des Deutschen*, 2nd ed., Tübingen, 1969.

Lockwood, W. B., *Historical German Syntax*, Oxford, 1968.

Lockwood, W. B., *An Informal History of the German Language*, 2nd ed., London, 1976.

Paul, H., *Deutsche Grammatik*, 5 vols., Halle, 1916–20.

Penzl, H., *Vom Urgermanischen zum Neuhochdeutschen*, Berlin, 1975.

Polenz, P. von, *Geschichte der deutschen Sprache*, Berlin, 1970.

Raad, A. A. van, Voorwinden, N. T. J., *Die historische Entwicklung des Deutschen*, Culemborg, Cologne, 1973.

Tschirch, F., *Geschichte der deutschen Sprache*, 2 vols., Berlin, 1966 (2nd ed. 1971) –1969.

Waterman, J. T., *A History of the German Language*, 2nd ed., Seattle, 1976.

Wilmanns, W., *Deutsche Grammatik*, 3 vols., Strasbourg, 1897–1906.

INDEX